12th International Conference on Computational Semantics (IWCS 2017)

Short Papers

Montpellier, France
19 – 22 September 2017

Editors:

Claire Gardent
Christian Retore

ISBN: 978-1-5108-5283-9

Proceedings of **IWCS 2017 short papers volume, ACL anthology W17-69xx.**

12th International Conference on Computational Semantics, Montpellier 19-22 September 2017

Edited by Claire Gardent (CNRS, LORIA Nancy) & Christian Retoré (Université de Montpellier & LIRMM)

Out of the 66 short submissions we received, 35 were selected. They have been completed by 9 of the 37 long submissions that were accepted as short papers. Thus 44 short papers were presented as posters preceded by a lightning talk and are included as 8 page papers in this volume. They are listed below. We thank the authors for their submissions, as well as the program committee listed below for their help with the reviews and the selection process.

Claire Gardent & Christian Retoré

First Name	Last Name	Affiliation
IWCS PROGRAM COMMITTEE		
Claire	**GARDENT (co-chair)**	**CNRS LORIA Nancy**
Christian	**RETORÉ (co-chair)**	**Université de Montpellier et LIRMM**
Rodrigo	AGERRI	IXA NLP Group, UPV/EHU
Nicholas	ASHER	IRIT-CNRS Toulouse
Timothy	BALDWIN	The University of Melbourne
Daisuke	BEKKI	Ochanomizu University
Emily M.	BENDER	University of Washington
Raffaella	BERNARDI	University of Trento
Gemma	BOLEDA	Universitat Pompeu Fabra
António	BRANCO	University of Lisbon
Chris	BREW	Digital Operatives
Paul	BUITELAAR	Insight - National University of Ireland, Galway
Harry	BUNT	Tilburg University
Aljoscha	BURCHARDT	DFKI
Stergios	CHATZIKYRIAKIDIS	CLASP University of Gothenbourg
Ivano	CIARDELLI	ILLC - Universiteit van Amsterdam
Philipp	CIMIANO	Bielefeld University
Vincent	CLAVEAU	IRISA - CNRS
Dick	CROUCH	A9
Montse	CUADROS	Vicomtech-IK4
Philippe	DE GROOTE	INRIA Nancy
Valeria	DE PAIVA	Nuance Comms
Rodolfo	DELMONTE	Universita' Ca' Foscari
Pascal	DENIS	INRIA
Marc	DYMETMAN	Xerox Research Centre Europe
Markus	EGG	Humboldt-Universität Berlin
Katrin	ERK	Univ Texas
Arash	ESHGHI	Heriot-Watt University
Raquel	FERNANDEZ	University of Amsterdam
Tim	FERNANDO	Trinity College Dublin
Claire	GARDENT	CNRS/LORIA Nancy
Jonathan	GINZBURG	Université Paris-Diderot (Paris 7)
Iryna	GUREVYCH	Technische Universität Darmstadt
Aurelie	HERBELOT	University of Trento
Agata	JACKIEWICZ	Université Paul Valéry Montpellier
Makoto	KANAZAWA	National Institute of Informatics
Dimitri	KARTSAKLIS	University of Cambridge
Ralf	KLABUNDE	Ruhr-Universitt Bochum
Shalom	LAPPIN	CLASP, University of Gothenburg
Zhaohui	LUO	Royal Holloway College, University of London
Louise	MCNALLY	Universitat Pompeu Fabra
Marie-Francine	MOENS	KU Leuven
Richard	MOOT	CNRS (LaBRI) & Bordeaux University
Erwan	MOREAU	Trinity College Dublin
Alessandro	MOSCHITTI	Qatar Computing Research Institute
Larry	MOSS	Indiana University Mathematics Department
Shashi	NARAYAN	University of Edinburgh
Vincent	NG	University of Texas at Dallas
Malvina	NISSIM	University of Groningen
Ekaterina	OVCHINNIKOVA	KIT, Karlsruhe & ICT, Uni Heidelberg
Alexis	PALMER	University of North Texas
Denis	PAPERNO	CNRS LORIA Nancy
Laura	PEREZ-BELTRACHINI	Free University of Bozen-Bolzano / LORIA
Paul	PIWEK	The Open University
Thierry	POIBEAU	LaTTiCe-CNRS
Christopher	POTTS	Department of Linguistics, Stanford University
Violaine	PRINCE	Université de Montpellier & LIRMM-CNRS
Matthew	PURVER	Queen Mary University of London
James	PUSTEJOVSKY	Brandeis University
Livy	REAL	IBM Research
Christian	RETORE	Université de Montpellier & LIRMM-CNRS
German	RIGAU	IXA Group, UPV/EHU
Laura	RIMELL	University of Cambridge
Stephen	ROLLER	The University of Texas at Austin
Michael	ROTH	Saarland University
Mehrnoosh	SADRZADEH	Queen Mary University of London
David	SCHLANGEN	Bielefeld University
Sabine	SCHULTE IM WALDE	Universität Stuttgart
Rolf	SCHWITTER	Macquarie University
Joanna Ut-Seong	SIO	Nanyang Technological University
Mark	STEEDMAN	University of Edinburgh
Matthew	STONE	Rutgers
Mary	SWIFT	IBM Watson
Stefan	THATER	Saarland University
Tim	VAN DE CRUYS	IRIT & CNRS
Benjamin	VAN DURME	HLTCOE, Johns Hopkins University
Eva Maria	VECCHI	University of Cambridge
Shan	WANG	The Education University of Hong Kong
Roberto	ZAMPARELLI	Università di Trento

Contents of IWCS 2017 short papers (available on ACL Anthology)

Towards Universal Semantic Tagging

Lasha Abzianidze
CLCG, University of Groningen
l.abzianidze@rug.nl

Johan Bos
CLCG, University of Groningen
johan.bos@rug.nl

Abstract

The paper proposes the task of universal semantic tagging—tagging word tokens with language-neutral, semantically informative tags. We argue that the task, with its independent nature, contributes to better semantic analysis for wide-coverage multilingual text. We present the initial version of the semantic tagset and show that (a) the tags provide semantically fine-grained information, and (b) they are suitable for cross-lingual semantic parsing. An application of the semantic tagging in the Parallel Meaning Bank supports both of these points as the tags contribute to formal lexical semantics and their cross-lingual projection. As a part of the application, we annotate a small corpus with the semantic tags and present new baseline result for universal semantic tagging.

1 Introduction

Part-of-speech (POS) tagging represents one of the most popular Natural Language Processing (NLP) tasks, especially when it comes to syntactic parsing. It is proven by practice that the information about POS-tags makes syntactic parsing easier. An independent nature of the task and its lower complexity (compared to syntactic parsing) make POS tagging a perfect preprocessor for syntactic parsing.

But to what extent is POS-tag information useful for semantic parsing—obtaining semantic representations of natural language texts? Trying to answer this question in favor of POS-tags, we take a stand of a semantic parsing approach that heavily relies on them. One of such approaches is the formal compositional semantics driven by syntactic derivations of Combinatory Categorial Grammar (CCG, Steedman 2001), where a meaning representation is derived by composing formal meaning representations of lexical items (Bos et al., 2004; Lewis and Steedman, 2013; Mineshima et al., 2015).[1] Since lexical items come with fully fledged semantics, obviously, assigning correct lexical semantics is crucial for this approach. This is the place where POS-tags come into play by providing lexical information helping to determine lexical semantics. For example, given a POS-tag NN (singular or mass noun) or JJ (adjective)[2], it is possible to assign the desired lexical semantics to the modifiers in (1). But there are cases where POS-tags fall short of providing sufficient information for lexical semantics. For instance, regardless of their semantics, quantifiers get the same tag DT (determiner). Hence one needs to check the lemma of a determiner in order to define its semantics in (2).

$$
\frac{\text{beer}^{\text{NN}} \text{ / transparent}^{\text{JJ}}}{N/N} \quad \frac{\text{bottle}^{\text{NN}}}{N} \text{ (1)} \qquad \frac{\text{no}^{\text{DT}} \text{ / every}^{\text{DT}}}{NP/N} \quad \frac{\text{man}^{\text{NN}}}{N} \text{ (2)}
$$

$\lambda px.\, beer(x) \wedge p(y) \wedge for(y,x)$ if pos=NN $\quad \lambda x.\, bottle(x)$ $\qquad$ if lemma='no' $\lambda pq.\, \neg \exists x (p(x) \wedge q(x)) \quad \lambda x.\, man(x)$

$\lambda px.\, transparent(x) \wedge p(x)$ if pos=JJ $\qquad$ if lemma='every' $\lambda pq.\, \forall x (p(x) \rightarrow q(x))$

Formal semantics of a content word usually involves a symbol corresponding the lemma. This is the case for each lexical item in (1) and (2) except for the quantifiers. But when dependence of lexical semantics on a lemma is beyond a simple substitution, i.e., one needs to verify a lemma to define lexical semantics, then this case fails to generalize across different languages. For example, assigning lexical

---

[1]Similarly, the semantic parsing based on dependency structures (Reddy et al., 2016, 2017) also rely heavily on POS-tags.

[2]Throughout the paper the Penn Treebank POS-tags (Marcus et al., 1993), widely accepted in the NLP community, will be assumed unless otherwise stated.

semantics to quantifiers based on their lemma does not scale up for multilingual semantics. On the other hand, the treatment of common nouns in (1) and (2) generalizes for a multilingual case by using a simple assignment:

$$[\![\langle w, \text{pos} = \text{NN}, \text{category} = N\rangle]\!] = \lambda x.\, \textsc{sym}(x) \tag{3}$$

where $\textsc{sym}$ is a lexical predicate, usually a lemma, corresponding to the word w.

In order to compensate the shortcomings of POS tagging for semantic parsing, we propose a new NLP task, called *Universal Semantic Tagging* or *Semantic Tagging* in short.[3] The task represents a standard sequence tagging problem where each word token gets a language-neutral semantic tag, in short *sem-tag*. Sem-tags carry information that better characterizes lexical semantics than POS-tags do. We will show that the semantic tagging not only improves over POS tagging but also subsumes the task of Named Entity (NE) classification. We argue that importance of the task for (cross-lingual) semantic parsing is comparable to the one POS tagging has for syntactic parsing.

The rest of the paper is organized as follows. First, we further motivate the idea behind semantic tagging—how it includes semantic virtues of POS-tags and Named Entity (NE) classes; Then we present the current version of the semantic tagset. To show application of semantic tagging in semantic parsing, we describe its use in the Parallel Meaning Bank (PMB) project[4] (Abzianidze et al., 2017), where the sem-tags help to determine formal lexical semantics. We also present a baseline result for semantic tagging on a small annotated corpus. In the end, the paper discusses possible directions of future research on semantic tagging.

2   Motivation for Semantic Tagging

The information about POS-tags and NE classes do contribute to determine lexical semantics to some extent, but they are not sufficiently informative. One of the goals of the semantic tagging is to incorporate semantic virtues of these two tasks and fill gaps in semantic modeling by adding new categories.

In a tagging task, a sequence of characters that takes a tag is called a *word token*, or simply a *token*. Definition of a token may vary depending on a tagging task and its application. We find the concepts of token for POS tagging and semantic tagging somewhat different. For example, *"20-year-old man from New Zealand"* represents five tokens for POS tagging while we consider six token version *"20 year old man from New_Zealand"* more suitable for semantic analysis.[5] Hereafter, when talking about semantic tagging, tokens should be understood as meaningful atoms.

In addition to the examples from the previous section, POS-tags fail to disambiguate lexical semantics of series of word tokens. For example, reflexive and emphasizing pronouns get the same POS-tag PRP. The conjunctions *and*, *or* and *but* are all POS tagged as coordinating conjunctions (CC).[6] A comma can have several semantic functions, e.g., Arivazhagan et al. (2016) distinguishes nine semantic roles including apposition, location or listing. Both infinitival and prepositional uses of *to* are POS tagged as TO (Santorini, 1990, p. 5). Semantics of the determiner *any* needs to be disambiguated in context. The auxiliary verbs (e.g., *do* and *have*) and content verbs obtain similar POS-tags based on their syntactic features. This complicates to determine whether a verb introduce an event entity or not. The relative pronouns *which* and *that* both get the WDT POS-tag regardless of their restrictive or non-restrictive behaviour. It is natural to distinguish semantics of intersective adjectives (e.g., *ill* and *dead*) from subsective ones (e.g., *skillful* and *professional*), but this is impossible to do with the single POS-tag JJ. The above-mentioned partial list clearly shows that POS-tags are not sufficient for fine-grained (formal) lexical semantics.

---

[3] Since semantics of linguistic expressions is language independent to a large extent, we find *universal* redundant from a semantic perspective. On the other hand, from an NLP perspective, we would like to emphasize the universal (i.e., cross-lingual) nature of the task.

[4] http://pmb.let.rug.nl

[5] In general, we assume a fixed multiword expression as one token if it is semantically non-compositional and has an obscure syntactic structure. Such multiword tokens include proper names (e.g., *Alfred_Nobel* and *European_Union*), numerical expressions (e.g., *ten_thousand* and *10_000*), and function phrases like *as_well_ as*, *each_other*, and *so_that*.

[6] Moreover, there are at least two semantic usages of *and* one might want to distinguish: distributive and collective readings.

For wide-coverage semantic analysis one needs to identify NEs, detect their type, and model their semantics appropriately. The information extraction community has been actively working on the problem of NE classification and designed annotation schemas. For example, the named entity task at MUC-7 (Chinchor and Robinson, 1998) distinguished three general classes of NEs, where each of them contain several types: entity names (person, organization, location), temporal expressions (date and time) and number expressions (money and percentage). These types of NEs are motivated by downstream applications of information extraction. For a fine-grained semantic analyses, one might go beyond this standards. For example, one of such moves, following to Doddington et al. (2004), is to distinguish the locations without political or social groups (e.g., seas, parks and mountains) from those with them, i.e. geo-political entities such as villages, cities, countries, etc. Also one can introduce new NE classes, for instance, the classes for events (e.g., *9/11* and *World War II*) and artifacts (e.g., *Ubuntu 12.04 LTS*) or generalize existing ones, for example, go beyond monetary currency and percentage and cover the measure words like *meter* and *kilogram*.

In the next section we present an inventory of the universal semantic tags which incorporates semantic merits of POS-tags and named entity classes, fill the gaps in semantic annotation, and represents one unified tagset aiming to facilitate cross-lingual semantic parsing.

3   The Universal Semantic Tagset

The universal semantic tagset aims to provide general cross-lingual description for lexical semantics of all sorts of word tokens. It significantly differs from POS tagset, which is not semantically motivated, and generalizes over NE classes as the latter only covers the words of a particular type. The current version of the semantic tagset (v0.7) is given in Table 1, a revised version of the tagset (v0.6) presented in Bjerva et al. (2016).[7] The sem-tags are organized into 13 coarse-grained semantic classes each having its own meta-tag. This division is informal as many sem-tags easily qualify for several classes. We designed the tagset in a data-driven fashion while bearing in mind formal semantic properties of tokens. The employed corpus consists of several parallel corpora of various genres spanning over four languages (see Sec. 4).

Before we characterize the sem-tags, let us explain how the tags can or cannot be interpreted. A sem-tag of a token describes a semantic contribution of the token with respect to the meaning of the source expression. In this way, the principle of semantic compositionality underlies the semantic tagging. Later, in Sec. 4, an application shows how to interpret a sem-tag as an unspecified semantic schema/recipe. In general, sem-tags are not responsible for encoding a syntactic function of a token; For example, concrete quantities and colors get QUC and COL regardless of being a nominal modifier or a head of a noun phrase.[8] Moreover, currently sem-tags do not separate adjectives and adverbs but treat them as properties. The information about thematic roles are not also provided by the sem-tags. In principle, sem-tags provide the semantic information that complements thematic roles, syntax and lemma. Due to the abstraction from syntactic and lemma-related information, sem-tags are suitable for cross-lingual application.

The semantic classes ATT, COM, NAM, EVE and UNE cover both open and closed class words while the rest of the classes focus on the closed class words. The sem-tags that model closed class words make two major contributions: (i) semantically disambiguate highly ambiguous words that usually belong to closed class words, and (ii) act as an umbrella term for cross-lingual variants of a word and opens the door to multilingual semantic tools.

Let us first describe the groups of sem-tags covering closed class words. The anaphoric tags encompass definite articles and types of pronouns. They distinguish emphasizing pronouns (EMP) from reflexive

---

[7]Major revisions concern the classes of named entity (NAM), attributes (ATT), events (EVE), deixis (DXS) and tense (TNS). In contrast to the tagset v0.6, the current tagset excludes 15 tags and includes 13 new ones. More details about the changes are explained below.

[8]In contrast to this, depending on a syntactic context a color can get the NN or JJ POS-tag in the Penn Treebank (Santorini, 1990, p. 12): *The plants are dark green/*JJ vs *The plants are a dark green/*NN. It is also needless to say that sem-tags do not distinguish singular or non-3rd person verb forms, unlike the POS-tags.

Table 1: The Universal Semantic Tagset v0.7: 73 sem-tags grouped into 13 meta-tags. The sem-tags are accompanied with the examples where several highly ambiguous tokens come with a _{context}. The new sem-tags of v0.7 wrt v0.6 are marked with an asterisk.

Meta	Tag	Description and examples	Tag	Description and examples	Meta
ANA anaphoric	PRO	anaphoric & deictic pronouns: *he, she, I, him*	NOT	negation: *not, no, neither, without*	**MOD** modality
	DEF	definite: *the, lo^{IT}, der^{DE}*	NEC	necessity: *must, should, have to*	
	HAS	possessive pronoun: *my, her*	POS	possibility: *might, could, perhaps, alleged, can*	
	REF	reflexive & reciprocal pron.: *herself, each_other*	SUB	subordinate relations: *that, while, because*	**DSC** discourse
	EMP	emphasizing pronouns: *himself*	COO	coordinate relations: *so, {,}, {;}, and*	
ACT speech act	GRE	greeting & parting: *hi, bye*	APP	appositional relations: *{,}, which, {(}, {—}*	
	ITJ	interjections, exclamations: *alas, ah*	BUT	contrast: *but, yet*	
	HES	hesitation: *err*	PER	person: *Axl_Rose, Sherlock_Holmes*	**NAM** named entity
	QUE	interrogative: *who, which, ?*	GPE	geo-political entity: *Paris, Japan*	
ATT attribute	QUC*	concrete quantity: *two, six_million, twice*	GPO*	geo-political origin: *Parisian, French*	
	QUV*	vague quantity: *millions, many, enough*	GEO	geographical location: *Alps, Nile*	
	COL*	colour: *red, crimson, light_blue, chestnut_brown*	ORG	organization: *IKEA, EU*	
	IST	intersective: *open, vegetarian, quickly*	ART	artifact: *iOS_7*	
	SST	subsective: *skillful surgeon, tall kid*	HAP	happening: *Eurovision_2017*	
	PRI	privative: *former, fake*	UOM	unit of measurement: *meter, \$, %, degree_Celsius*	
	DEG*	degree: *2 meters tall, 20 years old*	CTC*	contact information: *112, info@mail.com*	
	INT	intensifier: *very, much, too, rather*	URL	URL: `http://pmb.let.rug.nl`	
	REL	relation: *in, on, 's, of, after*	LIT*	literal use of names: *his name is John*	
	SCO	score: *3-0, grade A*	NTH*	other names: *table 1a, equation (1)*	
COM comparative	EQU	equative: *as tall as John, whales are mammals*	EXS	untensed simple: *to walk, is eaten, destruction*	**EVE** events
	MOR	comparative positive: *better, more*	ENS	present simple: *we walk, he walks*	
	LES	comparative negative: *less, worse*	EPS	past simple: *ate, went*	
	TOP	superlative positive: *most, mostly*	EXG	untensed progressive: *is running*	
	BOT	superlative negative: *worst, least*	EXT	untensed perfect: *has eaten*	
	ORD	ordinal: *1st, 3rd, third*	NOW	present tense: *is skiing, do ski, has skied, now*	**TNS** tense & aspect
UNE unnamed entity	CON	concept: *dog, person*	PST	past tense: *was baked, had gone, did go*	
	ROL	role: *student, brother, prof., victim*	FUT	future tense: *will, shall*	
	GRP*	group: *John {,} Mary and Sam gathered, a group of people*	PRG*	progressive: *has been being treated, aan_het^{NL}*	
DXS deixis	DXP*	place deixis: *here, this, above*	PFT*	perfect: *has been going/done*	
	DXT*	temporal deixis: *just, later, tomorrow*	DAT	full date: *27.04.2017, 27/04/17*	**TIM** temporal entity
	DXD*	discourse deixis: *latter, former, above*	DOM	day of month: *27th December*	
LOG logical	ALT	alternative & repetitions: *another, different, again*	YOC	year of century: *2017*	
	XCL	exclusive: *only, just*	DOW	day of week: *Thursday*	
	NIL	empty semantics: *{.}, to, of*	MOY	month of year: *April*	
	DIS	disjunction & exist. quantif.: *a, some, any, or*	DEC	decade: *80s, 1990s*	
	IMP	implication: *if, when, unless*	CLO	clocktime: *8:45_pm, 10_o'clock, noon*	
	AND	conjunction & univ. quantif.: *every, and, who, any*			

ones (REF). Other types of determiners like indefinite articles, demonstratives, and quantifiers (most of which get the DT pos-tag) are covered by existential (DIS), universal (AND), place deixis (DXP) and vague quantity (QUV) sem-tags. Besides place deixis, there are sem-tags for temporal and discourse deixis (Löbner, 2013, Ch. 4). In addition to the sem-tags for subordinated (SUB) and coordinated (COO) discourse relations, there are separate tags APP and BUT for appositional and contrasting relations. Phrasal conjunctions and other discourse relations that have relatively transparent formal logical semantics are singled out by the logical sem-tags DIS, IMP, and AND. Tokens with vacuous semantics are tagged with NIL. Such tokens might include punctuations, infinitival *to*, and *of* from pseudo-partitives, e.g., *two liters of water*. The LOG class also includes the tags ALT and XCL covering words with semantics involving inequality. Given these sem-tags, a comma might be tagged with NIL, APP, AND, or DIS depending on its semantic contribution. Relative pronouns of restrictive and non-restrictive relative clauses get AND and APP respectively.

Accounting for modal words in semantics is crucial as they often block certain entailments. For this reason, the tagset has dedicated tags for tokens with modal functions, including a tag NOT for negative lexical items. In contrast, the Penn Treebank POS-tagset distributes most of negative items among adverbs, prepositions and determiners. Unlike the POS-tags, the sem-tags distinguish tense and aspect marking auxiliary verbs (TNS) from content (EVE) and modal (MOD) ones.

Since date and time expressions play an important role is downstream applications and have been a target of several shared tasks, the tagset has fine-grained sem-tags for them: DAT and CLO are designed for the full date and time formats while the rest marks (unspecified) components of the date format. We also design special sem-tags for speech acts.

The attributive and comparative classes mostly cover words like adjectives, adverbs, quantities and words derived from them. Since both adjectives and adverbs can be seen as modifiers (of entities and events) from a semantic perspective, sem-tags do not differentiate them.[9] The sem-tags distinguish concrete QUC and vague QUV quantities (which were previously merged in a single quantity sem-tag in v0.6). There are separate tags for intersective, subsective and privative adjectives. The adjective like *alleged* that are neither subsective nor privative are tagged with the modal sem-tag POS. Adverbs are usually tagged as intersective. DEG marks adjectives that subcategorize for degrees , e.g., *10cm long* or *2 years old*, as they are not subsective. From comparative sem-tags, we would like to mention EQU which covers words with interpretation of (tense-free) equality.

The tagset makes fine-grained distinction of proper names. In addition to the standard NE tags PER and ORG, following LDC (2008), geographical locations are divided into geo-political entities (geographical regions defined by political and/or social groups, GPE) and the rest of geographical entities (GEO). To link individuals to the NEs they originate from, we use GPO. Units in measure phrases are tagged with UOM as they act like NEs.[10] UOM generalizes over the standard NE class for currency and percentage.

The event sem-tags account for semantics of content verbs that introduce Davidsonian event entities. EXS marks a content verb without tense or aspect (including nominalizations and gerunds) while the other sem-tags in EVE additionally encode tense or aspect. Currently, the sem-tags in EVE are motivated by English, German, Dutch and Italian. The sem-tags for unnamed entities divide nouns into concepts (CON), roles (ROL), and collective/group nouns (GRP). Moreover, ROL also covers relational nouns while GRP marks collective operators too.

The examples of semantically tagged tokenized texts are given below. In (4), *tall* is marked with DEG as it is not affirmative—the question is not asking weather the green monster is tall. The sem-tags in (6) and (7) disambiguate existential and universal semantics of *any* and *a*. Notice that the latter is tagged with AND as *$ 100 a day* is semantically equivalent to *$ 100 each day*. More examples of semantically tagged text can be accessed online via the PMB Explorer.[11]

$$
\text{How}^{\text{QUE}}\ \text{tall}^{\text{DEG}}\ \text{is}^{\text{NOW}}\ \text{the}^{\text{DEF}}\ \text{green\_monster}^{\text{ART}}\ \text{at}^{\text{REL}}\ \text{Fenway}^{\text{GEO}}\ \text{?}^{\text{QUE}} \tag{4}
$$

$$
\text{My}^{\text{HAS}}\ \text{sister}^{\text{ROL}}\ \text{went}^{\text{EPS}}\ \text{to}^{\text{REL}}\ \text{the}^{\text{DEF}}\ \text{United\_States}^{\text{GPE}}\ \text{to}^{\text{SUB}}\ \text{study}^{\text{EXS}}\ \text{English}^{\text{CON}}\ \text{.}^{\text{NIL}} \tag{5}
$$

$$
\text{Any}^{\text{AND}}\ \text{contribution}^{\text{CON}}\ \text{was}^{\text{PST}}\ \text{appreciated}^{\text{EXS}}\ \text{but}^{\text{BUT}}\ \text{we}^{\text{PRO}}\ \text{have}^{\text{NOW}}\ \text{n't}^{\text{NOT}}\ \text{got}^{\text{EXT}}\ \text{any}^{\text{DIS}}\ \text{.}^{\text{NIL}} \tag{6}
$$

$$
\text{He}^{\text{PRO}}\ \text{himself}^{\text{EMP}}\ \text{can}^{\text{POS}}\ \text{earn}^{\text{EXS}}\ \text{\$}^{\text{UOM}}\ \text{100}^{\text{QUC}}\ \text{a}^{\text{AND}}\ \text{day}^{\text{UOM}}\ \text{.}^{\text{NIL}} \tag{7}
$$

4 Applications and Results

The idea of the universal semantic tagging was originally motivated by the goals of the PMB project (Bos, 2014; Abzianidze et al., 2017): (i) compositionally derive formal meaning representations for wide-coverage English text (Bos, 2009), and (ii) project the meaning representations to Dutch, German and Italian translations via word alignments (Evang and Bos, 2016). These requirements challenge semantic competence and cross-lingual scalability of the universal semantic tagging.

A high quality large-scale semantic lexicon is crucial for the PMB as both projection and derivation of

---

[9]Moreover, some languages like Dutch and German make little grammatical distinction between adverbs and adjectives.

[10]It seems unnatural to treat them as predicates and therefore license entailments using the WordNet hypernymy relations: *he ran five kilometers* $\Rightarrow$ *he ran five metric linear units*.

[11]http://pmb.let.rug.nl/explorer/

meaning representations starts from lexical items. The semantic tagset plays a crucial role in development and organization of the lexicon. In particular, in the PMB, Boxer (Bos, 2008, 2015) interprets a sem-tag as a mapping from CCG categories (augmented with thematic roles) to a formal semantic schema which is further specified by a token-related predicate/constant symbol and thematic roles (if any). The function behind the EXS tag is partially depicted in (8):

$$
\text{EXS} = \left\{
\begin{array}{rcl}
S\backslash_{R_1} NP & \mapsto & \lambda P\, r.\, P\big(\lambda x.\ \boxed{\begin{array}{l} e \\ \hline \text{SYM}(e) \quad R_1(e,x) \end{array}} ; r(e)\big) \\[3ex]
(S\backslash_{R_1} NP)/_{R_2} NP & \mapsto & \lambda Q\, P\, r.\, P\Big(\lambda x.\, Q\big(\lambda y.\ \boxed{\begin{array}{l} e \\ \hline \text{SYM}(e) \quad R_1(e,x) \quad R_2(e,y) \end{array}} ; r(e)\big)\Big)
\end{array}
\right\}
\tag{8}
$$

In order to collect large semantically annotated data via bootstrapping, we prepared initial silver and gold datasets for system training and testing respectively. The datasets are part of the PMB, where the gold data is manually checked and consists of 2.4K English sentences (14.6K tokens) while the silver data (457K tokens) consists of the PMB documents that are tagged by the neural semantic tagger of Bjerva et al. (2016) and have some manual corrections. For the data collection via bootstrapping, we initially employ the tri-gram based TnT tagger (Brants, 2000) rather than data-hungry neural models. After training TnT on the silver data, it correctly tagged 86.89% of tokens in the gold data: almost 5% improvement over the most frequent tag per-word baseline (82.18%). This accuracy seems promising for bootstrapping application.[12]

Besides the application in the PMB, Bjerva et al. (2016) showed that using sem-tags as auxiliary information significantly improves English Universal Dependencies POS tagging. Given that Boxer and similar semantic parsing scenarios are commonly used (Mineshima et al., 2015; Beltagy et al., 2016; Lewis and Steedman, 2013), semantic tagging will help those researches to shift to a cross-lingual level. Additionally, multilingual semantic parsing approaches might also benefit from semantic tagging. For example, sematic tags can help UDEPLAMBDAReddy et al. (2017) to decrease efforts of looking up lexical information for several words, e.g., quantifiers and negation markers.

5   Conclusion

We have proposed a novel NLP task that contributes to wide-coverage cross-lingual semantic parsing. Tagging tokens with universal semantic tags represents an independent task that unifies and generalizes over semantic virtues of POS-tagging and NE recognition. The expressive semantic tagset allows disambiguation of various semantic phenomena. Besides their application in semantic parsing, already demonstrated in the PMB project, sem-tags can contribute to other NLP tasks, e.g. POS tagging, or research lines rooted in compositional semantics.

In contrast to POS tagsets (Marcus et al., 1993; Petrov et al., 2012) augmented with morphological/universal features (Sylak-Glassman, 2016; Nivre et al., 2016), the semantic tagset is less expressive from a morphological perspective. On the other hand, the tagset is leaner and models several semantic phenomena, e.g., roles (ROL), subsectives (SST), privatives (PRI), and degrees (DEG), that are beyond morphology. Compared to the standard NE classes (Sang and Meulder, 2003), the named entity class (NAM) of the tagset is broader. The annotations of temporal expressions at TempEval (UzZaman et al., 2013) and MUC-7 (Chinchor and Robinson, 1998) differ from semantic tagging in terms of granularity: they annotate entire time expressions (e.g., *August of 2014*) while the semantic tagset opts for a more compositional analysis.

In future research, we plan to annotate more data with the help of human annotators, automatically tag large monolingual data via bootstrapping, further improve cross-lingual projection of sem-tags, and prepare an annotation guideline for semantic tagging. Elaboration of compositional semantics in the PMB might lead to an additional refinement of the semantic tagset. For example, one can distinguish

---

[12]This result of the TnT tagger is not directly comparable to the result (83.6%) of the neural semantic tagger reported by Bjerva et al. (2016) since the experiments differ in terms of training/test data and the semantic tagset.

genders or animacy for better pronoun resolution or mark plurality information for better semantic analysis.

Acknowledgements

This work has been supported by the NWO-VICI grant "Lost in Translation Found in Meaning" (288-89-003). We also wish to thank the three anonymous reviewers for their helpful comments.

References

Abzianidze, L., J. Bjerva, K. Evang, H. Haagsma, R. van Noord, P. Ludmann, D.-D. Nguyen, and J. Bos (2017, April). The parallel meaning bank: Towards a multilingual corpus of translations annotated with compositional meaning representations. In *Proceedings of the 15th Conference of the European Chapter of the Association for Computational Linguistics: Volume 2, Short Papers*, Valencia, Spain, pp. 242–247. Association for Computational Linguistics.

Arivazhagan, N., C. Christodoulopoulos, and D. Roth (2016). Labeling the semantic roles of commas. In *Proceedings of the Thirtieth AAAI Conference on Artificial Intelligence, February 12-17, 2016, Phoenix, Arizona, USA.*, pp. 2885–2891.

Beltagy, I., S. Roller, P. Cheng, K. Erk, and R. J. Mooney (2016). Representing meaning with a combination of logical and distributional models. *Computational Linguistics 42*(4), 763–808.

Bjerva, J., B. Plank, and J. Bos (2016). Semantic tagging with deep residual networks. In *Proceedings of COLING 2016, the 26th International Conference on Computational Linguistics: Technical Papers*, Osaka, Japan, pp. 3531–3541.

Bos, J. (2008). Wide-coverage semantic analysis with boxer. In J. Bos and R. Delmonte (Eds.), *Semantics in Text Processing. STEP 2008 Conference Proceedings*, Research in Computational Semantics, pp. 277–286. College Publications.

Bos, J. (2009). Towards a large-scale formal semantic lexicon for text processing. In C. Chiarcos, R. Eckart de Castilho, and M. Stede (Eds.), *From Form to Meaning: Processing Texts Automatically. Proceedings of the Biennal GSCL Conference 2009*, pp. 3–14.

Bos, J. (2014). Semantic annotation issues in parallel meaning banking. In *Proceedings of the Tenth Joint ACL-ISO Workshop on Interoperable Semantic Annotation (ISA-10)*, Reykjavik, Iceland, pp. 17–20.

Bos, J. (2015). Open-domain semantic parsing with Boxer. In B. Megyesi (Ed.), *Proceedings of the 20th Nordic Conference of Computational Linguistics (NODALIDA 2015)*, pp. 301–304.

Bos, J., S. Clark, M. Steedman, J. R. Curran, and J. Hockenmaier (2004). Wide-coverage semantic representations from a CCG parser. In *Proceedings of the 20th International Conference on Computational Linguistics (COLING 2004)*, Geneva, Switzerland, pp. 1240–1246.

Brants, T. (2000). Tnt: A statistical part-of-speech tagger. In *Proceedings of the Sixth Conference on Applied Natural Language Processing*, ANLC '00, Stroudsburg, PA, USA, pp. 224–231. Association for Computational Linguistics.

Chinchor, N. and P. Robinson (1998). Appendix e: Muc-7 named entity task definition (version 3.5). In *Seventh Message Understanding Conference (MUC-7): Proceedings of a Conference Held in Fairfax, Virginia, April 29 - May 1, 1998*.

Doddington, G., A. Mitchell, M. Przybocki, L. Ramshaw, S. Strassel, and R. Weischedel (2004, May). The automatic content extraction (ace) program tasks, data, and evaluation. In *Proceedings of the Fourth International Conference on Language Resources and Evaluation (LREC-2004)*, Lisbon, Portugal. European Language Resources Association (ELRA).

Evang, K. and J. Bos (2016). Cross-lingual learning of an open-domain semantic parser. In *Proceedings of COLING 2016, the 26th International Conference on Computational Linguistics: Technical Papers*, Osaka, Japan, pp. 579–588.

LDC (2008). *ACE (Automatic Content Extraction) English Annotation Guidelines for Events* (Version 6.6 2008.06.13 ed.).

Lewis, M. and M. Steedman (2013). Combined distributional and logical semantics. *Transactions of the Association of Computational Linguistics 1*, 179–192.

Löbner, S. (2013). *Understanding Semantics, Second Edition*. Understanding Language. Taylor & Francis.

Marcus, M. P., M. A. Marcinkiewicz, and B. Santorini (1993). Building a large annotated corpus of english: The penn treebank. *Computational Linguistics 19*(2), 313–330.

Mineshima, K., P. Martínez-Gómez, Y. Miyao, and D. Bekki (2015, September). Higher-order logical inference with compositional semantics. In *Proceedings of the 2015 Conference on Empirical Methods in Natural Language Processing*, Lisbon, Portugal, pp. 2055–2061. Association for Computational Linguistics.

Nivre, J., M.-C. de Marneffe, F. Ginter, Y. Goldberg, J. Hajic, C. D. Manning, R. McDonald, S. Petrov, S. Pyysalo, N. Silveira, R. Tsarfaty, and D. Zeman (2016, may). Universal dependencies v1: A multilingual treebank collection. In N. C. C. Chair), K. Choukri, T. Declerck, S. Goggi, M. Grobelnik, B. Maegaard, J. Mariani, H. Mazo, A. Moreno, J. Odijk, and S. Piperidis (Eds.), *Proceedings of the Tenth International Conference on Language Resources and Evaluation (LREC 2016)*, Paris, France. European Language Resources Association (ELRA).

Petrov, S., D. Das, and R. McDonald (2012, may). A universal part-of-speech tagset. In N. C. C. Chair), K. Choukri, T. Declerck, M. U. Doan, B. Maegaard, J. Mariani, A. Moreno, J. Odijk, and S. Piperidis (Eds.), *Proceedings of the Eight International Conference on Language Resources and Evaluation (LREC'12)*, Istanbul, Turkey. European Language Resources Association (ELRA).

Reddy, S., O. Täckström, M. Collins, T. Kwiatkowski, D. Das, M. Steedman, and M. Lapata (2016). Transforming Dependency Structures to Logical Forms for Semantic Parsing. *Transactions of the Association for Computational Linguistics 4*, 127–140.

Reddy, S., O. Täckström, S. Petrov, M. Steedman, and M. Lapata (2017). Universal semantic parsing. *CoRR abs/1702.03196*.

Sang, E. F. T. K. and F. D. Meulder (2003). Introduction to the conll-2003 shared task: Language-independent named entity recognition.

Santorini, B. (1990). Part-Of-Speech tagging guidelines for the Penn Treebank project (3rd revision, 2nd printing). Technical report, Department of Linguistics, University of Pennsylvania, Philadelphia, PA, USA.

Steedman, M. (2001). *The Syntactic Process*. Cambridge, Ma., USA: The MIT Press.

Sylak-Glassman (2016). The composition and use of the universal morphological feature schema (Unimorph schema). Technical report, Johns Hopkins University.

UzZaman, N., H. Llorens, L. Derczynski, J. Allen, M. Verhagen, and J. Pustejovsky (2013, June). Semeval-2013 task 1: Tempeval-3: Evaluating time expressions, events, and temporal relations. In *Second Joint Conference on Lexical and Computational Semantics (*SEM), Volume 2: Proceedings of the Seventh International Workshop on Semantic Evaluation (SemEval 2013)*, Atlanta, Georgia, USA, pp. 1–9. Association for Computational Linguistics.

Propbank Annotation of Danish Noun Frames

Eckhard Bick
Institute of Language and Communication
University of Southern Denmark
`eckhard.bick@mail.dk`

Abstract

This paper presents a frame annotation scheme for Danish nouns, with VerbNet-derived frames and semantic roles covering both frame arguments and satellites. The scheme was implemented as a new module for a Danish frame tagger and applied to a 90,000-token Danish treebank with ongoing manual revision. In addition to explicit frames, Constraint Grammar rules are used to map free semantic roles on noun dependents without pre-defined frames, using general syntactic-semantic context clues. We discuss the annotation scheme and present a statistical breakdown and linguistic evaluation of the assigned noun frames and adnominal roles in the corpus.

1   Introduction

There is a long linguistic tradition of frame and role annotation for verbal predications, rooted in verb sense classifications on the one hand (e.g. Levin 1993), and the concept of semantic roles (also called thematic or case roles, Fillmore 1968) on the other. In a frame-based framework, verb categories and semantic roles are seen as interdependent, and predications are annotated for both, usually involving both valency-bound arguments and free (adverbial) satellites of a given verb. Two crucial resources in the area are FrameNet (Baker et al. 1998, Ruppenhofer et al. 2010) and PropBank (Palmer et al. 2005). The former is more lexicographical in its conception and focuses on a one-by-one exhaustive description of individual frames, the latter offers exhaustive proposition annotation of running corpus sentences, with an eye on applications such as Machine Learning (ML).

For Danish, both a FrameNet and a frame tagger (DanGram) have been published (Bick 2011), but unlike some work on larger languages, e.g. the German Salsa corpus (Rehbein et al. 2012), these Danish tools addressed only verbal frames, largely ignoring nominal predications. The work presented here strives to resolve this problem in a three-pronged fashion, with automatic corpus annotation based on (a) systematic derivation of noun frames from verb frames, (b) lexicographical treatment of argument-carrying nouns and (c) free role-mapping rules based on semantic noun classes and syntactic triggers.

2   De-verbal noun frame derivation

Rather than define separate frames for nouns, we think that frames have a sufficient level of abstraction to work across not only syntactic, but also morphological/POS variants. We therefore use the frame inventory of the Danish FrameNet, with around 500 categories[1], as is. For verbs themselves, morphological variation covers participles and gerunds, and allows verbs to fill adjectival or adverbial slots while still retaining their arguments, with parallel constructions in Danish and English, e.g. *the new book, published by Elsevier in 2012,* where the frames arguments are distributed across the head (”book” - TH/theme and the dependents of the participle: ”Elsevier” (AG/agent) and 2012 (LOC-

---

[1]   cf. http://framenet.dk

TMP/temporal location). For noun slots, like English, Danish can use infinitive clauses (*To visit Paris without visiting the Louvre is a weird thing to do*), but inflectional nominalization of verbs (with -n: *råbe - råben* [shout]) is very rare: *Hans evige råben efter mere øl* (his constant shouting for more ale). However, Danish has two common and reasonably productive derivational morphemes, *-else* and *-(n)ing* that can be employed for nominalization. The verb's original arguments can optionally be retained and will appear in either genitive or post-nominal PP slots, with the former typically inheriting the subject role, and the latter inheriting object and adverbial roles:

1. Firmaets §AG overraskende **udfasning** /V:udfase/ af bonusordninger §PAT [the company's surprising curb on bonus schemes]

2. **fornyelse** /V:forny/ af offentlige bygninger [repair of public buildings]

3. **opsigelse** /V:opsige/ [cancellation]

As a first step to adapt the DanGram Frametagger[2] for noun frames, we therefore exploited derivational analysis to retrieve verbal frames for -else/-ing nouns where a corresponding verb form could be found by stripping the suffix. In order to increase lexical precision, we excluded nouns that had semantic-class tags[3] incompatible with actions, activities, events and processes, such as *følelse* [emotion, not "to feel"] or *forretning* [shop, not "to do business"]. Unlike English, Danish very productively uses morphological compounding (i.e. without space), and deverbal nouns can morphologically incorporate their arguments, both subjects (*kvindesvømning* [women swimming]), objects (*atomspaltning* [atom cleaving]) and adverbials (*dialysebehandling* [dialysis treatment]). For such compound nouns with a second part ending in *-else/ing*, we applied the act/event condition to both the second part and the noun as a whole (if tagged). In addition, compounds with semantic class differences between whole and second part were deemed unsafe.

In loan words, Danish also allows the Latin equivalent of its native -else/-ing derivation, where *-ere* verbs correspond to *-ion/-ation* nouns: *adoptere - adoption, approksimere - approksimation*. Not least in the scientific domain, these words constitute a sizeable section of the lexicon, and many *-ere* verbs have been moved into the common domain, taking *-else/-ing* suffixes and allowing productive prefixation, e.g. *afnazificere/-ing* ["denazify"], *detailregulere/-ing* ["regulate in detail"]. While adding the -ere/-ation derivation to the frametagger did improve coverage, there is a substantical risk of gaps due to irregular stemming, e.g. the phonetically motivated c/k shift in *kvalificere - kvalifikation* [qualify - qualification], making the method less automatic and more dependent on derivational lexicon entries.

3   Lexicon scheme for nominal frames

Apart from proofreading automatic derivational analysis and entering verb stems for irregular *-ation* nouns, we also introduced the option of entering complete nominal frames into the lexicon from scratch. This solution is obviously much more labour-intensive, but allows the treatment of argument-taking nouns without any de-verbal morphological clue.

Each noun frame entry (FN) lists first the corresponding verb frame and then a slash-separated list of possible semantic role arguments[4] (marked §) with their slot filler conditions (1-5). We distinguish between primary conditions and secondary, optional subconditions (present in 1-3). Primary conditions are placed before the role concerned, secondary condition after it. The former are syntactic slot conditions (left/genitive position, self and bound preposition lexeme), the latter are categorial

---

[2]   https://visl.sdu.dk/visl/da/parsing/automatic/parse.php

[3]   DanGram uses - and tags - a shallow ontology of around 200 so-called semantic prototypes, among them <act> [+CONTROL,+PERFECTIVE, <activity> [+CONTR,-PERF], <event> [-CONTR,+PERF] or <process> [-CONTR,-PERF]

[4]   The Danish FrameNet foresees about 35 argument-capable roles and an additional 15 satellite roles

conditions concerning semantic class. Form conditions such as 'icl' (non-finite clause) or 'fcl' (finite clause) can be used both instead of a preposition condition or as a subcondition on the argument of the preposition (4).

1. hjælp - FN:**help**/til§BEN'all/til§FIN'act/fra§AG [help for/with]

2. krav - FN:**demand**/p§TH/om§ACT/til§REC'H/til§TP'all [demand for/to]

3. betaling - FN:**pay**/af§REC'H/af§CAU'act/for§CAU/til§REC/med§INS [payment to/for]

4. hensyn - FN:**adjust**/til§BEN [consideration]

5. ret - FN:**allow**/til§ASS/icl§ACT [a right to]

We created a new module for the DanGram Framtagger identifying nominal frames by trying to match conditions on argument slots and then assigning the corresponding semantic roles and tagging instantiated verb frames on the noun in question. If an NP has a human genitive dependent, agent role (§AG) will be used as a fall-back if no genitive condition with another role is found the lexical frame entries for the noun itself or, if relevant, its derivational verbal base. A special case of deverbal nouns are cases, where the noun denotes not the predicating core of the frame (as in -*else/ing*), but rather one of the arguments, usually the subject. Even without a realized predicator, such nouns still evoke their frame and will take genitive or preposition arguments representing other roles in the frame, as in the *hosting*-frame for *vært*, where the word itself is the agent (self§AG), while events and beneficiaries can be added as genitive [gen] or with the preposition for:

1. vært - FN:socializeO/self§AG/for,gen§BEN'H/for,gen§EV'occ [host for/to sb/an event]

4   Free role mapping

As for verbs, some PP dependents of nouns are not valency-bound by their head (arguments), but simple free satellites (adjuncts), with a low selection preference for a specific noun or frame. Thus, the majority of nouns can take a location complement, and most nouns with a deverbal component allow time complements. In these cases, a semantic role can be assigned to the adjunct complement, but no specific frame will be triggered by doing so, leaving the head noun untagged. Consider the following examples from our corpus, all of which contain an §EXT (extension) role complement mediated by the preposition *på*:

1. *nedskæringer på 750 millioner* [cuts amounting to 750 million] - frame: decrease

2. *håndteringsbeløb* på 50 kroner [a handling fee of 50 crowns] - compound, frame: cost

3. *fedtindhold* på 0,5% [a fat content of 0.5%]

4. *ikke så interessant efter 11 bind på 2 timer* [not so interesting after 11 volumes in 2 hours] - implied frame: read

These cases exhibit a cline from strongest-bound complement (1) to weakest-bound complement (4). Thus, in (1) the *decrease*-frame is recoverable from a verbal template *skære ned på*, which inherently implies a degree/extension of "cutting down". In (2), no verb is recoverable, but compound analysis reveals a second part noun *beløb* [amount], that has a frame listed in the lexicon, and a semantic class implying measurability. The second part of the compound (3), on the other hand (*indhold* [content]), evokes the *containing* frame, that only loosely implies degree, and only in connection with the first part (*fedt* [fat]). In (4), finally, the real predication (frame *read*) is elliptic, and only implied by a potential reading object (*bind* [volumes]). For (1) and (2), our corpus annotation task can rely on lexicon information, once the frame-carrying lexeme is identified. For (3) and (4), however, role mapping has to be performed without identifying a frame first. For this, we use Constraint Grammar mapping rules relying on the semantic class of the role carrier and its head preposition. Even where no semantic class is available, the degree/extension role can often be inferred from modifiers (numbers) or even hinted at by inflexion (plural), as long as the trigger-preposition (*på*) is present and linked to a noun.

The rule below maps the EXT role (extension) on nouns of class <unit>[5], if they have the right preposition as parent (p) and a noun LINKed as grandparent, and if the immediate left context (-1) is either a numeral (NUM) or a fraction word (NUM-FRACT) preceded (-1) by a number or the article "en".

MAP (§EXT) TARGET N-UNIT (p ("på" PRP) LINK p N)
    ((-1 NUM) OR (-1 NUM-FRACT LINK -1 NUM OR ("en"))) ;

5   Results

Our noun frame scheme and annotator module were developed as part of a larger Propbank project for Danish, and applied to a 87,000-token treebank automatically pre-annotated with morphosyntactic tags, (ambiguous) semantic class potential for nouns and dependency links. The corpus is based on the larger, sentence-randomized Korpus2010 (Asmussen 2015) and covers a variety of both printed, electronically published and described sources, among them national newspapers (15%) and magazines (58%), blogs (8.5%), chat fora (2.5%), parliamentary speeches (10.5%) and various Internet sources (6%), such as a recipe website. While the Propbank is subject to revision at all levels of annotation, and will contain full mark-up for all verbal frames, we are here only concerned with noun frames and their distribution.

Our method tagged 9.6% (1342) of the about 15,000 nouns in the corpus as frame carriers, and identified 4477 ad-nominal roles. Of these, about 30% were linked to (and identified through) a noun frame, while the remaining 70% were assigned by free mapping rules. About half (2300) of the adnominal role carriers were themselves nouns, 26% were clauses (especially relative clauses), and 13% names. Predictably, we found a clear tendency for some roles to be frame-projected arguments (ACT, RES, CAU, TH, PAT) while others were mostly identified by free mapping rules (ATR, ID, LOC, ORI, EXT).

Tag	role	% all	% frame arg
ATR	attribute	27.11	4.9
LOC	location	14.2	7.2
TH	theme	9.0	67.9
TP	topic	7.0	38.8
ID	identity	6.4	6.3
PAT	patient	4.0	65.5
AG	agent	3.3	29.5
BEN	beneficiary	3.0	48.1
ORI	origin	2.9	23.1
FIN	purpose	2.7	63.4
HOL	whole	2.1	77.4
ACT	action	2.1	90.3
CAU	cause	2.0	69.7
EXT	extension	1.9	26.5
RES	result	1.5	80.9

Table 1: Semantic role distribution

---

[5]   Note that the rule uses not the /unit/ tag itself, but a set, N-UNIT, which has been defined elsewhere in the grammar and allows the inclusion of other classes that unit itself, such as currency or containers, or even the addition of individual words, like the English-inspired fod [foot], which is not an ordinary Danish unit

The identified noun frames covered 741 different lexemes, amounting to a type/token ratio of about 1:2, indicating a higher lexeme spread than for verbs (type/token ratio of 1:8), probably due to the fact that both frequent and infrequent verbs are frame carriers, while many frequent nouns are not. All in all, 255 different frames were found, covering about half the frame inventory in the Danish FrameNet. Table 2 lists the most frequent noun frames, and for each of them, the three most frequent lexeme realisation. As can be seen, some frames are dominated by a single lexeme, while others have a more even lexeme spread. *be_part* and *run_obj* are examples of frames, where the carrier token often is itself a frame participant (i.e. deserving a role tag in its own frame), but most carrier words (and not only the 50% or so of verb-derived *-else/ing* words) function as predicators for their frame and can only carry role tags for a higher-level, containing frame.

Frame	n	lexemes
be_part	57	del 44, halvdel 5, led 2
investigate	40	undersøgelse 30, forskning 3, analyse 2
run_obj	39	formand 12, leder 5, forvaltning 4
future_having	35	mulighed 32, udbud 2, anvisning 1
decide	31	bestemmelse 12,regel 8,afgørelse 6
discuss	30	debat 9, samtale 4, forhandling 4
relate	29	forhold 9, spørgsmål 6, relation 5
cause	28	årsag 7, grund 6, konsekvens 5
adjust	26	regulering 9,omstilling 7,hensyn 5
explain	25	forklaring 8, eksempel 7, redegørelse 6
create	24	udvikling 9, udmøntning 7, fremstilling 3
allow	24	ret 7, adgang 5, godkendelse 3
tell	23	oplysning 11, historie 4, meddelelse 2
assess	22	vurdering 16, beregning 3
pay	20	råd 4, udgift 3, ressource 3
help	19	grundlag 9, støtte 3, hjælp 3

Table 2: Frame distribution

Since manual revision of the noun frames is work in progress, it is difficult to say how many frames we missed, but inspection indicates that 20% of the ad-nominal roles assigned by free mapping were in fact arguments rather than satellites,warranting a frame tag on their head noun. Given that certain roles are more likely to be arguments than others, these could be flagged for prioritized inspection, if linked to a frameless head. Another potential indicator for false-negatives are non-transparent nouns (i.e. excluding Danish equivalents of "kind [of]", "lot [of]", "handful" etc.) that did not receive any role-tag. A low figure of 5% for this category indicates a good coverage for our method, not least because every second of such nouns is a simple genitive modifying a non-deverbal noun, with a very low chance of being a role carrier.

6   Conclusions and outlook

We have shown how a combined method of verbo-nominal derivation, lexical argument-slotfiller information and ontology-based role mapping rules can be used to extend annotation of a Danish Propbank from verbal to nominal frames with a reasonable coverage. Our automatic annotation allows lexeme- and category-based statistics amenable to linguistic information and conducive to an informed prioritization of future manual revision work. Thus, a first layer of noun frame annotation will be available in the upcoming 2017 release of the Danish Propbank.

References

Asmussen, Jørg. 2015. *Corpus Resources & Documentation*. Det Danske Sprog- og Litteraturselskab, http://korpus.dsl.dk

Bick, Eckhard. 2011. A FrameNet for Danish. In: *Proceedings of NODALIDA 2011*, May 11-13, Riga, Latvia. NEALT Proceedings Series, Vol. 11, pp. 34-41. Tartu: Tartu University Library.

Baker, Collin F. Baker; J. Fillmore; J. Charles; John B. Lowe. 1998. The Berkeley FrameNet project. In *Proceedings of the COLING-ACL*. Montreal, Canada

Fillmore, Charles J. 1968. The case for case. In Bach & Harms (Ed.): *Universals in Linguistic Theory*. New York: Holt, Rinehart, and Winston. 1-88.

Palmer, Martha; Dan Gildea; Paul Kingsbury. 2005. The Proposition Bank: An Annotated Corpus of Semantic Roles. *Computational Linguistics, 31:1.*, pp. 71-105, March, 2005.

Rehbein, Ines; Josef Ruppenhofer; Caroline Sporleder; Manfred Pinkal. 2012. Adding Nominal Spice to SALSA - Frame-Semantic Annotation of German Nouns and Verbs. *Proceedings of KONVENS 2012*, Vienna. pp. 89-97.

Ruppenhofer, Josef; Michael Ellsworth; Miriam R. L. Petruck; Christopher R. Johnson; Jan Scheffczyk. 2010. *FrameNet II: Extended Theory and Practice*. http://framenet.icsi.berkeley.edu/

Deep Learning of Binary and Gradient Judgements for Semantic Paraphrase

Yuri Bizzoni
University of Gothenburg
yuri.bizzoni@gu.se

Shalom Lappin
University of Gothenburg
shalom.lappin@gu.se

Abstract

We treat paraphrase identification as an ordering task. We construct a corpus of 250 sets of five sentences, with each set containing a reference sentence and four paraphrase candidates, which are annotated on a scale of 1 to 5 for paraphrase proximity. We partition this corpus into 1000 pairs of sentences in which the first is the reference sentence and the second is a paraphrase candidate. We then train a DNN encoder for sentence pair inputs. It consists of parallel CNNs that feed parallel LSTM RNNs, followed by fully connected NNs, and finally a dense merging layer that produces a single output. We test it for both binary and graded predictions. The latter are generated as a by-product of training the former (the binary classifier). It reaches 70% accuracy on the binary classification task. It achieves a Pearson correlation of .59-.61 with the annotated gold standard for the gradient ranking candidate sets.

1 Introduction

Paraphrase identification is an area of research with a long history. Approaches to the task can be divided into supervised methods, such as (Madnani et al., 2012), currently the most commonly used, and unsupervised techniques (Socher et al., 2011).

While many approaches of both types use carefully selected features to determine similarity, such as string edit distance (Dolan et al., 2004)) or longest common subsequence (Fernando and Stevenson, 2008), several recent supervised approaches apply Neural Networks to the task (Filice et al., 2015; He et al., 2015), often linking it to the related issue of semantic similarity (Tai et al., 2015; Yin and Schütze, 2015).

Traditionally, paraphrase detection has been formulated as a binary problem. Corpora employed in this work contain pairs of sentences labeled as *paraphrase* or *non-paraphrase*. The most representative of these corpora, such as the Microsoft Paraphrase Corpus (Dolan et al., 2004), conform to this paradigm.

This approach is different from the one adopted in semantic similarity datasets, where a pair of words or sentences is labeled on a gradient classification system. In some cases, semantic similarity tasks overlap with paraphrase detection, as in Xu et al. (2015) and in Agirre et al. (2016). Xu et al. (2015) is one of the first works that tries to connect paraphrase identification with semantic similarity. They define a task where the system generates both a binary judgment and a gradient score for sentences pairs.

We present a new dataset for paraphrase identification which is built on two main ideas: (i) Paraphrase recognition is a gradient classification task. (ii) Paraphrase recognition is an ordering problem, where *sets of sentences* are ranked by similarity with respect to a reference sentence.

While the first assumption is shared by some of the work we have cited here, our corpus is, to the best of our knowledge, the first one constructed on the basis of the second claim.

We believe that annotating sets of sentences for similarity with respect to a reference sentence can help with both the learning and the testing processes in paraphrase identification.

We use this corpus to test a neural network architecture formed by a combination of Convolutional Neural Networks (CNNs) and Long Short Term Memory Recurrent Neural Networks (LSTM RNNs). We test this model on two classification problems: (i) binary paraphrase classification, and (ii) paraphrase ranking. We show that our system can achieve a significant correlation to human paraphrase judgments on the ranking task as a by-product of supervised binary learning.

2   A New Type of Corpus for Paraphrase Recognition

At this stage our corpus is formed of 250 sets of five sentences. In each set, the first sentence is the reference sentence, while the remaining four sentences are labeled on a 1-5 scale, based on their degree of paraphrase similarity with respect to the reference sentence. This is on analogy with the annotation frame used for SemEval Semantic Similarity tasks (Agirre et al., 2016). Every group of 5 sentences illustrates (possibly different) graduated degrees of paraphrasehood relative to the reference sentence. Broadly, our labels represent the following categories: (1) Two sentences are completely unrelated. (2) Two sentences are semantically related, but they are not paraphrases. (3) Two sentences are weak paraphrases. (4) Two sentences are strong paraphrases. (5) Two sentences are (type) identical.

The following example illustrates these ranking labels.

- Ref. sent: *A woman feeds a cat*

    - A woman kicks a cat. *Score: 2*
    - A person feeds an animal *Score: 3*
    - A woman is feeding a cat. *Score: 4*
    - A woman feeds a cat . *Score: 5*

- Ref. sent: *I have a black hat*

    - Larry teaches plants to grow. *Score: 1*
    - I have a red hat . *Score: 2*
    - My hat is night black ; pitch black. *Score: 3*
    - My hat's color is black. *Score: 4*

While the extremes of our scale (1 and 5) are relatively rare in our corpus, we focus on the intermediate cases of paraphrase, from non-paraphrases with some semantic similarity (2) to non type-identical strong paraphrases (4).

We believe that this annotation scheme is particularly useful. While it sustains graded semantic similarity labels, it also provides sets of semantically related elements, each one of which can be scored or ordered independently from the others. Therefore, the reference sentence can be tested separately for each sentence in the set in a binary classification task. In the test phase, this annotation schema allows us to observe how a system represents the similarity between two sentences by taking the scores of two candidates as points of relative proximity to the reference sentence.

Our examples above indicate that a binary classification can be misleading because it conceals the different levels of similarity between competing candidates.

We find instead that framing paraphrase recognition as an ordering problem allows a more flexible evaluation of a model. It permits us to evaluate the relative proximity of several candidate paraphrases to the reference sentence independently of the particular paraphrase score that the model assigns to each candidate in the set.

For example, the sentence *A person feeds an animal* can be considered to be a loose paraphrase of the sentence **A woman feeds a cat**, or alternatively, as a semantically related non-paraphrase. Which of these conclusions we adopt depends on our decision concerning how much content sentences need to share in order to be classified as paraphrases. By contrast, it would be far fetched to suggest that *A woman kicks a cat* is a better or even equally strong paraphrase for **A woman feeds a cat**. Similarly, the sentences **I have a black hat** and *My hat is night black* can be considered to be loose paraphrases, or semantically related non-paraphrases. But *I have a red hat* cannot plausibly be taken as more similar in meaning to **I have a black hat** than *My hat is night black*.

The core of this dataset was built from various parts of the Brown Corpus (Francis and Kucera, 1979), mainly from the news and narrative sections. For each sentence, we introduced raw paraphrases by round trip machine translation from English through Swedish, German, Spanish and Japanese, back to English. This process yielded paraphrases, looser relations of semantic relatedness, and non-paraphrases.

One of the authors then manually annotated each set of five sentences and corrected grammatical infelicities. We also introduced more interesting syntactic and semantic variation. For example we manually constructed many cases of negation and passive/active mood switch. This allows us to test paraphrase over a wider range of syntactic and lexical semantic constructions. Similar manually generated elements were often substituted as candidate paraphrases to round-trip generated candidates judged to be of little interest for the task. So, for example, we frequently had several strong paraphrases produced by round-trip translation, resulting in groups of three or four strong candidates for a reference sentence, and we replaced several of these with our own alternatives.

A number of shorter examples produced by the authors were also added to the corpus. These are intended to test the performance of the system for specific semantic relations, such as antinomy (*I have a new car – I have an old car*), expansion (*His car is red – His car has a characteristic red colour*) and subject–object permutation (*A white blanket covered her mouth – Her mouth covered a white blanket*).

One of the authors assigned the 1-5 ratings for each sentence in a reference set. We naturally regard this as a "weak" point in our dataset. As we discuss in the Conclusion, we intend to use crowd sourcing to obtain more broadly based and reliable speaker annotation for our examples.

Our corpus has the advantage of being suitable for both training a binary classifier and developing a model to predict gradient paraphrase judgments. For the former, we simply consider every score over a given gradient threshold label as 1, and scores below that threshold as 0. For gradient classification we use all the scoring labels to test the correlation between a system's ordering performance and our human judgments. We will show how, once a model has been trained for a binary detection task, we can check its performance on the gradient ordering task.

3   A DNN for Paraphrase Classification

For classification and gradient judgment prediction we constructed a deep neural network. Its architecture consists of three main components:

1. Two encoders that learn the representation of two sentences separately

2. A unified layer that merges the output of the encoders

3. A final set of fully connected layers that work on the merged representation of the two sentences to generate a judgment.

The encoder for each pair of sentences taken as input is composed of two parallel Convolutional Neural Networks and LSTM RNNs, feeding two sequenced fully connected layers.

The first layer of our encoders is a CNN with 50 filters of length 5. CNNs have been successfully applied to problems in computational semantics, such as text classification and sentiment analysis (Lai et al., 2015), as well as to paraphrase recognition (Socher et al., 2011). In this part of our model, the encoder learns a more compact representation of the sentence, with reduced vector space dimensions and features. This permits the NN to focus on the information most relevant to paraphrase identification.

We use an "Atrous" Convolutional Neural Network (Giusti et al., 2013; Chen et al., 2016). An "Atrous" CNN is a modified form of Convolutional Network designed to reduce the risk of losing important information in max pooling. In the case of a standard CNN, max pooling will perform a reduction of the output of the convolutional layer, selecting only some information contained in it. In the case of image processing, for example, a 2x2 max pooling on the so-called "map" returned by the convolutional layer will create a smaller map that does not contain information from the entire original map, but only from a specific region of such map, or mirroring a specific pattern in the original image: for example, all the patches whose upper left corner lies on even coordinates on the map (Giusti et al., 2013). This way of processing information can undermine the results when complex inputs are involved. An Atrous network fragments the map returned by the max pooling layer, so that each fragment contains information independent of the other fragments, and each reduced map contains information from all the patches of the input. This is a good strategy for speeding up processing time by avoiding redundant computation.

The output of each CNN is passed through a max pooling layer to an LSTM RNN. Since the CNN and the max pooling layer perform discriminative reduction of the input dimensionality, we can run a large LSTM RNN model (50 smart cells) without substantial computational cost. In this phase of processing, the vector dimensions of the sentence representation is further reduced, with relevant information (hopefully) conserved and highlighted, particularly for the sequential structure of the data. Each encoder is completed by two successive fully connected layers of dimensions 50 and 300, respectively, that produces a vector representation for an input sentence in the pair. The first one has a .5 dropout rate.

The 300 dimensional outputs of the two encoders are then passed to a layer that merges them into a single vector. We found that simple vector concatenation was the best option for performing this merge. To measure the similarity of two sequences our model only makes use of the information contained in the merged version of the encoders' output. We did not use a device in the merging phase to assess similarity between two sequences. The merging layer feeds the concatenated input to a series of five fully connected layers. The last layer applies a sigmoid function to produce the classifier judgment. While the sigmoid function performs well for binary classification, it returns a gradient over its input, thus generating an ordering of values for the ranking task.

These three kinds of Neural Network capture information in different ways. They can be combined to achieve a better global representation of sentence input. Specifically, while a CNN can reduce the spectral variance of input, an LSTM RNN is designed to model its sequential dimension over time. The CNN manages to reduce the input's dimensionality while keeping the ordering information of the original sentence. This information will then be processed by the LSTM RNN, which is particularly well suited for handling words sequenced through time.

Also, an LSTM RNN's performance can be strongly improved by providing it with better features (Pascanu et al., 2014). In our case this is accomplished by the CNN. The densely connected layers create clearer, more separable final vector representations of the data. To encode the original sentences we used Word2Vec embeddings pre-trained on Google News (Mikolov et al., 2013).

Table 1 gives the binary accuracy, and ranked ordering Pearson correlation performance of our model, over 10 fold validation, after 200 epochs.

Table 2 presents accuracy and F1 for different versions of our model. The baseline is the model's performance without any training. We compute the baseline by relying solely on the pre-loaded Word2Vec lexical embedding content of the words' distributional vectors to obtain a semantic similarity judgment. No learning from our corpus annotation is involved. The sentence's vectors are still reduced to a single vector through the LSTM layer, but this is done without corpus based supervision or training.

4   Binary Classification Task

To use our corpus for a binary classification task we map each set of five sentences into a series of pairs, where the first element is the reference sentence and the second element is one of the four remaining sentences. Gradient labels are then replaced by binary ones. We consider all labels higher than 2 as positive judgments (Paraphrase) and all labels equal to or lower than 2 as negative judgments (Non-Paraphrase). We train our model with these labels for a binary classification task.

We split our corpus into a training and a test set, making sure that the two sets contained completely distinct reference-candidate pairs. While a small minority of reference sentences is the same in train and test, their candidate paraphrases are always different.

We ran the training phase for 200 epochs, keeping the order of the input fixed (due to curriculum learning issues). Training on 761 pairs of sentences and testing on 239 pairs, we reached an average

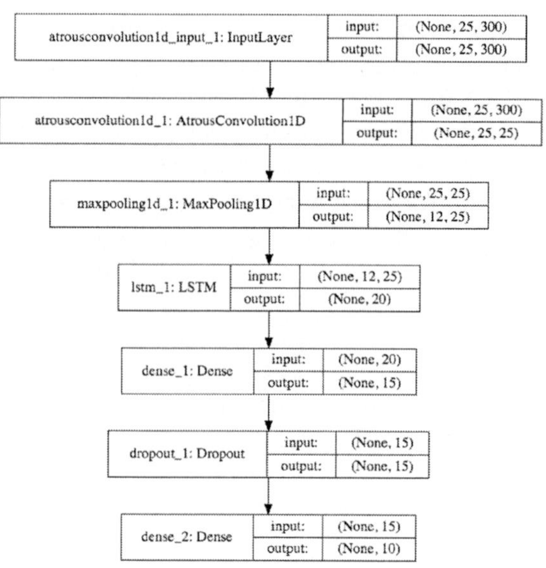

Figure 1: Example of an encoder. A padded input of fixed length is passed to a CNN, a max pooling layer, a single LSTM RNN, and finally two fully connected layers separated by a dropout layer of 0.5. The input's and output's shape is indicated in brackets for each layer

accuracy of 70.0 over 10 fold cross-validation. We see that our architecture learned to recognize different semantic and syntactic phenomena with a promising level of accuracy, although it is not state of the art in paraphrase recognition for systems trained on large corpora, such as the Microsoft Paraphrase Corpus (Ji and Eisenstein, 2013). [1]

A small corpus may cause instability in results. Interestingly, we found that our DNN is able to generalize consistently on the following patterns:

- **Negation**. This is a rich man's world – This is not a rich man's world. *Non-Paraphrase*;

- **Subject–Object permutation**. The man follows the wolf – The wolf follows the man. *Non-Paraphrase*;

- **Active–Passive relation**. A white blanket covered her mouth – Her mouth was covered with a white blanket. *Paraphrase*;

- **Various cases of loose paraphrase** The man follows the wolf – The person follows the animal. *Paraphrase*.

However, our model had trouble with several others cases, some due to its lack of relevant world knowledge, and others because of its limited capacity for semantically driven inference. These include:

- **Time expressions**. It was morning – It was noon. *Non-Paraphrase*;

- **Some cases of antinomy**. This is not good – This is bad. *Paraphrase*;

- **Space expressions**. Some years ago I was going to school when I met a man – Some years ago I was going to church when I met a man. *Non-paraphrase*.

Predictably, the model has difficulty in learning a pattern or a phrase when it is under represented in the training data. In some cases, the effect of data scarcity can be observed in an "overfit weighting" of specific words. We believe that these idiosyncrasies can be overcome through training on a larger set.

---

[1]This is to be expected, given the specific nature of the task and the small dimensions of our dataset. It is also worth noting that, while sentences in the Microsoft Paraphrase Corpus are generally longer, our corpus contains a much larger variety of syntactic and semantic patterns, including "more difficult" cases, like passive-active change and negation.

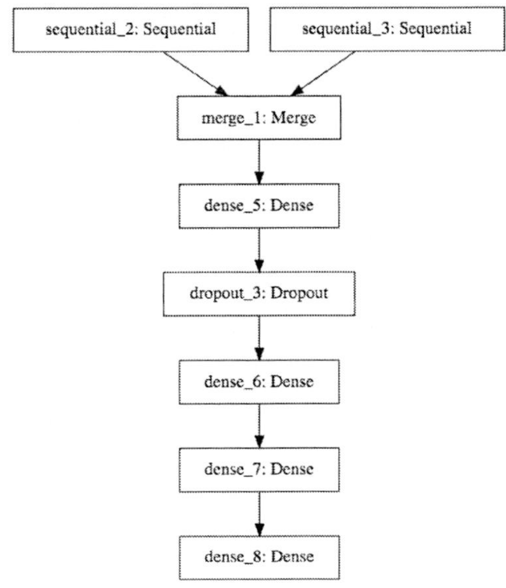

Figure 2: A more abstract representation of our full model. Sequential 2 and sequential 3 are encoders of the kind specified in Figure 1. Their outputs are concatenated in merge 1 and fed to a series of dense layers. Dropout 3 has a rate of 0.2

We observe that, on occasion, the model's errors are in the gray area between clear paraphrase and clear non-paraphrase. Here the correctness of a label is not obvious. For example, the pair *I am so sleepy I can barely stand – I am sleep deprived* can be considered to be a loose paraphrase pair, or they can be taken as an instance of non-paraphrase.

5   Paraphrase Ordering Task

Once the DNN has learned representations for binary classification, we can use it to rank the sentences of the test set in order of paraphrase proximity. We apply the sigmoid value distribution for the candidate sentences in a set of five (the reference and four candidates) to determine the ranking. To do this we use the original structure of our dataset, composed of sets of five sentences.

First, we attribute a similarity score to all pairs of sentences (reference sentence and candidate paraphrase) in a set. This is the similarity score learned in the binary task, which is determined by the sigmoid function applied on the output of our DNN. In this case, we don't "round" the judgment, as we are not seeking a 0,1 output.

We compute the average Pearson correlation on all sets of the test corpus to check the extent to which the ranking that our algorithm produces matches our gradient annotation. We found comparable and meaningful correlations between our ranking and the ordering that our model predicts. These correlations indicate that our model achieves an encouraging level of accuracy in predicting our gradient annotations for the candidate sentences in a set, using the weights learned for a binary classification task.

This task differs from the binary classification task in several important respects. In one way, it is easier. A non-paraphrase can be misjudged as a paraphrase and still fall in the right order within a ranking. In another sense, it is more difficult. Strict paraphrases, loose paraphrases, and semantically similar non-paraphrases have to be ordered in accord with human judgment patterns, which is a more complex task than simple binary classification.

Our gradient ranking system allows us to have a more nuanced view concerning some of the issues that arise in pairwise paraphrase labeling that we pointed out at the end of the previous section.

The existence of a correlation between our annotation ordering and our model's predictions is a by-product of supervised binary learning. Since we are re-using the representations learned for the binary

k	Accuracy		k	Pearson
1	70.10		1	.51
2	67.01		2	.63
3	79.38		3	.59
4	73.20		4	.62
5	67.01		5	.61
6	72.92		6	.72
7	66.67		7	.59
8	75.79		8	.67
9	64.21		9	.54
10	73.68		10	.67

Table 1: Accuracy (*on the binary task*) and Pearson Correlation (*on the ordering task*) Over Ten Fold Validation Testing after 200 epochs. The accuracy reported in the paper is an average over these results.

Model	Accuracy	F1
Baseline (without training)	42.1	59.3
Our model	**78.0**	74.6
Encoders without LSTM	65.9	68.9
Encoders without ACNN	69.5	50.8
Just one layer after concatenation	73.0	70.0
Using CNN instead of ACNN	76.6	76.0
ACNN with 10 filters	70.4	68.1
LSTM with 10 filters	69.0	71.3
Without dropouts	72.6	71.0
Merging via multiplication	72.6	71.1
Encoders without dense layers	72.2	71.7

Table 2: Accuracy for different versions of the model after 200 epochs. Each model ran on our standard train and test data, *without* our performing cross-validation.

task in order to perform a new task, we consider it a form of transfer learning from a supervised binary context (assigning a 0/1 value to a pair of sentences) to an unsupervised ordering problem (ranking a set of sentences). In this case, our corpus allowed us to perform double transfer learning. First, we use word embeddings trained to maximize single words' contextual similarity, in order to train on a supervised binary paraphrase dataset. Then, we use the representations acquired in this way to perform an ordering task for which the DNN has not been trained.

The fact that ranked correlations are sustained through binary paraphrase classification is not an obvious result. A model trained on {0,1} labels could "polarize" its scores to the point where no meaningful ordering would be available. Had this happened, a good performance in a binary task would actually conceal the loss of important semantic information. Xu et al. (2015), discussing the relation of paraphrase identification to the recognition of semantic similarity, observe that there is no necessary connection between binary classification and prediction of gradient labels, and that an increase in one can even produce a loss in the other.

6 Conclusions and Future Work

We present a new kind of corpus to evaluate paraphrase identification and we construct a novel type of DNN architecture for a set of paraphrase classification tasks. We show that our model learns an effective representation of sentences for such paraphrase tasks.

Our corpus' design is based on the assumption that paraphrase ranking is a useful way to approach the paraphrase identification problem. We show how this kind of corpus can be used for supervised learning of binary classification, for multi-class classification, and for gradient judgment prediction.

The neural network architecture that we propose encodes each sentence in a low dimensional representation, combining a CNN, an LSTM RNN, and two densely connected neural layers. The two output representations of the encoders are then merged through concatenation, and fed to a series of densely connected layers.

While binary classification is directly learned in the training phase, our model also yields a robust correlation to human judgments in the ordering task through the softmax sigmoid distributions generated for binary classification. While the model learns to classify two sentences as paraphrases or non-paraphrases, it retains enough information to assign gradient values to members of sets of sentences in a way that correlates significantly with our annotation.

Our model doesn't use any "alignment" of the data. The encoders' representations are simply concatenated. This gives our DNN considerable flexibility in modeling patterns such as subject–object permutation (*The man follows the wolf – The wolf follows the man*), and sentence expansions (*A man eats the food – There is a man and he eats the food*). It can also create complications where a simple alignment of two sentences might suffice to identify a similarity. We will experiment with the addition of some form of alignment to our model in future work.

We will be experimenting with crowd sourcing to obtain more reliable annotation of our corpus. We will also be expanding the corpus to encompass a wider range of syntactic and semantic patterns, and to include a significantly larger number of reference + candidate sets. Finally, we will be looking at alternative DNN architectures, particularly those with attentional components, in an effort to improve the performance of our models for both the binary classification and gradient judgment prediction tasks.

7   Acknowledgments

We are grateful to three anonymous reviewers for helpful comments and suggestions on an earlier draft of this paper. The research reported in this paper was supported by a grant from the Swedish Research Council for the establishment of the Centre for Linguistic Theory and Studies in Probability (CLASP) at the University of Gothenburg. We would also like to thank our colleagues at CLASP at the University of Gothenburg for useful discussion of many of the ideas presented here. We are solely responsible for any errors which may remain in this paper.

References

Agirre, E., C. Banea, D. M. Cer, M. T. Diab, A. Gonzalez-Agirre, R. Mihalcea, G. Rigau, and J. Wiebe (2016). Semeval-2016 task 1: Semantic textual similarity, monolingual and cross-lingual evaluation. In *Proceedings of the 10th International Workshop on Semantic Evaluation, SemEval@NAACL-HLT 2016, San Diego, CA, USA, June 16-17, 2016*, pp. 497–511.

Chen, L., G. Papandreou, I. Kokkinos, K. Murphy, and A. L. Yuille (2016). Deeplab: Semantic image segmentation with deep convolutional nets, atrous convolution, and fully connected crfs. *CoRR abs/1606.00915*.

Dolan, B., C. Quirk, and C. Brockett (2004). Unsupervised construction of large paraphrase corpora: Exploiting massively parallel news sources. In *Proceedings of the 20th International Conference on Computational Linguistics*, COLING '04, Stroudsburg, PA, USA. Association for Computational Linguistics.

Fernando, S. and M. Stevenson (2008). A semantic similarity approach to paraphrase detection. *Computational Linguistics UK (CLUK 2008) 11th Annual Research Colloqium*.

Filice, S., G. Da San Martino, and A. Moschitti (2015). *Structural representations for learning relations between pairs of texts*, Volume 1, pp. 1003–1013. Association for Computational Linguistics (ACL).

Francis, W. N. and H. Kucera (1979). Brown corpus manual. Technical report, Department of Linguistics, Brown University, Providence, Rhode Island, US.

Giusti, A., D. C. Ciresan, J. Masci, L. M. Gambardella, and J. Schmidhuber (2013). Fast image scanning with deep max-pooling convolutional neural networks. In *Image Processing (ICIP), 2013 20th IEEE International Conference on*, pp. 4034–4038. IEEE.

He, H., K. Gimpel, and J. Lin (2015, September). Multi-perspective sentence similarity modeling with convolutional neural networks. In *Proceedings of the 2015 Conference on Empirical Methods in Natural Language Processing*, Lisbon, Portugal, pp. 1576–1586. Association for Computational Linguistics.

Ji, Y. and J. Eisenstein (2013). Discriminative improvements to distributional sentence similarity. In *In EMNLP*, pp. 891–896.

Lai, S., L. Xu, K. Liu, and J. Zhao (2015). Recurrent convolutional neural networks for text classification. In *Proceedings of the Twenty-Ninth AAAI Conference on Artificial Intelligence*, AAAI'15, pp. 2267–2273. AAAI Press.

Madnani, N., J. Tetreault, and M. Chodorow (2012). Re-examining machine translation metrics for paraphrase identification. In *Proceedings of the 2012 Conference of the North American Chapter of the Association for Computational Linguistics: Human Language Technologies*, NAACL HLT '12, Stroudsburg, PA, USA, pp. 182–190. Association for Computational Linguistics.

Mikolov, T., I. Sutskever, K. Chen, G. S. Corrado, and J. Dean (2013). Distributed representations of words and phrases and their compositionality. In C. J. C. Burges, L. Bottou, M. Welling, Z. Ghahramani, and K. Q. Weinberger (Eds.), *Advances in Neural Information Processing Systems 26*, pp. 3111–3119. Curran Associates, Inc.

Pascanu, R., C. Gulcehre, K. Cho, and Y. Bengio (2014). *How to construct deep recurrent neural networks*.

Socher, R., E. H. Huang, J. Pennington, A. Y. Ng, and C. D. Manning+ (2011). Dynamic Pooling and Unfolding Recursive Autoencoders for Paraphrase Detection. In *Advances in Neural Information Processing Systems 24*.

Tai, K. S., R. Socher, and C. D. Manning (2015). Improved semantic representations from tree-structured long short-term memory networks. *CoRR abs/1503.00075*.

Xu, W., C. Callison-Burch, and B. Dolan (2015, June). Semeval-2015 task 1: Paraphrase and semantic similarity in twitter (pit). In *Proceedings of the 9th International Workshop on Semantic Evaluation (SemEval 2015)*, Denver, Colorado, pp. 1–11. Association for Computational Linguistics.

Yin, W. and H. Schütze (2015). Convolutional neural network for paraphrase identification. In *NAACL HLT 2015, The 2015 Conference of the North American Chapter of the Association for Computational Linguistics: Human Language Technologies, Denver, Colorado, USA, May 31 - June 5, 2015*, pp. 901–911.

Living a discrete life in a continuous world:
Reference in cross-modal entity tracking

Gemma Boleda[1] Sebastian Padó[2] Nghia The Pham[3] Marco Baroni[4]
[1]Universitat Pompeu Fabra
[2]Institut für Maschinelle Sprachverarbeitung, Universität Stuttgart
[3]Center for Mind/Brain Sciences, University of Trento
[4]Facebook Artificial Intelligence Research, Paris
gemma.boleda@upf.edu, pado@ims.uni-stuttgart.de,
thenghia.pham@unitn.it, mbaroni@fb.com

Abstract

Reference is a crucial property of language that allows us to connect linguistic expressions to the world. Modeling it requires handling both continuous and discrete aspects of meaning. Data-driven models excel at the former, but struggle with the latter, and the reverse is true for symbolic models.

This paper (a) introduces a concrete referential task to test both aspects, called cross-modal entity tracking; (b) proposes a neural network architecture that uses external memory to build an *entity library* inspired in the DRSs of DRT, with a mechanism to dynamically introduce new referents or add information to referents that are already in the library.

Our model shows promise: it beats traditional neural network architectures on the task. However, it is still outperformed by Memory Networks, another model with external memory.

1   Introduction

Language combines discrete and continuous facets, as exemplified by the phenomenon of *reference* (Frege, 1892; Abbott, 2010): When we refer to an object in the world with the noun phrase *the mug I bought*, we use content words such as *mug*, which are notoriously fuzzy or vague in their meaning (Van Deemter, 2012; Murphy, 2002) and are best modeled through continuous means (Boleda and Herbelot, 2016). Once the referent for the mug has been established, however, it becomes a linguistic entity that we can manipulate in a largely discrete fashion, retrieving it and updating it with new information as needed (*Remember the mug I bought? My brother stole it!* Kamp and Reyle, 1993). Put differently, managing reference requires two distinct abilities:

1. The ability to *categorize*, that is, to recognize that different entities are equivalent with regard to some concept of interest (e.g. two mugs, two instances of the "things to take on a camping trip" category; Barsalou, 1983). This implies being able to aggregate seemingly diverse objects.
2. The ability to *individuate*, that is, to keep entities distinct even if they are similar with regard to many attributes (e.g. two pieces of pink granite that were collected in different national parks). This implies being able to keep seemingly similar things apart.

Data-driven, continuous models are very good at categorizing, but not at individuating, and the reverse holds for symbolic models (Boleda and Herbelot, 2016). Our long-term research goal is to build a **continuous computational model of reference** that emulates discrete referential mechanisms such as those defined in DRT (Kamp and Reyle, 1993); here we present initial work towards that goal, with two specific contributions.

Our first contribution is an experimental task (and associated dataset), **cross-modal entity tracking**, that tests the ability of computational models to refer successfully in a setting where they are required to both categorize and individuate entities. The task presents different entities (represented by pictures) repeatedly, each time with a different, linguistically conveyed attribute (e.g. a given mug is presented once with the attribute *bought* and once with *stolen*). The category label ("mug") is not given at exposure time. The task is to choose the picture of the entity that corresponds to a linguistic query that combines category information with attribute information (e.g. simulating "the mug that was bought and stolen"), among the set of all the entities presented in a given sequence. The sequences in each datapoint of our dataset contain confounders that make the task challenging: Other entities with the same category but only one matching attribute (e.g. a different mug that was bought and stored), and other entities with the same attributes but a different category (e.g. a chair that was bought and stolen). Therefore, the task requires models to 1) correctly categorize entities, recognizing which images belong to the category in the query (something that is hard for symbolic models), 2) individuate and track them, being able to distinguish among different entities based on visual and linguistic cues provided at different time steps (something that is hard for continuous models).

In DRT terms (Kamp and Reyle, 1993), each entity exposure either introduces a new discourse referent or updates the representation of an old referent with new information. To solve the task successfully, the model needs to decide, for each incoming exposure, whether to aggregate it with a previously known referent (in DRT, this means introducing an equation between two referents), or to treat it as a new referent.

Our second contribution is a neural network architecture with a module for referent representations: **DIstributed model of REference, DIRE**. DIRE uses the concept of *external memory* from deep learning (Joulin and Mikolov, 2015; Graves et al., 2016) to build an entity library for an exposure sequence that conceptually corresponds to the set of DRT discourse referents, using similarity-based reasoning on distributed representations to decide between aggregating and initializing entity representations. In contrast to symbolic implementations of DRT (Bos, 2008), which manipulate discourse referents on the basis of manually specified algorithms, DIRE learns to make these decisions directly from observing reference acts using end-to-end training. We see our paper as a first, modest step in the direction of data-driven learning of DRT-like behavior, and are of course still far from learning anything resembling a fully fledged DRT system.

2   Cross-modal Entity Tracking: Task and Data

Task.   Imagine an office, with a desk where there are three mugs and other objects. Adam tells Barbara that he just bought two of the mugs and he particularly likes the one on the right. Later they are in the kitchen, and Adam, busy preparing coffee, asks Barbara: "Remember the mugs I bought? Could you please bring the one I like?". To pick the right mug from the office, Barbara must correctly categorize the objects on the desk (identify which ones are mugs) and individuate them via their properties (singling out the one Adam is asking for). Also, she must combine visual and linguistically conveyed properties of the objects: Visual properties tell her which ones are mugs, the properties that Adam told her about help her pick the right one. Our *cross-modal entity tracking task* emulates this kind of situation. Our current study uses a simplified version of the task that allows us to carefully control all the variables involved.

We operationalize the task as one of pointing to real-life pictures of objects. Figure 1 shows a simplified example. We sample six entities belonging to two categories (in the example, where only three entities are shown, barkeepers and soldiers). Each entity is represented by one image (that is, barkeeper A is always represented by the same image). We also sample different attributes, which are compatible with both categories (in the example, "instructed", "evaluated", "amused"). In the exposure phase, we present each entity (image) twice at different time steps, each time with one of the attributes. In this phase, the category of the entity in the image is not given to the model, only the images are. At query time, we use a linguistic query with one category (e.g., "barkeeper") and two attributes (e.g., "instructed and evaluated"). The task is to retrieve the image of the entity that corresponds to the query. To solve it, it is not enough to rely on categorization or object labeling (in the actual task, there are always three entities belonging to the category in the query), nor is it enough to rely on attribute information (there will always be three entities for each attribute, and two for the combination of attributes in the query). Note that one important simplification we make, with respect to a real-life scenario, is that an entity is always represented by the

Figure 1: Cross-modal tracking task (actual datapoints contain 12 exposures and 6 images to pick from).

very same image. The current setup is nevertheless already very challenging for current models, as the experiments below will show. Indeed, to succeed in the task a model must correctly associate the category in the query with images of the right object, it must develop a mechanism to index entities based on the images representing them, and it must learn to correctly accumulate over time the different attributes to be stored with each entity.

The task is related to coreference resolution (see Poesio et al., 2017, for a recent survey), but focuses on identifying language-external objects from images rather than mentions of a referent in text; to Visual Question Answering (Antol et al., 2015), but it cannot be solved with visual information alone; and to Referring Expression Generation (Krahmer and Van Deemter, 2012), but involves identification rather than generation.

Dataset.   We have constructed a dataset for the task containing 40k sequences for training, 5k for validation and 10k for testing.[1] It is assembled on the basis of 2k object categories with 50 ImageNet[2] images each, sampled from a larger dataset (Lazaridou et al., 2015). These are natural images, which makes the task challenging. The object categories given in the queries are those specified in ImageNet.

We build a set of linguistic attributes for each object by first extracting the 500 most associated, and thus plausible, syntactic neighbors for the category according to the DM resource (Baroni and Lenci, 2010). This excludes nonsensical combinations such as *repair:dog*. We further retain only (relatively) abstract verbs taking the target item as direct object.[3] This is because (a) concrete verbs are likely to have strong visual correlates that could conflict with the image (cf. *walk dog*); and (b) referential expressions routinely successfully mix concrete and abstract cues (e.g., *the dog I own*). We remove all verbs with a score over 2.5 (on a 1–5 scale) in the concreteness norms of Brysbaert et al. (2014).

We then construct each sequence as follows. First, we sample two random categories, and three random entities (distinct images) for each category (total: six entities). We then sample three attributes compatible with both categories, giving us three attribute sets of size two (a1+a2, a1+a3, a2+a3) to associate with the entities. We create a completely balanced set of exposures by randomly pairing up each of the three entities of each category with each of the three attribute sets. Since this process gives us two exposures for each entity (one with the first attribute, one with the second), it yields a sequence of twelve exposures. The query is a random combination of a category and two attributes, guaranteed to match exactly one entity.

3   The DIRE Model

The core novelty of our model, DIRE (for DIstributed model of REference), is a method to dynamically construct an *entity library*, conceptually inspired in 1) the DRSs of DRT,[4] and 2) Joulin and Mikolov

---

[1]Available at `http://www.ims.uni-stuttgart.de/forschung/ressourcen/korpora/dire`.

[2]`http://imagenet.stanford.edu`

[3]We use the base form of verbs rather than the past participle for simplicity.

[4]DRSs represent many types of information; as explained above, here we focus on entity-related information.

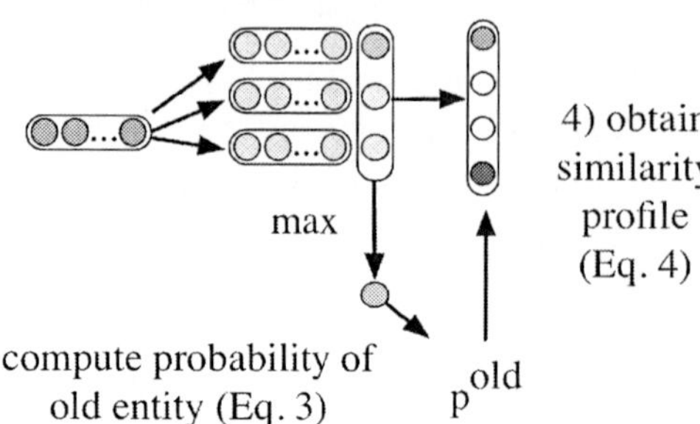

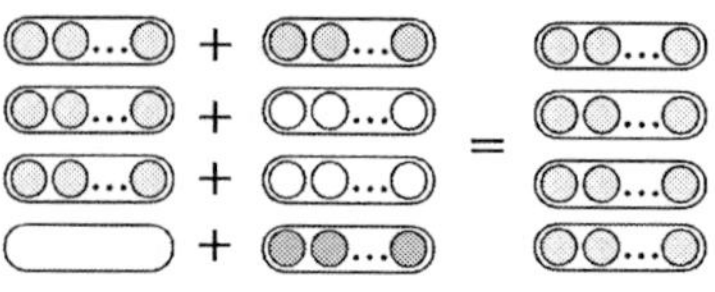

Figure 2: Building the DIRE entity library.

(2015) and Graves et al. (2016), who simulate discrete memory-building operations in a differentiable continuous setup.[5] The model is a feed-forward network enhanced with a dynamic memory (the entity library), as well as mechanisms to interact with it.

The entity library is updated after reading an input exposure by either creating a new entity slot for the exposure, or adding the exposure contents to an existing entity slot. This decision is based on the similarity between the current input and the entities already in the library. This generic mechanism (Section 3.1) can be applied in any setting that accumulates information about entities over time. We explain how we use it for our cross-modal tracking task in Section 3.2.

3.1 Building the DIRE Entity Library

Figure 2 depicts the entity library building mechanism. The input to the model is a set of subsequent exposures $x_1, x_2, \ldots, x_n$ which are represented by vectors $\mathbf{u}_1, \mathbf{u}_2, \ldots, \mathbf{u}_n$. At the t-th exposure, the entity library is updated to state $\mathbf{E}_t$ as follows. The first exposure vector $\mathbf{u}_1$ is added to the entity library as is (Equation 1). For $\mathbf{u}_{i>1}$, we obtain a similarity profile $\mathbf{s}_i$ by taking its dot product with the entity vectors in the library (Equation 2; note that $\mathbf{s}_i$ has $i - 1$ dimensions):

$$\mathbf{E}_1 = \mathbf{u}_1^\mathsf{T} \tag{1}$$
$$\mathbf{s}_i = \mathbf{E}_{i-1}\mathbf{u}_i \tag{2}$$

The maximum similarity to an existing entity, $s_i^{max} = \max(\mathbf{s}_i)$, cues whether x_i is an instance of an entity that has already been encountered before. We transform s_i^{max} into p_i^{old}, the probability that exposure x_i corresponds to an "old" entity, as follows (with the scalar w, b parameters shared across all exposures for $i > 1$):

$$p_i^{old} = \sigma(ws_i^{max} + b) \tag{3}$$

The entity library is updated by "soft insertion" (Joulin and Mikolov, 2015) of the current exposure vector $\mathbf{u}_i$ into the library. Concretely, we add the vector to each entity in the library, weighted by the

---

[5]While we developed DIRE, Henaff et al. (2016) proposed a similar architecture; we leave a comparison to future work.

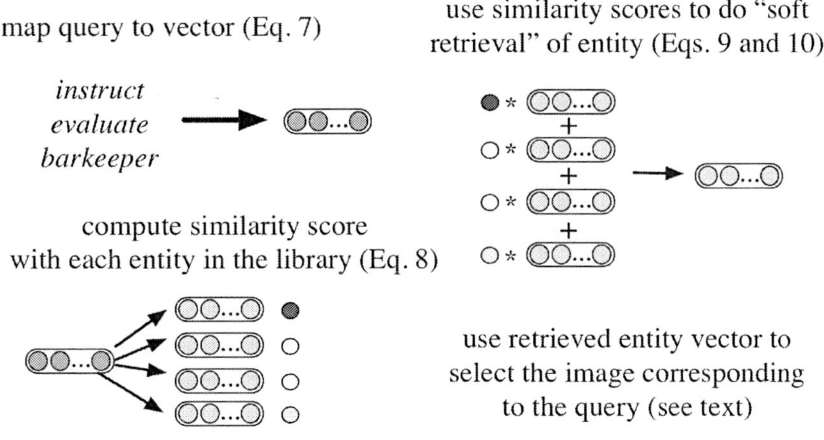

Figure 3: Querying the DIRE entity library.

probability that the current exposure is an instance of that entity. For the $i - 1$ existing entities, this probability is obtained by distributing the p_i^{old} mass across them, according to their probability of being the matching entity, conditional on the exposure being old. The latter probability is estimated by softmax-normalizing the similarity profile $\mathbf{s}_i$ from above. The probability that x_i is new is obviously $1 - p_i^{old}$. This results in the following distribution, where $\|$ stands for concatenation:

$$\mathbf{z}_i = p_i^{old} * \text{softmax}(\mathbf{s}_i) \| (1 - p_i^{old}) \tag{4}$$

Note that z_i has one value more than the current number of stored entities, expressing the probability that the current exposure instantiates a new entity.

The entity library is then updated as:

$$\mathbf{U}_i = \mathbf{z}_i \mathbf{u}_i^\top \tag{5}$$

$$\mathbf{E}_i = (\mathbf{E}_{i-1} \| \mathbf{0}) + \mathbf{U}_i \tag{6}$$

Thus, we insert a 0 vector of the same dimensionality as the $\mathbf{u}_i$ vectors at the end of the library, initializing a blank slot to store a new entity. As a consequence, the library in its end state will always contain as many entity vectors as exposures. However, we expect those inserted for exposures of old entities (that is, when $p_i^{old} \approx 1$) to be near zero, and removable from the library along the lines of Graves et al. (2016).

3.2   Cross-modal Entity Tracking with DIRE

We use DIRE for the cross-modal entity tracking task as follows (see Figure 3). Given pre-trained image and verbal attribute representations, we first derive a multimodal representation $\mathbf{u}_i$ for each exposure x_i and update the entity library as explained in Section 3.1. The linguistic query is mapped to the same multimodal space where entities live, and the most relevant entity is retrieved. Finally, the images the model has to choose from (candidate set) are also mapped to multimodal space, and the correct answer is picked based on their similarity with the retrieved entity. We share the same $\mathbf{V}$ projection across all images (in the exposures as well as in the candidate set at query time), a single $\mathbf{A}$ projection for the verbal attributes (in the exposures and in the query), and a matrix $\mathbf{C}$ for the category name in the query. Details on each of the steps follow.

Multimodal Mapping.   Exposures are linearly mapped to a multimodal space combining visual and linguistic information, building the $\mathbf{u}_i$ vector by separately embedding each image vector $\mathbf{i}_i$ and attribute vector $\mathbf{a}_i$ using a matrix $\mathbf{V}$ for images[6] and a matrix $\mathbf{A}$ for linguistic attributes[7] and adding up the result (Equation 7). Storage takes place by feeding the $\mathbf{u}_i$ vectors sequentially to the entity library (cf. Section 3.1).

$$\mathbf{u}_i = \mathbf{V}i_i + \mathbf{A}a_i \tag{7}$$

Query and Retrieval. To select the best entity match for the query, we compute a "soft retrieval" operation inspired by Sukhbaatar et al. (2015). To query the entity library, we first map the query (a linguistic referring expression, consisting of one noun and two attributes) to multimodal space. We embed the attribute vectors $\mathbf{a}_1^q$, $\mathbf{a}_2^q$ with the matrix $\mathbf{A}$ learned during storage and the noun vector $\mathbf{c}$ with matrix $\mathbf{C}$, and we sum the result (Eq. 8). The query vector $\mathbf{q}$ lives in the same space as the entity vectors, which enables similarity computations.

$$\mathbf{q} = \mathbf{C}c + \mathbf{A}a_1^q + \mathbf{A}a_2^q \tag{8}$$

We then retrieve the entity representation that matches the query, by first computing the similarity of the mapped query $\mathbf{q}$ to each entity vector $\mathbf{e}_i$ through a normalized dot product, $\mathbf{g}$ (Eq. 9), and then using those similarities as weights to perform a "soft retrieval" of the entity that best matches the query, summing up the vectors in the entity library multiplied by $\mathbf{g}$ (Eq. 10). Note that if only one entity is significantly similar to the query (so that the corresponding entry in the similarity profile tends to 1, while all other entries tend to 0), this is equivalent to retrieving that entity.

$$\mathbf{g} = \text{softmax}(\mathbf{E}_n \mathbf{q}) \tag{9}$$
$$\mathbf{r} = \mathbf{E}_n^{\mathsf{T}} \mathbf{g} \tag{10}$$

Picking the Right Image. Finally, we use the retrieved entity representation, $\mathbf{r}$, to pick among the k images that represent the entities. We map the candidate image vectors $\mathbf{d}_1 \ldots \mathbf{d}_k$ to multimodal space using the same visual matrix $\mathbf{V}$ as above. We compare the query with each of the images using a dot product, again obtaining a similarity profile, that we softmax-normalize to obtain the final probability distribution that will give us the candidate image, namely, the one corresponding to the argmax of the probability distribution. Note that we need a probability distribution because we use a cross-entropy cost function when training the model.

The whole architecture is differentiable, allowing end-to-end training by gradient descent; in particular, the cross-modal mapping is learned as the model learns to refer.[8] At the same time, it emulates discrete-like operations like insertion and retrieval of entity representations, that, in frameworks such as DRT, are performed entirely in symbolic terms, and are manually coded in the DRT system Boxer (Bos, 2008). This has the advantage that the entity representations can be continuous, enabling their matching with continuous representations of language as well as cross-modal reasoning (for instance, using *cup* for something that a different speaker calls *mug*, or mixing visual and linguistically conveyed information). The model is rather parsimonious, with parameters limited to three mapping matrices ($\mathbf{V}$, $\mathbf{A}$, $\mathbf{C}$) and the bias and weight terms for p^{old}.

4   Experiments

Experimental details. Images are represented by 4096-dimensional vectors produced by passing images through the pre-trained VGG 19-layer CNN of Simonyan and Zisserman (2015) (trained on the ILSVRC-2012 data), and extracting the corresponding activations on the topmost fully connected layer.[9] Linguistic

---

[6]Size $v \times m$, where v is the size of the image vector and m the multimodal dimensionality.

[7]Size $t \times m$, where t is the size of the attribute vector. Both matrices, V and A, are learned.

[8]Note that the input vectors for images are only visual, and those for nouns and attributes are only textual.

[9]We use the MatConvNet toolkit, http://www.vlfeat.org/matconvnet.

Baseline		Standard models		DIRE				MemN			
Random	0.17	FF	0.27	1m	0.64	2m	0.65	1m-1h	0.59	2m-1h	0.67
		RNN	0.28					1m-2h	0.67	2m-2h	**0.69**
								1m-3h	0.30	2m-3h	0.30

Table 1: Tracking results (accuracy on test set).

representations are given by 400-dimensional cbow embeddings from Baroni et al. (2014), trained on about 2.8 billion tokens of raw text. We map to a 1K-dimensional multimodal space. The parameters of **DIRE** are estimated by stochastic gradient descent with 0.09 learning rate, 10 minibatch size, 0.5 dropout probability, and maximally 150 epochs (here and below, hyperparameter values as in Baroni et al., 2017).

As competitors, we train standard feed-forward (**FF**) and recurrent (**RNN**) networks which have no external memory, using two 300-dimensional hidden layers and sigmoid nonlinearities. We also implement the related Memory Network model (**MemN**; Sukhbaatar et al., 2015). Like DIRE, MemN controls a memory structure, but stores each input exposure separately in the memory. At the same time, MemN can perform multiple "hops" at query time. Each hop consists in soft-retrieving a vector from the memory, where the probing vector is the sum of the input query vector and the vector retrieved in the previous hop (null for the first hop). Conceptually, DIRE attempts to merge different instances of the same entity at input processing time, whereas MemN stores each piece of input separately and aggregates relevant information at query time. MemN can thus use the query to guide the search for relevant information. At the same time, it does not optimize the way in which it stores information in memory. Another difference with DIRE is that MemN uses *two* sets of mapping matrices: One to derive the vectors used at query time, the other for the vectors used for retrieval. We employ the same hyperparameters for MemN (also multimodal vector size) as for our model.

Results. Table 1 shows that DIRE outperforms the standard networks (FF and RNN) by a large margin, confirming the importance of a discrete memory structure for reference tracking. If we make the MemN architecture completely comparable to our model (with one matrix and one hop, MemN-1m-1h), our model achieves higher results (0.64 for DIRE-1m, 0.59 for MemN-1m-1h), which indicates that the basic architecture of the model holds promise. However, MemN outperforms DIRE when using two matrices, two hops (0.67 MemN-2m-1h/MemN-1m-2h vs. 0.65 DIRE-2m), or both (0.69 MemN-2m-2h). For MemN, this seems to be the upper bound, as increasing to three hops greatly harms results (see last row).

Further analysis suggests that DIRE successfully addresses the two challenges set out in the introduction: (i) It learns to categorize: Only for 8% of the datapoints does the model pick an image of the wrong category, and these are cases where confounders belong to visually similar or related categories to the target (*cottage-chalet, youngster-enthusiast, witch-potion*). It is worth noting that the model learns to categorize directly from reference acts: At exposure time, the image is not provided with a category label, so the model needs to induce the category as part of solving the reference task. (ii) DIRE also learns to individuate by combining visual and linguistically-conveyed information: The similarity of the exposure to the query goes to near-zero when the attribute is wrong, even when the category is the same. Together, these two properties make it able to ground linguistic expressions to entities represented in images. However, the entity creation mechanism still needs to be fine-tuned, as currently DIRE creates a new entity vector for nearly every exposure. More work is needed for this crucial part of the model.

5 Discussion

Providing a continuous model of reference that can emulate discrete reasoning about entities is an ambitious research programme. We have reported on work in progress on such a model, DIRE, which, unlike Memory Networks, and emulating formal approaches such as DRT within an end-to-end neural architecture, is designed to make decisions as to how to store the information *at input processing time*, in a way that aids further reasoning, namely, organizing it by entity. Results suggest that merging complementary aspects of DIRE and MemN could be fruitful. We have also presented a new task, cross-modal entity tracking, that tests the categorization and individuation capabilities of computational models, and a challenging dataset for the task.

Our project is related to several areas of active research. Reference is a classic topic in philosophy of language and linguistics (Frege, 1892; Abbott, 2010; Kamp and Reyle, 1993; Kamp, 2015); emulating discrete aspects of language and reasoning through continuous means is a long-standing goal in artificial intelligence (Smolensky, 1990; Joulin and Mikolov, 2015), and recent work focuses on reference (Baroni et al., 2017; Herbelot, 2015; Herbelot and Vecchi, 2015); grounding language in perception (Chen and Mooney, 2011; Bruni et al., 2012; Silberer et al., 2013), as well as reference and co-reference (Krahmer and Van Deemter, 2012; Poesio et al., 2017) are important subjects in Computational Linguistics. Our programme puts these different strands together.

Acknowledgments: We thank Angeliki Lazaridou for help producing the visual vectors used in the paper. This project has received funding from the European Research Council (ERC) under the European Union's Horizon 2020 research and innovation programme (grant agreement No 715154; AMORE); EU Horizon 2020 programme under the Marie Skłodowska-Curie grant agreement No 655577 (LOVe); ERC 2011 Starting Independent Research Grant n. 283554 (COMPOSES); DFG (SFB 732, Project D10). We also gratefully acknowledge the support of NVIDIA Corporation with the donation of GPUs to U. Trento and U. Pompeu Fabra. This paper reflects the authors' view only, and the EU is not responsible for any use that may be made of the information it contains.

References

Abbott, B. (2010). *Reference.* Oxford, UK: Oxford University Press.

Antol, S., A. Agrawal, J. Lu, M. Mitchell, D. Batra, C. Lawrence Zitnick, and D. Parikh (2015). VQA: Visual Question Answering. In *Proceedings of ICCV*, Santiago de Chile, Chile.

Baroni, M., G. Boleda, and S. Padó (2017). Show me the cup: Reference with continuous representations. In *Proceedings of CICLing (International Conference on Computational Linguistics and Intelligent Text Processing)*.

Baroni, M., G. Dinu, and G. Kruszewski (2014). Don't count, predict! a systematic comparison of context-counting vs. context-predicting semantic vectors. In *Proceedings of ACL*, Baltimore, MD, pp. 238–247.

Baroni, M. and A. Lenci (2010). Distributional Memory: A general framework for corpus-based semantics. *Computational Linguistics 36*(4), 673–721.

Barsalou, L. W. (1983). Ad hoc categories. *Memory & Cognition 11*(3), 211–227.

Boleda, G. and A. Herbelot (2016). Formal distributional semantics: Introduction to the special issue. *Computational Linguistics 42*(4), 619–635.

Bos, J. (2008). Wide-coverage semantic analysis with Boxer. In *Proceedings of the 2008 Conference on Semantics in Text Processing*, pp. 277–286. Association for Computational Linguistics.

Bruni, E., G. Boleda, M. Baroni, and N. K. Tran (2012). Distributional semantics in technicolor. In *Proceedings of the 50th Annual Meeting of the Association for Computational Linguistics*, Jeju Island, Korea, pp. 136–145.

Brysbaert, M., A. B. Warriner, and V. Kuperman (2014). Concreteness ratings for 40 thousand generally known English word lemmas. *Behavior Research Methods 46*, 904–911.

Chen, D. and R. Mooney (2011). Learning to interpret natural language navigation instructions from observations. In *Proceedings of AAAI*, San Francisco, CA, pp. 859–865.

Frege, G. (1892). Über Sinn und Bedeutung. *Zeitschrift für Philosophie und philosophische Kritik 100*, 25–50.

Graves, A., G. Wayne, M. Reynolds, T. Harley, I. Danihelka, A. Grabska-Barwińska, S. Gómez Colmenarejo, E. Grefenstette, T. Ramalho, J. Agapiou, A. P. Badia, K. Moritz Hermann, Y. Zwols, G. Ostrovski, A. Cain, H. King, C. Summerfield, P. Blunsom, K. Kavukcuoglu, and D. Hassabis (2016). Hybrid computing using a neural network with dynamic external memory. *Nature 538*(7626), 471–476.

Henaff, M., J. Weston, A. Szlam, A. Bordes, and Y. LeCun (2016). Tracking the World State with Recurrent Neural Networks. https://arxiv.org/abs/1612.03969.

Herbelot, A. (2015). Mr Darcy and Mr Toad, gentlemen: distributional names and their kinds. In *Proceedings of the 11th International Conference on Computational Semantics*, London, UK, pp. 151–161. Association for Computational Linguistics.

Herbelot, A. and E. M. Vecchi (2015). Building a shared world: mapping distributional to model-theoretic semantic spaces. In *Proceedings of the 2015 Conference on Empirical Methods in Natural Language Processing*, Lisbon, Portugal, pp. 22–32. Association for Computational Linguistics.

Joulin, A. and T. Mikolov (2015). Inferring algorithmic patterns with stack-augmented recurrent nets. In *Proceedings of NIPS*, Montreal, Canada.

Kamp, H. (2015). Entity Representations and Articulated Contexts: An Exploration of the Semantics and Pragmatics of Definite Noun Phrases. Ms. University of Stuttgart.

Kamp, H. and U. Reyle (1993). *From Discourse to Logic: Introduction to Model-theoretic Semantics of Natural Language, Formal Logic and Discourse Representation Theory*. Dordrecht: Kluwer.

Krahmer, E. and K. Van Deemter (2012). Computational generation of referring expressions: A survey. *Computational Linguistics 38*(1), 173–218.

Lazaridou, A., N. Pham, and M. Baroni (2015). Combining language and vision with a multimodal skip-gram model. In *Proceedings of NAACL*, Denver, CO, pp. 153–163.

Murphy, G. (2002). *The Big Book of Concepts*. Cambridge, MA: MIT Press.

Poesio, M., R. Stuckardt, and Y. Versley (2017). *Anaphora Resolution: Algorithms, Resources, and Applications*. Springer. In press.

Silberer, C., V. Ferrari, and M. Lapata (2013). Models of semantic representation with visual attributes. In *Proceedings of ACL*, Sofia, Bulgaria, pp. 572–582.

Simonyan, K. and A. Zisserman (2015). Very deep convolutional networks for large-scale image recognition. In *Proceedings of ICLR Conference Track*, San Diego, CA. Published online: http://www.iclr.cc/doku.php?id=iclr2015:main.

Smolensky, P. (1990). Tensor product variable binding and the representation of symbolic structures in connectionist networks. *Artificial Intelligence 46*, 159–216.

Sukhbaatar, S., A. Szlam, J. Weston, and R. Fergus (2015). End-to-end memory networks. In *Advances in Neural Information Processing Systems 28*, pp. 2440–2448. Montral, Canada.

Van Deemter, K. (2012). *Not exactly: In praise of vagueness*. Oxford University Press.

Indexicals and Compositionality: Inside-Out or Outside-In?

Johan Bos
University of Groningen
`johan.bos@rug.nl`

Abstract

Two different approaches to the compositional semantics of indexicals are compared. The outside-in approach uses λ-abstraction and is heavily lexicalised. The inside-out approach treats indexicals by presupposition resolution. The former is relatively simple to implement and deals in a natural way with multiple occurences of indexicals. The latter is more complex, but has potential to deal with a wider range of indexical phenomena. However, it needs to be constrained in a practical implementation as it over-generates.

1 Introduction

Indexicals, linguistic expressions such as *I*, *you*, *today* that are highly sensitive to context, pose a challenge for compositional semantics, because their interpretation is highly context-sensitive. Sentences such as (1), demonstrating direct speech, and (2), showcasing reported speech, have similar meaning (the second entails the first, but not vice versa, as John might have uttered different words to indicate that he left). Hence, an algorithm developed for compositional semantics should predict this entailment.

(1)   **John said that he left.**

(2)   **John said, "I leave".**

In semantic parsing it is considered to be advantaguous to use a systematic, compositional approach, as it scales up to implementations that require robustness and wide coverage. There are various theoretical approaches to the interpretation of indexicals (Schlenker, 2004; Maier, 2009). In this paper I compare two different theories, in order to evaluate which of the two is more suitable for wide-coverage semantic parsing.

The first approach is what I dub an "outside-in" approach: once a proposition is contextualised, indexicals inside it are resolved with the information from outside (the context). I think this approach can be characterized as Kaplanian (Kaplan, 1989), although the implementation that I present here is new – as far as I know. The second approach is an "inside-out" approach: it deals with indexicals by treating them as an anaphoric species of presuppositional nature, finding antecedents outside in the surrounding context. This approach finds its roots in the *presupposition as anaphora* theory (Van der Sandt, 1992), and has been worked out in detail for indexicals by Zeevat (1999), Maier (2009) and Hunter (2013).

2 Methodology

The comparison of the two approaches is carried out in the framework of Discourse Representation Theory (DRT). Unlike standard DRT (Kamp and Reyle, 1993), I assume a neo-Davidsonian approach with an inventory of thematic roles similar to that of VerbNet (Kipper et al., 2008). The basic assumption is that sentences such as (1) and (2) have the meanings that are represented by the Discourse Representation Structures (DRS) shown in (3) and (4), thereby predicting that the latter entails the former.

(3) $[\![(1)]\!] =$

x s p
person(x) named(x, "John")
say(s) agent(s,x) topic(s,k)
p: $\boxed{\begin{array}{l} e \\ \hline \text{leave}(e) \ \text{agent}(e,x) \end{array}}$

(4) $[\![(2)]\!] =$

x s p
person(x) named(x, "John")
say(s) agent(s,x) topic(s,p) p = "I leave"
p: $\boxed{\begin{array}{l} e \\ \hline \text{leave}(e) \ \text{agent}(e,x) \end{array}}$

In the remainder of this paper, the two approaches are compared by giving a compositional analysis of (2) using the basic machinery of the λ-calculus. I will use $[\![.]\!]_{oi}$ to denote meanings for natural language expressions from the outside-in approach, and $[\![.]\!]_{io}$ to denote meanings from the inside-out method. In cases where there is no distinction in meaning between the two approaches the subscript will be dropped. As we will see, the two approaches have completely different ways to deal with indexicals, but will eventually – for this simple example, at least – produce the same meaning representation.

3   Approach I: Contextualising Indexicals Outside-In

The basic idea of this approach is to use a distinct set of indexed variables that denote indexical meanings. This must be a finite set, and for the purposes of this paper we can take this to be a small set of free variables $i_{speaker}$, i_{hearer} and i_{now}. These free variables are introduced in the lexical semantics of indexical expressions. For instance, the first-person pronoun *I* will get the following meaning representations ($\oplus$ denotes merging of DRSs):

(5) $[\![\mathbf{I}]\!]_{oi} = \lambda p.(\boxed{\begin{array}{l} x \\ \hline x = i_{speaker} \end{array}} \oplus p(x))$

In (5) an explicit discourse referent is introduced for the first-person pronoun. It is unclear to me whether this is necessary from a theoretical point of view, as eventually, the free, indexical variables will be substituted by variables bound by discourse referents provided by the context in which the indexical expression is analysed. Therefore, I assume a simplified (but logically equivalent) lexical meaning for the first-person pronoun in (6).

(6) $[\![\mathbf{I}]\!]_{oi} = \lambda p.p(i_{speaker})$

Suppose we combine the meaning in (6) with the meaning of an intransitive verb (7). This will yield the DRS (8). Note that the resulting DRS contains the free variable $i_{speaker}$. It is free because it is not contextualised yet. Quotation is a way to close the boundaries of a proposition and make it sensitive to the context. This is done in (9) by λ-abstracting over all indexed variables (for the sake of simplicity we just do it here for the free variable representing the *speaker*).

(7) $[\![\mathbf{leave}]\!] = \lambda x.\boxed{\begin{array}{l} e \\ \hline \text{leave}(e) \ \text{agent}(e,x) \end{array}}$

(8) $[\![\mathbf{I\ leave}]\!]_{oi} = [\![\mathbf{I}]\!]_{oi}([\![\mathbf{leave}]\!]) = \boxed{\begin{array}{l} e \\ \hline \text{leave}(e) \ \text{agent}(e,i_{speaker}) \end{array}}$

(9) $[\![\text{"I leave"}]\!]_{oi} = \lambda i_{speaker}.[\![\mathbf{I\ leave}]\!]_{oi} = \lambda i_{speaker}.\boxed{\begin{array}{l} e \\ \hline \text{leave}(e) \ \text{agent}(e,i_{speaker}) \end{array}}$

Now we are ready to provide the context, as the quotation of the reported speech in (2) is the direct object of the transitive verb (10). Here, $\mathcal{P}$ is a function that returns the phonetic form that triggered the meaning representation. Function application then will yield (11), resolving the indexical; combining this with (12) will give the desired DRS (4).

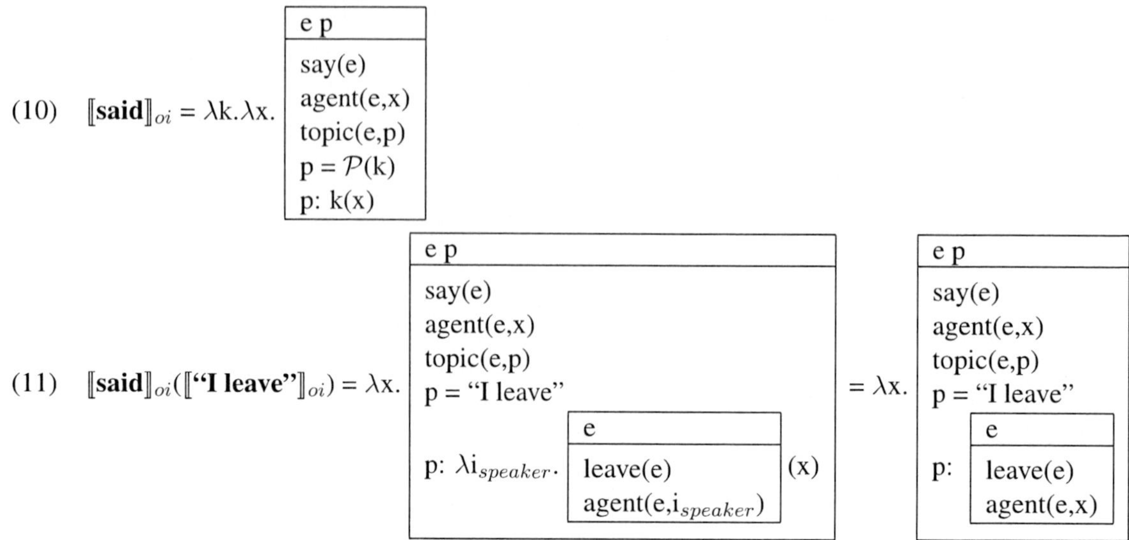

In sum: this approach assumes a small finite set of variables distinct from the usual set of first-order variables. It further assumes that contextualisation is dealt with in the lexicon, by expressions that indicate reported speech. No special, new machinery is required: the λ-calculus can deal with it all.

4 Approach II: Contextualising Indexicals Inside-Out

In the second approach, resolution of indexicals is considered to be part and parcel of an existing presupposition projection algorithm. Hence, indexicals are viewed as presupposition triggers and are lexically represented as such. I assume a projection theory similar to that of Van der Sandt (1992) and Hunter (2013). Presuppositional material is separated from assertive information using the $*$ operator, following Venhuizen et al. (2013). Consider now the lexical entries for the presupposition triggers in (12) and (13).

$$(12)\quad [\![\mathbf{John}]\!] = \lambda p.(\boxed{\begin{array}{l} x \\ \hline \text{person(x)}\ \ \text{named(x, "John")} \end{array}} * p(x))$$

$$(13)\quad [\![\mathbf{I}]\!]_{io} = \lambda p.(\boxed{\begin{array}{l} i\ s\ k \\ \hline \text{agent(s,i)} \\ \text{topic(s,k)} \end{array}} * p(i))$$

The indexical presupposition of the first-person pronoun is here, closely following Hunter (2013), a complex proposition of a speech event, its agent, and its topic. Combining this with the intransitive verb (7) yields a meaning representation (14) with the presupposition that there is some speech act with the speaker co-referring with the agent of the "leaving" event. The question is what role quotation plays in the second approach. For now I assume the quotes don't alter the meaning in the inside-out theory of indexicals (if it would, it would need to do so by adding some semantic information to the DRS), and hence we can state the equation in (15).

$$(14)\quad [\![\mathbf{I\ leave}]\!]_{io} = [\![\mathbf{I}]\!]_{io}([\![\mathbf{leave}]\!]) = \boxed{\begin{array}{l} i\ s\ k \\ \hline \text{agent(s,i)} \\ \text{topic(s,k)} \end{array}} * \boxed{\begin{array}{l} e \\ \hline \text{leave(e)} \\ \text{agent(e,i)} \end{array}}$$

$$(15)\quad [\![\text{"I leave"}]\!]_{io} = [\![\mathbf{I\ leave}]\!]_{io}$$

Now consider the lexical meanings for the speech reporting verb in the inside-out approach (16). It differs from (10) because it does not have to alter its argument. Instead, it will combine with (15) to produce (17).

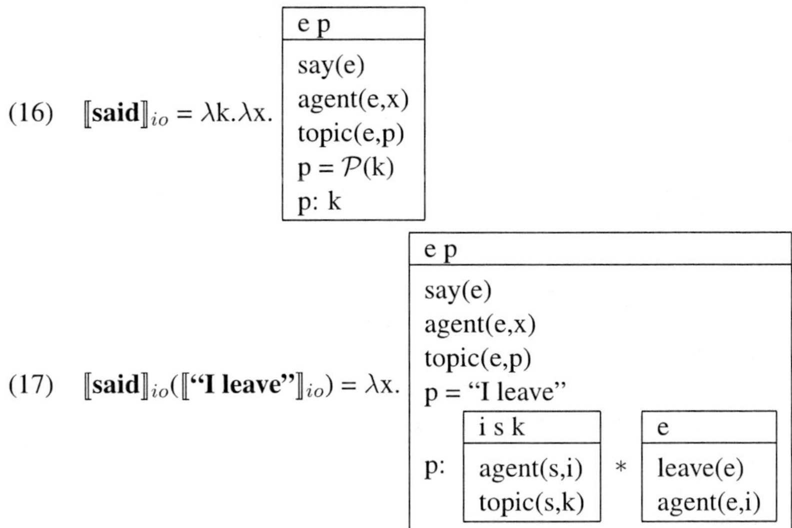

(16) $[\![\mathbf{said}]\!]_{io} = \lambda k.\lambda x.$

(17) $[\![\mathbf{said}]\!]_{io}([\![\text{``I leave''}]\!]_{io}) = \lambda x.$

Combining (17) with (12) will yield (18), a *proto*-DRS, using the terminology of Van der Sandt (1992), with two presuppositions that need to be resolved. The first presupposition triggered by the proper name "John" cannot be resolved by linking it to an accessible antecedent, so it will be accommodated. The second, indexical presupposition can be resolved in the context as the "saying" event provides a suitable antecedent. This will yield, then, a DRS equivalent to (4).

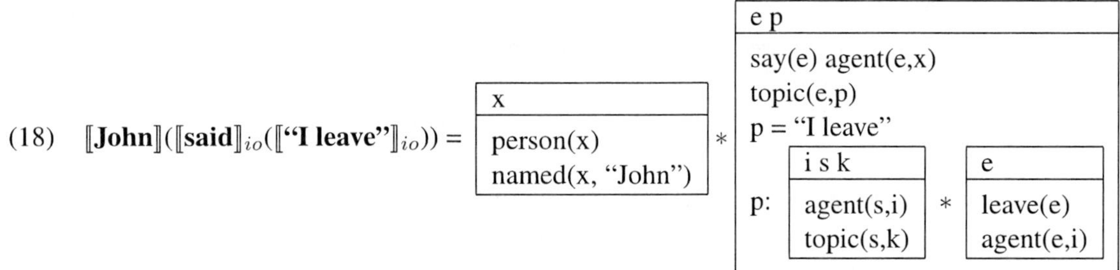

(18) $[\![\mathbf{John}]\!]([\![\mathbf{said}]\!]_{io}([\![\text{``I leave''}]\!]_{io})) =$

In sum: this approach requires a rich lexical representation for indexicals. It further assumes that contextualisation is dealt with during the presupposition projection. No special, new machinery is required, as one needs to deal with presuppositions anyway in a formalism aiming at a wide coverage of linguistic expressions. However, to constrain the resolution of indexicals it is required that particular rules need to be added to the algorithm (there could be several potential antecedents for an indexical presupposition, but only one can be correct; local accommodation needs to be banned). This has also been recognized by advocates of the inside-out approach (Zeevat, 1999; Maier, 2009; Hunter, 2013), who propose various extensions to the presupposition resolution algorithm to include indexicals.

5   Comparing the Approaches

Both approaches lead to the same meaning representation, but the way in which the composition process evolves is radically different (Table 1). In the Kaplanian outside-in approach, λ-abstraction is used to contextualizs indexicals. In the Van der Sandtian inside-out framework, indexicals are contextualised under the umbrella of presupposition resolution. Neither of the approaches uses new machinery: λ-abstraction and function application is used in the general process of semantic composition, and presupposition projection is required to deal with the large variety of presupposition triggers (such as names, definite descriptions, factuals, and so on).

Table 1: Comparing the two approaches to indexical interpretation.

	Approach I: Outside-In	**Approach II: Inside-Out**
Origin	Kaplan (1989)	Zeevat (1999); Maier (2009); Hunter (2013)
Representation	Simple	Complex
Machinery	$\lambda *$	$\lambda *$
Resolution	λ	$*$
Knowledge	Lexical	External
Quoted Speech	plays an important role	not considered
Extra	indexed variables	dedicated resolution strategies

Arguably, the meaning representations of the outside-in approach are way simpler. The inside-out approach does not require a distinct set of indexed variables, but needs to impose dedicated rules in the presupposition projection algorithm to deal with indexicals. It is also unclear how the latter incorporates direct speech in the meaning representation, for it seems to be important to steer the resolution of indexical presuppositions. Consider, for instance the following contrasting pair of examples:

(19)   John said that Mary said, "I am happy".

(20)   John said, "Mary said I am happy".

Clearly, (19) and (20) differ in meaning. The outside-in approach will deal with this in a straightforward way. The inside-out approach will face a difficulty here, as the proto-DRS for the two sentences will be identical since quotes are ignored in the DRS.

Another issue are sentences with multiple occurrences of indexicals, as "I love my dog." Here the outside-in approach takes advantage of the fact that both the personal pronoun and the possessive introduce the same free indexical variable. The inside-out approach needs to guarantee that both presuppositions that are invoked, will be resolved to the same antecedent.

6   Conclusion

It is perhaps attractive to have one mechanism that covers all kind of contextual phenomena. But there are many kinds of contextual phenomena each showing quite different types of behaviour. Although Maier (2009); Hunter (2013) argue that viewing indexicals as a type of presupposition solves some of the puzzles to do with bound pronouns, it also requires a complex implementation of the presupposition projection algorithm. A simple Kaplanian approach, as presented in this paper, might well be a good alternative for the purpose of wide-coverage semantic parsing: it is easy from a representational point of view, and cheap to implement. This is also the choice of analysis in the Parallel Meaning Bank, a large semi-automatically annotated corpus of DRSs for four languages (Abzianidze et al., 2017).

Acknowledgements

I would like to thank Lasha Abzianidze for comments on an earlier version of this paper. I am also grateful to the three anonymous reviewers for their comments — they helped to improve this paper considerably. In particular I would like to express my gratitude to Reviewer 3, who pointed out a little flaw in the semantic analysis that I presente in the draft version of this paper. I managed to fix problem this in the present version. This work was funded by the NWO-VICI grant "Lost in Translation Found in Meaning" (288-89-003).

References

Abzianidze, L., J. Bjerva, K. Evang, H. Haagsma, R. van Noord, P. Ludmann, D.-D. Nguyen, and J. Bos (2017). The parallel meaning bank: Towards a multilingual corpus of translations annotated with compositional meaning representations. In *Proceedings of the 15th Conference of the European Chapter of the Association for Computational Linguistics*, Valencia, Spain, pp. 242–247.

Hunter, J. (2013). Presuppositional indexicals. *Journal of Semantics 30*(3), 381–421.

Kamp, H. and U. Reyle (1993). *From Discourse to Logic; An Introduction to Modeltheoretic Semantics of Natural Language, Formal Logic and DRT*. Dordrecht: Kluwer.

Kaplan, D. (1989). Demonstratives. In J. Almog, J. Perry, and H. Wettstein (Eds.), *Themes From Kaplan*, pp. 481–563. Oxford University Press.

Kipper, K., A. Korhonen, N. Ryant, and M. Palmer (2008). A large-scale classification of English verbs. *Language Resources and Evaluation 42*(1), 21–40.

Maier, E. (2009). Proper names and indexicals trigger rigid presuppositions. *Journal of Semantics 23*, 253–315.

Schlenker, P. (2004). Person and binding: a partial survey. *Italian Journal of Linguistics/Rivista di Linguistica 16*(1), 155–218.

Van der Sandt, R. A. (1992). Presupposition Projection as Anaphora Resolution. *Journal of Semantics 9*, 333–377.

Venhuizen, N., J. Bos, and H. Brouwer (2013). Parsimonious semantic representations with projection pointers. In *Proceedings of the 10th International Conference on Computational Semantics (IWCS 2013) – Long Papers*, Potsdam, Germany, pp. 252–263.

Zeevat, H. (1999). Demonstratives in discourse. *Journal of Semantics 16*(4), 279–313.

A Semantically-Based Computational Approach to Narrative Structure

Rodolfo Delmonte
Ca' Foscari University of Venice
(delmont@unive.it)

Giulia Marchesini
Ca' Foscari University of Venice
(giuliamarches@gmail.com)

Abstract

In this paper we will define narrative structure as characterized by a basic element, the *narreme*, which is here described as the basic unit of narrative structure, the smallest possible unit of the story. We annotated a full novel – "The Solid Mandala" (1966) by Nobel laureate Patrick White – combining two approaches: one is related to sentiment and opinion mining, including deeper aspects connected to event factuality and subjectivity, and the other focuses on evaluative features derived from the Appraisal Theory framework. After characterizing the style, we will show the main significant events of the plot as they emerge from the distribution of deep semantic features. Narreme boundaries will be identified by presence of specific speech acts, change of point of view, and movement in spatio-temporal coordinates through flashbacks. An experiment with our system of text understanding, GETARUNS, has been carried out to test its ability to automatically identify narremes.

1 Introduction

According to Collier (1992) (hence GC92) Patrick White characterizes the plot of his books through the use of deep linguistic features: in particular, an accurate choice of words, syntactic structures, and semantic features is used to highlight specific portions of the role of each character in the narrative depending strictly on his/her personality traits and on the structure of the story. White's style remains always the same for all characters and sequences of events, but it varies its qualifying linguistic elements according to the point of view, to the events in the lives of the characters, and to the relationships in the storyline portrayed in the novel.

In order to make our narratological approach more transparent, we will here provide a brief summary of the main theme of "The Solid Mandala". Our novel tells the story of the life of twins Arthur and Waldo Brown, of their family, and of their neighbour, Mrs Poulter, all living in a suburb of Sydney. Waldo Brown is an appropriate example of many other important characters of Patrick White's novels, as well. He is the representative of the intellectual who failed to become an artist or even to accomplish anything of significance, ending up being a simple clerk in a municipal library. His life is empty of events and positive emotions. He is educated and despises his community, which he considers too uninteresting and uncultured for him to be a part of. This voluntary isolation translates in a general growing resentment and in open hostility towards his twin brother, who is completely different from him and yet always a constant in his life. Arthur and Waldo could not be more diametrically opposed. This opposition is specifically crafted to portray and therefore study two basic drives: intellect and intuition. We find in Waldo every characteristic of the academic individual driven by intellect, as we said before; in Arthur, instead, there is a more "feminine" intuition which is often painted as direct result of his weak wits. Contrary to his brother, Arthur is far from studious and clever: it is often difficult to understand him even from his point of view, and this does not seem to hold particular meaning for him. He has difficulty speaking and expressing himself, even though some of his thoughts are deeper and more significant than Waldo's. He loves others, even and mostly the brother who despises him and considers him an handicap. Most of all, he is completely, almost unbelievably good, always humble and helpful in his simple way of living.

This complex story was manually divided by Collier into *narremes* [1] and chronologically reorganized in order to reconstruct what in narratology is defined as *fabula*. This was limited to those units that have "event character"(GC92,p.36), "or which are processes or event-sequences of clearly demarcated duration". Narremes as entities are also defined as follows: "these narrative units might equally well be termed functions (at the level of the story, fabula, or recite) and motifs (at the levels of narrative, sujet, or discourse)". Each of them covers one independent event as narrated by a single point of view or by more than one [2]

For our study we created a new subdivision of the novel into narremes, partly following the approach suggested by Collier, but implementing 131 narremes to account for all events in the story, contrary to his total of 124. Four temporal blocks of narremes were selected: Childhood, Adulthood, Old Age and After Waldo's Death – this one only in Arthur's point of view.

As a first quantitative outline of the novel, we present here a short table indicating the main entities as they have been derived from the counts of tokens in each of the 131 narremes – or story units.

Quant.Data	Toks.Arthur	Annots.Arthur	Toks.Waldo	Annots.Waldo	Toks.Others	Annots.Others
SUM	54312	4060	66365	4894	32771	2208
MEAN	848.625	63.437	1106.083	81.567	1092.367	73.6
ST. DEV.	1040.998	82.528	1700.591	106.066	653.367	37.477

Table 1: Distribution per main characters of tokens, annotations, and their standard deviation

We also report in a second table general overall data to evaluate differences. As can be noticed, values of standard deviation are higher than the mean indicating a great irregularity in data distribution. However values for non protagonists, under "Others" are more regular thus marking a neat difference from the rest.

Items	Total	Mean	St.Deviation
Tokens	120,249	917.9	1149.3
Annotations	8616	65.78	84.26

Table 2: Number of tokens (including punctuation), annotations, and their standard deviation

Without considering punctuation, the total number of tokens is 106,935, the total of the types 9,419, and the type/token ratio is 0.0881. The repetition rate is very high, as can be gathered from the so-called Vocabulary Richness index. Coverage of 50% of the total text tokens is reached after first 70 entries in the Rank list. The lower portion of the Rank List, made up of Rare Words appearing only 3/2/1 times, is made of 6848 types. In the novel, Waldo is explicitly mentioned 1063 times, while Arthur 985, slightly less. This difference is also apparent in the distribution of tokens and annotations, as shown above in Table 1. The only case in which st.dev. is lower than the mean is in the distribution of annotations for other less important characters. As to presence of female and male characters, the pronoun "he" is used 2641 times, and "she" 1225 times. The two most prominent female characters of the story, Dulcie Feinstein and Mrs Poulter, are mentioned 282 and 277 times respectively. "Mrs", however, is mentioned 640 times: if compared to "Mr", appearing only 213 times, which makes women's role in the story highly important.

---

[1] As has been defined in Bonheim (2000) (pp. 1-11) and in Dorfman (1969). See also Wittmann (1975).

[2] Quoting Collier, "Some of the narremes could have been divided further, others perhaps merged where they are adjacent. The reader-response principles upon which the selection of narremes was made are at once simple and complex. They derive from the relative salience of given events to the reader's eye (after at least a second reading), and from the less overt pressure exerted by the presence of manifold details, leitmotifs and echoes or the microstructure level." Collier (1992), p. 37

In the second part of the paper we will describe the algorithm used in the experiment that we carried out to try and find narremes boundaries. The output was derived from a system for text understanding called GETARUNS, which has been used lately for event discovery and semantic similarity challenges. The novel is made up of sentences which by way of an homology (see Bal (1987)) are assumed to correspond to the linguistic content of the novel itself. Event units are expressed by eventive words – verbs, deverbal nouns, non-stative adjectives – and in our system they represent an action, a transition from one state to another. The system has been used to automatically detect and annotate event structures of news articles for the Event Workshop 2013 [3].

2   Highlighting Events in the Narrative Structure

Investigating the distribution of annotations throughout "The Solid Mandala" can also mean taking a closer look at differences and similarities in style amongst the narremes. The original structure of the novel, in fact, makes it difficult for the readers to judge the impact of earlier events on later occurrences at a first glance, and complicates the *sujet* – how events are presented in order to produce an emotive reaction from the reader - with a complex system of memories and triggers.

On the contrary, starting from the *fabula* – the logical sequence of events semantically related in space and time - is an easier way to compare events between themselves. Two premises on the peculiar characteristics of the narremes are in order. It is essential to keep in mind that there are two main kinds of narremes: some are tied to the actional present, and others are connected to memories, which can be either presented as such or directly connected to other narremes without explicit markers. Another relevant aspect is that not all the narremes have the same length, but they depend on the matching event. Some are consistent parts of the narration and cover many pages, while others are only made up of one or two sentences, implying disparity in word counts. At a first glance this difference could seem a problem for the analysis, but it really only shows how the author favored some events in the narrative, giving them a higher level of importance.

As anticipated, it is possible to identify three main stages of life for the twins Waldo and Arthur, each precisely represented by a certain number of narremes. They are:

- Childhood and youth (28 narremes)

- Adulthood (69 narremes)

- Old age (19 narremes)

This count only excludes narremes in which Mrs Poulter represents the point of view, and Arthur's narremes after Waldo's death. This arbitrary distinction aims to give better insight on the lifestyle of the two brothers and on how it changes throughout the years and decades.

2.1   The Density of Semantic Features Highlights *Significant Events*

We considered semantic features (see Bos and Delmonte (2008)) as the main elements used to link the style and the personality of the three main characters. They are the twins Waldo and Arthur Brown, each narrating one of the two main sections of the book, and their neighbour Mrs Poulter, who instead narrates the shorter first and last sections corresponding to prologue and epilogue. As for the annotation task itself, it was organized in three main meta-tags and a number of hierarchically related more specific ones, as shown in the table below. The annotation scheme is original and based on characteristics of the XML markup standard (elements, attributes and values). Our three high level features, the meta-tags, are *uncertainty*, *subjectivity* and *judgement*. Additionally, we annotated with the element *negative* all negative forms in the novel. Table 3 illustrates the hierarchy of the various features, with the attributes represented in italics and the values in normal text. [4].

---

[3] The 1st Workshop on EVENTS: Definition, Detection, Coreference, and Representation, HLT-NAACL, Atlanta

[4] We omit comments on the features because all detailed information about semantic features annotation are reported in a companion paper by the same authors in a workshop in this conference (see Delmonte and Marchesini (2017))

Uncertainty	Subjectivity	Judgement
Non-factual	*Psychology*	*Social-esteem*
Seeming	Perception	Positive/Negative
Gnomic	Precognition	*Social-sanction*
Concessive	Cognition	Positive/Negative
Conditional	PerformWill	
DefDesire	*Affect-emot*	
Will	Positive/Negative	
Possibility	*Affect-inclin*	
Ability	Positive/Negative	
Obligation	*Affect-secur*	
Assumption	Positive/Negative	
	Affect-satisf	
	Positive/Negative	

Table 3: Hierarchy of deep semantic features used in the annotation

Narreme length and number of annotations are both markers signaling importance. Even without a complex analysis, it is apparent that some events are fundamental for the story: we call these narremes "significant events". Significant events are characterized by a dense co-occurrence of stylistic features in more general terms, as well. In the two following Figures, we show the inter-relation between number of words annotated as a ratio of the total number of tokens. The areas of main concentration of the features are coincident with the ones that have been defined as "significant events" and are respectively: 1st area: 23-27; 2nd area: 42-45; 3rd area: 53-55; 4th area: 63-68; 5th area: 74-79b; 6th area: 92-94 + U2-U3; 7th area: 103-110; 8th area 121-125. As can be easily noticed, the peaks coincide with significant events, detected through individual assignment of relevant traits. The two diagrams below show how in some narremes the number of annotations is higher than in others. It was mentioned before that the length of the units plays an important role in many cases: to longer narremes are normally, but not consistently, associated more occurrences of each semantic trait.

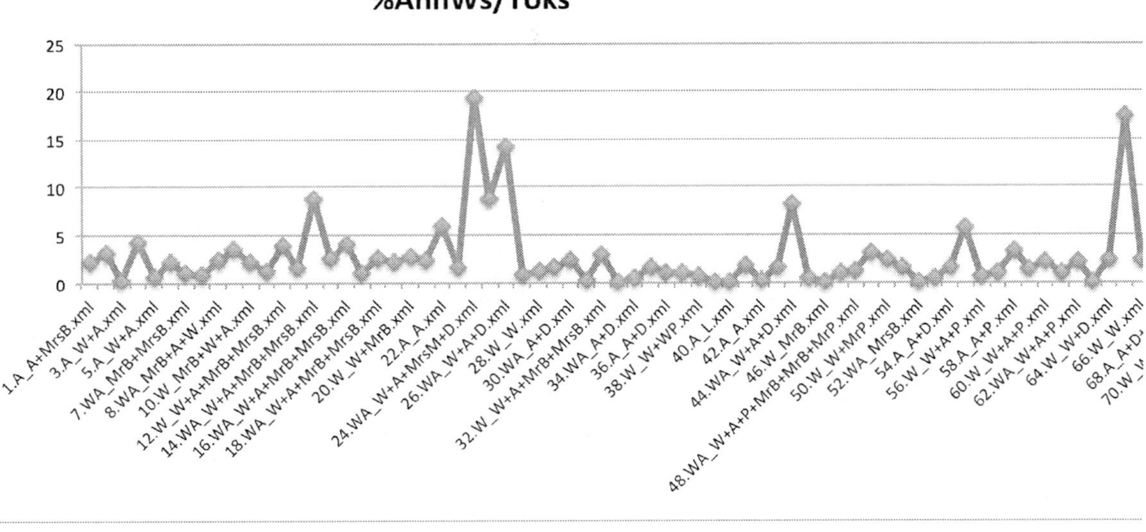

Figure 1: Distribution of words annotated in each narreme as a ratio of total tokens - first half of the novel

Narreme 104 - belonging to Waldo's section - represents the beginning of the actional present in

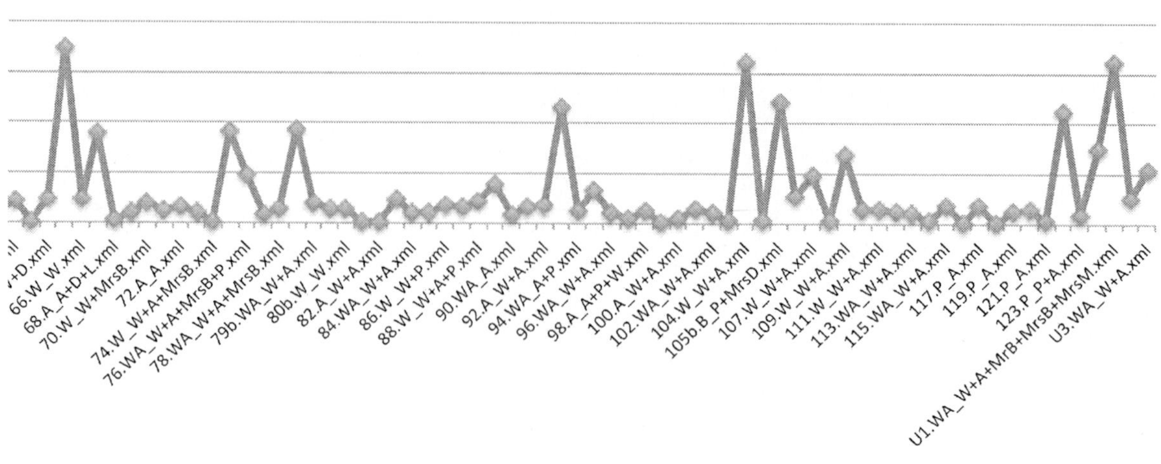

Figure 2: Distribution of words annotated in each narreme as a ratio of total tokens - second half of the novel

the *fabula*. Everything before this point is in the past and is constituted by memories. From here on, the events of the *fabula* follow the twins through Waldo's last days and, later, in Arthur's disorganized escape to Sydney. If we examine this section from a perspective involving the *sujet*, on the other hand, this is the first time in the novel that we meet Waldo as a narrator. The beginning of narreme 104 is in fact the beginning of the second section of the novel, Waldo's, immediately after the prologue-section "In the Bus". It covers roughly sixteen pages between 23 and 61, all in the first part of Waldo's section, and functions as a starting point for the stream of memories that comes afterwards. Interestingly, if we take into consideration the first segment of Arthur's narremes according to the *sujet* – first part of narreme 2, narreme 1, and then second part of narreme 2 – we notice something similar. In this case, strictly limiting the analysis at Arthur's section, the *sujet* almost coincides with the *fabula*, and we find an unusually high number of annotations if compared to most of the other narremes.

3 GETARUNS: a System for Text Understanding and Narreme Encoding

GETARUNS [5], the system for text understanding developed at the University of Venice, is organized as a pipeline which includes two versions of the system: what we call the Partial and the Deep GETARUNS. They work in a backoff policy: there are in fact three interconnected parsers, and they are activated in order to prevent failure. The system has a middle module for semantic interpretation and discourse model construction cast into Situation Semantics, and a higher module where reasoning and generation take place.

The system is based on the LFG theoretical framework and has a highly interconnected modular structure. The output of grammatical modules is fed onto the Binding Module, which activates an algorithm for anaphoric binding. Antecedents for pronouns are ranked according to grammatical function, semantic role, inherent features and their position at f-structure. Eventually, this information is added into the original f-structure graph and then passed on to the Discourse Module (hence DM).

---

[5]The system has been tested in STEP competition (see Bos and Delmonte (2008)), and can be downloaded in two separate places. The partial system called VENSES in its stand-alone version is available at http://www.aclweb.org/aclwiki/index.phptitle=Textual_Entailment_Resource_Pool. The complete deep system is available both at http://www.sigsem.org/wiki/STEP_2008_shared_task:_comparing_semantic_representations, and at http://project.cgm.unive.it/html/sharedtask/

GETARUNS has a linguistically based semantic module which is used to build up the DM. Semantic processing is strongly modularized and distributed amongst a number of different submodules. They in turn take care of Spatio-Temporal Reasoning, Discourse Level Anaphora Resolution, and other subsidiary processes, like Topic Hierarchy, which cooperate to find the most probable antecedent of coreferring and cospecifying referential expressions when creating semantic individuals. These are then asserted in the DM, which is at this point the only knowledge representation here used to solve nominal coreference. The system employs two resolution submodules working in sequence: the first one is run whenever a free sentence external pronoun is spotted; the second one takes the results of the first submodule and checks for nominal anaphora. They have access to all data structures contemporarily and pass the resolved pair of anaphor-antecedent to the following modules. Semantic Mapping is performed in two steps: at first is created a Logical Form, which is a structural mapping from DAGs onto unscoped well-formed formulas. These are then turned into situational semantics informational units, infons, which may become facts or sits. Each unit has a relation, a list of arguments, which in our case receive their semantic roles from lower processing – a polarity, a temporal and a spatial location index.

All entities and their properties are asserted in the DM with the relations in which they are involved; in turn the relations may have modifiers - sentence-level adjuncts – and the entities may have modifiers and attributes, as well. Each entity has a polarity and a couple of spatio-temporal indices linked to main temporal and spatial locations (if any exists). Otherwise they are linked to a presumed time reference derived from tense and aspect computation. On the second occurrence of the same nominal head the semantic index is recovered from the history list and the system checks whether it is the same referring expression and has non-conflicting attributes or properties. In all other cases a new entity is asserted in the DM, being however computed as included in (a superset of) or by (a subset of) the previous entity.

3.1 Coreference Links

In this section we briefly present the addition to the GETARUNS system added for the purpose of this task. The annotation of each narreme is shown in a XML file obtained with the following steps:

1. The GETARUNS system provides a deep analysis of each narreme on a sentence-by-sentence basis. At the end of this preliminary analysis, markables are collected and all semantic information is attached to each word in the sentence. With this system we collected all verbs, eventive nominals, and possible eventive modifiers. This is done in two steps:

1a. At the end of parsing, each word of the sentence is associated to its lemma. General semantic categories are collected from the analysis, as well.

1b. The system provides the steps required for building the Discourse Model, i.e. where entities, relations and properties are asserted along with their attributes. Semantic indices are assigned to each new entity, and previous mentions receive the previously assigned indices. At this point the contents of the Discourse Model are associated to each word in the sentence.

2. At the end of the analysis of the narreme the system collects all markables, which are internally made of four elements: markable index, word, lemma, semantic index (extracted from the Discourse Model) or a generic indicator of eventuality for all verbs.

3. The complete Discourse Model is searched to create a list of all entities, relations and properties, this time with spatio-temporal coordinates, relations and polarity – as documented in situation semantics. Additional information is derived in this phase from WordNet, FrameNet or SumoMilo, and is made available to the coreference algorithm. Another component activated at this point is sentiment analysis, which computes affective labels associated to each markable – if possible – and classifies each markable into three different classes: positive, negative or neutral.

4. The coreference algorithm works as follows: for each markable it checks all possible coreference links, at first only on the basis of inherent semantic features – wordform and lemma identity; then semantic similarity is measured on the basis of a number of lexically-based similarity criteria, without statistical measures. Searching WordNet synsets, we assign a score according to whether the markables are directly contained in the same synset or not. A different score is assigned if their relation can be inferred from the hierarchy.

5. After collecting all possible coreferential relations between semantically validated markables, we proceed to filter out all inconsistent or incompatible links according to three criteria: - first criterion: diverse sentiment polarity - second criterion: different argument structure - third criterion: non-related spatio-temporal relations Both argument structure and spatio-temporal relations are collected in the discourse structure, which also contains dependence relations expressed by discourse relations in discourse structure, temporal logical relations – as computed from an adaptation of Allen's algorithm –, and a point of view computed on the basis of presence of "reportive" verbs – direct speech, reported speech, reported indirect speech. Another selected criterion relates to the nature of semantic similarities as computed by the system: values below a certain threshold indicate that the coreference was chosen on the basis of weak similarity. This last point is based on thesauri classification.

4   Computing Narreme Boundaries

As said above, narreme boundaries are identified by the presence or absence of specific speech acts, by changes in the point of view, and by movements in spatio-temporal coordinates through flashbacks. The module looking for narremes tries to individuate their boundaries, taking as input the analysis of the text at a syntactic and semantic level. To evaluate results, it makes use of the ranges of all narremes as they were manually identified through start and sentence numbers. More in detail, the input is made of the following semantic information: - the list of entities evaluated as main, secondary and potential topics of discourse by the specialized centering algorithm with Topic Hierarchy, which works on the output of the anaphora resolution modules (see Grosz and Sidner (1986) Grosz et al. (1995)); - the list of discourse structures computed one for each clause, containing information on discourse moves, relations and main predicates in each clause.

At first the algorithm creates clusters of clauses around each entity in a sequence; it then keeps only the ones constituting frequently mentioned entities, or characters of the story. It eventually extracts another subset of clauses, this time characterized by the fact that the main predicate is included in a list of speech acts – verbs like "decide", "discover" etc., and those introducing direct discourse like "say", "ask", "tell" etc. Clusters are a function of four variables: Topic linguistic description - which may be subject to different types of mentions identified and unified under the same Semantic Identifier in the Discourse Model; Topic Type, in a hierarchy including Expected, Potential, Secondary and Main; Discourse Move - one among three (Up, Down, Level) - which are computed by the Discourse Structure module and assigned to a Clause identifier; Clause Relevance, one of two possibilities, Foreground or Background - computed on the basis of Tense, Aspect and Factuality again associated to a Clause Identifier.

At this point the algorithm has all the information it needs to decide whether two adjacent clusters may be unified into a single one or be left separate. If the second case is true, the boundary is individuated in the clause following the last one of each cluster, by matching the list of speech-act-related clauses or examining the distance between the two adjacent clusters [6] .

4.1   A Close Look at the Narreme Clustering Algorithm

We report here below the higher portion of the algorithm for narreme identification written in Prolog. In order to make the algorithm testable, we split the novel into 4 separate sections obeying criteria indicated above. The algorithm starts by loading system output for a given section of the novel and then the sentence range associated to each narreme as computed manually in order to make evaluation possible. Then it loads the structures of each clause computed at discourse level which are made up

---

[6]Our method is different from previous attempts at text segmentation, but is also similar in some aspects. It is different from plot-units segmentation proposed by Lehnert (1995) and lately by Goyal et al. (2010) which is solely based on affect and mental states of characters. It is different from Topic based segmentation purported by Hearst (1997) in its TextTiling system, and lately attempted in literary texts by Kazantseva and Szpakowicz (2012), because topics alone are not sufficient cue for our novel. It is also different from the approach proposed in Swanson et al. (2014) where the authors elaborate an annotation scheme at clause-level with an analysis based on Labov (1997) which distinguishes three types of clauses for narrative labeling: Action, Orientation and Evaluation. These are then used to create plot units

by a SentenceNumber, a ClauseNumber, the main verbal predicate, the Relevance computed and the Discourse Move. As a second element of the computation, the algorithm loads all topics as they have been computed by the coreference module and the topic hierarchy module. Topics are collected by their Semantic unique Identifier in the Discourse Model, the Topic Head, and the Clause number.

```
findallnarremes :-
    consult ( systemoutput1 ) ,
    consult ( sents_range ) ,
    findall ( Nsen-Cl-Pred-Relv-DsMv,  (
            sd_structure ( Nsen , Cl , Sbj , DsRel , Tens , Pred , Relv , DsMv , Move )
            ) , AllMovess ) ,
    reverse ( AllMovess , AllMoves ) ,
    findall ( SemId-Head-Cl , (
            topic ( Cl , Type , SemId ) ,
            topps ( Ty ,  Cls ,  Head ,  SemId , [ P , G , N , Sf , Sr ] )
            ) , AllCharss ) ,
    sort ( AllCharss , AllChars ) ,
    unifyallChars ( AllChars , Uniques ) ,
    eliminacharsminors ( Uniques , MainChars ) ,
    elaborate_output ( AllMoves , MainChars ) .
```

As a first step, the system unifies all Topics or Characters of the novel by their frequency - in number of clauses in which they are present-, choosing the most frequent ones, thus indirectly selecting the protagonists. Minor characters are filtered and deleted from the list. The net result is a list of protagonists with their Semantic identifier and all clauses in which they appear, which is accompanied by all moves - in the variable AllMoves - in discourse structure and passed to the call "elaborate output".

```
elaborate_output ( AllMoves , MainChars ): -
    clusteringchars ( MainChars , Clusters ) ,
    createclusters ( AllMoves , Clusters , Created ) ,
    extractculminated ( AllMoves , Culminated ) ,
    countranges ( 1 , Created , Outputs ) ,
    searchadjacents ( Culminated , Outputs , Output ) ,
    tell ( allranges ) ,
    writeoutputall ( Output ) ,
    told ,
    ! .
```

The final call of the algorithm does the following actions. It finds clusters of events associated to the main character/s. The first call "clusteringchars" decomposes the single list of clauses related to a single character into a set of ClauseNo-TopicHead-SemIdentifier triples, in order to reconstruct the "fabula"-based sequence of events per each protagonist. Then "createclusters" associates discourse level information and sentence number to each TopicHead thus make a quadruple, SentNumb-ClauseNo-TopicHead-Move. Then it creates a cluster by unifying in the same sublist all quadruples which have a Clause Number smaller than a threshold computed on the basis of the difference between the current clause number and the new one. This difference has been set to 7. In this way clusters may contain clauses referrable to same or different character/s as long as they are close enough. The following call, "extractculminated" chooses those discourse structures that have "culminated" verb predicates associated, i.e. special events that can mark the beginning of a new narreme and that will be used to individuate narreme boundaries. "Countranges" filters those clusters which are too small, i.e. smaller than 10 elements. Eventually the last call "searchadjacents" glues clusters which are close enough into one single "narreme" also checking whether the beginning and end are suitable.

Results from the analysis of the output of the whole of Waldo's and Arthur's chapters indicate an accuracy of 48%, which is the best result obtained with various attempts using different weights on the data available. In particular, we tried at first to make the choice of the ending boundary dependent on the presence of a new entity being asserted as Potential Topic, i.e. having entered the Entity List for the first time. Then we modified the algorithm to take into account presence of a clause with a predicate included in the list of speech acts. We eventually combined the two choices and got the best result, which is still however below 50%.

5   Conclusion

In this paper we focused on the analysis of a novel, "The Solid Mandala" (1966) by Nobel laureate Patrick White, annotating its whole text with semantic features. In addition, we manually subdivided the text into narremes, basing our work on the reconstruction of the *fabula* seen in Collier (1992). The problematic aspect of White's style is that it merges plot characteristics – connected to the *fabula* – with character traits. As a consequence, feelings, emotions and actions of the narrating characters are all deeply intertwined with the plot and the narrated events.

    We tried an automatic extraction of narremes from the output of a system for text understanding, which is strongly semantically driven. Results are still however below the 50% threshold, suggesting that the level of difficulty of the task is extremely high.

References

Bal, M. (1987). *Narratology*. Toronto: University of Toronto Press.

Bonheim, H. (2000). Shakespeare's narremes. *Shakespeare Survey: Shakespeare and narrative 53*.

Bos, J. and R. Delmonte (2008). *STEP '08 - Proceedings of the 2008 Conference on Semantics in Text Processing*. Semantics. London: College Publications.

Collier, G. (1992). *The Rocks and Sticks of Words Style, Discourse and Narrative Structure in the Fiction of Patrick White*. Amsterdam Atlanta: Editions Rodopi B. V.

Delmonte, R. and G. Marchesini (2017). A semantically based computational approach to the annotation of narrative style. In *Proceedings of IWCS, International Workshop on Computational Semantics*, Stroudsburg, PA, USA, pp. 1–12. ACL.

Dorfman, E. (1969). *The narreme in the medieval romance epic: An introduction to narrative structures*. University of Toronto Press.

Goyal, A., E. Riloff, and H. D. III (2010). Automatically producing plot unit representations for narrative text. In *Proceedings of the 2010 Conference on Empirical Methods in Natural Language Processing - EMNLP 2010*, Stroudsburg, PA, USA. ACL.

Grosz, B., A. K. Joshi, and S. Weinstein (1995). Centering: A framework for modeling the local coherence of discourse. *Computational Linguistics 21*(2).

Grosz, B. and C. Sidner (1986). Attention, intentions, and the structure of discourse. *Computational Linguistics 12*(3).

Hearst, M. A. (1997). Texttiling: Segmenting text into multi-paragraph subtopic passages. *Computational Linguistics 23*.

Kazantseva, A. and S. Szpakowicz (2012). Topical segmentation: a study of human performance. In *Proceedings of Human Language Technologies: The 2012 Annual Conference of the NAACL*, Stroudsburg, PA, USA, pp. 211–220. ACL.

Labov, W. (1997). Some further steps in narrative analysis. *Journal of narrative and life history 7*, 395–415.

Lehnert, W. G. (1995). Plot units and narrative summarization. *Cognitive Science 5*(4), 293–331.

Swanson, R., E. Rahimtoroghi, T. Corcoran, and M. A. Walker (2014). Identifying narrative clause types in personal stories. In *Proceedings of the SIGDIAL 2014 Conference*, Stroudsburg, PA, USA, pp. 171–180. ACL.

Wittmann, H. (1975). Thorie des narrèmes et algorithmes narratifs. *Poetics 4*(1), 19–28.

Graph Databases for Designing High-Performance Speech Recognition Grammars

Maria Di Maro
Università degli Studi di Napoli Federico II
mdimaro17@gmail.com

Marco Valentino
Università degli Studi di Napoli Federico II
m.valentino91@gmail.com

Anna Riccio
Università degli Studi di Napoli 'L'Orientale'
ariccio@unior.it

Antonio Origlia
Università degli Studi di Padova
antonio.origlia@unipd.it

Abstract

The present paper reports on the advantages of using graph databases in the development of dynamic language models in Spoken Language Understanding applications, such as spoken dialogue systems. First of all, we introduce Neo4J graph databases and, specifically, MultiWordNet-Extended, a graph representing linguistic knowledge. After this first overview, we show how information included in graphs can be used in speech recognition grammars to automatically extend a generic rule structure. This can be the case of linguistic elements, such as synonyms, hypernyms, meronyms and phonological neighbours, which are semantically or structurally related to each other in our mental lexicon. In all the AI based approaches depending on a training process using large and representative corpora, the probability to correctly predict the creativity a speaker can perform in using language and posing questions is lower than expected. Trying to capture most of the possible words and expressions a speaker could use is extremely necessary, but even an empirical, finite collection of cases could not be enough. For this reason, the use of our tool appears as an appealing solution, capable of including many pieces of information. In addition, we used the proposed tool to develop a spoken dialogue system for museums and the preliminary results are shown and discussed in this paper.

1 Introduction

While research on Natural Language Understanding is still investigating how to reliably interpret unconstrained user utterances, practical applications that are now common on mobile devices, like virtual assistants, heavily rely on utterance templates to provide their services. Such language models can be dynamically loaded depending on the situation so that the speech recognition engine becomes biased towards the set of utterances the underlying dialogue system is able to manage. For relatively small and well-defined dialogue domains, using this kind of language model appears to be a practical choice for application developers. The problems posed by language variability, however, do not only impact the functionality of spoken dialogue systems at run time: developing grammar-based language models can be a time-consuming and error-prone task by itself. Taking advantage of structured linguistic knowledge to overcome this aspect of dialogue systems design has led, in the past, to the use of linguistic ontologies to automatically expand the set of terms accepted by the speech recognition system (Milward and Beveridge, 2003). Using lexical ontologies to represent the knowledge a machine has to process is something which has been investigated in early years: WordNet (Miller, 1993), (Fellbaum, 1998) was used in machine translation (Knight, 1993), information extraction (Burke et al., 1995), automatic text summarisation (Chaves, 2001) and domain-specific dialogue systems management (Snae and Bruckner, 2008). In previous works, the preferred way of using ontological knowledge in dialogue systems appears to be based on the use of explicit reference to the classes defined in the taxonomy. This, however, implies that ontologies supporting the dialogue domain must already exist or be constructed before the system can take advantage from it. Modern approaches to data representation, however, use powerful querying languages to extract knowledge that is not explicitly structured in the ontological organisation by the presence of dedicated classes. Moreover, it appears that, while the interest towards using ontologies in dialogue systems is well-established, there has been a less significant effort towards the definition of a common way to merge grammar definitions supporting ontological expansions. In this paper, we present a formal language to describe ontologically-enriched language models. This language is obtained by expanding the W3C Speech Recognition Grammar Specification (SRGS) XML standard (Hunt and McGlashan, 2003) with an item dedicated to queries directed towards knowledge bases returning lists of words. In our work, we generalise the use of ontologies by proposing the integration with a graph database, which can represent ontologies as well as other forms of data representation based on objects and relationships among objects. The paper is organised as follows: in Section 2 we describe the Neo4J graph database (Webber, 2012), which is the system we consider for knowledge representation in our work, and highlight the advantages it poses for dialogue systems support. In the same Section, we also describe a specific Neo4J database hosting different types of linguistic information ranging from morphology to phonology. In Section 3, we describe the extended SRGS language we designed while, in Section 4, we present some use cases of interest. In the closing Section 5, we show the results we got in testing a spoken dialogue system using the designed grammars, in order to prove its quality.

2 Neo4J Graph Database

Neo4J[1] is a no-SQL database adopting a graph-based representation of data. Its approach is very similar to the Resource Description Framework (RDF), which is often adopted for Linked Open Data. Neo4J and RDF representations can be both graphically described using nodes and arcs but there is a fundamental difference in the focus put on graph elements. While RDF is edge-centred, graph databases are node-centred. Furthermore, graph databases also explicitly distinguish *properties* from relationships and both nodes and relationships can be specified with labels, which are close to the concept of class in ontologies. Another important difference lies in the way the two approaches provide access to the hosted data. RDF can be queried using inference rules to extract implicit information from the explicit relationships. Graph databases are more suited to graph traversing and path finding. Choosing one over the other may depend on the application but, in the domain of grammars for dialogue systems, the more natural way of representing data is an advantage to keep the specified domains clear. Neo4J, in particular, has developed a powerful, and yet clear, querying language - Cypher - that makes heavy use of ASCII graphical characters to build its syntax. Among the most important ones, round brackets are used to specify nodes, square brackets for relationship labels, ASCII arrows to link nodes specifying arcs orientations (if necessary), and curly brackets to specify for properties. Being ontologies, it is straightforward to think of the linguistic organisation proposed in Wordnets as graphs. In our work, we adopt a Neo4J conversion of a wordnet for Italian that has been extended to include phonological data. We will present how Cypher can be used to extend grammar templates using linguistic and domain knowledge.

2.1 MutiWordNet-Extended

MultiWordNet-Extended (MWN-E) (Origlia et al., 2017) is a Neo4J database representing part of the Italian lexicon. It combines linguistic resources, specifically MultiWordNet (Pianta et al., 2002), Morph-it (Zanchetta and Baroni, 2005), TreeTagger (Schmid et al., 2007; Schmid, 2013) and the ISTC pronunciation dictionary (Cosi et al., 2001). The resulting database is a collection of data concerning semantic relations between lemmas. Relationship types cover both morpho-syntactic and phonological aspects. All the words contained in the database are taken from MultiWordNet and stored as nodes. They are given a morpho-syntactic label, such as NOUN, VERB, ADVERB or ADJECTIVE and are linked to SYNSET nodes by means of the semantic relationship BELONGS_TO. Synsets are then linked to one another with

---

[1] https://neo4j.com/product/

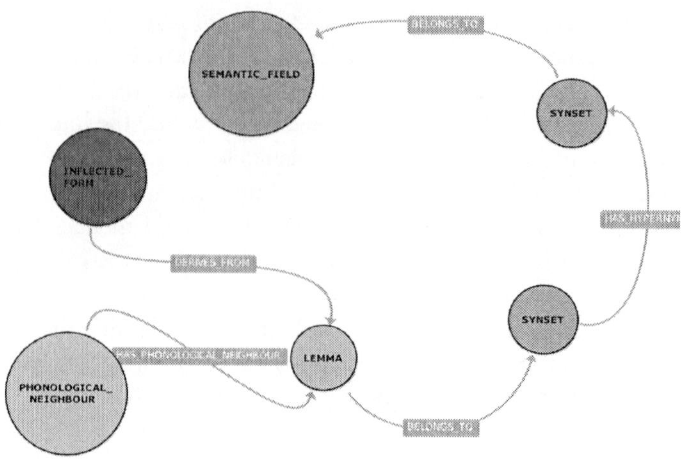

Figure 1: Nodes and relationships in MWN-E

an hypernymic relation and to SEMANTIC_FIELD nodes with a BELONGS_TO connection. By explicating this relationships, a semantic annotation is carried out. MultiWordNet, by itself, is not a complete representation of the language knowledge. For example, including the most common inflected forms and their phonological transcription makes it possible to use the same database to combine phonological and semantic information. To extend MultiWordNet this way, a procedure to import morpho-syntactic data using Morph-it and TreeTagger was adopted to add data like gender, number and inflection types for derived forms. Also, the ISTC pronunciation dictionary, was used to import phonological transcriptions in SAMPA format, including syllabification and accent position. Inflected forms are represented as new nodes, linked to their lemmas using a DERIVES_FROM relationship. Also, phonological neighbourhoods were computed and represented using HAS_PHONOLOGICAL_NEIGHBOUR connections. This kind of connection has a property describing the phonological distance (i.e. the Minimum Edit Distance between the SAMPA trascriptions) to distinguish homophones from actual neighbours. Figure 1 shows the general organisation of the database. Using MWN-E can be essential for a developer to easily create a language model including sets of words with a connected meaning, without having to write them manually. An example may be the need of encompassing the synonyms of a word used in a particular semantic field, as shown in the following query (1).

```
MATCH (n:NOUN {word: 'automobile'})-[:BELONGS_TO]->(m:SYNSET)<-[:BELONGS_TO]-(k:NOUN),
(m)-[:BELONGS_TO]->(j:SEMANTIC_FIELD {name: 'Tourism'})
RETURN distinct n.word, k.word
```
(1)

With this query we want to look for synonyms of the word *automobile* ('car') belonging to the semantic field 'Tourism'. Synonyms that are found are *auto*, *autovettura*, *vettura*, and *macchina*. They are part of a synset, which we can refer to in a grammar, without explicitly specify each lemma. In the next sections, it will be exemplified how we integrated Neo4J queries within a standard language for speech recognition grammars and we will show some examples of spoken dialogue systems taking advantage of this knowledge.

3   Speech Recognition Grammars and our extension proposal

Language data are formalised in order to let a machine be able to understand natural language and to actively produce it in giving answers, as far as a spoken dialogue system is concerned. This data can be organised in a grammar. The W3C standard we refer to in this paper is the Speech Recognition Grammar Specification (SRGS). This standard has been developed to allow Automatic Speech Recognition (ASR) engines to output the semantic interpretation of the matched pattern instead of the raw transcription. This is an important advantage for spoken dialogue systems as they can instruct ASR modules to *expect* specific word patterns and to present a structured interpretation of the obtained input to be provided to the dialogue manager. This results in reduced latency, as linguistic analysis chains working on raw strings are avoided, and in a more definite separation between dialogue management and input management. A speech recognition grammar $G = \{R_1, R_2, ...R_n\}$ is a finite set of rules. Each R_i generates a set A_i of utterances associated to semantic labels S_i so $R_i \vdash A_i, S_i$. Given a collection of semantic relations $X = \{x_1, x_2...x_n\}$, the tool described in this paper aims at expanding each R_i in a grammar G, according to $x_i \in X$, in order to produce a new grammar G' where the set of generated utterances A_i is included in A'_i. More formally:

$$T(G, X) = G' \mid \forall R'_i \in G', \quad R'_i \vdash A'_i, S_i \to A_i \subseteq A'_i$$

In SRGS, XML is used to describe what the ASR engine should expect. It is, then, possible to specify how the matched pattern should be returned to the dialogue manager in terms of semantic interpretation by using the W3C Semantic Markup Language (SML) (Van Tichelen and Burke, 2007). When combined, these two languages allow a dialogue manager to instruct and ASR engine to provide the semantic interpretation corresponding to actions and parameters it can handle in its current state. Listing all words accepted in a specific position, however, can be time-consuming for the dialogue designer. In the following example, suppose we want to match the regular expression pattern "dipingere .* quadro" ('do .* painting') against a generic output "PAINT" the dialogue manager can handle. Suppose we also want to accept all possible synonyms of the verb *dipingere* ('to paint') and of the noun *quadro* ('painting'). Using SRGS, we would obtain the following

```
1  <rule id="Query" scope="public">
2      <tag> out.QueryType="NONE"</tag>
3      ...
4      <ruleref uri="#PAINT" /> <tag> out.QueryType=rules.PAINT</tag>
5      ...
6  </rule>
7
8  <rule id="PAINT">
9      <ruleref special="GARBAGE"/>
10     <one-of>
11         ...
12         <item>dipingere</item>
13         <item>raffigurare</item>
14         ...
15     </one-of>
16     <ruleref special="GARBAGE"/>
17     <one-of>
18         ...
19         <item>quadro</item>
20         <item>dipinto</item>
21         ...
22     </one-of>
23  </rule>
```

Lists of synonym words, however, can be obtained by querying the MWN-E database. We therefore use an attribute *query* for the generic tag *item* to indicate that the item should be substituted with a list of alternative words, thus obtaining the more compact representation

```
1  <rule id="Query" scope="public">
2      <tag> out.QueryType="NONE"</tag>
3      ...
4      <ruleref uri="#PAINT" /> <tag> out.QueryType=rules.PAINT</tag>
5      ...
6  </rule>
7
8  <rule id="PAINT">
9      <ruleref special="GARBAGE"/>
10     <item query="MATCH ({word:"dipingere"})-[:BELONGS_TO]->()<-[:BELONGS_TO]-(m) RETURN m.
           word">dipingere</item>
```

```
11    <ruleref special="GARBAGE"/>
12    <item query="MATCH (({word:"quadro"}))-[:BELONGS_TO]->()<-[:BELONGS_TO]-(m) RETURN m.word">
         quadro</item>
13 </rule>
```

In this example, the Cypher query identifies all the nodes that have a BELONGS_TO relationship with the same synset the node having the value *dipingere* is part of, thus obtaining synonyms. Of course, this is not anymore an SRGS compliant XML document. A dialogue manager using these SRGS *templates* should be equipped with a simple software module to obtain an SRGS compliant XML document that can be passed to an ASR engine.

4   Case Study: Spoken Dialogue System for Cultural Heritage

Imagine you want to create a spoken dialogue system able to understand questions about artworks contained in a museum. Instead of writing all the possible words occurring in a particular syntactic structure to express a concept, we can include queries in our grammars. Speech recognition grammars were built in a way that made them suitable to represent structurally different questions expressing the same meaning. In the example (1), about materials, the rule contains different synonyms of the verb *utilizzare* ('to utilise'), such as *adoperare* ('to employ'), *usare* ('to use'), *impiegare* ('to use') and their inflected forms. Similarly, in the example (2), the synonyms of the word *periodo* ('period'), such as *contesto* ('context'), *epoca* ('epoch'), *secolo* ('century'), *milieu* and the inflected forms of the verb *vivere* ('to live') were encapsulated in the same rule, enabling the system to automatically understand different expressions of the same question:

(1)   *Quali materiali utilizza l'artista?*   'Which materials did the artist use?'

(2)   *In che periodo è vissuto l'artista?*   'In which period did the artist live?'

For example, the question in example (1) can be modelled as follows:

```
1  <item>
2     <item>
3        <one-of>
4           <item>che</item>
5           <item>quali</item>
6        </one-of>
7     </item>
8     <ruleref special="GARBAGE"/>
9     <item>materiali</item>
10    <ruleref special="GARBAGE"/>
11    <item query="MATCH (n:VERB {word:'usare'})-[:BELONGS_TO]->(s:SYNSET)
12         MATCH (:SEMANTIC_FIELD {name: 'Factotum'})<-[:BELONGS_TO]-(s)<-[:BELONGS_TO]-(k:
              VERB)<-[:DERIVES_FROM]-(q:VERB) RETURN distinct q.word">usare</item>
13    <ruleref special="GARBAGE"/>
14    <item>artista</item>
15 </item>
```

By simply including a query like **MATCH (n:VERB {word:'usare'})-[:BELONGS_TO]-> (s:SYNSET), MATCH (:SEMANTIC_FIELD {name: 'Factotum'})<-[:BELONGS_TO]-(s)<-[:BELONGS_TO]-(k:VERB)<-[:DERIVES_FROM]-(q:VERB) RETURN distinct q.word**, it was possible to get an extended grammar encompassing all the synonyms and the inflected forms of the verb *usare* ('to use'), in order to be able to correctly process different expression of the same question. The obtained extended grammar is shown in the below xml code:

```
1  <rule>
2     <item>
3        <one-of>
4           <item>usare</item>
5           <item>uso</item>
6           <item>usi</item>
7           <item>usa</item>
```

```
8              ...
9              <item>utilizzare</item>
10             ...
11             <item>impiegare</item>
12             ...
13             <item>adoperare</item>
14             ...
15         </one-of>
16     </item>
17 </rule>
```

Other content and formal information can be included by referring to MWN-E. As far as semantic aspects are concerned, we consider meronymic and hyperonymic relationships. Meronymy is concerned with part-whole relationships at a semantic level, meaning that entities are not only physically but also conceptually connected (Croft and Cruse, 2004). Speakers conceptualise reality and create specific significant associations between concepts, as a result that not each part of a whole can have relevance. Some entities are so relevant that can be used to refer to the whole they are part of. Part-whole associations are contained in the graph database MWN-E and including them can be useful to cover all the possible utterances a speaker can produce in a creative way. Suppose a speaker wants to ask the system a question on the painting "Tamara in a Green Bugatti" by Tamara de Lempicka, as in the example (3):

(3)   *Chi è il personaggio al volante? = Chi è il personaggio nell'auto?*
         'Who is the subject behind the wheel?' = 'Who is the subject in the car?'

This variation can be ruled by using a query, as in (2), including all the parts a car is made up of:

```
MATCH (n:NOUN{word: 'auto'})-[:BELONGS_TO]->(l)-[:HAS_PART]->(m)-[:BELONGS_TO]-(g)<-
[:BELONGS_TO]-(p)<-[:BELONGS_TO]-(h)
MATCH (p:SYNSET)-[:BELONGS_TO]->(g:SEMANTIC_FIELD{name: 'Mechanics'})              (2)
MATCH (m:SYNSET)-[:BELONGS_TO]->(g:SEMANTIC_FIELD{name: 'Mechanics'})
RETURN n.word, l.word, m.word, g.word, p.word, h.word
```

It is interesting to notice that meronymy is mainly concerned with conceptual relationships belonging to the same conceptual domain; for this reason, this kind of relation, as opposed to metaphors, can be better represented and formalised within an ontology.

Another important information to include is the relationship between general and specific words. Words with a general meaning, also known as hypernym, express concepts which are easily accessible to speakers (Feldman, 2013). For this reason, these words correspond to the basic level of categorisation (Rosch, 1976). Hypernymic words are, therefore, more frequently used, even when we want to refer to something which can be linguistically specified. Supposing we want to model the lexical variety concerning a particular frame, such as ART, we surely need specific terms, but being able to automatically include their hypernym is important to avoid misrecognitions. For instance, *pittore* ('painter) is the exact term used to refer to the author of a painting, but the basic term *artista* ('artist') can also be used to refer to the same concept. These terms are indeed related by an hypernymic relation in our database. Another example concerning hyperonymy can refer to the relation between *tela* ('canvas') and *quadro* ('painting'), which are interchangeable in some contexts, such as *Chi è l'autore di questa tela?* ('Who is the author of this canvas?') and *Chi è l'autore di questo quadro?* ('Who is the author of this painting'). In MWN-E they are related to each other by means of an hypernymic relationship, in that *tela* is an hyponym of *quadro*. For this reason, this information can be also included in our grammars.

Phonological neighbourhoods can, instead, be useful to work with words that *sound* similar. In the case of logopedic applications, for example, phonological neighbours can be used to develop dialogue systems to test the capability of distinguishing consonantic traits, in people with speech disorders. Since the speech recogniser could misunderstand some similar words, phonological neighbours can be here used to improve the quality of the recognition, as we will see in the next Section.

	Artist's name	Artist's place	Artist's time	Materials	Techniques	Painting's Time	Style	Iconography	Painting's place	Painting's name	Aim/Function	Dimension	Realisation time	Legends	Commission	Elements	Economic value
Artist's name	14																
Artist's place	1	19															
Artist's time			15														
Materials				12													1
Techniques					16					2							
Painting's time			3			17										1	
Style							18								1		1
Iconography								15	1		1					1	
Painting's place									16								
Painting's name	1					1			1	15							
Aim/Function	1										14						
Dimension												16					1
Realisation time													16				
Legends				1										13			
Commission															12		
Elements																12	
Economic value																	10
NC	3	1	2	7	4	2	2	5	2	3	5	4	4	7	7	6	7
%Correct Classification	70%	95%	75%	60%	80%	85%	90%	75%	80%	75%	70%	80%	80%	65%	60%	60%	50%
%Incorrect Classification	30%	5%	25%	40%	20%	15%	10%	25%	20%	25%	30%	20%	20%	35%	40%	40%	50%

Figure 2: Confusion Matrix showing the classification results

5 Results and Discussions

To verify the quality of the described extended grammars, we tested them in the pipeline of a spoken dialogue system. Specifically, the test intends to verify if the system is able to understand the belonging class of posed questions. The suggested classes were *Artist's name, Artist's place, Artist's time, Materials, Techniques, Painting's time, Style, Iconography, Painting's place, Painting's name, Aim/Function, Dimension, Realisation time, Legends, Commission, Elements* and *Economic value*. 10 testers were shown two paintings and were requested to ask for information about them. In particular, they had to ask 2 questions per class, a simple and a more complex one. In total, we were able to analyse 340 questions in this test. This was important to prove that the system was able to understand the meaning of a question, in order to map the correct answer on the right semantic class. Identifying the correct class can be seen as a conceptual hinge between the received input and the output to be generated, and a well-formed grammar is the key part of this process. In order to verify the performance of the designed grammars an experimental system setup was built. A 3D scene, designed with Unreal Engine 4, was designed to show the considered paintings to the users. The Kinect 2.0 was applied as speech recogniser, adopting grammars modelled through the SRGS standard. The test that we carried out shows that, by using our grammar, the confusion between the classes is low (19 questions out of 340), as shown in the confusion matrix in Figure 2. This is easily possible, since the classes are well described by means of the automatic extension to all the semantic and grammatical relations of the few included words used to express a particular concept.

To get a deeper insight, we can divide the classes into three groups, according to their precision:

- 7 high-performance classes (in green): for the classes *Artist's Place, Techniques, Painting's Time, Style, Painting's Place, Dimension* and *Realisation Time* the classification was correct in the 80%-100% of the cases;

- 6 medium-performance classes (in blue): for the classes *Artist's Name*, *Artist's Time*, *Iconography*, *Painting's Name*, *Aim/Function* and *Legends* the classification was correct in the 65%-75% of the cases;

- 4 low-performance classes (in red): for the classes *Materials*, *Commission*, *Elements* and *Economic value* the classification was correct in the 50%-60% of the cases.

The modelled questions were mostly well classified by the system, but some questions (71 out of 340) were not recognised at all, because some of them were not included in the grammar, for further empirical collections are still needed. Most of the non-recognised questions belong to the last 4 low-performance classes. As a matter of fact, for these classes a lot of questions asked were not included in our grammars, for they were not prototypical. For example, the question *Ha un valore molto alto?* ('Does the painting have a high economic value?') was not recognised because not included, since the modelled questions were mostly wh-questions and not yes/no questions. Even though we were able to automatically include a lot of pieces of information using our tool, we still need to list all the possible syntactic structures. Further implementations of the grammars expect the possibility to structure the SRGS in an even more general way, in that we could automatically include FrameNet information in it (Ruppenhofer et al., 2010). In FrameNet each word is indeed semantically and syntactically described. The reference to a particular semantic frame could be used to include all the pieces of information expressed by the words used in that frame. Another problem of misrecognitions was caused by phonologically similar words. For example, *Che valore ha l'opera?* ('Which is the value of the artwork?') was understood by the speech recogniser as *Che colore adopera?* ('Which colour was used?'), since *valore-colore* and *opera-adopera* are phonological neighbours. Using the phonological information included in MWN-E will be necessary to avoid this kind of misrecognition in the future.

Despite the on-going improvements, we can assert that the concision of the grammar structure, clarified in the examples, and the rapidity of database reaction (less than a second) make clear the advantages of using this automatic module instead of exclusively relying on the manual one. While the expertise with the Cypher language is still an asset to guarantee the speed of compiling, the impossibility to think of any possible related word would consistently be time-consuming without the use of such database. Moreover, we think that the use of grammars is the most appropriate choice for specific domain applications, instead of using a general purpose ASR. Especially apps mostly take advantage from this approach, since their functions are well-defined. In such contexts, an ex post linguistic analysis on strings containing unpredictable information would be less convenient, considering that ASRs can be taught what to expect. As a result, our specific-purpose aimed application better relies on grammars whose performances are increased through an automatised extension module of analysis.

6 Conclusions

We presented an extension to the SRGS language for grammar models specification to integrate knowledge hosted by a graph database in dialogue management systems. We showed how Cypher queries can be used to generate lists of words complying to complex patterns involving morpho-syntactic and phonological constraints. The resulting SRGS documents provide a compact and easy-to-manage representation of the rules and can significantly reduce the time needed to design dialogue management. Future work will concentrate on using SRGS templates and the automatic conversion module to deploy virtual assistants for interactive cultural heritage tours.

Acknowledgements

This paper has been developed within the framework of CHROME (*Cultural Heritage Resources Orienting Multimodal Experience* - PRIN 2015 MIUR), an ongoing Italian project on technologies for cultural heritage. Antonio Origlia's work is supported by Veneto Region and European Social Fund (grant C92C16000250006).

References

Burke, R., K. Hammond, and J. Kozlovsky (1995). Knowledge-based information retrieval from semi-structured text. In *Working Notes from AAAI Fall Symposium on AI Applications in Knowledge Navigation and Retrieval*, pp. 19–24.

Chaves, R. P. (2001). Wordnet and automated text summarization. In *NLPRS*, pp. 109–116.

Cosi, P., F. Tesser, R. Gretter, C. Avesani, and M. Macon (2001). Festival speaks italian! *7th European Conference on Speech Communication and Technology*.

Croft, W. and A. Cruse (2004). *Cognitive Linguistics*. New York: Cambridge University Press.

Feldman, L. B. (2013). *Morphological Aspects of Language Processing*. Taylor & Francis.

Fellbaum, C. (1998). *WordNet: An Electronic Lexical Database*. Cambridge: MA: MIT.

Hunt, A. and S. McGlashan (2003). Speech recognition grammar specification version 1.0. Technical report, W3C.

Knight, K. (1993). Building a large ontology for machine translation. In *Proceedings of the workshop on Human Language Technology*, pp. 185–190. Association for Computational Linguistics.

Miller, G. A. (1993). Wordnet: A lexical database for english. *Communications of the ACM 38*(11), 39–41.

Milward, D. and M. Beveridge (2003). Ontology-based dialogue systems. In *Proc. 3rd Workshop on Knowledge and reasoning in practical dialogue systems (IJCAI03)*, pp. 9–18. Citeseer.

Origlia, A., G. Paci, and F. Cutugno (2017). Mwn-e: a graph database to merge morpho-syntactic and phonological data for italian. In *Proc. of Subsidia*, pp. to appear.

Pianta, E., L. Bentivogli, and C. Girardi (2002). *MultiWordNet: developing an aligned multilingual database*, pp. 293–302.

Rosch, E. (1976). Structural bases of typicality effects. *Journal of Experimental Psychology: Human Perception and Performance*, 491–502.

Ruppenhofer, J., M. Ellsworth, M. R. L. Petruck, C. R. Johnson, and J. Scheffczyk (2010). *FrameNet 2: Extended Theory and Practice*.

Schmid, H. (2013). Probabilistic part-of speech tagging using decision trees. In *New methods in language processing*, pp. 154. Routledge.

Schmid, H., M. Baroni, E. Zanchetta, and A. Stein (2007). The enriched treetagger system. In *proceedings of the EVALITA 2007 workshop*.

Snae, C. and M. Bruckner (2008). Foods: a food-oriented ontology-driven system. In *Digital Ecosystems and Technologies, 2008. DEST 2008. 2nd IEEE International Conference on*, pp. 168–176. IEEE.

Van Tichelen, L. and D. Burke (2007). Semantic interpretation for speech recognition version 1.0. Technical report, W3C.

Webber, J. (2012). A programmatic introduction to neo4j. In *Proceedings of the 3rd Annual Conference on Systems, Programming, and Applications: Software for Humanity*, SPLASH '12, New York, NY, USA, pp. 217–218. ACM.

Zanchetta, E. and M. Baroni (2005). Morph-it! a free corpus-based morphological resource for the italian language. In *PROCEEDINGS OF CORPUS LINGUISTICS*, Birmingham, UK. University of Birmingham.

Bigger does not mean better!

We prefer specificity

Emmanuelle Dusserre, Muntsa Padró

Eloquant, Grenoble, France
{emmanuelle.dusserre, muntsa.padro}@eloquant.com

Abstract. This paper studies the applicability of word2vec to the task of extracting similar words from small, domain-specific data. Results show that, even though the general tendency of the community is to focus on using more and more data, the specificity of the corpus has much more influence on word2vec results than its size. Actually, when the goal is to automatically detect similar words that are domain specific, it is necessary to have a corpus that correctly represents the use of those specific words more than to have huge amounts of data unrelated to the targeted language.

Keywords: word2vec; semantic extraction; taxonomy; domain-specific data; customer relation management

1. Introduction

Dealing with the automatic extraction of related terms is a trending topic on Natural Language Processing (NLP) area. From synonym extraction, ontology creation or automatic gazetteer building, this is a challenging task approached by many in many publications and shared tasks.

This paper presents a set of experiments on finding similar words in very specific domains. This work is framed on a bigger project on performing classification of customer reviews for different companies in the Customer Relationship Management (CRM) domain. To enrich the classification system, a taxonomy that assigns a semantic tag to the terms that are relevant to the domain was developed. Currently, this is a manual work that is very time consuming, especially given that CRM domain is in fact a combination of sub-domains, or business sectors. This means that every time the data from a company operating in a new sector is to be treated, the taxonomy needs to be enriched to cover the terms specific to the new sector. Doing that manually is demanding in time and resources, and it is difficult to assure a good coverage, so the present study explores how to automatize this step. Thus, this paper proposes to use a small existing taxonomy developed by hand, and to automatically enrich it with terms that are semantically similar to the words already present in the taxonomy, we call them the seed words.

This paper presents an approach to extract related terms in domain-specific corpora by using distributional hypothesis [6], which permits to extract words which share similar contexts and consequently same senses. Specifically, word2vec ([13]) caught our attention because of its impressive performances in semantic extraction tasks in many works of NLP.

The key point of this study is the very reduced size of the domain-specific corpus. Even though it is a limitation for this kind of tool, these experiments show that size is not the only parameter that matters. Indeed, in the present case, we obtained better results with a small, specific corpus than with a huge, general domain amount of words.

2. Related work

The automatic extraction of similar terms is a task widely covered in the literature. Word-context matrices based on vector space models proved their efficiency. For instance, [10] proposed Latent Semantic Analysis (LSA), and obtained high results on the Test of English as a Foreign Language (TOEFL). This approach was used by many afterwards, such as [11] or [7].

Vector space models also contributed a lot to automatic thesaurus generation. The pioneer was probably [3] who generated automatically global thesauri by using a discrimination value model of [14] and the complete-link clustering algorithm. Also, we can cite [5], who introduced an automatic method to create a thesaurus from a raw corpus.

However, word-context matrices techniques are well-known to need a lot of data to obtain good results. Most of experiments have been realized on huge corpora surpassing billions of words. Nevertheless, in [5] the authors built a method using specific statistical analysis techniques for small datasets combining it with a system of semantic class constitution and topic detection. The goal of their study was to achieve automatically lexical semantic information on small corpora to help languages with few resources.

In the recent last years, the apparition of word2vec [13] permitted to create vectors using artificial neural networks. This allowed to fasten the system and to use more data. Many works have been conducted with word2vec with the intention of finding related words ([2, 12]).

Some works tried to compare traditional methods, such as LSA, with word2vec. For instance, [1] observed that word2vec is better than LSA on bigger corpora from a dream database. But, since they started to reduce corpora, LSA outperformed word2vec.

The work presented in this paper follows the previously mentioned lines on distributional hypothesis to extract related words. However, we do not know antecedent works using distributional hypothesis based on artificial neural networks on such small, domain-specific corpora. Indeed, one important factor in this study is the super-specificity of the data we dealt with.

3. Methodology

3.1. Finding most related words

As explained before, in order to improve document classification for customer reviews in different sectors, the classifier is enriched with semantic information. In previous work, a taxonomy has been developed to tag terms that are relevant to the CRM domain. For example, "operator" or "advisor" are tagged as *Interlocutor* or "phone" is tagged as *Product* in a telecommunications sector while "tire" has the same tag in a car-related activity. This semantic information is used as a feature in order to build a generic classification system based on the semantic tags more than on the lemmas.

Thereby, when the classifier needs to be adapted to a new sector, the relevant terms need to be added to the correct branch of the taxonomy, to be assigned to the correct semantic tag. To extract lists of similar words we use word2vec, and aim at placing similar words in the same branch of the taxonomy.

The basic idea is to compute vectors representing the context of the words in the corpus, and then compute the distance between each word and the seed words using the cosine of these vectors. Then, a threshold is applied and all words with a cosine above the threshold are considered as neighbors of the seed words, and thus, related words.

In this work, word2vec is ran to obtain the vectors that allow the computation of the closest neighbors of the seed words. To build the matrices and compare the results, the study is conducted on two corpora, presented in next section.

To evaluate performances of the method a gold standard was elaborated (section 3.3), and compared with the Random Indexing (RI) [8], a classical distributional algorithm.

3.2. Corpora

Two corpora are used in this work to build word embeddings using word2vec:
a. A CRM domain-specific corpus constituted with more than 35, 000 French customer reviews about a telecommunication company, amounting a total of 557, 676 words. Idiosyncrasies of this corpus are typical of CRM domain: texts are very short, one or two sentences per review, and the language used contains abbreviations and many spelling mistakes which add complexification to the treatment.

b. A word2vec model elaborated by J.P. Fauconnier[1] was used with the intention to compare domain specific and generic corpora on frWac corpus. It contains 1.6 billion of words crawled from the Web and POS-tagged and lemmatized with TreeTagger[2].

3.3. Gold standard

To evaluate the results of the experiments, a gold-standard was developed. It contains a set of seed words and their closest neighbors, and allows us to calculate the precision, the recall and the f-measure for each word2vec output.

To create the gold-standard, the first step was to pre-select set of nouns belonging to the taxonomy, this is the seed words. These nouns follow several criteria: (a) Belonging to the telecommunication sub-domain. (b) Having a frequency superior to five in the telecommunication corpus. (c) Select only one seed word for semantically close words. For instance, we choose *téléphone* and did not selection *mobile* because they can be synonyms.

The second step was to manually choose, with two linguists, the closest words to each seed word. These words are synonyms or also orthographical variations, and have a frequency superior to five in the telecommunication corpus too.

The totality of the gold-standard contains 97 words, with 18 seed words. A seed word can have one to nine neighbors. Even though it is difficult to say that the gold-standard is exhaustive and it is quite small, it contains the most relevant words for the sector so it allows us to study the behavior of the proposed method in the task of enriching our domain-dependent taxonomy.

Table 1 shows an extract of the gold-standard, in the first column there are the seed words, and in the second column there are their closest neighbors chosen by the two linguists.

Table 1. Extract of the gold-standard

Seed words	Neighbors
télé	*télévision tv tele television*
magasin	*boutique agence magazin*
message	*sms mail mms commentaire texto*
téléphone	*fixe portable mobile smartphone phone telephone tel*

3.4. Experiment

Word2Vec can be used with two architectures: Skip Gram Negative Sampling (SGNS) and Continuous Bag of Words (CBOW), both based on a prediction system that works with a neural network where words are represented by vectors. In the present case, experiments were conducted with SGNS architecture that is, according to [13], better for semantic relations.

Word2vec disposes of several parameters that can be adapted to improve the results such as the window size, the layer size or the number of iteration on the corpus. For the present experiments, it was decided to use a window size of 2 words, 400 dimensions for the vectors and 5 iterations on the corpus.

Several experiments were performed to study the performances and limitations of word2vec when applied to CRM domain. (a) Compare lemmatized corpus with PoS tagged corpus. (b) Test different sizes of the telecommunication corpus (using only part of the corpus to simulate lack of data). (c) Compare results on the telecommunication corpus with the frWac corpus to see the impact of the corpus size and corpus specificity. (d) Compare results obtained with Word2Vec and Random Indexing.

For each configuration, the list of closest neighbors for seed words was generated with word2vec. Different tests were conducted with different thresholds between 0.1 and 0.6, meaning that all words which are above the threshold are considered neighbors of the seed word (thus, semantically close). The different configurations performances were computed by using the gold-standard, over which was calculated micro-averaged Precision, Recall and F1.

---

[1] Fauconnier, J.-P. web site : http://fauconnier.github.io/#data

[2] TreeTagger: tool for annotating text with part-of-speech and lemma information. French version provided by Achim Stein. http://www.cis.uni-muenchen.de/~schmid/tools/TreeTagger/

4. Results

4.1. Part-of-speech tagging

Adding PoS-tagging on the system allowed to conserve only nouns inside word2vec outputs, and to create finer grained contexts. Figure 1 shows the f-measure evolution in terms of the threshold, using the telecommunication corpus just lemmatized or PoS-tagged (via TreeTagger). As we can observe, adding PoS systematically lead to better performances, since it allows to keep in the output only the nouns, thus some noise was reduced.

Figure 1 Comparison of f-measures on entire corpus with and without PoS

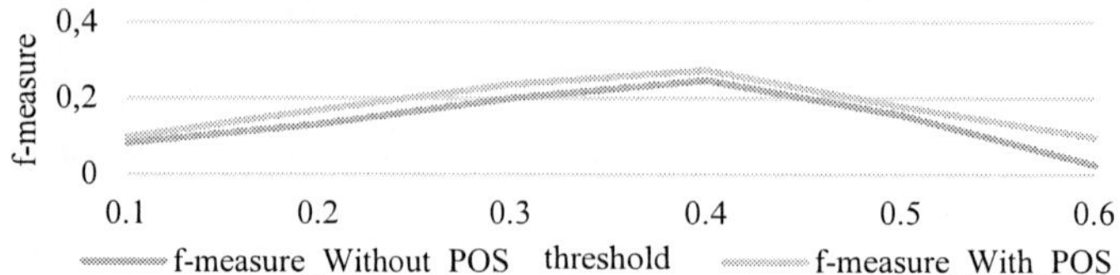

4.2. Corpus size and specificity

Two experiments were performed to see the influence of the corpus size on word2vec. (a) The telecommunication corpus was split in three sub-corpora, one quarter, half and three quarters. (b) The results were compared with the vectors learned with the frWac corpus, which contains much more data, but which is not specific to the studied domain.

Figure 2 shows, as expected, that reducing the telecommunication corpus produces a loss in the performance of the system. The smallest f-measure, by far, was surprisingly reached with the model built on frWac corpus, even if this corpus is almost 2,000 times bigger than the telecommunication corpus. Thus, in-domain corpus allows to better learn semantic similarity than a huge amount of words, so in this study, specificity is more important than size.

Figure 2 Comparison between the different sizes of corpus

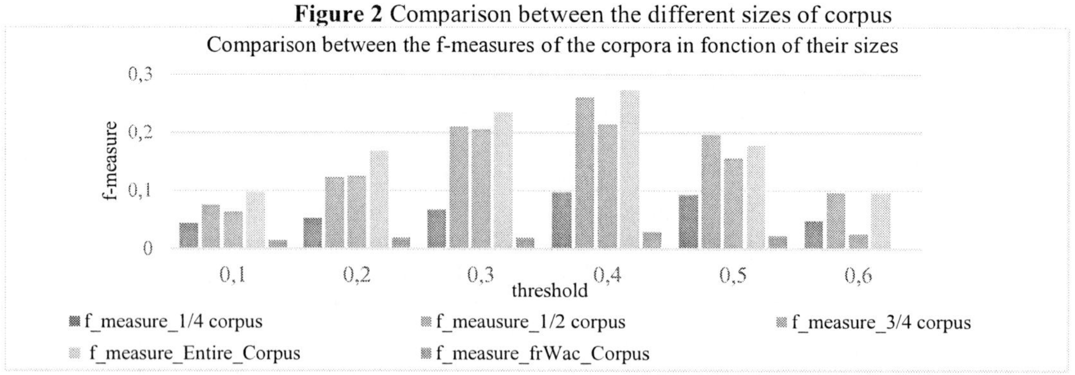

5. Discussion

In Table 2, the best results obtained on the telecommunication and the frWac corpus, plus the results using Random Indexing algorithm on the telecommunication corpus are presented.

Table 2. Comparison between the best results of Word2vec and Random Indexing

	Threshold	Precision	Recall	F1
Word2Vec with Telecommunication corpus	0.40	0.34	0.23	0.27
Word2Vec with frWac corpus	0.30	0.02	0.03	0.02
RI with telecommunication corpus	0.80	0.06	0.32	0.10

Table 2 indicates that word2vec with telecommunication corpus generated the best results with a f-measure reaching 0.27 while other systems are much below. Note that best results for RI are obtained with a much higher threshold than word2vec. This is because RI has a different method to compute the vectors that generates high cosines, even if the number of returned neighbors is similar.

It seems important to explain why results obtained have a very low f-measure (never over 0.3). This is mainly due to the requirements of the gold standard. On the one hand, words were selected for the gold standard only if the linguists decided that they were very close to the seed words. Thus, it is possible that a seed word has only one neighbor in the gold standard. On the other hand, the gold standard contains low frequency words, only words with frequency below five were ignored, thus the method fails to extract words with low frequency what producing a low final performance.

Table 3 presents a sample of word2vec results. In the first column, there are the seed words, in the second and third columns there is the word2vec output: correctly extracted words (true positives) and words not expected by the gold standard (false positives). The last column shows the words expected in the gold standard not generated by word2vec (false negatives).

Table 3. Word2vec's outputs instances for a threshold equal to 0.4

Seeds	True Positives	False Positives	False Negatives
ligne			*adsl réseau*
problème	*panne probleme*		*pb question bug incident*
box	*décodeur boxe decodeur*	*adsl tv wifi pc*	
conseiller	*personne intervenant interlocuteur*		*conseillère équipe demoiselle personnel collaborateur correspondant*

As presented in the Table 3, some seed words, such as *ligne* [*line*], do not have any neighbors. This means that there is no word which have a cosine superior to 0.4 in the corpus according to word2vec, probably due to the lack of data. Otherwise, for words such as *box* all expected words are retrieved, with a perfect Recall, even though some false positives are also introduced. Note that nevertheless, those unexpected words are not semantically far from the seed word. This shows that word2vec is able to correctly capture in-domain, semantically related words.

Overall, the first steps of this study are satisfying. A manual analyze of the results points that even though the results are not perfect and the f-measure is low, the list of related words is quite adequate, and could be used as a good basis to enrich the existing taxonomy.

6. Conclusion and Further Work

In this work, word2vec was used to extract domain-specific related terms from very small corpora. The results obtained show that corpus specificity is an important parameter for extraction of neighbors when using word2vec, even more than the size of the corpus. Results suggest that it is possible to get satisfactory results with small data for domain-specific words. Even if the f-measure is low, results are promising and can be helpful to enrich the taxonomy. This brings a gain that is not negligible on this task and opens the door to quickly adapting the classification system to new sectors, even though some manual revision is advised in the current setup.

As further work, the same experiments will be conducted with other business sectors, as e-commerce or car insurance. Also, an extrinsic evaluation will be performed to enrich automatically the taxonomy with word2vec and then study the results before and after the enrichment. In this way, we will study the real impact of the automatic enrichment of the taxonomy. Also, the gold standard will be increased to have statistical results more reliable, and we plan to try the CBOW architecture which has, according to some studies[3], good results on small corpora.

---

[3]   CBOW studies: https://www.tensorflow.org/tutorials/word2vec

7. References

1. Altszyler, E., Mariano, S., & Fernández Slezak, F.: Comparative study of LSA vs Word2vec embeddings in small corpora: a case study in dreams database. CoRR abs/1610.01520 (2016)
2. Baroni, M., Dinu, G. & Kruszewski, G.: Don't count, predict! A systematic comparison of context-counting vs. context-predicting semantic vectors. In Proceedings of the 52nd Annual Meeting of the Association for Computational Linguistics (Volume 1: Long Papers), pages 238–247, Baltimore, Maryland, June. Association for Computational Linguistics. (2014)
3. Crouch, C.-J.: A cluster-based approach to thesaurus construction. In Proceedings of the 11th Annual International ACM SIGIR Conference, pp. 309-320, Grenoble France. (1988)
4. Curran, J.-R., & Moens, M.: Improvements in automatic thesaurus extraction. In Unsupervised Lexical Acquisition: Proceedings of the Workshop of the ACL Special In-terest Group on the Lexicon (SIGLEX), pp. 59-66, Philadelphia, PA. (2002)
5. Grefenstette, G.: Explorations in Automatic Thesaurus Discovery. Kluwer. (1994)
6. Harris, Z.: Distributional structure. Word, 10(23):146–162. (1954)
7. Hofmann, T.: Probabilistic Latent Semantic Analysis, Uncertainty in Artificial Intelligence. (1999)
8. Karneva, P., Kristofersson, J. & Holst, A.: Random Indexing of text samples for Latent Semantic Analysis. Proceedings of the 22nd annual conference of the cognitive science society. New Jersey: Erlbaum. (2000)
9. Kato, R. & Goto, H.: Categorization of web news documents using word2vec and deep learning. Proceedings of the 2016 International Conference on Industrial Engineering and Operations Management Kuala Lumpur, Malaysia, March 8-10, (2016)
10. Landauer, T.-K. & Dumais, S.-T.: A solution to Plato's problem: The latent semantic analysis theory of acquisition, induction, and representation of knowledge. Psychological Review, Vol 104(2), Apr 1997, 211-240. (1997)
11. Landauer, T.-K., Foltz, P.-W. & et Laham, D.: « Introduction to Latent Semantic Analysis », Discourse Processes, vol. 25, p. 259-284, (1998)
12. Levy, O., Goldberg, Y. & Dagan, I..: Improving Distributional Similarity with Lessons Learned from Word Embeddings. Transactions of the Association for Computational Linguistics. (2015)
13. Mikolov, T., Corrado, G., Chen, K. & Dean, J.: Efficient Estimation of Word Representations in Vector Space. Proceedings of the International Conference on Learning Representations, (ICLR 2013), p. 1–12. (2013a)
    Rossignol, M. & Sébillot, P.: Automatic acquisition of lexical semantic information using medium to small corpora. (2008)
14. Salton, G., Wong, A. & Yang, C.-S.: A vector space model for automatic indexing. Communications of the ACM, v.18 n.11, p.613-620, Nov. (1974)

Utilizing Automatic Predicate-Argument Analysis
for Concept Map Mining

Tobias Falke and Iryna Gurevych

Research Training Group AIPHES and UKP Lab
Department of Computer Science, Technische Universität Darmstadt
`https://www.aiphes.tu-darmstadt.de`

Abstract

Concept maps can be used to provide concise and structured summaries of documents. Motivated by their usefulness in many application scenarios, several approaches have been suggested for concept map mining, the automatic extraction of concept maps from text. However, a major bottleneck of previous work is the common pattern-based approach used to extract concepts and relations from documents which is either limited in coverage or requires a laborious definition of large sets of patterns. Drawing upon recent advances in automatic predicate-argument analysis, we propose to replace pattern-based extraction by using predicate-argument structures. Our experiments compare three different representations with previous work and show that using predicate-argument structures leads to a better extraction performance while being much easier to use.

1   Introduction

A *concept map* is a labeled graph showing *concepts* as nodes and *relations* between them as edges (Novak and Gowin, 1984). They were invented by education researchers in the 1970s and have since been applied in many scenarios, including the usage as a teaching tool (Edwards and Fraser, 1983; Roy, 2008), writing assistance (Villalon, 2012), structure for information repositories (Briggs et al., 2004; Richardson and Fox, 2005) and concise text representation (Valerio et al., 2012). Recently, they have also been proposed as a representation in the context of multi-document summarization and document exploration (Falke and Gurevych, 2017a,b). Their advantages are the concise presentation of central terms and the explicit visualization of relationships. Figure 1 shows an example.

Concept map mining is the automatic generation of concept maps from natural language text. Several approaches have been proposed (see §3). Typically, they extract a set of candidate concepts and relations from given documents and then select a subset of them to construct a concept map. During the extraction, most previous work applies hand-written patterns to extract labels from syntactic representations. As an example, consider the following sentence:

(1) Joseph Novak invented concept maps.

To extract "Joseph Novak" and "concept maps" as concept labels, patterns extracting nsubj- and dobj-dependencies are needed to find the relevant spans when a dependency representation is given. However, these patterns cannot extract anything from the passive variant of the sentence because the relevant tokens now have another grammatical function:

(2) Concept maps were invented by Joseph Novak.

An additional set of patterns would be necessary to handle (2). Due to the syntactic variety of natural language, these pattern-based approaches are either limited in coverage or require a very large and carefully designed set of patterns that covers every possible way in which a proposition can be expressed.

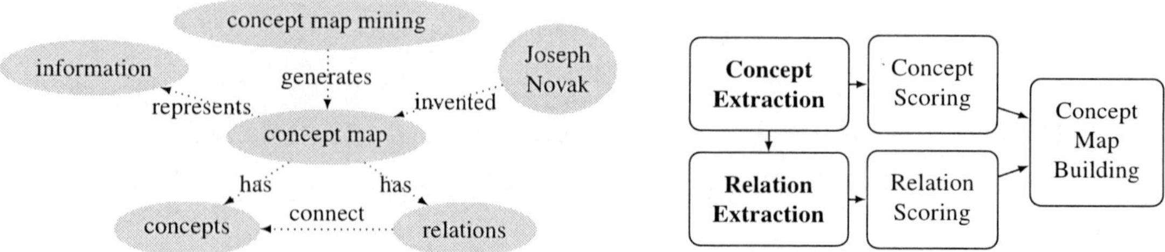

Figure 1: A concept map about concept maps.   Figure 2: Common concept map mining approach.

To eliminate the high manual effort associated with pattern definition, we propose to utilize semantic instead of syntactic representations as they already abstract away from many syntactic variations. Continuing the example, the binary predicate *invented(Joseph Novak; concept maps)* is a semantic representation for both (1) and (2), requiring no separate handling of the cases. Using such a unified representation based on predicates and arguments, concept map mining approaches no longer need to carefully define large sets of patterns, but can instead make use of existing semantic analysis tools.

In this work, we analyze three different representations that improve upon pure syntactic representations by different degrees: Open Information Extraction (OpenIE) (Banko et al., 2007), identifying predicates and arguments in a sentence, PropS (Stanovsky et al., 2016), which additionally unifies a certain amount of syntactic variations, and Semantic Role Labeling (SRL) (Hajič et al., 2009), mapping predicates and arguments to an abstract, semantic representation.

We describe how these representations can be used and present several experiments comparing them to previous work. As a result, we find that the suggested methods are competitive or even better while requiring no patterns to be defined. This finding has the potential to drastically simplify the development of concept map mining systems in the future, because they can rely on readily available tools for predicate-argument analysis and can focus on subsequent pipeline tasks. In addition, to the best of our knowledge, this is also the first comparative study of concept and relation extraction methods that have been suggested for concept map mining in previous work.

2   Task

Given input documents and a size restriction, extractive *concept map mining* creates a concept map $M = (C, R)$ where every node in C represents a concept, designated by a unique label, and R contains directed edges that connect pairs of concepts with a label such that the resulting proposition describes the concepts' relationship. A concept can be an object, event or abstract idea. All labels for concepts and relations should be taken from the documents and the map has to satisfy the size restriction which defines the maximal number of concepts and relations in the map. Under these constraints, the goal is to select concepts and relations that describe a maximal amount of the document's content. The size restriction controls how much the information should be compressed.

3   Related Work

Several attempts have been made to automatically construct concept maps as defined above (Qasim et al., 2013; Villalon, 2012; Valerio and Leake, 2006, inter alia). Zubrinic et al. (2012) provide a comprehensive survey of work on this task. Figure 2 shows the typical pipeline approach in previous approaches. First, potential labels for concepts and relations are extracted from the documents. Then, they are scored or ranked and a subset is selected and connected to build the final concept map.

In this work, we focus on the extraction part of the pipeline (bold in Figure 2), as this is the step where predicate-argument structures can be leveraged to simplify the syntax-pattern-based strategies of previous work. We briefly present the latter in the following sections.

Concept Extraction   The goal of concept extraction is to create a set of potential concept labels, called concept candidates. Ideally, this set is as small as possible while containing all desired phrases. Valerio and Leake (2006) suggest to use constituency parse trees and extract minimal noun phrases from them, i.e. noun phrases that do not cover shorter noun phrases. Both Qasim et al. (2013) and Villalon (2012) work with dependency parse trees and defined patterns to extract phrases from them. While there are slight differences between their patterns, all try to capture single noun tokens, noun compounds and combinations of nouns with adjectives, prepositions and conjunctions. Similar patterns on syntax or part-of-speech sequences were used in other work (Zouaq and Nkambou, 2009; Rajaraman and Tan, 2002; Kowata et al., 2010; Zubrinic et al., 2012).

Relation Extraction   During relation extraction, phrases describing the relationship between pairs of concept candidates have to be identified in the text. Following their concept extraction approach, Valerio and Leake (2006) identify verb phrases that connect two concept candidates, whereas Villalon (2012) uses tokens on the shortest path between the candidates in a simplified dependency graph. A pattern-based extraction from dependencies and part-of-speech sequences was also suggested (Qasim et al., 2013; Zouaq and Nkambou, 2009; Rajaraman and Tan, 2002). Olney et al. (2011) use the output of an SRL system and are thus close to this work. However, they focus on a variant of the task where relations are restricted to a fixed domain-specific set of 30 labels, creating less expressive concept maps.

In the next section, we show how the definition of these patterns for both concept and relation extraction can be made obsolete by leveraging existing predicate-argument analysis tools.

4   Concept and Relation Extraction from Predicate-Argument Structures

The intuition for using predicate-argument structures is that a proposition formed by a relation and its concepts in a concept map, e.g. *concept map - has - concepts*, is very similar to a predicate derived by a predicate-argument analysis of a sentence. Therefore, we study how useful different predicate-argument analysis tools are for the extraction of concepts and relations.

Given an input sentence, we want to derive a set P of binary predicates $pred(arg_1, arg_2)$, each of them representing a proposition. We use different existing systems to obtain this set and illustrate their representations for the following example sentence:

(3) Concept maps, which were invented by Joseph Novak, represent concepts and their relationships.

OpenIE   The first type of representation we consider is OpenIE. OpenIE systems extract tuples that represent basic binary propositions from a given sentence. Every tuple consists of a relation phrase and two arguments, making the representation very close to concepts and their relations. We use OpenIE-4, a state-of-the-art system.[1] With that system, the extracted tuples P_{OIE} obtained for (3) are:

1. were invented (concepts maps; by Joseph Novak)

2. represent (concept maps; concepts and their relationships)

PropS   As a second approach, we use PropS, a rule-based converter that turns dependency trees into typed predicate-argument graphs (Stanovsky et al., 2016). In addition to identifying predicates and arguments, it also canonicalizes the representation of propositions, e.g. by unifying variations such as active and passive or copula and appositive constructions. Note that the OpenIE approach does not go that far and only identifies predicate-argument structures.

PropS also classifies predicate-argument relations with a small set of labels such as *subj* and *dobj*. Since it does not try to match any tokens against an inventory of senses or frames, the representation will

---

[1] `https://github.com/knowitall/openie`, state-of-the-art according to Stanovsky and Dagan (2016b)

always cover the full content of a given sentence, as opposed to the SRL representation discussed in the next section. For (3), PropS yields the following representation:

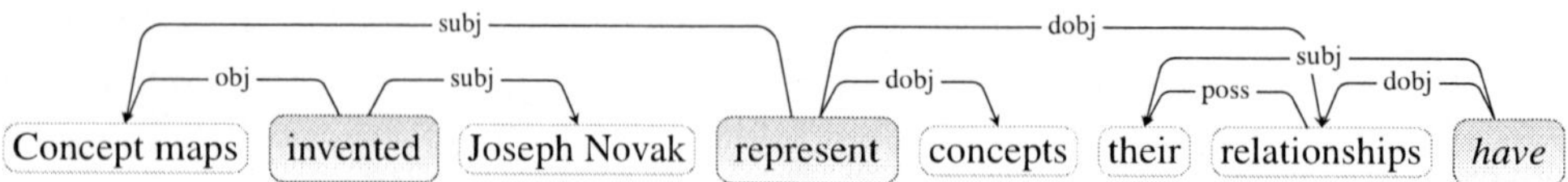

To create the set of binary predicates P_{PropS}, we traverse the graph from every predicate node and select as its arguments the subgraphs of the directly connected argument nodes. We remove unary predicates and break down higher-arity predicates by creating all possible pairs except if they have the same edge label (e.g. two objects). Thus, we obtain the following binary predicates for (3):

1. invented (Joseph Novak; concept maps)

2. represent (concept maps; concepts)

3. represent (concept maps; their relationships)

SRL   As the third method, we apply semantic role labeling using Mate Tools (Björkelund et al., 2009), which is freely available and was one of the best in the CoNLL 2009 shared task (Hajič et al., 2009). We prefer PropBank-style SRL (Palmer et al., 2005) over FrameNet and VerbNet because of its robustness and maturity. In a sentence, it marks verbs with their PropBank frame, identifies subtrees in the dependency representation of the sentence as arguments and labels them with a role:

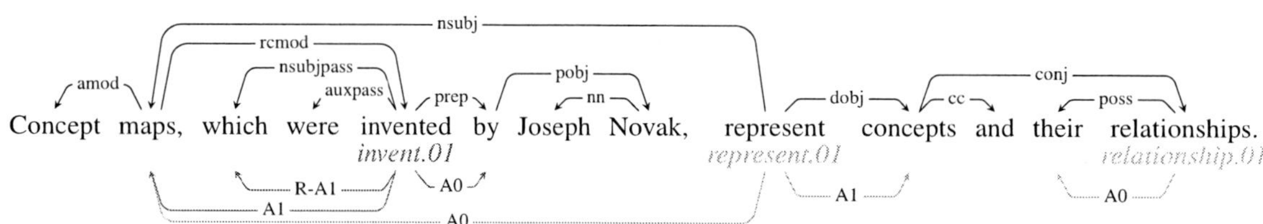

This approach is the most sophisticated type of analysis in our study, trying to map a natural language sentence to another layer of abstract semantic representation defined by the frame and role inventory. While being the most powerful representation, it also has disadvantages: First, spans of roles are strictly bound to full subtrees in the dependency parse, as shown in the example, where the relative clause becomes part of the A0-role of "represent". And second, predicates and arguments that are not covered by the inventory of frames and roles cannot be represented.

To obtain the set of binary predicates P_{SRL}, we ignore a predicate completely if it has just one argument, otherwise, we form a binary predicate for every pair of arguments. For (3), this yields the following predicates:

1. invented (concept maps; by Joseph Novak)

2. represent (concept maps which were invented by Joseph Novak; concepts and their relationships)

Given binary predicates P_x derived from a predicate-argument structure $x \in \{OIE, SRL, PropS\}$, concept and relations can be extracted by simply using all arguments of the predicates as the set of concept candidates C_x and the predicates themselves as relation candidates R_x, where each of the latter is associated with two concept candidates as given by the predicate. We intentionally do not further reduce or refine this set with any additional heuristics to assess the out-of-the-box applicability of predicate-argument structures for concept map mining.

Dataset	Maps	Gold Concept Maps				Source per Map	
		Concepts	Length	Relations	Length	Documents	Length
EDUC	30	25.0 ± 0.0	3.2 ± 0.5	25.2 ± 1.3	3.2 ± 0.5	40.5 ± 6.8	97880
BIOLOGY	165	7.0 ± 4.1	1.2 ± 0.5	3.5 ± 3.0	1.9 ± 1.2	1.0 ± 0.0	2621
ACL	230	11.0 ± 5.5	1.8 ± 0.9			1.0 ± 0.0	4987

Table 1: Corpus statistics for the datasets used in experiments. All measures are averages per map and corresponding standard deviations; length values are measured in number of tokens.

5   Datasets

In our experiments, we use corpora of documents paired with gold standard concept maps to evaluate the extraction performance of different approaches. We utilize one recently published dataset and additionally create two other by semi-automatically matching existing maps with corresponding documents.

The first dataset, called EDUC, provides manually created concept maps for clusters of web documents on educational topics. It was created using crowdsourcing and expert annotators and has been recently published by Falke and Gurevych (2017a). In contrast to the other datasets used in this study, this corpus represents a multi-document concept map mining setting, with on average 41 documents and a consequently high number of tokens as the input for a single concept map.

For the second dataset, BIOLOGY, we followed Olney et al. (2011) and used a collection of 464 concept maps produced by experts as teaching materials for biology.[2] The maps were created independently from a text. We matched them automatically with corresponding articles in Wikipedia and manually corrected wrong assignments. Every map is a star-like graph centered around a central concept, e.g. *protein*, and hence has a similar topical focus as an encyclopedic article.

As the third dataset, ACL, we used the ACL RD-TEC 2.0 corpus (QasemiZadeh and Schumann, 2016). It consists of 300 abstracts taken from papers in the ACL Anthology in which two annotators marked terms with a specialized meaning. As abstracts are usually good summaries of a paper, these terms tend to be the central concepts discussed in the papers. We used Apache Tika[3] to extract the full texts, excluding the abstracts, from the PDF version of the corresponding papers. These texts were then used with the annotated concepts as the gold concepts. Note that we cannot use this corpus to evaluate relation extraction, as such annotations are not available.

Table 1 compares the introduced datasets. EDUC represents a multi-document setting, while the other two only have one document per map. However, as this study is focused on the extraction part of concept map mining, this difference is of minor importance. The table also shows that EDUC has the biggest concepts maps with also slightly longer labels for concepts and relations, while the other two datasets, with smaller maps, offer more instances due to the automatic creation approach.

6   Experiments

We conducted several experiments to study the usefulness of the presented predicate-argument analysis tools. In the first two experiments we focus on the recall of different methods during extraction and then turn to the subsequent selection step and corresponding precision evaluations. For all experiments, we preprocessed the documents with components of DKPro Core (Eckart de Castilho and Gurevych, 2014), using tokenization, part-of-speech tagging and constituency parsing from the Stanford NLP tools and Snowball for stemming. Constituency parse trees were converted into collapsed and propagated dependencies (de Marneffe and Manning, 2008).

---

[2] http://web.archive.org/web/20120106232123/http://www.biologylessons.sdsu.edu/ta/toc.html (see *Lesson SemNet* for the different topics)

[3] https://tika.apache.org/

Approach	BIOLOGY			ACL			EDUC		
	Yield	Recall %	Length	Yield	Recall %	Length	Yield	Recall %	Length
Noun Tokens	51.53	75.61	1.0	48.99	42.48	1.0	167.38	25.07	1.0
Valerio/Leake	69.50	69.60	2.2	77.53	62.21	2.3	406.53	**55.73**	2.4
Qasim et al.	74.61	61.46	2.3	78.04	74.39	2.3	467.15	48.13	2.4
Villalon	60.75	**76.37**	2.3	69.10	**76.09**	2.3	351.85	51.20	2.5
OpenIE	44.53	41.80	4.9	41.99	28.67	5.3	277.70	**58.00**	5.9
SRL	66.28	50.99	4.2	77.21	44.14	5.0	481.59	46.93	6.5
PropS	76.55	**73.50**	3.2	55.87	**58.41**	3.7	451.20	46.27	4.3

Table 2: Concept extraction performance by dataset. For a definition of the metrics, please refer to the text. Bold indicates best recall per group. Concept length given as average number of tokens.

6.1 Concept Extraction

Experimental Setup To evaluate the coverage of different concept extraction strategies, we compared their sets of concept candidates C with the concepts C_G of the gold maps. For every approach, we measured the covered gold concepts with recall $R = |C \cap C_G|/|C_G|$ and used candidate yield $Y = |C|/|C_G|$ to indicate over-generation and thus selection difficulty.[4] Metrics are averages over maps. Concept labels are matched after stemming to allow for morphological variants, e.g. *concept map* and *concept maps*. As a baseline, we applied a strategy that extracts all noun tokens. From previous work, we included the noun phrase strategy of Valerio and Leake (2006) and, as representatives for dependency patterns, the patterns of Qasim et al. (2013) and Villalon (2012) (see §3).

Recall and Yield Table 2 reports results on the three datasets. Out of the different tools used to obtain predicate-argument structures, we observe the highest recall using PropS on two datasets and OpenIE on the other. From previous work, Villalon's method shows the best results on two datasets, while Valerio/Leake's method is best on EDUC. Overall, we conclude that concept extraction based on predicate-argument structure is competitive, giving slightly better (EDUC) or slightly worse (BIOLOGY) results, except for the performance on the ACL datasets. With regard to yield, predicate-argument structures are even more competitive, producing less candidate concepts in most cases. For all approaches, the yield correlates with the size of the input documents, producing most concepts on the EDUC dataset.

One interesting fact is that on EDUC the best performing method, among previous work as well as predicate-argument structures, differs from the one on the other two datasets. The reason is that the concept labels in this corpus tend to be longer, including more complex noun phrases and also verbal phrases describing activities, while concept labels are mostly single nouns in BIOLOGY or noun compounds in ACL. This explains the generally lower recall and better performance of approaches focusing on full noun phrases rather than nouns and noun compounds.

Analyzing the results on the ACL corpus, we found that the automatic extraction of text from the PDFs produced very data, causing a lot of the dependency parses to be of low quality due to wrong sentence segmentation. Interestingly, while this reduced the performance of all approaches using predicate-argument structures, it did not influence the methods from previous work. We hypothesize that these approaches are more robust against these parsing errors because they only extract from dependencies locally, while the other approaches globally process the full parse to derive predicate-argument structures.

Added Concepts We further compared the concept candidate set extracted by the best approach from previous work with those produced by predicate argument structures. To assess whether the latter identified previously uncaptured concepts, we joined both sets and compared the combined recall against the method from previous work alone. In all cases, predicate-argument structures extract at least some concepts that are not covered by previous approaches, with the best approach adding 6.90 (BIOLOGY),

---

[4]At the current pipeline step, all potential concepts in the text are extracted, while a subset of reasonable size is selected later (Figure 2). Hence, precision and F-scores are rather meaningless; we only report yield. We focus on precision in §6.3.

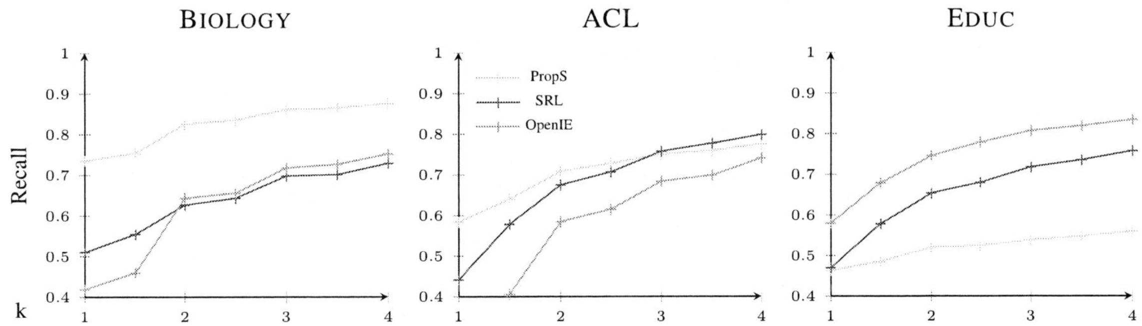

Figure 3: Concept extraction recall for inclusive matches at increasing thresholds k.

5.81 (ACL) and 15.20 (EDUC) points of recall. This shows the predicate-argument structures are not only competitive but can also be used to extend the coverage of previous methods.

Concept Length   Finally, we looked at the length of extracted concept labels. As Table 2 shows, the extractions made by previous work tend to be around 2.3 tokens long, while the arguments of predicate-argument structures are up to three times as long. In order to assess whether missing concepts might be present in these longer arguments, we defined a new evaluation metric: An extracted concept c and gold concept c_G match inclusively at k if c_G is contained in c and c is at most $k \cdot |c_G|$ token long. Figure 3 shows the corresponding recall when increasing k. For all three approaches, but especially for SRL and OpenIE, the recall increases dramatically when considering longer arguments. This indicates that the concept extraction performance could be further improved by learning how to reduce longer arguments to the desired parts. Corresponding techniques have been studied, e.g. (Stanovsky and Dagan, 2016a; Stanovsky et al., 2016), however, this step is not trivial as it has to be truth-preserving.

6.2   Relation Extraction

Experimental Setup   In our second experiment, we analogously evaluated different relation extraction approaches. To ensure a fair comparison independent of concept extraction, all strategies, including previous work, used gold concepts. Again, we computed candidate recall and yield as our metrics, counting relations that were extracted with a correct label for the correct pair of gold concepts. To account for the fact that some approaches extract complex phrases, e.g. including prepositions, while others extract only single tokens, we used a lenient matching criterion, requiring that the stemmed heads of the relation phrases have to match. Hence, *is located in* and *located* are considered a match. From previous work, we included the verb phrase extraction of Valerio and Leake (2006), the shortest path method of Villalon (2012) and the pattern-based approach of Qasim et al. (2013) (see §3).

Results   As shown in Table 3, the shortest path method of Villalon is the best performing method from previous work, however, it also creates a comparably large candidate set. Using predicate-argument structures, we see a substantial improvement on both datasets, and again, PropS performs well on BIOLOGY and OpenIE on EDUC. Note that on both datasets even the other method is on par with Villalon while producing a substantially smaller amount of candidates. We found that the low recall of Valerio/Leake and Qasim's method is due to the small coverage of the patterns, whereas Vilallon's method is very noisy and extracts many meaningless relation phrases. On the other hand, predicate-argument structures benefit from their main advantage in this evaluation: Since all extractions are made on the level of propositions, every concept has at least one meaningful relation to another concept.

With regard to the length of the extracted relation labels (not shown in the table), we found a similar picture: Villalon's method provides very long labels (4.5 token), as it extracts arbitrarily long paths from the dependency structure. SRL yields the shortest labels (1.0), since predicates are restricted to a single

Approach	BIOLOGY		EDUC	
	Yield	Recall %	Yield	Recall %
Valerio/Leake	2.02	17.75	2.70	8.32
Qasim et al.	1.43	8.08	2.24	3.30
Villalon	9.64	**32.34**	17.28	**21.53**
OpenIE	3.52	31.63	6.47	**25.76**
SRL	4.22	17.57	11.60	17.97
PropS	6.48	**40.95**	11.62	21.20

Table 3: Relation extraction performance.

	BIOLOGY	ACL	EDUC
	Precision@k	Precision@k	Precision@k
Valerio/Leake	29.46	17.75	**15.07**
Qasim et al.	24.99	19.47	14.27
Villalon	**32.60**	**20.34**	14.80
OpenIE	21.52	10.45	**15.33**
SRL	24.11	14.67	13.20
PropS	**28.86**	**16.61**	14.27

Table 4: Concept selection performance (in %).

token by design, while PropS finds a bit longer ones (1.5), including additional auxiliaries and light-verb constructions, and OpenIE extracts the longest labels (2.86), also containing prepositions as in *was made for*. Considering both recall and the style of labels, we found OpenIE to be most useful for this step.

6.3 Concept Selection

Finally, we present a third experiment on concept scoring. While we found predicate-argument structures to be superior for relation extraction in terms of both recall and yield, the picture is less clear for concepts. By analyzing selection performance, we try to shed more light on how useful certain trade-offs between recall and yield are.

Experimental Setup We used the concept candidate sets obtained with the different methods studied in §6.1, assigned a score to each candidate, selected the top-k candidates and compared them to the gold concepts. We set k to the number of gold concepts $|C_G|$ and measured Precision@k. As the score, we use the frequency of the label in the documents, a metric that has been previously proposed to find important concepts (Valerio and Leake, 2006). Note that we are mainly interested in the difference between candidate sets and not the absolute selection performance. Before scoring the candidates, we grouped them by comparing stemmed labels and chose the most frequent label as the representative.

Results Table 4 shows the selection precision of all extraction methods. As expected, the performance closely resembles the picture obtained from the extraction experiment: If the recall is higher after extraction, precision is also higher after the selection. However, an interesting exception is for example PropS and SRL on EDUC: While SRL has a slightly higher extraction recall (46.93 vs. 46.27), PropS selects more relevant concepts (13.20 vs. 14.37), which might be due to the lower extraction yield of PropS.

7 Conclusion

We compared the usefulness of three different approaches for predicate-argument analysis for concept map mining. Comparing them to several previous methods specifically developed for concept map mining, we found that they substantially improve relation extraction while being very competitive with regard to concept extraction. PropS representations are particularly good to capture short noun-focused concepts whereas longer and more complex concepts are more reliably extracted with OpenIE. Considering the good performance and the ease of use – as opposed to manually defining syntactic patterns – future work on concept map mining should rely on ready-to-use predicate-argument analysis for extraction.

Acknowledgments

This work has been supported by the German Research Foundation as part of the Research Training Group "Adaptive Preparation of Information from Heterogeneous Sources" (AIPHES) under grant No. GRK 1994/1.

References

Banko, M., M. J. Cafarella, S. Soderland, M. Broadhead, and O. Etzioni (2007). Open Information Extraction from the Web. In *Proceedings of the 20th International Joint Conference on Artifical Intelligence*, Hyderabad, India, pp. 2670–2676.

Björkelund, A., L. Hafdell, and P. Nugues (2009). Multilingual semantic role labeling. In *Proceedings of the Thirteenth Conference on Computational Natural Language Learning*, Boulder, CO, USA, pp. 43–48.

Briggs, G., D. A. Shamma, A. J. Cañas, R. Carff, J. Scargle, and J. D. Novak (2004). Concept Maps Applied to Mars Exploration Public Outreach. In *Concept Maps: Theory, Methodology, Technology. Proceedings of the First International Conference on Concept Mapping*, Pamplona, Spain, pp. 109–116.

de Marneffe, M.-C. and C. D. Manning (2008). The Stanford typed dependencies representation. In *Proceedings of the 22nd International Conference on Computational Linguistics*, Manchester, United Kingdom, pp. 1–8.

Eckart de Castilho, R. and I. Gurevych (2014). A broad-coverage collection of portable NLP components for building shareable analysis pipelines. In *Proceedings of the Workshop on Open Infrastructures and Analysis Frameworks for HLT*, Dublin, Ireland, pp. 1–11.

Edwards, J. and K. Fraser (1983). Concept maps as reflectors of conceptual understanding. *Research in Science Education 13*(1), 19–26.

Falke, T. and I. Gurevych (2017a). Bringing Structure into Summaries: Crowdsourcing a Benchmark Corpus of Concept Maps. In *Proceedings of the 2017 Conference on Empirical Methods in Natural Language Processing*, Copenhagen, Denmark.

Falke, T. and I. Gurevych (2017b). GraphDocExplore: A Framework for the Experimental Comparison of Graph-based Document Exploration Techniques. In *Proceedings of the 2017 Conference on Empirical Methods in Natural Language Processing*, Copenhagen, Denmark.

Hajič, J., M. Ciaramita, R. Johansson, D. Kawahara, M. Martí, L. Màrquez, A. Meyers, J. Nivre, S. Padó, J. Štěpánek, P. Straňák, M. Surdeanu, N. Xue, and Y. Zhang (2009). The CoNLL-2009 Shared Task: Syntactic and Semantic Dependencies in Multiple Languages. In *Proceedings of the Thirteenth Conference on Computational Natural Language Learning*, Boulder, CO, USA, pp. 1–18.

Kowata, J. H., D. Cury, and M. C. Silva Boeres (2010). Concept Maps Core Elements Candidates Recognition from Text. In *Concept Maps: Making Learning Meaningful. Proceedings of the 4th International Conference on Concept Mapping*, Vina del Mar, Chile, pp. 120–127.

Novak, J. D. and D. B. Gowin (1984). *Learning How to Learn*. Cambridge: Cambridge University Press.

Olney, A., W. Cade, and C. Williams (2011). Generating Concept Map Exercises from Textbooks. In *Proceedings of the 6th Workshop on Innovative Use of NLP for Building Educational Applications*, Portland, OR, USA, pp. 111–119.

Palmer, M., D. Gildea, and P. Kingsbury (2005). The Proposition Bank: An Annotated Corpus of Semantic Roles. *Computational Linguistics 31*(1), 71–106.

QasemiZadeh, B. and A.-K. Schumann (2016). The ACL RD-TEC 2.0: A Language Resource for Evaluating Term Extraction and Entity Recognition Methods. In *Proceedings of the 10th International Conference on Language Resources and Evaluation*, Portorož, Slovenia, pp. 1862–1868.

Qasim, I., J.-W. Jeong, J.-U. Heu, and D.-H. Lee (2013). Concept map construction from text documents using affinity propagation. *Journal of Information Science 39*(6), 719–736.

Rajaraman, K. and A.-H. Tan (2002). Knowledge discovery from texts: A Concept Frame Graph Approach. In *Proceedings of the Eleventh International Conference on Information and Knowledge Management*, McLean, VA, USA, pp. 669–671.

Richardson, R. and E. A. Fox (2005). Using concept maps as a cross-language resource discovery tool for large documents in digital libraries. In *Proceedings of the 5th ACM/IEEE-CS Joint Conference on Digital Libraries*, Denver, CO, USA, pp. 415.

Roy, D. (2008). Using Concept Maps for Information Conceptualization and Schematization in Technical Reading and Writing Courses: A Case Study for Computer Science Majors in Japan. In *IEEE International Professional Communication Conference (IPCC 2008)*, Montreal, Canada, pp. 1–12.

Stanovsky, G. and I. Dagan (2016a). Annotating and Predicting Non-Restrictive Noun Phrase Modifications. In *Proceedings of the 54th Annual Meeting of the Association for Computational Linguistics*, Berlin, Germany, pp. 1256–1265.

Stanovsky, G. and I. Dagan (2016b). Creating a Large Benchmark for Open Information Extraction. In *Proceedings of the 2016 Conference on Empirical Methods in Natural Language Processing*, Austin, Texas, pp. 2300–2305.

Stanovsky, G., I. Dagan, and M. Adler (2016). Specifying and Annotating Reduced Argument Span Via QA-SRL. In *Proceedings of the 54th Annual Meeting of the Association for Computational Linguistics*, Berlin, Germany, pp. 474–478.

Stanovsky, G., J. Ficler, I. Dagan, and Y. Goldberg (2016). *Getting More Out Of Syntax with PropS*. arXiv:1603.01648.

Valerio, A. and D. B. Leake (2006). Jump-Starting Concept Map Construction with Knowledge Extracted from Documents. In *Proceedings of the 2nd International Conference on Concept Mapping*, San José, Costa Rica, pp. 296–303.

Valerio, A., D. B. Leake, and A. J. Cañas (2012). Using Automatically Generated Concept Maps for Document Understanding: A Human Subjects Experiment. In *Proceedings of the 5th International Conference on Concept Mapping*, Valetta, Malta, pp. 438–445.

Villalon, J. J. (2012). *Automated Generation of Concept Maps to Support Writing*. PhD Thesis, University of Sydney, Australia.

Zouaq, A. and R. Nkambou (2009). Evaluating the Generation of Domain Ontologies in the Knowledge Puzzle Project. *IEEE Transactions on Knowledge and Data Engineering 21*(11), 1559–1572.

Zubrinic, K., D. Kalpic, and M. Milicevic (2012). The automatic creation of concept maps from documents written using morphologically rich languages. *Expert Systems with Applications 39*(16), 12709–12718.

Contextual Characteristics of Concrete and Abstract Words

Diego Frassinelli, Daniela Naumann, Jason Utt, and Sabine Schulte im Walde
Institut für Maschinelle Sprachverarbeitung
Universität Stuttgart
[frassinelli|naumanda|uttjn|schulte]@ims.uni-stuttgart.de

Abstract

In this work we investigate commonalities and differences between the semantic representations of concrete and abstract words using human judgments and distributional semantics. We tackle the following questions: a) Does distributional similarity imply similarity in concreteness vs. abstractness? b) How do concrete and abstract context words co-occur with concrete and abstract words? c) Are our contextual models in line with existing theories of meaning representation? Our studies show that both distributionally similar words as well as distributionally co-occurring words come from the same range of concreteness vs. abstractness scores, partly challenging existing theories of semantic representation.

1   Introduction

The literature on conceptual representation has extensively debated about the nature of concrete concepts, but much less has been said about abstract concepts and about the similarities and differences between these two classes (Murphy, 2002). Multiple studies support the hypothesis that concrete concepts are directly grounded in the sensory-motor system, while abstract concepts are mapped to concrete concepts in order to be processed (Barsalou and Wiemer-Hastings, 2005; Hill et al., 2014; Pecher et al., 2011). Distributional semantics represents a very powerful approach to investigate word meaning in a data-driven fashion: the Distributional Hypothesis states that we can infer the meaning of a word by looking at the linguistic contexts it co-occurs with (Harris, 1954; Firth, 1957; Turney and Pantel, 2010). The resulting word representation, as a vector of co-occurrences of a word with the surrounding contexts, has been shown to be cognitively plausible (Miller and Charles, 1991; Lenci, 2008).

The aim of this work is to quantitatively investigate similarities and differences between concrete and abstract words by analysing the concreteness vs. abstractness of their respective linguistic contexts. Based on the literature, both concrete and abstract words should primarily co-occur with concrete words (i.e., their core semantic representation should mainly incorporate concrete words).

After describing the materials used, we will report three studies where: 1) we investigate the concreteness vs. abstractness of distributionally similar words, 2) we analyse the concreteness nature of co-occurring context words at type level, and 3) at token level.

2   Materials

For our studies, we selected nouns from the Brysbaert et al. (2014) collection of concreteness ratings for 40,000 English words. In this collection, each word was evaluated by at least 25 participants on a scale from 1 (abstract) to 5 (concrete). Given that participants were not aware of the part-of-speech of the word they were rating, we automatically assigned each word its more frequently occurring POS in the corpus. We focused our analyses on nouns because they are usually easier to classify according to their concreteness compared to adjectives and verbs. In total we had 9,241 nouns covered in an extensive selection of behavioural measures, such as valency scores (Warriner et al., 2013) and reaction times (Balota et al., 2007) which we aim to include in further analyses.

We used the selected nouns both as targets and as context words, and created a symmetric noun–noun co-occurrence matrix relying on a $\pm$ 20 word window in the ENCOW14A corpus, a collection of 16-billion English tokens extracted from the web (Schäfer, 2015). In this way, each co-occurence is represented by a score (counts or positive LMI, cf. Evert (2004)). In addition, we ensure information about the concreteness scores for both the targets and the context words.

All the statistical analyses reported in this paper use linear mixed effects models (LME, Baayen et al. (2008)) with centered continuous predictors, implementing a maximal random effects structure as suggested by Barr et al. (2013).

3   Study 1: Investigating concreteness in distributionally similar words

In this study we investigate if distributionally similar words are also similar in their concreteness vs. abstractness scores. After computing the cosine similarity between each pair of target words using positive LMI transformation, we determined the nearest neighbours (NNs) for each target. Table 1 reports the top 8 NNs of the concrete word "lemon" (concreteness: 5.00) and the abstract word "belief" (concreteness: 1.19). The NNs are ordered by cosine similarity. The distributionally most similar words of the very concrete word "lemon" are, on average, also very concrete (6 out of 8 words have concreteness scores > 4). The two outliers "zest" and "concentrate" are ambiguous words with extremely different concreteness scores (e.g., "zest" means both "enthusiasm" and "skin"). In contrast, 4 of the 8 NNs of "belief" are very abstract words with concreteness scores < 2. Its remaining NNs have a mid-range concreteness value and refer to specific groups of people associated by similar believes (e.g., "sect").

Rank	NN	Similarity	Concreteness	Rank	NN	Similarity	Concreteness
-	**lemon**	-	**5.00**	-	**belief**	-	**1.19**
1	zest	0.831	2.27	1	spirituality	0.700	1.07
2	pineapple	0.756	4.94	2	atheist	0.642	2.93
3	cranberry	0.680	4.96	3	morality	0.634	1.47
4	ginger	0.617	4.92	4	superstition	0.593	2.07
5	grapefruit	0.601	4.96	5	sect	0.583	3.52
6	garnish	0.596	4.11	6	faith	0.561	1.63
7	concentrate	0.585	2.48	7	believer	0.546	2.73
8	orange	0.585	4.66	8	moral	0.539	1.69

Table 1: Top 8 NNs and their concreteness scores for the targets "lemon" and "belief", sorted by cosine.

In a second step, we selected the top 2 to 16 NNs and averaged over their concreteness scores. Figure 1 presents these averages aggregated by the concreteness score of the corresponding targets (9 bins spanning .5 changes in score). The plot clearly shows that while increasing the concreteness score of the target (different lines), also the average concreteness ratings of the NNs increase (y-axis). An LME analysis indicates that this increase in the ratings associated with the increase of the target's concreteness is statistically significant ($\beta_{concretenessTarget} = 0.22$, p<.001). On average, there are no significant differences between the different ranks (p=0.94); however, there is a significant reduction in the ratings while increasing the number of NNs of highly concrete targets ($\beta_{concretenessTarget:rank} = -0.001$, p<.001).

Finally, we computed the neighbourhood density of each target (Sagi et al., 2009). Higher density scores indicate higher similarity between the vectors of the NNs and the vector of the corresponding target. Table 2 reports means and standard deviations of the neighbour density for each target concreteness bin. The right-most column reports the regression estimates of the pairwise comparison of each bin with its predecessor and the adjusted p-values. The analysis shows a higher neighbourhood density for the more extreme scores, both for concrete and abstract targets.

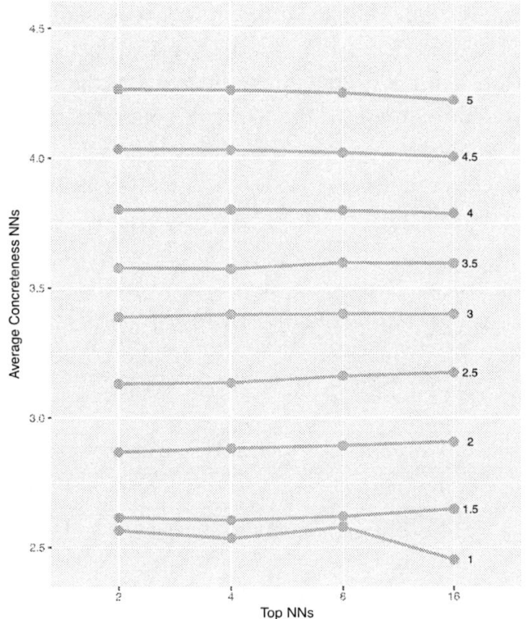

Figure 1: Study 1 - Average concreteness scores of the top 2-16 NNs grouped by the concreteness of the targets. The connection lines are not meaningful, but useful for visualisation purposes.

Figure 2: Study 2 - The five lines indicate the average concreteness scores of context words while decreasing their association with the target (2 to 256 co-occurring contexts words).

Concreteness	Density	SD	Estimate
1.0	0.468	0.083	
1.5	0.400	0.129	$\beta = -0.067$ ***
2.0	0.388	0.139	$\beta = -0.012$ ***
2.5	0.383	0.141	$\beta = -0.005$ *
3.0	0.393	0.144	$\beta = +0.009$ ***
3.5	0.391	0.147	$\beta = -0.002$ n.s.
4.0	0.402	0.147	$\beta = +0.012$ ***
4.5	0.415	0.146	$\beta = +0.013$ ***
5.0	0.434	0.145	$\beta = +0.019$ ***

Table 2: Average neighbourhood density and standard deviation (SD) for targets grouped in 9 bins according to their concreteness score. The `Estimate` column reports regression estimates and adjusted p-values comparing each bin with the previous one (e.g., 1.0 vs. 1.5).

To summarise, the main outcomes of this first study are: 1) distributionally similar words have a similar range of concreteness scores; 2) words with extreme concreteness scores have high neighbourhood density and are, on average, more similar to each other than mid-range words.

4   Study 2: Investigating the concreteness of context words at type level

In this study we shift our attention to the nature of the co-occurring context words. According to the Distributional Hypothesis, co-occurring words are essential elements for the definition of a word's meaning. For this reason, we investigate the concreteness patterns emerging from context words, in order to better understand the distributions of concrete and abstract words.

We grouped the targets into nine bins according to their concreteness ratings and we averaged the concreteness ratings of their first 2 to 256[1] most associated co-occurring context words (positive LMI scores). Figure 2 displays the outcome of this aggregation. An LME analysis indicates that the increase in the concreteness of the target corresponds to a significant increase in the average concreteness of its context words ($\beta_{concretenessTarget}$=.189, p<.001). The negative slopes of the lines in the plot indicate that less strongly associated context words are also less concrete ($\beta_{frequencyContext}$ = -.030, p< .001). This pattern is more pronounced for the contexts of concrete targets ($\beta_{concretenessTarget:frequencyContext}$ =-.005, p< .001).

Table 3 reports the 8 most frequent contexts of the words "lemon" and "belief", and the context concreteness scores, sorted by LMI association. The 8 strongest co-occurring words of "lemon" are all extremely concrete (> 4.2), except for "zest" (see Study 1). Concreteness scores of the co-occurring words of "belief" are medium-low, with the exception of "people".

Rank	Context	LMI	Concreteness	Rank	Context	LMI	Concreteness
-	**lemon**	-	**5.00**	-	**belief**	-	**1.19**
1	juice	47483.09	4.89	1	religion	154436.20	1.71
2	cup	27489.34	5	2	faith	85432.29	1.63
3	orange	21673.45	4.66	3	people	70812.64	4.82
4	sugar	15692.91	4.87	4	system	51274.14	2.94
5	dip	14138.21	4.22	5	freedom	31881.66	2.34
6	teaspoon	13608.63	4.76	6	practice	31808.87	2.52
7	zest	12910.50	2.27	7	value	30652.17	1.62
8	fruit	11633.53	4.81	8	attitude	30372.21	1.97

Table 3: 10 most associated contexts for the targets "belief" and "lemon" sorted by their positive LMI.

Overall, this second study highlights that target and context words share similar concreteness scores. Moreover, the concreteness of the contexts decreases with decreasing LMI association; and, in general, concrete words have more variability in the concreteness of their contexts compared to abstract words.

5 Study 3: Investigating the concreteness of context words at token level

In the previous study we only treated contexts as word types sorted by association score, but we did not completely exploit the informativeness of their co-occurrence strength. In order to analyse the distribution of concrete and abstract context words at token level, we now represent each target as a 9-dimensional concreteness vector, having one dimension per concreteness rating. Each dimension is the sum of frequencies of each context word having a specific concreteness rating, normalised by the total number of context words with the same score. In order to have all the values in the range 0-1, we normalised the scores in each cell again by the total amount of context words that each target has. For example, Table 4 reports the percentage of contexts with concreteness scores from 1 to 5 for "lemon" and "belief". "Lemon" has a very high proportion of contexts with a concreteness of 5.0 (44%); while "belief" has 47% of its contexts with a concreteness score of 1 and 1.5.

	1	1.5	2	2.5	3	3.5	4	4.5	5
lemon	0.08	0.03	0.04	0.05	0.04	0.06	0.10	0.16	**0.44**
belief	0.18	**0.29**	0.16	0.10	0.08	0.07	0.04	0.04	0.04

Table 4: Percentage of tokens in each context bin for the words "lemon" and "belief".

---

[1] As discussed in Polajnar and Clark (2014), MI models achieve their best performance in semantic similarity tasks with vectors of 240 dimensions.

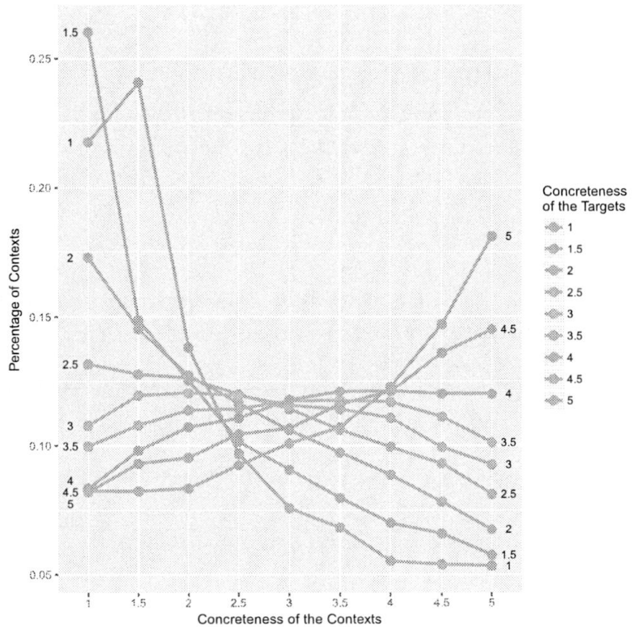

Figure 3: Study 3 - The five lines show the percentage of context words with a certain concreteness score averaged by the concreteness of their target.

Figure 3 shows an extremely clear picture. It reports the average number of contexts with a specific concreteness score (x-axis) grouped by the concreteness of the targets they co-occur with (different lines). Very concrete targets (e.g., pink and violet lines) have a clear preference for very concrete contexts (positive slope); on the other hand, very abstract words (red and yellow lines) show a clear preference for very abstract contexts (negative slope). The peak of the lines is steeper for abstract words than for concrete ones: compared to abstract words, concrete words seem to co-occur with words with different concreteness scores, still showing a clear preference for very concrete contexts.

Overall, Study 3 supports the evidence from the previous two studies: also at the token level, concrete words co-occur more frequently with concrete words, and abstract words co-occur primarily with abstract words.

6   Conclusion

Overall, the three studies show consistent results. Concrete words tend to co-occur with other concrete words, while abstract words tend to co-occur with abstract words. Moreover, concrete words seem to have more variable contexts in terms of their concreteness scores, compared to abstract words that seem to have a strong preference for abstract contexts with very low concreteness scores.

Our insights regarding concrete words are fully aligned with multiple studies in the literature (Barsalou and Wiemer-Hastings, 2005; Hill et al., 2014; Pecher et al., 2011). On the other hand, they seem to disagree with the grounding hypothesis for abstract words: in our studies, abstract words do not share the same context as concrete words. The importance of this research is threefold: it depicts a very consistent picture in the behaviour of concreteness measures from a distributional perspective; it also indicates some limitations of the behavioural measures adopted (e.g., average concreteness score for polysemous words); and it does not align with the existing psycholinguistic literature and thus provides a promising different perspective into the analysis of concrete and abstract concepts.

Acknowledgments

The research was supported by the DFG Collaborative Research Centre SFB 732 (Diego Frassinelli, Sabine Schulte im Walde, Jason Utt), and the DFG Heisenberg Fellowship SCHU-2580/1 (Sabine Schulte im Walde). We also thank the two anonymous reviewers for their comments.

References

Baayen, R. H., D. J. Davidson, and D. M. Bates (2008). Mixed-effects modeling with crossed random effects for subjects and items. *Journal of Memory and Language 59*(4), 390–412.

Balota, D. A., M. J. Yap, M. J. Cortese, K. A. Hutchison, B. Kessler, B. Loftis, J. H. Neely, D. L. Nelson, G. B. Simpson, and R. Treiman (2007). The English Lexicon Project. *Behavior Research Methods 39*(3), 445–459.

Barr, D. J., R. Levy, C. Scheepers, and H. J. Tily (2013). Random effects structure for confirmatory hypothesis testing: Keep it maximal. *Journal of Memory and Language*, 1–51.

Barsalou, L. W. and K. Wiemer-Hastings (2005). Situating abstract concepts. In D. Pecher and R. Zwaan (Eds.), *Grounding cognition: The role of perception and action in memory, language, and thinking*, Chapter 7, pp. 129–163. New York: Cambridge University Press.

Brysbaert, M., A. B. Warriner, and V. Kuperman (2014). Concreteness ratings for 40 thousand generally known English word lemmas. *Behavior Research Methods 46*(3), 904–11.

Evert, S. (2004). The statistical analysis of morphosyntactic distributions. In *Proceedings of the 4th International Conference on Language Resources and Evaluation*, pp. 1539–1542.

Firth, J. R. (1957). *Papers in Linguistics 1934-51*. London, UK: Longmans.

Harris, Z. (1954). Distributional structure. *Word 10*(23), 146–162.

Hill, F., A. Korhonen, and C. Bentz (2014). A quantitative empirical analysis of the abstract/concrete distinction. *Cognitive Science 38*(1), 162–177.

Lenci, A. (2008). Distributional semantics in linguistic and cognitive research. *Rivista di Linguistica 20*(1), 1–31.

Miller, G. A. and W. G. Charles (1991). Contextual correlates of semantic similarity. *Language and Cognitive Processes 6*(1), 1–28.

Murphy, G. L. (2002). *The Big Book of Concepts*. London: MIT Press.

Pecher, D., I. Boot, and S. Van Dantzig (2011). Abstract concepts. Sensory-motor grounding, metaphors, and beyond. *Psychology of Learning and Motivation - Advances in Research and Theory 54*, 217–248.

Polajnar, T. and S. Clark (2014). Improving distributional semantic vectors through context selection and normalisation. In *Proceedings of the 14th Conference of the European Chapter of the Association for Computational Linguistics*, pp. 230–238.

Sagi, E., S. Kaufmann, and B. Clark (2009). Semantic density analysis: Comparing word meaning across time and phonetic space. In *Proceedings of the EACL Workshop on GEMS: GEometical Models of Natural Language Semantics*, pp. 104–111.

Schäfer, R. (2015). Processing and querying large web corpora with the COW14 architecture. In *Proceedings of the 3rd Workshop on Challenges in the Management of Large Corpora*, pp. 28–34.

Turney, P. D. and P. Pantel (2010). From frequency to meaning: Vector space models of semantics. *Journal of Artificial Intelligence Research 37*, 141–188.

Warriner, A. B., V. Kuperman, and M. Brysbaert (2013). Norms of valence, arousal, and dominance for 13,915 English lemmas. *Behavior Research Methods 45*(4), 1191–1207.

Surprisal and Satisfaction: Towards an Information-theoretic Characterization of Presuppositions with a Diachronic Application

Remus Gergel, Martin Kopf-Giammanco, Julia Masloh
Saarland University
{remus.gergel, martin.kopf, julia.masloh}@uni-saarland.de

Abstract

The paper offers a pilot study concerned with presuppositions in historical data, which are identified and annotated on the basis of six triggers, viz. three for additives, and three for factives. It brings together information extraction and annotation on (A) the satisfaction/binding and (B) information-theoretic surprisal values of presuppositions. An initial (naive) hypothesis is that the two lines of investigation converge, but this only turned out to be the case for factives in the data inspected. The work conducted relates two strands of research: information theory (Shannon 1948, Fankhauser et al. 2014, Degaetano-Ortlieb et al. 2016) and the semantic theory of presuppositions (Stalnaker 1973, Heim 1983, Schwarz 2014, 2016). Furthermore, the study begins to connect two methodological points relevant for studies concerned with the diachronic evolution of meaning and structure but not approached jointly so far: syntactically parsed data and information-theoretically calculated predictors on semantic phenomena. Using such tools, the paper offers an initial description, a discussion of methodological issues, and some empirical results such as the existence of two crystallizing major classes of triggers during the Early Modern English period, which may be indicative of the distinction between informative and run-of-the-mill presuppositions. While the focus of the paper is on the early modern period (that is, roughly, the sixteenth and the seventeenth century), a short outlook on Late Modern English (the subsequent two centuries) is offered.

1 Background

This paper reports a pilot study concerned with the extraction of information-theoretic surprisal values (Shannon, 1948, Fankhauser et al., 2014, Degaetano-Ortlieb et al., 2014, Degaetano-Ortlieb et al. 2016). We conducted the bulk of the work described in what follows on the basis of syntactic corpora such as Kroch et al. (2004), Kroch et al. (2016). Empirically, we have pursued a two-pronged metric consisting of surprisal values as well as the rate of overt textual satisfaction applied to the topic of presuppositions in a genre-balanced randomized sample of tokens of Early Modern English (Kroch et al. 2004). The context-annotation of presupposition satisfaction was manual and double-checked team-internally, thus adapting previous basic techniques (cf. Spenader 2002, Poesio & Vieira 1998, Venhuizen 2015) to the necessities of working with earlier philological traditions ('old language' and its conventions). This means, inter alia, that we could not rely on naive annotators in the same way that synchronic studies can. But why proceed with syntactically parsed corpora when investigating a semantic phenomenon? A benefit of using surprisal calculation on a syntactic parse in our case turned out to be, quite trivially, that the searched categories and phrases which were searched could be identified more precisely to then undergo semantic and information-theoretic scrutiny. The associates of presupposition triggers could be identified better for the calculation of surprisal values. To clarify the terminology we use, consider (1) and (2):

(1)   Sally *knows* that Abby left late.

(2)   Peter juggled, *too*.

The factive verb *know* and the additive adverb *too* are presupposition triggers. For simplicity, we call the constituents – the denotations of which help us reconstruct the presupposition – 'associates'. For (1), that's the clause headed by the complementizer *that* (i.e. the CP in usual syntactic terminology) *that Abby left late*. For factive predicates, we then have clauses as associates. For (2), however, an ambiguity arises – either *Peter* or *juggled* could be an associate. Pitch accent could resolve this, but we don't have such information in most cases in the historical data. However, if the preceding context contains e.g. another predicate which is asserted of Peter (such as *danced*), then the associate must be *juggled*. The toy example already illustrates the fact that the associate can vary with respect to its syntactic category. The syntactic parse together with the contextual scanning of the discourse semantics allow us to determine it. In our data for additives, the associate varied between the following categories: adjectival phrases (AP), clausal constituents (e.g. CP/IP in one common terminology, though not much hinges on the labeling), noun phrases (NP), verb phrases (VP) and prepositional phrases (PP). The issue is obvious. Some notion of a structured tree and precise categories are needed. Determining surprisal values of an associate requires in a first step circumscribing the associate as precisely as possible. Even for factives, where hardly any such ambiguity is involved, a syntactic parse is of help to determine surprisal calculation (for details of which cf. section 3.2).

The larger goal in the background of our current endeavor is twofold: (A) to prepare the ground to get a systematic understanding of how presuppositions behave in language change (paths of other side messages, invited inferences, implicatures etc. have of course been much more studied); (B) to combine, in an initial attempt, advances in two areas of modern historical research – viz. syntactically parsed corpora and the extraction of Shannonian information density – in order to derive the effects of the well-defined notion of surprisal on linguistic change.

2   Presuppositions in Historical Data

Research on presuppositions has seen rich theoretical paradigms over the decades and it has recently gained additional momentum due to synchronic experimental studies engaging in theoretical issues (Schwarz, 2007, 2014, 2015, 2016a,b, Tiemann et al., 2011, Bade, 2014, 2016, DeVeaugh-Geiss et al., 2015, Jayez& Reinecke, 2016, Tonhauser, 2016, Djärv et al., to appear). Despite the increasing body of research, corpus-based (and clearly, even less: information-theoretic) as well as the historical-developmental properties of presuppositions have only scarcely been approached (unlike studies on implicatures in semantic change, which are too numerous to mention within present confines). Diachronic studies dealing with the topic are Eckardt (2009) and Schwenter & Waltereit (2010). Upon closer inspection Schwenter & Waltereit concentrate on implicatures which can arise once a presuppositional item is already in place (e.g. interesting dialectal readings parasitic on *too*) and do not (claim to) have a corpus-based study. It is essential, however, to distinguish between presuppositions and other types of inferences as the experimental work cited above shows. Eckardt posits the APO (*Avoid Pragmatic Overload*) tendency, as a possible driving maxim of semantic change; we see large potential in APO, primarily with regard to implicatures, but we are generally of the opinion that such principles should be founded not only on the basis of interesting theoretical considerations and the analysis of individual examples, but also of wide systematic corpus studies (cf., e.g., Beck and Gergel, 2015, for a pertinent corpus-based semantic account of a presupposition trigger, though without measures of overt satisfaction or information-theoretic notions).

3 Methods

3.1 Data

The choice of data for this pilot study was guided by a selection of six potential triggers of presuppositions from the PPCEME corpus (Kroch et al., 2004). It contains three sub-periods – E1, E2, E3 – which are delimited chronologically as follows:

> E1: 1500 – 1570
>
> E2: 1570 – 1640
>
> E3: 1640 – 1710

Furthermore, for each text the meta-information regarding its year of composition is available, so segmentation into other intervals than the ones given by the corpus three-fold division itself was possible. An interesting measure at the period is of 50-year intervals. Using unigrams as units, models are created for each 50-year interval. These allow us to track usage change over time while preserving the context information of a given unit.

The triggers themselves were chosen in such a way as to have a reasonable number of occurring tokens in the corpus. We aimed at a randomized selection of 100 tokens per trigger. To detect diachronic developments we often focused on the first and the third sub-period of Early Modern English; that is, E1 and E3. We chose three additive adverbs/particles – *too, also, even* – and three verbs – *know, find* and *see*. The verbs were required to have clausal complements.

3.2 Surprisal Calculation on Syntactically Parsed Data

Our primary understanding of surprisal is information-theoretic (Fankhauser et al., 2014, Degaetano-Ortlieb et al., 2016). The general definition of surprisal is the formula in (I), while the one in (II) gives the average surprisal (AvS).

$$S(unit) = -log_2 p(unit|context) \tag{I}$$

$$AvS(unit) = \frac{1}{|unit_i|} \times -\sum_i log_2 p(unit_i|context_i) \tag{II}$$

We adapted Degaetano et al.'s method to syntactically parsed corpora by calculating the mean average over the terminal nodes included in the constituents in which we were interested, i.e. the associates of the triggers. During pre-processing, the corpus files had been sliced into 50-year sections (following Degaetano et al. - other choices are possible, but we could not detect any crucial difference so far). For every 50-year slice, the AvS for every single unit ('word') was calculated with the context represented by the three preceding words/items. After calculating the 50-year models, the AvS values were aligned with the terminal nodes in parsed files of the PPCEME. Notice, hence, that the technology we have used did not initially hinge on the syntactic representation per se, but that such representations turned out to be advantageous in comparison with corpora that lack syntactic structures given the precise enclosure of different types of associate phrases (cf. also the discussion in section 1 above). Searches in the syntactic corpus were conducted using *CorpusSearch* (http://sourceforge.net/projects/corpussearch/), *CQPweb* for the surprisal-annotated corpus and we have used *R* for the calculations and plots.

3.3 Context-Based Semantic Annotation

We drew on two lines of research here. On the one hand, e.g. Beck, et al. (2009), and Gergel and Beck (2015) show that identifying the salient presuppositions in historical data is feasible and such efforts offer the prospects of ascertaining sometimes meaningful trajectories. Our historical handling of the data is similar. Additionally following Spenader's (2002) synchronic study (among others), we kept track not only of which presuppositions were salient for the extracted token-context pairs, but also whether the presuppositions were assigned to specific types. The basic possibilities were: (i) was the presupposition in each individual case given, i.e. satisfied overtly through direct textual evidence or (ii) was it not given (and potentially to be accommodated)? A third category we took into account was (iii) that the presupposition was inferable. See below for additive adverbs and factive verbs and their respective categories – (3) & (4) for *Given*, (5) & (6) for *Inferred*, (7) & (8) for *New*. The triggers are italicized throughout and the underlined parts in (5) indicate clues for presuppositional inference - thus, while there is no directly mentioned notion of mistrust preceding the presupposition trigger, this can be inferred from the tyrant's unwillingness to be shaved by anyone. In (6) the entire sequence of operations described is intended to yield the result in the complement of the verb.

(3)   Yes, Sir, She has a Daughter by Sir Charles [...]. She has a Son *too* by her first Husband Squire
        Sullen, [...];   (FARQUHAR-E3-H,3.98)

(4)   The first time that his Strength was known, was by his Mothers going to a Rich Farmers House,
        [...]/[...] so when Tom began to *know* that he had more strength then twenty Men had, he then
        began to be Merry with Men, and very tractable,[...].   (PENNY-E3-P1,34.198[...]/PENNY-E3-
        P1,35.249)

(5)   What misery was in the life of <u>Dionyse</u> the tyrant of Cicile ? Who <u>knowing that his people desired
        his distruction</u> , for his rauine and crueltie , <u>wold nat be of any man shauen</u> , but first caused his
        owne doughters to clippe his berde , and afterwarde he *also* mistrusted them, [...].
                                                                               (ELYOT-E1-P1,157.119)

(6)   Multiply the Sine of the Latitude giuen by the total Sine, and diuide the product by the comple-
        ment of y=e= said Latitude that done, multiply the quotient by the Sine of the sunnes declination,
        and diuide the product by the Sine of the complement of the declination, and the quotient thereof
        will shew the signe of the ascentionall difference: and by working according to this rule youshal
        find that when the Sunne is entred 3'3. into Taurus, at which time his declination is 11. degrees,
        4'1. as hauebeen said before the ascentionall difference will be 15. degrees , 2'1.   (BLUNDEV-
        E2-P1,54V.114-BLUNDEV-E2-P1,55R.119)

(7)   MISS.: Pray, Father, what do you intend to do with him, hang him?
        SIR TUN: That, at least, Child.
        NURSE: Ay, and it's e'en too good for him *too*.   (VANBR-E3-P2,74.582)

(8)   Thus we *see*, that most Resinous Gums [...] do also, being moderately solicited by heat [...] emit
        steams.   (BOYLE-E3-H)

4 Results

4.1 Overt Satisfaction in Context, Inferred Information, and New Information

The adverbs investigated ('additive particles') had the ratios reported in Table 1 below. Table 2 below subsequently summarizes the findings for the factive verbs *know, find,* and *see*. Recall that E1 and E3 are the first and the last subperiod of Early Modern English, respectively, on which we concentrated in our search for variation.

	E1 #	E1 %	E3 #	E3 %
also				
given	45	91.84	49	96.08
new	1	2.04	1	1.96
inferred	3	6.12	1	1.96
even				
given	10	25.00	24	50.00
new	29	72.50	22	45.83
inferred	1	2.50	2	4.17
too				
given	46	92.00	40	81.63
new	4	8.00	3	6.12
inferred	0	0.00	6	12.24

Table 1: Adverbial selection of pilot study

As is evident from Table 1, the additives *also* and *too* in particular display very high rates of overt satisfaction (i.e. givenness) in the corpus data. The adverbial uses of *even* are distinct as they have a more balanced division between given and new information. Table 2, by contrast, illustrates the very high - and increasing - rate of new information in the potential factive verbs during the Early Modern period:

	E1 #	E1 %	E2 #	E2 %	E3 #	E3 %
know						
given	9	18.75			6	12.76
new	34	70.83	not included		41	87.24
inferred	5	10.42			0	0.00
find						
given	0	0.00	0	0.00	1	2.44
new	3	75.00	17	80.95	39	95.12
inferred	1	25.00	4	19.05	1	2.44
see						
given	4	12.50	4	12.50	1	3.33
new	20	62.50	24	75.00	26	86.67
inferred	8	25.00	4	12.50	3	10.00

Table 2: Verbal selection of pilot study

4.2   Surprisal values

The surprisal values obtained for the six types of potential presuppositions were translated into boxplot-diagrams. We calculated such suprisal values on the basis of the methods outlined in 3.2 both for the triggers themselves and the associates. For space reasons, we reproduce the more informative figures for the associates in this short paper. Thus figure 1 (cf. below) provides insight into the distinct behaviors of both additive adverbs and factive verbs regarding the surprisal values of their associates (cf. section 5 Discussion). The temporal axis includes the period (i.e. crucially E1 vs. E3 for each individual trigger). Notice what distinguishes the two classes. While for the verbs (cf. figures 1d to 1f), we witness significantly more surprising values for the new occurrences, this is not borne out for the additive adverbs in general (cf. figures 1a to 1c).

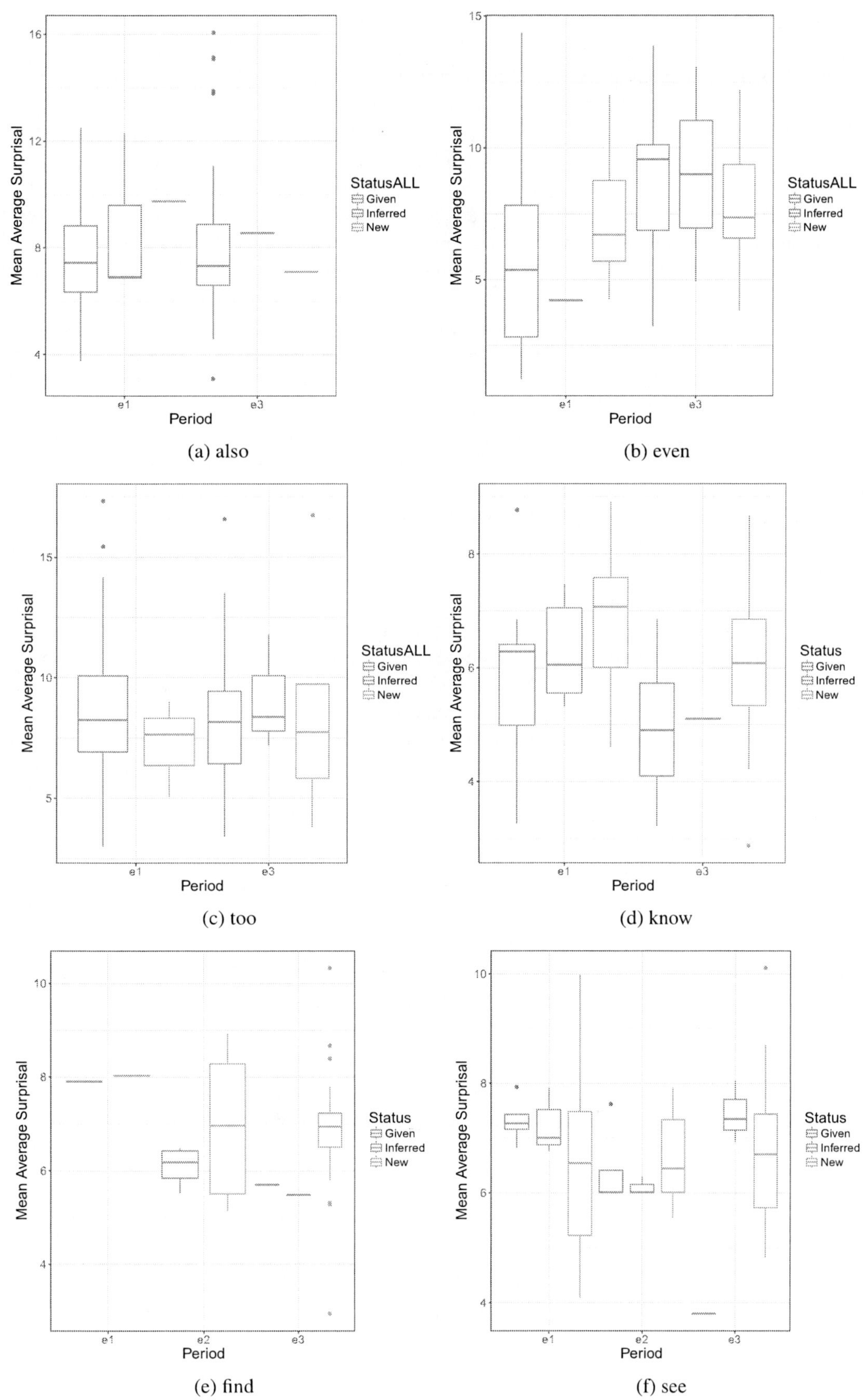

Figure 1: PSP triggers - factive verbs & additive adverbs; mean average surprisal of assoc. elements

5 Discussion

The triggers showed an interestingly distinct behavior in the two classes with respect to overt satisfaction, with the additive adverbs requiring satisfaction considerably more frequently, and in particular *too* and *also*. This is consonant with synchronic findings (Spenader 2002) made for Present-day English. The observation, then, nourishes the idea that, unlike implicatures, presuppositions partially together with their satisfaction signatures are comparatively resilient over time, pace Eckardt's (2009) theoretically interesting take. And the degree of distinctive satisfaction behavior in different classes is an indicator. Presuppositions are, however, not entirely static. First, recall that our current database only contains Early Modern English (with a brief excursus on Late Modern English explained below) and more is being done by extending the database in several respects, including on a wider span on the diachronic axis. Second, an interesting behavior can be culled from the behavior of factives in our window of observation: the territory of 'new' presupposition continuously increases during Early Modern English. This leads us to explore the idea that 'informative' presuppositions (Prince 1978, Tonhauser 2015), which arguably do not require satisfaction, may be an increasing category in English (at particular times). It will be interesting to compare the ratio of presuppositional change-of-state verbs, another candidate for so-called informative presuppositions, in a follow-up study. For space reasons, we also leave out a discussion of yet another interesting type of trigger in this short paper - viz. cleft constructions - the evolution of which we investigate in a study parallel to the one which is the focus of this short paper and for which a similar increase of the *New* category can be observed over time (cf. Gergel, Kopf-Giammanco and Watkins 2017).

While the focus of this paper has been on two trigger groups during the Early Modern English period, we mention some possible extensions and caution against too strong generalizations both across trigger classes and within groups when the timespan is extended. There are, for instance, differences between clefts and e.g. the factive verb *know* on the basis of what we have been able to see so far. While the increasing tendency for clefts to express new information seems to carry on the basis of observations reported in Gergel, Kopf-Giammanco, and Watkins (2017), a similar tendency for *know* is only observable in Early Modern English, while during Late Modern English the tendency is reversed (cf. Table 3 below).

	L1 #	L1 %	L3 #	L3 %
know				
given	8	16.00	13	26.00
new	32	64.00	28	56.00
inferred	10	20.00	9	18.00

Table 3: Verbal selection in extended study

And additives part way again. From an incipient inquiry into Late Modern English, we observe that *also* shows almost a mirror image of the factive verb *know*. That is, a decreasing tendency for new information first and a subsequent slight increase for it in Late Modern English; cf. Table 4 (synonymous *too* is less clear in this respect):

	L1 #	L1 %	L2 #	L2 %	L3 #	L3 %
also						
given	44	84.89	42	82.31	42	84.00
new	3	5.85	3	5.92	4	8.00
inferred	5	9.26	6	11.77	4	8.00
too						
given	34	68.00	33	67.08	33	62.50
new	10	20.00	10	20.58	8	15.74
inferred	6	12.00	6	12.33	11	21.76

Table 4: Adverbial selection in extended study

The inclusion of surprisal values is a potential additional predictor of distinct classes and a longer-term goal of such work can be to implement this more broadly, more reliably, and with improved measurements. An interesting information-theoretic asymmetry between the classes studied already emerges on the basis of the current findings from Early Modern English. While a particular tendency could be ascertained for factives in the data studied, namely that the presuppositions which are overtly satisfied (and specifically given) are less surprising than the new ones, the tendency was not visible for additives. Initial observations towards a fuller account are as follows: first, the syntax of additives is more flexible. Second, the 'given' part can have a higher degree of variation in the case of additives. Third, additional pragmatic inferences often arise parasitic on additive presupposition markers. Overall, however, notice that an important caveat is in order. The current notion of surprisal, while legitimate in diachronic studies and perhaps more generally due to a current lack of more suitable tools for tackling long-range dependencies (of which presuppositions are a clear case) needs to be drastically improved. On closer inspection, it may be in fact surprising that given information turns out to be less surprising for the Early Modern verbs studied in view of the type of measurement used. We do not have a better measurement tool at this point, but would like to hint at a possible direction based on the distance between trigger and its associate (in cases in which there is one); cf. Gergel, Kopf-Giammanco and Watkins (2017) for an initial testing of distance measurements.

We conclude by stressing the necessity of two objectives in the field (in our view): first, broad and systematic studies of explicit presupposition satisfaction in corpora including historical ones, towards which we take an initial step; second, the methodologically interesting possibility, which we have implemented in a first instantiation, of combining (A) information theory (e.g. via surprisal values), (B) data from syntactically parsed corpora, and (C) context-based annotation of meaning. One goal is as follows: given a group of potential trigger words (we again use the term 'potential' because historically you first have to test whether the trigger is genuine), find out to what extent the time-consuming philological task (C) can be approximated on the basis of combining (A) and (B) applied to that trigger group. Clearly, more (also) of the footwork of type (C) in terms of training ground needs to be done, before a reasonable answer to the general problem can be offered.

References

Bade, N. (2014). Obligatory implicatures and the presupposition of "too". In *Proceedings of Sinn und Bedeutung 18*, Bayonne and Vitoria-Gasteiz, pp. 42–59.

Bade, N. (2016). *Obligatory presupposition triggers in discourse*. Dissertation, Universität Tübingen.

Beck, S., P. Berezovskaya, and K. Pflugfelder (2009). The use of *again* in 19th-century English versus present-day English. *Syntax 12-3*, 193–214.

Beck, S. and R. Gergel (2015). The diachronic semantics of English *again*. *Natural Language Semantics 23,3*, 157–203.

Degaetano-Ortlieb, S., P. Fankhauser, H. Kermes, E. Lapshinova-Koltunski, N. Ordan, and E. Teich (2014). Data mining with shallow vs. linguistic features to study diversification of scientific registers. In *Proceedings of the 9th edition of the Language Resources and Evaluation Conference (LREC 2014)*, Reykjavik, Iceland.

Degaetano-Ortlieb, S., H. Kermes, A. Khamis, and E. Teich (2016). An information-theoretic approach to modeling diachronic change in scientific English. *Selected Papers from Varieng - From Data to Evidence (d2e)*.

Degaetano-Ortlieb, S. and E. Teich (2016). Information-based modeling of diachronic linguistic change: from typicality to productivity. In N. Reiter, B. Alex, and K. A. Zervanou (Eds.), *Proceedings of the 10th SIGHUM Workshop on Language Technology for Cultural Heritage, Social Sciences, and Humanities. Association for Dorothee Pesch Computational Linguistics (ACL)*, Berlin.

DeVeaugh-Geiss, J., M. Zimmermann, E. Onea, and A.-C. Boell (2015). Contradicting (not-)at-issueness in exclusives and clefts: an empirical study. *Semantics and Linguistic Theory 25*, 373–393.

Djärv, K., J. Zehr, and F. Schwarz (tba). Cognitive vs. emotive factives: an experimental differentiation. In *Proceedings of Sinn und Bedeutung 21*, Edinburgh, pp. 42–59.

Eckardt, R. (2009). APO: Avoid pragmatic overload. In J. Visconti and M.-B. M. Hansen (Eds.), *Current Trends in Diachronic Semantics and Pragmatics*, pp. 21–42. London: Emerald.

Fankhauser, P., J. Knappen, and E. Teich (2014). Exploring and visualizing variation in language resources. In N. C. C. Chair), K. Choukri, T. Declerck, H. Loftsson, B. Maegaard, J. Mariani, A. Moreno, J. Odijk, and S. Piperidis (Eds.), *Proceedings of the Ninth International Conference on Language Resources and Evaluation (LREC'14)*.

Gergel, R. and S. Beck (2015). Early Modern English 'again': A corpus study and semantic analysis. *English Language and Linguistics 19(1)*, 27–47.

Gergel, R., M. Kopf-Giammanco, and J. Watkins (2017). Annotating presuppositional information in historical corpora. In *Talk at 23rd International Conference on Historical Linguistics, San Antonio, Texas*.

Heim, I. (1983). On the projection problem for presuppositions. In *Proceedings of WCCFL 2*, Stanford University, Stanford, California, pp. 114–125.

Jayez, J. and R. Reinecke (2016). Presuppositions and salience: An experimental approach. In *Proceedings of Semantics and Linguistic Theory 26*, University of Texas, Austin, pp. 601–619.

Kermes, H., S. Degaetano-Ortlieb, A. Khamis, J. Knappen, and E. Teich (2016, May 23-28). The Royal Society Corpus: From uncharted data to corpus. In *Proceedings of the LREC*, Portoroz, Slovenia.

Kroch, A., B. Santorini, and L. Delfs (2004). *The Penn-Helsinki Parsed Corpus of Early Modern English (PPCEME)* (First ed.). Department of Linguistics, University of Pennsylvania. Release 3.

Kroch, A., B. Santorini, and A. Diertani (2016). *The Penn-Helsinki Parsed Corpus of Early Modern English (PPCEME)* (Second ed.). Department of Linguistics, University of Pennsylvania. Release 1.

Poesio, M. and R. Vieira (1998). A corpus-based investigation of definite description use. *Computational Linguistics 24*, 183–216.

Prince, E. (1978). A comparison of wh-Clefts and it-clefts in discourse. *Language 54*, 883–906.

Schwarz, F. (2007). Processing presupposed content. *Journal of Semantics 24*, 373–416.

Schwarz, F. (2014). Presuppositions are fast, whether hard or soft - evidence from the visual world. *Semantics and Linguistic Theory 24*, 1–22.

Schwarz, F. (Ed.) (2015). *Experimental perspectives on presuppositions*. Berlin: Springer.

Schwarz, F. (2016a). Experimental work in presupposition and presupposition projection. *Annual Review of Linguistics 2*, 273–292.

Schwarz, F. (2016b). Presuppositions, Projection, and accommodation- theoretical issues and experimental approaches. Draft submitted to Handbook of Experimental Semantics and Pragmatics.

Schwenter, S. and R. Waltereit (2010). Presupposition accommodation and language change. In K. Davidse, L. Vandelanotte, and H. Cuyckens (Eds.), *Subjectification, Intersubjectification and Grammaticalization*, pp. 75–102. Berlin: Mouton de Gruyter.

Shannon, C. A mathematical theory of communication. *Bell System Technical Journal 27*.

Spenader, J. (2002). *Presuppositions in spoken discourse*. Dissertation, University of Stockholm.

Stalnaker, R. (1973). Presuppositions. *Journal of Philosophical Logic 2*, 447–457.

Tiemann, S., M. Schmid, N. Bade, B. Rolke, I. Hertrich, H. Ackermann, and S. Beck (2011, May 23-28). Psycholinguistic evidence for presuppositions: On-line and off-line data. In *Proceedings of Sinn und Bedeutung*, Volume 15, Saarland University, pp. 581–597.

Tonhauser, J. (2015). Are 'informative presuppositions' presuppositions? *Language and Linguistics Compass 9*, 77–101.

Venhuizen, N. J. (2015). *Projection in Discourse: A data-driven formal semantic analysis*. Ph. D. thesis, University of Groningen.

Incorporating visual features into word embeddings:
A bimodal autoencoder-based approach

Mika Hasegawa
Waseda University
mika@pcl.cs.waseda.ac.jp

Tetsunori Kobayashi
Waseda University
koba@waseda.jp

Yoshihiko Hayashi
Waseda University
yshk.hayashi@aoni.waseda.jp

Abstract

Multimodal semantic representation is an evolving area of research in natural language processing as well as computer vision. Combining or integrating perceptual information, such as visual features, with linguistic features is recently being actively studied. This paper presents a novel bimodal autoencoder model for multimodal representation learning: the autoencoder learns in order to enhance linguistic feature vectors by incorporating the corresponding visual features. During the runtime, owing to the trained neural network, visually enhanced multimodal representations can be achieved even for words for which direct visual-linguistic correspondences are not learned. The empirical results obtained with standard semantic relatedness tasks demonstrate that our approach is generally promising. We further investigate the potential efficacy of the enhanced word embeddings in discriminating antonyms and synonyms from vaguely related words.

1 Introduction

The efficient learning and the effective exploitation of a distributed representation of words, phrases, and sentences are active research topics in NLP (Bengio et al., 2013; Mikolov et al., 2013). Theoretically supported by the concept of grounded cognition (Barsalou, 2008) and technically endorsed by the progress of deep learning techniques, this line of research has been further pursued in order to incorporate perceptual information, such as visual features, into linguistic embeddings (Silberer and Lapata, 2014; Bruni et al., 2014; Kiela and Bottou, 2014; Kiela et al., 2016). The resulting semantic representation is often referred to as *multimodal semantic representation*.

Two fundamental requirements, however, may not have been fulfilled simultaneously: (1) the *zero-shot representation learning* of words, and (2) the exploitation of existing useful resources. It should be noted that zero-shot representation learning in the context of the present research means a computational process for obtaining an appropriate multimodal representation even for a word for which direct visual-linguistic correspondences have not been learned. In this paper, a bimodal autoencoder[1] model, named ViEW (visually enhanced word embeddings), is proposed for incorporating visual features into existing word embeddings.

This architecture facilitates bimodal representation learning from the given visual-linguistic correspondences. In the training, the autoencoder learns to reproduce a linguistic word embedding vector, while having an additional input vector (of the same dimensionality) that represents the corresponding visual features. During the runtime, by exploiting the trained neural network parameters, the autoencoder can construct a visually enhanced word embedding even for a word for which direct visual-linguistic correspondences have not been learned. It should be noted here that these visual and linguistic features could be drawn from independently developed existing resources.

The experimental results demonstrate that our model exhibits state-of-the-art performances in standard semantic relatedness tasks, some of which innately contain zero-shot instances. We further discuss

---

[1] Autoencoders are generally used in representation learning; after training, the compact representation of an input data can be obtained from one of the hidden layers. A bimodal autoencoder is a type of autoencoder that takes two types of inputs and has one output (or more).

the potential efficacy of the enhanced word embeddings in discriminating antonyms and synonyms from vaguely related words.

2   Related work

The approaches to multimodal representation learning can be primarily classified by the method of information fusion or integration. In addition, so-called *zero-shot representation learning* is an important factor for characterizing an approach.

Among the several researches on multimodal semantic representation, only two of them are summarized here. Bruni et al. (2014) applied singular value decomposition (SVD) to a word-feature matrix, where each word is represented by the concatenation of a linguistic vector and the corresponding visual vector. The linguistic vectors are generated using the Strudel method (Baroni et al., 2010), and the visual vectors are obtained by applying a conventional feature-extraction method that relies on the local features of bag-of-visual-words (BoVW). Kiela and Bottou (2014) simply used vector concatenation, in which the visual features were extracted from a convolutional neural network (CNN), and the linguistic features were Word2Vec (Mikolov et al., 2013) word embeddings. These works pioneered this research direction by developing methods to combine or integrate linguistic and visual features; however, they suffered from the inability to handle zero-shot representation learning.

Zero-shot representation learning, in the context of the present research, indicates a computational process for achieving an appropriate multimodal representation even for a word for which direct visual-linguistic correspondences have not been learned. This concept may have originated in the field of computer vision (Lampert and Harmeling, 2009) and has been a continuously active research topic. It is crucial in computer vision and other research areas as well, given a potential situation in which sufficient annotations for all possible categories or concepts cannot be expected.

In order to tackle the zero-shot learning problem in the context of multimodal representation learning, Lazaridou et al. (2015) proposed the multimodal skip-gram (MMSG) model that extends the original skip-gram model (Mikolov et al., 2013) by incorporating visual features. More specifically, a restricted set of words in the training text corpus is accompanied with the corresponding images, and the model builds word vectors by learning to *jointly* predict linguistic and visual features. The joint objective enables the propagation of visual information to representations of words for which no direct visual evidence is available in the training, and hence, the model can realize zero-shot image labeling and retrieval. However, it should be noted that this framework requires a joint learning process, which means that independently developed existing linguistic or visual features cannot be used.

As in (Lazaridou et al., 2015), our ViEW model addresses the zero-shot representation learning problem but does not adopt a joint-learning approach. This allows us to fully exploit the existing independently developed linguistic and visual resources. The heart of the proposed approach is a bimodal autoencoder that integrates bimodal inputs by maintaining a specially designed loss function that is described afterward. It should be mentioned here that Silberer and Lapata (2014) have already adopted a similar architecture (in a sense). Their architecture, however, integrates modality-dependent autoencoders in a hidden layer, which means that the multimodal representations can only be built for pairs of visual and linguistic inputs. This means that the autoencoder cannot cope with zero-shot representation learning. Recently, a literature (Kodirov et al., 2017) that proposed an autoencoder architecture for zero-shot learning was published in a computer vision conference. Although the architecture is apparently similar to our ViEW model, their primary input/output is a visual feature instead of a linguistic feature.

3   ViEW model

Figure 1 schematizes the neural network architecture of the ViEW model, which is essentially a multi-layer autoencoder for linguistic input/output (shown in blue) with an additional visual input (shown in orange). This means that the network primarily attempts to minimize the error between the linguistic input (as represented in a hidden layer) and output ($Loss_{ling}$), while simultaneously minimizing the error

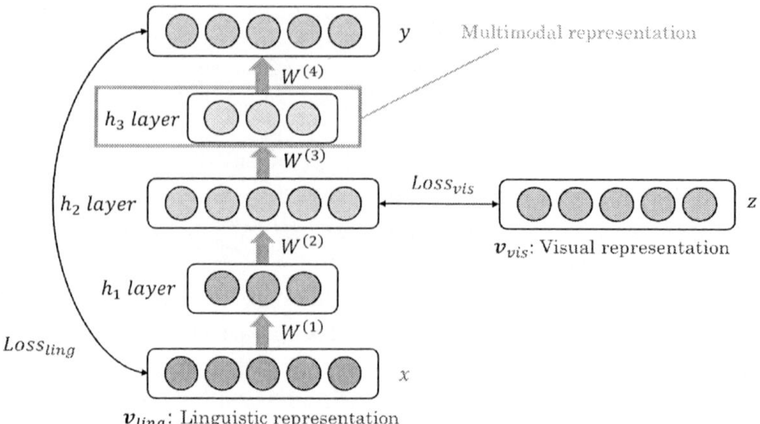

Figure 1: Architecture of the ViEW model.

between the linguistic input and the visual input ($Loss_{vis}$). The rationale behind the architecture is that if a pair of linguistic features are similar, the corresponding visual feature vectors would also be similar. We can expect that a visually enhanced representation could be obtained from the hidden layers (shown in green), even for a word for which direct visual-linguistic correspondences have not been learned.

In particular, during the training time, two losses (L_{ling} and L_{vis}) are simultaneously optimized in order to minimize the mean square errors (MSEs). L_{ling} measures the error between the input and output linguistic representations, whereas L_{vis} indicates the error between the visual and the hidden-layer (h2) representations.

$$L = \delta_{ling} L_{ling} + \delta_{vis} L_{vis} \tag{1}$$

$$L_{ling} = \sum_{k=1}^{n} \left(x^{(k)} - y^{(k)} \right)^2 \tag{2}$$

$$L_{vis} = \sum_{k=1}^{n} \left(h_2^{(k)} - z^{(k)} \right)^2 = \sum_{k=1}^{n} \left((\tanh(W^{(2)} x_1 + b^{(2)}))^{(k)} - z^{(k)} \right)^2 \tag{3}$$

$$x_n = \tanh\left(W^{(n)} x_{n-1} + b^{(n)} \right) \tag{4}$$

In the formulation, $x = \{x^{(1)}, ..., x^{(n)}\}$ and $y = \{y^{(1)}, ..., y^{(n)}\}, \in \mathbb{R}^{d_{ling} \times n}$ denote the sequences of linguistic input and output representations respectively; $z = \{z^{(1)}, ...z^{(n)}\} \in \mathbb{R}^{d_{vis} \times n}$ represents the sequence of visual representations, and n is the number of trained word–image pairs. In addition, δ_{ling} and δ_{vis} are hyper-parameters that balance the linguistic and visual components[2].

During the runtime, only a linguistic representation (word-embedding vector) is fed into the network, and the network performs a forward computation by employing the trained parameters. We adopt the h3-layer vectors, rather than the h2-layer vectors as the multimodal semantic representation. This decision was made because the h2-layer vectors might be too influenced by visual features, whereas the h3-layer vectors could more mildly incorporate the visual features[3], and hence, they are more suitable as a semantic representation that can be used in a variety of linguistic semantic tasks.

It should be mentioned that the dimensionalities of the h2-layer vector and visual feature vector must be identical, as we compute the MSE between them. In order to maintain this constraint, we have experimented with several methods for reducing the dimensionality of the visual feature vector (described in section 4.3.2).

---

[2] In the experiments, we adopted equal weights that were determined after a rough parameter search.

[3] We conducted a series of experiments to confirm this: the results obtained with the h2-layer vectors were consistently worse than those obtained with the h3-layer vectors.

4 Experimental setup

4.1 Task and the evaluation measure

We evaluate the performance of the achieved multimodal representations using standard semantic relatedness tasks (Gabrilovich and Markovitch, 2007; Budanitsky and Hirst, 2006), which would enable us to compare our results with that of previous works. As semantic relatedness covers a wider range of lexical or semantic relationships between words than semantic similarity, the relatedness tasks may be more suitable for assessing the performance of multimodal semantic representations, which would encode our implicit perceptual knowledge. We mainly employ the MEN (Bruni et al., 2014) dataset and assess the performance by measuring the Spearman's rank correlation coefficients between the MEN's gold ratings and the predicted relatedness.

4.2 Test dataset

The MEN dataset was specifically developed for evaluating multimodal semantic models (Bruni et al., 2014). In addition, we used the SimLex-999 (Hill et al., 2015) and the SemSim/VisSim (Silberer and Lapata, 2014) datasets to further investigate the applicability of the proposed model in other datasets having different characteristics.

- MEN: This dataset includes 3,000 word pairs created from 751 distinct words. Each pair in the dataset was given a semantic relatedness score in the range of [0, 1]. It contains highly semantically related pairs (e.g., *beach/sand* rated as 0.96) as well as low-scored pairs (e.g., *bakery/zebra* rated as 0). Each word in the dataset was assigned a part of speech (POS) tag: verb, adjective, or noun.
- SimLex-999: This is a dataset of 999 word pairs that is used for assessing the ability of a semantic model in capturing semantic similarity, rather than semantic relatedness or association. As the authors argue and several empirical results suggest, this dataset poses challenges to the most models based on the distributional hypothesis.
- SemSim/VisSim: This is a dataset of 7,576 word pairs, each of which is annotated using not only semantic similarities (SemSim) but also visual similarities (VisSim), so that the user can compare the performances of her/his model in predicting different types of similarities.

4.3 Features

As described in section 3, our ViEW model can consume existing visual and linguistic features. In the experiments, we prepared both these types of features as detailed below. It should be noted that these processes are completely independent from the construction and application of the ViEW model.

4.3.1 Linguistic features

We extracted 300-dimensional word embeddings by applying the skip-gram model (Mikolov et al., 2013). The text corpus used was enwiki9[4], which consisted of a collection of the first 10^9 bytes of text from the Wikipedia 2009 dump. We adopted the following hyper-parameters: the window size was set as five, and the frequency threshold for inclusion was five.

4.3.2 Visual features

In order to obtain the visual representation of a word, GoogLeNet (Szegedy et al., 2015) was used to analyze the corresponding images and derive the visual feature vector. GoogLeNet is well known owing to its deep neural network structure and its superior performance, which was demonstrated in the ImageNet Large Scale Visual Recognition Competition (ILSVRC2014). Kiela et al. (2016) states that GoogLeNet balances its performance and memory-efficiency. We constructed a 1024-dimensional

---

[4]http://mattmahoney.net/dc/textdata.html

visual feature vector for a word by averaging the resulting hidden-layer vectors obtained from the 50–100 corresponding images. As the source of the images, we used the following image datasets. Their utility and problems were examined in the experiments.

- ImageNet (Krizhevsky et al., 2012)[5]: It is a collection of 14 million high-quality images assigned to 21K WordNet synsets. Generally, the target object associated with a synset is depicted at the center of an image, which means that the obtained visual feature chiefly represents the target concept. Therefore, the images are clean but the dataset only contains images associated with concrete concepts.
- ESP-Game dataset (von Ahn and Dabbish, 2004)[6]: It contains 100K images, each of which has multiple labels assigned through "game with a purpose." This means that (1) the object associated with an image label is not necessarily the primary visual component in the image, and (2) an image label does not always have a corresponding visual object in the image. Thus, the images in the ESP-Game dataset are obviously noisier (in terms of target word) as compared to the ImageNet images. However, it is expected that this dataset may provide useful visual co-occurrence information in some cases. Furthermore, it should be noted that the images are associated not only with concrete nouns but also with adjectives and verbs.

Dimensionality reduction: As mentioned in section 3, the dimensionality of an h2-layer vector and that of the visual feature vector must be identical. This means that if we require a 300-dimensional h2-layer vector, the corresponding 1024-dimensional visual feature vector extracted from a CNN hidden layer must be reduced in order to match its dimensionality. In order to perform this task, we have applied two methods: the use of a principal component analysis (PCA) and that of an autoencoder (AE). The results obtained on using these two methods were compared with those obtained in the case of no dimensionality reduction (RAW setting). In the RAW setting, the dimensionality of the h2-layer vector was 1024 rather than 300, which implies that the multimodal representations might be sparse.

5 Results and discussion

5.1 Results: non-zero-shot settings

Although the zero-shot representation learning is the main focus of the present work, the efficacy of the proposed model should primarily be evaluated in a setting in which all the words in a test dataset have undergone the bimodal training process. This setting is henceforth referred to as "non-ZS." Table 1 displays the overall results for the non-ZS setting for which a portion of the MEN dataset was employed. The size of the portion used varies depending on the coverage of the images in the exploited image source. Around 23% and 42% of the words in the MEN dataset were accompanied with the corresponding images with the ESP-Game and ImageNet, respectively. The table also compares the following models: linguistic, visual, and multimodal; the multimodal models are further classified by the method used for the dimensionality reduction of the visual features.

Table 1 demonstrates that the multimodal representation enabled by the ViEW model is superior to that of the unimodal models. It also shows that ImageNet yielded better results, thus demonstrating the superiority of this image source. However, interestingly, the ViEW model seems to compensate for the problems with the ESP-Game image source well: the difference in the Spearman coefficient between the two image sources is smaller in the case of the MM as compared to the visual unimodal model. It should be further noted that PCA was a better method for visual feature dimensionality reduction, particularly in this setting.

Table 2 compares our results with those of related works, showing that the ViEW model (with PCA dimensionality reduction) almost achieves state-of-the-art performances.

---

[5]http://image-net.org
[6]http://hunch.net/~jl/

Model	Dimensionality reduction	ESP-Game	ImageNet
Linguistic	-	0.75	0.74
Visual	RAW	0.56	0.62
	PCA	0.56	0.63
	AE	0.57	0.60
Multimodal	RAW	0.75	0.76
	PCA	**0.76**	**0.78**
	AE	0.75	0.77

Table 1: ViEW model results for the non-ZS setting (MEN dataset).

Model	ESP-Game	ImageNet
ViEW (PCA)	0.76	**0.78**
Kiela and Bottou (2014)	0.72	0.70
Bruni et al. (2014)	**0.78**	-
Lazaridou et al. (2015): MMSG-A	-	0.74
Lazaridou et al. (2015): MMSG-B	-	0.76

Table 2: Comparison of the non-ZS results (MEN dataset).

5.2 Results: zero-shot including settings

Table 3 summarizes the results for the settings for which the entire test dataset is used. We refer to this setting as "ZS," because it inherently includes words without the corresponding trained images (zero-shot conditions). As shown in the table, the ViEW model exhibited a superior performance with the MEN dataset, which is our primary dataset. In contrast, the MMSG models (MMSG-A and MMSG-B) (Lazaridou et al., 2015) achieved better results with the other datasets, such as SimLex-999, SemSim, and VisSim, which indicates that there exist issues to be further explored with the ViEW model.

Model	MEN (100%)	SimLex-999 (100%)	SemSim (100%)	VisSim (100%)
ViEW (PCA)	**0.76**	0.34	0.68	0.55
MMSG-A	0.75	0.37	**0.72**	**0.63**
MMSG-B	0.74	**0.40**	0.66	0.60

Table 3: Comparison of the ZS results with four datasets.

5.3 Results: POS breakdown

As previously mentioned, the MEN dataset accommodates some words whose part-of-speech (POS) is not a noun. Table 4 thus breaks down the MEN results by POSs, and demonstrates that the overall results are dominated by nouns. Furthermore, the degradation in nouns between the non-ZS and ZS conditions is not very significant, which indicates that, in general, more noun concepts, such as concrete objects, can be depicted in images. However, the ZS results for adjectives were unanticipatedly better than the non-ZS results. We could expect to some extent that the semantic information propagated to adjectives from the modified nouns that could be concrete. Nevertheless, this would be yet another issue that requires further investigation. It should be noted that the verb results were not reliable owing to the small number of instances.

Model		Noun (2005 pairs)		Adjective (96 pairs)		Verb (29 pairs)	
		ZS	non-ZS (21%)	ZS	non-ZS (66%)	ZS	non-ZS (31%)
Ling.		0.75	0.76	0.60	0.44	0.37	0.78
Vis.		-	0.57	-	0.64	-	-0.20
MM	RAW	0.75	0.77	0.64	0.53	0.37	0.78
	PCA	0.76	0.78	0.64	0.54	0.38	0.73
	AE	0.75	0.77	0.63	0.53	0.36	0.73

Table 4: POS breakdown of the MEN dataset results (Image source: ESP-Game).

5.4 Discussion: antonyms and synonyms

It is often argued that text-based distributional/distributed representations hardly distinguish synonyms from other semantically related words. This is natural because these approaches rely heavily on contextual similarities. One of these typical relation types is antonymy: antonyms are frequently predicted as highly similar or related. In this subsection, we examine the potential efficacy of the multimodal representation in discriminating antonyms and synonyms from vaguely related words.

Among the pairs of antonymous adjectives defined in WordNet, we could assign the ViEW multimodal representations to 4,172 pairs by employing ImageNet as the image source. Table 5 shows the examples of k-neighbor words retrieved for some adjectives: "rural," "cold," and "happy." Similarly, we assigned multimodal representations to 106,472 synonymous noun pairs.

Word	MM (ImageNet)	MM (ESP-Game)	Ling.
rural	**countryside**, urbanised, **homesteads** **farmers**, urban	countryside,heckmondwike, urbanised **crofting**,smalandian	urban,exurban,urbanizing **suburban**,**countryside**
cold	**freeze**, warmed, smothered **freezing**, grit	**freezing**,thawing,**cool** bloodedness, **colder**	bloodedness, warm warmed, **clammy**, **cool**
happy	newlyweds, darlin, **glad** merrily, wistful	**cheerful**, **glad**, sentimental waifs, goodnight	doggone, **happier**, bummed derkins, hooky

Table 5: Comparison of k-neighbor words ($k = 5$) for some adjectives.

By using the Word2Vec word embedding vectors and multimodal vectors, we compared the similarity ranks obtained for these representations. As summarized in Table 6, some of the antonymous pairs had low ranks, and several of the synonymous pairs were ranked relatively higher, which is promising. These results may imply the potential efficacy of the multimodal representation in propagating visual information even to visually novel words and in filtering semantically related but perceptually irrelevant words or concepts.

	#ranked lower	#ranked equal	#ranked higher
Antonyms	**2,082** (50%)	283 (7%)	1,807 (43%)
Synonyms	38,928 (37%)	226 (1%)	**66,338** (62%)

Table 6: Changes in the similarity ranks of antonyms/synonyms (ImageNet).

5.5 Discussion: comparison of the image sources

Kiela et al. (2016) comprehensively compared deep visual representation learning techniques, in which a range of image datasets was investigated. Both ImageNet and ESP-Game were the targets of the survey, and the paper concluded that "The ESP Game dataset does not appear to work very well and is best avoided. If we have the right coverage, then ImageNet gives good results, ..." In order to visually compare the nature of the visual features obtained respectively from ImageNet and ESP-Game, Figure 2 displays two-dimensional visualizations of the obtained vectors. t-SNE (Maaten and Hinton, 2008) was applied in the visualization. Each of the labels in these figures represents the centroid of a target word. On comparing these figures, it is observed that the centroids for semantically related words are relatively closely located in both cases, but the dispersion is more evident for the features obtained from the ESP-Game dataset. These differences may be attributed to the difference in the nature of the datasets as discussed in the previous section. That is, the images in ImageNet are clean in terms of the depiction of a target concept, whereas ESP-Game images are generally noisy.

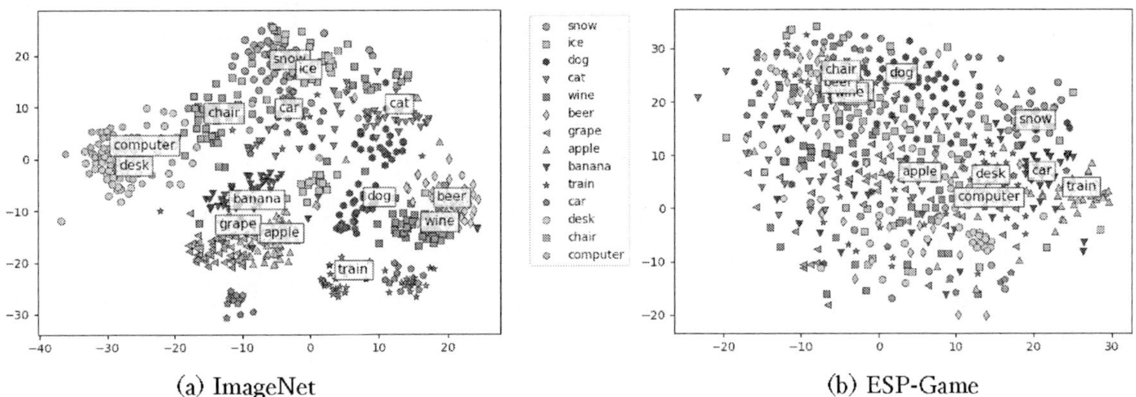

(a) ImageNet   (b) ESP-Game

Figure 2: t-SNE visualization of image features.

This insight was already confirmed by the results of our experiments. However, the differences in performance (Spearman coefficients) were not very significant as expected, particularly when employed with the multimodal models. This may be partly attributed to the nature of the ESP-Game dataset: visual co-occurrences would have been captured relatively well, and this might have contributed to enhancing the linguistic representations, which form the basis of the multimodal representations.

6 Concluding remarks

This paper presented a novel bimodal autoencoder model for incorporating visual features into existing word embeddings. Although the empirical results were generally promising, there is still room for improvement and exploration. We would like to incorporate more features, such as POS, semantic class, and abstractness/correctness (Kiela et al., 2014), into the neural network structure. We intend to develop a method for extracting effective features in order to capture *dynamics* from videos; this may be vital in representing the visual meaning of motion verbs and the like. Another potential research direction could involve the evaluation of the utility of multimodal representations in downstream applications, such as cross-modal mapping/retrieval.

Acknowledgment

The present research was supported by the JSPS KAKENHI Grant Number JP17H01831.

References

Baroni, M., B. Murphy, E. Barbu, and M. Poesio (2010). Strudel: A corpus-based semantic model based on properties and types. *Cogn. Sci. 34*(2), 222–254.

Barsalou, L. W. (2008). Grounded cognition. *Annu. Rev. Psychol. 59*(August), 617–645.

Bengio, Y., A. Courville, and P. Vincent (2013). Representation Learning : A Review and New Perspectives. *IEEE Trans. Pattern Anal. Mach. Intell. 35*, 1798—1828.

Bruni, E., D. Gatica-perez, N. K. Tran, and M. Baroni (2014). Multimodal distributional semantics. *J. Artif. Intell. Res. 49*(December), 1–47.

Budanitsky, A. and G. Hirst (2006). Evaluating WordNet-based Measures of Lexical Semantic Relatedness. *Comput. Linguist. 32*(1), 13–47.

Gabrilovich, E. and S. Markovitch (2007). Computing semantic relatedness using wikipedia-based explicit semantic analysis. *IJCAI Int. Jt. Conf. Artif. Intell.*, 1606–1611.

Hill, F., R. Reichart, and A. Korhonen (2015). SimLex-999: Evaluating Semantic Models with (Genuine) Similarity Estimation. *Comput. Linguist. 41*(4), 665–695.

Kiela, D. and L. Bottou (2014). Learning Image Embeddings using Convolutional Neural Networks for Improved Multi-Modal Semantics. *EMNLP 2014*, 36–45.

Kiela, D., S. Clark, A. L. Ver, S. Clark, M. Baroni, B. Murphy, E. Barbu, and M. Poesio (2016). Comparing Data Sources and Architectures for Deep Visual Representation Learning in Semantics. *EMNLP 2016 34*(2), 447–456.

Kiela, D., F. Hill, A. Korhonen, and S. Clark (2014). Improving Multi-Modal Representations Using Image Dispersion : Why Less is Sometimes More. *ACL 2014*.

Kodirov, E., T. Xiang, S. Gong, and Q. Mary (2017). Semantic Autoencoder for Zero-Shot Learning. *IEEE Conf. Comput. Vis. Pattern Recognit.*, 3174–3183.

Krizhevsky, A., I. Sutskever, and G. E. Hinton (2012). ImageNet Classification with Deep Convolutional Neural Networks. *Adv. Neural Inf. Process. Syst.*, 1–9.

Lampert, C. H. and S. Harmeling (2009). Learning To Detect Unseen Object Classes by Between-Class Attribute Transfer. *IEEE Conf. Comput. Vis. Pattern Recognit.*.

Lazaridou, A., T. P. Nghia, and M. Baroni (2015). Combining Language and Vision with a Multimodal Skip-gram Model. *NAACL 2015*, 153–163.

Maaten, L. V. D. and G. Hinton (2008). Visualizing Data using t-SNE. *J. Mach. Learn. Res. 9*, 2579–2605.

Mikolov, T., I. Sutskever, K. Chen, G. Corrado, and J. Dean (2013). Distributed Representations of Words and Phrases and their Compositionality. *Proc. NIPS 9*, 1–9.

Silberer, C. and M. Lapata (2014). Learning Grounded Meaning Representations with Autoencoders. *Proc. 52nd Annu. Meet. Assoc. Comput. Linguist. (Volume 1 Long Pap.*, 721–732.

Szegedy, C., W. Liu, Y. Jia, P. Sermanet, S. Reed, D. Anguelov, D. Erhan, V. Vanhoucke, and A. Rabinovich (2015). Going deeper with convolutions. *Proc. IEEE Comput. Soc. Conf. Comput. Vis. Pattern Recognit. 07-12-June*, 1–9.

von Ahn, L. and L. Dabbish (2004). Labeling images with a computer game. *Proc. 2004 Conf. Hum. factors Comput. Syst. - CHI '04*, 319–326.

Feedback relevance spaces:
The organisation of increments in conversation

Christine Howes
University of Gothenburg, Sweden
`christine.howes@gu.se`

Arash Eshghi
Heriot-Watt University, UK
`a.eshghi@hw.ac.uk`

Abstract

Feedback such as backchannels and clarification requests can occur subsententially, demonstrating the incremental nature of grounding in dialogue. However, although such feedback *can* occur at any point within an utterance, it typically does not do so, tending to occur at *feedback relevance spaces* (FRSs). We provide a low-level, semantic processing model of where feedback ought to be licensed. The model can account for cases where feedback occurs at FRSs, and how it can be integrated or interpreted at non-FRSs using the predictive, incremental and interactive nature of the formalism. This model shows how feedback serves to continually realign processing contexts and thus manage the characteristic divergence and convergence that is key to moving dialogue forward.

1 Introduction

Dialogue is co-constructed by multiple interlocutors with the traditional split between *speaker* and *hearer* inadequate to describe how this proceeds. Even in monological contexts (e.g. lectures), listeners provide frequent feedback to demonstrate whether or not they have *grounded* the conversation thus far (Clark, 1996), i.e. whether something said can be taken to be understood. To achieve this grounding, we produce relevant next turns, or backchannels (e.g. 'mm', as in (1):5144,[1] or 'yeah' (1):5146) including non-linguistic cues (e.g. nods).[2] Other responses indicate processing difficulties or lack of coordination and signal a need for repair ((1):5158) (Bavelas et al., 2012). Further, feedback affects how the conversation unfolds even when it does not contribute any semantic content, with listeners' choice of backchannels shaping narratives (e.g. 'mm' or 'crikey!' (1):5152) (Bavelas et al., 2000; Tolins and Fox Tree, 2014).

As seen in (1):5148, backchannels do not just occur at the ends of sentences or turns, but can occur subsententially. Grounding thus occurs incrementally, before a complete proposition has been produced or processed. Despite this, evidence suggests that there are places within and between turns where backchannels are salient. These *backchannel relevance spaces* (BRSs: Heldner et al., 2013), are analogous to but more common than transition relevance places (TRPs) – places where the turn may shift between speakers (Sacks et al., 1974). Feedback is optional at these points, and there are many reasons why any given BRS might not contain a backchannel or other feedback (e.g. individual variation). There may also be subtle nonverbal feedback which further complicates efforts to automatically predict where backchannels occur in dialogue. For practical dialogue systems, the positioning of backchannels is crucial. However although using low-level features (Cathcart et al., 2003; Gravano and Hirschberg, 2009) may allow a dialogue model to sound 'more human', it can't provide any insight into why feedback occurs where it does. Further, models in which feedback incorporates reasoning about the intentions or goals of one's interlocutor (Visser et al., 2014; Buschmeier and Kopp, 2013; Wang et al., 2011) presuppose a level of complexity that is unnecessary in natural conversation (Gregoromichelaki et al., 2011).[3]

---

[1]Examples are all taken from dialogue KB2 in the British National Corpus (BNC: Burnard, 2000).

[2]Although we believe that our analysis also applies to non-verbal feedback, in this paper we focus on verbal feedback.

[3]We are not claiming that people never use higher level reasoning – both in terms of general dialogue or in terms of appropriate backchannel placement – just that it is not necessary that they do so. This is especially clear from dialogues with young children who do not yet have higher-level mind reading skills, but still produce appropriate backchannel behaviour. We

However, despite evidence that speaker switch *can* occur at any point in a turn, even within syntactic constituents (Purver et al., 2009; Howes et al., 2011) feedback does not appear to be appropriate just anywhere. Evidence using different paradigms such as avatar studies (Poppe et al., 2011) or audio of dialogues with backchannels moved from their actual position (Kawahara et al., 2016) suggests that randomly placed backchannels disrupt the flow of dialogue, are rated as less natural and decrease rapport.

	A	5143	He did mashed potatoes
	J	5144	Mm.
	A	5145	cabbage, savoy cabbage, carrots ⟨pause⟩ and he'd cu- cut them like I always cut them cos they were only them little baby carrots so, what I do I slice them down
	J	5146	Yeah.
	A	5147	you know, down middle like
	J	5148	Yeah.
	A	5149	into quarters so I do them longer
	J	5150	Yeah.
	A	5151	and he'd done them like that in microwave for eight minutes ⟨pause⟩ and er, done sprouts ⟨pause⟩ then he'd put this meat pie in oven
(1)	J	5152	Crikey!
	A	5153	and er, done onion gravy!
	J	5154	Mm mm!
	A	5155	I says, ooh this gravy's lovely!
	J	5156	Yeah!
	A	5157	He says er, yeah he said I did some onion, and then, I got some of them, you know
	J	5158	Granules?
	A	5159	yeah, put some of that in
	J	5160	Mm.
	A	5161	he says, I put a bit a ⟨pause⟩ Italian mixed herbs in middle of meat pie in my hand, put [them]
	J	5162	[Mm.] [⟨laugh⟩]
	A	5163	[and a bit] of Bovril.

2 Modelling feedback relevance spaces (FRSs)

In this section we briefly outline the formal tools used. Eshghi et al. (2015) provide a low-level semantic model of feedback integration in dialogue, and here we extend the model to explain why feedback tends to occur at certain points in an utterance. The model accounts for cases where feedback occurs at FRSs, and also provides an account of how feedback at inappropriate points can be integrated or interpreted.

2.1 Dynamic Syntax and Type Theory with Records

Dynamic Syntax (DS: Kempson et al., 2001; Cann et al., 2005) is an action-based grammar formalism, which models the word-by-word incremental processing of linguistic input. DS models the linear construction of *interpretations* without an independent level of syntactic representation, such that the output for any given string of words is a semantic tree representing predicate/argument structure. DS lends itself to the analysis of dialogue (Purver et al., 2006; Kempson et al., 2016, a.o.) as there is no stipulation for a separate parsing/production module, and speaker and hearer actions are the same; except that the current speaker has a more advanced goal-tree that subsumes the current tree. Recently, DS has been integrated

acknowledge that this means that models that include extra features such as acknowledger confidence (Visser et al., 2014) may capture an additional level of complexity over and above our notion of where backchannels are semantically licensed – indeed, the inclusion of such features may help explain when 'infelicitously' placed backchannels are interpretable (see Section 2.4, below) or what type of backchannel is more appropriate at a certain point.

with Type Theory with Records (TTR: Cooper, 2005) to provide the formalism in which semantic representations are couched (Eshghi et al., 2012; Eshghi, 2015; Purver et al., 2011) – see e.g. Fig. 1. TTR, with its rich notions of underspecification and sub-typing has proven crucial in (1) subsentential, incremental specifications of utterance content; (2) specifications of richer notions of dialogue context (Purver et al., 2010; Ginzburg, 2012); and (3) models of grammar learning and dialogue systems (Eshghi et al., 2013; Eshghi and Lemon, 2014; Kalatzis et al., 2016).[4]

Tree nodes in DS-TTR correspond to terms in the lambda calculus, decorated with labels expressing their semantic type and semantics; beta-reduction determines the type and formula at a mother node from those at its daughters (Figure 1). Trees can be *partial*, with unsatisfied *requirements* (e.g. $?Ty(e)$ is a requirement for development to $Ty(e)$) and contain a *pointer*, $\diamond$, labelling the node under development. Grammaticality is defined as processability in a context: the successful incremental construction of a tree with no outstanding requirements using all information given by the words in a string.

The parsing process is defined in terms of conditional *actions*: procedural specifications for monotonic semantic tree update. *Computational actions* are general structure-building principles; and *lexical actions* are language-specific actions induced by parsing particular lexical items. All actions take the form of 'macros' to provide update operations on semantic trees, instantiated as IF..THEN..ELSE rules which yield semantically transparent structures when applied (e.g. see Fig. 3).

Computational actions form a small, fixed set of macros. Some encode the properties of the lambda calculus and the logical tree formalism (the logic of finite trees; LOFT: Blackburn and Meyer-Viol, 1994): e.g. THINNING, which removes satisfied requirements, and COMPLETION, which moves the pointer up and out of a sub-tree once all requirements therein are satisfied. Others reflect the fundamental predictivity and dynamics of DS. These apply optionally whenever their preconditions are met, but are not triggered by lexical input. The successful parse of a word w_1 amounts to finding a sequence of computational actions (possibly empty) that leads to a tree which satisfies the preconditions of the lexical actions for w_1. The parse search process/history can thus be represented as a Directed Acyclic Graph (DAG), with (partial) semantic trees as nodes, and actions as edges, i.e. transitions between trees.

Fig. 1 shows "John arrives", parsed incrementally, starting with the axiom tree, T_0, and ending with a complete tree. The intermediate step shows the effect of COMPLETION, which moves the pointer up and out of a complete node - this process is central in our explanation of FRSs.

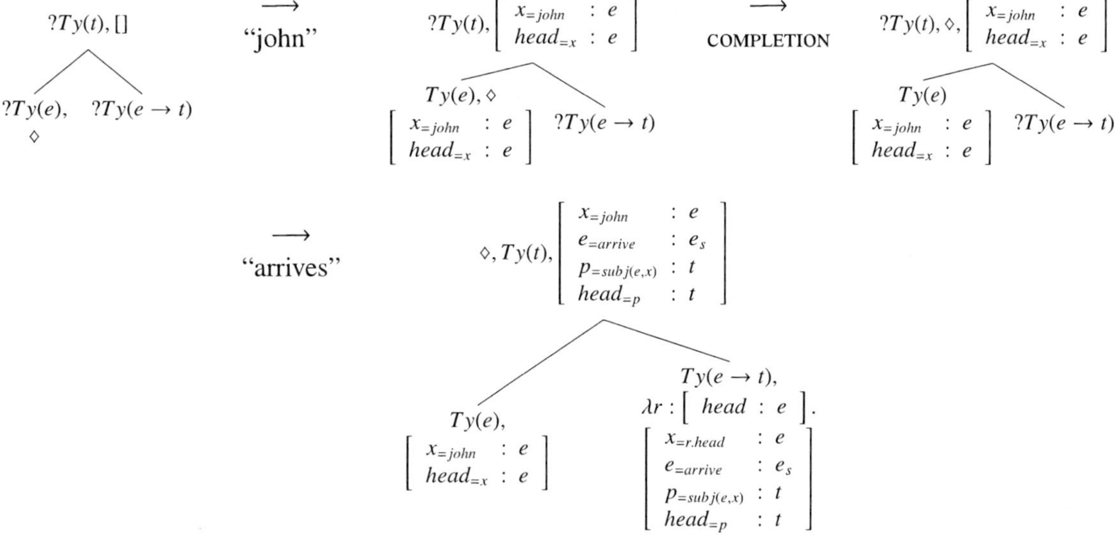

Figure 1: Incremental parsing in DS-TTR: *"John arrives"*

---

[4]Implementation of DS-TTR and the feedback model: https://bitbucket.org/dylandialoguesystem/

2.2 Context and the integration of feedback in DS

In DS, context, required for processing various forms of context-dependency – including pronouns, VP-ellipsis, self-repair and short answers – is the parse search DAG (Sato, 2011; Eshghi et al., 2012; Kempson et al., 2015). We take a coarse-grained view of the DAG with edges corresponding to words (sequences of computational action followed by a lexical action) rather than single actions, and dropping abandoned parse paths (see Hough, 2015, for details) - Fig. 2 shows an example.

As Eshghi et al. (2015) show, grounding (the integration into context of positive and negative feedback) can be captured using the context DAG, augmented with two *coordination pointers*: the *self-pointer*, ♦; and the *other-pointer*, ◊, marking where the speaker and hearer have each reached. Any utterance causes DAG pointer movement: the self-pointer tracks where the speaker has got to in production, and the other-pointer tracks where the listener has given feedback for reaching. This model accounts for negative and positive feedback. Negative feedback, e.g. clarification requests, causes branching in the DAG, where the current path is abandoned and another branch constructed – subsequent positive feedback realigns the two pointers. Contrarily, positive feedback e.g. backchannels and utterance continuations do not create new branches, but move the other-pointer forward on the current path.

Dialogue	**Context-final Semantics**	**A's Context After Dialogue**

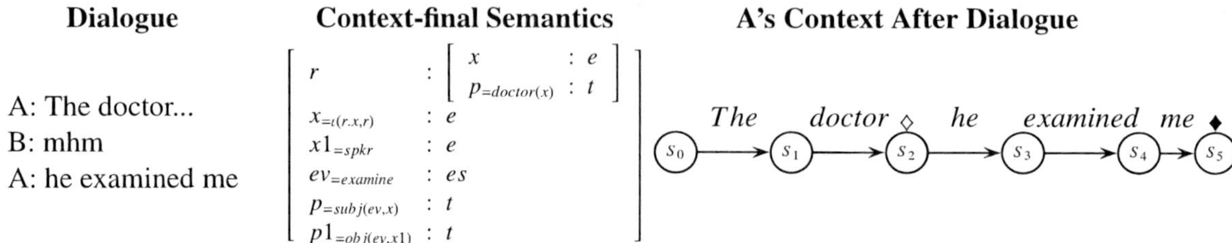

$$\left[\begin{array}{l} r \quad : \left[\begin{array}{l} x \quad : e \\ p_{=doctor(x)} : t \end{array} \right] \\ x_{=\iota(r.x,r)} \quad : e \\ x1_{=spkr} \quad : e \\ ev_{=examine} \quad : es \\ p_{=subj(ev,x)} : t \\ p1_{=obj(ev,x1)} : t \end{array} \right]$$

Figure 2: Backchannels as movement of context DAG coordination pointers. From A's perspective.

Fig. 2 shows a simple example of how a backchannel is integrated: this is A's context after processing the dialogue. After producing the first utterance, A's self-pointer, ♦, is on s_2, the right-most node of the DAG so far. B's backchannel provides positive feedback, thus moving A's other-pointer, ◊, to the same node, grounding "the doctor". A's subsequent continuation creates new edges, and moves her self-pointer to the new right-most node. At this point, A's new utterance needs feedback from B to be grounded: divergence of pointer positions thus represents 'forward momentum' in conversation. According to this model, the intersection of the path back to root from the self- and other-pointers is taken to be grounded.

This puts structural, surface forms of context-dependency at the centre of the explanation of participant coordination and feedback in dialogue: various forms of context-dependent expression, from the weakest – backchannels, which have no semantic content, to the strongest – utterance continuations, all serve to narrow down the otherwise mushrooming space of possible processing paths for interpretation. Their pervasiveness in dialogue is therefore not coincidental, but strategic, and serves to make interpretation in dialogue *locally* computationally tractable.

2.3 Feedback Relevance Spaces

Extending the model in Eshghi et al. (2015), we take backchannels to signal (when produced), or trigger (when parsed) COMPLETION. Feedback is therefore salient when a sub-tree has just been completed, i.e. when a semantic functor and argument have *both* been processed; for example, a backchannel is not normally licensed after a determiner (before the noun has been encountered) or after e.g. "John went to".

Fig. 3 shows the lexical entry for backchannels. This action ensures that after parsing a backchannel, we end up with a maximally complete tree. Specifically, for a backchannel to be parsable, we should not be on a node that is type-incomplete or on a node that is complete when its sister node is also complete - i.e. if more tree completion (BETA-REDUCTION, THINNING and COMPLETION) can still be done. This mechanism has been tested in the Dynamic Syntax implementation (Eshghi et al., 2011; Eshghi, 2015).

mhm $\left|\begin{array}{lll} \text{IF} & ?Ty(X) \\ \text{THEN} & \texttt{abort} \\ \text{ELSE} & \text{IF} & \langle\uparrow_0\downarrow_1\rangle\exists x.Tn(x) \\ & & \langle\uparrow_0\downarrow_1\rangle\neg\exists x.?x \\ & & \neg\exists x.?x \\ & \text{THEN} & \texttt{abort} \\ & \text{ELSE} & \texttt{do-nothing} \end{array}\right.$

Figure 3: Lexical Entry for a backchannel

This allows us to explain feedback that comes after a semantic unit of information, thus grounding it. Further, it predicts that parse paths leading to further qualification become less likely when followed by a backchannel (e.g. in "A: Matt, B: mmm", A is less likely to further qualify/extend 'Matt'). A lack of feedback at such points is interactionally relevant. Elaboration should be more likely if no feedback is provided (e.g. A: Matt [no feedback], my brother ...). In dialogue, speakers often prompt or look for feedback using non-verbal behaviours such as gaze (Hjalmarsson and Oertel, 2012) and intonation (Gravano and Hirschberg, 2009). We hypothesise that this type of cue should occur at (or just before) points in the dialogue where COMPLETION can occur.

2.4 Feedback at non FRSs

In our model, there are two possibilities for when feedback is produced at a point where it ought not be appropriate. The first is that the listener is lagging behind the speaker and has produced the feedback late. This may reflect the time taken for the listener to integrate the information into their interpretation – 'correct' placement of feedback at FRSs will require some element of prediction, analogously to how turn-taking occurs with such precise timing indicating that people predict upcoming TRPs (de Ruiter et al., 2006, a.o.). In this case, feedback can be interpreted as grounding the most recent increment (informational unit) – i.e. moving ones other-pointer to the most recent position in the DAG at which COMPLETION could have occurred.

The second, more interesting, possibility is where feedback is produced early. In this case, feedback seemingly precedes the completion of a semantic unit, which ought to be impossible. However, early feedback may be licensed where the completion is highly predictable. This is due to two key components of DS; i) predictability, which comes about from lexical and computational actions that induce more tree structure with requirements for fixed decorations as well as the reuse of actions and ii) the parity between parsing and production in DS. As shown in DS accounts of cross-person completions (Purver et al., 2010; Eshghi et al., 2012), a listener may switch to being a speaker at any point in the interpretation of an utterance, provided that they have a more advanced goal tree in mind. We propose that exactly the same mechanisms are exploited in cases of early feedback; in (2):211, for example, J's continuation is so predictable (it is a repetition of prior material; "got a lot on") that A does not have to wait for it in order to interpret the complete utterance (including the unuttered material that A has predicted will come next) but can instead rerun the actions she has already used. Similarly, in (1):5158, J can produce a completion of A's prior turn that also functions as a clarification request. This analysis is supported by a text chat experiment in which producing candidate completions as clarifications turns out to be a fairly common strategy in response to artificially truncated turns – particularly when the part of speech of the upcoming material is predictable, and the context is sufficiently constrained (Howes et al., 2012).

	J	210	her mum really she's got a lot on, she'll have a lot on cos she's got to prepare for that wedding, you know what you're like when you, [you've got]
(2)	A	211	[Mm]
	J	212	you know if you want, want to be doing things [don't you get out of house and that]
	A	213	[Yeah, pre- preparing for a wedding, yeah]

3 Conclusions

We have presented an analysis of feedback in dialogue using DS-TTR, which unifies the dialogue phenomena of backchannels, clarifications and completions in terms of their grounding actions. All these phenomena occur subsententially, and serve to signal how the dual processes of divergence and convergence that are crucial to successful interaction are managed locally, in a way that makes the search space tractable at a given point in an exchange.

We have hypothesised that FRSs are interactionally relevant parts of a utterance, analogous to TRPs, and that these are based on low-level semantic criteria. Further, we speculate that when feedback such as backchannels occurs at points other than FRSs it gets interpreted as if it had done so – either because the feedback is late and grounding the previous informational unit, or because it's early and the (rest of the) informational unit is predictable.

We have provided a precise, formal model of backchannels, their licensing, and effect. The evidence presented in this paper, while consistent with our model, is thus far circumstantial. We are therefore planning some corpus and experimental studies that directly bear on the clear empirically testable predictions provided by our model.

This work has implications for the production and interpretation of human-like feedback in dialogue systems; not just based on unanalysed features (which may result in accurate placement), but because they have successfully compiled a semantic unit at the point at which they produce or parse feedback.

Acknowledgements

Work on this paper was supported by two project grants: *Incremental Reasoning in Dialogue (IncReD)* VR (2016-01162); and *Babble: Domain-general methods for learning natural spoken dialogue systems* EPSRC (EP/M01553X/1).

References

Bavelas, J. B., L. Coates, T. Johnson, et al. (2000). Listeners as co-narrators. *Journal of personality and social psychology 79*(6), 941–952.

Bavelas, J. B., P. De Jong, H. Korman, and S. S. Jordan (2012). Beyond back-channels: A three-step model of grounding in face-to-face dialogue. In *Proceedings of Interdisciplinary Workshop on Feedback Behaviors in Dialog*.

Blackburn, P. and W. Meyer-Viol (1994). Linguistics, logic and finite trees. *Logic Journal of the Interest Group of Pure and Applied Logics 2*(1), 3–29.

Burnard, L. (2000). *Reference Guide for the British National Corpus (World Edition)*. Oxford University Computing Services.

Buschmeier, H. and S. Kopp (2013). Co-constructing grounded symbols–feedback and incremental adaptation in human-agent dialogue. *KI-Künstliche Intelligenz 27*(2), 137–143.

Cann, R., R. Kempson, and L. Marten (2005). *The Dynamics of Language*. Oxford: Elsevier.

Cathcart, N., J. Carletta, and E. Klein (2003). A shallow model of backchannel continuers in spoken dialogue. In *Proceedings of the tenth EACL conference*, pp. 51–58. Association for Computational Linguistics.

Clark, H. H. (1996). *Using Language*. Cambridge Univ Press.

Cooper, R. (2005). Records and record types in semantic theory. *Journal of Logic and Computation 15*(2), 99–112.

de Ruiter, J., H. Mitterer, and N. Enfield (2006). Projecting the end of a speaker's turn: A cognitive cornerstone of conversation. *Language 82*(3), 515–535.

Eshghi, A. (2015). DS-TTR: An incremental, semantic, contextual parser for dialogue. In *Proceedings of the 19th SemDial workshop on the semantics and pragmatics of dialogue (goDial)*.

Eshghi, A., J. Hough, and M. Purver (2013). Incremental grammar induction from child-directed dialogue utterances. In *Proceedings of the 4th Annual Workshop on Cognitive Modeling and Computational Linguistics (CMCL)*, pp. 94–103. ACL.

Eshghi, A., J. Hough, M. Purver, R. Kempson, and E. Gregoromichelaki (2012). Conversational interactions: Capturing dialogue dynamics. In S. Larsson and L. Borin (Eds.), *From Quantification to Conversation: Festschrift for Robin Cooper on the occasion of his 65th birthday*, Volume 19 of *Tributes*, pp. 325–349. London: College Publications.

Eshghi, A., C. Howes, E. Gregoromichelaki, J. Hough, and M. Purver (2015). Feedback in conversation as incremental semantic update. In *Proceedings of the 11th International Conference on Computational Semantics (IWCS)*, London, UK. ACL.

Eshghi, A. and O. Lemon (2014). How domain-general can we be? Learning incremental dialogue systems without dialogue acts. In *Proceedings of Semdial 2014 (DialWatt)*.

Eshghi, A., M. Purver, and J. Hough (2011). Dylan: Parser for dynamic syntax. Technical report, Queen Mary University of London.

Ginzburg, J. (2012). *The Interactive Stance: Meaning for Conversation*. Oxford University Press.

Gravano, A. and J. Hirschberg (2009). Backchannel-inviting cues in task-oriented dialogue. In *INTERSPEECH*, pp. 1019–22.

Gregoromichelaki, E., R. Kempson, M. Purver, G. J. Mills, R. Cann, W. Meyer-Viol, and P. G. T. Healey (2011). Incrementality and intention-recognition in utterance processing. *Dialogue and Discourse 2*(1), 199–233.

Heldner, M., A. Hjalmarsson, and J. Edlund (2013). Backchannel relevance spaces. In *Nordic Prosody: Proceedings of XIth Conference, Tartu 2012*, pp. 137–146.

Hjalmarsson, A. and C. Oertel (2012). Gaze direction as a back-channel inviting cue in dialogue. In *IVA 2012 workshop on Realtime Conversational Virtual Agents*, Volume 9.

Hough, J. (2015). *Modelling Incremental Self-Repair Processing in Dialogue*. Ph. D. thesis, Queen Mary University of London.

Howes, C., P. G. T. Healey, M. Purver, and A. Eshghi (2012). Finishing each other's ... responding to incomplete contributions in dialogue. In *Proceedings of the 34th Annual Meeting of the Cognitive Science Society (CogSci 2012)*, pp. 479–484.

Howes, C., M. Purver, P. G. T. Healey, G. J. Mills, and E. Gregoromichelaki (2011). On incrementality in dialogue: Evidence from compound contributions. *Dialogue and Discourse 2*(1), 279–311.

Kalatzis, D., A. Eshghi, and O. Lemon (2016). Bootstrapping incremental dialogue systems: using linguistic knowledge to learn from minimal data. In *Proceedings of the NIPS 2016 workshop on Learning Methods for Dialogue*, Barcelona.

Kawahara, T., T. Yamaguchi, K. Inoue, K. Takanashi, and N. Ward (2016). Prediction and generation of backchannel form for attentive listening systems. In *Proc. INTERSPEECH*, Volume 2016.

Kempson, R., R. Cann, A. Eshghi, E. Gregoromichelaki, and M. Purver (2015). Ellipsis. In S. Lappin and C. Fox (Eds.), *The Handbook of Contemporary Semantics*. Wiley-Blackwell.

Kempson, R., R. Cann, E. Gregoromichelaki, and S. Chatzikiriakidis (2016). Language as mechanisms for interaction. *Theoretical Linguistics 42*(3-4), 203–275.

Kempson, R., W. Meyer-Viol, and D. Gabbay (2001). *Dynamic Syntax: The Flow of Language Understanding*. Blackwell.

Poppe, R., K. P. Truong, and D. Heylen (2011). Backchannels: Quantity, type and timing matters. In *International Workshop on Intelligent Virtual Agents*, pp. 228–239. Springer.

Purver, M., R. Cann, and R. Kempson (2006). Grammars as parsers: Meeting the dialogue challenge. *Research on Language and Computation 4*(2-3), 289–326.

Purver, M., A. Eshghi, and J. Hough (2011, January). Incremental semantic construction in a dialogue system. In J. Bos and S. Pulman (Eds.), *Proceedings of the 9th International Conference on Computational Semantics*, Oxford, UK, pp. 365–369.

Purver, M., E. Gregoromichelaki, W. Meyer-Viol, and R. Cann (2010). Splitting the 'I's and crossing the 'You's: Context, speech acts and grammar. In *Proceedings of the 14th SemDial Workshop on the Semantics and Pragmatics of Dialogue*, pp. 43–50.

Purver, M., C. Howes, E. Gregoromichelaki, and P. G. T. Healey (2009, September). Split utterances in dialogue: A corpus study. In *Proceedings of the 10th Annual SIGDIAL Meeting*, London, UK, pp. 262–271. Association for Computational Linguistics.

Sacks, H., E. Schegloff, and G. Jefferson (1974). A simplest systematics for the organization of turn-taking for conversation. *Language 50*(4), 696–735.

Sato, Y. (2011). Local ambiguity, search strategies and parsing in Dynamic Syntax. In E. Gregoromichelaki, R. Kempson, and C. Howes (Eds.), *The Dynamics of Lexical Interfaces*. CSLI Publications.

Tolins, J. and J. E. Fox Tree (2014). Addressee backchannels steer narrative development. *Journal of Pragmatics 70*, 152–164.

Visser, T., D. Traum, D. DeVault, and R. op den Akker (2014). A model for incremental grounding in spoken dialogue systems. *Journal on Multimodal User Interfaces 8*(1), 61–73.

Wang, Z., J. Lee, and S. Marsella (2011). Towards more comprehensive listening behavior: beyond the bobble head. In *Intelligent Virtual Agents*, pp. 216–227. Springer.

Modeling Quantification with Polysemous Nouns

Laura Kallmeyer
Heinrich-Heine-Universität Düsseldorf
`kallmeyer@phil.hhu.de`

Rainer Osswald
Heinrich-Heine-Universität Düsseldorf
`osswald@phil.hhu.de`

1 Introduction

Babonnaud et al. (2016) introduce a framework for modeling systematic polysemy that combines Lexicalized Tree Adjoining Grammar (LTAG) with frame semantics and Hybrid Logic (HL). The components of the syntax-semantics interface are elementary LTAG trees paired with frame descriptions that are expressed by possibly underspecified HL formulas. A brief review of this framework will be given in Section 2 below. In Babonnaud et al. (2016), an inherently polysemous noun such as 'book', which provides referential access to both a physical and an informational object, is assumed to refer to entities of type *phys(ical)-obj(ect)* which have an attribute CONTENT whose value is of type *information*. That is, the semantic type of 'book' is a subtype of the complex type *phys-obj* $\wedge$ $\langle$CONTENT$\rangle$*information* or *info(rmation)-carrier* for short (cf. Section 3 below). The physical aspect and the informational aspect are then addressed in different ways in contexts such as 'read the book', 'carry the book', 'master the book' or 'a heavy book on magic'. The verb 'read', for instance, is analyzed as denoting a complex event that consists of two components, the perception of the physical aspect and the comprehension of the informational aspect (following Pustejovsky 1998), and thus combines with both aspects of 'book'. By comparison, the verb 'master' calls for a grammatical object that denotes an entity of type *information* or *info-carrier* and semantically selects only the informational aspect in the latter case.

Treating books as physical information carriers in this way gives rise to the following "quantification puzzle" as noted in Asher and Pustejovsky (2005, 2006); see also Asher (2011). While (1a) poses no problem since the domain of quantification consists of physical entities, it not obvious how to cope with (1b), which is naturally interpreted as quantifying over all contents of the books in the library.

(1)   a.   John carried off every book in the library.
      b.   John read every book in the library.

Since the library may own more than one copy of a book, there is not necessarily a one-to-one correspondence between the physical books in the library and the book contents. It is not even necessary that John used a copy from the library at all. The solution proposed in Section 4 retains the idea that a book basically denotes a physical object which has informational content associated to it. To this end, this basic representation will be embedded in an underspecified representation which allows the referential index of the NP to refer to the physical or to the informational component of the basic structure.

2 LTAG, Frames and Hybrid Logic

Babonnaud et al. (2016) follow Kallmeyer et al. (2015, 2016) in modeling the syntax-semantics interface by combining LTAG with frame semantics. More concretely, every elementary syntactic tree is paired with a frame description formulated in Hybrid Logic (Areces and ten Cate, 2007). Frames are semantic graphs with labeled nodes and edges, as in Fig. 1, where nodes correspond to entities (individuals, events, ...) and edges to (functional or non-functional) relations between these entities. In Fig. 1 all relations except *part-of* are functional. Frames can be formalized as extended typed feature structures

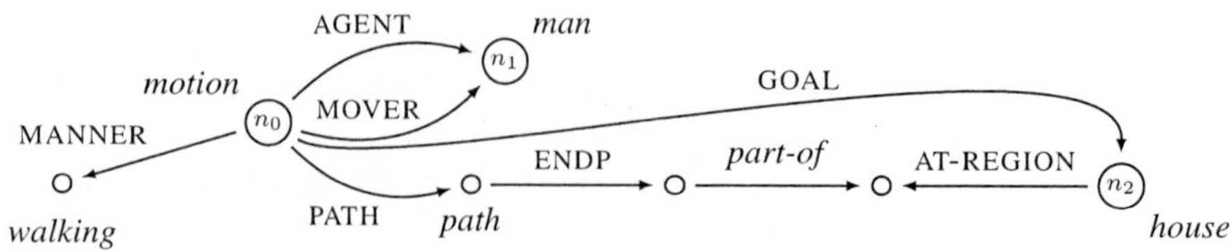

Figure 1: Frame for 'the man walked to the house' (adapted from Kallmeyer and Osswald (2013))

and specified as models of a suitable logical language (Kallmeyer and Osswald, 2013). In order to enable quantification over entities or events, Kallmeyer et al. (2016) propose to use Hybrid Logic (HL), an extension of modal logic. HL formulas have the following syntax: Let Rel = Func $\cup$ PropRel be a set of functional and non-functional *relation symbols*, Type a set of *type symbols*, Nom a set of *nominals* (node names), and Nvar a set of *node variables*, with Node = Nom $\cup$ Nvar. Then *formulas* are defined as Forms ::= $\top \mid p \mid n \mid \neg\phi \mid \phi_1 \wedge \phi_2 \mid \langle R \rangle \phi \mid \exists\phi \mid @_n\phi \mid \downarrow x.\phi \mid \exists x.\phi$, with $p \in$ Type, $n \in$ Node, $x \in$ Nvar, $R \in$ Rel and $\phi, \phi_1, \phi_2 \in$ Forms. Moreover, $\forall\phi \equiv \neg\exists(\neg\phi)$, $\phi \rightarrow \psi \equiv \neg(\phi \wedge \neg\psi)$ and $\phi \vee \psi \equiv \neg(\neg\phi \wedge \neg\psi)$, as usual. A *model* is a triple $\langle M, (R^M)_{R \in \mathsf{Rel}}, V \rangle$ where M is a non-empty set (of "nodes"), each R^M is a binary relation on M, and V is a function (the *valuation*) from Type $\cup$ Nom to $\wp(M)$ such that $V(i)$ is a singleton for every nominal i. An *assignment* g is a function from Nvar to M; the assignment g_v^x differs from g at most on x, and $g_v^x(x) = v$. The following examples illustrate the notions of satisfaction and truth with reference to the frame structure in Fig. 1; see Kallmeyer et al. (2015, 2016) for more details and a formal definition. The formula *motion*, a type symbol, is true at the node denoted by the nominal n_0 in the structure of Fig. 1. Formula $\langle R \rangle \phi$ is true at a node if the relation R^M holds between that node and a node at which ϕ is true. For example, $\langle \text{AGENT} \rangle man \wedge \langle \text{MANNER} \rangle walking \wedge \langle \text{PATH} \rangle \langle \text{ENDP} \rangle \top$ is true at n_0. (Notice that since HL does not distinguish between functional and non-functional edge labels, functionality has to be enforced by additional constraints.) There are different ways to express existential quantification in HL, namely $\exists\phi$ and $\exists x.\phi$. Formula $\exists\phi$ is true at node v if there exists a node v' at which ϕ holds. For instance, $\exists house$ is true at all nodes of the example structure. Formula $\exists x.\phi$ is true at v if there is a v' such that ϕ is true at v under an assignment of x to v'. E.g., $\exists x. \langle \text{PATH} \rangle \langle \text{ENDP} \rangle \langle \text{part-of} \rangle (x \wedge region) \wedge \exists(house \wedge \langle \text{AT-REGION} \rangle x)$ is true at n_0. Besides quantification, HL also allows us to use nominals or variables to refer to nodes via the @ operator: $@_n\phi$ is true at a node if ϕ is true at n. The $\downarrow$ operator allows us to assign the current node to a variable: $\downarrow x.\phi$ is true at v if ϕ is true at v under the assignment g_v^x. E.g., $\langle \text{PATH} \rangle \langle \text{ENDP} \rangle \langle \text{part-of} \rangle (\downarrow x.region \wedge \exists(house \wedge \langle \text{AT-REGION} \rangle x))$ is true at n_0.

A Lexicalized Tree Adjoining Grammar (LTAG; Joshi and Schabes 1997; Abeillé and Rambow 2000) consists of a finite set of *elementary trees*. Larger trees are derived via *substitution* (replacing a leaf with a tree) and *adjunction* (replacing an internal node with a tree). An adjoining tree has a unique *foot node* (marked with an asterisk), which is a non-terminal leaf labeled with the same category as the root of the tree. When adjoining such a tree to some node n of another tree, in the resulting tree, the subtree with root n from the original tree is attached at the foot node of the adjoining tree. Non-terminal nodes in LTAG are usually enriched with feature structures (Vijay-Shanker and Joshi, 1988): Each node has a top and a bottom feature structure (except substitution nodes, which have only a top). Features can be shared within elementary trees. In a substitution step, the top of the root of the new tree unifies with the top of the substitution node; in an adjunction, the top of the root of the adjoining tree unifies with the top of the adjunction site and the bottom of the foot of the adjoining tree unifies with the bottom of the adjunction site. Furthermore, in the final derived tree, top and bottom unify in all nodes.

In line with previous proposals of how to add semantics to LTAG, we pair each elementary tree with a semantic representation that consists of a set of HL formulas which can contain holes and which can be labeled. In other words, *hole semantics* (Bos, 1995) is applied to HL and these underspecified formulas are linked to the elementary trees. Composition is triggered by the syntactic unifications using interface features on the syntactic trees (cf. Gardent and Kallmeyer 2003; Kallmeyer and Romero 2008). As an example consider the derivation in Fig. 2 where the two NPs are substituted into the two argument slots

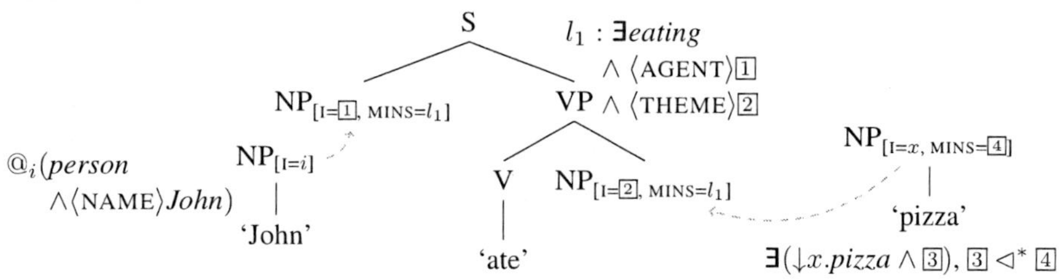

Figure 2: Derivation of 'John ate pizza'

in the 'ate' tree. The interface features I on the NP nodes make sure that the contributions of the two arguments feed into the AGENT and THEME nodes of the frame structure. Furthermore, an interface feature MINS is used for providing the label of the $\exists(eating...)$ formula as minimal scope to a possible quantifier. The feature unifications on the syntactic tree lead to $\boxed{1} = i$, $\boxed{2} = x$ and $\boxed{4} = l_1$. As a result, when collecting all formulas, we obtain the underspecified representation (2a).

(2)   a. $@_i(person \wedge \langle$NAME$\rangle John)$, $l_1: \exists(eating \wedge \langle$AGENT$\rangle i \wedge \langle$THEME$\rangle x)$, $\exists(\downarrow x.pizza \wedge \boxed{3})$, $\boxed{3} \triangleleft^* l_1$
        b. $@_i(person \wedge \langle$NAME$\rangle John)$, $\exists(\downarrow x.pizza \wedge \exists(eating \wedge \langle$AGENT$\rangle i \wedge \langle$THEME$\rangle x))$

The relation $\triangleleft^*$ links holes to labels: $h \triangleleft^* l$ signifies that the formula labeled l is a subformula of h. In (2a), the $\exists(eating...)$ formula, labeled l_1, has to be part of the nuclear scope of the quantifier (hole $\boxed{3}$). Disambiguating such underspecified representations consists of "plugging" the labeled formulas into the holes while respecting the given constraints. (2a) has a unique disambiguation, namely $\boxed{3} \rightarrow l_1$. This leads to (2b), which is then interpreted conjunctively.

3   Basic analysis of polysemous nouns

We will now sketch the analysis of Babonnaud et al. (2016) of inherently polysemous nouns such as 'book' and their composition with verbs such as *read*. The noun 'book' carries two meaning aspects in that it can denote a physical object ('the book is heavy') or an informational content ('the book is interesting'). Babonnaud et al. (2016) assume that the semantic frame associated with 'book' contains two nodes of type *information* and *phys-obj*, respectively, with an explicit relation between them: The physical aspect of the frame is taken to be its referential node, which is linked via a CONTENT attribute to the information it carries. The type *book* is a subtype of *info-carrier*, which in turn is a subtype of *phys-obj* and which has a $\langle$CONTENT$\rangle$ attribute whose value is of type *information*.

The verb 'read' allows for the direct selection of the dot object *book* as complement (cf. Pustejovsky, 1998) but also enables coercion of its complement from type *information* ('read the story') as well as from type *phys-obj* ('read the blackboard'). Babonnaud et al. (2016) assume an event node of type *reading* with attributes PERC(EPTUAL)-COMP(ONENT) and MENT(AL)-COMP(ONENT), whose values are respectively of type *perception* and *comprehension*. These nodes represent the decomposition of the activity of reading into two subevents, the action of looking at a physical object (the perception) and the action of processing the provided information (the comprehension). Moreover, the *perception* node has an attribute STIMULUS of type *info-carrier*, and the *comprehension* node has an attribute CONTENT whose value is the information being read, which coincides with the value of CONTENT attribute of the *info-carrier* node. The fact that the argument contributed by the object can be either the stimulus of the perception (*phys-obj*) or its content is captured by a disjunction.

A sample analysis is given in Fig. 3. The label of the HL formula coming with 'read' is provided as potential minimal scope for quantifiers at the NP slots. The determiner 'the' is treated as an existential quantifier, disregarding the presuppositions it carries. The label of the formula associated with 'book' is made available via an interface feature P (for "proposition"). Due to the two scope constraints, this proposition will be part of the restriction of the quantifier (i.e., part of the subformula at $\boxed{4}$) while the 'read' formula will be part of the nuclear scope, i.e., part of the subformula at $\boxed{5}$. Substitutions and

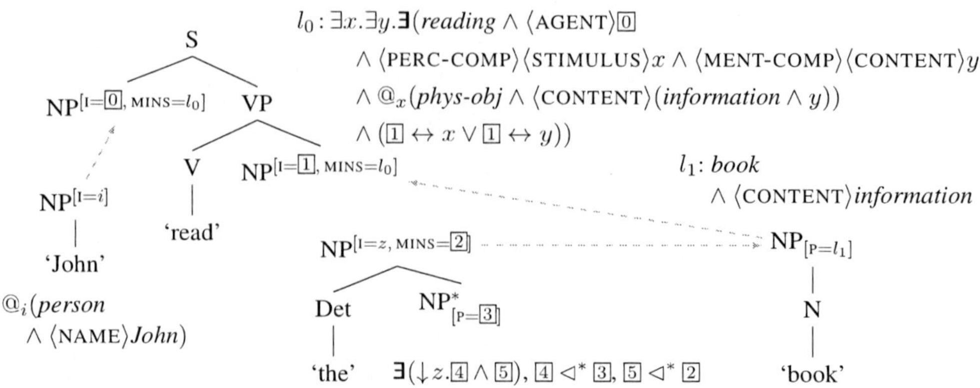

Figure 3: Derivation for 'John read the book'

adjunctions lead to the unifications $\boxed{0} = i$, $\boxed{1} = z$, $\boxed{2} = l_0$ and $\boxed{3} = l_1$ on the interface features. The result is the underspecified representation in (3), which has to be disambiguated by the mapping $\boxed{4} \mapsto l_1$, $\boxed{5} \mapsto l_0$. Since *information* and *phys-obj* are incompatible, it follows that $z \leftrightarrow x$ and $\neg(z \leftrightarrow y)$.

(3) $@_i(person \wedge \langle\text{NAME}\rangle John)$, $\exists(\downarrow z.\boxed{4} \wedge \boxed{5})$,
    l_0: $\exists x.\exists y.\exists(reading \wedge \langle\text{AGENT}\rangle i$
        $\wedge \langle\text{PERC-COMP}\rangle\langle\text{STIMULUS}\rangle x \wedge \langle\text{MENT-COMP}\rangle\langle\text{CONTENT}\rangle y$
        $\wedge @_x(phys\text{-}obj \wedge \langle\text{CONTENT}\rangle(information \wedge y)) \wedge (z \leftrightarrow x \vee z \leftrightarrow y))$,
    l_1: $book \wedge \langle\text{CONTENT}\rangle information$,
    $\boxed{4} \lhd^* l_1$, $\boxed{5} \lhd^* l_0$

4   Polysemous nouns and quantification

A problem of the approach described above concerns the decision to provide the *phys-obj* node of the book frame as an argument in a predicate argument structure. As explained in the introduction, this is problematic in examples like (1b) ('John read every book in the library') where the noun interacts with a quantifier in such a way that the quantifier's restriction concerns specific pairs of physical objects and associated information content but the predicate the quantifier scopes over applies only to the latter. The natural reading of (1b) is that for every book in the library, John read a (possibly different) copy of that book, i.e., John read some book with the content of that book. Simply changing the nodes provided for predicate-argument composition to the information content does not work either, as shown in (1a) ('John carried off every book in the library') where 'carried off' applies to the physical objects.

    As a solution, we revise the entry of 'book' such that it explicitly provides an underspecified I feature at the syntax-semantics interface ($\text{I} = \boxed{8}$ in Fig. 4a)) and the value of this feature can either be a variable referring to the *phys-obj* node or a variable referring to the *information* node (expressed by the disjunction $\boxed{8} \leftrightarrow u \vee \boxed{8} \leftrightarrow v$). The restriction of the adjoining quantifier (variable $\boxed{4}$) has to embed the entire formula contributed by the 'book' tree (i.e., the formula labeled l_1), while the formula that characterizes the *book* frame (label l_4) has to be provided as well for further modification, for instance by 'in the library' (interface feature P). This latter formula is embedded under the formula labeled l_1 (constraint $\boxed{11} \lhd^* l_4$). The derivation of (1b) is given in Fig. 4a). The result of combining the trees for the complex NP 'every book in the library' is shown in Fig. 4b). It is underspecified with respect to whether the variable z introduced by the quantifier refers to the *book* node or to the *information* node. The frame structure contributed by the NP is, however, still the *phys-obj* node with a CONTENT attribute of type *information*, as in the basic analysis presented in Section 3. As a result of the entire derivation, we obtain the frame description in (4), in particular $\boxed{1} = z$. Disambiguating the scope constraints leads to the plugging $\boxed{4} \rightarrow l_1$, $\boxed{5} \rightarrow l_0$. But the disjunction $z \leftrightarrow x \vee z \leftrightarrow y$ cannot be resolved, i.e., we are not

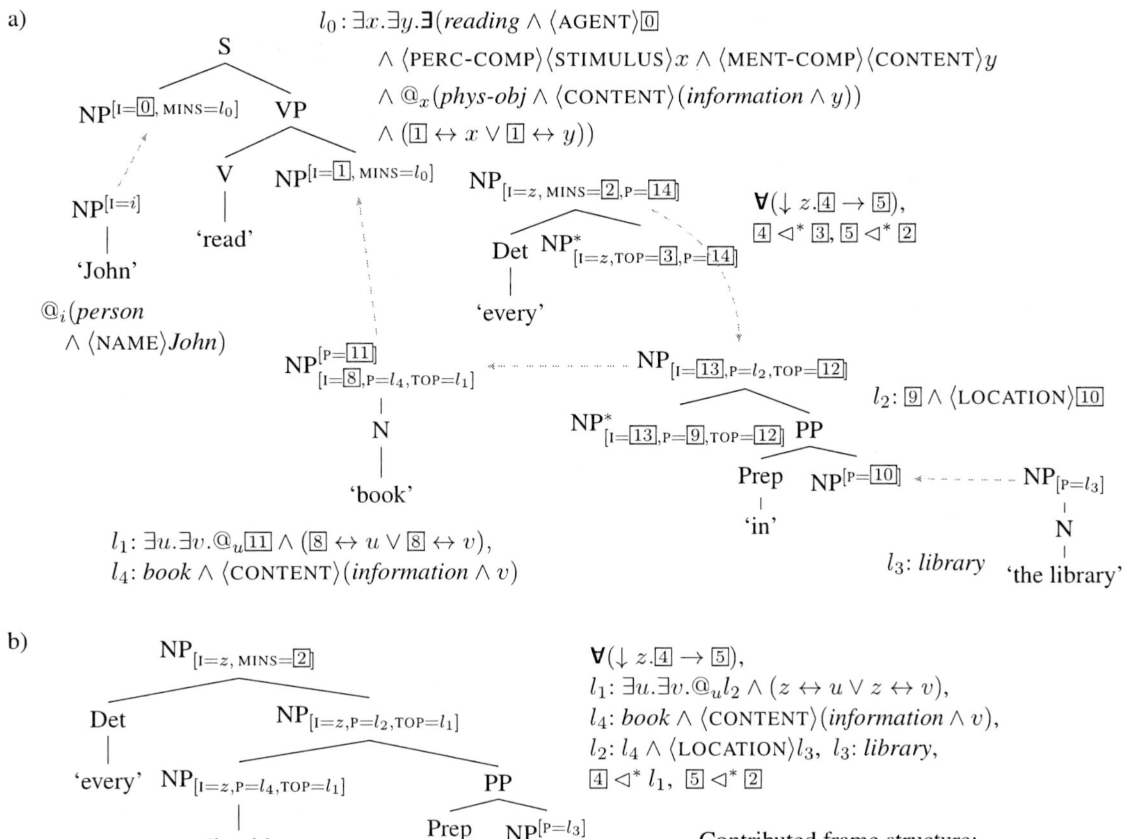

Figure 4: (a) Derivation for (1b); (b) result of deriving 'every book in the library'

able to disambiguate between quantification over the physical objects (option $z \leftrightarrow x$ which would imply $z \leftrightarrow u$) on the one hand and information content ($z \leftrightarrow y$ and $z \leftrightarrow v$) on the other hand, since 'read' allows for both argument types. In a case like (1a), a disambiguation towards the first option takes place.

(4) $\forall(\downarrow z.\boxed{4} \rightarrow \boxed{5})$,
  $l_1: \exists u.\exists v.@_u(book \wedge \langle \text{CONTENT}\rangle(information \wedge v) \wedge \langle \text{LOCATION}\rangle library)$
      $\wedge(z \leftrightarrow u \vee z \leftrightarrow v)$,
  $l_0: \exists x.\exists y.\mathbf{\exists}(reading \wedge \langle \text{AGENT}\rangle i \wedge \langle \text{PERC-COMP}\rangle\langle \text{STIMULUS}\rangle x \wedge \langle \text{MENT-COMP}\rangle\langle \text{CONTENT}\rangle y$
      $\wedge@_x(phys\text{-}obj \wedge \langle \text{CONTENT}\rangle(information \wedge y))$
      $\wedge(z \leftrightarrow x \vee z \leftrightarrow y))$,
  $@_i(person \wedge \langle \text{NAME}\rangle John)$,
  $\boxed{4} \triangleleft^* l_1, \boxed{5} \triangleleft^* l_0$

5 Copredication and quantification

A crucial property of the proposed analysis is that we do not assume separate nodes for dot objects. In a quantificational NP involving *book*, we therefore have to quantify either over the physical objects or over the information contents. This might pose problems for cases of copredication as in (5).

(5) a. John destroyed every book in the library that Mary had mastered

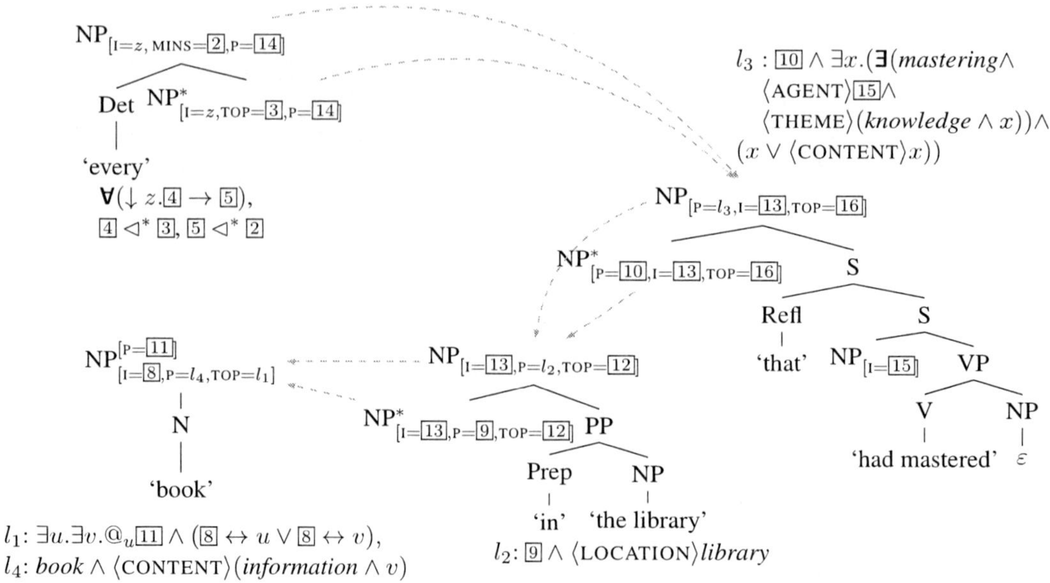

$l_3 : \boxed{10} \wedge \exists x.(\exists(mastering \wedge \langle \text{AGENT} \rangle \boxed{15} \wedge \langle \text{THEME} \rangle (knowledge \wedge x)) \wedge (x \vee \langle \text{CONTENT} \rangle x))$

$l_1: \exists u. \exists v. @_u \boxed{11} \wedge (\boxed{8} \leftrightarrow u \vee \boxed{8} \leftrightarrow v),$
$l_4: book \wedge \langle \text{CONTENT} \rangle (information \wedge v)$

$l_2: \boxed{9} \wedge \langle \text{LOCATION} \rangle library$

Figure 5: Derivation for *every book in the library that _ had mastered*

 b. John mastered and then destroyed every book in the library.
 c. Mary mastered every book$_i$ in the library before John destroyed it$_i$.

Note that the analyses of coordination as in (5b) and also of anaphoric reference as in (5c) are still open questions in LTAG. Concerning (5a), the predicate *destroy* clearly is a predication over the physical objects while the predicate *master* takes the informational content as argument. In the following, we will detail the analysis of (5a) in order to show that disambiguating towards one of the two options in the context of one predication does not necessarily exclude predicating in a different place over the other component.

Fig. 5 gives the derivation of *every book in the library that _ had mastered*. As in the examples in the preceding sections, we have features P and TOP on the NP nodes. The value of P is the label of the frame description contributed by the (complex) noun without considering the case of quantification. The value of TOP gives the label of the formula that characterizes the possible "entry points" into this frame (in our case the physical object node and the information node). Once these formulas are introduced via the noun, any further predication can access the frame itself via the P feature and extend its description. This is the case for *in the library* (as already in Fig. 4), and the predication *that Mary had mastered* works similarly (see the tree-frame pair on the right of Fig. 5). In other words, the relative clause headed by *mastered* adjoins to the NP above the *in the library* PP and simply adds another conjunct to the frame description that holds at the physical object node of the *book* frame.

A crucial feature of the frame description associated with *master* is that its THEME argument has to be of type *knowledge* (which is a subtype of *information*) and it is either the frame modified by the relative clause or the value of the CONTENT attribute of this frame (see also Babonnaud et al., 2016, for similar examples of copredication). This disjunction accounts for the coercion effect in (5a) since it allows *master* to predicate over the value of the CONTENT attribute of the modified *book* frame. Because of this, (5c) and probably also (5b) are not problematic. Even though the predicate *destroy* requires that the variable of the quantification is the physical object, the predicate *master* still has access to the informational component via the CONTENT attribute.

6 Futher issues

As Asher (2011) points out, the relation from books as physical objects to books as informational units is not necessarily functional because of omnibus editions. Likewise, the content of a single novel can be spread over several physical volumes. For this reason, Asher posits dot objects as entities of their own right which are related to their physical and informational aspects by appropriate elaboration relations. However, the problem just mentioned is more complicated since it can happen with multi-volume editions of collected works that one novel is distributed over two volumes and that the second volume contains another novel in addition to the final part of the first novel. This means that if we want to quantify over books understood as novels, which may have once been published as single volumes, the only way to cope with situations like the one just described is to quantify over the elements of an appropriate segmentation of a (mereological) sum of the CONTENT values of the (physical) books in the library.

A related topic concerns the interaction of copredication and counting as illustrated in the examples in (6), which are taken from Gotham (2017).

(6)   Three informative books are heavy.

In order to be true, sentence (6) seems to require three different copies of books with different informational contents. That is, an appropriate representation of (6) must be able to encode the constraints that the three books have different informational content and that they are different physical objects. We leave the analysis of such examples within our framework for future work.

Another interesting issue arises in examples like (7), which make explicit that reading a book does not necessarily require to stick to a single copy. In general, it is possible to switch between different physical copies including instantiations on electronic devices such as ebook readers and the like.

(7)   Mary read the heavy book on magic. She read part of it on her ebook reader for convenience.

If we want to build the variability of the physical carrier into our approach while preserving the idea that reading consists of a perception and a comprehension component, we need to zoom into the course of the reading event and describe it as consisting of different subevents, each of which is bound to a certain physical information carrier. To this end, we need to extend our model by some version of the homomorphic event-to-object relation that comes with incremental themes.

Our analysis of copredication described in Section 5 assumes that copredication is flexible in the sense that picking an attribute as argument (for instance the CONTENT) does not mean that the original root node is no longer accessible. In many cases, this makes the right predictions. However, there seem to be cases where a predication over one aspect blocks the other meaning aspects for further access; compare, for instance, the examples in (8) taken from Retoré (2014):

(8)   a.   Liverpool is spread out and voted (last Sunday).
       b.   # Liverpool voted and won (last Sunday).

Retoré (2014) models coercion within the framework of the Montagovian Generative Lexicon (Mery et al., 2007), which is a many-sorted higher order predicate calculus where the lexical entries associated with words are finite sets of λ-terms, one of them being the principal λ-term. Coercion is triggered by type mismatch, and one of the optional λ-terms is used in this case, which changes the type of either the predicate or the argument. Some of these type shifts are specified as rigid in the lexicon, which means that they block coercion to other types. Our system shares with the Montagovian Generative Lexicon the assumption of a rich type system and of functional relations between the different instances of these types present in the meaning of a word. We will look more closely into examples of copredication and its interaction with quantification in future work, in particular into the question of flexibility/rigidity of coercive shifts.

References

Abeillé, A. and O. Rambow (2000). Tree Adjoining Grammar: An Overview. In A. Abeillé and O. Rambow (Eds.), *Tree Adjoining Grammars: Formalisms, Linguistic Analysis and Processing*, pp. 1–68. CSLI.

Areces, C. and B. ten Cate (2007). Hybrid logics. In P. Blackburn, J. V. Benthem, and F. Wolter (Eds.), *Handbook of Modal Logic*, Volume 3 of *Studies in Logic and Practical Reasoning*, Chapter 14, pp. 821–868. Elsevier.

Asher, N. (2011). *Lexical Meaning in Context. A Web of Words.* Cambridge: Cambridge University Press.

Asher, N. and J. Pustejovsky (2005). Word meaning and commonsense metaphysics. Manuscript, available at semanticsarchive.net/Archive/TgxMDNkM/.

Asher, N. and J. Pustejovsky (2006). A type composition logic for generative lexicon. *Journal of Cognitive Science 6*, 1–38.

Babonnaud, W., L. Kallmeyer, and R. Osswald (2016). Polysemy and coercion – a frame-based approach using LTAG and Hybrid Logic. In M. Amblard, P. de Groote, S. Pogodalla, and C. Retoré (Eds.), *Logical Aspects of Computational Linguistics, 9th International Conference*, Lecture Notes in Artificial Intelligence 10054, pp. 18–33. Berlin: Springer.

Bos, J. (1995). Predicate logic unplugged. In P. Dekker and M. Stokhof (Eds.), *Proceedings of the 10th Amsterdam Colloquium*, pp. 133–142.

Gardent, C. and L. Kallmeyer (2003). Semantic Construction in FTAG. In *Proceedings of EACL 2003*, Budapest, pp. 123–130.

Gotham, M. (2017). Composing criteria of individuation in copredication. *Journal of Semantics 34*, 333–371.

Joshi, A. K. and Y. Schabes (1997). Tree-Adjoining Grammars. In G. Rozenberg and A. Salomaa (Eds.), *Handbook of Formal Languages*, pp. 69–123. Berlin: Springer.

Kallmeyer, L., T. Lichte, R. Osswald, S. Pogodalla, and C. Wurm (2015, August). Quantification in Frame Semantics with Hybrid Logic. In R. Cooper and C. Retoré (Eds.), *Type Theory and Lexical Semantics*, ESSLLI 2015, Barcelona, Spain.

Kallmeyer, L. and R. Osswald (2013). Syntax-driven semantic frame composition in Lexicalized Tree Adjoining Grammars. *Journal of Language Modelling 1*(2), 267–330.

Kallmeyer, L., R. Osswald, and S. Pogodalla (2016). *For*-adverbials and aspectual interpretation: An LTAG analysis using hybrid logic and frame semantics. In C. Piñón (Ed.), *Empirical Issues in Syntax and Semantics EISS*, Volume 11.

Kallmeyer, L. and M. Romero (2008). Scope and situation binding in LTAG using semantic unification. *Research on Language and Computation 6*(1), 3–52.

Mery, B., C. Bassac, and C. Retoré (2007). A montagovian generative lexicon. In L. Kallmeyer, P. Monachesi, G. Penn, and G. Satta (Eds.), *12th conference on Formal Grammar (FG 2007)*, Dublin, Ireland. CSLI Publications.

Pustejovsky, J. (1998). The semantics of lexical underspecification. *Folia Linguistica 32*(3–4), 323–348.

Retoré, C. (2014). The Montagovian Generative Lexicon ΛTy_n: a type theoretical framework for natural language semantics. In *TYPES: International Workshop on Types and Proofs for Programs, April 2013, Toulouse, France*, pp. 202–229.

Vijay-Shanker, K. and A. K. Joshi (1988). Feature structures based tree adjoining grammar. In *Proceedings of COLING*, Budapest, pp. 714–719.

Textual Inference: getting logic from humans

Aikaterini-Lida Kalouli
University of Konstanz
Aikaterini-Lida.Kalouli@uni-konstanz.de

Livy Real
University of São Paulo
livyreal@gmail.com

Valeria de Paiva
Nuance Communications
valeria.depaiva@nuance.com

Abstract

This paper describes a manual investigation of the SICK corpus, which is the proposed testing set for a new system for natural language inference. The system provides conceptual semantics for sentences, so that entailment-contradiction-neutrality relations between sentences can be identified. The investigation of the SICK corpus was a necessary task to check the quality of the testing data which is to be used as a golden standard for the new system. This checking also provides crucial insights for the implementation of the components of the system. The investigation showed that the human judgements used in the building of the SICK corpus can be erroneous, in this way deteriorating the quality of an otherwise useful resource. We also show that detecting the relationship between some pairs of the SICK corpus requires more than just lexical semantics, which provides us with guidelines and intuitions for our further implementation.

1   Introduction

This paper describes our manual investigation of the SICK corpus[1] by Marelli et al. (2014), which is to be used as a testing baseline for a new system for natural language inference (NLI). SICK is a corpus containing pairs annotated for their degree of similarity and for the inference relation between the sentences of each pair, i.e. entailment, contradiction, neutrality. The long-term goal is to be able to provide conceptual semantics for sentences so that entailment-contradiction-neutrality relations between sentences can be identified.

In order to evaluate this testing set (and future ones), we explore a preliminary pipeline that is open source and free to use and which we will expand by providing our own representations and implementation. We put different tools together and investigate which kinds of improvements are needed in each of those components so that the evaluation and verification of the corpus is efficient and successful. Investigating the testing data can give us insights on issues that need to be taken into account when we build the components of the new NLI system. By looking into a corpus such as SICK we can see what humans consider entailment-contradiction-neutrality and we can obtain clues on where a logic based pipeline might fail because of the lack of encyclopedic knowledge or the lack of higher reasoning mechanisms that humans possess. Additionally, investigating the test corpus can show us to what extent the off-the-self components can be used as-are or need improvements. Last but not least, by verifying the testing set we can be sure that it can be used as a golden standard for the new system and thus serve as a reliable baseline.

In what follows we briefly refer to the different components of this pipeline, describe the SICK corpus and then raise some issues on how to define textual entailment based on SICK. The main part of this work is a preliminary analysis of these problems, our suggestions for improving them and an investigation of other phenomena of the corpus, which are not discussed in Marelli et al. (2014).

---

[1]Available at http://clic.cimec.unitn.it/composes/sick.html.

2   The framework

The preliminary pipeline is based on dependency parsing provided by the Stanford Parser, in particular universal dependencies (UD). The Stanford parser can produce enhanced universal dependencies (Schuster and Manning (2016)), which are more semantic than conventional universal dependencies. Enhanced dependencies augment the information present in the basic dependency structure by adding more explicit syntactic relations and labels that facilitate many kinds of semantic transformations. Our pipeline also uses tools for lexical semantics. We make use of Princeton WordNet [2] as described in Fellbaum (1998) as a repository of word senses. For disambiguation of senses we use the JIGSAW algorithm[3] by Basile et al. (2007). Thirdly, we use the mappings from Wordnet to SUMO [4] by Niles and Pease (2001) which provide us with traditional knowledge representation concepts. These resources should give us a baseline knowledge representation semantics and we integrate them to see how much we can get back from this preliminary pipeline for our purposes of checking the SICK data.

For the ultimate system, we use the same tools to rewrite (syntactic representations of the) sentences into their semantic representations. Depending on the form of those rewritten conceptual semantics the last stage of the system will be implemented, which will be responsible for inference and reasoning, integrating some of the ideas from the PARC Bridge blueprint by Bobrow et al. (2007), but also combining state-of-the-art machine-learning techniques.

To test the quality of the preliminary pipeline and to see to what extent our lexical resources suffice or how and where they need to be improved, we need a simple, common-sense corpus, meaning a corpus which contains simple sentences about concrete, everyday, common events or activities. Since SICK was built to contain such common-sense sentences, it seemed ideal for our kind of testing. To verify the quality of the SICK data and to confirm our choice of corpus, we manually investigated it, checking what the human annotators considered inference relations and how they codified them. Before diving into the analysis, we define what we mean by entailment, contradiction and neutrality. We take entailment to be the semantic relation between sentence A and sentence B, where sentence A entails sentence B, if whenever A is true, then B must also be true. Contradiction is the semantic relation where sentence A contradicts sentence B if whenever A is true, then B cannot be true. If neither of those two relations holds for sentences A and B, then we say that sentence A is neutral with respect to B because there can be a world where both sentences hold or not.

3   The corpus

SICK (Sentences Involving Compositional Knowledge) by Marelli et al. (2014) is an English corpus, created to provide a benchmark for compositional extensions of Distributional Semantic Models (DSMs). DSMs approximate the meaning of words using vectors, which summarize the patterns of co-occurrence of words in corpora. SICK includes 9840 sentence pairs that are rich in the lexical, syntactic and semantic phenomena that compositional DSMs are expected to account for (e.g. lexical variation phenomena, impact of negation, etc.) but do not require dealing with other aspects of existing sentential data sets (e.g. named entities, temporal phenomena, etc.) that are not within the main scope of compositional distributional formal semantics. The curators of the corpus also made an effort to reduce the amount of encyclopedic world-knowledge needed to interpret the sentences.

The SICK corpus was created from captions of pictures talking about daily activities and non-abstract entities. Therefore, such pictures should "only" require concrete, common-sense concepts since they do not include many actions or actors or a too complicated description. With this setting, SICK becomes an ideal corpus for testing the off-the-shelf lexical resources.

The set of SICK pairs may seem large, but these sentences were "expanded" from a core set, which was normalized to restrict the linguistic phenomena and also to make sure that complete sentences and not

---

[2]Available at http://wordnet.princeton.edu/.

[3]Available at https://github.com/pippokill/JIGSAW.

[4]Available at http://www.adampease.org/OP/.

just caption-phrases were included. The SICK creators describe the process as follows: each normalized sentence was used to generate three new sentences based on a set of rules, such as adding passive or active voice, adding negations, etc. Each sentence was then paired with all of those three generated sentences. According to the authors, a native speaker eliminated odd and ungrammatical sentences. To repeat an example from Marelli et al. (2014), the caption *The turtle followed the fish* was normalized to the sentence *The turtle is following the fish* and expanded to the three sentences *The turtle is following the red fish*, *The turtle isn't following the fish* and *The fish is following the turtle*. After de-duplication, we have 6076 unique sentences combined in the different pairs. Also the lexical items involved are limited to less than two thousand lemmas of content words.

Each pair of sentences in the SICK corpus was annotated by Amazon Mechanical Turkers [5] to show their degree of similarity and their semantic relationship, namely entailment, contradiction and neutrality. The semantic relationships were annotated in both directions, meaning that annotators described the relation of sentence A with respect to sentence B and conversely, the relation of sentence B with respect to sentence A. Then, each pair was given one of the labels *ENTAILMENT, CONTRADICTION, NEUTRAL* based on the judgement of the majority of the annotators. However, the annotators were not told that the sentences came from captions and they were only given examples of the three kinds of inference relation as guides. Crowdsourcing techniques can be useful for such annotation tasks. However, the quality and consistency of these annotations can be poor. When looking at the corpus to investigate what humans considered entailment and contradiction, we realized that there were many troublesome annotations. Hence we decided to delve deeper into the corpus to find the reasons for those incorrect annotations and to manually correct the mistaken ones.

4   The problematic pairs

Contradictions in logic are symmetric; if proposition A is contradictory to B, then B must be contradictory to A. This is not what happens with the annotations of SICK. From our processing of the corpus [6] we have many asymmetrical pairs:

- 8 pairs $AeBBcA$, meaning that A entails B, but B contradicts A;

- 327 pairs $AcBBnA$, meaning that A contradicts B, but B is neutral with respect to A;

- 276 pairs $AnBBcA$, meaning that A is neutral with respect to B, but B contradicts A.

In total 611 pairs out of 9840 are annotated in a way that logically does not make sense. These may seem few (6%) but since the sentences chosen ought to describe simple, common-sense situations and since these wrong annotations are not even self-consistent, this is a cause for concern. The ones where A entails B, but B contradicts A are the worst ones. In fact, we find surprising that the creators of the corpus decided to label pairs of this category as *ENTAILMENT*. If A entails B, but B contradicts A we have a logical contradiction, an absurd situation. The unidirectionality can work for $AeBBnA$, because such a relation is possible in logic: a sentence A can entail B and sentence B might be neutral with respect to A because it does not make any commitments about A. However, for the category $AeBBcA$, if sentence B contradicts A it can never be the case that A entails B; there must be a mistake somewhere in the annotation. Both other asymmetrical sets are also logically inconsistent and hence disturbing. Thus, it is important to verify why these occur. After all, the corpus is supposed to have been simplified and checked manually, to a large extent.

We manually looked into 108 of those 611 wrongly annotated pairs to discover what the mistakes were and see if those cases offer us insights for the task at hand. First off, we have the obvious case of mistaken annotations of different referents within the same pair, already discussed in Marelli et al. (2014). Since the annotators were not given information on where the sentences came from or what their

---

[5]Crowdsourcing platform avalaible at `https://www.mturk.com/mturk/welcome`.

[6]Available at `https://github.com/kkalouli/SICK-processing/tree/master/pairs`.

frame of reference was, they did not have any kind of context to judge the sentences. Therefore, we see examples such as in the pair A = *An Asian woman in a crowd is not carrying a black bag. B = An Asian woman in a crowd is carrying a black bag.* The annotators decided that A contradicts B and that B is neutral with respect to A. It is clear that the same woman cannot at the same time be carrying a black bag and not carrying it, but there might be one woman carrying a bag and another one not carrying a bag. We might simply be talking about different women. This corpus design flaw seems to have created much confusion for the annotators. These mistakes seem to be the most common ones within the corpus, as 81 out of the 108 cases we looked at were of this nature. This lack of specific reference means that all contradiction pairs in which both sentences have indefinite determiners or in which one of the sentences has an indefinite determiner and the other one does not have a universal quantifier need to be checked as well. Contradictions need a common reference background, as already argued in Zaenen et al. (2005) and de Marneffe et al. (2008), and since there was none, it might be the case that we find more wrong annotations among the contradictions that we have not checked.

But not all problems are of this kind. We discovered pairs that contain an ungrammatical sentence, e.g., *The black and white dog isn't running and there is no person standing behind.* Although the grammatical errors are not dramatic, we can assume that each annotator mentally fixes the ungrammaticality in a different way, thus creating different relations and annotations. In this example, we could add an *it* at the end of the sentence or remove *behind* altogether and depending on that decision the sentence pair might have a different relation. Moreover, there is the case of nonsensical sentences, e.g., *A motorcycle is riding standing up on the seat of the vehicle.* (did they forget to add *rider* after motorcycle?), over which it is hard to reason. Thus, it might be reasonable to exclude such sentences from the corpus.

Another common issue within the SICK annotations is the difference between contradictory and alternative concepts. When someone says *Three civilians died in the incident* and someone else says *No civilians died in the incident* and there is a single referent for the incident in question, you have a true contradiction. Both sentences cannot be true in any possible world. But when concepts are alternative to others, the annotator may have a problem deciding whether they are contradictory or not. For example, for the pair A = *The lady is cracking an egg into a bowl. B = The lady is cracking an egg into a dish.*, the annotators decided that A entails B, but B is contradictory to A. Clearly, a *bowl* is a sub-type of *dish*, as any bowl is a dish (a container), that is round and deep, so the entailment is easy to see. But why did the annotators decide that being a dish is contradictory to being a bowl? One reason could be that *bowl* and *dish* are considered alternatives (bowls are deep, dishes are flat) and therefore these were judged as contradictory.

Similar to this example, but harder to detect is the pair A = *The man is aiming a gun. B = The man is drawing a gun.*, for which the annotators decided that A entails B, but B is contradictory to A. The rationale seems to be that to aim a gun, you first need to draw it from the holder, so aiming a gun entails having drawn it beforehand. This is similar to the example that every bowl is primarily a dish and then a specific kind of dish. But *drawing the gun* does not contradict *aiming the gun*, as *drawing the gun* is a sub-concept or a precondition, we could say, of *aiming the gun*.

Another interesting case is the pair A = *There is no man on a bicycle riding on the beach. B = A person is riding a bicycle in the sand beside the ocean.* This seems to be about what the definition of a *beach* should be. The question might be whether a beach is some "sand beside the ocean" or not. There are beaches in seas, lakes and rivers too, for sure. There are stone beaches, as well. So, what do we take a beach to be?

Furthermore, there were sentences among the 611 pairs that were simply wrongly annotated. We could not tell what the reason for the wrong label was. The pair A = *The blond girl is dancing behind the sound equipment. B = The blond girl is dancing in front of the sound equipment.*, was marked as A contradicts B and B is neutral with respect to A. This cannot be the case because we should be talking about the same blond girl which is either in front or behind the sound equipment, for the same observer. Thus, B should also contradict A. It seems that other testsuites of the RTE (Recognizing Textual Entailment [7]) task had similar problems with pairs that can only be classified as "plain errors"

---

[7] https://www.aclweb.org/aclwiki/index.php?title=Recognizing_Textual_Entailment

and no apparent reason for the mistakes can be found (Zaenen et al. (2005)).

Thus, to be able to use SICK as a real golden standard, we need to make sure that whatever is in the corpus is correct, as if humanly checked. In order to achieve this, we need a good understanding of what kinds of inferences are included in such a corpus and also of the kinds of mistakes that are found in there. Therefore, we started to check the corpus, by cleaning the entailment section included in it. We are making it available at `https://github.com/kkalouli/SICK-processing`.

We consider the category of pairs where A entails B and B is neutral with respect to A ($AeBBnA$). It is natural to start with this category as it is required to judge the others. The investigation of the wrong pairs showed us that it is easier to say if something entails something else, rather than to say that it contradicts it, because you need to check for more parameters in order to make the second decision. That is we need to decide whether the entities in the two sentences are co-referents or not, whether there can be a possible world where the two sentences can be true, etc. Our goal was to check all 9640 pairs and create our own "healthy" corpus, to begin with. For now, we simply investigate the 1513 pairs in the $AeBBnA$ class and try to collect the kinds of mistakes found, the reasons that could have led to them and also the kinds of inference involved in them.

5 Cleaned entailments

On total, we deemed 178 of the 1513 pairs as wrong, almost 12% of the pairs. Most of these mistakes were similar to the ones already discussed. The most common ones being the "plain" errors (148 can be categorized as such), the ungrammatical sentences (found in 8 pairs), the nonsensical sentences (found in 3 pairs) and the referents issue (found in 2 pairs). There are also sentences (found in 4 pairs) that do not really refer to common-sense concepts, as they were supposed to according to the design of the corpus, and this influences the annotations. For example, how do you really reason over and annotate a pair containing a sentence about *singing hamsters* since a singing hamster is not really in your every day experience?

Apart from those, we have the issue of compound nouns, in particular, of deverbal adjectives modifying nouns, such as in the pair A = *The microphone in front of the talking parrot is being muted. B = A parrot is speaking.* If the *talking parrot* is a parrot that is talking right now, then A entails B and B is neutral to A. But if the *talking parrot* refers to the parrot's general ability to talk (rather than that the parrot is talking right now), then A should be neutral with respect to B and B should be neutral with respect to A.

There is also the traditional problem of what Partee (2010) calls "privative adjectives" (4 examples found). These are adjectives that contradict the noun they modify, e.g. a fake gun is not a gun. Consider the pair A = *A cartoon airplane is landing. B = A plane is landing.* A cartoon airplane is not a proper airplane, the same way a toy car is not a car. Thus, A cannot entail B and should rather be neutral with respect to B as B is neutral with respect to A.

Additionally, there are still the expected issues with ambiguous sentences – at least, 5 pairs can be categorized as such – as in the pair A = *Two bikes are being ridden by two people. B = Two people are riding a bike.* Here, sentence B is underspecified in a way that does not allow us to judge if the two people are together riding one bike or if they are each riding their own bike. One might expect that such ambiguities will not be encountered in a corpus like SICK which ought to contain simple, common-sense sentences. Nevertheless, it seems that language cannot avoid ambiguity even in its simplest forms. This shows that even a basic, preliminary effort for an inference system will have to be able to deal with such basic ambiguities from the beginning.

We also observed that some definitions are cultural (observed in 2 pairs). A representative example is the pair A = *Different teams are playing football on the field. B = Two teams are playing soccer.* Depending on whether sentence A talks about American football or not, we can say that it entails B or not. If we are talking about American football, then sentence A does not entail sentence B.

We were also able to observe the kinds of inference intended by the corpus creators. Since the corpus was expanded from an initial core set of sentences, through semi-automatic transformations, e.g. conversion of passive to active voice, synonyms of words, addition of adjective modifiers, etc., these kinds of inference are all there (Marelli et al. (2014) provide their complete list of expansions). Apart from those, however, we made a couple of other observations. Firstly, we found pairs where the entailment is based on more than basic lexical semantics. The pair *A = One man is turning on the microwave. B = The buttons of a microwave are being pushed by a man.* is an example. For this pair we need to infer that turning on the microwave requires the pushing of some buttons and that therefore some button must have been pushed. Such inferences are more than what Wordnet and SUMO can give us, off-the-shelf. Similar cases of explicit world-knowledge were already observed by Zaenen et al. (2005) and indicate that our proposed pipeline might have to find other ways to add some basic forms of world knowledge. Another interesting issue is related to agentive nouns, such as *swimmer*. Everyone who swims is a swimmer, but is everyone who poses for a photo a model? We found many pairs where this linguistic phenomenon seems to have an impact on human judgements. For example, the annotators may say *A man is wearing a purple shirt and black leather chaps and is posing for the camera* entails *A model is wearing a purple shirt and black leather chaps and is posing for the camera.* However, we do not think that a model is anyone who poses for a photo, but only the ones who are doing that intentionally (for money or not). Hence it should not be the case that *A* entails *B*, for any man. The dictionary we use, Wordnet, will not necessarily map *man* to *model*, as these annotators seem to have done. Since Wordnet is the resource we are using to link lexical knowledge to world knowledge, and since its first analysis contradicts some of the human judgements, we cannot take for granted that the whole analysis will be correctly done by Wordnet. For the example of *swimmer* we could use the Wordnet relation *derivated-by* that relates *swimmer* to *swim*, but in the case of *pose* and *model*, there is no explicit relation between these synsets. However, if we consider the glosses offered by Wordnet, we might be able to get that inference, see synset `http://compling.hss.ntu.edu.sg/omw/cgi-bin/wn-gridx.cgi?synset=10324560-n`, where *model* is described as "person who poses for a photographer or painter or sculptor". Even if Wordnet does offer both senses for *model*, it is unlikely that it would get the same sense as the annotators have because for other humans such as ourselves this is not an obvious relation.

6 Conclusions

Our manual investigation of the SICK corpus was an important preliminary step to check both the kinds of inference that we want to have and to detect the mistakes that can appear within the corpus design as well as the mistakes that humans can make when annotating inferences. On the one hand, the investigation helped us conceptualize the limits of lexical semantics. Even a simple, common-sense corpus as SICK contains sentences that cannot be captured by the semantics given by Wordnet and SUMO and therefore our preliminary pipeline may also need more than that. Moreover, world-knowledge has to be integrated in a way that does not conflict with lexical semantics. On the other hand, the wrong cases we found motivate us to think through the special challenges that semantics pose and whether and how these can be handled in an automatic system. We will need more sophisticated solutions for sentences whose interpretation needs more context, for deverbal and privative adjectives, for alternative vs. contradictory concepts, for the underspecificity of some of the definitions of concepts, etc. Our next step will be to provide a baseline corpus of basic entailments and contradictions, based on SICK, which can then be used as a reliable golden standard. For that we would like to use the strengths of our preliminary pipeline. Together with the completion of this task, we will focus on the other components of our system.

References

Basile, P., M. de Gemmis, A. L. Gentile, P. Lops, and G. Semeraro (2007, June). Uniba: Jigsaw algorithm for word sense disambiguation. In *Proceedings of the Fourth International Workshop on Semantic Evaluations (SemEval-2007)*, Prague, Czech Republic, pp. 398–401. Association for Computational Linguistics.

Bobrow, D. G., B. Cheslow, C. Condoravdi, L. Karttunen, T. H. King, R. Nairn, V. de Paiva, C. Price, and A. Zaenen (2007). Parc's bridge and question answering system. In *Proceedings of the Grammar Engineering Across Frameworks Workshop (GEAF 2007)* .

de Marneffe, M.-C., A. N. Rafferty, and C. D. Manning (2008). Finding contradictions in text. In *Proceedings of ACL-08*.

Fellbaum, C. (1998). *WordNet: An Electronic Lexical Database (Language, Speech, and Communication)*. The MIT Press.

Marelli, M., S. Menini, M. Baroni, L. Bentivogli, R. Bernardi, and R. Zamparelli (2014). A SICK cure for the evaluation of compositional distributional semantic models. In *Proceedings of LREC 2014*.

Niles, I. and A. Pease (2001). Toward a Standard Upper Ontology. In C. Welty and B. Smith (Eds.), *Proceedings of the 2nd International Conference on Formal Ontology in Information Systems (FOIS-2001)*, pp. 2–9.

Partee, B. H. (2010). Privative adjectives: Subsective plus coercion. In *Presuppositions and Discourse: Essays Offered to Hans Kamp*, pp. 273–285. Brill.

Schuster, S. and C. D. Manning (2016). Enhanced English Universal Dependencies: An improved representation for natural language understanding tasks. In *Proceedings of the Tenth International Conference on Language Resources and Evaluation (LREC 2016)*.

Zaenen, A., L. Karttunen, and R. Crouch (2005). Local textual inference: can it be defined or circumscribed? In *Proceedings of the ACL workshop on empirical modeling of semantic equivalence and entailment*, pp. 31–36. Association for Computational Linguistics.

Situating Word Senses in their Historical Context with Linked Data

Fahad Khan

CNR - Istituto di Linguistica Computazionale "A. Zampolli", Pisa, Italy

`fahad.khan@ilc.cnr.it`

Jack Bowers

Austrian Academy of Sciences (ACDH), Vienna, Austria

`Jack.Bowers@oeaw.ac.at`

Francesca Frontini

Praxiling UMR 5267 CNRS, Université Paul-Valéry, Montpellier, France

`francesca.frontini@univ-montp3.fr`

Abstract

In this article we present a Semantic Web-based model for creating lexical resources in which the diachronic and, more broadly, contextual dimensions of word meaning can be explicitly represented as part of a graph-based data structure. We start by discussing why Linked Data is the right publishing approach for such diachronic datasets. We then describe our model, lemonEty, which utilizes the ontology engineering technique of perdurants in order to model lexical entries as dynamic processes. Next we go onto explain how to represent etymologies using our model, and in particular how to associate temporal information with word senses, taking examples from two different lexicographic resources. In addition, we will show how our model deals with cognates and attestations.

1 Introduction

Ontologies can be used to enrich computational lexical resources in numerous different ways, the most obvious of which is by using ontological entities to describe the semantics of individual lexical entries. In addition to this however ontologies can also be used to help describe and to reason about how languages change and evolve; and in particular, they allow us to model word meaning change. In this article our focus will be on lexical and ontological datasets for the **Semantic Web**, that is **linked data** datasets. This choice was made for various reasons, not the least of which is the fact that the Linked Data (LD) publishing paradigm has made it easier than ever before to link together different, individual datasets. This has, in turn, served to highlight the many benefits of augmenting single resources with (semantically specified) links to other datasets. Working with linked data also offers up access to a host of different Semantic Web tools and languages, amongst which: a dedicated Knowledge Representation language (OWL), an expressive query language (SPARQL) along with a semantic web rule language (SWRL). There can, however, be certain drawbacks to publishing datasets as Linked Data. One of the most restrictive of these relates to the fact that Linked Data best practices require that datasets be published using the standard RDF model, meaning that they must in effect be modeled as sets of subject-predicate-object (S-P-O) triples. This restriction to unary and binary relations prevents us from directly adding extra arguments to binary predicates in order to model n-ary relations for any n greater than 2. And so we cannot just specify the temporal validity of RDF statement representing an S-P-O triple by adding a time argument to P. This can be a particular problem as temporal information is a core part of many lexical datasets, especially those dealing with etymological data.

A number of solutions to the problem of representing n-ary relations in RDF have already been proposed each of which carries its own particular advantages and disadvantages. One popular solution, and the one which we adopt in this paper, is to model entities as *perdurants*, that is, as entities with an inherent temporal extent: effectively treating them as processes that unfold through time.

Unlike static entities, so called *endurants* – which retain their essential (identifying) properties at any of the different points in time in which they exist – looking at a 'snapshot' of a perdurant at any given point in time only gives us a part of the entity. So for example take a lexical entry, l, and two lexical senses $s1$, $s2$, such that l has the sense $s1$ during interval $i1$, and $s2$ during interval $i2$. We would like represent this as follows, *sense(l, s1, i1)* and *sense(l,s2,i2)*. But since the sense relation is binary we can't express the temporal duration of $s1$ and $s2$ in this way. Instead if we view $s1$ and $s2$ as perdurants then we can associate them with the respective temporal intervals $i1$ and $i2$ so that they are classified among the properties of $s1$ and $s2$. The particular approach to perdurants which we take up in this article is the *fluent* approach proposed by Welty and Fikes (Welty and Fikes (2006)) and subsequently modified by Krieger (Krieger (2014)). In the latter, relations that were formerly represented as holding between entities modelled as endurants now hold between time slices of those same entities modelled as perdurants. So for example if in the original, non-diachronic version of an ontology relation, *employeeOf* was specified as holding between an entity, p, of type *Person*, and an entity, c, of type *Company*, then according to Welty and Fikes' approach to perdurants we create two new entities $p@t1$ and $c@t1$ which are temporal parts of p and c respectively and therefore of type *TemporalPart*, both with the temporal extent of $t1$, with *employeeOf* now holding between $p@t1$ and $c@t1$ instead of between p and c. Krieger's approach simplifies this by allowing these time slices to be typed according to the original classes, so that $p@t1$ is now also of type Person (as is p) and c@t1 of type Company (as is c). In this way we don't need to change the type of *employeeOf* to make it a relation between entities of type *TemporalPart*.

In what follows we will apply the perdurantist approach to representing etymological information. Briefly, we will define a class called *Etymon* which consists of time slices of the class *LexicalEntry* (with the latter class belongs to the RDF-based lexicon model *lemon*[1]), where, as per the Krieger approach to perdurant modeling, the class *Etymon* is a subclass of *LexicalEntry*. We will also define a class *Etymology* which represents the evolution through time of the salient properties of a lexeme. Finally we explicitly represent lexicographic attestations using a class called *Attestation*. We hope to show that these new classes together with their related properties permit us to explicitly situate word senses temporally as well as to clearly represent statements and hypotheses *about* senses, within the framework of the RDF data model.

2 Modeling Diachronic/Etymological Lexical Data

The diachronic dimensions of lexical data have been somewhat neglected in models for the representation of lexicons up till now, although they are partly dealt with in the TEI dictionary module [2]. Work has also been carried out in the past on the best way of representing etymological information in LMF (Salmon-Alt (2006)), and detailed proposals for an extension of TEI that deal with etymologies have recently been made (Bowers and Romary (2016)). The de-facto standard for representing lexical datasets as linked data is lemon (McCrae et al. (2011)), the design of which was heavily influenced by LMF, something that is readily apparent from a comparison of lemon with the LMF core model. One of the main ways in which lemon differs from LMF, however, aside from simply having fewer classes and properties in its core model and basic extensions, is in its modeling of lexical semantics. In lemon, members of the class *LexicalEntry* are linked to ontological items which represent the extension (as opposed to intension) of these entries via a *LexicalSense* object. These *LexicalSense* objects are intended as reified pairings of a lexical entry with an ontological item representing one of the meanings of the entry in question.

The core of the lemon model is presented below in Fig. 1.

In contrast to LMF or TEI, lemon's approach to representing word meaning was explicitly designed with linked data in mind. However neither lemon nor its successor Ontolex-lemon have any relations or classes that specifically deal with diachronic information[3]. In previous work we proposed an extension of lemon called lemonDia that allowed the representation of diachronic semantic data (Khan et. al. 2016). At the core of this extension was the idea of modeling senses of lexical entries as perdurants. However, we did not take into consideration the interaction between the meaning of a word and other, non-semantic, properties. This can be a real limitation since it often occurs that multiple properties of a word change at the around the same time. For instance, the pronunciation and/or

---

[1] For the specifications of this model see https://www.w3.org/2016/05/ontolex/
[2] http://www.tei-c.org/release/doc/tei-p5-doc/it/html/DI.html
[3] Although there is currently a proposal to discuss such an extension on the ONTOLEX mailing list.

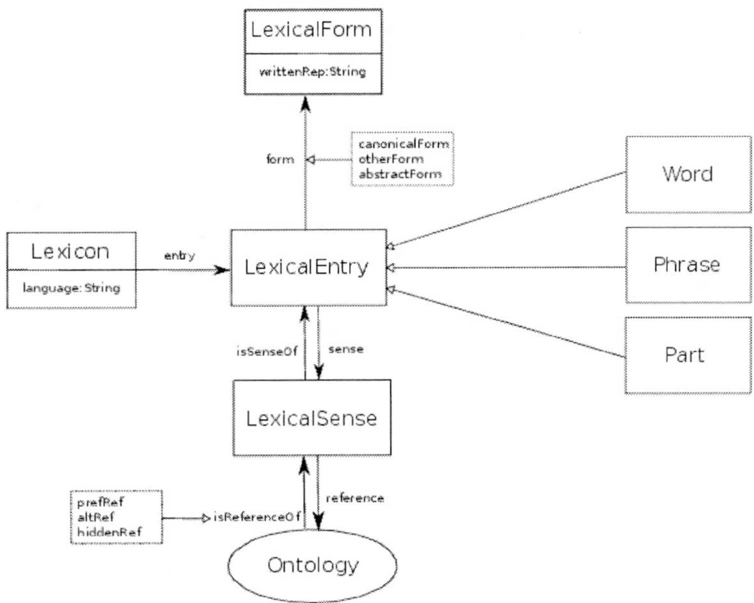

Figure 1: lemon model core diagram.

orthography of a word may change or vary over a span of time during which a new sense of that same word may come into use. In order to remedy this, we present, in the next section, an extension of lemon, lemonEty, that applies the perdurantist approach to the whole lexical entry, instead of just the sense or any other single aspect of an entry's profile (e.g. grammatical, phonetic, etc.). Another issue which quickly comes up in modeling etymological data is how to properly represent textual attestations where these provide strong evidence for the use of a word with a particular sense. Indeed if one views etymologies as scientific hypotheses tracing out a word's origin and the evolution of its many senses, then it is intuitively obvious that we should be able to model attestations as pieces of evidence. We will look at how our approach can help in modeling this too.

3   Representing Etymological Sense Data using lemonEty

Before we move on to describing the model itself, a brief note on working with temporal data. As we have already mentioned, one of the main advantages of publishing datasets as linked data is the ready availability of useful tools and standards. In the case of the knowledge representation language, OWL, this includes open source inference engines that permit us to reason over OWL datasets: something that is especially attractive when it comes to temporal data since there exist a number of vocabularies and SWRL rule sets for working with such data[4]. One difficulty that quickly becomes apparent in this context however is that we rarely have precise dates temporally delimiting a given linguistic phenomenon; instead the intervals we work with tend to be highly underspecified. Although the lack of precise dates can indeed hamper our ability to make temporal inferences on data, we are still able to carry out *qualitative*, as opposed to *quantitative*, reasoning, using Allen relations, e.g., *before*, *meets*, *overlaps*, to make basic inferences as to how different intervals stand with respect to each other (Allen (1983)). Thus even if we do not know *exactly* which years, or even in which centuries a word was used with a certain sense, we will likely have an idea of some broader interval of time in which this interval of use is contained. For example, we might specify a period representing Middle English delimited by the years 1100AD and 1500AD, as its respective start and end point; the time intervals associated with word meanings can then be be specified as overlapping or being contained within this period. Having the possibility of specifying time intervals with respect to their mutual relations instead of being constrained into always giving specific years or centuries, helps us deal with the vagueness and ambiguity of the temporal information that we find

---

[4]See for instance https://github.com/sbatsakis/TemporalRepresentations

in many pre-existing lexical resources. Any inferences that we run over such data will effectively take this vagueness into consideration. But it's not always enough. For instance how do we represent a preposition such as "circa" when referring to a year or a century, an expression that has a fairly 'fuzzy' definition in natural language? Somewhere along the line we have to make an interpretation of such phases in our formal language and then ensure that this interpretation is consistent across a dataset. Such interpretations should be stated explicitly either in the documentation or in the resource itself, preferably both.

3.1 Etymology Examples

In order to explain how our model works and some of the ideas behind it we will look at the encoding of some concrete examples. We will take the entry for the word 'girl' from two different lexical sources. The first is the online etymology dictionary[5]:

> *'girl (n.) c. 1300, gyrle "child, young person" (of either sex but most frequently of females), of unknown origin. One guess [OED] leans toward an unrecorded Old English *gyrele, from Proto-Germanic *gurwilon-, diminutive of *gurwjoz (apparently also represented by Low German gære "boy, girl," Norwegian dialectal gorre, Swedish dialectal gurre "small child," though the exact relationship, if any, between all these is obscure), from PIE *ghwrgh-, also found in Greek parthenos "virgin." But this involves some objectionable philology. Liberman (2008) writes:*
>
> *Girl does not go back to any Old English or Old Germanic form. It is part of a large group of Germanic words whose root begins with a g or k and ends in r. The final consonant in girl is a diminutive suffix. The g-r words denote young animals, children, and all kinds of creatures considered immature, worthless, or past their prime.*
>
> *Another candidate is Old English gierela "garment" (for possible sense evolution in this theory, compare brat). A former folk-etymology derivation from Latin garrulus "chattering, talkative" is now discarded. Like boy, lass, lad it is of more or less obscure origin. "Probably most of them arose as jocular transferred uses of words that had originally different meaning" [OED]. Specific meaning of "female child" is late 14c. Applied to "any young unmarried woman" since mid-15c. Meaning "sweetheart" is from 1640s. Old girl in reference to a woman of any age is recorded from 1826. Girl next door as a type of unflashy attractiveness is recorded by 1953.'*

The second lexical source is the important early 20th century work 'An etymological dictionary of the English language' compiled by Walter Skeat (Skeat 1910):

> *GIRL, a female child, young woman. (E.) ME. gerle, girle, gyrle, formerly used of either sex, and signifying either a boy or girl. In Chaucer, C.T. 3767 (A 3769) gerl is a young woman; but in C.T. 666 (A 664), the pl. girles means young people of both sexes. In Will. of Palerne, 816, and King Alisander, 2802, it means 'young women;' in P. Plowman, B. i.33, it means 'boys;' cf. B. x. 175. Answering to an AS. form *gyr-el-, Teut. *gur-wil-, a dimin. form from Teut. base *gur-. Cf. NFries. gör, a girl; Pomeran. goer, a child; O. Low G. gör, a child; see Bremen Wörtebuch, ii. 528. Cf. Swiss gurre, gurrli, a depriciatory term for a girl; Sanders, G. Dict. i. 609, 641; also Norw. gorre, a small child (Aasen); Swed. dial. gårrä, guerre (the same). Root uncertain. Der. girl-ish, girl-ish-ly, girl-ish-ness, girl-hood*

We will model several of the salient pieces of etymological information contained in the preceding two lexical entries for the word 'girl' – which we will refer to as (a) and (b), respectively – using lemonEty.

3.2 LemonEty

In our perdurantist approach to etymological data we associate objects of the class *Etymon* with a lemon *LexicalEntry*, where *Etymon* objects are modeled as time slices of *LexicalEntry* objects. In other words etymons are bundles of lexical properties that hold throughout a certain interval of time; these properties can be phonetic, phonological, orthographic, morphosyntactic, or semantic. We

---

[5]"Girl". Online Etymology Dictionary. Retrieved April 14, 2017. http://www.etymonline.com/index.php?term=girl

can then specify the relationships between different *Etymon* objects and their associated properties by including links between them; these links are represented as reified *EtymologicalLink* objects. *EtymologicalLink* objects are associated with a given *Etymology* object which represents one version of the history of a *LexicalEntry*. A *LexicalEntry* can have more than one *Etymology* associated with it. Fig. 2 presents the core of the lemonEty module in diagrammatic form[6].

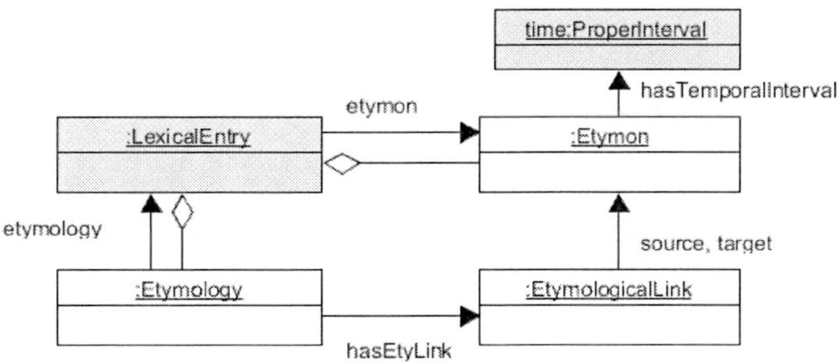

Figure 2: lemonEty core diagram.

In order to capture more specific kinds of etymological relationship we have defined a number of subtypes of *EtymologicalLink* such as *SenseShift* and *Inheritance*. In cases of sense shift we can also create a link between the two *Etymon* senses.

At this point we should clarify the different roles that the *Etymon* and *Etymology* classes play in our model since on first glance it may seem redundant or confusing to include both when presumably only one is really necessary: the answer is that they play different roles. The role of *Etymon* is to represent various different periods in the 'lifespan' of a word during which the word is represented as being stable for certain properties such as the fact that it has only one single sense. This *Etymon* object then will have a temporal interval which delimits its validity in time. A lexical entry can have more than one *Etymon* representing different stages of the word's existence. Objects of the class *Etymology* on the other hand serve to describe the arrangement of these different etymons; etymologies, even though they are the etymologies of single lexical entries, can bring together etymons belonging to different lexical entries in describing the origin of a word. But then, why wouldn't it be enough just to have relations between single objects of the class *Etymon* without introducing the class *Etymology*? The answer is that *Etymology* objects serve to describe different hypotheses as to a word's origins and development; each such object reifies the history or evolution of a lexical entry and allows us to refer to it and to predicate different properties of it, such as for example when the etymology was proposed and by whom. We will now look at the lemonEty representation of (part of) the (a) example above.

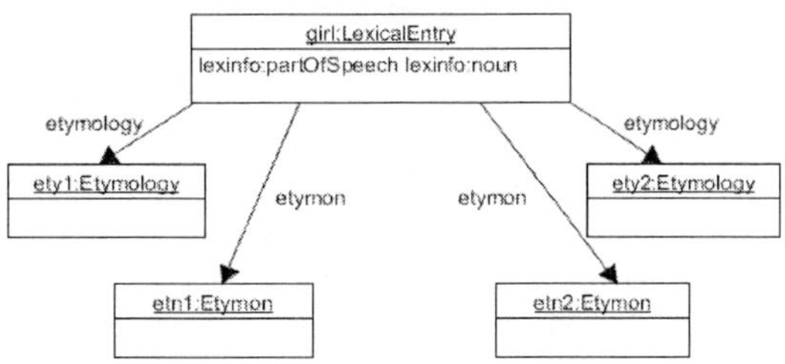

Figure 3: Girl example

In Fig. 3 the word 'girl' has two etymons, *etn1* and *etn2*, representing two different stages in the word's evolution. There are also two different etymology objects, *ety1* and *ety2* which represent two separate versions of the history and development of the word. Note that although we haven't shown

---

[6]In the diagrams which follow we colour classes and individuals that are from non-lemonEty vocabularies in grey.

this in Fig. 3, we can also associate textual information from the original lexical entry as string values to objects of the class *Etymon* and *LexicalSense* using the *gloss* data property which we have defined.

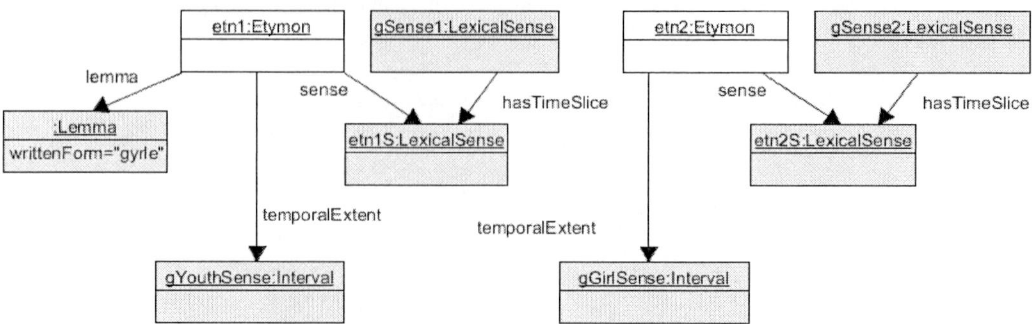

Figure 4: Two *Etymon* individuals

Fig. 4 illustrates the two different objects of class *Etymon*, *etn1* and *etn2* assigned to 'girl' in Fig. 3. The first etymon, *etn1*, corresponds to the first sentence of the entry (The sentence starting with 'c.1300...'). Although we haven't added temporal information to the diagram (for reasons of space) we can specify the *gYouthSense* interval using the OWL Time relation *intervalContains*[7]; we have chosen to represent *gYouthSense* as being contained within an interval with a lower bound of 1250AD and an upper bound of 1350AD (this is our interpretation of 'circa 1300')[8]. The second etymon, *etn2*, represents the narrower sense of 'girl' which is still in contemporary use. We can give the interval *gGirlSense* a lower bound of 1350AD (our interpretation of "late 14th century") and leave it unbounded from the top. Note that each sense of an etymon (in this case *etn1S* and *etn2S*) is a time slice of one of the senses of the lexical entry object (*gSense1* and *gSense2*). Note also that since the original entry did not explicitly mention the existence of a 'narrowing' relationship between the two senses *etn1S* and *etn2S*, we haven't added an explicit *EtymologicalLink* object of type *shiftNarrowing*, even though this would have been a reasonable interpretation to make. Similarly we haven't made a finer division of the second etymon on the basis of the subsequent broadening of the sense of 'girl' in the 15th century, nor have we created new etymons tracking the changes in the written form of the word or additional morphosyntactic changes. The former is for reasons of space; the latter because this information was not included in the original entry which we were modeling. The example reveals how quickly one comes up against multiple ambiguities when representing etymological data from legacy lexical resources in a formal model like RDF.

In Fig. 5 we have given a lemonEty representation of the first etymology given in (a). We represent the etymology using an *Etymology* object, *ety1*, which points to reified etymological links between etymons that in this case belong to different lexical entries. The etymons in Fig. 5 are all linked together with the property *Inheritance*, which is a subproperty of *EtymologicalLink*. In future refinements of our model, we will allow for the addition of confidence measures to members of the class *Etymology* by associating a numerical value or a value from a set of confidence values {low, medium, high} to each etymology object. The second lexical entry, (b), gives a number of attestations for the two different senses of the word 'girl' including a citation apiece from the Canterbury Tales, attestations from Piers Plowman, as well as the translation from French of Guillaume de Palerne ("William of Palerne"). These attestations function as evidence for the use of words and allow us to relate word sense data to information from external bibliographic and historical databases. Again, the graph structure of RDF, along with the fact that RDF requires a universal identifier (URI) for each resource that is dereferenceable using the HTTP protocol, makes this reasonably straightforward. In the present case we would like to link word senses to their attestations which we link in turn to bibliographic and historical datasets. If we can access triples via this second dataset that tell us when the text was (approximately) written, then we have effectively linked up the original lexical sense

---

[7] https://www.w3.org/TR/owl-time/#time:intervalContains

[8] This is our interpretation of the temporal phrase 'circa'. While it's indeed hard to avoid making such interpretations when representing such data in a computationally useful format, it is important however is to make sure that such assumptions are readily accessible to potential users of the resources, possibly as part of the resource's metadata.

with evidence about when that sense was used. Although there is currently a lack of LOD datasets that contain high-quality, well-curated bibliographic, biographical or historical data, there does seem to be a strong impetus towards the creation of such datasets, especially for use in Digital Humanities' contexts.

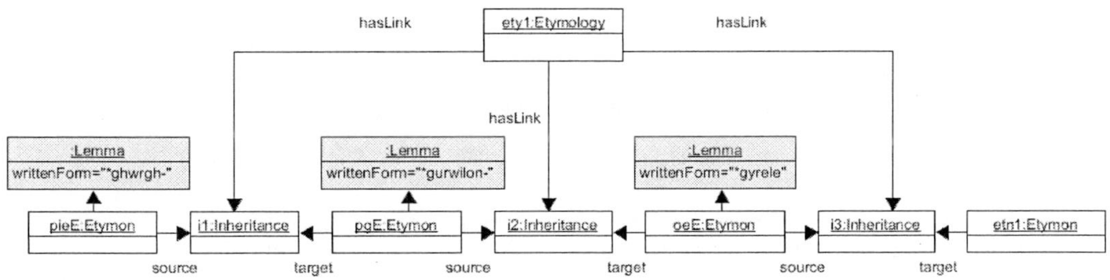

Figure 5: *Etymology* individual.

Based on our previous work on modeling lexicographic resources (Khan et. al. 2017) we decided to add an *Attestation* class to our model. Objects of *Attestation* are linked to objects of the class *LexicalSense* using the object property *attestation*; these *Attestation* objects can then be linked to texts, textual fragments, or corpora, using already existing vocabularies such as CITO (Peroni and Shotton, 2012). So then, to return to our examples, and assuming that we've already created the *LexicalEntry* and *Sense* objects for the entry, similar to those we showed in Fig. 3, we can create an etymon representing the period of time in which 'girl' had both senses, girl and youth, using lemonEty as in Fig. 6. Note that we have specified that the interval of time in which the word *girl* had both meanings is included in the interval of Middle English[9], this is our interpretation based on the text of the entry for the purposes of the encoding, although one might argue that this information isn't actually specified in the text itself.

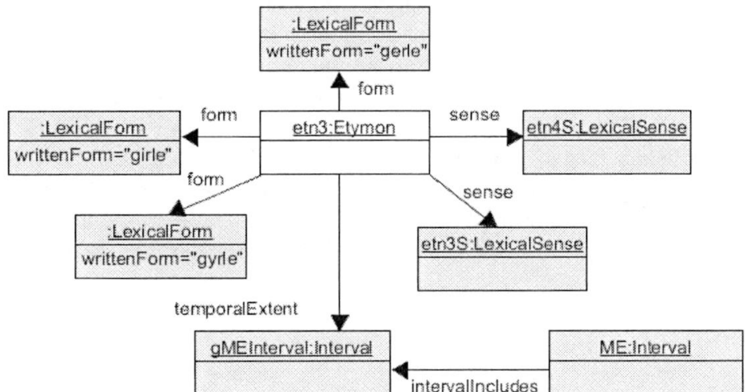

Figure 6: Attested *Etymon*.

We can represent the fact that each of the two senses has an attestation in the Canterbury Tales using the attestation relation which links each sense to a specific object of the type *Attestation* as in Fig. 7.

Here we can specify the immediate context of the word in question, assuming that we have already specified that *etn3S* and *etn4S* are time slices of senses with references *dbpedia:girl* and *dbpedia:youth* respectively. We also assume that the CITO property *citesAsEvidence* points to a

---

[9]We can use the time span associated with the ISO 639-3 language code for Middle English: http://www-01.sil.org/iso639-3/documentation.asp?id=enm

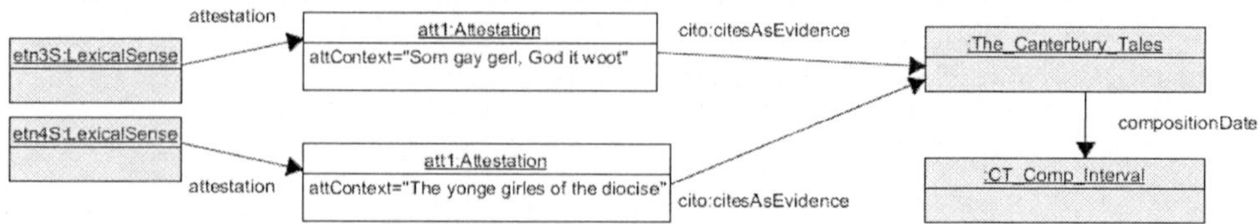

Figure 7: An attestation in the Canterbury Tales.

dataset containing information about the text and its date of composition as in the diagram. Finally, in Fig. 8, we show how to link a lexical entry with its cognates, taking three of the cognates from the girl (a) example. Our model contains the symmetric *hasCognate* object property which links together an object of type *LexicalEntry* with objects of type *Cognate*, which is a subtype of *LexicalEntry* itself[10].

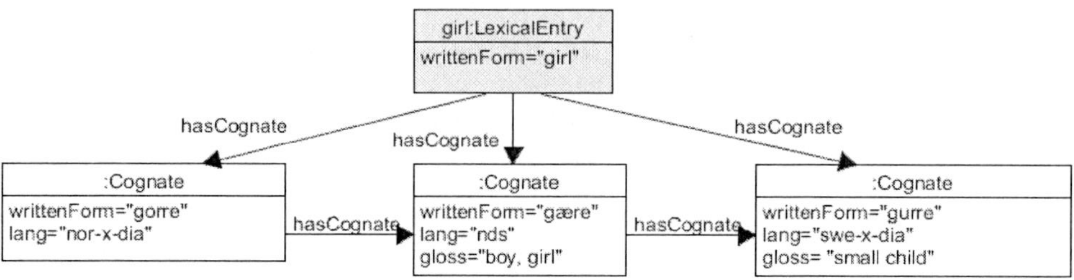

Figure 8: Cognates of girl.

By rendering explicit many of the etymologically (and in general the diachronically) salient aspects of the original textual data we are able to represent etymological lexical information in a way that makes it easier to query and, in general, more computationally actionable and accessible than it might otherwise have been as free text. We chose to make certain theoretical entities explicit classes in our model (such as the classes *Etymon* and *Etymology*) because we felt potential consumers of such lexical datasets would find it useful to have the possibility of querying for these classes and searching for different attributes belonging to them (and here it should be pointed out that the second author is a domain expert in lexicography). The fact that we have have chosen the popular RDF data framework also ensures interoperability for datasets encoded using our new model.

4 Conclusion

In this article we have presented an RDF-based model for representing lexical data using a perdurantist approach in order to make the diachronic aspects of the data more accessible. We have applied the model to some concrete examples from the domain of etymology to illustrate its viability. We are currently testing the lemonEty model by using it to encode a large and varied number of test examples from various sources. Although certain parts of the model will likely undergo subsequent changes, the core elements, as we have presented them in this article, are intended to be stable. The model we have presented is specifically based on RDF, and takes advantage of several features of the RDF framework that may not be as relevant for other standards, and so we would like, in further work, to identify a core set of classes and properties for encoding etymological/diachronic data that could be common to lemonEty as well as LMF and TEI.

---

[10]The language tags for Norwegian and Swedish ("nor-x-dia") and ("swe-x-dia") respectively combine the ISO 639-3 tags with a private tag denoted by "-x-", followed by "dia" as per BCP 47 (Phillips and Davis (2009)). This is necessary in order to express the underdefined dialect varieties of these languages mentioned by the author of the entry.

References

Allen, J. F. (1983). Maintaining Knowledge About Temporal Intervals. *Communications of the ACM 26 November 1983*, 832–843.

Bellandi, A., F. Boschetti, A. M. Del Grosso, A. F. Khan, and M. Monachini (2017 to appear). Provando e riprovando modelli di dizionario storico digitale: collegare voci, citazioni, interpretazioni. In *AIUCD 2017 – Book of Abstracts, 24-28 January 2017*, Rome, Italy.

Bowers, J. and L. Romary (2016). Deep encoding of etymological information in TEI. *TEI. Journal of the Text Encoding Initiative* (10). Available at `https://doi.org/10.4000/jtei.1643`.

Khan, F., J. E. Díaz-Vera, and M. Monachini (2016). Representing Polysemy and Diachronic Lexico-Semantic Data on the Semantic Web ? In *Proceedings of the Second International Workshop on Semantic Web for Scientific Heritage co-located with 13th Extended Semantic Web Conference (ESWC 2016), Heraklion, Greece, May 30th, 2016.*, Volume V-1595, pp. 37–46.

Krieger, H.-U. (2014). A Detailed Comparison of Seven Approaches for the Annotation of Time-Dependent Factual Knowledge in RDF and OWL. In *Proceedings of the 10th Joint ACL-ISO Workshop on Interoperable Semantic Annotation (held in conjunction with LREC 2014)*. European Language Resources Association.

McCrae, J., D. Spohr, and P. Cimiano (2011). Linking lexical resources and ontologies on the semantic web with lemon. In *The semantic web: research and applications*, Extended Semantic Web Conference, pp. 245–259. Springer.

Peroni, S. and D. Shotton (2012, December). FaBiO and CiTO: Ontologies for describing bibliographic resources and citations. *Web Semantics: Science, Services and Agents on the World Wide Web 17*, 33–43.

Phillips, A. and M. Davis (2009). *BCP 47, RFC 5646 – Tags for Identifying Languages*. IETF. Published: BCP 47 Standard, see http://www.rfc-editor.org/rfc/bcp/bcp47.txt.

Salmon-Alt, S. (2006). Data structures for etymology: towards an etymological lexical network. *Bulletin de linguistique appliquée et générale 31*, 101–112.

Skeat, W. W. (1910). *An etymological dictionary of the English language. (4th ed.)*. Oxford Clarendon Press.

Welty, C. and R. Fikes (2006). A Reusable Ontology for Fluents in OWL. In *Proceedings of the 2006 Conference on Formal Ontology in Information Systems: Proceedings of the Fourth International Conference (FOIS 2006)*, Amsterdam, The Netherlands, The Netherlands, pp. 226–236. IOS Press.

An Object-oriented Model of Role Framing and Attitude Prediction

Manfred Klenner

Computational Linguistics, University of Zurich, Switzerland

`klenner@cl.uzh.ch`

1   Introduction

According to Rashkin et al. (2016) and other researchers, a text not only reveals the attitudes of the discourse referents dealt with in the text, but it also indicates how they are framed by the text author. Do they play a positive or negative role in the exposed narrative? We call this the author's role framing. While the attitudes tell us who is for or against who (pro and con relations), the role framing indicates who is a beneficiary or a victim etc. of the situation described. Both, attitude and role framing depend on the factuality status of the described situations. For instance, if A hopes that B helps C, than A has a positive attitude towards C, but neither is C is beneficiary nor is there an attitude of B towards C. The reason is that *hope* is a non-factive verb and *help*, thus, non-factual. If we were told that A *might* hope that B helps C, nothing follows at all, since now even *hope* in non-factual.

Not only verbs like *hope*, but also nouns like *destruction* and predicatively used adjectives like e.g. *angry* in *Trump is angry that our neighbors are hurting Wisconsin and other border states* indicate attitude. Here, Trump and Canada (neighbors) are adversaries, but Trump is pro Wisconsin, which is framed as a victim. Moreover, constructions like *It is sad that* .. clearly reveal the stance of the author towards an event and - as a consequence - towards the participants of this event. So in the end, we are able to derive the author's stance, the proclaimed attitudes among referents and the role framing that comes with a text. We introduce an object-oriented model realized in Python to deal with these topics. An empirical evaluation is presented concerning predicatively used adjectives.

2   Attitude Prediction and Role Framing

A verb might express an attitude between an opinion source and target role. It also sometimes frames a particular role in terms of a positive or negative effect the filler of the role receives in an affirmative usage of the verb. If A helps B, A has a positive attitude towards B and B is a beneficiary since he actually receives help. The author is committed to the truth of what he writes and the reader is entitled to draw conclusions on that basis. Verbs, nouns and adjectives subcategorizing for a complement clause pose a commitment on it regarding the truth of the subclause. Among others, Nairn et al. (2006) and Karttunen (2012) have described the different kinds of verb-specific commitments. They called it *verb implicatures*. The crucial point is that truth commitment and negation give rise to factuality, counterfactuality and non-factuality. While non-factuality blocks any inference, counterfactuality inverts the attitude and the effects of the verb. Our model does not explicitly ascribe factuality, we just use the equivalent notion of truth commitment in combination with negation. In sum, the attitude expressed and the role framing depends on the meaning of the matrix verb, its truth commitment on the subclause and the affirmative status of both, the matrix verb and the subclause verb. This is, mutatis mutantis, true for nouns and predicatively used adjectives as well.

There is wide range of phenomena, from verbs that are falsehood committing if affirmatively used and truth committing if negated (*forget*) to verbs with opposite commitments (*manage*). There are factive verbs which commit the truth in any case and non-factive verbs that do not cast a commitment at all (truth or falsehood). See e.g. Karttunen (2012) for the details. Keep in mind, that this not only holds for verbs, but for nouns and adjectives as well. For the ease of presentation, however, we explicate the underlying principles with reference to verbs.

The intuition behind our approach for attitude prediction and role frameing can be illustrated by a couple of simple examples: if A is *against* something that is bad/good for B, then A is for/against B. If A is *for* something that is bad/good for B, then A is against/for B. This is true for the affirmative usage. In order to deal with negation, we just switch the labels (invert them): A *against* (matrix) verb is turned into a *for* verb if negation is present and vice versa. A *bad-for* (subclause) verb is turned into *good-for* if negation is present and vice versa.

We call predicates subcategorizing for a clausal complement *disapprove* predicates if they express an opposition of the opinion holder towards the subclause event (e.g *criticize, is_shocked*). The complementary class are *approve* predicates (e.g. *hope,is_amused*). Verbs with a positive or negative effect on the patient role (e.g. *promote,hurt*) are called *good-for* and *bad-for* verbs, cf. Deng and Wiebe (2015).

Here is an example with negation: A appreciates that B was not promoted. *Appreciate* is an approve verb, *promote* is a good-for (patient) verb, but since negated this turns into a bad-for verb. Approving something that is bad-for someone means to have a negative attitude towards them.

Table 1 shows the composition principles applied to subclause embeddings where the matrix verb is a disapprove verb (e.g. *regret*) and the subclause verb is a good-for verb (e.g. *promote*). An affirmative use (aff == 1) of both, the matrix and the subclause verb leads to a con relation (A regrets that B gets promoted). Negation (aff == 0) switches the value (see the *derived* columns in Tab.1: disapprove $\rightarrow$ approve and good-for $\rightarrow$ bad-for). Any other constellation (e.g. an approve matrix verb and a bad-for subclause verb) can easily be derived from that table.

#	matrix	aff	derived	subclause	aff	derived	attitude
1	A disapproves	1	A disapprove	good-for B	1	good-for B	A con B
2	A disapproves	1	A disapprove	good-for B	0	bad-for B	A pro B
3	A disapproves	0	A approve	good-for B	1	good-for B	A pro B
4	A disapproves	0	A approve	good-for B	0	bad-for B	A con B

Table 1: Principles of the Combination of a Disapprove and a Good-for Verb

We use the verb lexicon of Klenner et al. (2017). For each verb frame we thus know whether it is an approve or disapprove verb (if it takes a complement clause) or whether it is a good-for or bad-for verb (verbs with a patient role). For clauses subcategorizing verbs moreover their commitment (truth, falsehood, no commitment) is specified - for both, the affirmative and the negated usage. We have modelled about 60 German adjectives in order to evaluate our object-oriented prototype. Our system consists of a dependency parser (cf. Sennrich et al. (2009)) and rules for predicate argument extraction[1].

3   An Object-oriented Model in Python

A sentence is represented in Python by dictionaries where the grammatical functions are the keys. Fig. 1 shows the representation for the example sentence *The senate is shocked that the minister helps the president to cheat the people*[2]. For readability, subclauses get their own dictionary variable (c2 and

```
s={'subj':'senate','main':'is_shocked','neg':'no','comp':c2}
c2={'subj':'minister', 'verb':'help','neg':'no','obj':'president','comp':c3}
c3={'subj':'president', 'verb':'cheat','neg':'no','obj':'people'}
```

Figure 1: Representation of the Input Sentence as a Python Dictionary

---

[1]In this paper, we use grammatical functions instead of semantic roles.

[2]We provide an English example, the German version works much like the English one.

c3). The interpretation is triggered by instantiating the main predicate of the matrix clause. We call: eval(s['main'])(s,'t') where *s* is the sentence and *t* means truth committed (affirmative use, no modals present). Interpretation is an outside-in instantiation of the predicates denoted by the verbs, nouns and adjectives of the clauses. Each predicate class has methods to determine attitude and role framing. The polar roles *opinion source* and *opinion target* are set depending on the predicate: two variables, source and target, are used to store the particular grammatical functions that realize these polar roles. Fig. 2

```
class is_shocked(disapprove):
1    def __init__(self,sent,com):
2        self.sc=eval(sent['comp']['verb'])(sent['comp'],'t')
3        self.attitude(sent,self.sc,com)
```

Figure 2: Definition of *is_shocked*

shows the definition of the disapprove predicate *is_shocked*. Both, the disapprove and approve class set the (logical) subject to be the opinion source (i.e. source = 'subj'). The init method has (besides self) two parameters, the sentence and a truth commitment. The commitment that *is_shocked* casts on its subclause is - in any case - *t* (truth commitment), since *is_shocked* is factive. We, thus, directly instantiate (line 2) the subclause verb (sent['comp']['verb'] gives *help*) with the whole subclause (i.e. sent[comp]) and *t* as truth commitment. This call leads to the evaluation of the embedded clause (*help*). The attitude expressed by *is_shocked* is predicted by the method *attitude* in line 3 (self.sc is the instance of *help*, providing access to the source and target of that verb instance).

```
class help(approve, atnan, goodfor):
1    def __init__(self,sent,com):
2        self.sc=eval(sent['comp']['verb'])
3                      (sent['comp'],self.propagates(sent['comp']['neg'],com))
4        self.attitude(sent,self.sc,com)


class atnan:
     def propagates(self,neg,com):
1        if com == 'n': return 'n'
2        elif com == 'f' and neg == 'yes': return 't'
3        elif com == 'f' and neg == 'no':  return 'n'
4        elif com == 't' and neg == 'no':  return 't'
5        elif com == 't' and neg == 'yes': return 'n'
```

Figure 3: Definition of *help*(upper part) and of *propagate*(lower part)

Fig. 3 shows the definition of the approve verb *help*. The opinion target is given by the direct object. This is the contribution of the class *goodfor* (i.e. target='obj', not shown). The truth commitment *help* casts on its subclause depends on the truth commitment it receives from the embedding predicate (here *is_shocked*) and the verb signature and the affirmative status of *help*. The method *propagate* (see Fig. 3 lower part) determines this. *com* is the commitment of the matrix predicate, while *neg* refers to the affirmative status of the embedded verb, here *help*. The class *atnan* models how the truth commitment of the embedding predicate influences the truth commitment of the embedded predicate given that it is truth committing if affirmative (at) and has no commitment if negated (nan, thus the class *atnan*).

If *help* is embedded under *n* (*com* == 'n') which means *no commitment*, like in *A hopes that B helps to free C*, *n* is returned (line 1), i.e. *free* receives no commitment. If it is embedded under negation with a falsehood commitment *f* (line 2) like in *A refuses not to help to free c*, *t* is returned, *free* is truth committed and so on. How commitments propagate depend on the verb (class). According to line 5, no commitment is set if the predicate (*help*) is negated and embedded in a truth committing verb like in *A criticizes that B not helps C to free D*. (i.e. it is unknown whether D is freed by C or not). This is in contrast to verbs like *manage* where the same constellation leads to *f* (*A criticizes that B not manages to free D*).

```
class cheat(badfor):
    def __init__(self,sent,com):
        if com=='t' and sent['neg']=='no': negactor(sent[self.source])
        self.direct-attitude(sent,com)
```

Figure 4: Definition of *cheat*

Fig. 4 shows the definition of *cheat*, a *badfor* verb. The truth commitment wrt. our example is 't' and since it is used affirmatively (i.e. it is factual) the source (self.source = president) is classified as a negative actor (*negactor*). *cheat* expresses a direct (negative) attitude between the source and the target.

```
class badfor:
1     def direct-attitude(self,sent,com):
2         if sent['neg'] == 'no' and com == 't':
3             con(sent[self.source],sent[self.target])
4             negaffected(sent[self.target])
5         elif sent['neg'] == 'yes' and com == 't':
6             pro(sent[self.source],sent[self.target])
7             posaffected(sent[self.target])
. . . .
```

Figure 5: Definition (partial) of *badfor*

The method *direct-attitude* of *badfor* (see Fig. 5) sets a con relation between the source and target in an affirmative context (neg=='no') under a truth commitment 't'. The target then receives a negative effect (*negaffected*). If negated (still under 't'), a pro relation is set and the target is said to be positively affected (*posaffected*). *pro, con, negaffected and posaffected* are for bookkeeping, they store instances and relations.

```
class disapprove(subj-source):
    def indirect-attitude(self,sent,sc,com):
1         if com=='t' and sent['neg'] == 'no'
2             con(sent[self.source],sent[self.comp][sc.source])
3             if sent[self.comp]['neg'] == 'yes':
4                 if isinstance(sc,goodfor):
5                     pro(sent[self.source],sent[self.comp][sc.target])
6                 if isinstance(sc,badfor):
7                     con(sent[self.source],sent[self.comp][sc.target])
8             elif sent[self.comp]['neg'] == 'no':
9                 if isinstance(sc,badfor):
10                    pro(sent[self.source],sent[self.comp][sc.target])
11                if isinstance(sc,goodfor):
12                    con(sent[self.source],sent[self.comp][sc.target])
. . . .
```

Figure 6: Definition (partial) of *disapprove*

While goodfor and badfor verbs express a direct attitude of the verb's source towards the verb's target, approve and disapprove predicates cast an indirect attitude of the source of the matrix predicate on the source (and the target) of the subclause predicate. Fig. 6 shows the (partial) definition of *disapprove*, which inherits from the class *subj-source* (not shown), which just tells that subject is the opinion source (source='subj'). The disapprove class defines the class method *indirect-attitude*. It serves two purposes: the attitude between the source of the matrix predicate and the source of the subclause is determined (here e.g. *con*, line 2). In our example, the disapprove predicate *is_shocked* yields a con relation (line 2) with sent[self.source]=senate and sent[self.comp][sc.source]=sent[self.comp][subj]=minister which establishes: con(senate,minister). If the embedded verb is an instance of goodfor (i.e. has a target, not in our case), then a pro relation between the source (of the matrix predicate) and that target (of the subclause predicate) is set like in e.g. *A criticizes that B not promotes C*. In sum: we get a negactor (president), a negaffected entity (people), three con relations (senate, minster), (minister,people) and (president,people) and a pro relation (minister,president). Other attitudes, namely con(senate,president) and pro(senate,people) are indirectly derivable, e.g. by rules like con(?x,?y) and con(?y,?z) then pro(?x,?z) which gives us pro(senate,people).

4   Related Work

The goal of the rule-based approach of Deng and Wiebe (2014), Deng et al. (2014) and Deng and Wiebe (2015) is to detect entities that are in a positive (PosPair) or negative (NegPair) relation to each other. Rules are realized in the framework of Probabilistic Soft Logic, where the rule weights depend on the output of the preprocessing pipeline, i.e. two SVM classifiers and three existing sentiment analysis systems. The model of Deng and Wiebe (2015) also copes with event-level sentiment inference, however truth commitment is not taken into account. Also, role framing does not play any role in their framework.

Rashkin et al. (2016) have presented an elaborate model that is meant to explicate the relations between all involved entities: the reader, the writer, and the entities referred to by a sentence. Also, the internal states of the referents and their values are part of the model. Their resource, called connotation frames (see also Choi et al. (2016)), was created by crowdsourcing , the model parameters (e.g. values for positive and negative scores) are average values. In contrast, the resources we use and the one we have additionally created are manually specified. Truth commitment etc. is not taken into account in their model.

Klenner and Clematide (2016) introduce a rule-based system for German realized with Description Logic and SWRL. The (numerous) rules also take the affirmative and factuality status of the sentence into account. The goal is to instantiate relations (con and pro) expressing the attitudes of entities towards each other. Recently, Klenner et al. (2017) have revised and augmented their model which now also induces a reader and writer perspective. Our model is meant to solve the attitude prediction and role framing tasks set by Klenner et al. (2017). It is aimed to especially solve cope with a new class of inference indicators, namely predicatively used adjectives.

5   Empirical Evaluation

The focus of this paper lies on predicatively used adjectives. We used the polarity lexicon described in Clematide and Klenner (2010) in order to generate expamples where an adjective is combined with a personal pronoun and a subclause comprising a verb from Klenner and Amsler (2016). For instance, the German version of the sentence *it is provocative that they ignore him* is part of the set of 100 sentences we used. We annotated these sentences wrt. to the attitudes between the virtual writer of such a sentence and the virtual referents (*they,him*). We did neither annotate the attitude between the referents nor the role framing (e.g. *they against him* and *victim(him)*), since these inferences come from the verbs not the adjectives. In other words, we were wondering whether the reasoning scheme that worked for verbs and nouns also worked (without modifications) for adjectives. It turned out that such a model overgenerates. Recall is 100%, but precision is about 83%. The reason is the model predicts an attitude towards the target in each and every case. Given *it is sad that they hurt him*, a positive attitude of the virtual writer of that sentence towards *him* is (correctly) predicted. But this is not so clear in the following sentences: *it is stupid that they cheat him* and *it is jaunty that they laugh at him*. Here, the focus seems to lie much more on the attitude towards the source of the subclause (here *they*). There are also interesting examples where the adjective seems to suppress the attitude normally expressed by the embedded verb. For instance, in *He is responsible that she abandoned her plans* a con relation between *she* and *plan* is incorrect. However, if we replace *responsible* with *happy* such an inference was valid. This inference blocking is not yet covered by our model.

6 Conclusions

We have introduced a prototype of an object-oriented model implemented in Python for attitude prediction and role framing. Compared to previous approaches, our model is lean and it deals not only with predictions derived from verbs and nouns, but also with predicative constructions where an adjective has an effect and a truth commitment on its subcategorized clause. Our claim is that lexical resources are still valuable and that they even are, especially for the kind of reasoning we are interested in, indispensable. Our empirical evaluation revealed that our model is in part overgeneral. We believe that crowdsourcing experiments might help to get a clearer picture of the underlying principles.

References

Choi, E., H. Rashkin, L. Zettlemoyer, and Y. Choi (2016). Document-level sentiment inference with social, faction, and discourse context. In *Proceedings of the 54th Annual Meeting of the Association for Computational Linguistics (ACL)*, Berlin, Germany, pp. 333–343.

Clematide, S. and M. Klenner (2010). Evaluation and extension of a polarity lexicon for German. In *Proceedings of the First Workshop on Computational Approaches to Subjectivity and Sentiment Analysis (WASSA)*, Lisbon, Portugal, pp. 7–13.

Deng, L. and J. Wiebe (2014). Sentiment propagation via implicature constraints. *Meeting of the European Chapter of the Association for Computational Linguistics (EACL-2014)*.

Deng, L. and J. Wiebe (2015). Joint prediction for entity/event-level sentiment analysis using probabilistic soft logic models. In *Proceedings of the Conference on Empirical Methods in Natural Language Processing (EMNLP)*, Lisbon, Portugal, pp. 179–189.

Deng, L., J. Wiebe, and Y. Choi (2014). Joint inference and disambiguation of implicit sentiments via implicature constraints. *Proceedings of COLING*.

Karttunen, L. (2012). Simple and phrasal implicatives. In *Proceedings of the First Joint Conference on Lexical and Computational Semantics - Volume 1: Proceedings of the Main Conference and the Shared Task, and Volume 2: Proceedings of the Sixth International Workshop on Semantic Evaluation*, SemEval '12, Stroudsburg, PA, USA, pp. 124–131. Association for Computational Linguistics.

Klenner, M. and M. Amsler (2016). Sentiframes: A resource for verb-centered German sentiment inference. In *Proceedings of the Tenth International Conference on Language Resources and Evaluation (LREC)*, Portoro, Slovenia, pp. 2888–2891.

Klenner, M. and S. Clematide (2016). How factuality determines sentiment inferences. In I. T. Claire Gardent, Raffaella Bernardi (Ed.), *Proceedings of *SEM 2016: The Fith Joint Conference on Lexical and Computational Semantics*, Berlin, Germany, pp. 75–84.

Klenner, M., D. Tuggener, and S. Clematide (2017). Stance detection in Facebook posts of a German right-wing party. In *Linking Models of Lexical, Sentential and Discourse-level Semantics (LSDSem)*.

Nairn, R., C. Condoravdi, and L. Karttunen (2006). Computing relative polarity for textual inference. In *Proceedings of Inference in Computational Semantics (ICoS 5)*, Buxton, England, pp. 67–75.

Rashkin, H., S. Singh, and Y. Choi (2016). Connotation frames: A data-driven investigation. In *Proceedings of the 54th Annual Meeting of the Association for Computational Linguistics (ACL)*, Berlin, Germany, pp. 311–321.

Sennrich, R., G. Schneider, M. Volk, and M. Warin (2009). A new hybrid dependency parser for German. In *Proceedings of the German Society for Computational Linguistics and Language Technology (GSCL)*, Potsdam, Germany, pp. 115–124.

Argument Structure and Referent Systems

Marcus Kracht
Bielefeld University
marcus.kracht@uni-bielefeld.de

Yousuf Aboamer
Bielefeld University
yousuf.aboamer@uni-bielefeld.de

1   Introduction

We describe here a theory of semantic composition, which integrates referent systems into argument structure. The main idea is that argument structure is the key component in linguistic signs, and that it provides the interface between syntax and semantics. To make this idea work for language, referent systems as defined in Vermeulen (1995) have been used. Referent systems (RS) are based on the idea that the identity of variables *across different representations* is irrelevant (see also Fine (2007)). Thus, whether or not two variables must be taken to be coreferential in the formation of a syntactic constituent must be effected by encoded linguistic cues, be they word order or a particular word form. This basic insight started the present investigation. Many adaptations had to be made in order to make the basic idea compatible with the requirements of natural language.

In RSs the natural merge operation in semantics makes all variables occurring free in the respective representations disjoint. Thus, in contrast to an idea promoted in Zeevat (1989), where variables shared across representations are taken to be pointing to the same object, here this is treated as an unwarranted assumption. In natural languages, however, there are clearly defined circumstances in which certain variables need to be identified during the merge operation, for example when a head is merged with its complement. The way this is done in RSs is that this fact is *explicitly* encoded by means of a shared name. This name is taken from a specified set of names.

This idea has been the starting point of the current theory. This theory takes it that argument structures are lists of argument identification statements (AISs), that need to be discharged one by one in order to reach the phrase level. A discharge is obtained by matching a single variable from the argument structure in both the functor and its argument. This match is subject to several conditions: (i) the variables occur in particular AISs that are visible during match, (ii) the variables have matching names, and (iii) no morphological conditions are violated.

In the present paper we shall simplify the actual theory in order to concentrate on its main engine, the argument structure. In particular, we shall not say much about the morphology. The theory is fully implemented, see the section on implementation for source code.

2   Semantic Structures

Semantic units are called signs. A *sign* is a triple $\langle m, \alpha, \Delta \rangle$, where m is a morpheme (= a set of morphs), α an argument structure and Δ a DRS. Both argument structures and morphs have a combinatorics, that is to say, they specify some number of arguments and modes how they will combine with them. Each morph in m has as many arguments as α. The sign combines any number of morphs that have the same semantics into a single morpheme. This accounts in particular for allomorphy, but may also be used for portmanteau realisation.

A *morph* is a pair $\mathfrak{m} = (\mathfrak{g}, \mathcal{A})$, where $\mathfrak{g}$ is its exponent, typically a string, and $\mathcal{A}$ a vector of so-called selectors (the length of which is called the dimension of $\mathfrak{m}$). The selectors state the number and morphological kind of arguments that the morph requires and in which way their exponents are to be combined with the exponent of the head. If exponents are strings, then we can state (i) that the argument is required to follow the head (the head is looking right for its argument), or (ii) that the argument is required to precede the head (head is looking left). Such statements are given for each argument independently; thus, it may be stated that the subject is to the left, while the direct object is to the right.

The name space is given as follows. We take a finite set A of *attributes*, and a finite set V of *values*, together with a function $o : A \rightarrow \wp(V)$. $o(n)$ is the set of *admissible values* for n (see Gazdar et al. (1988)). A legal *attribute value structure* (AVS) is a set of pairs (n, s), where $n \in A$ and $s \subseteq o(n)$. The sets represent underspecification. An absent name can be added in the form $(n, o(n))$. Thus we may see a legal AVS as a function $f : A \rightarrow \mathcal{P}(V)$ such that for all $n \in A$, $f(n) \subseteq o(n)$. A particular role is played by pairs $(n, \varnothing)$, which we write $(n, \star)$. $\star$ represents the *absence* of a value. A pair (n, s) *matches* a pair (n', s') iff (a) $n = n'$; (b) $s \cap s' \neq \varnothing$ (in which case $s \neq \varnothing$ and $s' \neq \varnothing$) or $s = s' = \varnothing$. Two legal AVSs f and g are *unifiable* if for all $n \in A$ $f(n)$ and $g(n)$ match. In that case, the unification is $(f \cap g)$, the pointwise intersection. A *name* is a fully specified AVS, that is, $f(n)$ is either a singleton or $\star$ for any given n.

In the sequel we use *functor* in place of *head*. When a functor F combines with an argument A, we require that there always be a semantic object, a variable, that needs to be shared between them. (This is called the *main variable*.) The mechanism will be spelled out below. Both the functor and the argument contain an argument structure. Let α be the AVS of the functor and β be the argument structure of the argument. The merge is denoted by $\alpha \bullet \beta$. An *argument structure* is a sequence of argument identification statements (AISs). An *AIS* takes the form

$$(x : \delta : \Sigma :: P)$$

where

1. x is a variable;

2. δ is a diacritic;

3. Σ is a pair of AVSs;

4. P is a pair of parameter AVSs.

We first spell out merge in case α and β contain single AISs: $\alpha = \langle \mu \rangle$, $\beta = \langle \nu \rangle$, where

$$\mu = (x : \delta : \Sigma :: P), \qquad \nu = (y : \epsilon : \Xi :: Q).$$

The diacritic δ contains specific instructions on merge. They specify among other whether x is supplied by the functor or not (we speak of the variable being *exported* or not, indicated by the presence or absence of the diacritic $\triangle$) and whether it is to be supplied by the argument or not (we speak of a variable being *imported* or not, indicated by the presence or absence of the diacritic $\triangledown$). This is a fourfold alternative; yet, since x is in the functor it must be imported by the functor. This reduces the space to two choices: if the functor does not export the variable, the AIS μ will be removed after merge. If it does, the merge $\mu \bullet \nu$ will replace it. This reproduces the argument/adjunct distinction (though it is more general since import names may be changed).

The argument variable y is likewise accompanied by a diacritic, ϵ. As the argument must export its variable, we are left with two options: ν is either importing y or not. In the latter case, the argument structure is not saturated, a case to which we shall return below.

Σ is a pair of AVSs. The first of these determines under which name the variable is imported, the second under which name the variable is exported. If the diacritic says "no export" then the second AVS is left empty (and is omitted in the notation); likewise when the diacritic says "no import" the first AVS is left empty (or is simply omitted). Abstractly speaking, when a variable is both imported and exported, the functor specifies a function from import names to (sets of) export names. However, this function is restricted. The export name is actually underspecified, and so is the import name. Thus, the function is actually undefined or returns the same set of export names. However, the export AVS may contain a special value ✓ for an attribute, in which case the function returns the same value, ie is the identity. Thus the pair

$$[(case, \{nom, acc\}], [(case, ✓)]]$$

returns $[(case, \{nom\})]$ given $[(case, \{nom\})]$ and $[(case, \{acc\})]$ given $[(case, \{acc\})]$. However,

$$[(case, \{nom, acc\}], [(case, \{nom, acc\})]]$$

returns $[(case, \{nom, acc\})]$ for both inputs. This situation is quite frequent. For example, if an adjective A composes with a noun N that can either be nominative or accusative, then if the noun is accusative, so is the complex $[A\,N]$, and if the noun is nominative, so is the complex $[A\,N]$. Thus, the indeterminacy is only in the noun, and the indeterminate value is being passed up "as is", without adding indeterminacies for the new constituent.

The merge is simply function composition. For AVSs, this is spelled out as follows.

$$\Sigma = (f_1, g_1), \qquad \Xi = (f_2, g_2).$$

Primarily, f_1 and g_2 must be unifiable. If so, a new pair of AVSs is being computed. The details are straightforward, but tedious.

With the combination of Σ and Ξ defined, we turn to P and Q. Likewise, they consist of two parts, which are now parameter AVSs. These are sets of statements of the form (π, x), where π is some name (taken from a given set of parameter names), and x a variable. If $P = (U, V)$, and $Q = (U', V')$, then parameters will be unified during merge iff there is a name π such that U contains (π, x) and V' contains (π, y) (where y is potentially a different variable).

When all components match, we first get a pair of substitutions σ_1 and σ_2. The first substitution is to be executed on the first sign (the functor) and the second substitution is to be executed on the second sign (the argument). This substitution is effected on the semantics as well as the argument structure (main variable and parameter AVSs alike). After that a new sign is computed by:

1. applying each morph of the functor to each morph of the argument and keeping only the successful combinations;

2. computing the merge of the argument structures; and

3. taking the union (= Zeevat-merge) of the new DRSs.

We emphasise that the substitutions will unify variables on the basis of the AVSs alone. Thus, if the functor contains x as main variable and the argument contains $y \neq x$, and the merge succeeds, we will have $\sigma_1(x) = \sigma_2(y)$. However, if they do not get identified, then $\sigma_1(x) \neq \sigma_2(y)$. Likewise, if the first sign contains x and so does not the second, then $\sigma_1(x) \neq \sigma_2(x)$ *unless they are identified under merge*. This is a desired outcome.

Crucially, the number of arguments that are needed in morphology is the same as the number of arguments given by the argument structure. This says nothing else but that each time a syntactic nexus is established, some semantic merge must be performed—and conversely.

Here is a simple case of how this works. A verb may contain a specification of its subject in the following form.

$$/rennen/ : (x : \nabla : \begin{bmatrix} \text{pers} : \{1, 3\} \\ \text{num}: \quad \{pl\} \\ \text{case}:\{nom\} \end{bmatrix} ::)$$

This says that the variable x is imported under merge under the name nominative-1st-plural or nominative-3rd-plural (a third option, that this is the infinitive, has been omitted). A pronoun in turn can contain the following

$$\text{/wir/}: (y : \triangle: \begin{bmatrix} \text{pers}: & \{1\} \\ \text{num}: & \{pl\} \\ \text{case}: \{nom\} \end{bmatrix} ::)$$

In that case the AISs merge successfully, and the complex has an empty argument structure. Moreover, the substitutions will be arranged such that $\sigma_1(x) = \sigma_2(y)$. Thus, the constituent /wir rennen/ is well formed, since they have the argument structures displayed above. By contrast, the following is not well-formed: /uns rennen/, even if the pronoun is given the following argument structure:

$$\text{/uns/}: (x : \triangle: \begin{bmatrix} \text{pers}: & \{1\} \\ \text{num}: & \{pl\} \\ \text{case}: \{acc\} \end{bmatrix} ::)$$

This is because accusative case blocks identification under merge, irrespective of the actual variable chosen.

3 Merge and Fusion

So far we have only talked about the case of a single AIS in each argument structure. Now we need to go full scale. First, say that an argument structure is *saturated* if none of its AISs imports a variable. There are now two kinds of merge: *proper merge* and *fusion*. Fusion is marked option. In a proper merge the argument structure of the complement is saturated. In a fusion it is not. The diacritic (in addition to the above fourfold choice) states whether the particular AIS allows for fusion.

Second, it is theoretically possible to identify several variables under merge. A merge is called n-ary if exactly n AISs are merged at the same time. A *monadic merge* is a 1-ary merge. A *polyadic merge* is an n-ary merge with $n > 1$. This option is used on control constructions. In the sentence /Bert persuaded Mary to leave./ it is Mary who does the leaving, while in /Bert promised Mary to leave./ it is Bert. This is accomplished by assigning the infinitive /to leave/ its semantic arguments, including the actor. However, the actor is not imported, it is exported on a par with the the event variable. Thus, when the higher verb identifies the event variable, it will also identify the actor. In this case, it can choose to either make it the same as the subject (in the case of /promise/) or the same as the theme (in the case of /persuade/).

Third, when the argument structures contain several AISs, access conditions apply. Suppose that

$$\alpha = (\mu_1, \mu_2, \cdots, \mu_k)$$

and that

$$\beta = (\nu_1, \nu_2, \cdots, \nu_\ell).$$

Then in a monadic merge

1. ν_1 must export a variable; and

2. for the largest (!) j such that $\mu_j \bullet \nu_1$ succeeds the following holds:

   - the global option of E-access is valid and $j = k$; or
   - the global option of G-access is valid and for no $i > j$, the variable of ν_i is a barrier.

In a polyadic merge, we inspect ν_2 for the next exported variable, and try to see if some μ_i, $i < j$, imports it. And so on.

To explain this, we need to resort to diacritics again. In a diacritic, a further specification is being made: whether the AISs can be skipped in merge or not (in the latter case it is a *barrier*). Now, a grammar is *E-access* if all AISs are barriers. A grammar is otherwise *G-access*.

To explain this notion, consider a language with case markers. Say a verb has an argument structure of the following form (think a verb in a language with subject agreement):

$$/\text{zumuten}/ : (x : \nabla : \begin{bmatrix} \text{pers}: \{1,3\} \\ \text{num:} \quad \{pl\} \\ \text{case}: \{nom\} \end{bmatrix} \; ::), (y : \nabla : [\; \text{case}: \{acc\} \;] \; ::), (z : \nabla : [\; \text{case}: \{dat\} \;] \; ::)$$

An NP that is marked for dative case can merge in both access conditions. For the last of the AISs matches the case of the NP. An NP with accusative can match only if it is allowed to skip the dative. An NP with nominative case can match only if it is allowed to skip both the dative and the accusative. So, given that arguments are to the left, under E-access only the following is grammatical:

NP-nom NP-acc NP-dat V

Given G-access and no variable is a barrier, we get 6 possibilities:

NP-nom NP-acc NP-dat V
NP-nom NP-dat NP-acc V
NP-acc NP-nom NP-dat V
NP-acc NP-dat NP-nom V
NP-dat NP-nom NP-acc V
NP-dat NP-acc NP-nom V

If word order is different, then matters can become more involved. For example, if only the nominative NP is to the left, there are only two patterns left:

NP-nom V NP-acc NP-dat
NP-nom V NP-dat NP-acc

In this way one can account for different word order patterns in languages. In Latin all word orders are well formed (though some may be dispreferred), while in English only one is permitted (/John gave a book to Mary/). German patterns like Latin, however verb-second complicates matters substantially.

4   Agreement

Grammar formalisms can be largely divided into those that base themselves on agreement (HPSG) and those that base themselves on cancellation (Categorial Grammar). The present framework combines cancellation with agreement. It performs *cancellation under agreement*. Thus, it is similar to some variant of UCG (unification categorial grammar, Calder et al. (1988)), however its categorial apparatus is greatly reduced.

It takes its motivation from the fact that agreement is one of the main inputs in deciding the association between variables across constituents. In many languages this is case; however, head marking regimes also exist. For example, in German a verb displays subject agreement. This fact not only regiments the proper form of the subject, as in the case of */uns rennen/ above. It also helps to disambiguate sentences as in /Uns haben die Fragen geholfen./ "The questions were helpful for us.". The fact that the pronoun in first position, /uns/, is in the accusative, means that it cannot be subject. German allows for G-type access, so accusative NP may be sentence initial. On the other hand, /die Fragen/ ("the questions") may be both nominative and accusative. It turns out that only when

we decide them to be nominative is the sentence grammatical. This is borne out, assuming the following.
(1) The verb /helfen/ has the argument structure

$$
/\texttt{helfen}/ : (x : \nabla : \left[\begin{array}{ll} \text{pers}: & \{1,3\} \\ \text{num}: & \{pl\} \\ \text{case}: & \{nom\} \end{array}\right] ::), (y : \nabla : [\ \text{case}:\{acc\}\ ] ::)
$$

(2) The NP /die Fragen/ has two separate argument structures:

$$
/\texttt{die Fragen}/ : (x :\Delta: \left[\begin{array}{ll} \text{pers}: & \{3\} \\ \text{num}: & \{pl\} \\ \text{case}: & \{acc\} \end{array}\right] ::)
$$

and

$$
/\texttt{die Fragen}/ : (x :\Delta: \left[\begin{array}{ll} \text{pers}: & \{3\} \\ \text{num}: & \{pl\} \\ \text{case}: & \{nom\} \end{array}\right] ::)
$$

(3) The pronoun /uns/ has the structure

$$
/\texttt{uns}/ : (x :\Delta: \left[\begin{array}{ll} \text{pers}: & \{1\} \\ \text{num}: & \{pl\} \\ \text{case}: & \{acc\} \end{array}\right] ::)
$$

(We do not display the morphology here, for it is quite complicated.) Choosing a single entry in (2) with underspecified case gives the wrong result.

The calculus admits as many marking patterns for a verb as there are arguments that it takes. Therefore, it is possible to have no agreement (Chinese), subject agreement (German), subject and object agreement (Mordvin), and more. Similarly, adjectives may exhibit agreement with the noun they modify.

5 Parameters

The parameters are another important feature. Recall that an AIS contains a pair (U, V) of parameter AVSs. These consist of pairs (π, x), where x is a variable and π a parameter name. There is no prohibition for a variable to occur both as a parameter and as a main variable of the AIS. Also, variables may be assigned different parameter rules in import and in export AVSs.

A particularly instructive use of parameters is the phenomenon of sequence-of-tense (Abusch (1997), Ogihara (1996)). Recall that languages differ in how they use morphological tenses in subordinate clauses. Some languages require subordinate clauses to use nonpresent when the superordinate clause is in the past: /John said that he was ill./. Others require present tense if the subordinate clause is cotemporaneous with the event of the main clause. Russian is such a language. The phenomenon is explained as follows. Choose two parameter names, ρ ("reference time") and ε ("event time"). Put the argument structure of /said/ as

$$
(e :\Delta: [\ \ ] :: \left[\begin{array}{l} \rho{:}\,t \\ \varepsilon{:}t' \end{array}\right]), (x : \nabla : [\ \ ] ::), (e' : \nabla : [\ \ ] :: [\ \ ], [\ \rho{:}t'\ ])
$$

(irrelevant detail omitted) and in the semantics the statement $t' < t$ is added as well. Now, present tense may either be deictic (in which case it states that the event takes place at reference time) or it may be relational, in which case the event takes place at the event time of the higher predicate. To implement this, we give it the following argument structure:

$$
(e :\Delta: [\ \ ] :: \left[\begin{array}{l} \rho{:}\,t \\ \varepsilon{:}t' \end{array}\right])
$$

with $t = t'$. The idea is this. A verb of saying has a complement, and this complement needs to be situated in time. The higher verb decides whether the reference time of the embedded clause is its own reference time, or whether it is taken to be its event time. The first choice is realised in English. Reference time is not shifted. The second choice is realised in Russian. Reference time is shifted, because it is set to the event time of the higher clause.

We may combine this with a more fully fledged account of tense and aspect (as of Klein (1994)), but the core insight is as explained above, only that one more parameter is added and the choice of identification is multiplied further.

Time points are by far not the only parameters. From the evidence provided in Schlenker (2003) also worlds and speaker roles are shiftable, and therefore assume parameter roles. There are more: properties (to account for adjectives), locations, and even experiencers, eg for expressions of taste, see Kneer et al. (2017).

6 Implementation

Absent copying, the formalism leads to what is known as Multicomponent CFGs (Seki et al. (1991)). If copying is allowed, depending on further restrictions, the full power of Literal Movement Grammars can be achieved, equivalent to PTIME parseability (Groenink (1997), Kracht (2003)). Unlike Mel'cuk (2000) it is completely surface oriented.

The calculus has been faithfully implemented (in OCaml) and can be downloaded at

wwwhomes.uni-bielefeld.de/mkracht/referent/

This site contains the complete description together with a user manual as well as the source code and dictionaries for Hungarian nouns and basic Latin morphology.

Data is stored in a special XML-format. It handles UTF-8. Output can be rendered into XML or LaTeX and then shown via standard DVI or PDF viewers. This ensures high quality output. Based on a dictionary, one can either merge entries, or parse strings. The parser is a chart parser adapted for discontinuity. Morphs may be empty, but a special rank function ensures that this does not lead to infinite loops. The system has not primarily been designed for speed but to faithfully compute according to the theory. A chart parser has been chosen to determine all possible parses.

As an example we show here the entry of the verbal root /tang/ "to touch" of the Latin dictionary (as given in the online resource).

Id:tang

$$\mathbf{*}.(\circ,0)./\texttt{tac}/\langle\,[\ \text{BASE} : p; \text{LEVEL} : r; \text{STEM} : c\ ] : 0\,\rangle$$
$$\mathbf{*}.(\circ,0)./\texttt{tang}/\langle\,[\ \text{BASE} : a; \text{LEVEL} : r; \text{STEM} : c\ ] : 0\,\rangle$$
$$\mathbf{*}.(\circ,0)./\texttt{tetig}/\langle\,[\ \text{BASE} : f; \text{STEM} : c\ ] : 0\,\rangle$$

$\langle e0 : \triangle :$	$\begin{bmatrix} \text{ASP} & : & * \\ \text{CAT} & : & \nu \\ \text{MOOD} & : & * \\ \text{TENSE} & : & * \\ \text{TRS} & : & 2 \\ \text{VOICE} & : & * \end{bmatrix}$	$:: \begin{bmatrix} \text{gf2} & : & \text{x1} \\ \text{gf1} & : & \text{x0} \end{bmatrix} \rangle$

e0; x0; x1

touch$'$(e0); agt$'$(e0) = x0;   thm$'$(e0) = x1.

Parse terms:
$\mathbf{*}$.tang : mr104
$\mathbf{*}$.tang : mr105
$\mathbf{*}$.tang : mr106

The first line is the identifier, an arbitrarily chosen string. The next lines specify the morphs. There are in total three morphs, corresponding to the three stems: /tang/, /tetig/, and /tact/. Each of them is accompanied by some morphological properties. Colours are used to highlight identical arguments across morphs and the argument structure.

Below that are found three boxes. The first contains the argument structure, the second the semantics (a DRS with head section and body), and finally a box containing the parse terms for the morphs. Three are listed, coindexed (by the stars of different shape) with the morphs given upstairs. Notice that the parse terms record the identifier as well as the morph contained in the entry.

The argument structure of a root is minimal: it exports an event variable, e. The category is specified as v (verbal) and the transitivity as 2. All other attributes have no value. The parameter AVS lists two parameters (for agent and theme).

7   Conclusion

The design criterion of this calculus has been to derive the complexity of phenomena from an interaction of several components, each of which are quite simple. In the morphology, we allow for discontinuous constituents, and each part can specify a limited context condition. Morphs are composed by piecing together the discontinuous parts in a specified manner. Allomorphy is explained by the fact that morphs specify context conditions; different morphs under the same morpheme may thus compete for the contexts.

The semantic algorithm is independent of this, however. It only takes into account whether the morphemes can be combined or not. Thus, in contrast to Morrill (2017), the discontinuity is not reflected in the categorical system. The main driver of semantic composition, by contrast, is the argument structure, which combines morphosyntactically supplied specification (AVSs) with semantic names of variables.

The third component, the semantics proper, is yet again independent. It is subjected to substitution before merge, where the substitution is calculated from the merge of argument structures.

The presented calculus is quite powerful. It has been designed to deal with the semantics in combination both with morphology and syntax. We do not draw a line between purely syntactic or purely morphological formation. Thus, there is no commitment to the lexical integrity principle. For example, it can be shown that case marking in Hungarian is best viewed as phrasal affixation. We have omitted the details of morphological analysis here. It is possible to decompose full paradigms (eg the nominal paradigm in Hungarian, the verbal paradigm in Latin) and give them the correct semantics, calculated bottom up.

The link with overt morphology and syntactic features is theoretically arbitrary. This is a drawback, which the calculus shares however with the overwhelming majority of frameworks. Further work is needed. We would ideally like to propose eg that in a language without overt gender marking (like Finnish or Hungarian) no attribute for gender exists. However, at this point, it is not prohibited to posit one, and not even mandatory that it have only one value.

References

Abusch, D. (1997). Sequence of tense and temporal *de re*. *Linguistics and Philosophy 20*, 1–50.

Calder, J., E. Klein, and H. Zeevat (1988). Unification Categorial Grammar: A Concise Extendable Grammar for Natural Language Processing. In *Proceedings of COLING 12, Budapest*, pp. 83–86.

Fine, K. (2007). *Semantic relationism*. London: Blackwell.

Gazdar, G., G. Pullum, R. Carpenter, T. Hukari, and R. Levine (1988). Category structures. *Computational Linguistics 14*, 1–19.

Groenink, A. (1997). *Surface without Structure. Word Order and Tractability Issues in Natural Language Analysis*. Ph. D. thesis, University of Utrecht.

Klein, W. (1994). *Time in Language*. London: Routledge.

Kneer, M., A. Vicente, and D. Zeman (2017). Relativism about predicates of personal taste and perspectival plurality. *Linguistics and Philosophy 40*, 37–60.

Kracht, M. (2003). *Mathematics of Language*. Berlin: Mouton de Gruyter.

Mel'cuk, I. (1993 – 2000). *Cours de Morphologie Générale*, Volume 1 – 5. Les Presses de l'Université de Montréal.

Morrill, G. V. (2017). Grammar logicised: relativisation. *Linguistics and Philosophy 40*, 119–163.

Ogihara, T. (1996). *Tense, Attitudes and Scope*. Dordrecht: Kluwer.

Schlenker, P. (2003). A Plea for Monsters. *Linguistics and Philosophy 26*, 29–120.

Seki, H., T. Matsumura, M. Fujii, and T. Kasami (1991). On multiple context–free grammars. *Theoretical Computer Science 88*, 191–229.

Vermeulen, K. F. M. (1995). Merging without mystery or: Variables in dynamic semantics. *Journal of Philosophical Logic 24*, 405–450.

Zeevat, H. (1989). A compositional approach to Discourse Representation Theory. *Linguistics and Philosophy 12*, 95–131.

Communicating and Acting:
Understanding Gesture in Simulation Semantics

Nikhil Krishnaswamy[1], Pradyumna Narayana[2], Isaac Wang[3], Kyeongmin Rim[1], Rahul Bangar[2], Dhruva Patil[2], Gururaj Mulay[2], Ross Beveridge[2], Jaime Ruiz[3], Bruce Draper[2], and James Pustejovsky[1]

[1]Dept. of Comp. Sci., Brandeis University, Waltham, MA, USA
[2]Dept. of Comp. Sci., Colorado State University, Fort Collins, CO, USA
[3]Dept. of Comp. and Info. Sci. and Eng., University of Florida, Gainesville, FL, USA
{nkrishna,krim,jamesp}@brandeis.edu, {prady,rahul.bangar,dkpatil,guru5,
ross.beveridge,draper}@colostate.edu, {wangi,jaime.ruiz}@ufl.edu

Abstract

In this paper, we introduce an architecture for multimodal communication between humans and computers engaged in a shared task. We describe a representative dialogue between an artificial agent and a human that will be demonstrated live during the presentation. This assumes a multimodal environment and semantics for facilitating communication and interaction with a computational agent. To this end, we have created an embodied 3D simulation environment enabling both the generation and interpretation of multiple modalities, including: language, gesture, and the visualization of objects moving and agents performing actions. Objects are encoded with rich semantic typing and action affordances, while actions themselves are encoded as multimodal expressions (programs), allowing for contextually salient inferences and decisions in the environment.

1   Introduction

In order to facilitate collaborative communication between a human and a computational agent, we have been working to integrate a multimodal model of semantics (*Multimodal Semantic Simulations, MSS*) with a real-time visual recognition system for identifying human gestures. The language VoxML, Visual Object Concept Modeling Language (Pustejovsky and Krishnaswamy, 2016), is used as the platform for multimodal semantic simulations in the context of human-computer communication. Gestural input is recognized in real time by a convolutional neural net-based machine vision system networked to the simulation environment, which is configured for joint activity and communication between a human and a computational agent. This involves the integration of inputs from speech, gesture, and action, as mediated through a dialogue manager (DM) that tracks discourse and situational context variables embodied in a shared situated simulation. Hence, the dynamic of human-computer interaction changes from giving and receiving orders to a *peer-to-peer conversation*.

We explore this idea in the context of the blocks world. In particular, we consider a scenario in which one person (the *builder*) has a table with blocks that another person (the *signaler*) can see. We also assume the builder and signaler can see each other. The signaler is then given a pattern of blocks, and their job is to get the builder to recreate the pattern. While blocks world is obviously not a real-world application, it serves as a surrogate for any cooperative task where both partners share a workspace.

Our system design and gesture vocabulary are taken primarily from an elicitation study, similar to that introduced in Wobbrock et al. (2009) but with differences in the way gestures are elicited. The purpose of the study underlying our gesture vocabulary (Wang et al., 2017a,b) was to analyze the natural dyadic communication used by two people when engaging in solving a collaborative task.

We asked pairs of participants to collaboratively build different pre-determined structures using wooden blocks. Participants were put in separate rooms with similar setups. Each participant stood in front of a table facing a TV screen on the opposite end of the table. Microsoft Kinect v2 sensors were

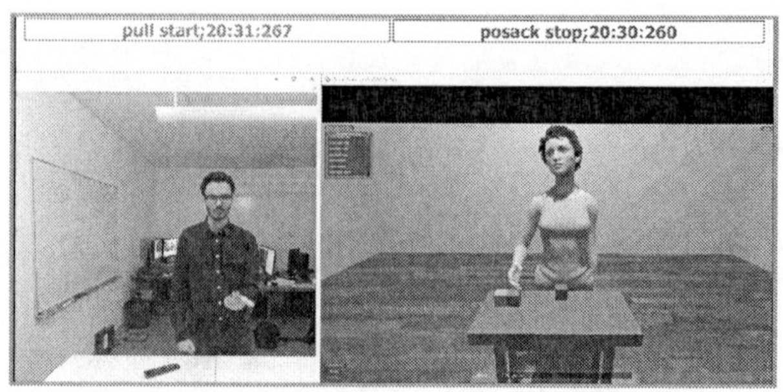

Figure 1: Prototype peer-to-peer interface

also set up on the opposite end, facing the participant. We developed software to stream live video (and audio) from the Kinect sensors between the two setups so that participants could communicate with each other as if they were facing each other at opposite ends of the same table. The Kinect sensors were also used to record the experiment, providing us with RGB video, depth data, and motion capture skeletons.

One participant was given the role of builder and was provided with a set of 12 wooden cubes (with 4-inch sides). The other participant was given the role of signaler and was given an image of an arrangement, or layout, of these blocks. The signaler was assigned the task of communicating to and directing the builder to replicate the layout; the builder needed to respond to the signalers commands by placing and arranging the blocks on the table. The table acted as a shared workspace, as blocks placed on the table could be seen by both participants (although from opposite perspectives). Not all 12 blocks were used for every layout, and the signaler was not allowed to show the layout to the builder.

Since we wanted to observe natural communication in action, participants were also not allowed to talk or strategize beforehand, and no instruction on how to speak/gesture was given from the experimenter. A trial began when the experimenter presented a new block layout to the signaler and ended when the participants replicated the block layout. Communication between the two varied across three conditions:

(1) the signaler and builder could both see and hear each other;

(2) the signaler and builder could see but not hear each other;

(3) the signaler could see the builder (and therefore the blocks on the table), but the builder can only hear the signaler.

In our working prototype human-computer system, the signaler is a person and the builder is an avatar, with a virtual table and virtual blocks. The signaler can see a graphical projection of the virtual world, and communicates to the avatar through gestures. The avatar communicates back through language (text or speech), gesture, and action in the form of moving blocks (cf. Figure 1). In particular, we took initial inspiration for the system design from the setup within the elicitation study where the participants could only see but not hear each other, removing the audio channel entirely and forcing them to rely on gestures to communicate, in order to assess the impact that gesture had on the communication. Therefore the initial setup only allowed the signaler to communicate though gesture, and subsequent refinements have introduced speech and language input to the signaler's capability, increasing the level of communicative symmetry in the interaction.

2   Related Work

Multimodal interfaces combining language and gesture are found in the literature since Bolt's "Put-that-there" system (1980), which anticipated some of the issues discussed herein, including the use of deixis to disambiguate references, and also inspired a community surrounding multimodal integration (e.g., Dumas et al. (2009); Kennington et al. (2013); Turk (2014)).

The psychological motivation for multimodal interfaces, as epitomized by Quek et al. (2002), holds that speech and gesture are coexpressive and processed partially independently, and therefore complement each other. Using both modalities increases human working memory and decreases cognitive load (Dumas et al., 2009), allowing people to retain more information and learn faster.

Visual information has been shown to be particularly useful in establishing common ground (Clark and Wilkes-Gibbs, 1986; Clark and Brennan, 1991; Dillenbourg and Traum, 2006; Eisenstein et al., 2008b,a), or mutual understanding that enables further communication. Other research in HCI additionally emphasizes the importance of shared visual workspaces in computer-mediated communication (Fussell et al., 2000, 2004; Kraut et al., 2003; Gergle et al., 2004), highlighting the usefulness of non-verbal communication in coordination between humans (Cassell et al., 2000; Cassell, 2000).

Brennan et al. (2008) shows that allowing for shared gaze increased performance in spatial tasks in paired collaborations. Multimodal systems of gaze and speech have also been studied in interaction with robots and virtual avatars (Andrist et al., 2017; Mehlmann et al., 2014; Skantze et al., 2014). However, few systems have centered the use of language and gesture in collaborative and communicative scenarios.

Communicating with computers becomes even more interesting in the context of shared physical tasks. When people work together, their conversation consists of more than just words. They gesture and they share a common workspace (Lascarides and Stone, 2006, 2009b; Clair et al., 2010; Matuszek et al., 2014). Their shared perception of this workspace is the context for their conversation, and it is this shared space that gives many gestures, such as pointing, their meaning (Krishnaswamy and Pustejovsky, 2016a). The dynamic computation of discourse (Asher and Lascarides, 2003), furthermore, becomes more complex when multiple modalities are at play. Fortunately, embodied actions (such as coverbal gestures) do not seem to violate coherence relations (Lascarides and Stone, 2009a).

Many of the components used here will be familiar, in role if not in details. Visual gesture recognition has long been a challenge (Jaimes and Sebe, 2007; Madeo et al., 2016). Gesture recognition in this system is facilitated by Microsoft Kinect depth sensing (Zhang, 2012) and ResNet-style deep convolutional neural networks (DCNNs) (He et al., 2016) implemented in TensorFlow (Abadi et al., 2016).

The avatar and her virtual blocks world are implemented with VoxSim, a semantically-informed reasoning system previously described by Krishnaswamy and Pustejovsky (2016b) that allows the avatar to react to gestural events with both actions and words.

3 Communicating through Gesture, Language and Action

The system operates in real time, allowing the human signaler to gesture to the avatar. In return, the avatar can gesture, speak with the words also printed on screen, or communicate through actions by moving blocks. This system, the human/avatar blocks world (HAB) allows us to explore peer-to-peer communication between people and computers.

While the HAB implementation relies on many components, here we focus on the real-time gesture recognition module, which recognizes gestures by the signaler, the grounded semantics module (VoxSim), which determines the avatar's response to gestures, and the interplay between them. VoxSim is described in Subsection 3.1, gesture recognition is described in Subsection 3.2, while the interactions between the two are described in Subsection 3.3.

3.1 VoxSim

The HAB system's virtual world is built on the VoxSim platform (Krishnaswamy and Pustejovsky, 2016a,b), an open-source, semantically-informed 3D visual event simulator implemented in the Unity game engine (Goldstone, 2009) that leverages game engine graphics processing, UI, and physics to operationalize events described in natural language within a virtual environment.

VoxSim maps natural language event semantics through a dynamic interval temporal logic (DITL) (Pustejovsky and Moszkowicz, 2011) and the modeling language VoxML (Pustejovsky and Krishnaswamy, 2016). VoxML encodes qualitative and geometrical knowledge about objects and events that is presupposed in linguistic utterances but not made explicit, in a visual modality. This includes information about symmetry or concavity in an object's geometry, the relations resulting from an event, the qualitative relations described by a positional adjunct, or behaviors *afforded* by an object's *habitat* (Pustejovsky, 2013; McDonald and Pustejovsky, 2014) associated with the situational context that enables or disables certain actions that may be undertaken using the object. Such information is a natural extension of the lexical semantic typing provided within Generative Lexicon Theory (Pustejovsky, 1995), cf. also Asher (2011), towards a semantics of embodiment. This allows the HAB system to determine which regions, objects, or parts of objects may be indicated by gestures such as deixis or action referentials, and the natural language interface allows for human-understandable disambiguation. Object motion and agent motion are compositional in the VoxML framework, allowing VoxSim to easily separate them in the virtual world, so the gesture used to refer to an action (or program) can be directly mapped to the action itself, establishing a shared context grounded from the perspective of both the human and the computer program.

3.1.1   Dialogue Manager

Avatar-directed dialogue serves to manage the flow of control through either requesting disambiguation in the previously-established context, acknowledging receipt of a gesture, or expressing completion of an action. Dialogue output from the avatar is usually accompanied by a complementary gesture, such as deixis of a block or region, or enactment of a program over an object. The dialogue manager (DM) maintains a queue of possible outputs based on what additional information the avatar needs to know to complete its next action, including unique disambiguating attributes of the blocks (e.g., distinguishing color) or disambiguating labels of the actions (e.g., possible relational interpretations of a gesture, relative to the table or a block). It then composes questions or statements based on these qualities, in order to give the human signaler the most complete amount of information needed to interpret the received gestures.

For instance, when presented with a gesture indicating a region of the table that currently contains a green block and a red block, the dialogue manager takes the possible entities indicated (here, the set of two blocks), and calculates those attributes unique to each one (here, distinct colors). The avatar can then present the human with questions of the form *"Are you pointing to the* [COLOR] *block?"* that the human can answer either in the affirmative or negative, in order to communicate their intent. This same process can be used to disambiguate the particulars of actions, such as requesting clarification about the location to which a block is intended to be moved. Some specific examples of this are discussed in Sections 3.3 and 3.4.

While having the avatar explicitly ask if the human is indicating a particular block or action is one way of replicating a naturalistic interaction, having this repetitive process be the only way of resolving ambiguity does not exercise the variety of methods humans would use with each other in the same task. Particularly, if many options must be iterated through before the avatar arrives at the intended one, then the interaction risks becoming tedious. To this end, it may often be more useful and more naturalistic for the avatar to ask an open-ended question that the human can answer using one of their available modalities. For example when presented with an ambiguous block choice, the avatar might instead ask the human "Which block?" to which the human can respond with some distinguishing attribute as has already been determined for the possible blocks under question, such as relative orientation or color. Something like relative orientation can be easily communicated through gesture, as in the context of the question very coarse-grained directional deixis can suffice to distinguish the "left" block from the "right" block or the "near you" block from the "near me" block. An attribute like color cannot be easily communicated through gesture, but we have been working on integrating speech input on the human's side, and so a question such as "Which block?" could be answered with "The red one" or simply "red," and VoxSim can map that attribute to the block in the scene that has it. The addition of speech recognition to the human's input, and speech synthesis to the avatar's output parallels the gesture recognition capability and the animated avatar gesture generation in VoxSim, bringing a measure of symmetry to the communication in both modalities.

3.2   Gesture Recognition

The gesture recognition module independently labels five body parts. The left and right hands are both labeled according to their pose. The system is trained to recognize 34 distinct hand gestures in depth images, plus an "other" label, used for hands at rest or in unknown poses. Hand poses are directional, such that pointing down is considered a different pose than pointing to the right. Head motions are classified as either nod, shake or other based on a time window of depth difference images. Finally, the left and right arms are labeled according to their direction of motion, based on the skeleton pose estimates generated by the Microsoft Kinect (Zhang, 2012).

Real-time gesture recognition is spread across 6 processors, as shown in Figure 2: *Kinect Host* segments hands and head data from skeleton data gathered from the Kinect atop the signaler's monitor, producing 3 depth streams; *Right Hand Pose*, *Left Hand Pose*, and *Head Motion* are each ResNet-style deep convolutional neural networks (DCNNs) (He et al., 2016) on nVidia Titan X GPUs; *Arm Motion* labels arm directions from skeleton data; *Gesture Fusion* collects the hand, arm and head labels and fuses them using finite state machines to detect gestures.

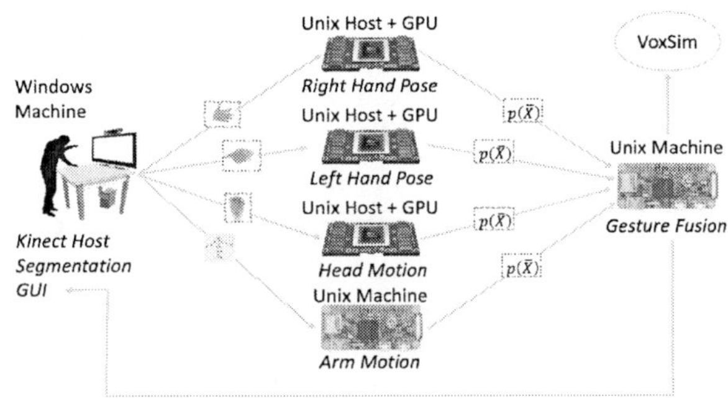

Figure 2: The architecture of the real-time gesture recognition module

3.3   Gestures & VoxSim

VoxSim receives gestural "words" from the gesture recognizer, and interprets them at a contextually-wrapped compositional semantic level. For the moment, interface is limited to seven such "words" chosen due to their frequent occurrence in the elicitation study described in Section 1:

1. Engage. Begins the task when the signaler steps up to the table, and ends it when they step back.

2. Positive acknowledge. A head nod or a "thumbs up" pose with either or both hands. Used to signal agreement with a choice by the avatar or affirmative response to a question.

3. Negative acknowledge. A head shake, "thumbs down" with either or both hands, or palm-forward "stop" sign. Signals disagreement with a choice by the avatar or negative response to a question.

4. Point. Pointing (deixis) includes the direction of the hand and/or arm motion: one or two of front, back, left, right, up, or down. Indicates a region or block(s) in that region.

5. Grab. A "claw," mimicking grabbing a block. Tells the avatar to grasp an indicated block.

6. Carry. Moving the arm in a direction while the hand is in the grab position. "Carry up" can be thought of as *pick up*, while "carry down" is equivalent to *put down*.

7. Push. A flat hand moving in the direction of the open palm. Like "carry," but without the up or down directions. A beckoning motion signals the avatar to push a block toward the signaler.

Importantly, the semantics of each of these gestures is *compositional* and *context-dependent*. The "directional" gestures, that is "point," "carry," and "push," require a direction for a complete interpretation. Pointing provides the indexicals or "nouns" that are used as arguments for subsequent action gestures or "verbs."

Context is typically introduced through objects or possible objects indicated. For example, "grab" has a distinct interpretation in the blocks world context, but could be interpreted and enacted differently over a different set of objects, particularly if those objects afford grasping in a manner different from the claw-like hand position used with small blocks.

All gestures are interpreted in the current context, which is established by previously undertaken actions by both the human and the avatar. For instance, if at the beginning of the scene, the human first makes the "grab" gesture as described above, and has not indicated a block which they intend the avatar to grasp, the gesture is not provided with enough context to be completely interpreted and the avatar must return with a question of uncertainty; she cannot, from the information provided by the gesture and current context, determine what is meant. If the human begins by pointing to a region of the table, the context makes it necessary to look for potential blocks that must be indicated. If no blocks exist in that area of the table the avatar must say she doesn't know what the human means to indicate; if more than one block exists there, she must ask for clarification. Examples of these ambiguities are discussed below and in Section 3.4.

The avatar can communicate its interpretation and intent to the human in multiple modalities. The human can see the avatar enacting a command in context when it moves blocks in the virtual world. The avatar can also communicate through gesture, for example by reaching toward a block. Finally, the avatar can speak to the signaler through text or speech output, to initiate requests for clarification if necessary.

When VoxSim receives a semantic gesture from the recognition module, it parses the meaning of the gesture in the context of the current state occupied by the avatar and the blocks. For example, if the humans points to the right and the avatar is currently holding a block, then the gesture may be a request to move the block to the right. Alternatively, if the avatar is not currently holding a block, the same gesture may indicate a block on the right side of the table for the next action.

Gestural ambiguities are common. If there are two blocks on the right side of the table and the signaler points to the right, which block do they mean? Similarly, a gesture to put a block down may be ambiguous: should the avatar put the block down on top of the block below it, or next to it?

When presented with ambiguous gestures, VoxSim asks the signaler to choose among the possible interpretations. VoxSim orders the options according to a set of heuristics derived from common human intentions observed in the aforementioned elicitation studies. For example, if the options are to put a red block on top of a blue block or next to it, VoxSim favors the stacking option. It will ask the signaler if the first option is the desired choice (e.g., "Should I put the red block on top of the blue block?"). It will iterate through the options until it receives a positive acknowledgement or runs out of options, in which case it tells the signaler that it does not understand and waits for a new gesture.

3.4 Building a Three-block Staircase

Figure 3 depicts the process of building a three-block staircase, an example scenario as can be demonstrated using the HAB system. In Frame A, the signaler, having engaged the avatar in the task, points to the left, which the avatar interprets as indicating the blue block and gestures to that block, in acknowledgment. In Frame B, having directed the avatar to move the blue back away from her, the signaler points to the right. This is ambiguous, since there are two blocks there, so the avatar asks if the signaler means the red block. The signaler shakes his head, so the avatar asks about the green block. The signaler nods, then directs the avatar to push the green block toward him. The signaler points to the blue block, then gestures to slide it to the right (Frame C). The avatar asks for disambiguation: should it slide the block all the way to the green block? The signaler gives this option a thumbs up (Frame D).

Initiative continues to switch. The signaler indicates the red block and directs the avatar to pick up and move it. Frame E shows him performing a "carry" gesture up and away from himself. He then lowers his arm to indicate putting the block down. Placement is again ambiguous – should the red block

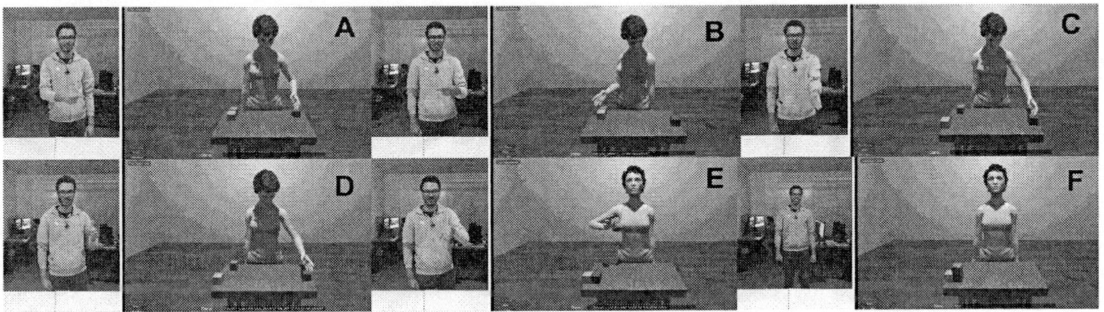

Figure 3: An example of building a staircase in HAB

go on the blue block, the green block, or the table top? The avatar asks and resolves these questions, and Frame F shows the completed staircase.

4   Conclusion and Future Directions

In this paper we have demonstrated the semantics and architecture underlying a multimodal peer-to-peer interface that interprets natural gestures in the context of a shared perceptual task and uses a mixed initiative dialogue. The result is symmetric communication between a human and a virtual avatar on a shared task with a common goal, facilitated by the shared context created through linguistic, gestural, and visual modalities, that highlights certain dynamics of multimodal communication, including:

- Judiciously determining when to have the avatar seek confirmation from the human as opposed to having it confirm every action;
- Gestural communication from the avatar to the human, such as gesturing toward a potentially-indicated block or region to seek confirmation, as doing nothing suggests to the human that no gesture was received by the system;
- A common coordinate system when using deixis as a gestural "referring expression," so that directions like "forward"/"back" or "left"/"right" have a common interpretation to both parties.

The HAB system's current implementation as demonstrated is limited to a vocabulary of well-defined gestures that appeared frequently in the human-subject elicitation studies discussed in Section 1. This demonstration serves to show how very basic actions can be mapped through a dynamic event semantics that interprets both natural language utterances and gestures, to facilitate the completion of a shared task and to communicate a goal from a human to a computer.

Further work to be undertaken primarily involves making interactions enabled through the HAB system more naturalistic. With the addition of speech recognition and generation to the avatar side, we are more closely approaching a true symmetry of communication between the interlocutors, and so in order to increase the variety of instruction and action that can be communicated between them, we need to increase the range of gesture semantics the system can process and compose. We will begin with other common gestures that occurred frequently in the aforementioned elicitation studies. These include the introduction of scalars, such as cardinal numbers (indicated by fingers and indexicals) and spacing (as indicated by space between the hands). This might map to a linguistic utterance such as "place three blocks *this far* apart," where "three" is accompanied by three raised fingers and "this far" is accompanied by separated hands indicating a distance. In the near term, we are also researching the inclusion of iterated actions, i.e., a palm-extended "push" hand continually moving over the same short interval, such as might represent an utterance of "a little more" or "keep going." This allows more fine-grained control over the placement of blocks and speed of motion.

We are also exploring approaches to performing automatic compositions of motions from primitives, including approaches based on machine learning (cf. Dubba et al. (2015); Do and Pustejovsky (2017)) and analogical reasoning (cf. Chen and Forbus (2017)). Such composition-based approaches would allow the agent to be taught a behavior with a given label, and then replicate it, e.g., following the instructions given in the example scenario in Section 3.4, label the resulting structure a "staircase," and then instruct the agent to build another staircase or "build another one."

Finally, by extending the virtual environment to robotics, wherein a real robotic agent enacts actions in an environment isomorphic to the simulated environment, the simulated environment provides a context within which new concepts can be grounded (cf. Paul et al. (2016)).

This system, and the addition of gestural interpretation to VoxSim demonstrates a viable platform for cooperating with computational agents in a new way, by creating a common ground that the human and machine partners can share for demonstrating individual and common knowledge, action, and planning. Together, they take the steps to complete tasks through mixed initiative conversations.

Acknowledgements

We would like to thank the reviewers for their insightful comments. We have tried to incorporate their suggestions where possible. This work was supported by Contract W911NF-15-C-0238 with the US Defense Advanced Research Projects Agency (DARPA) and the Army Research Office (ARO). Approved for Public Release, Distribution Unlimited. The views expressed herein are ours and do not reflect the official policy or position of the Department of Defense or the U.S. Government. All errors and mistakes are, of course, the responsibilities of the authors.

References

Abadi, M., P. Barham, J. Chen, Z. Chen, A. Davis, J. Dean, M. Devin, S. Ghemawat, G. Irving, M. Isard, et al. (2016). Tensorflow: A system for large-scale machine learning. In *Proceedings of the 12th USENIX Symposium on Operating Systems Design and Implementation (OSDI). Savannah, Georgia, USA.*

Andrist, S., M. Gleicher, and B. Mutlu (2017). Looking Coordinated: Bidirectional Gaze Mechanisms for Collaborative Interaction with Virtual Characters. In *Proceedings of the 2017 CHI Conference on Human Factors in Computing Systems*, CHI '17, New York, NY, USA, pp. 2571–2582. ACM.

Asher, N. (2011). *Lexical meaning in context: A web of words*. Cambridge University Press.

Asher, N. and A. Lascarides (2003). *Logics of conversation*. Cambridge University Press.

Bolt, R. A. (1980). *"Put-that-there": Voice and gesture at the graphics interface*, Volume 14. ACM.

Brennan, S. E., X. Chen, C. A. Dickinson, M. B. Neider, and G. J. Zelinsky (2008, March). Coordinating cognition: The costs and benefits of shared gaze during collaborative search. *Cognition 106*(3), 1465–1477.

Cassell, J. (2000). *Embodied conversational agents*. MIT press.

Cassell, J., M. Stone, and H. Yan (2000). Coordination and context-dependence in the generation of embodied conversation. In *Proceedings of the first international conference on Natural language generation-Volume 14*, pp. 171–178. Association for Computational Linguistics.

Chen, K. and K. D. Forbus (2017). Action recognition from skeleton data via analogical generalization. In *Proc. 30th International Workshop on Qualitative Reasoning*.

Clair, A. S., R. Mead, M. J. Matarić, et al. (2010). Monitoring and guiding user attention and intention in human-robot interaction. In *ICRA-ICAIR Workshop, Anchorage, AK, USA*, Volume 1025.

Clark, H. H. and S. E. Brennan (1991). Grounding in communication. In L. Resnick, L. B., M. John, S. Teasley, and D (Eds.), *Perspectives on Socially Shared Cognition*, pp. 13–1991. American Psychological Association.

Clark, H. H. and D. Wilkes-Gibbs (1986, February). Referring as a collaborative process. *Cognition 22*(1), 1–39.

Dillenbourg, P. and D. Traum (2006). Sharing solutions: Persistence and grounding in multimodal collaborative problem solving. *The Journal of the Learning Sciences 15*(1), 121–151.

Do, T. and J. Pustejovsky (2017). Learning event representation: As sparse as possible, but not sparser. In *Proc. 30th International Workshop on Qualitative Reasoning*.

Dubba, K. S., A. G. Cohn, D. C. Hogg, M. Bhatt, and F. Dylla (2015). Learning relational event models from video. *Journal of Artificial Intelligence Research 53*, 41–90.

Dumas, B., D. Lalanne, and S. Oviatt (2009). Multimodal interfaces: A survey of principles, models and frameworks. *Human machine interaction*, 3–26.

Eisenstein, J., R. Barzilay, and R. Davis (2008a). Discourse topic and gestural form. In *AAAI*, pp. 836–841.

Eisenstein, J., R. Barzilay, and R. Davis (2008b). Gesture salience as a hidden variable for coreference resolution and keyframe extraction. *Journal of Artificial Intelligence Research 31*, 353–398.

Fussell, S. R., R. E. Kraut, and J. Siegel (2000). Coordination of Communication: Effects of Shared Visual Context on Collaborative Work. In *Proceedings of the 2000 ACM Conference on Computer Supported Cooperative Work*, CSCW '00, New York, NY, USA, pp. 21–30. ACM.

Fussell, S. R., L. D. Setlock, J. Yang, J. Ou, E. Mauer, and A. D. I. Kramer (2004, September). Gestures over Video Streams to Support Remote Collaboration on Physical Tasks. *Hum.-Comput. Interact. 19*(3), 273–309.

Gergle, D., R. E. Kraut, and S. R. Fussell (2004). Action As Language in a Shared Visual Space. In *Proceedings of the 2004 ACM Conference on Computer Supported Cooperative Work*, CSCW '04, New York, NY, USA, pp. 487–496. ACM.

Goldstone, W. (2009). *Unity Game Development Essentials*. Packt Publishing Ltd.

He, K., X. Zhang, S. Ren, and J. Sun (2016). Deep residual learning for image recognition. In *Proceedings of the IEEE Conference on Computer Vision and Pattern Recognition*, pp. 770–778.

Jaimes, A. and N. Sebe (2007). Multimodal human–computer interaction: A survey. *Computer vision and image understanding 108*(1), 116–134.

Kennington, C., S. Kousidis, and D. Schlangen (2013). Interpreting situated dialogue utterances: an update model that uses speech, gaze, and gesture information. *Proceedings of SIGdial 2013*.

Kraut, R. E., S. R. Fussell, and J. Siegel (2003, June). Visual Information As a Conversational Resource in Collaborative Physical Tasks. *Hum.-Comput. Interact. 18*(1), 13–49.

Krishnaswamy, N. and J. Pustejovsky (2016a). Multimodal semantic simulations of linguistically underspecified motion events. In *Spatial Cognition X: International Conference on Spatial Cognition*. Springer.

Krishnaswamy, N. and J. Pustejovsky (2016b). VoxSim: A visual platform for modeling motion language. In *Proceedings of COLING 2016, the 26th International Conference on Computational Linguistics: Technical Papers*. ACL.

Lascarides, A. and M. Stone (2006). Formal semantics for iconic gesture. In *Proceedings of the 10th Workshop on the Semantics and Pragmatics of Dialogue (BRANDIAL)*, pp. 64–71.

Lascarides, A. and M. Stone (2009a). Discourse coherence and gesture interpretation. *Gesture 9*(2), 147–180.

Lascarides, A. and M. Stone (2009b). A formal semantic analysis of gesture. *Journal of Semantics*, ffp004.

Madeo, R. C. B., S. M. Peres, and C. A. de Moraes Lima (2016). Gesture phase segmentation using support vector machines. *Expert Systems with Applications 56*, 100–115.

Matuszek, C., L. Bo, L. Zettlemoyer, and D. Fox (2014). Learning from unscripted deictic gesture and language for human-robot interactions. In *AAAI*, pp. 2556–2563.

McDonald, D. and J. Pustejovsky (2014). On the representation of inferences and their lexicalization. In *Advances in Cognitive Systems*, Volume 3.

Mehlmann, G., M. Häring, K. Janowski, T. Baur, P. Gebhard, and E. André (2014). Exploring a Model of Gaze for Grounding in Multimodal HRI. In *Proceedings of the 16th International Conference on Multimodal Interaction*, ICMI '14, New York, NY, USA, pp. 247–254. ACM.

Paul, R., J. Arkin, N. Roy, and T. M. Howard (2016). Efficient grounding of abstract spatial concepts for natural language interaction with robot manipulators. In *Robotics: Science and Systems*.

Pustejovsky, J. (1995). *The Generative Lexicon*. MIT Press, Cambridge, MA.

Pustejovsky, J. (2013). Dynamic event structure and habitat theory. In *Proceedings of the 6th International Conference on Generative Approaches to the Lexicon (GL2013)*, pp. 1–10. ACL.

Pustejovsky, J. and N. Krishnaswamy (2016, May). VoxML: A visualization modeling language. In N. C. C. Chair), K. Choukri, T. Declerck, S. Goggi, M. Grobelnik, B. Maegaard, J. Mariani, H. Mazo, A. Moreno, J. Odijk, and S. Piperidis (Eds.), *Proceedings of the Tenth International Conference on Language Resources and Evaluation (LREC 2016)*, Paris, France. European Language Resources Association (ELRA).

Pustejovsky, J. and J. Moszkowicz (2011). The qualitative spatial dynamics of motion. *The Journal of Spatial Cognition and Computation*.

Quek, F., D. McNeill, R. Bryll, S. Duncan, X.-F. Ma, C. Kirbas, K. E. McCullough, and R. Ansari (2002). Multimodal human discourse: gesture and speech. *ACM Transactions on Computer-Human Interaction (TOCHI) 9*(3), 171–193.

Skantze, G., A. Hjalmarsson, and C. Oertel (2014, November). Turn-taking, feedback and joint attention in situated human-robot interaction. *Speech Communication 65*, 50–66.

Turk, M. (2014). Multimodal interaction: A review. *Pattern Recognition Letters 36*, 189–195.

Wang, I., P. Narayana, D. Patil, G. Mulay, R. Bangar, B. Draper, R. Beveridge, and J. Ruiz (2017a). EGGNOG: A continuous, multi-modal data set of naturally occurring gestures with ground truth labels. In *To appear in the Proceedings of the 12th IEEE International Conference on Automatic Face & Gesture Recognition*.

Wang, I., P. Narayana, D. Patil, G. Mulay, R. Bangar, B. Draper, R. Beveridge, and J. Ruiz (2017b). Exploring the use of gesture in collaborative tasks. In *Proceedings of the 2017 CHI Conference Extended Abstracts on Human Factors in Computing Systems*, CHI EA '17, New York, NY, USA, pp. 2990–2997. ACM.

Wobbrock, J. O., M. R. Morris, and A. D. Wilson (2009). User-defined Gestures for Surface Computing. CHI '09, New York, NY, USA, pp. 1083–1092. ACM.

Zhang, Z. (2012). Microsoft kinect sensor and its effect. *IEEE MulitMedia 19*, 4–10.

Ambiguss, a game
for building a Sense Annotated Corpus for French

Mathieu Lafourcade
LIRMM, 161, rue ADA 34392
Montpellier Cedex 5 - France
lafourcade@lirmm.fr

Nathalie Le Brun
Imagin@t
France
imaginat@imaginat.fr

Summary : This paper presents Ambiguss, a Game With A Purpose designed both to collect ambiguous sentences and build a Sense Annotated Corpus. It also generates a lexicon of polysemous words associated with the glosses that illustrate the different meanings. Early evaluations indicate that the approach is relevant and efficient.

1   Introduction

Evaluating a WSD task is a challenge at least as difficult as developing the task itself. Manually constructing a corpus of ambiguous sentences is a difficult and tedious task. Such a corpus is even more complex to produce if in each sentence, each ambiguous word is associated with its correct meaning. In addition to finding/imagining the sentence, it is necessary to have a word sense lexicon to associate the correct meaning with each ambiguous word, and such a resource may not be available in any given language. Secondly, referring to a given meaning might be tricky. This can be done by associating a meaning number, but in such a case, the lexicon must be provided along with the corpus. Another method would be to represent the correct meaning of the ambiguous word by a gloss, i.e. a word or group of words that intuitively refers to its correct meaning. A classic example could be *bank > river* and *bank > money*; the glosses *river* and *money* refer to two possible meanings of the word *bank*. Anyway, to define the glosses, i.e. to choose the word that best illustrates the meaning of a word is another pitfall: Indeed, it seems that there is not always a strong agreement between people for such a task.

Collect lexical data by crowdsourcing through games is a new trend since few years. The question that arises is to properly identify what kind of data can be collected in the domain of Natural Language Processing and Semantic computing. The postulate is that the semantic information understandable by the native speakers can be collected in this way. Furthermore, the type of semantically ambiguous sentence in which we are interested here, refers mostly to common sense knowledge (to be tackled with knowledge bases in the spirit of (Lenat, 1995)). This type of knowledge is intuitive and easy to infer for speakers, but definitively difficult to model to develop an Artificial Intelligence that would perform properly WSD.

This paper presents the design of a Gwap (Game With A Purpose) called *Ambiguss,* whose goal is twofold. On one hand, this game allows collecting ambiguous sentences created by players. On the other hand, these sentences are proposed to other players who must select from a list of glosses the one that corresponds to the correct meaning of each ambiguous word of the sentence. First, we show that the concept of Gwap is adapted to the production of Sense Annotated Corpus. Then we describe a novel Gwap designed to build a Sense Annotated Corpus. We conclude with a shallow evaluation of the first data collected.

2   From GWAPs to Sense Annotated Corpora

How could we relate and apply the idea of Gwap to the production of a Sense Annotated Corpus?

With the advent of Gwaps and more generally crowdsourcing approaches, one observe a fundamental shift in language resources building that is going on now (see (Chamberlain *et al.*, 2013) for more details). If the use of crowdsourcing microworking platforms like Amazon Mechanical Turk can be questionable, both in terms of ethics and quality (Fort *et al.*, 2011), Gwaps represent a paradigm shift for the acquisition of lexical resources, which passes from hand-made by specialists to crowdsourced through entertainment by native speakers. However, creating an efficient GWAP involves principles and developments that are not that straightforward.

The concept of Gwap was first proposed by (von Ahn and Dabbish, 2004 and 2006) and is based on the idea that beyond the simple entertainment of players, a game can have a purpose, such as data acquisition or problem solving. Since then, the first principles defined by (von Ahn *et al.*, 2008) have given rise to Gwaps in various fields (see Lafourcade, *et al.*, 2015 for a survey). In (Chamberlain *et al.*, 2009), the Phrase Detectives game is proposed to solve coreferences in texts, which is conceptually quite close to construct a corpus of sense annotated sentences. Wordrobe (Venhuizen *et al.*, 2013) is a game for labeling word senses, but senses come from a predefined set (the Groningen Meaning Bank).

Besides being funny and addictive, the mandatory characteristics for a Gwap to be successful could be found by asking simple questions: what can we ask to players? How could we ask these things to players? The task of selecting the proper meanings of words contained in sentences is clearly within the reach of native speakers. But one may wonder if this is a fun enough task to give rise to a game, and entertaining enough so that players are willing to do it?

According to (Habert et al., 1998) a corpus is a collection of language related data which are selected and organized according to linguistic criteria so as to be used as samples (for evaluation, for instance). Amongst those corpora, there are the British National Corpus (Burnard, 1998) (100 million words) and the American National Corpus (Ide & Macleod, 2001) (20 million words). In a Sense Annotated Corpus each word is related to a word meaning, usually by means of a sense number linked to a specific database (see Vial *et al.*, 2017). For example, the corpus of the task number 7 of SemEval 2007 is annotated with the identifiers of Princeton WordNet 2.1 (Fellbaum and Miller, 1998). The English corpus for the task 13 of SemEval 2015 2015 (Moro & Navigli, 2015) is annotated with the identifier of version 3.0 of BabelNet. Building such corpus might be based on various motivations, the most obvious of them being to provide a basis for automatically evaluating WSD systems.

For the French language, there is no such corpus freely available. Furthermore, there is a strong need for a corpus that would not be directly dependent on a given database. Hence the interest of indicating the meaning of words by glosses rather than identifiers related to specific meanings of a specific resource. Evaluating the feasibility of developing a new GWAP designed to construct such a corpus sounds interesting. The main issues lie in the design of the game which must be addictive and efficient, and secondarily in the evaluation of the collected data.

3   Ambiguss, a game to collect Semantically Ambiguous Sentences

Ambiguss (`https://ambiguss.calyxe.fr/`) is a game to solve lexical ambiguities in sentences, but also to collect such semantically ambiguous sentences (SemAS). Although this might be the case with some collected sentences, Ambiguss is not designed to collect syntactically ambiguous sentences. Everything is designed so that players do only need common language knowledge. The game is aimed at native speakers, who are not expert in linguistics or grammar.

3.1   Playing ambiguous sentences

Once logged, the player is proposed a random sentence in which at least one word is highlighted. The purpose of the game is to select the proper meaning of each highlighted word, through an user interface menu that presents a list of several possible meanings. When done, the player has to click on the *Valider* (Eng. Validate) button, and then he gets the result (Figure 2). There is no time constraint in the game.

In Figure 1, an example of game is given. The words *rat* and *radis* are highlighted: this means they are polysemous and the player is invited to disambiguate them by choosing the correct meaning according to the sentence, as seen in the figure for the word *rat*, which has two possible meanings.

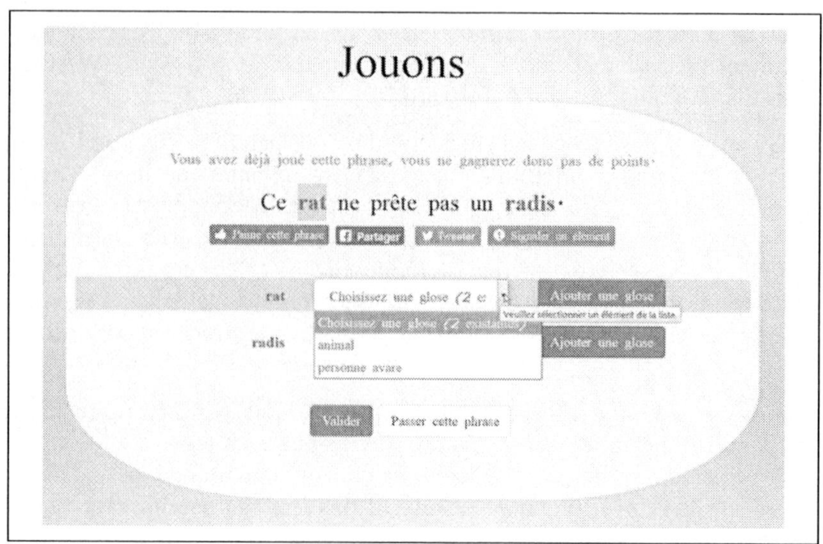

Figure 1: An Ambiguss play with the sentence *Ce rat ne prête pas un radis*.

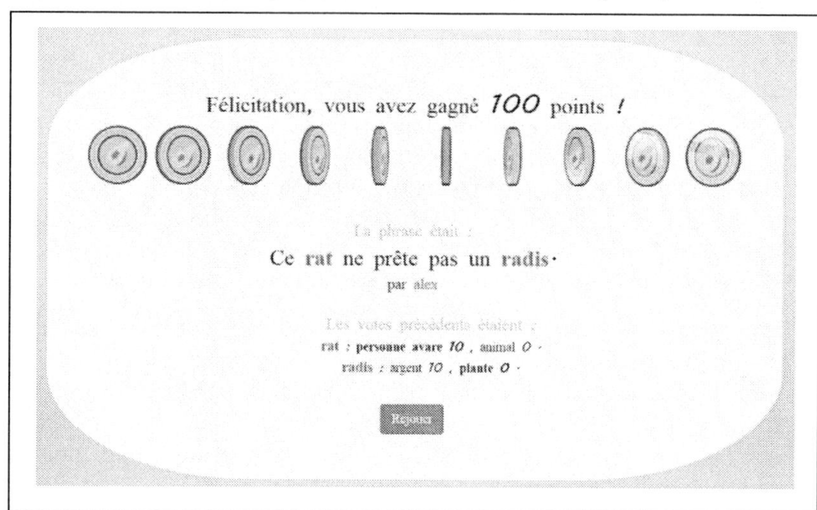

Figure 2: A screenshot of the game result. The player earns the same number of points and credits, here 100.

Players earn two types of rewards, *points*, only for fame, and *credits* that can be used for typical game actions, such as creating oneself an ambiguous phrase or adding a gloss: indeed, during the game, a player may add his own gloss, if he feels that none of the proposed ones is appropriate. The amount of points earned is related to the distribution of other player answers. (Of course, the main hypothesis, which is verified experimentally, is that *globally,* players provide the adequate answers).

3.2   Creating ambiguous sentences

The opportunity to create an ambiguous sentence is both a reward for good players and an incentive to play well, while being a way of spending the credits earned by playing. To do this, the player has to select the *"Créer"* menu and key in a sentence. He/she can then select one or more word(s) in this sentence and declare them as ambiguous. If an ambiguous word does not yet have glosses, he/she adds some to it to establish a list of possible meanings, and indicates what the correct gloss is for the term in the context of his/her sentence. These ambiguous words are those that will be highlighted and that another player will have to disambiguate in a game.

Although the user interface was deemed intuitive by the players, for now, only a small fraction of them (15%) has created sentences. It would seem that the fear of being judged through the quality of his own sentences might be deterrent to some players.

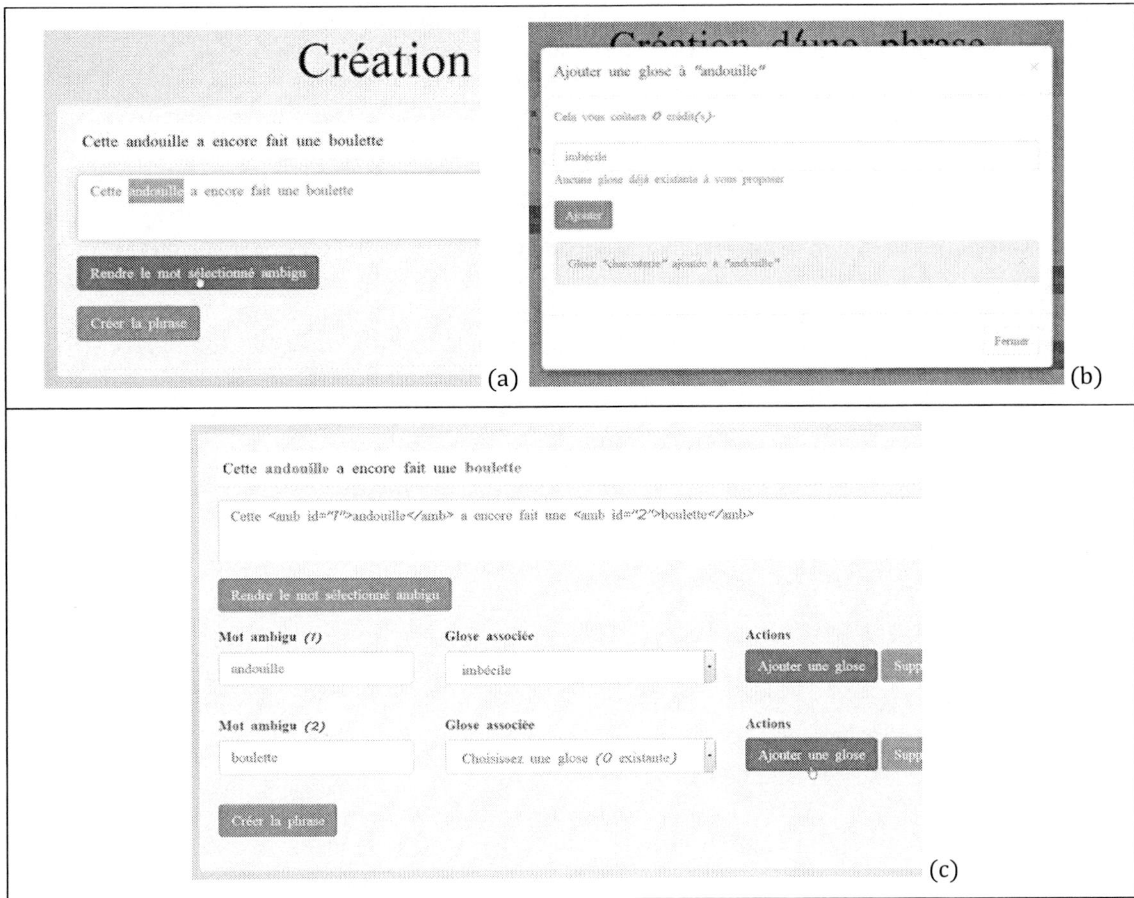

Figure 3: Screenshots of the different steps (a), (b), (c) of creating an ambiguous sentence. (a): Enter the sentence and select the ambiguous words. (b): add glosses for each ambiguous word. (c): Choose the correct gloss for each ambiguous word.

Why creating sentences? For greed and fame of course!

Each time a player earns *points* and *credits*, the creator of the sentence recovers 10% of the total. Hence, from a strict gaming point of view, players have a definite interest in creating sentences with many interesting ambiguities. When he/she plays, a player can pass over a sentence, if he/she finds it boring or nonsensical. Moreover, when playing, people can *like* a sentence (and share it on Facebook and Twitter). Having a high number of likes is an incentive for many players. Hence, they trend to produce interesting and funny sentences. Some of those sentences are "undecidable" in the absence of context, for example:

Je suis une fille.	*L'avocat est véreux*	*La petite brise la glace*	*Je loue un appartement*

In such cases, the interest of the game is to make emerge the preferred meaning, the one chosen by the majority of the players. But in some cases, a quite even number of votes for glosses is also possible.

The game proposes a multi-criteria ranking that orders players according to various parameters (number of points, number of sentences created, and number of *likes* obtained). Another ranking concerns the sentences and orders them according to the number of likes or the gains they have given to their creator. All this is designed to flatter and retain the player and thus intensify his contribution.

3.3 About the data collected

Ambiguss is still a prototype, but people have been asked from the beginning to serve as testers. By word of mouth, we reach after few weeks a total number of 64 players. Most of them have just played the disambiguation game, few daring to embark on the creation of sentences. A manual evaluation by expert in NLP concluded that 96% of the sentences are valuable for WSD evaluation as they are mostly good examples of semantic ambiguity related to common sense.

Number of sentences	354
Number of ambiguous words	524
Number of glosses	1556

Table 1: The amount of data collected with around 60 players in a few weeks.

Are the sentence properly disambiguated? Are the collected glosses correct?

So far, 100% of the sentences are disambiguated properly. More precisely, the gloss predominantly selected is the one that corresponds to the correct meaning in 100% of the cases. If we go into details, players achieve collectively a precision of 0.985. This means that it is very rare for a player to select a wrong meaning. Recall is not applicable in this context. Wrong glosses for a given term are never selected, but some glosses (4%) are not very representative of the meaning to be illustrated.

Reporting incorrect data

Players have access to an user interface button to indicate an incorrect item, whether it's a spelling mistake in a sentence or a gloss, a bad gloss, an absurd phrase, an ethical violation, and so on. The reporting mechanism allows self healing of the data and is very fast in practice (wrong data do not stay very long uncorrected).

3.4 Exporting the data

The data collected with Ambiguss are freely available to anyone. Two sets of data are available: the sentences, and the list of ambiguous terms with their glosses. The export format is JASON. For example, exporting the sentence *C'était un vol agréable malgré la distance* (Eng. It *was a pleasant flight/theft despite the distance.*) produces the following output :

```
{"phrase":"C'était    un    <amb    id=\"1\">vol<Vamb>    agréable    malgré    la
distance.","reponse":[{"motAmbigu":"vol","ordre":1,"nbRep":30,"gloses":[{"valeur":"crime","nb
Rep":"1"},{"valeur":"voyage","nbRep":"29"}]}]}
```

The sentence is given with inside annotations for indicating the ambiguous words. The field *"réponses"* (Eng. *Answers*) gives for each ambiguous word the distribution of the glosses proposed by the players. In the above example, 29 players answered *"voyage"* for the word *"vol"* and only 1 player proposed *"crime"*. Of course, this particular sentence can hold at least two interpretations, but only one sounds reasonably meaningful. Concerning the lexicon of terms and glosses, the export is also under a JASON form:

```
{"motAmbigu":"vol","gloses":["voyage","crime"]}
{"motAmbigu":"souris","gloses":["animal","objet","gigot","périphérique informatique","nana"]}
```

For the word *souris*, 5 glosses are proposed. It is most than probable that in many cases more glosses are proposed than the actual number of meanings. That is to say, for some meaning, several glosses are present. So, there would remain a task not foreseen by the game: to distribute the glosses for each polysemous word in equivalence classes. For example, in the case of *souris,* both glosses « *périphérique informatique* » and « *objet* » might probably refer to the same meaning.

4   Conclusion

We presented a game, called Ambiguss, designed for collecting ambiguous sentences along with player choices for the proper meanings. Another output of the game is that it builds a lexicon of polysemous words with their associated glosses. Although still in its testing phase, the game was judged *highly addictive* by many testers.

We have already collected several hundred semantically ambiguous sentences (for French). This corpus can be freely used as a reference for easily evaluating an automatic WSD process (or any relevant tasks). Word meanings are represented as glosses, which avoids the use of a dedicated semantic lexicon. The list of polysemous words and glosses is also freely accessible.

Acknowledgements

The Ambiguss game would not have existed without the dedication of the members of the TER M1 (Travail d'Etude et de Recherche, Master 1 en Informatique) student group IMNA, namely Isna, Melissa, Nicolas, and Alexandre. A big up for them.

References

VON AHN L., AND DABBISH L.   (2004). *Labelling Images with a Computer Game.* ACM Conference on Human Factors in Computing Systems (CHI). pp. 319-326, New York, NY, USA, 2004. ACM Press.

VON AHN, L., KEDIA, M., AND BLUM, M. (2006). *Verbosity: a game for collecting common-sense facts.* In Proceedings of ACM CHI 2006 Conference on Human Factors in Computing Systems, volume 1 of Games, pages 75–78, 2006.

VON AHN L., AND DABBISH L. (2008*). Designing Games With a Purpose.* Communication of the ACM, 51(8):58–67 August 2008.

BASILE V., BOS J., EVANG K., AND VENHUIZEN H. (2012). Developing a large semantically annotated corpus. *LREC 2012, Eighth International Conference on Language Resources and Evaluation*, May 2012, Istanbul, Turkey.

BURNARD L. (1998). *The British National Corpus*, The digital word, MIT Press Cambridge, MA,1998.

CHAMBERLAIN J, POESIO M, AND KRUSCHWITZ U. (2009). *A demonstration of human computation using the Phrase Detectives annotation game.* In HCOMP '09: Proceedings of the ACM SIGKDD Workshop on Human Computation pp. 23-24.

CHKLOVSKI T., AND GIL Y. (2005). *Improving the design of intelligent acquisition interfaces for collecting world knowledge from web contributors.* In Proceedings of K-CAP '05, pages 35–42.

FELLBAUM C. AND MILLER, G. editors. (1998). *Word-Net*. The MIT Press, 1998.

HABERT B., FABRE C. AND ISSAC F. (1998). *DE L'ECRIT AU NUMERIQUE. Constituer, normaliser et exploiter les corpus électroniques.* Number ISBN : 2-225-82953-5. Elsevier Masson.

FORT, K., ADDA, G., AND BRETONNEL COHEN, K. (2011). *Amazon Mechanical Turk: Gold mine or coal mine?* Computational Linguistics (editorial), 37(2):413–420.

IDE N., BAKER C. AND PASSONNEAU R. (2008). *Masc: the manually annotated sub-corpus of american english.* In Proceedings of the Sixth International Conference on Language Resources and Evaluation (LREC'08), Marrakech, Morocco: European Language Resources Association (ELRA). http ://www.lrec-conf.org/proceedings/lrec2008/.

IDE N. AND MACLEOD C. (2001). *The american national corpus: A standardized resource of American English.* In Proceedings of Corpus Linguistics 2001, volume 3.

LENAT D. (1995). *CYC: A large-scale investment in knowledge infrastructure.* Communications of the ACM, 38(11):33–38, 1995.

LAFOURCADE M., LE BRUN N. AND A. JOUBERT A. (2015). *Games with a Purpose (GWAPS)* ISBN: 978-1-84821-803-1 July 2015, Wiley-ISTE, 158 p.

LAFOURCADE M., AND JOUBERT A. (2010). *Computing trees of named word usages from a crowdsourced lexical network.* Investigationes Linguisticae, vol. XXI, pp. 39-56.

LAFOURCADE M., (2007). *Making people play for Lexical Acquisition.* In Proc. SNLP 2007, 7th Symposium on Natural Language Processing. Pattaya, Thailande, 13-15 December 2007, 8 p.

LAFOURCADE, JOUBERT A., SCHWAB D., AND ZOCK M. (2011). *Évaluation et consolidation d'un réseau lexical grâce à un assistant ludique pour le " mot sur le bout de la langue "* In proc of TALN'11, Montpellier, France, 27 juin-1er juillet 2011, pp. 295-306.

LIEBERMAN H., SMITH D., AND TEETERS A. (2007). *Common Consensus: A Web-based Game for Collecting Commonsense Goals Workshop on Common Sense for Intelligent Interfaces.* ACM International Conference on Intelligent User Interfaces (IUI-07), Honolulu, January 2007.

MORO A. AND NAVIGLI R. (2015). *Semeval-2015 task 13: Multilingual all-words sense disambiguation and entity linking.* In Proceedings of the 9th International Workshop on Semantic Evaluation (SemEval 2015), p. 288–297, Denver, Colorado : Association for Computational Linguistics.

NAVILI R. & PONZETTO S. P. (2010). *Babelnet: Building a very large multilingual semantic network.* In Proceedings of the 48th annual meeting of the association for computational linguistics, p. 216–225 : Association for Computational Linguistics (ACL).

RAGANATO A., CAMACHO-COLLADOS J., AND NAVIGLI R. (2017). *Word sense disambiguation : A unified evaluation framework and empirical comparison.* In Proceedings of the 15th Conference of the European Chapter of the Association for Computational Linguistics : Volume 1, Long Papers, p. 99–110, Valencia, Spain : Association for Computational Linguistics.

SAGOT B., FORT K., ADDA G., MARIANI J., AND LANG B. (2011). *Un turc mécanique pour les ressources linguistiques : critique de la myriadisation du travail parcellisé.*, Traitement Automatique des Langues Naturelles (TALN), Montpellier, France, 2011.

VIAL L., LECOUTEUX B. ET SCHWAB S. (2017). *Uniformisation de corpus anglais annotés en sens.* In proc of TALN 2017, 26 – 30 juin 2017, Orléans, 6 p.

VENHUIZEN N., EVANG K., BASILE V., AND BOS J. (2013). *Gamification for Word Sense Labeling.* Proceedings of the 10th International Conference on Computational Semantics (IWCS 2013), Mar 2013, Potsdam, Germany.

The Pragmatics of Indirect Commands in Collaborative Discourse

Matthew Lamm*
Stanford Linguistics
Stanford NLP Group
mlamm@stanford.edu

Mihail Eric*
Stanford Computer Science
Stanford NLP Group
meric@cs.stanford.edu

Abstract

Today's artificial assistants are typically prompted to perform tasks through direct, imperative commands such as *Set a timer* or *Pick up the box*. However, to progress toward more natural exchanges between humans and these assistants, it is important to understand the way non-imperative utterances can indirectly elicit action of an addressee. In this paper, we investigate command types in the setting of a grounded, collaborative game. We focus on a less understood family of utterances for eliciting agent action, locatives like *The chair is in the other room*, and demonstrate how these utterances indirectly command in specific game state contexts. Our work shows that models with domain-specific grounding can effectively realize the pragmatic reasoning that is necessary for more robust natural language interaction.

1 Introduction

A major goal of computational linguistics research is to enable organic, language-mediated interaction between humans and artificial agents. In a common scenario of such interaction, a human issues a command in the imperative mood—e.g. *Put that there* or *Pick up the box*—and a robot acts in turn (Bolt, 1980; Tellex et al., 2011; Walter et al., 2015). While this utterance-action paradigm presents its own set of challenges (Tellex et al., 2012), it greatly simplifies the diversity of ways in which natural language can be used to elicit action of an agent, be it human or artificial (Clark, 1996; Portner, 2007; Kaufmann and Schwager, 2009; Condoravdi and Lauer, 2012; Kaufmann, 2016). Most clause types, even vanilla declaratives, instantiate as performative requests in certain contexts (Austin, 1975; Searle, 1989; Perrault and Allen, 1980).

In this work, we employ machine learning to study the use of performative commands in the Cards corpus, a set of transcripts from a web-based game that is designed to elicit a high degree of linguistic and strategic collaboration (Djalali et al., 2011, 2012; Potts, 2012). For example, players are tasked with navigating a maze-like gameboard in search of six cards of the same suit, but since a player can hold at most three cards at a time, they must coordinate their efforts to win the game.

We focus on a subclass of performative commands that are ubiquitous in the Cards corpus: Non-agentive declaratives about the locations of objects, e.g. "The five of hearts is in the top left corner," hereafter referred to as *locatives*. Despite that their semantics makes no reference to either an agent or an action—thus distinguishing them from conventional imperatives (Condoravdi and Lauer, 2012)—locatives can be interpreted as commands when embedded in particular discourse contexts. In the Cards game, it is frequently the case that an addressee will respond to such an utterance by fetching the card mentioned.

Following work on the context-driven interpretation of declaratives as questions (Beun, 2000), we hypothesize that the illocutionary effect of a locative utterance is a function of contextual features that variably constrain the actions of discourse participants. To test this idea, we identify a set of 94 locative utterances in the Cards transcripts that we deem to be truly ambiguous, out of context, between

---

* Authors contributed equally

informative and command readings. We then annotate their respective transcripts for a simplified representation of the tabular common ground model of Malamud and Stephenson (2015). Here, we identify the common ground with the state of a game as reflected by the utterances made by both players up to a specific point in time. Finally, we train machine learning classifiers on features of the common ground to predict whether or not the addressee will act in response to the utterance in question. Through these experiments we discover a few very powerful contextual features that predict when a locative utterance will be interpreted as a command.

2   Related Work

The subject of indirect commands, of which the locative utterances we study are an example, has been extensively analyzed in terms of speech act and decision theory (Austin, 1975; Clark, 1979; Perrault and Allen, 1980; Allen and Perrault, 1980; Searle, 1989). In Portner's (2007) formal model, imperatives are utterances whose conventional effect updates an abstract "to-do list" of an addressee. More recent debate has asked whether this effect is in fact built into the semantics of imperatives, or if their directive force is resolved by pragmatic reasoning in context (Condoravdi and Lauer, 2012; Kaufmann, 2016).

The present work synthesizes these intuitions from the theory of commands with recent computational work on natural language pragmatics (Vogel et al., 2013, 2014; Degen et al., 2013) and collaborative dialogue (Chai et al., 2014). We are particularly influenced by previous work demonstrating the complexity of pragmatic phenomena in the Cards corpus (Djalali et al., 2011, 2012; Potts, 2012).

3   The Cards corpus

The Cards corpus is a set of 1,266 transcripts from a two-player, collaborative, web-based game. The Cards corpus is well-suited to studying the pragmatics of commands because it records both utterances made as well as the actions taken during the course of a game.

At the start of the game, player locations are randomly initialized on a two-dimensional, grid-style game board. Cards from a conventional 52-card deck are scattered randomly throughout the board. Players are prompted with the following task:

> Gather six consecutive cards of a particular suit (decide which suit together), or determine that this is impossible. Each of you can hold only three cards at a time, so youll have to coordinate your efforts. You can talk all you want, but you can make only a limited number of moves.

In addition to the fact that players can only hold three cards at a time, the game is further-constrained in ways that stimulate highly collaborative talk. In particular, while players can see their own location, they cannot see the locations of their partners and so must inquire about them. Players can only see cards within a small neighborhood around their respective locations, and so must explore the board to find relevant cards. Moreover, while some walls are visible, others are invisible and so lead to surprise perturbations in the course of exploring the gameboard.

4   Command types in the Cards Corpus

Commands in the Cards corpus can be coarsely divided into ones which make reference to an action with a second person agent, and those which do not.

The first of these categories is comprised of imperatives and a variety so-called performative commands: Utterances which act as commands in context but whose clause type is not conventionally associated with the effect of commanding (Clark, 1979; Searle, 1989; Wierzbicka, 1991). For example, with respect to picking up cards:

> pick it up!
> pick up the 9
> or hell, grab the 234 of D
> ok when you get here pick up the 8H
> i think you should pick up the 3h, 5h, and 8h
> so if you can find 5S,6S,7S that would be great

With respect to dropping (or not dropping) cards:

> drop the 2
> keepp the 3
> no dont drop it.)
> ok drop the 7 i guess
> get rid of 6d. i found 7h
> so if you come and drop the 8h and pick up the 6h we are good

With respect to conversational actions (some of these utterances are shortened for clarity):

> tell me where it is
> talk to me dude [...]
> tell me if you see 5 or 6
> don't just say "a lot of cards" [...]
> awesome let me know once you have it.

Imperatives and performatives that mention agents contrast with the lesser understood subclass of performative commands that are the focus of this work. Utterances like "The five of hearts is in the top corner" do not even encode an action with respect to the object mentioned, let alone an agent, but can nevertheless be used to elicit action of an addressee in certain contexts.

As a motivating example, consider the following exchange between two players describing their respective hands:

> P1: 3h, 4h and ks
> P2: i have a queen of diamonds and ace of club
> P2: we have a mess lol

Despite Player 2's concerns, a strategy emerges shortly thereafter when Player 1 finds an additional hearts card:

> P1: i have 3h,4h,6h
> P2: ok so we need to collect hearts then

At this point in the transcript, all that has been committed to the common ground is that Player 1 has a full hand of three proximal hearts cards that could be relevant to a winning strategy, and Player 2 has two non-hearts cards. This is the very next utterance in the exchange:

> P1: there is a 5h in the very top left corner

Player 2 is seen immediately hereafter to navigate to the top left corner, pick up the five of hearts, and confirm:

> P2: ok i got it :)

In this exchange, Player 2 appears to understand not only that the five of hearts is relevant to the winning strategy of six consecutive hearts, but also that it makes more sense for her to act on information about its location than it does for Player 1 to do so.

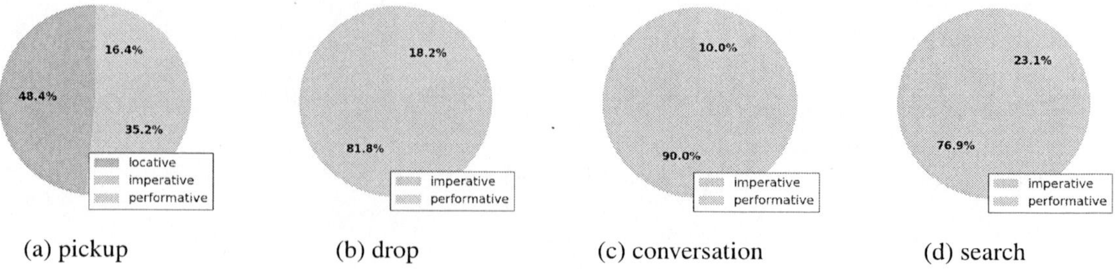

(a) pickup   (b) drop   (c) conversation   (d) search

Figure 1: For each action, the distribution of command types

This discourse encapsulates the collaborative reasoning pattern described by Perrault and Allen (1980). The speaker assumes that the addressee is a cooperative agent. Thus, the addressee shares in the goal of attaining a winning game state and will act in a way so as to realize that goal. Recognizing the fact that the speaker would have to drop cards relevant to the goal to pick up the card at issue, a cooperative addressee will infer that she *should* act by picking it up instead. In this way, locative utterances can be indirectly used as commands.

The distribution of command types for a subset of actions (*pickup*, *drop*, *conversation*, and *search*) is displayed in Figure 1. As depicted, for the majority of actions compelled by a speaker and taken by an addressee, the imperative is the predominant command strategy, followed by non-locative performatives. However locative commands appear to be the dominant strategy for eliciting card pickups in the corpus, constituting nearly half of all such commands observed.

This pattern demonstrates that for certain kinds of actions, it is quite natural to use the least direct, most context-dependent command strategy to elicit action of an addressee.

5   Common Ground Effects on the Directive Force of Locative Utterances

We seek to understand how the discourse context of a game can influence the interpretation of locative utterances as commands. We therefore construct a binary classification task whereby we test how the role of a locative utterance can be resolved in context, evidenced by the actions that are taken as follow-ups to the utterance. In our task, one label denotes addressee follow-up in the form of acting to pick up the card in question, signaling her intention to act, or asking a clarifying question about its whereabouts. The second label denotes that either the speaker acts on their own utterance or neither agent does.

5.1   Annotation Details

Using a random sample of 200 transcripts from the corpus, we identify instances where a locative utterance is made and we annotate the common ground up to this utterance. This yields 55 distinct transcripts constituting 94 utterances with this particular phenomenon.

Our common ground annotations include the following information about the game state as indicated by players' utterances: cards in the players hands, player location, known information about the existence or location of cards, strategic statements made by players about needed cards, and whether a player is able to act with respect to an at-issue card.

5.2   Experiments

Our aim in devising this task is to investigate connection between common ground knowledge and the illocutionary effects of locative utterances. We therefore train a standard logistic regression classifier and experiment with a few carefully designed features that encode constraints on player action, and which should hypothetically trigger the interpretation of locative utterances as indirect commands. We experiment with the following features:

170

Model	F_1
Random	23.5
Bigram	58.9
Edit Distance	62.5
Explicit Goal	76.2
Full Hand	**82.3**
Explicit Goal + Full Hand	77.7

Table 1: F_1 performance as reported on the test set. Note our baselines are italicized.

- **Edit Distance**: We use the minimal number of edits for an optimal solution as a feature. Given the cards in the players' hands at a given point in the game, we can define an optimal solution based on the number of edits that must be made to the hands to achieve that optimal solution. An edit is defined as either picking up or dropping a card, and each such action has a cost of 1. An optimal solution is defined as the one that requires the minimal number of edits given the current hands. For example, if player 1 has a 2H, 3H, and 4H and player 2 has a 6H and a 7H, the optimal solution is the 2H, 3H, 4H, 5H, 6H, and 7H. Such a solution requires a single edit because player 2 simply has to pick up a 5H. This feature seeks to capture the intuition that an addressee should tend to act with respect to a card when the edit distance is not particularly high and hence the game is near a winning state.

- **Explicit Goal**: This binary feature is triggered in two cases: 1) When the suit of card mentioned matches the agreed-upon suit strategy in the common ground and 2) When the card mentioned appears in the set of cards the addressee claims to need. This models the prediction that locative utterances are more likely to be indirect commands when they are relevant to a well-defined goal.

- **Full Hands**: This binary feature is triggered when the speaker has three cards of the same suit as the card mentioned, and which are associated with some winning six-card straight, but the addressee does not. This models the prediction that locative utterances are likely to be indirect commands when they provide information relevant to winning, but only the addressee can act as such.

Single-feature classifiers are compared against a number of baselines to help benchmark our predictive task. Our first baseline, which is context-agnostic, seeks to capture the intuition that the role of a locative utterance is entirely ambiguous when considered in isolation. This baseline predicts the agent follow-up using a Bernoulli distribution weighted according to the class priors of the training data.

The second baseline incorporates surface-level dialogue context via bigram features of all the utterance exchanged between players up to and including the locative utterance. We also experimented with a unigram baseline but found that its performance was inferior to that of the bigram.

5.3   Results

We test our common-ground features one at a time with our logistic regression model, as we are interested in seeing how successfully they encode agents' pragmatic inferences. We also combine the two best-performing common-ground features. We report the results of our experiments using an F_1 measure and a 0.8/0.2 train/test split of our data in Table 1.

We see that of our two baselines, the bigram model performs better. This bigram model also uses 2,916 distinct lexical features which makes it a highly overspecified model for our moderate data size.

We find that our single-feature context-sensitive models both significantly outperform our baselines. Our Explicit Goal feature outperforms the Edit Distance feature by about 14%, which indicates that locative utterances are often interpreted as commands in the presence of an explicit, common goal. The Full Hands feature outperforms the Explicit Goal feature by about 6%. This strongly suggests that constraints on speaker action play a role in determining the illocutionary effect of a locative utterance. An addressee of such an utterance will tend to act accordingly when their partner cannot pick up the card mentioned, and when the card in question brings them closer to winning the game. We find that combining the Explicit Goal and Full Hands features improved performance over only using the Explicit Goal feature but reduced overall performance. This could be because the two features encode some common information about the agents' pragmatic implicatures during the game, and hence their correlative effects tend to degrade the combined model performance.

6 Conclusion

In this work, we have performed an extensive study of command types as present in the Cards corpus. Using the corpus as a test bed for grounded natural language interaction among agents with a shared goal, we describe a variety of utterances that may function as indirect commands when regarded in context. In particular, locative utterances, which are not conventionally associated with command interpretations, are shown to operate as commands when considered in relation to situational constraints in the course of collaborative interaction. We develop a predictive task to show that models with carefully-designed features incorporating game state information can help agents effectively perform such pragmatic inferences.

7 Acknowledgments

The authors would like to thank Christopher Potts and all of the anonymous reviewers for their valuable insights and feedback.

References

Allen, J. F. and C. R. Perrault (1980). Analyzing intention in utterances. *Artificial intelligence 15*(3), 143–178.

Austin, J. L. (1975). *How to do things with words.* Oxford University Press.

Beun, R.-J. (2000). Context and form: Declarative or interrogative, that is the question. *Abduction, Belief, and Context in Dialogue: Studies in Computational Pragmatics 1*, 311–325.

Bolt, R. A. (1980). *Put-that-there: Voice and gesture at the graphics interface*, Volume 14. ACM.

Chai, J. Y., L. She, R. Fang, S. Ottarson, C. Littley, C. Liu, and K. Hanson (2014). Collaborative effort towards common ground in situated human-robot dialogue. In *Proceedings of the 2014 ACM/IEEE international conference on Human-robot interaction*, pp. 33–40. ACM.

Clark, H. H. (1979). Responding to indirect speech acts. *Cognitive psychology 11*(4), 430–477.

Clark, H. H. (1996). *Using language.* Cambridge: Cambridge University Press.

Condoravdi, C. and S. Lauer (2012). Imperatives: Meaning and illocutionary force. *Empirical issues in syntax and semantics 9*, 37–58.

Degen, J., M. Franke, and G. Jäger (2013). Cost-based pragmatic inference about referential expressions. In *CogSci.*

Djalali, A., D. Clausen, S. Lauer, K. Schultz, and C. Potts (2011, November). Modeling expert effects and common ground using Questions Under Discussion. In *Proceedings of the AAAI Workshop on Building Representations of Common Ground with Intelligent Agents*, Washington, DC. Association for the Advancement of Artificial Intelligence.

Djalali, A., S. Lauer, and C. Potts (2012). Corpus evidence for preference-driven interpretation. In M. Aloni, V. Kimmelman, F. Roelofsen, G. W. Sassoon, K. Schulz, and M. Westera (Eds.), *Proceedings of the 18th Amsterdam Colloquium: Revised Selected Papers*, Berlin, pp. 150–159. Springer.

Kaufmann, M. (2016). Fine-tuning natural language imperatives. *Journal of Logic and Computation*, exw009.

Kaufmann, S. and M. Schwager (2009). A unified analysis of conditional imperatives. In *Semantics and Linguistic Theory*, Volume 19, pp. 239–256.

Malamud, S. A. and T. Stephenson (2015). Three ways to avoid commitments: Declarative force modifiers in the conversational scoreboard. *Journal of Semantics 32*(2), 275–311.

Perrault, C. R. and J. F. Allen (1980). A plan-based analysis of indirect speech acts. *Computational Linguistics 6*(3-4), 167–182.

Portner, P. (2007). Imperatives and modals. *Natural Language Semantics 15*(4), 351–383.

Potts, C. (2012). Goal-driven answers in the Cards dialogue corpus. In N. Arnett and R. Bennett (Eds.), *Proceedings of the 30th West Coast Conference on Formal Linguistics*, Somerville, MA, pp. 1–20. Cascadilla Press.

Searle, J. R. (1989). How performatives work. *Linguistics and philosophy 12*(5), 535–558.

Tellex, S., P. Thaker, R. Deits, T. Kollar, and N. Roy (2012). Toward information theoretic human-robot dialog. In *Robotics: Science and Systems*, Volume 2, pp. 3.

Tellex, S. A., T. F. Kollar, S. R. Dickerson, M. R. Walter, A. Banerjee, S. Teller, and N. Roy (2011). Understanding natural language commands for robotic navigation and mobile manipulation.

Vogel, A., A. Gómez Emilsson, M. C. Frank, D. Jurafsky, and C. Potts (2014, July). Learning to reason pragmatically with cognitive limitations. In *Proceedings of the 36th Annual Meeting of the Cognitive Science Society*, Wheat Ridge, CO, pp. 3055–3060. Cognitive Science Society.

Vogel, A., C. Potts, and D. Jurafsky (2013, August). Implicatures and nested beliefs in approximate Decentralized-POMDPs. In *Proceedings of the 2013 Annual Conference of the Association for Computational Linguistics*, Stroudsburg, PA, pp. 74–80. Association for Computational Linguistics.

Walter, M. R., M. Antone, E. Chuangsuwanich, A. Correa, R. Davis, L. Fletcher, E. Frazzoli, Y. Friedman, J. Glass, and J. P. How (2015). A situationally aware voice-commandable robotic forklift working alongside people in unstructured outdoor environments. *Journal of Field Robotics 32*(4), 590–628.

Wierzbicka, A. (1991). *Cross-cultural pragmatics: the semantics of human interaction*. Berlin: Mouton de Gruyter.

Are *doggies* cuter than *dogs*?
Emotional valence and concreteness in
German derivational morphology

Gabriella Lapesa, Sebastian Padó, Tillmann Pross, and Antje Roßdeutscher
University of Stuttgart, Institute for Natural Language Processing
`[gabriella.lapesa,pado,tillmann.pross,`
`antje.rossdeutscher]@ims.uni-stuttgart.de`

Abstract

The semantic behavior of derivational processes has been investigated with compositional distributional models relating the meaning of base, affix, and derivative (e.g., *anti+capitalist* $\rightarrow$ *anticapitalist*). While broadly successful, these approaches model how the distributional behavior generally is affected by derivation. Meanwhile, their predictions can not be interpreted at the level of linguistic regularities. In this paper, we adopt an alternative approach and focus on the impact of derivation on finer-grained semantic properties of the base. We focus on (the psycholinguistically prominent) *emotional valence*, i.e., the speakers' positive/negative evaluation of the word referent. We present two case studies on German derivational patterns, combining distributional and regression analysis. We are able to establish the broad presence of valence effects in German derivation as well as strong interactions with concreteness.

1   Introduction

Morphological derivation (Plag, 2003) is a word formation process which combines *bases* (e.g., *Hund* – "dog") with *affixes* (e.g., the diminutive *-chen*) into new words (*Hündchen* "doggie"). The semantic properties of derivation have been extensively explored in theoretical linguistics, and a number of recent computational studies in compositional distributional semantics have modelled the mappings that hold between the vectors of bases, affixes, and derivatives (Lazaridou et al., 2013; Luong et al., 2013; Padó et al., 2016). What these studies crucially lack, though, is *interpretability*: typically, they model mappings in an embedding space, but have little to say about linguistic regularities such as systematic changes in *meaning components*.

In this paper, our goal is to do exactly that, namely investigate the effects of derivation on a specific meaning component, *emotional valence* (henceforth, valence), which quantifies the speaker's positive or negative affect towards the referent of a word. This choice is motivated by psycholinguistic considerations: Valence is very well established in the literature as having substantial effects on human language processing (Vinson et al., 2014; Kuperman et al., 2014; Snefjella and Kuperman, 2016). Since it is not clear that the effects on valence take place independently of other variables, we extend our analysis to include a set of other meaning components, most notably *concreteness*, a second prominent meaning component in psycholinguistics (cf. the references above). Both meaning components are also highly relevant for NLP: (Variants of) valence occur under the names of sentiment and polarity and form the basic variable of interest in sentiment analysis (Pang and Lee, 2008). Concreteness is exploited, among other things, for metaphor identification (Turney et al., 2011; Köper and Schulte im Walde, 2016b).

The questions we ask are (a) whether a derivative carries a significantly different valence from its base; and (b) whether there are interactions between valence and concreteness (i.e., whether valence shifts occur only in more concrete vs. abstract contexts). To the best of our knowledge, the effect of derivation on valence has not been explored in distributional semantics. Our work extends a couple of studies that consider the interaction between valence and concreteness: Mohammad et al. (2016) present a collection of ratings targeting emotion and metaphor; Hill and Korhonen (2014) explore the interplay between subjectivity and concreteness. From a purely linguistic perspective, valence is situated between semantics and pragmatics; despite the interest for the interplay between semantics and pragmatics in derivational morphology (Dressler and Barbaresi, 1998; Plag, 2003), there has been no attempt yet to integrate theoretical considerations and computational modeling.

Our contribution is twofold. First, computationally, we define a distributional procedure that quantifies the basis–derivative differences with respect to specific meaning components and aggregates these differences across a large vocabulary with a regression analysis. Second, linguistically, we present two case studies on German derivation. The first one focusses on a specific pattern (*über- (over-)* prefix verbs) and illustrates the integration of valence with a theoretically motivated manual subclass analysis. The second one targets a larger set of patterns without manual annotation. We establish a strong presence of valence effects in derivation, even where its role would have been not obvious (female forms are used in more positive contexts than their male counterparts). We also find an interaction with concreteness which characterizes a "classic" evaluative pattern, the diminutive *-chen* (see Jurafsky (1996) for a cross-linguistic overview of the semantic spectrum covered by diminutives), as well as a pattern which has a clear evaluative flavor, the adversative *anti-*.

2   Experimental Setup

Our goal is to analyse the role of *valence* as a meaning component that undergoes systematic changes between base and derived words. We proceed as follows: given a set of base-derived word pairs for a derivation pattern, we represent the words distributionally. Then we quantify valence and a set of auxiliary meaning components (concreteness, imageability, arousal) for each word using a lexicon-based approach. Finally, we perform a regression analysis to analyse the factors affecting valence.

Distributional Semantic Model   Since our assignment of meaning components is lexicon-based (see next paragraph), we require a distributional model with lexical dimensions. This precludes the use of neural embedding models (Mikolov et al., 2013). Instead, we use a count (bag-of-words) distributional model with lexical dimensions. It is extracted from SdeWaC (Faaß and Eckart, 2013), a 800M words German web corpus with a large target and context vocabulary (approx. 280k lemmatized open-class words). We adopt standard choices for the main parameters, namely a symmetrical 5-words context window and positive pointwise mutual information to transform raw counts.

Computing Meaning Components.   We employ the German Affective Norms (Köper and Schulte im Walde, 2016a). The dataset contains automatically generated scores for 350k German lemmas on a 0 to 10 scale for four psycholinguistically prominent meaning components: *valence*, the (un-) pleasantness associated with the word; *arousal*, the intensity of the emotion associated with it; *concreteness*, the extent to which the word's referent can be perceived; and *imageability*, the extent to which the word's referent can be perceived visually. While the scores on these four components can in principle be used 'as is' for words covered by the resource, we found that their quality can be crucially improved (see Section 3 for details) by defining a *context-based reweighing scheme*. We define the score assigned to a target word t on a given component as the weighted average of the scores of its context words c by computing the dot product between the (L1-normalized) distributional vector for t and the vector of Affective Norm Scores for all context words. For each component, we reduce the set of context words with scores belonging to the top and bottom quartile for this component.

Regression analysis.   To gain a systematic understanding of valence, we perform a linear regression analysis. Linear regression predicts a continuous dependent variable (here, the valence score) as a linear combination of weighted predictors. We considered (a), theoretically motivated subclasses of *über-* verbs (Study 1, Section 3) and derivational patterns (Study 2, Section 4); (b), the meaning dimensions annotated in the German Affective Norms (imageability, concreteness, arousal); (c), frequency effects, as is best practice. In a model selection step, we discarded imageability based on a collinearity analysis (strong correlation to concreteness) and added the interaction between class/pattern and the Affective scores that were significant for both studies. The final model is:[1]

$$
\begin{aligned}
\texttt{valence} \sim{}& \texttt{class/pattern} \\
&* \texttt{(concreteness + arousal)} \qquad (1) \\
&+ \texttt{freq\_base + freq\_derived}
\end{aligned}
$$

We trained three regression models to predict valence scores for base and derived words and to predict *differences* between valence scores for base and derived words.

3 Study 1: *über* prefix verbs

We investigate *über-* prefix verbs as an interesting object in lexical semantics: some *über* verbs (e.g., *überrennen*, "to overrun", *überschwemmen*, "to overflood",) encode a negative evaluation for events perceived as uncontrolled or uncontrollable (an excess reading, absent in the corresponding base terms *rennen*, "to run", *schwemmen*, "to float"). We build on a previous study of *über* prefix verbs (Pross and Roßdeutscher, 2015) that has produced a dataset of 74 *über* verbs and their corresponding bases manually selected to ensure that derived words are transparent with respect to their bases, at least in their dominant reading. Each pair was manually assigned to one of four theoretically motivated classes that differ by the contribution of *über-* to the interpretation of prefix verb:

- TRANSFER of an object from a source region to a goal region (16 pairs). Ex: *bringen, überbringen* ("to bring", "to deliver").

- APPLICATION of an object to another object (19 pairs). Ex: *kleben, überkleben* ("to paste", "to paste over").

- movement ACROSS some boundary or obstacle, which is conceptualized as a patient and in some cases undergoes change of state (18 pairs). Ex: *fahren, überfahren* ("to drive", "to drive (something) over").

- exceeding a certain threshold on a scale (MORE) provided by the base verb or by the usage context (21 pairs). Ex: *(be)werten, überbewerten* ("to value", "to overvalue").

We hypothesize that the ACROSS class is associated with negative valence, the others are neutral. We test the hypothesis by including the class in our regression model (cf. Equation (1)).

Results.   Table 1 summarizes the fit of the linear models in terms of their ability to explain the valences of base verbs (column "Base"), the valences of *über* prefix verbs (column "Derived"), and the differences between base and prefix verbs (column "Shift"). It shows both the total amount of variance accounted for and the contribution of individuals predictors, computed though Lindeman-Merenda-Gold (LMG) scores (Lindeman et al., 1980). The fit of the full models (between .60 and .74 adjusted R^2) is very good, and even though frequencies are a major predictor (as almost always), both semantic classes and other meaning components (concreteness, arousal) contribute nicely.

Table 2 shows coefficients for all predictors that are significant in at least one of the columns. In the following, we focus on the Shift results and give Base and Derived for comparison only. For Shift, a positive coefficient for a predictor means that derived words with a high value of the predictor exhibit a higher valence than their bases. Vice versa, a predictor with a negative coefficient will reduce the

---

[1]We use the R statistical environment. The asterisk in the formula represents the interaction between class/pattern and concreteness and arousal. Continuous predictors are scaled, categorical variables are sum-coded: effects are calculated with the grand mean of the groups as reference value. Frequencies are log-transformed.

Predictor	Shift	Derived	Base
Semantic Class	.031	.058	.072
Concreteness	.037	.051	.087
Arousal	.011	.002	.108
Class:Arousal	.088	.086	.004
Base frequency	.105	N/A	.498
Derived frequency	.384	.553	N/A
Adjusted R^2	.60 ***	.72 ***	.74 ***

Table 1: Study 1 model fit (explained variance)

Predictor	Shift	Derived	Base
APPLICATION	–	–	-.06 **
Concreteness	-.06 **	-.08 **	–
ACROSS:Arousal	-.13 ***	-.10 ***	–
Base frequency	.15 ***	N/A	-.15 ***
Derived frequency	-.20 ***	-.20 ***	N/A

Table 2: Study 1: Coefficients of predictors

valence scores of derived words associated with high values of it. Contrary to our expectations, there is no significant main effect for any semantic class in the Shift analysis, meaning that the verb classes at large do not differ in valence. We do however, specifically find an interaction between the ACROSS semantic class and arousal that is highly significant and has a negative sign. Thus, ACROSS bases do tend to acquire negative valence as you add *über-*, but only if they already carry high arousal, i.e., are "emotionally loaded" verbs. A second interesting observation is the negative main effect of concreteness. It shows that across all pairs in the dataset, negative valence shifts are more pronounced for concrete verbs (*fahren, überfahren* "drive, drive over") than for abstract verbs (*nehmen, übernehmen* "take, take over").

Finally, we return to a question from §2: is there a difference between using valence scores from the Affective Norms and (re-)computing them distributionally? We repeated the analysis above using the Affective Norms valence scores, and found a much lower model fit (only .21 adjusted R^2, compared to .60 as in Table 1) as well as an absence of significant effects. In sum, the distributional valence scores do a substantially better job.

4   Study 2: Other Derivation Patterns

Our second study extends the focus beyond *über-* to six other German within part-of-speech derivation patterns from a previous study (Kisselew et al., 2015):

- N→N, FEMALE: *-in* (80 pairs). Ex: *Bäcker, Bäckerin* ("baker", "female baker")

- N→N, DIMINUTIVE: *-chen* (80 pairs). Ex: *Schiff, Schiffchen* ("ship", "small ship")

- A→A, OPPOSED: *anti-* (80 pairs). Ex: *religiös, antireligiös* ("religious", "antireligious")

- A→A, NEGATIVE: *un-* (80 pairs). Ex: *dankbar, undankbar* ("grateful", "ungrateful")

- V→V, DIRECTED: *an-* (68 pairs). Ex: *sprechen, ansprechen* ("to speak", "to address")

- V→V, TRAVERSE: *durch-* (70 pairs). Ex: *gehen, durchgehen* ("to go", "to go through")

Here, our hypotheses are that DIMINUTIVE comes with a positive valence shift and ADVERSE and DIRECTIONAL with a negative valence shift.

Predictor	Shift	Derived	Base
Pattern	.082	.093	.076
Concreteness	.009	.001	.030
Arousal	.002	.006	.001
Pattern:Concreteness	.018	.009	.008
Base frequency	.135	N/A	.524
Derived frequency	.148	.277	N/A
Adjusted R^2	.38***	.37***	.63***

Table 3: Study 2 model fit (explained variance)

Predictor	Shift	Derived	Base
AN-	-.06 *	–	.04 ***
ANTI-	–	-.05 *	-.03 *
-IN	.06 *	.07 **	–
Concreteness	-.04 ***	–	-.01*
ANTI-:Concreteness	.07 **	.06 *	–
-CHEN:Concreteness	.04 *	–	–
Base frequency	.16 ***	N/A	-.16 ***
Derived frequency	-.17 ***	-.18 ***	N/A

Table 4: Study 2: Coefficients of predictors

Results. We again start with model fit (Table 4). While the fit is lower than in Study 1, the new dataset is much more varied. Thus, we consider the (highly significant) Adjusted R^2 of .38 as still very good. Again, frequency explains much of the variance, followed by the derivational pattern.

The coefficients in Table 4 again show that our hypotheses hold up only partially. A significant negative effect for the AN- pattern is explained by the corresponding results for the base verbs, which show a highly significant positive valence compared to all other patterns in the dataset. We do not find a main effect for -CHEN, but a positive interaction with concreteness: concrete objects (*Hund*, "dog") gain in valence through diminution (*Hündchen*, "doggie") while abstract objects do not or can even acquire a pejorative component (*Idee, Ideechen* "idea, little idea"). A comparable interpretation offers itself for ANTI- where again there is no main effect but an interaction with concreteness (compare the strongly negative *antisemitisch* with the neutral *antibiotisch*). A somewhat unexpected result is the positive main effect of the female pattern -IN. A possible interpretation is that the marked female forms, many of which are professions, are only chosen when the gender is relevant, which is supported by the occurrence of positive evaluative adjectives ("good", "skilled"). In this connection, our results are a contribution to the characterization of gender bias in language (cf., Terkik et al. (2016) for another example of such study). At any rate, a more detailed analysis of the contexts is required to understand this effect better. Lack of a negative effect for *über* shows that for certain patterns an approach which is based on semantic subclasses of the derived terms is necessary to detect valence shifts that are more fine-grained.

As in Study 1, there was an overall negative effect of concreteness; however, this time, arousal did not play any significant role (its interaction being specific to the semantic classes annotated in the *über* dataset).

5 Conclusion

In this study, we have applied a kind of "magnifying glass" approach: instead of attempting to characterize the meaning of a word as completely as possible from distributional evidence, we focus on a small set of specific meaning components centered around emotional valence, and investigated how the strength of these components is influenced by derivational word formation. We described a method that can be used to extract a data-driven analysis of valence shifts and their interactions with other variables: It maps distributional representations for the words onto a valence scale and uses regression analysis as a pattern mining framework. We showed that the method can use manual annotation when available (Study 1) but also scales to larger, automatically generated datasets (Study 2). Beyond valence, our approach is applicable to other meaning components. Our analysis has uncovered a number of novel observations, notably the modulation of emotional valence for prefix verbs encoding boundary crossing (Study 1) and the unexpected presence of a positive evaluative meaning nuance in the female pattern (Study 2), as well as interactions between factors (Study 1 and Study 2). In particular, we found a strong effect of concreteness in modulating emotional valence shifts in derivation.

Acknowledgments

We gratefully acknowledge funding of our research by the DFG, SFB 732 (project B9: Lapesa and Padó; project B4: Pross and Roßdeutscher).

References

Dressler, W. U. and L. M. Barbaresi (1998). Morphopragmatics. In J. B. Jef Verschueren, Jan-Olaf Östman and C. Bulcaen (Eds.), *Handbook of Pragmatics: 1997 Installment*. John Benjamins Publishing.

Faaß, G. and K. Eckart (2013). Sdewac – a corpus of parsable sentences from the web. In *Language Processing and Knowledge in the Web*, Volume 8105 of *Lecture Notes in Computer Science*, pp. 61–68. Springer Berlin Heidelberg.

Hill, F. and A. Korhonen (2014). Concreteness and subjectivity as dimensions of lexical meaning. In *Proceedings of ACL*, Baltimore, USA, pp. 725–731.

Jurafsky, D. (1996). Universal tendencies in the semantics of the diminutive. *Language 72*(3), 533–578.

Kisselew, M., S. Padó, A. Palmer, and J. Šnajder (2015). Obtaining a better understanding of distributional models of German derivational morphology. In *Proceedings of IWCS*, London, UK, pp. 58–63.

Köper, M. and S. Schulte im Walde (2016a). Automatically generated affective norms of abstractness, arousal, imageability and valence for 350000 German lemmas. In *Proceedings of LREC*, Portoroz, Slovenia, pp. 2595–2598.

Köper, M. and S. Schulte im Walde (2016b). Distinguishing literal and non-literal usage of German particle verbs. In *Proceedings of NAACL-HLT*, San Diego, USA, pp. 353–362.

Kuperman, V., Z. Estes, M. Brysbaert, and A. B. Warriner (2014). Emotion and language: Valence and arousal affect word recognition. *Journal of Experimental Psychology. General 143*(3), 1065–1081.

Lazaridou, A., M. Marelli, R. Zamparelli, and M. Baroni (2013). Compositional-ly derived representations of morphologically complex words in distributional semantics. In *Proceedings of ACL*, Sofia, Bulgaria, pp. 1517–1526.

Lindeman, R. H., P. F. Merenda, and R. Z. Gold (1980). *Introduction to Bivariate and Multivariate Analysis*. Glenview, IL, USA: Scott Foresman.

Luong, M.-T., R. Socher, and C. D. Manning (2013). Better word representations with recursive neural networks for morphology. In *Proceedings of CoNLL*, Sofia, Bulgaria, pp. 104–113.

Mikolov, T., K. Chen, G. Corrado, and J. Dean (2013). Efficient estimation of word representations in vector space. In *Proceedings of ICLR*, Scottsdale, AZ.

Mohammad, S. M., E. Shutova, and P. D. Turney (2016). Metaphor as a medium for emotion: An empirical study. In *Proceedings of STARSEM*, Berlin, Germany, pp. 23–33.

Padó, S., A. Herbelot, M. Kisselew, and J. Šnajder (2016). Predictability of distributional semantics in derivational word formation. In *Proceedings of COLING*, Osaka, Japan, pp. 1285–1296.

Pang, B. and L. Lee (2008). Opinion mining and sentiment analysis. *Foundations and Trends in Information Retrieval 2*(1–2), 1–135.

Plag, I. (2003). *Word-formation in English*. Cambridge Textbooks in Linguistics. Cambridge University Press.

Pross, T. and A. Roßdeutscher (2015). Measuring out the relation between conceptual structures and truth-conditional semantics. In *Selected papers from the Workshop "Bridging Formal and Conceptual Semantics"*, Düsseldorf.

Snefjella, B. and V. Kuperman (2016). It's all in the delivery: Effects of context valence, arousal, and concreteness on visual word processing. *Cognition 156*, 135–146.

Terkik, A., E. Prud'hommeaux, C. O. Alm, C. Homan, and S. Franklin (2016). Analyzing gender bias in student evaluations. In *Proceedings of COLING*, Osaka, Japan, pp. 868–876.

Turney, P. D., Y. Neuman, D. Assaf, and Y. Cohen (2011). Literal and metaphorical sense identification through concrete and abstract context. In *Proceedings of EMNLP*, Edinburgh, United Kingdom, pp. 680–690.

Vinson, D., M. Ponari, and G. Vigliocco (2014). How does emotional content affect lexical processing? *Cognition and Emotion 28*(4), 737–746.

Compositionality for perceptual classification

Staffan Larsson
Centre for Linguistic Theory and Studies in Probability (CLASP)
Department of Philosophy, Linguistics and Theory of Science, University of Gothenburg
sl@ling.gu.se

Abstract

We compare three approaches to compositional semantics for words that are modeled (in part) using perceptual classifiers: "meanings as sets", "meanings as transparent functions", and "meanings as opaque functions". The approaches are evaluated according to whether they fulfill a set of desiderata, including dealing with non-intersective compositionality, working with state of the art classifiers, and accounting for learning of perceptual meanings. We find that none of the current approaches fulfill all our desiderata.

1 Introduction

The idea of using classifiers in modeling perceptual meanings has recently received much attention in a variety of research fields, mostly if not exclusively focusing on visual domains. A couple of different overall approaches can be discerned, and in this paper we provide an overview and comparison of these approaches. Among perceptual domains[1] we count both visual and other domains. Among the visual domains, meanings of spatial terms and colour terms have so far received the most attention from the research community. In work on vagueness, the domain of height is often used.

By perceptual words we mean words with perceptual meanings. By perceptual meaning we mean the aspect of meaning of an expression e which enables an agent to decide, based on perceptual information derived from some situation s, whether e holds of (is true of, describes etc.) s. Of course, each individual perceptual domain has its own unique features and needs to be studied separately. However, by regarding perceptual meanings as a more or less uniform phenomenon, we are assuming that useful generalizations can be made across specific perceptual domains.

The general problem of compositionality for perceptual classification can be described as follows: Given an NL expression (phrase or sentence) e that includes $n \geq 2$ perceptual words (or subexpressions) $e_1, \ldots, e_n$, how can an agent decide whether e correctly describes a visual scene s? This minimally requires computing the meaning c of e and classifying a situation s as being described (or not) by c. The different approaches to compositionality for classifiers give different solutions to how this is to be done[2].

2 Desiderata on solution

In this section, we list a couple of possible desiderata on solutions to the problem of compositionality for perceptual meanings. For each feature, each approach will be marked with "+", "-" or "?". A "+" means that at least a proof of concept solution addressing the desideratum in question exists, and "-" means that no proof of concept exists. Unclear cases are marked "?".

A solution to the problem of compositionality for perceptual classification should...

---

[1] We use this term to mean something more specific than "sensory modality" (which include visual, auditory, tactile, olfactory, and taste modalities).

[2] Note that we are limiting our analysis to the modeling of perceptual words using classifiers, excluding e.g. vector space analyses of word meanings. While there may be some affinities, exploring these is left for future work

...handle intersective compositionality [COM]. Most work on compositionality for classifiers focuses on intersective compositionality, where a classifier c is composed from two classifiers c_1 and c_2 by saying that c classifies s positively to the extent that both c_1 and c_2 classify s positively. For example, we may assume that "light green" can be interpreted as "light and green", or that "upper right" means "upper and right".

...handle non-intersective compositionality [NON]. There seem to be cases where intersective compositionality does not work, and this is an area where the different approaches differentiate in interesting ways, as will be shown below. For example, "sort of green" probably does not mean "sort of and green" in the way that "light green" can be (possibly) modeled as meaning "light and green"[3].

...account for learning of perceptual meanings [LEA]. This amounts to updating classifiers based on sensory observations of visual scenes and associated linguistic descriptions. This can be done in different ways, e.g. from corpora or from interaction with humans.

...account for vagueness [VAG]. Given that there will always be some variation in human judgement (McMahan and Stone, 2015), one may also want a solution to account for (replicate or at least explain) the observed variability. This is especially relevant for vague judgements (which may possibly include all perceptual judgements)[4]

...work with state of the art classifiers [SOA]. There are many approaches to visual classification, and recently deep learning approaches have made great strides. It is of course an advantage if an account of compositionality for visual classifiers can benefit from these advances, and therefore it is desirable that the account is neutral to the type of classifier, as far as possible.

...connect perceptual meanings to other semantic phenomena [SEM]. For example, inference, quantification and modality. Being able to reason based on observations, bringing together perceptual and linguistic information, would presumably be useful in e.g. robotics. Reasoning about modality, e.g. distinguishing necessary, possible, impossible and actual states of affairs, can also be expected to be useful in many AI applications.

3 Existing approaches to compositionality for visual classifiers

In this section, we review and compare a few different approaches to the use of classifiers for judging whether a sentence holds of an observed situation.

3.1 Meanings as sets

In work on formal semantics in the context of perception in robots, several researchers (Matuszek et al., 2012; Krishnamurthy and Kollar, 2013) have used classifiers in conjunction with NL semantics based on first order logic (FOL) in the Possible Worlds Semantics (PWS) tradition (Montague, 1974).

The idea here is to apply all classifiers to all objects in the scene, producing a first order model where meanings of predicates are sets of referents (or n-tuples of referents in the case of n-place relations). This makes it possible to apply standard FOL compositional semantics to sentences, and to evaluate these using standard model-theoretic semantics.

---

[3]In general, it appears that (at least) adverbs that modify (perceptual) adjectives cannot be modeled using intersective compositionality.

[4]Vague words are often also context sensitive, so that e.g. a tall basketball player is generally taken to be taller than a tall person. However, the two phenomena are in principle independent. While accounting for context-sensitivity is a possible desideratum on accounts of perceptual semantics, we have not included it here.

The main advantage of this approach is that it is pretty straightforward and uses standard machinery of formal semantics, which means that inference, quantification etc. are taken care of **[SEM+]**. Note, however, that on this approach predicates are not evaluated against objective referents in a world (encompassing everything there is), but against mental and subjective representations of observed and classified referents in a specific situation (typically encompassing only a limited part of the world). This seems to depart from foundational assumptions of PWS and may possibly put into question existing accounts of e.g. quantification and modality. Another advantage is that there are no limits on the kinds of classifier that can be used **[SOA+]**.

Existing accounts of compositionality rely exclusively on set intersection. For example, Krishnamurthy and Kollar (2013) analyze "blue mug on table" as the intersection of the sets [blue], [mug] and [on-table][5]**[COM+]**. A problem for this approach, however, is non-intersective compositionality. Intersective compositionality will not work when a phrase containing more than one perceptual predicate cannot be analysed as a conjunction, and (as far as we know) there is currently no set-theoretic analysis of non-intersective compositionality **[NON-]**.

There is some work on learning and vagueness in the PWS tradition(Barker, 2002) which appears to be compatible with the meanings-as-sets approach and that may be applicable to perceptual semantics, although this remains to be shown **[LEA?, VAG?]**.

3.2   Meanings as transparent functions

In general, a parameterised function takes an input (domain) and a set of parameters, and yields an output (range). We distinguish *transparent* and *opaque* functions as follows. A transparent function is a parameterised function where the input and parameters have clear interpretations understandable to humans, and where the effects on the output of manipulating the parameters are predictable. For example, a simple threshold classifier (parameter: threshold) or a noisy threshold classifier (parameters: threshold, standard deviation). An *opaque function* is a parameterised function where the parameters do *not* have clear interpretations understandable to humans. Examples include most neural networks, including deep neural nets, and probability distributions collected from observations[6]. Note that the distinction is slightly vague and that there are borderline cases. For example, a n-input neuron with a threshold implements to a transparent linear classifier function in n-dimensional space.

Gapp (1994) models spatial concepts using cubic spline functions[7], essentially parameterized (transparent) functions mapping points in 3D space onto "degrees of applicability" in the interval $[0..1]$[8]. These functions are transparent in the sense that there is an observable and understandable connection between the function parameters and the resulting distribution of degrees of applicability across the spatial domain. McMahan and Stone (2015) model meanings of colour words as probability distributions over colour spaces. These distributions are represented by probabilistic thresholds derived from a corpus of colour descriptions. Transparent functions are also used for modeling perceptual concepts in Larsson (2011) (using "(to the) right" as a proof of concept) and Larsson (2013) (adding compositionality, exemplified by "far right" and "upper right") and incorporating vagueness (Fernández and Larsson, 2014) ("tall"). Here, the meaning of "(to the) right" is modeled as a two-input perceptron, which is transparent in the sense that it the connection between the parameters and the resulting classification results is understandable (with some effort). Specifically, the weights on the two inputs modify the slant of the line dividing "(to the) right" from "not (to the) right", while the threshold modifies the distance of this line from the centre.

On the approach taken in Larsson (2013), high-level logical aspects of meaning are represented together with low-level aspects (classifiers etc.) in a single representational system (Type Theory with

---

[5]We are here simplifying somewhat by not seeing "table" as a separate predicate, as done in the original.

[6]Note that if a probability distribution derived from observations is analysed using some kind of curve-fitting, it may become transparent.

[7]Cubic splines are constructed of piecewise third-order polynomials which pass through a set of control points (`http://mathworld.wolfram.com/CubicSpline.html`)

[8]Note that degrees of applicability do not form a probability distribution.

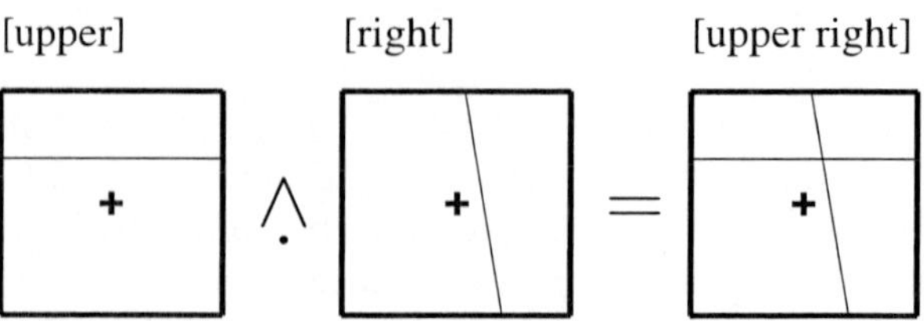

Figure 1: Intersective compositionality for "upper right" on the transparent functions approach

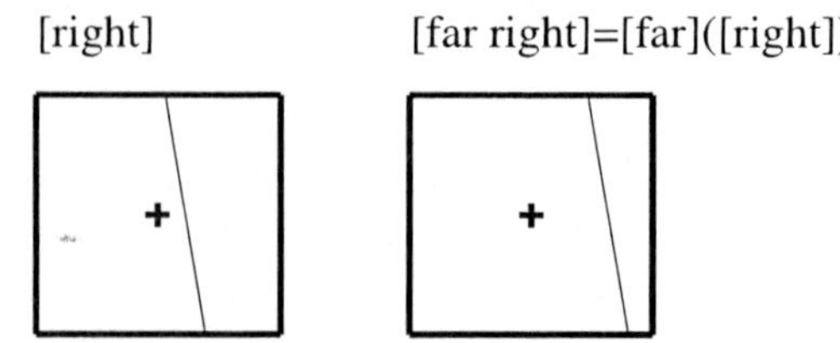

Figure 2: Non-intersective compositionality for "far right" on the transparent functions approach

Records or TTR (Cooper, 2012)). A wide variety of semantic phenomena have been described using TTR including modeling of intensionality and mental attitudes (Cooper, 2005), dynamic generalised quantifiers (Cooper, 2004), co-predication and dot types in lexical innovation, frame semantics for temporal reasoning, reasoning in hypothetical contexts (Cooper, 2011) and enthymematic reasoning (Breitholtz and Cooper, 2011) **[SEM+]**.

On the transparent function approach, intersective compositionality can be handled in various ways. Gapp (1994) analyses "between X and Y" as meaning (roughly) "in front of X and in front of Y, with X and Y facing each other", with the applicability score for a point being "between" an two facing objects X and Y computed as the arithmetic mean of the scores for p for "in-front-of X" and "in-front-of Y". As a proof of concept of intersective compositionality for transparent classifiers, Larsson (2013) shows how to compute the intersective meaning of "upper right" from the meanings of "upper" and "right" (see Figure 1). This is done by simply conjoining the classifiers for "upper" and "right" so that a point (in 2D space) is to the upper right iff it is "upper" and "(to the) right" **[COM+]**.

Larsson (2013) also provides a proof of concept of non-intersective compositionality for degree modifiers, accounting for "far" in "far right". The proposal is that "far" takes parameters of the "right" classifier and yields modified classifier for "far rightness" with an increased threshold (see 2). Together, these two examples indicate how both intersective and non-intersective can be handled in this version of the transparent functions approach **[NON+]**.

In Fernández and Larsson (2014), the above analysis is supplemented with an account of vagueness, using probabilistic TTR (Cooper et al., 2015). In line with Lassiter (2011), both Fernández and Larsson (2014) and McMahan and Stone (2015) uses a noisy threshold, and in Fernández and Larsson (2014) the meaning of "tall" is modeled as a transparent function parameterised by mean and standard deviation **[VAG+]**.

In Larsson (2013), learning is accounted for by modifying parameters of classifiers based on observed judgements (e.g. by a teacher in the case of supervised learning). One could also imagine how extending the corpus underlying the probabilistic thresholds in McMahan and Stone (2015) could result in updated thresholds, thus providing the basis for a learning mechanism. **[LEA+]**

On the downside, on this approach probability distributions are computed from transparent functions, which excludes deep learning, thus forcing the use of lower quality classifiers compared to the state of the art **[SOA-]**.

3.3   Meanings as opaque functions

As mentioned above, opaque functions are functions whose parameters (if any) are understandable to human interpreters. We believe that a couple of related approaches to meanings as classifiers can be seen as examples of this overall approach.

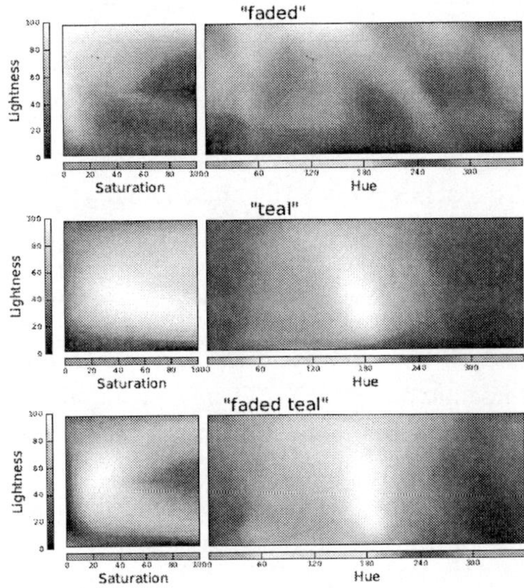

Figure 3: Intersective compositionality for "faded teal" on the opaque functions approach. Picture from Monroe et al. (2016).

Monroe et al. (2016) build on McMahan and Stone (2015) but, instead of explicitly computing thresholds, encode probability distributions implicitly in a recurrent neural network sequence decoder. Feeding a word sequence and a colour sample to this network yields the probability of the sequence as describing the colour sample, equal to the product of probabilities of each successive word in the sentence conditioned on the colour sample input and the preceding words. On this approach, classification is done by getting the probability for the point in conceptual space corresponding to the situation. This is similar to the approach of Logan and Sadler (1996), although the latter model "degrees of goodness" rather than probabilities. Monroe et al. (2016) includes an account of intersective compositionality for dealing with descriptions not found in the training set. If one ignores the word sequence probabilities, Monroe et al. (2016) can be interpreted as regarding intersective composition as equivalent to multiplying together probability distribution matrices (see Figure 3)[9]. Schlangen et al. (2016) model classifiers as neural networks taking feature representations of objects and returning "appropriateness score"; these classifiers presumably correspond (for visual space) to something like the "degrees of goodness" of Logan and Sadler. Intersective composition is done not on the classifier level (the matrices) but on the combined classifier outputs for an object described by words $w_1, \ldots, w_n$, by simple multiplicative composition (for nominal constructions). Åstbom (2017) shows that geometric mean provides a better analysis than arithmetic mean when composing a matrix for "upper and to the right" from matrices for "upper" and "to the right" [COM+].

Regarding non-intersective modifiers, the question is to what extent they can be represented as distributions of appropriateness scores or probabilities in perceptual spaces, and thus handled by the regular mechanisms of intersective compositionality. We have not been able to find any account of non-intersective compositionality on the opaque functions approach [NON-].

Perhaps the main advantage of this approach is that since it does not matter how probability distributions are encoded, deep learning can be used to yield high quality classifiers [SOA+]. Also, the distributions can be derived from observed judgements, possibly amended with a smoothing function [LEA+]. Furthermore, provided that vagueness can be modeled as probability distributions, this approach is well suited to model vagueness [VAG+].

---

[9]However, the output probability for a word in a multi-word sequence will also be conditioned on the previous words, which enables this approach at least in principle to learn a separate meaning for "teal" when it follows "faded", provided "faded teal" is the training corpus. Furthermore, since the output of the hidden layer of each node in an RNN is fed forward into the next node, they can also model more complex phenomena such as long distance dependencies.

Meanings as...	INT	NON	LEA	VAG	SOA	SEM
... sets	+	-	?	?	+	+
... transparent functions	+	+	+	+	-	+
... opaque functions	+	-	+	+	+	?

Table 1: How the different approaches satisfy the desiderata (INT=intersective compositionality, NON=non-intersective compositionality, LEA=learning perceptual meanings, VAG=accounting for vagueness, SOA=work with state of the art classifiers, SEM=connect to other semantic phenomena

Since this approach has not so far been connected with work on formal semantics, it is unclear to what extent it connects to other semantic phenomena. There is work on inference in deep neural networks (Kumar et al., 2015) but as of yet, many semantic phenomena (such as quantification, modality, intensional contexts, and co-predication) remain to be captured in terms of this approach **[SEM?]**. However, there seems to be no principled reason why one could not connect opaque function classifiers to TTR in the same way as has been done for transparent function classifiers (see above), yielding probabilistic type judgments.

4   Discussion

Table 1 shows an overview of our conclusions. The lack of an account of non-intersective compositionality is, on our view, a serious shortcoming of the "meanings as sets" approach. The main drawback of the "transparent functions" approach is that it does not work with state of the art classifiers, such as deep neural nets. The reason for this is of course that such classifiers are not transparent functions. Finally, insofar as compositionality in the "opaque functions" approach is limited to intersective compositionality, this means that none of the current approaches fulfill all our desiderata. The question is then if any of the approaches can be improved to satisfy all the desiderata, or if some kind of hybrid approach is needed. We hope to address this question in future work.

Acknowledgements

The author would like to thank to the anonymous IWCS reviewers whose perceptive comments helped improve this paper.

References

Åstbom, A. (2017). How function of objects affects geometry of spatial descriptions. a study of swedish and japanese. bachelors thesis.

Barker, C. (2002). The Dynamics of Vagueness. *Linguistics and Philosophy 25*(1), 1–36.

Breitholtz, E. and R. Cooper (2011). Enthymemes as rhetorical resources. In *Proceedings of the 15th Workshop on the Semantics and Pragmatics of Dialogue (SemDial 2011)*, Los Angeles (USA), pp. 149–157.

Cooper, R. (2004). Dynamic generalised quantifiers and hypothetical contexts. In *Ursus Philosophicus, a festschrift for Björn Haglund*. Department of Philosophy, University of Gothenburg.

Cooper, R. (2005). Austinian truth, attitudes and type theory. *Research on Language and Computation 3*, 333–362.

Cooper, R. (2011). Copredication, quantification and frames. In S. Pogodalla and J.-P. Prost (Eds.), *LACL*, Volume 6736 of *Lecture Notes in Computer Science*, pp. 64–79. Springer.

Cooper, R. (2012). Type theory and semantics in flux. In R. Kempson, N. Asher, and T. Fernando (Eds.), *Handbook of the Philosophy of Science*, Volume 14: Philosophy of Linguistics. Elsevier BV. General editors: Dov M. Gabbay, Paul Thagard and John Woods.

Cooper, R., S. Dobnik, S. Larsson, and S. Lappin (2015). Probabilistic type theory and natural language semantics. *LiLT (Linguistic Issues in Language Technology) 10*.

Fernández, R. and S. Larsson (2014). Vagueness and learning: A type-theoretic approach. In *Proceedings of the 3rd Joint Conference on Lexical and Computational Semantics (*SEM 2014)*.

Gapp, K.-P. (1994). Basic meanings of spatial relations: computation and evaluation in 3d space. In *Proceedings of the Twelfth AAAI National Conference on Artificial Intelligence*, pp. 1393–1398. AAAI Press.

Krishnamurthy, J. and T. Kollar (2013). Jointly Learning to Parse and Perceive : Connecting Natural Language to the Physical World. *Transactions of the Association for Computational Linguistics 1*, 193–206.

Kumar, A., O. Irsoy, J. Su, J. Bradbury, R. English, B. Pierce, P. Ondruska, I. Gulrajani, and R. Socher (2015). Ask me anything: Dynamic memory networks for natural language processing. *CoRR, abs/1506.07285*.

Larsson, S. (2011). The ttr perceptron: Dynamic perceptual meanings and semantic coordination. In *Proceedings of the 15th Workshop on the Semantics and Pragmatics of Dialogue (SemDial 2011)*, Los Angeles (USA).

Larsson, S. (2013). Formal semantics for perceptual classification. *Journal of Logic and Computation*.

Lassiter, D. (2011). Vagueness as probabilistic linguistic knowledge. In R. Nowen, R. van Rooij, U. Sauerland, and H. C. Schmitz (Eds.), *Vagueness in Communication*. Springer.

Logan, G. D. and D. D. Sadler (1996). A computational analysis of the apprehension of spatial relations.

Matuszek, C., N. FitzGerald, and L. Zettlemoyer (2012). A joint model of language and perception for grounded attribute learning. In *Proceedings of the 29th International Conference on Machine Learning*.

McMahan, B. and M. Stone (2015). A bayesian model of grounded color semantics. *Transactions of the Association for Computational Linguistics 3*, 103–115.

Monroe, W., N. D. Goodman, and C. Potts (2016). Learning to generate compositional color descriptions. *arXiv preprint arXiv:1606.03821*.

Montague, R. (1974). *Formal Philosophy: Selected Papers of Richard Montague*. New Haven: Yale University Press. ed. and with an introduction by Richmond H. Thomason.

Schlangen, D., S. Zarrie, and C. Kennington (2016). Resolving References to Objects in Photographs using the Words-As-Classifiers Model. In *Proceedings of the 54th Annual Meeting of the Association for Computational Linguistics (ACL 2016)*.

Dual Embeddings and Metrics for Relational Similarity

Dandan Li
U.S. Army Research Laboratory
`happydandan2016@gmail.com`

Douglas Summers-Stay
U.S. Army Research Laboratory
`douglas.a.summers-stay.civ@mail.mil`

Abstract

Abstract. In this work, we study the problem of relational similarity by combining different word embeddings learned from different types of contexts. The word2vec model with linear bag-of-words contexts can capture more topical and less functional similarity, while the dependency-based word embeddings with syntactic contexts can capture more functional and less topical similarity. We explore topical space and functional space simultaneously by considering these two word embeddings and different metrics. We evaluate our model on relational similarity framework, and report state-of-the-art performance on standard test collections.

1   Introduction

Measuring relational similarity between two word pairs plays important roles in natural language processing (NLP). The techniques for solving this problem can be applied to a variety of NLP tasks, such as query expansion, word sense disambiguation, machine translation, information extraction and question answering. Previous work addressing the problem can be roughly classified into three categories: (1) learning word embeddings from large collections of text using variants of neural networks (Mikolov et al. (2013a); Mikolov et al. (2013b); Mikolov et al. (2013c); Levy and Goldberg (2014)) or global matrix factorization (Deerwester et al. (1990); Turney (2012)); (2) extracting knowledge from existing semantic networks, such as WordNet (Yang and Powers (2005); Alvarez and Lim (2007); Hughes and Ramage (2007)) and ConceptNet (Boteanu and Chernova (2015)); (3) combining the above two models by various ways (Agirre et al. (2009); Zhila et al. (2013); Iacobacci et al. (2015); Summers-Stay et al. (2016)).

The empirical evidence shows that the word representations learned from neural network models do an especially good job in capturing not only attributional similarities between words but also similarities between pairs of words (Mikolov et al. (2013c)). Levy and Goldberg (2014) generalize the skip-gram model with negative sampling to include arbitrary word contexts and present the dependency-based word embeddings, which are learned from syntactic contexts derived from dependency parse-trees. Qualitative and quantitative analysis demonstrates that the word2vec model with linear bag-of-words contexts can yield broad topical similarity while the dependency-based word embeddings with syntactic contexts can capture more functional similarity. Turney (2012) is the first, to the best of our knowledge, to raise the word vector representations in a dual space and unify semantic relations and compositions by the dual-space model. The dual-space model consists of a domain space and a function space, where the domain or topic of a word is characterized by the nouns that occur near it and the function or role of a word is characterized by the syntactic context that relates it to the verbs that occur near it.

We detail our main contributions as follows. (1) In this paper, we use the word2vec model with linear bag-of-words contexts to capture the domain of a word, and the dependency-based word embeddings with syntactic contexts to characterize the function of a word. The broad contexts used in our model can provide richer information for measuring domain similarity (i.e., topic, subject, or field similarity) and function similarity (i.e, role, relationship, or usage similarity) than noun or verb-based patterns for contexts in Turney's (2012) model. (2) The two existing models for measuring relational similarity are: the directional similarity model (Zhila et al. (2013)) and the dual-space model consisting of domain and function space (Turney (2012)). Both models suffer some drawbacks. The directional similarity model explores the difference of two relationships in multiple topicality dimensions in the vector space. However, it ignores the spatial distances between word vectors, which can reveal the function similarity of words in function space. The dual-space model can measure the domain similarity and function similarity between words. However, it only computes the domain similarity between two single words and places less emphasis on the domain similarity between two relations. In this work, we propose a new dual-space model for measuring relational similarity, which combines the advantages of the two existing models. (3) We evaluate our model on relational similarity framework and report state-of-the-art performance on SAT analogy questions.

2   Related Work

Vector space models have a long, rich history in the field of natural language processing, where each word is represented as a real-valued vector in a continuous vector space. All these models depend in some way or another on the distributional hypothesis which states that words that occur in similar contexts tend to have similar meanings (Harris, 1954; Firth, 1957). There are the two main model families for learning word vectors: (1) global matrix factorization methods, such as latent semantic analysis, which generates embeddings from term-document matrices by singular value decomposition (Deerwester et al. (1990)); (2) neural network models, such as the skip-gram and continuous bag of words models of ()Mikolov et al. (2013a); Mikolov et al. (2013b); Mikolov et al. (2013c)), referred to as word2vec, which learn embeddings by training a network to predict neighboring words. Levy and Goldberg (2014) generalize the skip-gram model with negative sampling to include arbitrary word contexts, learn embeddings from syntactic contexts and demonstrate that the dependency-based embeddings can capture more functional similarity than the original skip-gram embeddings (word2vec).

Several algorithms have been proposed for solving SAT-style analogy questions. A good algorithm for recognizing analogies can also help to solve the classification problem of semantic relations, which has potential applications in machine translation, information extraction and word sense disambiguation. Quesada et al. (2004) propose LSA as a method to represent the relations between words and use a prediction to represent relation comparisons in the LSA semantic space. Veale (2004) considers the utility of the taxonomic structure of WordNet to the solution of SAT analogies. Turney and Littman (2005) show that the cosine metric in the Vector Space Model of information retrieval can be used to solve analogy questions and to classify semantic relations. Turney (2012) introduces a dual-space model, which consists of a space for measuring domain similarity and a space for measuring function similarity. The dual-space model has been applied to measuring relation similarity and compositional similarity.

3   Word Embeddings with Different Context Types

Word2vec (W2V) is one of the most popular word embedding methods that learn word vectors from raw text. It has two models for generating dense embeddings: the skip-gram model and the continuous bag-of-words (CBOW) model. The training objective of the skip-gram model is to predict each surrounding word in a context window of $2k$ words from the target word. So for $k = 2$, the contexts of the target word w_t are w_{t-2}, w_{t-1}, w_{t+1}, w_{t+2} and we are predicting each of these from the word w_t. However, a context window with a smaller size k may miss some important contexts while including some accidental ones. Recently, Levy et al. propose the dependency-based word embeddings (DEP), which generalize the skip-gram model with negative sampling, and move from linear bag-of-words contexts to syntactic contexts that are derived from automatically produced dependency parse-trees. Embeddings produced from different kinds of contexts can induce different word similarities. The original skip-gram embeddings can yield broad topical similarities, while the dependency-based word embeddings can capture more functional similarities (Levy et al., 2014).

4 Relational Similarity

Relational similarity measures the degree of correspondence between two relations (Jurgens et al. (2012)). The task can be modeled as an analogy problem, where given two pairs of words, *A:B* and *C:D*, the goal is to determine the degree to which the semantic relation between *A* and *B* is similar to that between *C* and *D*. We first introduce two types of existing models for relational similarity.

4.1 Directional Similarity Model

Zhila et al. (2013) propose a directional similarity model to evaluate the correspondence between relations. Given two pairs of words A:B and C:D, suppose (v_A, v_B) and (v_C, v_D) are the corresponding vectors of these words. Relational similarity of these two word pairs is defined as the cosine function between the two directional vectors of $(v_A - v_B)$ and $(v_C - v_D)$:

$$\text{Similarity}(A\!:\!B :: C\!:\!D) = \frac{(v_A - v_B) \cdot (v_C - v_D)}{||v_A - v_B|| ||v_C - v_D||}.$$

In this model, the relationship between two words is represented by the difference of corresponding two word vectors, which reveals the change from one word to the other in terms of multiple topicality dimensions in the vector space. From the geometric point of view, if two relationship vectors are relatively parallel (i.e., share the same direction), then the two word pairs can be considered as they have similar relations. They apply the model to the problem of relation classification which determines whether two pairs share the same relation. The goal here is to design a model for answering the more difficult SAT analogy questions. However, sometimes this directional similarity model can not measure the analogy problem correctly.

4.2 A Dual-Space Model

Why does the directional similarity model fail on some analogy questions? One possible reason is that the model depends on direction alone and ignores spatial distance between word vectors. Turney (2012) presents a dual-space model to unify semantic relations and compositions. The dual-space model consists of a domain space for measuring domain similarity and a function space for measuring function similarity. He gives a good example to explain this model. Consider the analogy example, *traffic:street :: water:riverbed*. *Traffic* and *street* share the same domain, the domain of *transportation*. *Water* and *riverbed* share the same domain, the domain of *hydrology*. On the other hand, *traffic* and *water* share the same function, the function of *flow*, and *street* and *riverbed* share the same function, the function of *carry*. The model can recognize that the semantic relation between *traffic* and *street* is analogous to the relation between *water* and *riverbed* by considering the combination of domain and function similarity. A general explanation for the model is, given an analogy A:B :: C:D, A and B, C and D have relatively high domain similarity in their respective domains; A and C, B and D have relatively high function similarity in respective function spaces.

4.3 A New Dual-Space Model: Refining the Directional Similarity Model and the Dual-Space Model

The directional similarity model (Zhila et al. (2013)) explores the difference of two relationships in multiple topicality dimensions in the vector space. However, it ignores the spatial distance between word vectors, which can reveal the function similarity of words in function space. The dual-space model (Turney (2012)) can measure both domain similarity and function similarity between words. However, it only computes the domain similarity between two single word vectors and places less emphasis on the domain similarity between two relations. Moreover, Turney's (2012) model uses only noun or verb-based patterns for contexts to model domain or function space. In this paper, we propose a novel dual-space model, which combines the advantages of the above two existing models. We use the word2vec-based directional similarity model to measure the similarity of two relations in domain space, and the dependency-based word embeddings to represent the word vector in function space. The two embeddings used in our model consider broader contexts than those in the original dual-space model, which can provide richer information for measuring domain similarity and function similarity.

A mathematical description of our dual-space model is given as follows:

Given two pairs of words A:B and C:D, suppose $V_{W2V(A)}$, $V_{W2V(B)}$, $V_{W2V(C)}$, $V_{W2V(D)}$ are the vectors of these words in domain space and $V_{DEP(A)}$, $V_{DEP(B)}$, $V_{DEP(C)}$, $V_{DEP(D)}$ are the vectors of these words in function space. Based on the directional similarity model (Zhila et al., 2013), we define the domain similarity of two pairs of words as follows:

$$\text{Similarity}_D(A\!:\!B::C\!:\!D) = \frac{(V_{W2V(A)} - V_{W2V(B)}) \cdot (V_{W2V(C)} - V_{W2V(D)})}{||V_{W2V(A)} - V_{W2V(B)}|| \, ||V_{W2V(C)} - V_{W2V(D)}||}.$$

The function similarity of A and C and the function similarity of B and D are defined respectively as follows:

$$\text{Similarity}_{F1}(A\!:\!C) = \frac{V_{DEP(A)} \cdot V_{DEP(C)}}{||V_{DEP(A)}|| \, ||V_{DEP(C)}||};$$

$$\text{Similarity}_{F2}(B\!:\!D) = \frac{V_{DEP(B)} \cdot V_{DEP(D)}}{||V_{DEP(B)}|| \, ||V_{DEP(D)}||}.$$

We design the method Similarity_{ADD} to combine the above similarities for relational similarity as follows, which satisfies that the combined similarity is high when the component similarities are high:

$$\text{Similarity}_{ADD}(A\!:\!B::C\!:\!D) = \frac{1}{3}(\text{Similarity}_D(A\!:\!B::C\!:\!D) + \text{Similarity}_{F1}(A\!:\!C) + \text{Similarity}_{F2}(B\!:\!D))$$

We give an SAT question in Table 1 to demonstrate how our compositional similarity works. An SAT analogy question consists of a target pair of words and five option pairs of words. The task is to select the option pair that "best expresses a relationship similar to that expressed in the original pair", as stated in the test's directions. We use the 300-dimensional W2V and DEP vectors available for downloading [1]. For the target pair *bruise:skin* in Table 1, our method Similarity_{ADD} (= 0.406) can recognize the correct answer *stain:fabric* although Similarity_D (= 0.189), Similarity_{F1} (= 0.539) and Similarity_{F2} (= 0.491) for the correct answer are all ranked second among five options.

bruise:skin	Similarity_D	Similarity_{F1}	Similarity_{F2}	$\textbf{Similarity}_{ADD}$
muscle:bone	0.023	0.457	**0.622**	0.367
smudge:blemish	-0.135	**0.540**	0.320	0.242
rash:allergy	**0.208**	0.358	0.370	0.312
layer:veneer	-0.091	0.273	0.468	0.216
stain:fabric	0.189	0.539	0.491	**0.406**

Table 1: Experimental results of four models on SAT question *bruise:skin*

5 Experiments and Evaluation

5.1 Relational Similarity Experiment

In the following experiments, we evaluate our approaches to solving analogies by a set of 374 SAT analogy questions, which is the same set of questions as was used in Turney's Dual-Space mode (Turney

---

[1] http://u.cs.biu.ac.il/~nlp/resources/downloads/embeddings-contexts/

(2012)). Precision and Recall are two standard performance measurements used for evaluation. The definitions of precision and recall are specified by (Turney and Littman (2005)). In all experiments, we use the 300-dimensional W2V and DEP vectors pretrained on a concatenation of three large, diverse English corpora, and those vectors are available for downloading [1].

Table 2 shows the experimental results of four approaches presented in Section 4.3 on the set of 374 analogy questions. Two questions are skipped because the vector for the target pair is not available in the collection. Since there are five options for each target pair of an SAT analogy question, random guessing would yield a recall of 20%. Domain similarity $Similarity_D$, function similarity $Similarity_{F1}$ and $Similarity_{F2}$ all perform much better than random guessing. Our compositional similarity model $Similarity_{ADD}$ in the dual space clearly outperforms $Similarity_D$, $Similarity_{F1}$ and $Similarity_{F2}$ in single domain or function space.

	$Similarity_D$ '13	$Similarity_{F1}$	$Similarity_{F2}$	$\mathbf{Similarity_{ADD}}$
Correct	170	139	144	**185**
Incorrect	202	233	228	187
Precision%	45.7	37.4	38.7	**49.7**
Recall%	45.5	37.2	38.5	**49.5**

Table 2: Experimental results on the set of 374 analogy questions

Table 3 splits out the results for different parts of speech of the 374 SAT questions, which include noun:noun, adjective:adjective, verb:verb, noun:adjective or adjective:noun, noun:verb or verb:noun, verb:adjective/adverb or adjective/adverb:verb. We compare the number of correct guesses of our model $Similarity_{ADD}$ with two existing models $Similarity_D$ (Zhila et al. (2013)) and Dual-Space model (Turney (2012))[2]. $Similarity_{ADD}$ works best on the questions with the labels noun:adjective and adjective:adjective. For the questions with the label verb:verb, $Similarity_D$ achieves the best performance. Dual-Space'12 outperforms other two models on the noun:noun, noun:verb and verb:adj/adv questions.

Parts of speech	Total	$\mathbf{Similarity_{ADD}}$	$Similarity_D$ '13	Dual-Space'12
noun:noun	192	95	93	**97**
noun:adj or adj:noun	66	**38**	28	35
noun:verb or verb:noun	54	23	20	**27**
adj:adj	24	**10**	8	9
verb:adj/adv or adj/adv:verb	21	10	9	**12**
verb:verb	17	9	**12**	11

Table 3: Experimental results on the 374 SAT questions labeled with different parts of speech

6 Conclusion and Future Work

In this work, we explore domain space and function space simultaneously by considering two kinds of word embeddings and different metrics. Word embeddings can capture topical and functional information of a word by using different types of contexts, however they are unable to model the words with multiple meanings accurately because a word is represented as just a single vector which carries a weighted average of different meanings. Existing lexical and knowledge databases, such as WordNet, ConceptNet and Cyc, can be modeled as graphs in which words are represented as the nodes and the relations between words are signified by the edges. These databases have more accurate information although their coverage of words and types of relations is usually limited. We plan to look at ways to combine our dual-space model with existing databases to improve the performance of our current system.

---

[2]In the paper (Turney (2012)), the number of questions labeled by noun:noun is 191, and the number of questions labeled by noun:verb or verb:noun is 55.

References

Agirre, E., Alfonseca, E., Hall, K., Kravalova, J., Pasca, M., and Soroa, A. (2009). A study on similarity and relatedness using distributional and wordnet-based approaches. In *NAACL '09 Proceedings of Human Language Technologies: The 2009 Annual Conference of the North American Chapter of the Association for Computational Linguistics*, pages 19–27, Boulder, Colorado.

Alvarez, M. A. and Lim, S. J. (2007). A graph modeling of semantic similarity between words. In *Proceedings of the Conference on Semantic Computing*, pages 355–362.

Boteanu, A. and Chernova, S. (2015). Solving and explaining analogy questions using semantic networks. In *Proceedings of the Twenty-Ninth AAAI Conference on Artificial Intelligence*, pages 1460–1466.

Deerwester, S., Dumais, S. T., Furnas, G. W., Landauer, T. K., and Harshman, R. (1990). Indexing by latent semantics analysis. *Journal of the Association for Information Science and Technology*, 41(6):391–407.

Hughes, T. and Ramage, D. (2007). Lexical semantic relatedness with random graph walks. In *Proceedings of EMNLP-CoNLL-2007*, pages 581–589.

Iacobacci, I., Pilehvar, M. T., and Navigli, R. (2015). Sensembed: learning sense embeddings for word and relational similarity. In *ACL-IJCNLP 2015 : The 53rd Annual Meeting of the Association for Computational Linguistics and the 7th International Joint Conference on Natural Language Processing of the Asian Federation of Natural Language Processing*, pages 95–105, Beijing, China.

Jurgens, D. A., Mohammad, S. M., Turney, P. D., and Holyoak, K. J. (2012). Semeval-2012 task 2: Measuring degrees of relational similarity. In **SEM 2012: The First Joint Conference on Lexical and Computational Semantics*, pages 356–364, Montreal, Canada.

Levy, O. and Goldberg, Y. (2014). Dependency-based word embeddings. In *Proceedings of the 52nd Anua Meeting of the Associations for Computational Linguistics (short papers)*, pages 302–308.

Mikolov, T., Chen, K., Corrado, G., and Dean, J. (2013a). Efficient estimation of word represen-tations in vector space. In *arXiv preprint arXiv: 1301.3781*.

Mikolov, T., Sutskever, I., Chen, K., Corrado, G. S., and Dean, J. (2013b). Distributed rep-resentations of words and phrases and their compositionality. In *Proceedings of the 26th International Conference on Neural Information Processing Systems*, pages 3111–3119, Nevada, USA.

Mikolov, T., Yih, W.-T., and Zweig, G. (2013c). Linguistic regularities in continuous space word repre-sentations. In *Proceedings of the 2013 Conference of the North American Chapter of the Association for Computational Linguistics: Human Language Technologies*, pages 746–751, Atlanta, Georgia, USA.

Quesada, J., Kintsch, W., and Mangalath, P. (2004). Analogy-making as prediction using relational information and lsa vectors. In *Proceedings of the 26th Annual Meeting of the Cognitive Science Society*, page 1623, Austin, TX.

Summers-Stay, D., Voss, C., and Cassidy, T. (2016). Using a distributional semantic vector space with a knowledge base for reasoning in uncertain conditions. *Biologically Inspired Cognitive Architectures*, 16:34–44.

Turney, P. D. (2012). Domain and function: A dual-space model of semantic relations and compositions. *Journal of Artificial Intelligence Research (JAIR)*, 44:533–585.

Turney, P. D. and Littman, M. L. (2005). Corpus-based learning of analogies and semantic relations. *Machine Learning*, 60(1-3):251–278.

Veale, T. (2004). Wordnet sits the sat: A knowledge-based approach to lexical analogy. In *Proceedings of the 16th European Conference on Artificial Intelligence (ECAI 2004)*, pages 606–612, Valencia, Spain.

Yang, D. and Powers, D. M. (2005). Measuring semantic similarity in the taxonomy of wordnet. In *Proceedings of the Twenty-eighth Australasian conference on Computer Science*, pages 315–322.

Zhila, A., Yih, W.-T., and Meek, C. (2013). Combining heterogeneous models for measuring relational similarity. In *Proceedings of NAACL-HLT*, pages 1000–1009.

Action Languages and Question Answering

Yuliya Lierler
University of Nebraska Omaha
`ylierler@unomaha.edu`

Daniela Inclezan
Miami University
`inclezd@miamioh.edu`

Michael Gelfond
Texas Tech University
`michael.gelfond@ttu.edu`

Abstract

This paper describes a methodology for designing Question Answering systems that utilize an action language $\mathcal{ALM}$ to allow inferences based on complex interactions of events described in texts. This methodology assumes the extension of the VERBNET lexicon with interpretable semantic annotations in $\mathcal{ALM}$ and specifies the use of several other NLP resources to produce $\mathcal{ALM}$ system descriptions for input discourses.

1 Introduction

In this paper, we propose a methodology for designing Question Answering (QA) systems that uses state-of-the-art techniques from the field of Natural Language Processing (NLP) complementing them with the latest advances from the field of Knowledge Representation and Reasoning (KRR).

The applicability of KRR for the design and implementation of QA systems was explored by Baral et al. (2004) who demonstrated the suitability of the KRR language Answer Set Prolog (ASP) (Gelfond and Lifschitz, 1991) for this purpose. Balduccini et al. (2008) continued this line of research and described a QA system with an intended wide coverage, based on KRR techniques and NLP tools. Todorova and Gelfond (2011; 2012) addressed the problem from a different angle. They focused on texts restricted to a *controlled* natural language tailored to *motion* verbs and concentrated on answering difficult questions requiring counting. Their knowledge base was written in a higher-level KRR language than ASP, a so-called *action language* called $\mathcal{ALM}$ (Inclezan and Gelfond, 2016).

The system by Todorova and Gelfond processed multiple-sentence texts exemplified by

$$\text{Ann went to the room.} \tag{1}$$

$$\text{Michael left the room.} \tag{2}$$

and derived inferences based on information in these sentences to answer questions such as

$$\textit{Is Michael inside the room (at the end of the story)?} \tag{3}$$

$$\textit{Is Ann inside the room (at the end of the story)?} \tag{4}$$

$$\textit{Is the room empty (at the end of the story)?} \tag{5}$$

In the sequel, we refer to the text composed of sentences (1) and (2) as the *MA* discourse.

Our goal is to build upon the methodology outlined by Todorova and Gelfond by putting more emphasis on the organization of KRR libraries and the NLP stages of QA. We remove some of the constraints assumed by their system: we do not limit ourselves to the motion verbs and we avoid a commitment to a controlled language. Our long term goal is to have a methodology that encompasses texts containing a large collection of action verbs (`go`, `give`, `put` exemplify the class of action verbs). In this paper, we test the feasibility of such a proposal by allowing change of possession verbs such as `grab`, `grasp`, `yank` in addition to motion verbs. Consider a discourse that contains the sentence

$$\text{Michael grasped the suitcase.} \tag{6}$$

uttered between sentences (1) and (2). We name it the *MAS* discourse. We illustrate that a system developed according to our methodology is able to infer that at the time when *Michael* was grasping *the suitcase*, its location was *the room* — the location of *Michael*, and that *the suitcase* is no longer in *the room* at the end of the described scenario.

The main feature of our approach is the use of $\mathcal{ALM}$ as a language for encoding the meaning of action verbs (i.e., the effects and constraints for the execution of the actions they denote). In addition, we propose to extend an NLP resource about verbs, VERBNET (Kipper-Schuler, 2005; Palmer, 2006), with $\mathcal{ALM}$ based semantic annotations. Other logic formalisms have been used for other NLP tasks (e.g., Recognizing Textual Entailment (NIST, 2008)), but unlike $\mathcal{ALM}$ they cannot perform temporal reasoning (MacCartney and Manning, 2007; Harmeling, 2009) or reasoning by cases (Bos and Markert, 2005). This makes them less suitable for answering questions about discourses describing sequences of events.

The paper is structured as follows. Section 2 starts by introducing the KRR action language $\mathcal{ALM}$ by illustrating how a knowledge engineer can utilize this language to formalize the scenarios described by the *MA* and *MAS* discourses and query the respective formalization. In the process, generic modules that capture the knowledge about such actions/verbs as `move`, `go`, and `grasp` are developed. Section 3 focuses on the methods that will allow us to automatically produce $\mathcal{ALM}$ descriptions that capture information present in discourses of interest by utilizing the arsenal of modern NLP lexicons and tools including VERBNET, PROPBANK (Palmer et al., 2005; Palmer, 2005), SEMLINK (Bonial et al., 2013b,a), Ontonotes Sense Groupings (CLEAR, 2008), LTH (Johansson and Nugues, 2007b,a), and CORENLP (Manning et al., 2014). We end with conclusions and future work.

2 The *MA* and *MAS* discourses formalized in $\mathcal{ALM}$

Action language $\mathcal{ALM}$ is a recent representative of KRR languages for modeling knowledge about domains in which changes are caused by the occurrence of actions. An important feature of $\mathcal{ALM}$ is its ability to capture the commonality of actions `go` and `leave` by defining them as instances of the same action class that we refer to as MOVE, and thus encode the relation that exists between the corresponding verbs.

We start by using $\mathcal{ALM}$ to formalize the domain behind the *MA* discourse. First, we use this example to illustrate the syntax and semantics of the language. Second, we demonstrate how the $\mathcal{ALM}$ framework can be used to perform inferences required to answer questions (3-5). The section concludes with the $\mathcal{ALM}$ formalization of the *MAS* discourse.

MA discourse via $\mathcal{ALM}$: There are several *informative pieces* in the *MA* discourse:
1. the discourse refers to actions of class MOVE through the use of verbs `go` and `leave`. This action class immediately brings about a set of axioms associated with it. For example, we are aware that it is impossible to move an object from a point if this object is not at this point.
2. three objects (entities, or instances) are introduced, to which we refer as `ann`, `michael`, and `room`; and two *events* (instances of actions): `ann` moves into `room` and `michael` moves out of `room`.
3. a sequence of event occurrences is given, i.e., *first* `ann` moves into `room`, and *next*, `michael` moves out of `room`.

Informative piece 1 or $\mathcal{ALM}$ module `basic_motion` **for modeling the** MOVE **action class:** In Figure 1 (LHS), we show the $\mathcal{ALM}$ module called `basic_motion`. This module is a general purpose description of knowledge/axioms about the MOVE action class. It describes how the location of objects is affected by occurrences of events of type MOVE.

Modules in $\mathcal{ALM}$ start with the declaration of *sorts* of objects relevant to the knowledge to be encoded. In `basic_motion`, we distinguish between `things` and discrete `points` in space. We declare these two sorts as special cases of the pre-defined root sort of $\mathcal{ALM}$ called `universe`. We also declare a sort called `agents`, denoting entities capable to move by themselves, as a subsort of `things`. The knowledge engineer then proceeds to specify the relevant action classes for the domain in

```
(LHS)                                        (RHS)
module basic_motion                          module basic_motion_verbnet
 sort declarations                            sort declarations
  things, points :: universe                   concrete :: universe
  agents :: things
  move :: actions                              escape :: actions
   attributes                                   attributes
    actor : agents                               theme : concrete
    origin, dest : points                        initial_location, destination : concrete
function declarations                        function declarations
 fluents                                      fluents
  basic                                        basic
   loc_in : things * points -> booleans         loc_in : concrete * concrete -> booleans
axioms                                       axioms
 occurs(X) causes loc_in(A,D)                 occurs(X) causes loc_in(A,D)
   if instance(X,move),                          if instance(X,escape),
      actor(X)=A,                                   theme(X)=A,
      dest(X)=D.                                    destination(X)=D.
 occurs(X) causes -loc_in(A,O)                occurs(X) causes -loc_in(A, O)
   if instance(X,move),                          if instance(X,escape),
      actor(X)=A,                                   theme(X)=A,
      origin(X)=O.                                  initial_location(X)=O.
 impossible occurs(X) if instance(X,move),    impossible occurs(X) if instance(X, escape),
                         actor(X)=A,                                   theme(X)=A,
                         origin(X)=O,                                  initial_location(X)=O,
                         -loc_in(A,O).                                 -loc_in(A,O).
 impossible occurs(X) if instance(X,move),    impossible occurs(X) if instance(X,escape),
                         actor(X)=A,                                   theme(X)=A,
                         dest(X)=D,                                    destination(X)=D,
                         loc_in(A,D).                                  loc_in(A,D).
```

Figure 1: LHS: $\mathcal{ALM}$ module `basic_motion` capturing knowledge about action class MOVE; RHS: the same module restated using the VERBNET lexicon terminology.

question. In module `basic_motion`, action class `move` is declared as a special case of the pre-defined sort `actions` with three attributes (i.e., intrinsic properties): attribute `actor` ranging over the sort `agents`, and attributes `origin` and `dest` (destination) ranging over `points`.

Next, properties (fluents and statics) related to the domain are declared. *Fluents* are properties that may be changed by actions; they are divided in $\mathcal{ALM}$ into *basic* and *defined*. Basic fluents normally maintain their previous values, unless the occurrence of an event causes their value to change. Defined fluents allow one to specify properties in terms of other properties. Properties are modeled via functions in $\mathcal{ALM}$ using syntax similar to the mathematical notation for functions. In the `basic_motion` module, the property of interest is the location `loc_in` of things, which may be affected by the occurrence of actions of type `move` and is thus declared as a basic fluent. Per its specification, it is a function that maps pairs of `things` and `points` into the pre-defined sort `booleans`.

$\mathcal{ALM}$ modules conclude with axioms about described action classes and properties. The first two rules in the `basic_motion` module capture the direct effects of actions of sort `move`. In particular, the first axiom states that after an occurrence of an instance of `move` its actor will be located at the destination. The second axiom states that after an occurrence of a `move` event the actor will no longer be at the origin. We note that symbol "-" is used to denote the classical negation symbol $\neg$. The last two statements describe when the action cannot be executed. In particular, the third and fourth axioms state that `move` cannot occur when the actor is not located at the specified origin, and when the actor is already at the destination, respectively.

Informative piece 2 or $\mathcal{ALM}$ system description for the *MA* discourse: In $\mathcal{ALM}$, we describe a given domain via a *system description* that consists of a *theory* — modules organized into a hierarchy, and a *structure* — definitions of instances. A system description captures a *transition diagram* that characterizes the behavior of the given domain. *Trajectories* in a transition diagram correspond to possible evolutions or scenarios in the domain. We illustrate these concepts by means of the `discourse_ma` system description presented in Figure 2 (LHS), which corresponds to the *MA* discourse.

The `discourse_ma` theory consists of the line `import module basic_motion` that can be

```
(LHS)                                      (RHS)
system description discourse_ma            system description discourse_ma_verbnet
  theory discourse_ma                        theory discourse_ma_verbnet
    import module basic_motion                 import module basic_motion_verbnet
                                               module drs_michael_and_ann
                                                 ann, michael, room :: universe
  structure discourse_ma                     structure discourse_ma_verbnet
    instances                                  instances
      ann  in agents                             r1 in ann,  concrete
      michael in agents                          r2 in room, concrete
      room in points                             r3 in michael, concrete
      e1 in move                                 e1 in escape
        actor = ann                                theme = r1
        dest = room                                destination = r2
      e2 in move                                 e2 in escape
        actor = michael                            theme = r3
        origin = room                              initial_location = r2
```

Figure 2: LHS: $\mathcal{ALM}$ system description capturing parts of the *MA* discourse using module `basic_motion`; RHS: the same system description restated using `basic_motion_verbnet`.

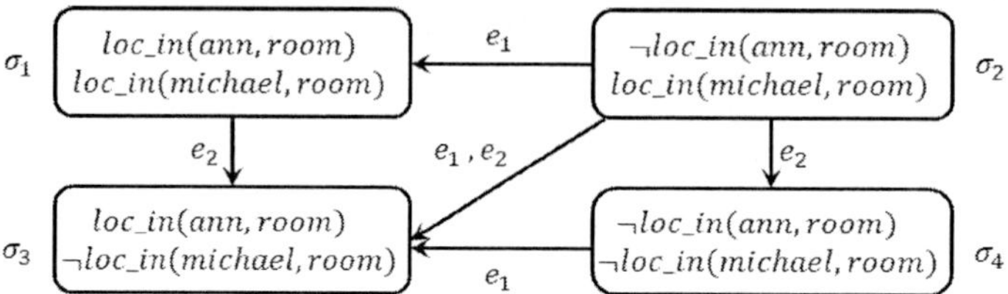

Figure 3: Transition diagram captured by the system description `discourse_ma`.

interpreted as a macro to denote that the $\mathcal{ALM}$ code describing "module basic_motion" has to be inserted in this place. The structure of `discourse_ma` declares instances `ann`, `michael`, and `room` so that the former two are of sort `agents`, whereas the latter is of sort `points`. The two events described in the *MA* discourse are represented as instances `e1` and `e2` of sort `move`. The `actor` of `e1` is instance `ann` and its `dest` is `room`, while the `actor` of `e2` is `michael` and its `origin` is `room`.

The system description `discourse_ma` defines the transition diagram T presented in Figure 3. It consists of four states labeled $\sigma_1 \cdots \sigma_4$, and five transitions labeled by actions e_1, e_2 that may take the dynamic system from one state to another. For example, the arc e_1 between states σ_2 and σ_1 says that the occurrence of e_1 may take the system from the former state to the latter. Note how action `e1` cannot occur in state σ_1 (due to the last axiom in `basic_motion`) and thus there is no arc in T going out of σ_1 and labeled e_1. The initial state of a system is associated with time step 0. Each arc in the transition diagram suggests an increment of a time step by one. A sequence $\tau_1 = \langle \sigma_2, e_1, \sigma_1, e_2, \sigma_3 \rangle$ constitutes a sample trajectory. This trajectory captures the following scenario: initially (time step 0), `ann` is not in `room`, whereas `michael` is in `room`; at time step 0, `ann` moves to (enters) `room`; at time step 1, `michael` moves from (leaves) `room`. A sequence $\tau_2 = \langle \sigma_2, e_2, \sigma_4, e_1, \sigma_3 \rangle$ exemplifies another trajectory of transition diagram T, whereas a sequence $\langle \sigma_1, e_1, \sigma_2, e_2, \sigma_4 \rangle$ is not a trajectory.

Informative Piece 3 or $\mathcal{ALM}$ histories: A particular domain scenario defines what we call a *history* (Gelfond and Khal, 2014) — a set of observations about fluents that hold in some states and events that happen at some states. Certain trajectories in the transition diagram encoded by a system description are compatible with a particular history, while others are not. We call the compatible trajectories *models* of a history. The *MA* discourse provides the following history: action `e1` happens first (at time 0), then `e2` happens (at time 1), which we abbreviate below

$$\{hpd(e1, 0), hpd(e2, 1)\}. \tag{7}$$

Given system description `discourse_ma`, trajectory τ_1 is the only model of this history. Thus the initial state of the story conveyed by the *MA* discourse must be σ_2 and the final one must be σ_3.

Answering questions (3-5): Model τ_1 of history (7) allows us to answer questions (3-5). The final

```
(a)
module grasping depends on basic_motion
  sort declarations
    carriables :: things
    grasp :: actions
      attributes
        grasper : agents
        grasped_thing : carriables
  function declarations
    fluents
      basic
        holding : agents * carriables -> booleans
      defined
        can_reach : agents * things -> booleans
axioms
  occurs(X) causes holding(A,C) if instance(X,grasp),
                                    grasper(X)=A,
                                    grasped_thing(X)=C.
  can_reach(A,C) if loc_in(A)=P, loc_in(C)=P.
  impossible occurs(X) if instance(X,grasp),
                          grasper(X)=A,
                          grasped_thing(X)=C,
                          holding(A,C).
  impossible occurs(X) if instance(X,grasp),
                          grasper(X)=A,
                          grasped_thing(X)=C,
                          -can_reach(A,C).
  loc_in(X,P) if loc_in(C,P), holding(X,C).
  loc_in(C,P) if loc_in(X,P), holding(X,C).
  -loc_in(X,P) if -loc_in(C,P), holding(X,C).
  -loc_in(C,P) if -loc_in(X,P), holding(X,C).
```

```
(b)
system description discourse_mas
  theory discourse_mas
    import module grasping
  structure discourse_mas
    instances
      ann in agents
      michael in agents
      suitcase in carriables
      room in points
      e1 in move
        actor = ann
        dest = room
      ea in grasp
        grasper = michael
        grasped_thing = suitcase
      e2 in move
        actor = michael
        origin = room
```

Figure 4: (a) $\mathcal{ALM}$ module defining action `grasp`; (b) System description for the *MAS* discourse.

state σ_3 of the trajectory τ_1 contains literal `-loc_in(michael, room)`, which translates into the answer *no* to question (3). State σ_3 contains `loc_in(ann, room)` that translates into answer *yes* to question (4). Presence of `loc_in(ann, room)` in state σ_3 translates into answer *no* to question (5).

Similarly, we can answer other questions: *Is Michael inside the room at the beginning of the story? Is Ann inside the room at the beginning of the story? Were Ann and Michael in the room together at some point? How many people were in the room when Ann walked in?* The initial state σ_2 of model τ_1 supports the answers *yes* and *no* to the first and the second questions, respectively. The positive answer to the third question is endorsed by the intermediate state σ_1 of τ_1. Initial state σ_2 encodes the situation preceding *Ann walking into the room*. It supports the answer *at least one* to the last question.

Automatically computing models of a history: Given the $\mathcal{ALM}$ system description and the history that correspond to a discourse in question, the task of computing models of this history relative to the system description can be automated. First, the system description is translated into a logic program under answer set semantics using the transformation defined by Inclezan and Gelfond (2016). Second, the history and a predefined module for temporal projection (Gelfond and Khal, 2014) are added to the produced logic program. Answer sets of the resulting program can be computed using an off-the-shelf ASP{f} solver CLINGO{F} available at `http://www.mbal.tk/clingof/`. Each answer set corresponds to a model of the given history. A prototype translator from $\mathcal{ALM}$ system descriptions and histories to logic programs is available at `http://tinyurl.com/z6n9fmx`.

***MAS* discourse via $\mathcal{ALM}$**: In order to model the *MAS* discourse, an $\mathcal{ALM}$ module that formalizes knowledge about actions of type GRASP is required. Figure 4 (a) presents a module called `grasping` that serves this purpose. It is adapted from (Inclezan and Gelfond, 2016), where it was used to illustrate the methodology of creating modular representations in $\mathcal{ALM}$ by encoding a classical *Monkey and Bananas* problem from the field of reasoning about actions and change. The first line of module `grasping` specifies the reuse of sorts and/or functions explicitly declared in module `basic_motion`. Specifically, this module reuses the fluent `loc_in` since the location of agents and things conditions what GRASP actions can be executed.

$\mathcal{ALM}$ **system description for the *MAS* discourse**: The system description for the *MAS* discourse, discourse_mas, is presented in Figure 4 (b). Its theory starts with an import statement for module grasping. Given that grasping depends on module basic_motion, the meaning of this $\mathcal{ALM}$ statement is that contents of both modules are copied into the theory of discourse_mas. Hence, within this system description we can instantiate events that are of type grasp or move. The fact that action classes grasp and move are interconnected in the definition of module grasping allows a knowledge engineer to model nontrivial interdependencies between actions. For example, an instance of action grasp causes its agent to hold a grasped object. Module grasping also encodes the knowledge that if an agent holds an object then the locations of the agent and object must be the same. These restrictions allow one to deduce that, when an instance of an action move occurs while the agent holds some object, then this object changes its location just as the agent does. The structure of the discourse_mas system description is defined similarly to that of discourse_ma.

History $\{hpd(e1,0), hpd(ea,1), hpd(e2,2)\}$ records the events described in discourse *MAS*. In all models of this history relative to discourse_mas (i) the location of entity suitcase is the same as that of entity michael (namely, entity room) before action instance e2 occurs; (ii) after event ea occurs michael is holding suitcase in all subsequent states; and (iii) after event e2 occurs michael is holding suitcase, and both michael and suitcase are not in room. All of these observations correspond to our expectations given the *MAS* discourse. Indeed, we infer that *the suitcase is no longer in the room* at the end of the story. Similarly, when *Michael* grasped *the suitcase*, its location was the same as the location of *Michael*, i.e., *the room*.

3 Automatic construction of $\mathcal{ALM}$ system descriptions from discourses

In the previous section we illustrated how a knowledge engineer may encode the information carried within the *MA* and *MAS* discourses in $\mathcal{ALM}$. We then discussed how these $\mathcal{ALM}$ formalizations can be used to automatically reason about these discourses. In this section, we present a proposal for automating the process of creating an $\mathcal{ALM}$ system description for an English discourse by relying on modern NLP tools such as LTH, CORENLP and existing lexical resources including Ontonotes Sense Groupings, VERBNET, PROPBANK, and SEMLINK. We stress the steps that have to be performed and how NLP tools and resources are to be used in those steps. The *MA* discourse is a running example in this section.

Stage 1 or Entity and relation extraction: The goal of this stage is to take an English discourse as an input and produce a so-called discourse representation structure (DRS) — a basic building block of Discourse Representation Theory (Kamp and Reyle, 1993). Figure 5 presents a DRS for the *MA* discourse. The top part of this DRS enumerates all of the entities, called discourse referents, that take part in the captured discourse (namely, $r1, r2$, and $r3$) as well as referents denoting events that the discourse describes (namely, $e1$ and $e2$). The bottom part of the DRS captures conditions on the entities and events that follow from the discourse. The events are encoded in Neo-Davidsonian style.

r1 r2 r3 e1 e2
entity(r1) entity(r2) entity(r3)
property(r1,ann) property(r2,room) property(r3,michael)
event(e1) event(e2)
eventType(e1,go.01) eventTime(e1,0) eventArgument(e1,a1,r1) eventArgument(e1,a4,r2)
eventType(e2,leave.01) eventTime(e2,1) eventArgumet(e2,a0,r3) eventArgument(e2,a1,r2)

Figure 5: Discourse representation structure for the *MA* discourse

To produce a DRS as exemplified, the first proposed step is to process discourse sentences using the LTH semantic role labeler. For sentences (1) and (2) of the *MA* discourse, LTH produces the output:

```
[A1 Ann] [V (go.01) went] [A4 to the room]
[A0 Michael] [V (leave.01) left] [A1 the room]
```

The examples above are annotated using the rolesets/labels of the predicates `go.01` and `leave.01` as defined in frame schemas of PROPBANK (version 1.7), where the suffix `01` indicates that Ontonotes Sense Groupings associates these predicates with senses 1 of verbs `go` and `leave`:

```
go.01: motion
  A1: entity in motion/goer    A2: extend    A3: start point    A4: end point
  AM-LOC: medium               AM-DIR: direction (usually up or down)
leave.01: move away from
  A0: entity leaving    A1: place left    A3: attribute/secondary predication
```

In the second step, we propose to process a given discourse using the Stanford CORENLP system. Among other NLP tasks, the CORENLP system can perform mention detection and coreference resolution. Given the *MA* discourse it is able to detect that there are three entities in the discourse: *Michael, Ann,* and *the room*, and that expressions *the room* in sentences (1) and (2) refer to the same entity.

In the third step, the output of systems LTH and CORENLP is combined to produce a DRS for the given input. Based on the output of CORENLP, entities $r1$, $r2$, and $r3$ that have a property of being *ann, room,* and *michael,* respectively, are added to the DRS. Similarly, events $e1$ and $e2$ are known to be of type `go.01` and `leave.01`, respectively, based on the output of LTH. Relation *eventArgument* is populated by using the role labels assigned by LTH. The time step for the events (encoded by *eventTime*) is provided based on chronological order of events mentioned in the discourse, which coincides with default readings of sentences (we disregard for now markers such as *before, after*).

Related NLP systems: System BOXER (Bos, 2008) is an open-domain NLP tool that, given a discourse constructs a respective DRS. However, the discourse representation structures constructed by BOXER omit ordering of events in the discourse (i.e., contain no counterpart to "eventTime" in Figure 5), as well as details on the roles played by event arguments. Also, named entity recognition and coreference resolution components of CORENLP perform better than BOXER.

Stage 2 or From discourse to an $\mathcal{ALM}$ system description or via PROPBANK to VERBNET to $\mathcal{ALM}$: The next question that we tackle is how to map entities, properties, and history present in a given DRS into the vocabulary of $\mathcal{ALM}$ modules that capture axioms about the actions denoted by verbs occurring in this DRS? For the *MA* discourse, this question translates into *how do we transition from the DRS in Figure 5 to an $\mathcal{ALM}$ scenario composed of a system description in Figure 2 and history (7)?*

In order to produce a system description and a history from a DRS, first we have to link two distinct PROPBANK predicates `go.01` and `leave.01` to the same $\mathcal{ALM}$ action class MOVE. Second, we ought to map the semantic roles prescribed by PROPBANK for these predicates to the arguments of action class MOVE as prescribed by the `basic_motion` module. Third, we have to link the entities mentioned in the given DRS in Figure 5 with the instances that compose the structure of the system description capturing this discourse. We will illustrate how these steps result in an $\mathcal{ALM}$ system description `discourse_ma_verbnet` presented in Figure 2 (RHS). It is easy to see that to a large extent the new system description is a syntactic modification of the `discourse_ma` system description in Figure 2 (LHS) that has been designed earlier to process the *MA* discourse. The `discourse_ma_verbnet` system description can be used in the same manner to answer questions about this discourse. Next, we present details on components required to automate the construction of this system description.

VERBNET **Lexicon**: We start by focusing on the first two of the described tasks: mapping PROPBANK predicates `go.01` and `leave.01` and their arguments into instances of the $\mathcal{ALM}$ action class MOVE and its attributes. We argue that it is possible to carry out such mappings in a systematic manner using theories developed by linguists pertaining to verb semantics. Levin (1993) proposed the grouping of verbs into classes based on their syntactico-semantic behavior in sentences. Verb lexicon VERBNET is organized into verb classes that extend and refine these by Levin. For instance, VERBNET class ESCAPE-51.1 contains among others verbs `go` and `return`. A direct subclass of ESCAPE-51.1 named ESCAPE-51.1-1 contains verb `leave`. Any subclass of a class in VERBNET inherits all of the features of its parent class, but also contains its specific entries. In addition to capturing the grouping information of the verbs, VERBNET provides the ontology of core thematic roles associated with each group.

Four (thematic) roles are identified with the classes ESCAPE-51.1 and 51.1-1: *theme*, *initial_location*, *destination*, and *trajectory*. Condition *concrete* represents (selectional) *restriction* that the arguments of the verbs of this class should satisfy to form semantically coherent sentences. Intuitively, in sentence (1) an entity corresponding to *Ann* serves the role *theme*, while an entity corresponding to *the room* serves the role *destination*. Both of these entities are of *concrete* kind/sort. Kipper-Schuler, Section 3.1.4 (2005) describes semantic annotations provided within VERBNET for each class. However, unlike $\mathcal{ALM}$ descriptions, these do not have formal semantics and are not computer interpretable in prescribed manner.

The $\mathcal{ALM}$ declaration of action class MOVE in Figure 1 (LHS) echoes the information present in VERBNET. We see how attribute `actor` of MOVE is declared of sort *agents*, whereas `origin` and `dest` are declared of sort *points*. Intuitively, attribute names such as `actor`, `origin`, and `dest` serve the role of thematic roles *theme*, *initial_location*, and *destination*, respectively. Sorts *agents* and *points* echo selectional restrictions and are designated to be of *concrete* kind by VERBNET. Figure 1 (RHS) presents the restatement of the `basic_motion` module in (LHS) of the same figure using VERBNET terminology and named `basic_motion_verbnet`. It differs from (LHS) by different name choices. The only non-syntactic change appears in sort declarations, where the (RHS) module defines a less specific sort hierarchy. *We envision an extended* VERBNET *that is augmented with $\mathcal{ALM}$ modules (such as* `basic_motion_verbnet`*), which provide $\mathcal{ALM}$-based semantic annotations for its verb classes. Then, the* VERBNET *lexicon can serve as a lookup table for finding relevant action classes and $\mathcal{ALM}$ modules while processing discourses. We believe that the creation of an extended* VERBNET *will be an important contribution to both the NLP and KRR communities.*

The SEMLINK **Project**: The last step to address is how to translate information about entities and events in a DRS into the $\mathcal{ALM}$ system description capturing a given discourse. Here, the missing piece of the puzzle is the SEMLINK project (Bonial et al., 2013b) that links together PROPBANK and VERBNET.

For instance, SEMLINK contains an entry suggesting that (i) the predicate `leave.01` is part of verb class 51.1-1 (a child of the class ESCAPE-15.1) (ii) the argument A0 of predicate `leave.01` is mapped to role *theme* of verb class 51.1-1, and (iii) the argument A1 of predicate `leave.01` is mapped to role *initial_location* of class 51.1-1. These mappings are sufficient for devising a translation from information in the DRS in Figure 5 about event $e2$ into the respective part of the structure of the $\mathcal{ALM}$ system description present in Figure 2 (RHS). Thus an event of type `leave.01` can be seen as an event of type ESCAPE-51.1 and in turn as an instance of action MOVE, which is captured by `escape` in the `basic_motion_verbnet` module presented in Figure 1 (RHS). Note that this also implies that module `basic_motion_verbnet` should be imported into the theory of this constructed system description. Similarly, SEMLINK contains a mapping for predicate `go.01` of PROPBANK to a respective class in VERBNET. Yet, argument A4 of `go.01` and role *destination* in VERBNET is missing in this mapping. Thus, SEMLINK has to be augmented to accommodate the mapping from A4 to *destination*. Nevertheless, SEMLINK provides a solid foundation for the PROPBANK-VERBNET connection.

4 Conclusions and Future Work

We proposed a methodology for building a QA system that uses KRR techniques related to the representation of actions. We focused on answering questions that require the specification of knowledge about actions. We argued that annotating the verb lexicon VERBNET with such knowledge specifications in the KRR language of $\mathcal{ALM}$ will allow us to utilize a variety of NLP tools. We showed that the use of *multiple* NLP resources provides us with the means to extract information from an input discourse sufficient to "populate" a respective $\mathcal{ALM}$ system description and history that in turn can be used to draw nontrivial inferences about the discourse in question. In the immediate future, we will evaluate our method on a collection of texts from project bAbI (Weston et al., 2016; Facebook Research, 2016) containing motion and change of possession verbs. In a long term, we plan to expand the VERBNET annotations to include other types of English verbs.

References

Balduccini, M., C. Baral, and Y. Lierler (2008). Knowledge Representation and Question Answering. In F. van Harmelen, V. Lifschitz, and B. Porter (Eds.), *Handbook of Knowledge Representation*, pp. 779–820. Elsevier.

Baral, C., M. Gelfond, and R. Scherl (2004). Using Answer Set Programming to Answer Complex Queries. In *Workshop on Pragmatics of Question Answering at HLT-NAAC2004*.

Bonial, C., K. Stowe, and M. Palmer (2013a). *SemLink.* https://verbs.colorado.edu/semlink/ [Accessed: 2017].

Bonial, C., K. Stowe, and M. Palmer (2013b). Renewing and revising semlink. In *Proceedings of The GenLex Workshop on Linked Data in Linguistics*.

Bos, J. (2008). Wide-coverage semantic analysis with boxer. In *Proceedings of the 2008 Conference on Semantics in Text Processing*, STEP '08, Stroudsburg, PA, USA, pp. 277–286. Association for Computational Linguistics.

Bos, J. and K. Markert (2005). Recognising textual entailment with logical inference. In *Proceedings of the Conference on Human Language Technology and Empirical Methods in Natural Language Processing*, HLT '05, Stroudsburg, PA, USA, pp. 628–635. Association for Computational Linguistics.

CLEAR (2008). *Ontonotes Sense Groups.* http://clear.colorado.edu/compsem/index.php?page=lexicalresources&sub=ontonotes [Accessed: 2017].

Facebook Research (2016). bAbI. https://research.fb.com/downloads/babi/ [Accessed: 2017].

Gelfond, M. and Y. Khal (2014). *Knowledge Representation, Reasoning, and the Design of Intelligent Agents: The Answer-Set Programming Approach.* Cambridge University Press.

Gelfond, M. and V. Lifschitz (1991). Classical Negation in Logic Programs and Disjunctive Databases. *New Generation Computing 9*(3/4), 365–386.

Harmeling, S. (2009, October). Inferring textual entailment with a probabilistically sound calculus*. *Nat. Lang. Eng. 15*(4), 459–477.

Inclezan, D. and M. Gelfond (2016). Modular action language. *TPLP 16*(2), 189–235.

Johansson, R. and P. Nugues (2007a). *Language Technology at LTH.* http://nlp.cs.lth.se/ [Accessed: 2017].

Johansson, R. and P. Nugues (2007b, June). Lth: Semantic structure extraction using nonprojective dependency trees. In *Proceedings of the Fourth International Workshop on Semantic Evaluations (SemEval-2007)*, Prague, Czech Republic, pp. 227–230. Association for Computational Linguistics.

Kamp, H. and U. Reyle (1993). *From discourse to logic*, Volume 1,2. Kluwer.

Kipper-Schuler, K. (2005). *VerbNet: A Broad-Coverage, Comprehensive Verb Lexicon.* Ph. D. thesis, University of Pennsylvania.

Levin, B. (1993). *English verb classes and alternations : a preliminary investigation.* University Of Chicago Press.

MacCartney, B. and C. D. Manning (2007). Natural logic for textual inference. In *Proceedings of the ACL-PASCAL Workshop on Textual Entailment and Paraphrasing*, RTE '07, Stroudsburg, PA, USA, pp. 193–200. Association for Computational Linguistics.

Manning, C. D., M. Surdeanu, J. Bauer, J. Finkel, S. J. Bethard, and D. McClosky (2014). *Stanford CoreNLP a suite of core NLP tools*. `http://stanfordnlp.github.io/CoreNLP/` [Accessed: 2017].

NIST (2008). Past RTE data. `https://tac.nist.gov/data/RTE/index.html` [Accessed: 2017].

Palmer, M. (2005). *Proposition Bank*. `http://verbs.colorado.edu/~mpalmer/projects/ace.html` [Accessed: 2017].

Palmer, M. (2006). *VerbNet*. `https://verbs.colorado.edu/~mpalmer/projects/verbnet.html` [Accessed: 2017].

Palmer, M., D. Gildea, and P. Kingsbury (2005, March). The proposition bank: An annotated corpus of semantic roles. *Computational Linguistics 31*(1), 71–106.

Todorova, Y. (2011). *Answering questions about dynamic domains from natural language using ASP*. Ph. D. thesis, Texas Tech University.

Todorova, Y. and M. Gelfond (2012). Toward Question Answering in Travel Domains. In *Correct Reasoning*, pp. 311–326.

Weston, J., A. Bordes, S. Chopra, A. M. Rush, B. van Merriënboer, A. Joulin, and T. Mikolo (2016). *Towards AI-Complete Question Answering: A Set of Prerequisite Toy Tasks*. `https://arxiv.org/pdf/1502.05698.pdf` [Accessed: 2017].

Using Neural Word Embeddings in the Analysis of the Clinical Semantic Verbal Fluency Task

Nicklas Linz, Johannes Tröger and Jan Alexandersson
German Research Center for Artificial Intelligence (DFKI), Germany
`<f>.<l>@dfki.de`

Alexandra König
Memory Center, CoBTeK - IA CHU Université Côte d'Azur, France
`akonig03@gmail.com`

Abstract

The *Semantic Verbal Fluency Task* is a common neuropsychological assessment for cognitive disorders: patients are prompted to name as many words from a semantic category as possible in a time interval; the count of correctly named concepts is assessed. Patients often organise their retrieval around semantically related clusters. The definition of clusters is usually based on hand-made taxonomies and the patient's performance is manually evaluated. In order to overcome limitations of such an approach, we propose a statistical method using distributional semantics. Based on transcribed speech samples from 100 French elderly, 53 diagnosed with *Mild Cognitive Impairment* and 47 healthy, we used distributional semantic models to cluster words in each sample and compare performance with a taxonomic baseline approach in a realistic classification task. The distributional models outperform the baseline. Comparing different linguistic corpora as basis for the models, our results indicate that models trained on larger corpora perform better.

1   Introduction

Verbal fluency is amongst the most widely adapted neuropsychological standard tests and is routinely applied in the asessment of neurocognitive disorders. Its subform, category fluency or *semantic verbal fluency* (SVF), demands the assessed person to produce as many different items from a given category as possible within a given time interval, e.g., "as many animals as possible in 60 seconds". A substantial number of clinical studies confirm the discriminative power of SVF for brain pathologies including Alzheimer's disease (AD) (Pakhomov et al., 2016; Raoux et al., 2008; Auriacombe et al., 2006), AD's probable predecessor amnestic *mild cognitive impairment* (MCI), schizophrenia (Robert et al., 1998), as well as focal brain lesions (Troyer et al., 1998). In order to differentiate between multiple pathologies, semantic measures have been established which serve as additional markers next to the raw fluency word count (Gruenewald and Lockhead, 1980; Troyer et al., 1997). There is a broad agreement that these semantic measures serve as indicators for underlying cognitive processes. On a behavioural level, words are spoken in spurts, forming temporal clusters. A cluster is followed by a pause, implying (1) the lexical search between clusters, and (2) retrieval of words within a cluster. On a cognitive level, this is interpreted as follows: executive search processes happen between temporal clusters, (1) *switching*, and semantic memory retrieval processes happen within temporal clusters, (2) *clustering*.

$$(cat \text{ - } dog) \text{ - } (cow \text{ - } horse)$$
$$(Cluster_1) \; Switch_1 \; (Cluster_2)$$

Temporal cluster are closely related to semantic clusters, as "words that comprise these temporal clusters tend to be semantically related" (Troyer et al., 1997, p. 139). Traditionally, semantic clusters are defined by predefined semantic subcategories. After clustering the words, the clusters' mean size and the number of switches between clusters are computed.

However, multiple studies investigating the same subject group report a great variance of cluster sizes and switch counts. This can be explained through the subjective clustering criterion (Troyer et al., 1997) which leaves some room for interpretation regarding the clustering and thereby directly affecting both measures, switches and cluster size. Statistical semantic analysis automatically and reliably providing clusters is a powerful solution to this problem.

This paper explores the possibility of using distributional semantics in the analysis of SVF tasks with a focus on clustering and switching patterns. This is in contrast to *taxonomic models* which are based on predefined subcategories and might not be able to capture the full complexity of semantic connections made by humans. We investigate the application and performance of word2vec (Mikolov et al., 2013) by which words are embedded into a vector space and where the cosine distance in this space is used as a metric for semantic similarity. This allows for an automatic identification of semantic clusters as well as the computation of switches and cluster size. To indicate the feasibility of this approach within the particular scenario of automated SVF analysis for clinical MCI detection, we compare a set of statistical classification experiments building upon multiple variations of word2vec models to an implementation of the taxonomic approach provided by Troyer et al. (1997).

2   Related Work

Recently, first computational approaches to analyse SVF have been proposed (Woods et al., 2016). The classical measure for SVF performance is word count per minute; sometimes the one minute is split into four 15s time frames. In qualitative analysis of SVF performance this count can be modelled as a combination of two components: the mean cluster size and the number of switches between clusters. The two measures relate to the word count as depicted below; The semantic clustering criterion is the main determiner for both measures. The following section will briefly discuss the two concurring approaches for semantic clustering: taxonomy/ subcategory-based semantic clustering and statistical clustering/ chaining.

$$\text{Word Count} = \text{Mean Cluster Size} \times (\text{Number of Switches} + 1)$$

2.1   Subcategory-based clustering

Troyer et al. (1997) first described a taxonomy-based semantic clustering approach, which despite obvious shortcomings is still extremely popular within clinical research (Troyer et al., 1998; Gomez and White, 2006; Bonner et al., 2010). In this approach words, i.e., animals, can belong to one or more predefined subcategories. The categories are based on living environment, zoological categories, and human use. A cluster is then defined as successively generated words belonging to the same subcategory. If a word could be assigned to two clusters, meaning it is part of the subcategory of the previous and the next cluster, it is counted as belonging to both. In case one cluster is contained by another one, only the bigger one is scored. Adaptations have been suggested, which extend the inclusion rules (Ledoux et al., 2014), the minimal cluster size (Robert et al., 1998), or the handling of repetitions and intrusions (Mueller et al., 2015). However, the fundamental mechanisms remain the same and some prominent limitations are: (1) recognising non-category based associations is not catered for: phonemically similar words (e.g. *donkey & monkey*) or animals that occur together in popular culture (e.g. *panther, crane & aardvark*, as in the cartoon series *The Pink Panther*); (2) human-made taxonomies are error prone and likely to be incomplete. In the Troyer et al. (1997) system, there is only one category for *water animals* and therefore, *frog* and *dolphin* appear in the same semantic cluster which may not capture the differences between both animals well; (3) there is a high effort to build a model for a new category which leads to usage within a single category. However, availability of different semantic categories (e.g., tools & supermarket) is of high clinical value for re-testing patients as it prevents confounding training effects.

For a detailed discussion, see Woods et al. (2016).

2.2 Statistical clustering and chaining

To avoid the above-mentioned shortcomings, statistical methods have been applied in order to obtain semantic clusters. However, careful revision of these approaches reveals that many do not actually implement semantic clustering, but rather what we would call *semantic chaining*. In semantic chains, the semantic chain adherence decision is solely based on the previous word.

chain: (*cat - dog - wolf*) - (*cow*) vs. cluster: (*cat - dog*) - (*dog - wolf*) - (*cow*)

To our knowledge, Hills et al. (2012) are the only authors who explicitly differentiates between a *static* and *fluid* switch model—a clustering and a chaining model. In this study, the model of Troyer et al. (1997) is used to evaluate clustering and chaining models. A chaining model is built on the basis of the BEAGLE (Jones and Mewhort, 2007) model, a holographic word embedding trained on Wikipedia. To the best of our knowledge, there has been no research into building a clustering model instead of a chaining one based on distributional semantics.

Ledoux et al. (2014) use Latent Semantic Analysis (LSA), based on the LSA website[1] of the Colorado University to compute similarity within clusters and between clusters, to verify their adaptation of Troyer's method. Woods et al. (2016) use Explicit Semantic Analysis (ESA) (Gabrilovich and Markovitch, 2009)—a vector embedding trained on co-occurrence of words in Wikipedia articles—to identify chaining behaviour for different demographics based on pairwise cosine similarity.

In summary, though very powerful for automation of SVF tasks, statistical approaches are only as good as the linguistic material they are trained on. Most approaches discussed above were trained on Wikipedia articles. However, this might not be the most suitable training material for a model that should capture semantic associations made by humans.

Therefore, we compare the discriminative performance of qualitative SVF parameters derived from statistical models based on word2vec to the approach by Troyer et al. (1997) as prominent baseline and subcategory-based approach. Additionally, we investigate the performance of two different text corpora as basis—the common Wikipedia-based approach vs. a less organised and less academic corpus. We also explore the performance of semantic clustering and semantic chaining implementations.

3 Methodology and Results

As authors before us, we are left with a lack of hard metrics to reliably compare the performance of semantic similarity models. Mikolov et al. (2013) propose a benchmark task for evaluating word2vec models, but it is not suitable to judge the applicability to our task. To get around this conundrum, we adhere to the following line of reasoning: Whatever approach performs best at our task at hand, that is discriminating between MCI and healthy subjects, is the approach we should use in analysis. This method is obviously limited by the amount of data that is available for evaluation, and results have to be interpreted with this in mind. We are going to compare two different distributional semantic models with different hyper parameters on a French data set.

3.1 Data

The corpus used consists of 100 samples from older persons: 53 patients diagnosed with MCI (M_{Age}=76.8 $\pm$7.2; 28F/ 25M; $M_{FluencyCount}$=14.63 $\pm$ 5.76) and 47 healthy control subjects (HC) with a subjective memory complaint (M_{Age}=72.4 $\pm$7.9; 40F/ 7M; $M_{FluencyCount}$=18.86 $\pm$ 5.57). Patients are given 60s to name as many animals as they can. All performances have been recorded and transcribed. The data have been collected in the context of the Dem@Care project (Karakostas et al., 2014).

---

[1] http://lsa.colorado.edu/

Table 1: Hyper parameters of trained word2vec models (CBoW=Continous Bag of Words; Skip=Skip-Gram Model), classification results for chaining and clustering implementations (Pre=Precision; Rec=Recall; F1=F_1 Score; highest values are marked in bold) and Pearson correlation coefficient between clustering and chaining-based features (switch counts=r_{Switch}; mean cluster size=r_{Size}).

Model	Size	Hyper parameters			Chain			Cluster			Correlation	
		Algorithm	Cutoff	Dimensionality	Pre	Rec	F1	Pre	Rec	F1	r_{Switch}	r_{Size}
FraWac	1.6 B	CBoW	100	200	0.75	0.79	**0.77**	**0.73**	0.80	0.76	0.90	0.87
		Skip	100	200	0.66	0.75	0.70	0.70	0.83	0.76	0.90	0.85
		Skip	100	500	0.72	0.72	0.72	0.68	0.68	0.68	0.91	0.88
		Skip	200	500	0.71	0.72	0.69	0.71	**0.84**	**0.77**	0.90	0.75
Wiki	600 M	CBoW	100	1000	0.67	0.71	0.69	0.67	0.75	0.71	0.99	0.95
		CBoW	200	1000	**0.77**	0.74	0.75	0.71	0.69	0.70	0.96	0.87
		Skip	100	1000	0.68	**0.80**	0.74	0.71	0.72	0.72	0.91	0.84
		Skip	200	1000	0.70	0.74	0.72	0.67	0.76	0.71	0.84	0.77
Troyer	-	-	-	-	-	-	-	0.71	0.74	0.72	-	-

3.2 Models

We compare a set of models, all of them learned using word2vec (Mikolov et al., 2013). Word2vec is a word-embedding based on a shallow, two-layer neural network trained to embed words in a vector space, where the cosine distance is a measure for semantic similarity. We compare models trained on two different linguistic corpora: (1) models based on the FraWac corpus (Baroni et al., 2009), a large corpus collected by a web crawler and (2) models based on a dump of the French Wikipedia. Pre-trained models are taken from here[2]. All varying word2vec hyper parameters are reported in Table 1. For all models, the context window was set to 5 tokens and negative sampling was used.

3.3 Clustering and Chaining

On the basis of these models and the cosine distance in the resulting vector space we compute semantic clusters/chains in the following way:

Let a_1, a_2, ..., a_n be the sequence of animals produced by patient p. Let $\vec{a_1}$, $\vec{a_2}$, ..., $\vec{a_n}$ be their representations in the vector space and let a_1, ..., a_{n-1} form a semantic cluster/chain. a_n is part of this cluster/chain if

Cluster   **Chain**

$$\left| \frac{\langle \vec{\mu}, \vec{a_n} \rangle}{\|\vec{\mu}\| \cdot \|\vec{a_n}\|} \right| > \delta_p \qquad\qquad \left| \frac{\langle \vec{a_{n-1}}, \vec{a_n} \rangle}{\|\vec{a_{n-1}}\| \cdot \|\vec{a_n}\|} \right| > \delta_p$$

with

$$\vec{\mu} = \frac{1}{n-1} \cdot \sum_{\vec{x} \in \{\vec{a_1}, ..., \vec{a_{n-1}}\}} \vec{x} \qquad\qquad \delta_p = \frac{n!}{(n-2)!} \cdot \sum_{\vec{x}, \vec{y} \in \{\vec{a_1}, ..., \vec{a_n}\}} \left| \frac{\langle \vec{x}, \vec{y} \rangle}{\|\vec{x}\| \cdot \|\vec{y}\|} \right|$$

One of the main problems of using distributional semantic models to determine clusters/chains is finding a sensible cut-off value δ. We decided to use the mean distance between any animal produced by a subject. An ad-hoc global cut-off value would be hard to determine, since similarity scores tend to vary a lot.

---

[2] http://fauconnier.github.io/

3.4 Classification

We train different classifiers, one for each model using Support Vector Machines (SVMs) with a radial basis kernel. This is mainly because we only have two features (Hsu et al., 2010). Moreover, since our data set is small, we perform a stratified 10-fold cross validation. As features we use the mean size of clusters identified and the number of switches between clusters. For results, see Table 1.

4 Discussion

This paper set out to compare the discriminative performance of qualitative SVF parameters derived from statistical models based on neural word embeddings with the traditional subcategory-based approach by Troyer et al. (1997). Therefore, we implemented Troyer's approach as a baseline deriving the semantic clustering criterion from predefined subcategories. We compared this to a group of statistical approaches based on a patient-dependent clustering criterion derived from word2vec models. Through both approaches, we automatically calculated mean cluster size and number of switches based on transcripts of two groups' SVF recordings: MCI and healthy controls. In order to examine both approaches' feasibility within the given scenario, we trained classifiers, showing results clearly in favour of the statistically derived feature set. This is in line with reported feasibility benefits of this approach (Woods et al., 2016; Hills et al., 2012). However, to the best of our knowledge, no study so far compared both approaches based on the discriminative performance they achieve, given a clinical classification scenario; so far, either one of both approaches has been used to validate the features derived by the other approach and vice versa. Nonetheless, maybe the most straight forward way of comparing both approaches is by applying them to a relevant clinical scenario—which SVF has actually been designed and used for—and deciding based on their performance in the classification task at hand.

Additionally, we investigate the performance of two different text corpora as basis for the word2vec models. Our results show that the classifiers using features based on the FraWac corpus models (Baroni et al., 2009) achieve higher F1 scores than the ones based on the Wikipedia models. Although it is difficult to derive a conclusion from this rather exploratory result, possible explanations might be that the FraWac corpus is simply larger, or that it represents a less (artificially) academic and therefore more natural linguistic resource.

Finally, considering different effects through semantic chaining vs. semantic clustering, we yield no interpretable results favouring either one of the implementations. Our experiments yield throughout high correlation indices between both implementations across both SVF dependent variables/ features: switch count & mean cluster size. This is in line with Hills et al. (2012), who also find no clear pattern.

5 Conclusion

To conclude, this paper presents a clinical application of neural word embeddings rendering a statistical approach to the traditionally manual analysis of semantic verbal fluency tasks. Our results demonstrate the feasibility and therefore economic validity of such an approach, having especially relevant implications for remote automatic screening applications like in Tröger et al. (2017). The strong dependency between both qualitative SVF measures, switch count & mean cluster size, and simple word count performance, still remains a challenge for understanding their respective diagnostic values. Future research should therefore explore measures which are based on the here-presented encouraging approach and which go beyond the triangular relation of SVF switches, cluster size and word count.

Acknowledgements

This research was partially funded by the EIT Digital Wellbeing Activity 17074, *ELEMENT*. The data was collected during the EU FP7 *Dem@Care* project, grant agreement 288199.

References

Auriacombe, S., N. Lechevallier, H. Amieva, S. Harston, N. Raoux, and J.-F. Dartigues (2006). A Longitudinal Study of Quantitative and Qualitative Features of Category Verbal Fluency in Incident Alzheimer's Disease Subjects: Results from the PAQUID Study. *Dementia and geriatric cognitive disorders 21*(4), 260–266.

Baroni, M., S. Bernardini, A. Ferraresi, and E. Zanchetta (2009). The WaCky Wide Web: A Collection of Very Large Linguistically Processed Web-Crawled Corpora. *Language Resources and Evaluation 43*(3), 209–226.

Bonner, M. F., S. Ash, and M. Grossman (2010). The New Classification of Primary Progressive Aphasia into Semantic, Logopenic, or Nonfluent/Agrammatic Variants. *Current Neurology and Neuroscience Reports 10*(6), 484–490.

Gabrilovich, E. and S. Markovitch (2009, March). Wikipedia-based Semantic Interpretation for Natural Language Processing. *J. Artif. Int. Res. 34*(1), 443–498.

Gomez, R. G. and D. A. White (2006). Using verbal fluency to detect very mild dementia of the Alzheimer type. *Archives of Clinical Neuropsychology 21*(8), 771 – 775.

Gruenewald, P. J. and G. R. Lockhead (1980). The Free Recall of Category Examples. *Journal of Experimental Psychology: Human Learning and Memory 6*, 225–240.

Hills, T. T., M. N. Jones, and P. M. Todd (2012, Apr). Optimal Foraging in Semantic Memory. *Psychol Rev 119*(2), 431–440.

Hsu, C.-W., C.-C. Chang, and C. jen Lin (2010). A Practical Guide to Support Vector Classification.

Jones, M. N. and D. J. Mewhort (2007, Jan). Representing Word Meaning and Order Information in a Composite Holographic Lexicon. *Psychol Rev 114*(1), 1–37.

Karakostas, A., A. Briassouli, K. Avgerinakis, I. Kompatsiaris, and M. Tsolaki (2014). The Dem@Care Experiments and Datasets: a Technical Report. Technical report, Centre for Research and Technology Hellas (CERTH).

Ledoux, K., T. D. Vannorsdall, E. J. Pickett, L. V. Bosley, B. Gordon, and D. J. Schretlen (2014). Capturing additional information about the organization of entries in the lexicon from verbal fluency productions. *Journal of Clinical and Experimental Neuropsychology 36*(2), 205–220.

Mikolov, T., I. Sutskever, K. Chen, G. S. Corrado, and J. Dean (2013). Distributed Representations of Words and Phrases and their Compositionality. In C. J. C. Burges, L. Bottou, M. Welling, Z. Ghahramani, and K. Q. Weinberger (Eds.), *Advances in Neural Information Processing Systems 26*, pp. 3111–3119. Curran Associates, Inc.

Mueller, K. D., R. L. Koscik, A. LaRue, L. R. Clark, B. Hermann, S. C. Johnson, and M. A. Sager (2015). Verbal Fluency and Early Memory Decline: Results from the Wisconsin Registry for Alzheimer's Prevention. *Archives of Clinical Neuropsychology 30*(5), 448.

Pakhomov, S. V., L. Eberly, and D. Knopman (2016). Characterizing cognitive performance in a large longitudinal study of aging with computerized semantic indices of verbal fluency. *Neuropsychologia 89*, 42 – 56.

Raoux, N., H. Amieva, M. L. Goff, S. Auriacombe, L. Carcaillon, L. Letenneur, and J.-F. Dartigues (2008). Clustering and switching processes in semantic verbal fluency in the course of Alzheimer's disease subjects: Results from the PAQUID longitudinal study. *Cortex 44*(9), 1188 – 1196.

Robert, P. H., V. Lafont, I. Medecin, L. Berthet, S. Thauby, C. Baudu, and G. Darcourt (1998). Clustering and switching strategies in verbal fluency tasks: Comparison between schizophrenics and healthy adults. *Journal of the International Neuropsychological Society 4*(6), 539–546.

Tröger, J., N. Linz, J. Alexandersson, A. König, and P. Robert (2017). Automated Speech-based Screening for Alzheimer's Disease in a Care Service Scenario. In *Proceedings of the 11th EAI International Conference on Pervasive Computing Technologies for Healthcare*, PervasiveHealth '17. ICST. in press.

Troyer, A. K., M. Moscovitch, and G. Winocur (1997). Clustering and Switching as Two Components of Verbal Fluency: Evidence From Younger and Older Healthy A dults. *neuropsychology 11*(1), 138.

Troyer, A. K., M. Moscovitch, G. Winocur, M. P. Alexander, and D. Stuss (1998). Clustering and switching on verbal fluency: the effects of focal frontal- and temporal-lobe lesions. *Neuropsychologia 36*(6), 499 – 504.

Troyer, A. K., M. Moscovitch, G. Winocur, L. Leach, and M. Freedman (1998). Clustering and switching on verbal fluency tests in Alzheimer's and Parkinson's disease. *Journal of the International Neuropsychological Society 4*(2), 137–143.

Woods, D. L., J. M. Wyma, T. J. Herron, and E. W. Yund (2016, 12). Computerized Analysis of Verbal Fluency: Normative Data and the Effects of Repeated Testing, Simulated Malingering, and Traumatic Brain Injury. *PLOS ONE 11*(12), 1–37.

Neural Disambiguation of Causal Lexical Markers
Based on Context

Eugenio Martínez-Cámara[†], Vered Shwartz[‡], Iryna Gurevych[†], Ido Dagan[‡]
[†]Ubiquitous Knowledge Processing Lab (UKP-TUDA)
Department of Computer Science, Technische Universität Darmstadt
[‡]Bar-Ilan University, Ramat-Gan, Israel
{camara, gurevych}@ukp.tu-darmstadt.de, vered1986@gmail.com,
dagan@cs.biu.ac.il

Abstract

Causation is a psychological tool of humans to understand the world and it is projected in natural language. Causation relates two events, so in order to understand the causal relation of those events and the causal reasoning of humans, the study of causality classification is required. We claim that the use of linguistic features may restrict the representation of causality, and dense vector spaces can provide a better encoding of the causal meaning of an utterance. Herein, we propose a neural network architecture only fed with word embeddings for the task of causality classification. Our results show that our claim holds, and we outperform the state-of-the-art on the AltLex corpus. The source code of our experiments is publicly available.[1]

1 Introduction

Causation is a psychological tool of humans to understand the world independently of language, and it is one of the principles involved in the construction of the human mental model of reality (Neeleman and van de Koot, 2012). Following the words of Reinhart (2002), causal relations are imposed by humans on input from the world, and the (computational) linguist's task is to understand what it is about language that enables speakers to use it to describe their causal perceptions.

Due to the importance of modelling causality, in this paper we present a study of the classification of the causal meaning of an utterance. The computational treatment of causality requires a computational definition, which should be grounded in a philosophical theory. There are two broad categories of theories modelling causality: dependency and production theories. The dependency theories define causality as a relation of dependence between two eventualities, and the counterfactual theory of Lewis (1973) is their main representative theory. Differently, production theories define causation as the transmission of forces with the sense that the transmission of the force of the causing event enables the provoked effect. In this case, the force dynamic theory of Talmy (1988) stands out.

The computational treatment of causality can be addressed by the study of the causal relation between a predicate and its arguments (lexical causality) or towards the analysis of the relation between propositions (propositional causality). Copley and Wolff (2014) argue that production theories may fit with lexical causality, because the transmission of a force may be better projected by the relation between a predicate and its arguments. Otherwise, propositional causality is explicitly projected by some lexical markers, such as *because*, that represent the dependency relation between propositions, so dependency theories may suit propositional causality.

We argue that the dependency theories restrict the phenomenon of causality, because they require the satisfaction of some conditions to establish the causal relation, hindering the representation of the human causal reasoning, which is sometimes based on assumptions instead of empirical evidences. In contrast,

---

[1]https://github.com/UKPLab/iwcs2017_disambiguation_causality_lexical_markers

"

production theories encompass those causal relations that are not founded on facts, can incorporate the general knowledge of humans into the model and may represent abstract causality. We additionally argue that the transmission of forces can be produced not only between the arguments of a predicate, but between the eventualities expressed in different propositions too. Thus, we follow the production theories, and we extend their definition in order to model propositional causality.

The computational treatment of causality could benefit from the existence of specific linguistic constructions of causality, and the matching of those linguistic constructions with any philosophical theory of causality. However, Neeleman and van de Koot (2012) assert that causation lacks of unarguable syntactic constructions, and Copley and Wolff (2014) conclude that there is not an agreement between the link of linguistic and philosophic theories of causation. Nonetheless, there are some lexical units that project the meaning of causality of an utterance. Those lexical units can be verbs (*cause*), prepositions (*because*), adverbs (*consequently*) or expressions like *as a result of*. However, those lexical markers are ambiguous, which means that they can also be used without a causal meaning. Moreover, the set of lexical markers with a causal meaning is not limited, which increases the need of their disambiguation.

Due to the lack of unambiguous linguistic construction of causality, we claim that the use of linguistic features may restrict the representation of causality meaning. Also, the use of dense vector spaces, roughly speaking word embeddings, can provide a better representation of causality, and can improve the disambiguation of the causal meaning of lexical markers. Hence, we propose a neural network architecture with two inputs as sequences of word embeddings, encoding the left and the right context of the lexical marker. We evaluate our proposal on the AltLex corpus (Hidey and McKeown, 2016), which is a corpus of causal relations signalled by lexical markers with a wider coverage of those kind of expressions than the Penn Discourse TreeBank Corpus (PDTB) (Prasad et al., 2008). Empirical results on the AltLex corpus show that our claim indeed holds and our system outperforms the state-of-the-art on that corpus.

2   Related Work

Previous works in the task of causal language classification are mainly focused on lexical or propositional causality, explicit causality and some of them were restricted to a narrow kind of syntactic constructions.

The works of Girju (2003); Riaz and Girju (2013, 2014) were focused on the classification of lexical causality conveyed between verbs and nouns. Recently, Kruengkrai et al. (2017) proposed a system for the classification of propositional causality in Japanese. The system incorporates background knowledge for enhancing the learning process through the use of multi-column convolutional neural networks.

Regarding the classification of explicit causality, Khoo et al. (1998) proposed a rule-based system grounded in regular expressions for the classification of explicit causal relations, whereas Mirza and Tonelli (2016) presented a supervised system based on the use of lexical, syntactic and semantic features from WordNet. The proposal of Bethard and Martin (2008) is similar to that of Mirza and Tonelli (2016), but it was focused only on conjunction constructions, namely conjoined events. The three approaches suffer from the ambiguity of the lexical markers, the limited coverage of the linguistic resources and the constraint to a specific syntactic construction.

In contrast, our proposal tries to cover lexical and propositional causality independently of whether it is explicit or implicit, and we do not restrict the study to a specific syntactic construction.

3   Causality classification

The next sections present the task definition (§ 3.1), the corpus (§ 3.2) and the proposed system (§ 3.3).

3.1   Definition

The cause dynamics model of Wolff (2007) is the main basis for our definition of causality, because we can adapt it to the causal language that we find on real data. The dynamics model states that causation is

Sentence	Type
(Cathay Pacific delayed both legs of its quadruple daily Hong Kong to London route)$_{e_1}$ [due to]$_l$ (this disruption in air traffic services.)$_{e_2}$	Explicit
The factory was not well equipped to handle (the gas)$_{e_1}$ (created by the sudden addition of water to the MIC tank.)$_{e_2}$	Implicit

Table 1: Explicit and implicit causal relations.

Sentence	Meaning
An undercroft is traditionally a cellar or storage room, often brick-lined and vaulted, and used for storage in buildings *since* medieval times.	Temporal
Additionally if one is to use a large scan range then sensitivity of the instrument is decreased due to performing fewer scans per second *since* each scan will have to detect a wide range of mass fragments.	Causal
In stark contrast to his predecessor, five days *after* his election he spoke of his determination to do what he could to bring peace.	Temporal
Bischoff in a round table discussion claimed he fired Austin *after* he refused to do a taping in Atlanta.	Causal

Table 2: Different meanings of the prepositions *since* and *after* taken from the AltLex corpus.

an interaction between two entities, namely *affector* and *patient*. This definition can be extended in order to fit our definition. The affector and the patient will be the causing (e_1) and the caused (e_2) events, and the interaction between them will correspond to the lexical marker (l) in case of explicit causal relations, and the context in implicit scenarios. Table 1 shows the difference between explicit and implicit causal relations. So, following the cause dynamics model of Wolff (2007), we define causality as $e_1 \xrightarrow[l]{CAUSE} e_2$. The next sentence from the test set used in our experiments is an example of our definition of causality:

> A government affidavit in 2006 stated that (the leak)$_{e_1}$ ([caused]$_l$ 558,125 injuries, including 38,478 temporary partial injuries and approximately 3,900 severely and permanently disabling injuries.)$_{e_2}$

The presence of a lexical marker does not ensure that the meaning of an utterance is causal, because they are usually ambiguous. An example is the adverb *since*, which can have a temporal or a causal meaning, as Table 2 shows.

We define the task of causality classification as a task composed of two subtasks: *causal meaning classification* and *causal arguments identification*. Given two events, the task of causal meaning classification is to disambiguate the causal meaning (Causal or Non Causal) of the relation of those two events. The task of causal argument identification focuses on the identification of the causing (e_1) and caused (e_2) events. We contribute to the first subtask.

3.2   Data

According to the definition of causal meaning classification, we need a corpus in which the events are annotated, as well as the lexical markers that can trigger the causal meaning in case of explicit relations, for the classification of the causal meaning of an utterance. Thus, our method requires that the input utterance is composed of the two events of the relation and optionally the lexical marker (e_1, l, e_2).

The AltLex corpus (Hidey and McKeown, 2016) meets the requirements of our task. The corpus was built on the idea that causality can be expressed by different types of linguistic constructions. This is validated by the fact that in PDTB there are explicit causal lexical markers, and other kinds of expressions that have a discourse meaning, which are called AltLex (Alternative Lexicalization). The relations signalled by an AltLex expression are a kind of implicit relation, in which the causal meaning is projected by an expression that is not part of common discourse connectives. The relations with an AltLex expression are those ones in which the annotators did not find an appropriate lexical marker to insert between

Corpus	Version	Causal	Non-Causal	Total
Training	non-bootstrapped	7,606	79,290	86,896
	bootstrapped	12,534	88,210	100,744
Dev.		181	307	488
Test		315	296	611

Table 3: Number of instances in the AltLex corpus.

	Non-Boots.	Boots.
Unambiguous in `Non Causal` class	7171	7673
Unambiguous in `Causal` class	922	1034
Ambiguous	121	147
Total	8214	8854
`Causal` in train, `Non Causal` in test	0	27
`Non Causal` in train, `Causal` in test	0	8

Table 4: Distribution of the lexical markers.

the events, because the meaning of the causal relation is entailed by an AltLex expression. From the existence of AltLex expressions in PDTB one can deduce that there are more expressions that entail the causal meaning of an utterance. Hence, the authors of the AltLex corpus developed a method to identify a larger amount of AltLex expressions that can trigger the causal meaning of an utterance. The corpus construction leveraged Simple Wikipedia by aligning sentences from Wikipedia that consist of unknown lexical causal markers with sentences from Simple Wikipedia that contain corresponding known lexical causal markers. The result was a set of sentences with expressions that trigger their causal meaning. Once a first set of causal and non-causal sentences were identified, a *bootstrapping* method was applied to enhance the corpus. We call the first version of the corpus "non-bootstrapped" and the second one "bootstrapped". The corpus statistics are in Table 3. More details in Hidey and McKeown (2016).

Since one feature of the corpus is the annotation of the lexical markers that may express causation, we studied their class distribution. Table 4 shows the class distribution of the lexical markers, as well as the number of unarguable ones and the number of lexical markers with mostly a different meaning in the training and the test set. According to Table 4, there are few ambiguous lexical markers: 121 in the "non-bootstrapped" corpus and 147 in the "bootstrapped" version. However, there is an important difference between the two versions of the corpus: the class distribution of the lexical markers in the training and test set is the same in the "non-bootstrapped" version, whereas in the "bootstrapped" version is not. This fact means that the instances of the "bootstrapped" version of the corpus present a higher difficulty for the classifier, because there are some lexical markers with a dissimilar class distribution in the training and test set. We show that our system works on those instances in § 4.3.2.

3.3 Disambiguation of the Causal Meaning

According to our definition of causality as the relation of two events ($e_1 \xrightarrow[l]{CAUSE} e_2$), we propose a neural network architecture with two inputs (see Figure 1). The first input matches the first event (e_1), and the second one corresponds to the lexical marker (l) and the second event (e_2), which are separated by a special character. In case there is no lexical marker (implicit relation), the second input is composed of a special character and the second event.

The classification starts with the tokenization of the two inputs. The lengths (n, m) of the instances of each input are not necessarily the same, so in order to make their lengths equal, three zero-padding strategies were assessed, namely the maximum, the mean and the mode of the lengths (t) of the components of the inputs (see Equation 1).

For each word, its corresponding word vector of 300 components (d) was looked up in the 840b cased Glove embeddings (Pennington et al., 2014). Subsequently, the concatenated word embeddings get passed through an encoding Long Short-Term

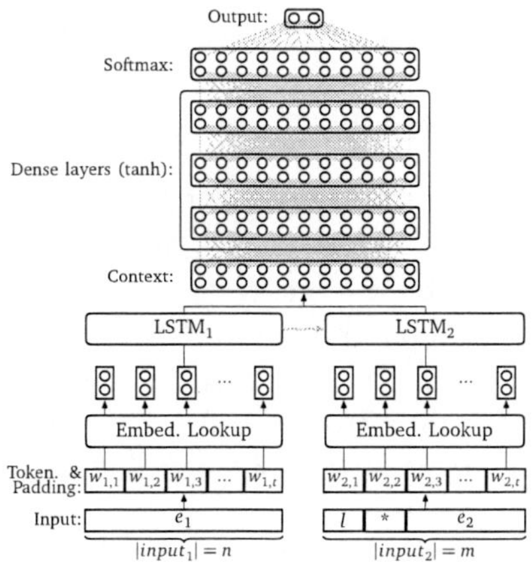

Figure 1: Neural model, where e_1 is the first event, l is the lexical marker and e_2 is the second event.

Memory (LSTM) recurrent neural network (RNN) (Hochreiter and Schmidhuber, 1997) layer. We decided to use LSTM because of its ability to encode sequential and contextual information (Melamud et al., 2016). We assume some sort of relation exists between e_1 and e_2, so we first evaluated the performance of the connection of the two LSTM layers through the initialization of the second LSTM with the end state of the first one (dashed arrow in Figure 1). We call this model "Stated_Pair_LSTM". We assessed the same model but without the connection of the two LSTMs for evaluating our assumption. We call it "Pair_LSTM" (no dashed arrow in Figure 1).

The two outputs of the encoding layer are transformed to a vector of length 100 by a dense layer with a *tanh* activation function. The context of the causal relation is represented by the concatenation of the two vectors (see Equation 2). The output of Equation 2 is processed by three dense layers activated by a *tanh* function. The last layer is composed of the *softmax* operation.

$$\forall e_1 \in \mathbb{R}^{n \times d}, \forall e_2 \in \mathbb{R}^{m \times d} \text{ and } r \in \{n, m\}$$
$$pad(e) : \mathbb{R}^{r \times d} \to \mathbb{R}^{t \times d} \tag{1}$$
$$t \in \{max(e), mean(e), mode(e)\}$$

$$\forall W \in \mathbb{R}^{100 \times nd} \text{ and } \forall b \in \mathbb{R}^{100}$$
$$vec(e) : \mathbb{R}^{n \times d} \to \mathbb{R}^{nd}$$
$$tanh(W \cdot e + b) \tag{2}$$
$$context : (vec(e_1), vec(e_2))$$

The performance of two learning optimizers with their default learning rates was evaluated, specifically Adadelta (Zeiler, 2012) and Adam (Kingma and Ba, 2015). Different values for dropout ($[0.5, 0.75]$) and L^2 regularization ($[8 \cdot 10^{-3}, 8 \cdot 10^{-6}]$) were evaluated to avoid overfitting.

4   Experiments and Results

As far as we know, the AltLex corpus has been only used in Hidey and McKeown (2016), so we consider their classification method as the state-of-the-art on that corpus. We have used the two versions of the corpus ("non bootstrapped" and "bootstrapped") in our experiments.

4.1   Baselines

We compare our proposal with two baselines. The first one (B1) assigns the most common class of each lexical marker in the training data, and it is similar to the baseline used in Hidey and McKeown (2016). The second baseline (B2) is the system of Hidey and McKeown (2016), which is based on SVM with a large set of features generated from the original parallel corpus and some lexical resources (WordNet, VerbNet and PropBank). Since relying on lexical resources restricts the recall of the system to their linguistic coverage, we propose a neural model fed only by a set of word embedding vectors.

4.2   Results

Table 5 displays the performance of the different configurations of our system and the baselines.[2] The precision, recall and F1 values were used to measure the performance of the system in the `Causal` class (C), and the accuracy to measure the overall performance of the system.

The performance of B1 defines a hard baseline for the two versions of the corpus, which might indicate that the training corpus is composed of few ambiguous causal connectives, which is expected given the statistics of the corpus in Table 4. However, the proposed systems outperform B1, which means that the systems learn beyond the class distribution of the lexical markers in the training data.

Those configurations that use Adadelta as optimizer outperform the system B2 in the "non bootstrapped" version of the corpus. The low value of precision of B2 means that it returns a large number of false positives. Rather, the high precision of our proposed approach indicates a good classification of sentences with unambiguous lexical markers, as it is expected since there are very few ambiguous lexical markers (see Table 4). The best configuration ("Pair_LSTM_Max_Adadelta") uses the `max` operation for

---

[2]For the sake of brevity, those systems that performed worse than the three baselines are not listed in Table 5.

Training corpus	Method	Precision C.	Recall C.	F1 C.	Accuracy
Non-bootstrapped	B1	68.92%	54.92%	61.13%	63.99%
	B2	70.28%	**77.60%**	73.76%	71.86%
	Stated_Pair_LSTM_Mean_Adadelta	**90.04%**	60.31%	72.24%	76.10%
	Stated_Pair_LSTM_Mode_Adadelta	89.23%	63.17%	73.97%	77.08%
	Pair_LSTM_Max_Adadelta	88.46%	65.71%	**75.40%**	**77.90%**
	Pair_LSTM_Mean_Adadelta	89.33%	63.80%	74.44%	77.41%
Bootstrapped	B1	74.38%	86.66%	80.05%	77.74%
	B2	77.29%	84.85%	80.90%	79.58%
	Stated_Pair_LSTM_Max_Adadelta	78.69%	84.44%	81.47%	80.19%
	Stated_Pair_LSTM_Mean_Adam	80.00%	82.53%	81.25%	80.36%
	Stated_Pair_LSTM_Mode_Adam	80.24%	82.53%	81.37%	80.52%
	Pair_LSTM_Max_Adadelta	78.07%	84.76%	81.12%	79.86%
	Pair_LSTM_Mean_Adadelta	78.48%	85.71%	81.94%	80.52%
	Pair_LSTM_Mean_Adam	**80.30%**	82.85%	81.56%	**80.68%**
	Pair_LSTM_Mode_Adam	77.24%	**87.30%**	**81.96%**	80.19%

Table 5: Results of the baselines and the different configurations of our neural model.

Trainig corpus	Method	Precision C.	Recall C.	F1 C.	Accuracy
Non-bootstrapped	B1	68.92%	54.92%	61.13%	63.99%
	B2	70.28%	77.60%	73.76%	71.86%
	Pair_LSTM_Max_Adadelta	88.46%	65.71%	75.40%	77.90%
	Pair_LSTM_0dense_Max_Adadelta	**88.84%**	65.71%	75.54%	78.06%
	Pair_LSTM_4dense_Mode_Adadelta	88.52%	**68.57%**	**77.28%**	**79.21%**
Bootstrapped	B1	74.38%	**86.66%**	80.05%	77.74%
	B2	77.29%	84.85%	80.90%	79.58%
	Pair_LSTM_Mean_Adam	80.30%	82.85%	81.56%	80.68%
	Pair_LSTM_2dense_Mode_Adam	79.57%	84.12%	81.79%	80.68%
	Pair_LSTM_0dense_Mean_Adam	80.74%	82.53%	81.63%	80.85%
	Pair_LSTM_1dense_Mean_Adam	80.18%	**86.49%**	81.80%	80.85%
	Pair_LSTM_4dense_Mode_Adam	80.06%	84.12%	**82.04%**	81.01%
	Pair_LSTM_0dense_Mode_Adadelta	**81.44%**	82.22%	81.83%	**81.17%**

Table 6: Results of the evaluation of the influence of the number of dense layers.

the zero-padding strategy and Adadelta as learning optimizer. Our proposal improves B2 by 2.13% and 7.72% according to F1 and accuracy respectively.

Our assumption about the relation of the meaning of the two inputs does not hold, due to the better performance of the architecture "Pair_LSTM" with both versions of the corpus. Accordingly, it is better to independently encode each argument and then to measure the relation between the arguments by using dense layers. When the "bootstrapped" version of the corpus is used as training data, the optimizer Adam returns more homogeneous results between precision and recall, which indicates a better disambiguation of different expressions of causality. Although B2 outperforms our method in terms of recall by 2.41%, overall our system performs better in terms of F1 score, as B2 tends to classify many instances as false positives. To conclude, the best configuration ("Pair_LSTM_Mean_Adam") uses the mean strategy for zero-padding and the optimizer Adam, and yields an improvement of 3.89% in precision over B2.

According to Conneau et al. (2017), the number of dense layers influences the performance of neural models in text classification tasks, so we also made that analysis in the task of causality classification. We evaluated the performance of the best neural model, "Pair_LSTM", with a different number of dense layers, specifically from 0 to 4. The results in Table 6 show that 1) the combination of four dense layers and mode as padding strategy substantially increases the results compared to "Pair_LSTM_Max_Adadelta" when the "non bootstrapped" corpus is used as training set, and 2) the efficiency of the method is also improved because the mode operation reduces the length of the input. When the "bootstrapped" version of the corpus is used as training data, the number of layers also influences the performance. In this case, the best performance is reached when no dense layers are used, and the mode operation is the non-zero padding strategy. This configuration is more efficient than "Pair_LSTM_Mean_Adam" because the length of the input vector of the model is shorter and less dense layers are used. Therefore, we conclude that the number of dense layers influences the performance of causality classification.

4.3 Analysis

In this section we present analyses of the proposed model from several points of views: an evaluation of the proposal in a balanced version of the datasets (§ 4.3.1), and a qualitative analysis of the classification of three different groups of lexical markers (§ 4.3.2).

4.3.1 Balanced Training Set

The Causal class is only the 8.7% and the 12.4% of all the instances in both versions of the corpus respectively (see Table 3). This big difference between the two classes may affect the performance of the classification, because it may separate the two classes and hence may ease the classification. So, we reduced the number of instances of the Non Causal by a factor of ten with the aim of evaluating our system with a more balanced dataset (see Table 8). The results of the evaluation of B1 and our best configurations are in Table 7. The results show that B1 follows a similar trend in the two versions of the corpus, which is a big difference between the precision and the recall. In contrast, our proposal not only outperforms the baselines, but it also yields a better balance between precision and recall. Our proposal significantly improves B1 according to McNemar's test ($p < 0.001$ and $p < 0.05$ respectively).

4.3.2 Distribution of Lexical Markers

Three groups of lexical markers were identified in the test set: 1) ambiguous lexical markers, those ones that are not in the training set or the difference of the probability to belong to each class is less than 10% according to their distribution in the training set (Ambiguous); 2) opposite meaning lexical markers, those ones whose probability distribution in the training set is opposite to their probability distribution in the test set (Opposite); and 3) the rest of lexical markers. We compare the performance of B2 and our best system in those clusters in order to know the strengths and weaknesses of our proposal.

Table 9 shows that B2 reaches a better performance with Ambiguous lexical markers, which means that we have to continue working on improving the representation of the context for the classification of unseen lexical markers. On the other hand, our neural model performs better with those lexical markers of the Opposite cluster, which means that our proposal rightly leverages the context of each lexical marker, and results in a higher capacity of generalization than B2. Our proposal also tends to classify better those instances with lexical markers that are not Ambiguous or Opposite.

Table 10 shows some instances from the test set of AltLex corpus whose lexical markers belong to the cluster Opposite, so they mostly have a different class in the training and the test set. Those examples are correctly classified by our best configuration ("Pair_LSTM_0dense_Mode_Adadelta") using the "bootstrapped" corpus as training data, and they are misclassified by B2. Table 10 shows the class of the instances in the training set (Training column) and in the test set (Test column), as well as the output of B2 and our proposal. The case of the verb *break* is noteworthy since *break* is a causative verb, and it mostly has a causative interpretation in the training data. However, there are other uses of *break* without a causal meaning, as the example shows in Table 10. *Make* is another example of a causative verb, and our proposal also correctly disambiguates it, while B2 does not. These positive results with causative verbs encourage us to research the subtleties of these kind of verbs. Due to the better performance of our proposal on the examples showed in Table 10 and the comparison of Table 9, we can conclude that our neural model learns beyond the class distribution of the training instances, so it has the ability of generalizing the causal meaning. The last conclusion allow us to confirm our claim, i.e. the use of linguistic features restricts the representation of causality, and a neural model only fed with word embeddings performs better in the task of causality classification.

Trainig corpus	Method	Precision C.	Recall C.	F1 C.	Accuracy
Non-bootstrapped	B1	63.70%	84.12%	72.50%	67.10%
	Pair_LSTM_4dense_Mode_Adadelta	**73.96%**	79.36%	**76.56%**	**74.95%**
Bootstrapped	B1	67.34%	94.28%	78.57%	73.48%
	Pair_LSTM_0dense_Mode_Adadelta	**72.27%**	88.57%	**79.60%**	**76.56%**

Table 7: Results of B1 and our best configurations with the downsampled version of the corpus.

Corpus	Causal	Non Causal	Total
Non-bootstrapped	7,606	7,929	15,534
Bootstrapped	12,534	8,821	21,354

Lexical markers	Total	B2	Our proposal
Ambiguous	344	303	284
Opposite	92	48	64
Rest	181	127	150

Table 8: Size of the reduced version of the AltLex corpus.

Table 9: Lexical markers correctly classified by B2 and our proposal using the bootstrapped corpus for training.

Sentence from the test set	Training	Test	B2	Our proposal
The United States decided to *break* off economic relations with Cuba (which means that they would stop buying things from them).	Causal	Non Causal	Causal	Non Causal
Although Roosevelt had promised *to keep* the United States out of the war, he nevertheless took concrete steps to prepare for war.	Causal	Non Causal	Causal	Non Causal
Mary spent the next 18 years in confinement, but proved too dangerous *to keep* alive, as the Catholic powers in Europe considered her, not Elizabeth, the legitimate ruler of England.	Causal	Non Causal	Causal	Non Causal
Greatly alarmed and with Hitler *making* further demands on the Free City of Danzig, Britain and France guaranteed their support for Polish independence; when Italy conquered Albania in April 1939, the same guarantee was extended to Romania and Greece.	Causal	Non Causal	Causal	Non Causal
They are purely written languages and are often *difficult* to read aloud.	Causal	Non Causal	Causal	Non Causal

Table 10: Some correctly classified examples by our best configuration that were misclassified by B2.

5 Conclusions and Future Work

We divided the task of causation classification into two subtasks: causal meaning classification and causal argument classification. The paper focused on the task of causal meaning classification, and we claim that the encoding of the two events of the relation is required for a suitable disambiguation of causality. We proposed an encoding system based on a neural network with two inputs, one for the first event and the other for the lexical marker and the second event. Our proposed system outperforms the state-of-the-art on the AltLex corpus. We also showed the success of the system in some non-causative sentences but with commonly causative verbs (see Table 10).

The task of causality classification lacks corpora not restricted to specific syntactic constructions (see § 2) and balanced corpora with a good coverage of causal instances (see § 4.3.1). Therefore, for future work, we plan the creation of a new corpus for the two subtasks of causality classification, namely causality disambiguation and causality argument classification.

Acknowledgements

This work was supported by the German Research Foundation through the German-Israeli Project Cooperation (DIP, grant DA 1600/1-1 and grant GU 798/17-1). Calculations for this research were conducted on the Lichtenberg high performance computer of the TU Darmstadt.

References

Bethard, S. and J. H. Martin (2008). Learning semantic links from a corpus of parallel temporal and causal relations. In *Proceedings of the 46th Annual Meeting of the ACL on Human Language Technologies: Short Papers*, HLT-Short '08, Stroudsburg, PA, USA, pp. 177–180. Association for Computational Linguistics.

Conneau, A., H. Schwenk, L. Barrault, and Y. Lecun (2017, April). Very deep convolutional networks for text classification. In *Proceedings of the 15th Conference of the European Chapter of the Association for Computational Linguistics: Volume 1, Long Papers*, Valencia, Spain, pp. 1107–1116. Association for Computational Linguistics.

Copley, B. and P. Wolff (2014). *Causation in Grammatical Structures*, Chapter Theories of causation should inform linguistic theory and vice versa, pp. 11–57. Oxford Scholarship Online.

Girju, R. (2003). Automatic detection of causal relations for question answering. In *Proceedings of the ACL 2003 Workshop on Multilingual Summarization and Question Answering - Volume 12*, MultiSumQA '03, Stroudsburg, PA, USA, pp. 76–83. Association for Computational Linguistics.

Hidey, C. and K. McKeown (2016, August). Identifying causal relations using parallel wikipedia articles. In *Proceedings of the 54th Annual Meeting of the ACL (Volume 1: Long Papers)*, Berlin, Germany, pp. 1424–1433. Association for Computational Linguistics.

Hochreiter, S. and J. Schmidhuber (1997, November). Long short-term memory. *Neural Comput. 9*(8), 1735–1780.

Khoo, C. S. G., J. Kornfilt, R. N. Oddy, and S. H. Myaeng (1998). Automatic extraction of cause-effect information from newspaper text without knowledge-based inferencing. *Literary and Linguistic Computing 13*(4), 177–186.

Kingma, D. P. and J. Ba (2015). Adam: A method for stochastic optimization. In *3rd International Conference for Learning Representations, San Diego, 2015*.

Kruengkrai, C., K. Torisawa, C. Hashimoto, J. Kloetzer, J.-H. Oh, and M. Tanaka (2017, February). Improving event causality recognition with multiple background knowledge sources using multi-column convolutional neural networks. In *Proceedings of the 31st AAAI Conference on Artificial Intelligence (AAAI-17)*, San Francisco, California, USA, pp. to appear.

Lewis, D. (1973). Causation. *Journal of Philosophy 70*(17), 556–567.

Melamud, O., J. Goldberger, and I. Dagan (2016). context2vec: Learning generic context embedding with bidirectional LSTM. In *Proceedings of the 20th SIGNLL Conference on Computational Natural Language Learning, CoNLL 2016, Berlin, Germany, August 11-12, 2016*, pp. 51–61.

Mirza, P. and S. Tonelli (2016, December). Catena: Causal and temporal relation extraction from natural language texts. In *Proceedings of COLING 2016, the 26th International Conference on Computational Linguistics: Technical Papers*, Osaka, Japan, pp. 64–75. The COLING 2016 Organizing Committee.

Neeleman, A. and H. van de Koot (2012, May). The linguistic expression of causation. In M. Everaert, M. Marelj, and T. Siloni (Eds.), *The Theta System: Argument Structure at the Interface*, pp. 20–51. Oxford University Press.

Pennington, J., R. Socher, and C. D. Manning (2014). Glove: Global vectors for word representation. In *Empirical Methods in Natural Language Processing (EMNLP)*, pp. 1532–1543.

Prasad, R., N. Dinesh, A. Leeand, E. Miltsakaki, L. Robaldo, A. Joshi, and B. Webber (2008, may). The penn discourse treebank 2.0. In *Proceedings of the Sixth International Conference on Language Resources and Evaluation (LREC'08)*, Marrakech, Morocco. European Language Resources Association (ELRA). http://www.lrec-conf.org/proceedings/lrec2008/.

Reinhart, T. (2002). *The Theta System: Syntactic Realization of Verbal Concepts*. Cambridge, Mass: The MIT Press.

Riaz, M. and R. Girju (2013, August). Toward a better understanding of causality between verbal events: Extraction and analysis of the causal power of verb-verb associations. In *Proceedings of the SIGDIAL 2013 Conference*, Metz, France, pp. 21–30. Association for Computational Linguistics.

Riaz, M. and R. Girju (2014, June). In-depth exploitation of noun and verb semantics to identify causation in verb-noun pairs. In *Proceedings of the 15th Annual Meeting of the Special Interest Group on Discourse and Dialogue (SIGDIAL)*, Philadelphia, PA, U.S.A., pp. 161–170. Association for Computational Linguistics.

Talmy, L. (1988). Force dynamics in language and cognition. *Cognitive Science 12*(1), 49–100.

Wolff, P. (2007). Representing causation. *Journal of experimental psychology: General 136*(1), 82.

Zeiler, M. D. (2012). ADADELTA: an adaptive learning rate method. *CoRR abs/1212.5701*.

Are *doggies* cuter than *dogs*?
Emotional valence and concreteness in
German derivational morphology

Gabriella Lapesa, Sebastian Padó, Tillmann Pross, and Antje Roßdeutscher
University of Stuttgart, Institute for Natural Language Processing
`[gabriella.lapesa,pado,tillmann.pross,`
`antje.rossdeutscher]@ims.uni-stuttgart.de`

Abstract

The semantic behavior of derivational processes has been investigated with compositional distributional models relating the meaning of base, affix, and derivative (e.g., *anti+capitalist* → *anticapitalist*). While broadly successful, these approaches model how the distributional behavior generally is affected by derivation. Meanwhile, their predictions can not be interpreted at the level of linguistic regularities. In this paper, we adopt an alternative approach and focus on the impact of derivation on finer-grained semantic properties of the base. We focus on (the psycholinguistically prominent) *emotional valence*, i.e., the speakers' positive/negative evaluation of the word referent. We present two case studies on German derivational patterns, combining distributional and regression analysis. We are able to establish the broad presence of valence effects in German derivation as well as strong interactions with concreteness.

1 Introduction

Morphological derivation (Plag, 2003) is a word formation process which combines *bases* (e.g., *Hund* – "dog") with *affixes* (e.g., the diminutive *-chen*) into new words (*Hündchen* "doggie"). The semantic properties of derivation have been extensively explored in theoretical linguistics, and a number of recent computational studies in compositional distributional semantics have modelled the mappings that hold between the vectors of bases, affixes, and derivatives (Lazaridou et al., 2013; Luong et al., 2013; Padó et al., 2016). What these studies crucially lack, though, is *interpretability*: typically, they model mappings in an embedding space, but have little to say about linguistic regularities such as systematic changes in *meaning components*.

In this paper, our goal is to do exactly that, namely investigate the effects of derivation on a specific meaning component, *emotional valence* (henceforth, valence), which quantifies the speaker's positive or negative affect towards the referent of a word. This choice is motivated by psycholinguistic considerations: Valence is very well established in the literature as having substantial effects on human language processing (Vinson et al., 2014; Kuperman et al., 2014; Snefjella and Kuperman, 2016). Since it is not clear that the effects on valence take place independently of other variables, we extend our analysis to include a set of other meaning components, most notably *concreteness*, a second prominent meaning component in psycholinguistics (cf. the references above). Both meaning components are also highly relevant for NLP: (Variants of) valence occur under the names of sentiment and polarity and form the basic variable of interest in sentiment analysis (Pang and Lee, 2008). Concreteness is exploited, among other things, for metaphor identification (Turney et al., 2011; Köper and Schulte im Walde, 2016b).

The questions we ask are (a) whether a derivative carries a significantly different valence from its base; and (b) whether there are interactions between valence and concreteness (i.e., whether valence shifts occur only in more concrete vs. abstract contexts). To the best of our knowledge, the effect of derivation on valence has not been explored in distributional semantics. Our work extends a couple of studies that consider the interaction between valence and concreteness: Mohammad et al. (2016) present a collection of ratings targeting emotion and metaphor; Hill and Korhonen (2014) explore the interplay between subjectivity and concreteness. From a purely linguistic perspective, valence is situated between semantics and pragmatics; despite the interest for the interplay between semantics and pragmatics in derivational morphology (Dressler and Barbaresi, 1998; Plag, 2003), there has been no attempt yet to integrate theoretical considerations and computational modeling.

Our contribution is twofold. First, computationally, we define a distributional procedure that quantifies the basis–derivative differences with respect to specific meaning components and aggregates these differences across a large vocabulary with a regression analysis. Second, linguistically, we present two case studies on German derivation. The first one focusses on a specific pattern (*über- (over-)* prefix verbs) and illustrates the integration of valence with a theoretically motivated manual subclass analysis. The second one targets a larger set of patterns without manual annotation. We establish a strong presence of valence effects in derivation, even where its role would have been not obvious (female forms are used in more positive contexts than their male counterparts). We also find an interaction with concreteness which characterizes a "classic" evaluative pattern, the diminutive *-chen* (see Jurafsky (1996) for a cross-linguistic overview of the semantic spectrum covered by diminutives), as well as a pattern which has a clear evaluative flavor, the adversative *anti-*.

2 Experimental Setup

Our goal is to analyse the role of *valence* as a meaning component that undergoes systematic changes between base and derived words. We proceed as follows: given a set of base-derived word pairs for a derivation pattern, we represent the words distributionally. Then we quantify valence and a set of auxiliary meaning components (concreteness, imageability, arousal) for each word using a lexicon-based approach. Finally, we perform a regression analysis to analyse the factors affecting valence.

Distributional Semantic Model   Since our assignment of meaning components is lexicon-based (see next paragraph), we require a distributional model with lexical dimensions. This precludes the use of neural embedding models (Mikolov et al., 2013). Instead, we use a count (bag-of-words) distributional model with lexical dimensions. It is extracted from SdeWaC (Faaß and Eckart, 2013), a 800M words German web corpus with a large target and context vocabulary (approx. 280k lemmatized open-class words). We adopt standard choices for the main parameters, namely a symmetrical 5-words context window and positive pointwise mutual information to transform raw counts.

Computing Meaning Components.   We employ the German Affective Norms (Köper and Schulte im Walde, 2016a). The dataset contains automatically generated scores for 350k German lemmas on a 0 to 10 scale for four psycholinguistically prominent meaning components: *valence*, the (un-) pleasantness associated with the word; *arousal*, the intensity of the emotion associated with it; *concreteness*, the extent to which the word's referent can be perceived; and *imageability*, the extent to which the word's referent can be perceived visually. While the scores on these four components can in principle be used 'as is' for words covered by the resource, we found that their quality can be crucially improved (see Section 3 for details) by defining a *context-based reweighing scheme*. We define the score assigned to a target word t on a given component as the weighted average of the scores of its context words c by computing the dot product between the (L1-normalized) distributional vector for t and the vector of Affective Norm Scores for all context words. For each component, we reduce the set of context words with scores belonging to the top and bottom quartile for this component.

Regression analysis.   To gain a systematic understanding of valence, we perform a linear regression analysis. Linear regression predicts a continuous dependent variable (here, the valence score) as a linear combination of weighted predictors. We considered (a), theoretically motivated subclasses of *über-* verbs (Study 1, Section 3) and derivational patterns (Study 2, Section 4); (b), the meaning dimensions annotated in the German Affective Norms (imageability, concreteness, arousal); (c), frequency effects, as is best practice. In a model selection step, we discarded imageability based on a collinearity analysis (strong correlation to concreteness) and added the interaction between class/pattern and the Affective scores that were significant for both studies. The final model is:[1]

$$\text{valence} \sim \text{class/pattern} \\ * \ (\text{concreteness} + \text{arousal}) \qquad (1) \\ + \ \text{freq\_base} + \text{freq\_derived}$$

We trained three regression models to predict valence scores for base and derived words and to predict *differences* between valence scores for base and derived words.

3 Study 1: *über* prefix verbs

We investigate *über-* prefix verbs as an interesting object in lexical semantics: some *über* verbs (e.g., *überrennen*, "to overrun", *überschwemmen*, "to overflood",) encode a negative evaluation for events perceived as uncontrolled or uncontrollable (an excess reading, absent in the corresponding base terms *rennen*, "to run", *schwemmen*, "to float"). We build on a previous study of *über* prefix verbs (Pross and Roßdeutscher, 2015) that has produced a dataset of 74 *über* verbs and their corresponding bases manually selected to ensure that derived words are transparent with respect to their bases, at least in their dominant reading. Each pair was manually assigned to one of four theoretically motivated classes that differ by the contribution of *über-* to the interpretation of prefix verb:

- TRANSFER of an object from a source region to a goal region (16 pairs). Ex: *bringen, überbringen* ("to bring", "to deliver").

- APPLICATION of an object to another object (19 pairs). Ex: *kleben, überkleben* ("to paste", "to paste over").

- movement ACROSS some boundary or obstacle, which is conceptualized as a patient and in some cases undergoes change of state (18 pairs). Ex: *fahren, überfahren* ("to drive", "to drive (something) over").

- exceeding a certain threshold on a scale (MORE) provided by the base verb or by the usage context (21 pairs). Ex: *(be)werten, überbewerten* ("to value", "to overvalue").

We hypothesize that the ACROSS class is associated with negative valence, the others are neutral. We test the hypothesis by including the class in our regression model (cf. Equation (1)).

Results. Table 1 summarizes the fit of the linear models in terms of their ability to explain the valences of base verbs (column "Base"), the valences of *über* prefix verbs (column "Derived"), and the differences between base and prefix verbs (column "Shift"). It shows both the total amount of variance accounted for and the contribution of individuals predictors, computed though Lindeman-Merenda-Gold (LMG) scores (Lindeman et al., 1980). The fit of the full models (between .60 and .74 adjusted R^2) is very good, and even though frequencies are a major predictor (as almost always), both semantic classes and other meaning components (concreteness, arousal) contribute nicely.

Table 2 shows coefficients for all predictors that are significant in at least one of the columns. In the following, we focus on the Shift results and give Base and Derived for comparison only. For Shift, a positive coefficient for a predictor means that derived words with a high value of the predictor exhibit a higher valence than their bases. Vice versa, a predictor with a negative coefficient will reduce the

---

[1]We use the R statistical environment. The asterisk in the formula represents the interaction between class/pattern and concreteness and arousal. Continuous predictors are scaled, categorical variables are sum-coded: effects are calculated with the grand mean of the groups as reference value. Frequencies are log-transformed.

Predictor	Shift	Derived	Base
Semantic Class	.031	.058	.072
Concreteness	.037	.051	.087
Arousal	.011	.002	.108
Class:Arousal	.088	.086	.004
Base frequency	.105	N/A	.498
Derived frequency	.384	.553	N/A
Adjusted R^2	.60 ***	.72 ***	.74 ***

Table 1: Study 1 model fit (explained variance)

Predictor	Shift	Derived	Base
APPLICATION	–	–	-.06 **
Concreteness	-.06 **	-.08 **	–
ACROSS:Arousal	-.13 ***	-.10 ***	–
Base frequency	.15 ***	N/A	-.15 ***
Derived frequency	-.20 ***	-.20 ***	N/A

Table 2: Study 1: Coefficients of predictors

valence scores of derived words associated with high values of it. Contrary to our expectations, there is no significant main effect for any semantic class in the Shift analysis, meaning that the verb classes at large do not differ in valence. We do however, specifically find an interaction between the ACROSS semantic class and arousal that is highly significant and has a negative sign. Thus, ACROSS bases do tend to acquire negative valence as you add *über-*, but only if they already carry high arousal, i.e., are "emotionally loaded" verbs. A second interesting observation is the negative main effect of concreteness. It shows that across all pairs in the dataset, negative valence shifts are more pronounced for concrete verbs (*fahren, überfahren* "drive, drive over") than for abstract verbs (*nehmen, übernehmen* "take, take over").

Finally, we return to a question from §2: is there a difference between using valence scores from the Affective Norms and (re-)computing them distributionally? We repeated the analysis above using the Affective Norms valence scores, and found a much lower model fit (only .21 adjusted R^2, compared to .60 as in Table 1) as well as an absence of significant effects. In sum, the distributional valence scores do a substantially better job.

4 Study 2: Other Derivation Patterns

Our second study extends the focus beyond *über-* to six other German within part-of-speech derivation patterns from a previous study (Kisselew et al., 2015):

- N→N, FEMALE: *-in* (80 pairs). Ex: *Bäcker, Bäckerin* ("baker", "female baker")

- N→N, DIMINUTIVE: *-chen* (80 pairs). Ex: *Schiff, Schiffchen* ("ship", "small ship")

- A→A, OPPOSED: *anti-* (80 pairs). Ex: *religiös, antireligiös* ("religious", "antireligious")

- A→A, NEGATIVE: *un-* (80 pairs). Ex: *dankbar, undankbar* ("grateful", "ungrateful")

- V→V, DIRECTED: *an-* (68 pairs). Ex: *sprechen, ansprechen* ("to speak", "to address")

- V→V, TRAVERSE: *durch-* (70 pairs). Ex: *gehen, durchgehen* ("to go", "to go through")

Here, our hypotheses are that DIMINUTIVE comes with a positive valence shift and ADVERSE and DIRECTIONAL with a negative valence shift.

Predictor	Shift	Derived	Base
Pattern	.082	.093	.076
Concreteness	.009	.001	.030
Arousal	.002	.006	.001
Pattern:Concreteness	.018	.009	.008
Base frequency	.135	N/A	.524
Derived frequency	.148	.277	N/A
Adjusted R^2	.38***	.37***	.63***

Table 3: Study 2 model fit (explained variance)

Predictor	Shift	Derived	Base
AN-	-.06 *	–	.04 ***
ANTI-	–	-.05 *	-.03 *
-IN	.06 *	.07 **	–
Concreteness	-.04 ***	–	-.01*
ANTI-:Concreteness	.07 **	.06 *	–
-CHEN:Concreteness	.04 *	–	–
Base frequency	.16 ***	N/A	-.16 ***
Derived frequency	-.17 ***	-.18 ***	N/A

Table 4: Study 2: Coefficients of predictors

Results. We again start with model fit (Table 4). While the fit is lower than in Study 1, the new dataset is much more varied. Thus, we consider the (highly significant) Adjusted R^2 of .38 as still very good. Again, frequency explains much of the variance, followed by the derivational pattern.

The coefficients in Table 4 again show that our hypotheses hold up only partially. A significant negative effect for the AN- pattern is explained by the corresponding results for the base verbs, which show a highly significant positive valence compared to all other patterns in the dataset. We do not find a main effect for -CHEN, but a positive interaction with concreteness: concrete objects (*Hund*, "dog") gain in valence through diminution (*Hündchen*, "doggie") while abstract objects do not or can even acquire a pejorative component (*Idee, Ideechen* "idea, little idea"). A comparable interpretation offers itself for ANTI- where again there is no main effect but an interaction with concreteness (compare the strongly negative *antisemitisch* with the neutral *antibiotisch*). A somewhat unexpected result is the positive main effect of the female pattern -IN. A possible interpretation is that the marked female forms, many of which are professions, are only chosen when the gender is relevant, which is supported by the occurrence of positive evaluative adjectives ("good", "skilled"). In this connection, our results are a contribution to the characterization of gender bias in language (cf., Terkik et al. (2016) for another example of such study). At any rate, a more detailed analysis of the contexts is required to understand this effect better. Lack of a negative effect for *über* shows that for certain patterns an approach which is based on semantic subclasses of the derived terms is necessary to detect valence shifts that are more fine-grained.

As in Study 1, there was an overall negative effect of concreteness; however, this time, arousal did not play any significant role (its interaction being specific to the semantic classes annotated in the *über* dataset).

5 Conclusion

In this study, we have applied a kind of "magnifying glass" approach: instead of attempting to characterize the meaning of a word as completely as possible from distributional evidence, we focus on a small set of specific meaning components centered around emotional valence, and investigated how the strength of these components is influenced by derivational word formation. We described a method that can be used to extract a data-driven analysis of valence shifts and their interactions with other variables: It maps distributional representations for the words onto a valence scale and uses regression analysis as a pattern mining framework. We showed that the method can use manual annotation when available (Study 1) but also scales to larger, automatically generated datasets (Study 2). Beyond valence, our approach is applicable to other meaning components. Our analysis has uncovered a number of novel observations, notably the modulation of emotional valence for prefix verbs encoding boundary crossing (Study 1) and the unexpected presence of a positive evaluative meaning nuance in the female pattern (Study 2), as well as interactions between factors (Study 1 and Study 2). In particular, we found a strong effect of concreteness in modulating emotional valence shifts in derivation.

Acknowledgments

We gratefully acknowledge funding of our research by the DFG, SFB 732 (project B9: Lapesa and Padó; project B4: Pross and Roßdeutscher).

References

Dressler, W. U. and L. M. Barbaresi (1998). Morphopragmatics. In J. B. Jef Verschueren, Jan-Olaf Östman and C. Bulcaen (Eds.), *Handbook of Pragmatics: 1997 Installment*. John Benjamins Publishing.

Faaß, G. and K. Eckart (2013). Sdewac – a corpus of parsable sentences from the web. In *Language Processing and Knowledge in the Web*, Volume 8105 of *Lecture Notes in Computer Science*, pp. 61–68. Springer Berlin Heidelberg.

Hill, F. and A. Korhonen (2014). Concreteness and subjectivity as dimensions of lexical meaning. In *Proceedings of ACL*, Baltimore, USA, pp. 725–731.

Jurafsky, D. (1996). Universal tendencies in the semantics of the diminutive. *Language 72*(3), 533–578.

Kisselew, M., S. Padó, A. Palmer, and J. Šnajder (2015). Obtaining a better understanding of distributional models of German derivational morphology. In *Proceedings of IWCS*, London, UK, pp. 58–63.

Köper, M. and S. Schulte im Walde (2016a). Automatically generated affective norms of abstractness, arousal, imageability and valence for 350000 German lemmas. In *Proceedings of LREC*, Portoroz, Slovenia, pp. 2595–2598.

Köper, M. and S. Schulte im Walde (2016b). Distinguishing literal and non-literal usage of German particle verbs. In *Proceedings of NAACL-HLT*, San Diego, USA, pp. 353–362.

Kuperman, V., Z. Estes, M. Brysbaert, and A. B. Warriner (2014). Emotion and language: Valence and arousal affect word recognition. *Journal of Experimental Psychology. General 143*(3), 1065–1081.

Lazaridou, A., M. Marelli, R. Zamparelli, and M. Baroni (2013). Compositional-ly derived representations of morphologically complex words in distributional semantics. In *Proceedings of ACL*, Sofia, Bulgaria, pp. 1517–1526.

Lindeman, R. H., P. F. Merenda, and R. Z. Gold (1980). *Introduction to Bivariate and Multivariate Analysis*. Glenview, IL, USA: Scott Foresman.

Luong, M.-T., R. Socher, and C. D. Manning (2013). Better word representations with recursive neural networks for morphology. In *Proceedings of CoNLL*, Sofia, Bulgaria, pp. 104–113.

Mikolov, T., K. Chen, G. Corrado, and J. Dean (2013). Efficient estimation of word representations in vector space. In *Proceedings of ICLR*, Scottsdale, AZ.

Mohammad, S. M., E. Shutova, and P. D. Turney (2016). Metaphor as a medium for emotion: An empirical study. In *Proceedings of STARSEM*, Berlin, Germany, pp. 23–33.

Padó, S., A. Herbelot, M. Kisselew, and J. Šnajder (2016). Predictability of distributional semantics in derivational word formation. In *Proceedings of COLING*, Osaka, Japan, pp. 1285–1296.

Pang, B. and L. Lee (2008). Opinion mining and sentiment analysis. *Foundations and Trends in Information Retrieval* 2(1–2), 1–135.

Plag, I. (2003). *Word-formation in English*. Cambridge Textbooks in Linguistics. Cambridge University Press.

Pross, T. and A. Roßdeutscher (2015). Measuring out the relation between conceptual structures and truth-conditional semantics. In *Selected papers from the Workshop "Bridging Formal and Conceptual Semantics"*, Düsseldorf.

Snefjella, B. and V. Kuperman (2016). It's all in the delivery: Effects of context valence, arousal, and concreteness on visual word processing. *Cognition 156*, 135–146.

Terkik, A., E. Prud'hommeaux, C. O. Alm, C. Homan, and S. Franklin (2016). Analyzing gender bias in student evaluations. In *Proceedings of COLING*, Osaka, Japan, pp. 868–876.

Turney, P. D., Y. Neuman, D. Assaf, and Y. Cohen (2011). Literal and metaphorical sense identification through concrete and abstract context. In *Proceedings of EMNLP*, Edinburgh, United Kingdom, pp. 680–690.

Vinson, D., M. Ponari, and G. Vigliocco (2014). How does emotional content affect lexical processing? *Cognition and Emotion* 28(4), 737–746.

Evaluation Metrics for Automatically Generated Metaphorical Expressions

Akira Miyazawa[†,‡]   Yusuke Miyao[†,‡]

[†,‡]The Graduate University for Advanced Studies / [†,‡]National Institute of Informatics
{miyazawa-a, yusuke}@nii.ac.jp

Abstract

This paper proposes metrics to evaluate the quality of automatically generated metaphors not restricted to similes. The metrics are metaphoricity, novelty, comprehensibility, and overall evaluation. First, we discuss their importance and necessity. Next, we show that it is feasible to evaluate them by crowdsourcing. The targets of the evaluation are 1,360 expressions, each of which consists of a noun taken from a list of 40 nouns and a verbal phrase taken from a list of 34 verbal phrases. Then, we analyze the results to check the validity of the metaphoricity, novelty, and comprehensibility, and clarify their relationship. Finally, we argue that high-ranked expressions in the overall evaluation are considered to be "good metaphors" by showing that they actually are metaphors and are preferred by a human judge.

1   Introduction

In natural language processing (NLP), there are three main tasks that deal with metaphors: *detection*, *comprehension*, and *generation*. Generation has been studied less intensively than the others, but it has many applications. In poetry and prose, a metaphor is a tool that gives originality to works by helping writers avoid the banality of the everyday usage of the language (Leech, 2014, Ch. 2). Politicians use metaphor to make their statements more persuasive (Charteris-Black, 2011, Ch. 2). Generally, using metaphors makes language more visual or emotional (Mohammad et al., 2016). Thus, a metaphor generating system that suggests metaphorical expressions based on genres, purposes, or objects that we want to describe would be beneficial.

Most of the studies of metaphor generation have focused on similes of some fixed form such as "*T* like *S*". However, metaphor (in a broad sense) or *trope* has many other subclasses such as metaphor in a narrow sense, metonymy, or synecdoche. Thus, for example, previous works were not able to determine which is better: "his despair overflows" and "despair fills him". In this study, we propose metrics to evaluate metaphors not restricted to similes that help us find "good" metaphors from possible candidates. In the experiment, we calculated the scores of each metric by crowdsourcing. This allowed us to collect and analyze how general readers feel about expressions on a large scale. Preferably, metrics should be calculated automatically for objectivity and scalability. We expect that this is possible but do not discuss specific ways of achieving automation in this paper.

The rest of the paper is arranged as follows. Section 2 introduces works on automatic generation of similes, and their evaluation method. In Section 3, we introduce three metrics: *metaphoricity, comprehensibility, novelty*, and *overall evaluation*, which is calculated from the other three metrics. In Section 4, we check that it is feasible to evaluate expressions in terms of the metrics by conducting crowdsourcing. The target expressions in the evaluation are made by combining a noun taken from a list of 40 nouns and a verbal phrase taken from 34 verbal phrases. Section 5 shows the results of the experiment, analysis on the validity of the metrics, and their relationship. Finally some conclusions are given in Section 6.

2   Related Work

Existing works on metaphor generation have focused on similes such as "*T* like *S*" (Abe et al., 2006; Kitada and Hagiwara, 2001). Words used in the position of *S* are called the *source* or *vehicle*, and *T* is called the *target* or *topic*. Kitada and Hagiwara (2001) suggested a system that finds a word for the source that can be used in a given sentence. For example, given a sentence "The moon was red", the system outputs "The moon was as red as the setting sun". It uses some scores to select the source from the candidates and one of them is metaphoricity. This is calculated from the affective similarity and categorical dissimilarity of the target and each candidate for the source. In the evaluation, they asked volunteers who used the system to rate how good the generated sentences were as metaphors. Abe et al. (2006) proposed a model that finds suitable nouns for the source according to the properties that the target word has. For example, their model suggests "grandchild" for *S* in "a character like *S*", when given the list of properties "young, innocent and fine character". They evaluated the generated phrases in terms of *adequacy*, *ease of visualization*, *amusingness*, and *novelty*.

Because these systems generate metaphors by filling templates of similes, metaphoricity has been ignored in the evaluation process. A problem here is that judging metaphoricity in a systematic way is difficult. In corpus linguistics, researchers also needed such a method to annotate words that are used metaphorically. For that purpose, Steen et al. (2010) created a detailed guideline called *MIPVU*. We followed this guideline to make the gold standard. The basic procedure of MIPVU is as follows. First, annotators determine the contextual meaning of the target word. Then, they look up the word in a dictionary and search for a more *basic meaning* than the contextual meaning. Basic meanings tend to be concrete and are easy to imagine, see, hear, feel, smell, or taste or are related to bodily action. If a more basic meaning exists, the contextual meaning differs from the basic meaning, and if it can be understood in comparison, then it is judged as a *metaphor-related word*.

In this study, we use metaphoricity, novelty and comprehensibility. We introduce and describe this issue in the next section. Adequacy in the work of Abe et al. (2006) is regarded as the same as comprehensibility in this paper. Because adequacy and ease of visualization are close values in the work of Abe et al. (2006), we do not use ease of visualization. Similarly, amusingness and novelty have similar scores in the work of Abe et al. (2006). Thus, we integrate amusingness into novelty. Our work is also different in that the number of target expressions in evaluation is much larger[1]. This enables us to analyze the relationship among metrics more precisely.

3   Metrics

In this study, we propose three metrics: metaphoricity, comprehensibility, and novelty. The reason we use multiple metrics is that the importance of each metric differs from application to application. For example, poems, proses, and novels need creativity. For these, novelty is important. In the case where no important feature is selected, we also propose overall evaluation after introducing the other three metrics.

3.1   Metaphoricity

Metaphoricity measures how metaphorical an expression is. As stated in the preceding section, existing studies on metaphor generation have focused on similes of forms such as "*T* like *S*". Therefore, they have not paid much attention to whether the generated expressions are metaphorical. However, this matters a great deal in the generation of general metaphors because generated expressions are not necessarily metaphorical. To solve this problem, we measure metaphoricity of expressions on a five-point scale. The reason we do not classify them into two classes, metaphorical or nonmetaphorical, is that we need to compare metaphoricity with the other metrics to investigate their relationship. We collect metaphoricity scores by asking simple questions of crowdworkers. After that, we check if the results are reliable by using MIPVU. We did not ask workers to make judgments according to MIPVU because it is for experts.

---

[1]Those in the work of Kitada and Hagiwara (2001) and Abe et al. (2006) are 226 and 15 respectively.

3.2 Novelty

Next, we introduce *novelty* to measure how novel an expression looks or sounds. It is hard to define "good expressions" in general. However, creativity or originality can be an important criterion and novelty is a tool to generate creative or original expressions (Leech, 2014, Ch. 2). An advantage of using novelty is that it is easier to evaluate than creativity or originality. In the evaluation of novelty, an evaluator gives the highest score if he or she has never heard of or used the target expression, and the lowest score if the expression is widely used and conventional. It may be possible to measure novelty by counting the number of occurrences of expressions. However, in this study, we use crowdsourcing to measure novelty so that we can compare it with other metrics in the same conditions.

3.3 Comprehensibility

The third metric is *comprehensibility*. This quantifies how easy it is to understand the meaning of expressions. It is necessary because we use novelty as a metric and nonsense phrases (e.g., "she drinks sleep") tend to be highly novel. Comprehensibility serves as a constraint to keep the generated result meaningful.

This metric is more important for metaphors than for similes. Metaphors are often harder to understand in that they require that the writer and readers share some kind of similarity between the source and target. For example, readers would conceive the Japanese sentence *"ano kaisya made ensyou-sita"* (the fire spread to that company) in a metaphorical sense only when they have a detailed context or already know that the concept FIRE is used in contemporary Japanese to describe the situation where many people accuse someone of misbehaving over the Internet. On the other hand, similes usually do not require such knowledge, because readers try to find some kind of similarity between the source and target when they notice that the expressions are similes by their syntactic form.

3.4 Overall Evaluation

It is expected that some users of metaphor generation systems do not know which metric is important. For them, we introduce one integrated metric called *overall evalutation*. While it can be defined in many ways, for simplicity,we calculate it by just adding the three metrics.

4 Experiment

We conducted crowdsourcing to verify the validity of the metrics and clarify the relation among them[2].

4.1 Target

In this study, the targets of evaluation are short expressions, each of which consists of one noun and verbal phrase. For example, the expression *"zouo ga afureru"* (hatred spills out) is made up of *"zouo"* (hatred) and *"X ga afureru"* (X spills out). In this paper, we use the symbol X as a placeholder for a noun. We also use the symbol Y or Z as an anonymous subject or object in English translations to make the distinction between transitive and intransitive verbs clear or make them sound more natural. For example, we translate the original Japanese phrase *"X ni hitasu"* into *"Y dips Z in X"*. The nouns are chosen from a list of 40 nouns. Most of them are related to emotion such as *"ai"* (love) or *"ikari"* (anger), while some unrelated nouns, such as *"neko"* (cat), are included for contrast. Verbal phrases are chosen from a list of 34 verbal phrases, and consequently we get $40 \times 34 = 1360$ expressions in total. All of the verbs in them are often used with *"mizu"* (water) and stand for physical actions such as *"X ga nagareru"* (X flows) rather than cognitive actions such as *"X ni tuite kangaeru"* (Y thinks about X).

Our method follows the method of Nabeshima (2011, Ch. 6). He made 336 expressions from 12 nouns and 28 verbs, and evaluated them in terms of the acceptability to examine the productivity and

---

[2]The result is available at `https://github.com/pecorarista/metaphor-evaluation-result`.

structural basis of *conceptual metaphors*: EMOTION IS WATER, WORDS ARE WATER, and MONEY IS WATER[3]. Each score of acceptability is the average of the scores given by 6 undergraduate students. The advantage of this method is that it can generate diverse expressions regarding metaphoricity, conventionality, or comprehensibility.

Our lists contain all the words that Nabeshima (2011) used. We added 28 nouns to the original list because it lacks words for specific types of emotion such as "*ai*" (love) while it includes more abstract words such as "*kanjou*" (emotion). We also added 6 verbal phrases that represent actions related to water and can be used metaphorically. For example, we added the phrase "*X wo kumitoru*" (*Y* scoops up *X*). It sometimes means "understand" or "consider" as in "*kimoti wo kumitoru*" (*Y* considers *Z*'s feelings).

4.2 Metrics

We asked workers to evaluate the metaphoricity, comprehensibility, and novelty of each expression on a scale of one to five. The choices for the lowest or highest score had short descriptions as the followings.

- **Metaphoricity**

  Do you feel that the expression is metaphorical?

  5. It seems to be metaphorical.
  1. It doesn't seem to be metaphorical.

- **Comprehensibility**

  Is the following expression easy to understand?

  5. I understand it without any problem.
  1. I don't understand it at all.

- **Novelty**

  Is the expression novel?

  5. It is so novel that I have never seen or heard it before.
  1. It is conventional and widely used.

4.3 Evaluator

We used the crowdsourcing platform *Yahoo! Crowdsourcing*, which is provided by Yahoo! Japan, to collect evaluators. Because the application form is written in Japanese, applicants are considered to be able to understand Japanese. We did not put any restriction on age, sex, or district of residence. However, each applicant was asked to pass a test to prove he or she was not a spammer. The test is to choose the correct part of speech of a given word. The answers given by applicants who failed the test are excluded from the results that we analyze later.

The total number of questions was 4,080, which is the product of the number of metrics and the number of expressions. We collected 10 workers for each question. The questions were divided into several *tasks*. A task is a collection of questions and a unit that crowdworkers apply. In a task, we asked each worker to answer 21 questions including one for the test. We restricted the number of applications of a worker to a task to one so that he or she did not answer the same questions multiple times. However, the restriction could cause a delay in collecting sufficient answers. Preparing multiple tasks solved the problems of duplicate answers and delay.

5 Analysis of Result

5.1 Analysis of Individual Metrics

By conducting the crowdsourcing, we got 10 scores for each expression and metric. After that, because Nabeshima (2011) evaluated the acceptability on a scale of 0 to 4, we subtracted 1 from every score so that we could compare the scores of comprehensibility to those of acceptability directly. Then, we calculated the average score of each expression and metric. We use this result in the following analysis.

---

[3] "*T* IS/ARE *S*" denotes a conceptual metaphor that maps a concept *S* to another concept *T*. See Lakoff (1993) for the details of conceptual metaphors.

Rank	Noun (X)	Verbal phrase	Score
1	*kotoba* (word)	*X ga huttou-suru* (*X* boils)	3.9
2	*kanjou* (emotion)	*X ni oboreru* (*Y* almost drowns in *X*)	3.8
3	*zetubou* (despair)	*X ga ahureru* (*X* overflows)	3.7
4	*oto* (sound)	*X ga simiru* (*X* soaks into *Y*)	3.6
5	*zetubou* (despair)	*X ga koboreru* (*X* spills out)	3.5
⋮			
1356	*koe* (voice)	*X wo kakeru* (*Y* sprays *X*)	0.0
1356	*mizu* (water)	*X wo susuru* (*Y* sips *X*)	0.0
1356	*mizu* (water)	*X ga huttou-suru* (*X* boils)	0.0
1356	*mizu* (water)	*X ga nagareru* (*X* flows)	0.0
1356	*mizu* (water)	*X wo nomu* (*Y* drinks *X*)	0.0

Table 1: High-ranked and low-ranked expressions in terms of metaphoricity.

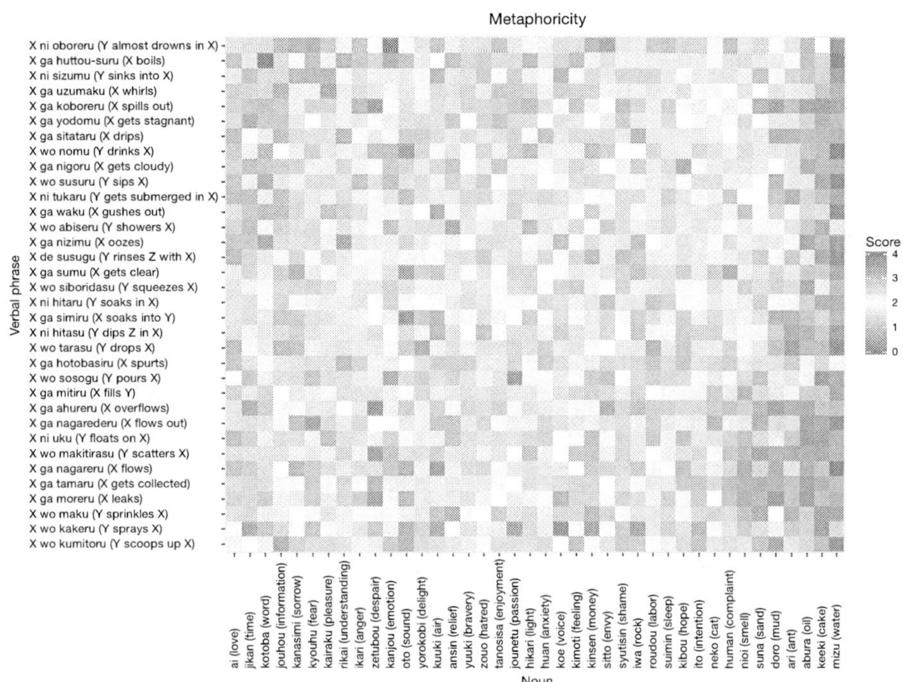

Figure 1: Scores of metaphoricity visualized in heat map. Nouns and verbal phrases are arranged in descending order of column- and row-wise sums of scores respectively.

First, we look at metaphoricity. As shown in Table 1, high-ranked expressions tend to contain a noun related to an emotion such as "*zetubou*" (despair). The complete ranking is available at the repository. It shows that 4 of the 10 expressions use "despair". On the other hand, most of the low-ranked expressions (9 of the bottom 10 expressions) consist of the noun "*mizu*" (water). Since each verb stands for a physical action related to water, they are not metaphorical. To check that high-ranked expressions were actually metaphorical, an author judged the top 10 expressions for their metaphoricity. The criterion is that an expression is metaphorical if its verb is a metaphor-related word in the sense of MIPVU. In the judging process, he used *Shin Meikai Kokugo Jiten* (a Japanese dictionary) to find basic and other meanings. As a result, 8 of the 10 expressions were metaphorical. He could not make judgments on the two expressions, "*kotoba ga huttou-suru*" (words boil)[4] and "*zetubou ga koboreru*" (despair spills out), because it was hard to understand their meanings.

Next, we examine the result of comprehensibility. Contrary to the case of metaphoricity, many high-ranked expressions consist of "*mizu*" (water) such as "*mizu de susugu*" (*Y* rinses *Z* with water) as partially

---

[4]We sometimes add an article "a(n)" or "the", or suffix "-(e)s" to the noun in translation to make it sound more natural; the number of the noun is usually not expressed explicitly in Japanese.

Rank	Noun (X)	Verbal phrase	Score
1	*ai* (love)	X *ni oboreru* (Y almost drowns in X)	4.0
1	*kanjou* (emotion)	X *wo kumitoru* (Y scoops up X)	4.0
1	*mizu* (water)	X *de susugu* (Y rinses Z with X)	4.0
1	*mizu* (water)	X *wo kakeru* (Y sprays X)	4.0
1	*mizu* (water)	X *wo susuru* (Y sips X)	4.0
		$\vdots$	
1356	*ari* (ant)	X *ga simiru* (X soaks into Y)	0.0
1356	*keeki* (cake)	X *wo sosogu* (Y pours X)	0.0
1356	*iwa* (rock)	X *wo susuru* (Y sips X)	0.0
1356	*ikari* (anger)	X *wo susuru* (Y sips X)	0.0
1356	*zouo* (hatred)	X *de susugu* (Y rinses Z with X)	0.0

Table 2: High-ranked and low-ranked expressions in terms of comprehensibility.

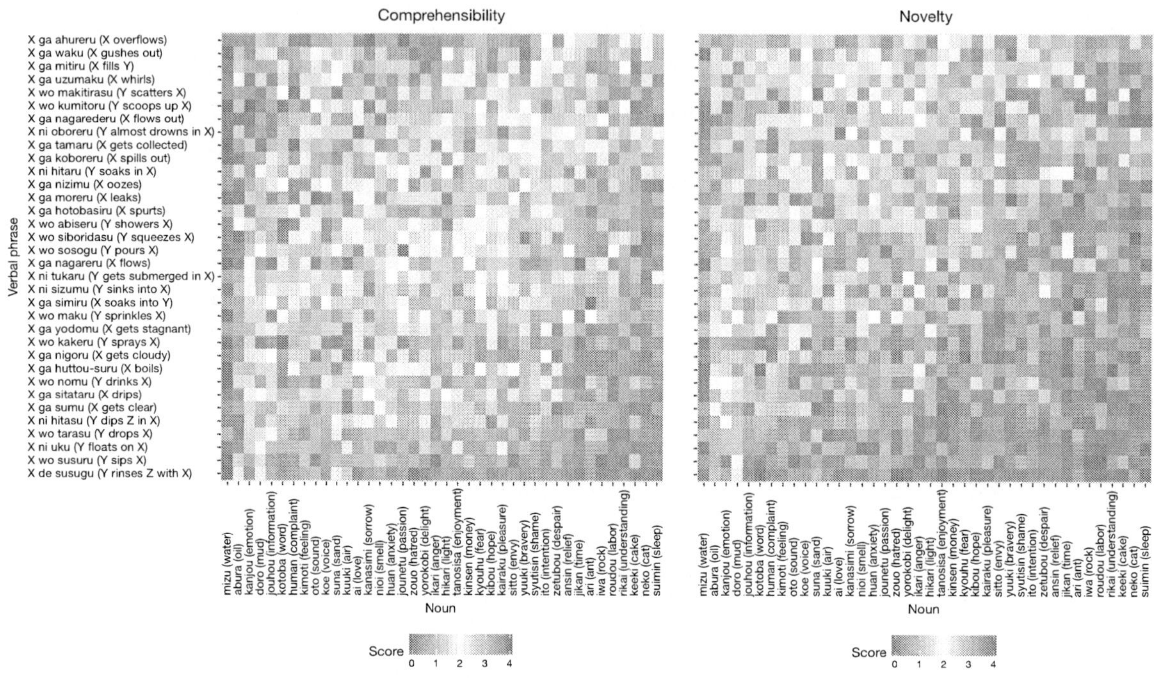

Figure 2: Scores of comprehensibility and novelty visualized in heat maps. Nouns and verbal phrases are arranged in descending order of column- and row-wise sums of comprehensibility.

shown in Table 2. On the other hand, low-ranked expressions tend to contain concrete objects (e.g., "ant" or "cake"). To confirm that our method actually captures how easy it is to understand the expression, we compare it to the acceptability reported in Nabeshima (2011). It is expected that the scores are close and show a similar tendency. First, when dealing with the common 336 expressions, we calculate the average of absolute differences of corresponding scores. The result is 0.64. It is less than one step of the scale of evaluation. Thus, it is considered to be minor. Next, we calculate the correlation coefficient between comprehensibility and acceptability. It is as high as 0.81 and means that they have a high positive correlation. As a result, we conclude that our evaluation on comprehensibility is as confident as that of Nabeshima (2011). The left graph of Figure 2 illustrates the scores of the expressions. Though nouns and verbal phrases were arranged by column- and row-wise sum, they form a dapple pattern. This implies that synonymous expressions have different grades of comprehensibility. For example, while "*kyouhu wo makitirasu*" (Y (disorderly) scatters fear) obtained 2.9, "*kyouhu wo maku*" (Y sprinkles fear) obtained 1.6. Analyzing this kind of discord is essential to examine the systematicity of metaphor and we succeeded in collecting the data for that purpose in a scalable and controllable way. We do not analyze such patterns in this paper, but will analyze them with the results in other domains.

Rank	Noun (X)	Verbal phrase	Score
1	*ari* (ant)	*X ga simiru* (X soaks into Y)	4.0
1	*neko* (cat)	*X wo siboridasu* (Y squeezes X)	4.0
1	*neko* (cat)	*X ga nagarederu* (X flows out)	4.0
1	*nioi* (smell)	*X ni uku* (Y floats on X)	4.0
1	*roudou* (labor)	*X wo susuru* (Y sips X)	4.0
⋮			
1353	*mizu* (water)	*X ga nagareru* (X flows)	0.0
1353	*mizu* (water)	*X ga waku* (X gushes out)	0.0
1353	*mizu* (water)	*X wo nomu* (Y drinks X)	0.0
1353	*jikan* (time)	*X wo kakeru* (Y sprays X)	0.0
1353	*kotoba* (word)	*X wo kakeru* (Y sprays X)	0.0

Table 3: High-ranked and low-ranked expressions in novelty.

Rank	Noun (X)	Verbal phrase	Score
1	*kuuki* (air)	*X ni sizumu* (Y sinks into X)	8.9
2	*kimoti* (feeling)	*X ga huttou-suru* (X boils)	8.8
3	*kyouhu* (fear)	*X ga nagaredaru* (X flows out)	8.7
4	*kanjou* (emotion)	*X ga huttou-suru* (X boils)	8.6
4	*syuutisin* (shame)	*X ga koboreru* (X spills out)	8.6
⋮			
1356	*keeki* (cake)	*X wo sosogu* (Y pours X)	4.0
1356	*mizu* (water)	*X ga huttou-suru* (X boils)	4.0
1356	*mizu* (water)	*X ga nagareru* (X flows)	4.0
1356	*mizu* (water)	*X wo nomu* (Y drinks X)	4.0
1360	*koe* (voice)	*X wo kakeru* (Y sprays X)	3.8

Table 4: High-ranked and low-ranked expressions in overall evaluation.

Finally, we look at novelty. Table 3 shows the opposite tendency. That is, many high-ranked expressions contain concrete objects, while many low-ranked expressions contain "*mizu*" (water). This is shown visually in Figure 2.

5.2 Relationships

To analyze the relationships among the three metrics, we calculate the correlation coefficients. The result is shown in Table 5. It reveals a strong negative correlation between comprehensibility and novelty. This is natural because we expect that comprehensible expressions get used more often and are more conventional. Thus, it may be possible to integrate one into the other. However, there are some expressions that achieve high scores in both comprehensibility and novelty such as "*human wo nomu*" (Y suppresses complaints; literally, Y drinks or swallows complaints) (comprehensibility: 3.3; novelty: 2.6) or "*syuutisin ga waku*" (shame gushes out) (comprehensibility: 3.1; novelty: 2.4). These are preferable when we want to generate expressions that are creative as well as comprehensible. Consequently, both comprehensibility and novelty are needed to retrieve such expressions.

5.3 Overall Evaluation

The high-ranked and low-ranked expressions in the overall evaluation are shown in Table 6. In high-ranked expressions, there are several expressions that are not common but are understandable. For example, we can understand "*kuuki ni sizumu*" (Y sinks into the air) by interpreting "the air" as "an atmosphere" or "an ambience", and "Y sinks into" as "Y gets depressed in". Similarly, we can comprehend the meaning of the expression "*kanjou ga huttou-suru*" (emotion boils) if we assume that "emotion" stands for a specific type of emotion such as "anger", "hatred", or "excitement". In Japanese, there are many idioms that describe such kinds of emotion by using words related to fire.

To examine the validity of the overall evaluation, we check if high-ranked expressions are actually "good metaphors". We define "good metaphors" as expressions that are metaphorical and "good", and

	Metaphoricity	Comprehensibility	Novelty
Metaphoricity	1.0	-0.19	0.28
Comprehensibility	-0.19	1.0	-0.92
Novelty	0.28	-0.92	1.0

Table 5: Correlation coefficients between metrics.

High-ranked expression [rank in overall evaluation]	Low-ranked expression [rank in overall evaluation]	Match
human wo nomu (*Y* drinks complaints) [23]	*abura wo kumitoru* (*Y* scoops up oil) [1087]	✓
ikari ga koboreru (anger spills out) [6]	*iwa ni oboreru* (*Y* almost drowns in a rock) [1117]	✓
syuutisin ga tamaru (shame gets collected) [44]	*syuutisin wo sosogu* (*Y* pours shame) [856]	✓
jouhou ga nigoru (information gets cloudy) [106]	*kuuki X wo makitirasu* (*Y* scatters the air) [212]	✓
kanasimi ga simiru (sorrow soaks into *Y*) [32]	*rikai ga nagareru* (understanding flows) [721]	✓
tanosisa ga uzumaku (enjoyment whirls) [81]	*human ni tukaru* (*Y* gets submerged in complaints) [1241]	−
kotoba ga nizimu (words ooze) [14]	*kyouhu ga nagareru* (fear flows) [307]	−
kanjou wo sosogu (*Y* pours emotion) [44]	*ito X ni tukaru* (*Y* gets submerged in intention) [654]	✓
huan ga nagarederu (anxiety flows out) [44]	*jounetu wo kumitoru* (*Y* scoops up passion) [165]	✓
jouhou ni oboreru (*Y* almost drowns in information) [23]	*abura ga tamaru* (oil gets collected) [1241]	✓

Table 6: Result of human evaluation. Column "Match" is checked if high-ranked expression is preferred by judge.

we define "good" as "making us more inclined to use". The process of examination was as follows. First, we divided all the expressions into two groups: the top 10% and bottom 90% in the overall evaluation. Then, we randomly picked one expression from each group and made 10 pairs. For evaluation, we asked a volunteer to choose the one from each pair that he prefers without caring about whether it is metaphorical. This volunteer is a graduate student in NLP, native speaker of Japanese, and has a basic knowledge of linguistics. In addition, we changed the border to 20%, 30%, 40%, and 50% to find the effective range.

The result of 10% is shown in Table 6. The volunteer preferred 8 high-ranked expressions in 10 pairs. We regard the overall evaluation as valid in that high-ranked ones are preferred in most cases. Changing the boundary to 20%, 30%, 40%, and 50% made only small changes in the number: 6, 6, 6, and 7. In the cases where the low-ranked ones are preferred, four cases had the nouns related to emotion only in the low-ranked ones. Three cases contained the high-ranked expressions that are hard to understand; the noun "rock" is used with incompatible verbal phrases. To make the preferred ones highly ranked in these cases, taking the abstractness or concreteness of the nouns into the overall evaluation would be effective.

Finally, an author judged if high-ranked expressions are actually metaphorical. Table 6 shows high- and low-ranked expressions divided by 10%. He followed MIPVU in making judgments in the same way as he did in checking the validity of metaphoricity. As a result, all but six expressions are metaphorical. Three of them are nonmetaphorical: *"nioi wo kakeru"* (*Y* sprays smell), *"abura ni sizumu"* (*Y* sinks into oil), and *"iwa wo nomu"* (*Y* drinks oil). The rest of the expressions are nonsense: *"?iwa ga sitataru"* (a rock drips)", *"?iwa ga nizimu"* (a rock oozes)", and *"?suna ga sitataru"* (sand drips)". All the expressions that are not metaphorical use concrete nouns. Thus, the situation will be improved by taking concreteness/abstractness into consideration in the overall evaluation.

In total, 33 of the 50 high-ranked expressions in Table 6 are preferred. Moreover, 44 of the 50 high-ranked expressions are metaphorical. Consequently, we conclude that the overall evaluation is valid in finding "good metaphors".

6   Conclusion

In this study, we proposed metrics to evaluate automatically generated metaphors not restricted to similes. Then, we actually evaluate expressions by crowdsourcing. The analysis of the result revealed the validity of the metrics and their relationship. Finally, we confirmed that high-ranked expressions in the overall evaluation are good metaphors. In future, we will apply the evaluation to an automatic metaphor generation system to help writers.

References

Abe, K., K. Sakamoto, and M. Nakagawa (2006). A computational model of metaphor generation process. In *Proceedings of the 28th Annual Meeting of the Cognitive Science Society*, pp. 937–942.

Charteris-Black, J. (2011). *Politicians and rhetoric: The persuasive power of metaphor*. Springer.

Kitada, J. and M. Hagiwara (2001). Figurative composition support system using electronic dictionaries (in Japanese). *Transactions of Information Processing Society of Japan 42*(5), 1232–1241.

Lakoff, G. (1993). The contemporary theory of metaphor.

Leech, G. N. (2014). *A linguistic guide to English poetry*. Routledge.

Mohammad, S. M., E. Shutova, and P. D. Turney (2016). Metaphor as a medium for emotion: An empirical study. In *Proceedings of the Fifth Joint Conference on Lexical and Computational Semantics (*Sem)*, Berlin, Germany.

Nabeshima, K. (2011). *Nihongo no metafā (in Japanese)*. Kurosio Publishers.

Steen, G. J., A. G. Dorst, J. B. Herrmann, A. Kaal, T. Krennmayr, and T. Pasma (2010). *A Method for Linguistic Metaphor Identification: From MIP to MIPVU*. John Benjamins Publishing.

Semantic Network Analysis of Contested Political Concepts

Paul Nulty
Centre for Research in Arts, Social Science and Humanities,
University of Cambridge
`pgn26@cam.ac.uk`

Abstract

This work presents methods for exploring the lexical environment of political concepts using inter-active network visualisations of corpus-derived grammatical relations and word associations. The conceptual relations consist of part-of-speech tagged words connected by typed, weighted, edges indicating the strength of relations between words, as measured by pointwise mutual information of different types of co-occurrences. An interactive animated interface allows users to adjust the node degree directly, or to specify edge-weight thresholds, and observe the resulting effect on the network. The system can be searched by neighbourhood sub-graphs ('ego graphs') of particular sets of query terms. The force-directed layout of the network highlights conceptual structure, as terms connected by many relations are drawn together, and the user can select which subsets of relations and sub-corpora to display. Community detection (cliques) and centrality measures provide addi-tional comparative measures of the use of contested concepts in diverse political communities. As an example of such a system for exploring the structure of political concepts, an implementation on com-ments from libertarian and socialist partisan online communities is presented. The work is motivated by the extensive theoretical treatment of political conceptual morphology but limited computational implementations extant in the literature.

1 Introduction

Distributional semantic methods that use aggregate syntactic and textual word co-occurrence behaviour have been applied successfully to many natural language processing tasks. These methods are often de-ployed as part of a pipeline to solve an engineering problem, and evaluated by classification or correlation performance against human judgements on sub-tasks. This paper focuses on a descriptive or exploratory application of the data generated from distributional semantic analysis, allowing researchers to examine terms of interest in aggregate contexts across different kinds of co-occurrence relations and association measures.

In the social sciences, concordance views, topic models, and dictionary analysis provide a simple digest of the use of particular words in digital text collections. Although not often discussed as a spe-cific method, in practice keyword search and snippet-views of large digital book collections are a widely used in historical and theoretical political research. The system described in this paper shows that inter-active tables and network diagrams may be used to present summaries of linguistic features and word associations that allow for a descriptive interpretation of how concepts are deployed in ordinary political discourse. This can serve as a level of analysis between a close reading of the whole text collection and a fully automated bag-of-words based classification, dictionary analysis, or concordance.

This paper emphasises political concept analysis as a particularly useful application of this kind of method, due to the extensive theory of political conceptual morphology but limited computational implementations extant in previous work.

1.1 Essentially contested politcal concepts

Political discourse provides an especially suitable domain for exploratory analysis of distributional se-mantic data. It has long been recognized that many political concepts are 'essentially contested concepts':

When we examine the different uses of these terms and the characteristic arguments in which they figure we soon see that there is no one use of any of them which can be set up as its generally accepted and therefore correct or standard use. (Gallie, 1955)

Researchers in political theory and intellectual history have emphasised the importance of understanding political concepts in their linguistic context(Skinner, 1969). Such studies primarily consist in close reading of primary texts produced by academics, intellectuals, and political actors, in addition to consideration of the social and cultural contexts of their time and place.

Following earlier work on the subject (Berlin, 1958; Skinner, 2012) a series of political theory articles discuss the distinction between negative and positive conceptions of liberty, in part by considering the syntactic valences and semantic affordances of the words themselves and their morphological variants (Gray, 1980; MacCallum, 1967; Oppenheim, 1961)

Koselleck (1989) discusses the historical origins of debates over voting rights by pointing to the semantic distinctions drawn by the terms *bürger* and *citoyen* in the eighteenth century. De Bolla (2013) traces the history of the concept of human rights through word use in eighteenth century corpora, and proposes a method and typology for conceptual analysis that captures variation in levels of abstraction and the rhetorical or ideational functions of concepts.

Freeden (1994) refines Gallie's notion of essential contestability by emphasising that particular instantiations of concepts ('conceptions') expressed in political discourse consist of 'empirically ascertainable and describable' as well as normative parts. This chimes with the descriptive goal and empirical methods commonly now employed by lexicographers to capture the meaning of words in general. Freeden and others (e.g. Finlayson (2007); Oppenheim (1983)) urge political theorists to investigate the structure of political concepts through their actual usage in text, with reference to structures such as a substantive core and optional peripheral components, or the roles filled by concepts as they are expressed in sentences. This approach has much in common with how word meaning is modelled by computational semantics (Jackendoff, 2010; Pustejovsky et al., 1993), though the two literatures are not connected. This does not assume that analytic treatment of linguistic context can resolve any 'true' or 'correct' meaning of a contested concept, but simply that usage reflects meaning as held by the community or ideology that produces the text.

Despite the history of interest in linguistic analysis in political theory and the history of intellectual thought, quantitative political science researchers generally treat text analysis as a means to an end, whereby the distribution of words into documents allows for measurement of attention to issues, or estimation of ideological positions. Bag-of-words techniques often suffice for this task, as it is generally observed that political actors tend to reveal ideology more often through relative issue emphasis than by expressing contrasting beliefs, desires, or intentions about the same issues (Budge, 2001).

Political document scaling methods solve a practical estimation problem — how similar is each document to the others in the corpus along particular ideological dimensions? (Slapin and Proksch, 2008; Laver et al., 2003). These inferred positions can then be used in statistical models of the political institutions or processes that produced the documents. With some exceptions (Monroe et al., 2008; Sagi et al., 2013), the intention is usually not to interpret the weights or parameter estimates of the model's linguistic features in order to investigate the relationship between the language used and the implied political position. Where topic models are applied to measure issue emphasis or attention, the goal is to incorporate these measurements into a wider model of political attention or an analysis of the effects of speeches focusing on particular topics. (Grimmer and Stewart, 2013; Grimmer, 2010; Quinn et al., 2010).

Computer scientists have applied more complex methods in order to recover ideological position from text: Iyyer et al. (2014) use recursive neural networks to detect political ideology compositionally, using crowd-sourced annotations of congressional debates. However, the focus is again to expedite the data-annotation process with machine learning, rather than to present and interpret the linguistic structures that give rise to ideological differences.

Given the ongoing significance of contested concepts in public debate (for an example treatment of the term *neoliberalism*, see (Ferguson, 2010)), a computationally-assisted comparative analysis of descriptive word meaning in various political communities can give insight into the nature of ideological disagreement and miscommunication. This work demonstrates that interactive visualisations and novel application of standard network analysis techniques such as community detection and centrality measures discover relevant ideological distinctions.

1.2 Previous work

Mixed-method approaches to text analysis in political science have made use of commercial software for manual coding or visualisation of dictionary or factor-analysis methods (Reinert, 1993) with word clouds or tables. In corpus linguistics and lexicography, perhaps the most widely used tool is the Sketch Engine (Kilgarriff et al., 2014), which presents tables summarising the selectional preferences of terms of interest gathered from dependency parsed corpora. Sketch Engine has been widely deployed in lexicography and the study of language learning, but less often for broader questions in social science (Blinder and Allen, 2015). In computational semantics, the Wordnet, Concept Net and generative lexicon projects specify the representation of concepts, but lack implementations of exploratory tools beyond presenting tables of the resulting structures, and derive their associations from 'universal' human curated databases, rather than automatically from ideologically partisan corpora.

Network representations of concepts are widely studied in cognitive science (Steyvers and Tenenbaum, 2005; Gruenenfelder et al., 2015). Lopes et al. (2010) describes a web-based interactive tool for exploring networks derived from bioinformatic data. Van Atteveldt (2008) describes an RDF-based system for representing and querying semantic network data from Dutch newspaper articles.

(Shneiderman and Aris, 2006) presents software for dynamically presenting network visualisations to allow the user control the density and visibility of nodes based on degree and node metadata, although the software is not yet publicly available [1].

2 Method

Conceptual structures are implied in text through both syntactic and non-syntactic relations. The type, attributes, and functional roles of a concept may be indicated through paradigmatic and syntagmatic grammatical relations, and also by general thematic textual co-occurrence counts as leveraged by topic models and document classification systems. The system described here implements network visualisations derived from both syntagmatic grammatical relations and textual co-occurrences. For both types of co-occurrence, the association between words is calculated using adjusted pointwise mutual information, with the context distribution smoothing method of Levy et al. (2015) used to reduce the impact of very infrequent co-occurrences.

The corpus used to construct the networks for figures in this paper and the linked R Shiny web applications is a collection of all comments from the *libertarian* and *socialism* communities on the website `reddit.com`. This data shows the contrasting way in which political concepts are deployed in natural discourse within self-selecting ideologically partisan communities. All comments from 2014-2015 with a positive rating of three or higher and containing at least two sentences are included. Reddit comments are public data available through an API provided by the website[2]

2.1 Word co-occurrence extraction

Grammatical relations are extracted with a syntactic dependency parser implemented in the SpaCy python package for natural language processing, accessed through the R spacyr package.[3] This parser has been shown to achieve state-of-the-art accuracy on part-of-speech tagging and dependency parsing evaluation datasets (Honnibal et al., 2015). To simplify the visualisation and try to focus on the

---

[1]`http://www.cs.umd.edu/hcil/nvss/#software`

[2]`https://www.reddit.com/dev/api/`

[3]`https://github.com/explosion/spaCy`, spacyr package: `https://github.com/kbenoit/spacyr`

most informative relations, the detailed dependency tagset is reduced to four general relation types, and functional categories (determiners and auxiliaries) and prepositional relations are excluded. The resulting relation types are conjunction, modification, verb-subject and verb-object. The type of semantic association is indicated by the colour of the edge, and the strength of association by the edge width. Non-syntactic associations are measured by counting co-occurrences within the same comment, but excluding co-occurrences within the same sentence. The intention is to properly separate the data gathered from sentential and non-sentential (document) relations.

2.2 Interactive network visualisation

The visualisation is implemented as an R Shiny web application. The figures in this section show screenshots from the network representatations displayed by the web app. These are 'neighbourhood' or 'ego' graphs of order two, that is, they show nodes within at most two edges from the focal node — an edge exists between two nodes if their PMI association is a above a user-specified threshold. The network is drawn using the R *visNetwork* package, using a force-directed algorithm (Fruchterman and Reingold, 1991), which models the network mechanically as repelling particles connected by springs. The result is that in a graph of suitable density and degree, nodes are spaced apart enough to be distinguished, but the edges pull together nodes into clusters that share many relations.

The figures in this section are illustrative only, intended to show the interface design and the general properties of the network. The application should be evaluated using the online interactive prototypes for the syntactic [4] and textual co-occurrence [5] data. The visNetwork package implements a drag, pan, and zoom enabled central widget, and this is combined with input boxes for search terms and sliders for setting the order of the neighbourhood graph, the maximum node degree, and the association score threshold.

Static images of these networks are of limited use when large enough to show structures larger than a few individual nodes — attempting to label all of the nodes makes them unreadable. If the number of nodes is reduced in order to make the labels legible, then the resulting network is too small to show interesting structure at a large or medium scale. Interpretation or exploration of these semantic networks is therefore best approached through an interactive interface which allows for adjustment in the scale and highlighting of particular neighbourhoods.

Figure 1 shows syntactic association graphs for the term *power* tagged as a noun for the socialism (left) and libertarian (right) communities. In the socialism community, the immediate neighbours of power are *priviledge, wealth, influence* (conjunction relations), *rule* (verb subject) and *labour* (modifier). For the libertarian community, the immediate neighbours are *corrupt, enforce, abuse, sell* (verb subject); *limit* (verb object), *wealth* and *influence* (conjunction).

---

[4]Syntactic co-occurrences: `http://52.207.96.220:3838/iwcs_app_syntax/`
[5]Textual co-occurrences `http://52.207.96.220:3838/iwcs_app_cooc/`

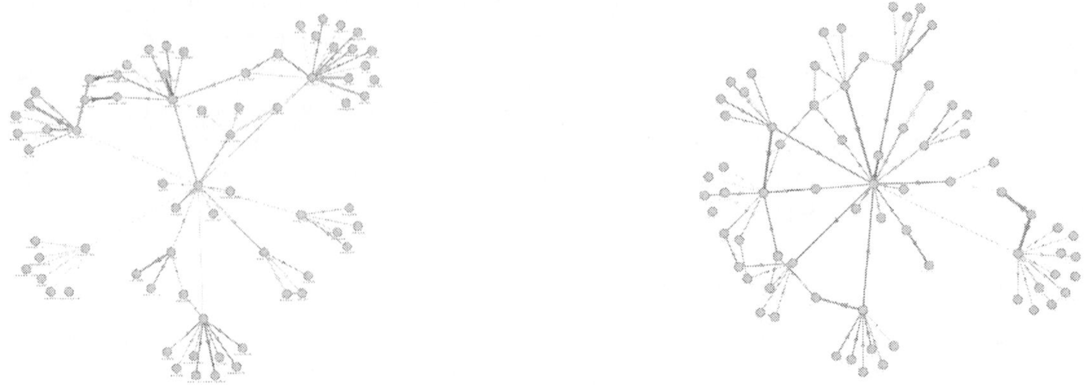

Figure 1: *power* (noun) in the socialism (left) and libertarian (right) subreddit

Figure 2 shows syntactic association graphs for the term *freedom* tagged as a noun for the socialism (left) and libertarian (right) communities. In the socialism community, the immediate neighbours of freedom are *democracy, wealth, equality* (conjunction relations), *attain* (verb subject) and *true, personal* (modifier). For the libertarian community, the immediate neighbours are *choose, associate, abridge, value, restrict* (verb object); *religious, personal* (modification), and *liberty* (conjunction).

Figure 2: *freedom* (noun) in the socialism (left) and libertarian (right) subreddit

Figure 3 shows the full interface for the textual co-occurrence relationships. The sliders on the left allow control of node degree, association score threshold, and the selection of variations of the PMI association measure. The concept shown is the verb 'plan', for the socialism subreddit, where the immediate neighbours are *enterprise, central, economy, innovation*, and *diet*.

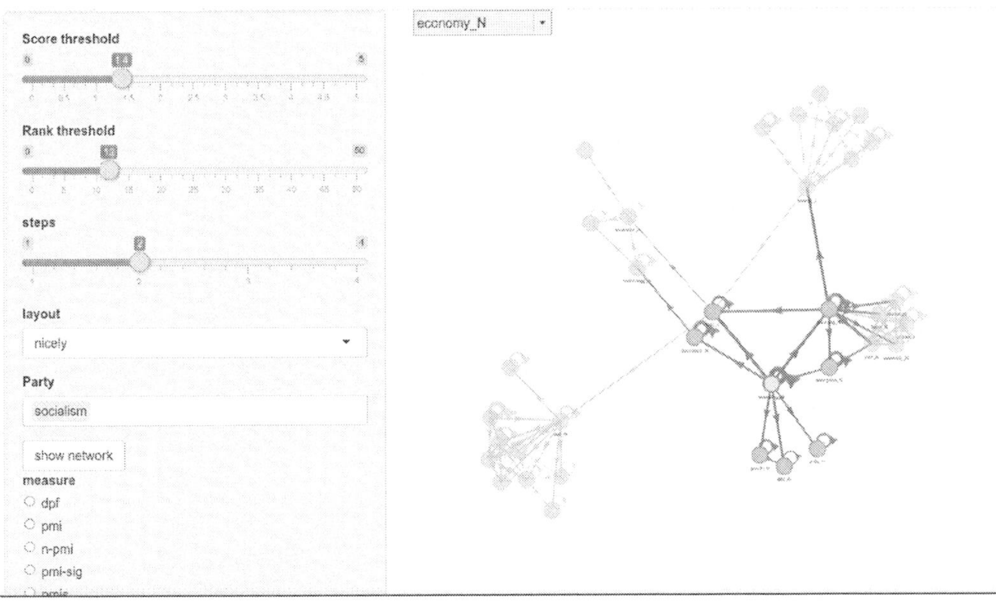

Figure 3: Interface for Shiny application for graph visualisation. Sliders control node degree, association score threshold, and word association measure calculation. The central node of the ego network is the verb *plan*.

Syntactic selectional preferences require an automated parser trained on comparable text, and therefore it is not appropriate to apply this analysis to historical text, especially with additional noise resulting from optical character recognition. However, general context-based co-occurrences may be extracted from historical texts. Figure 4 shows a joint neighbourhood network of the terms *freedom* and *liberty* from the 1795 – 1800 portion of the Eighteenth Century Collections Online corpus. Edges are associations based on sentence-level co-occurrences. The user can choose from a number of lexical association measures; in this case t-score associations are shown. Lexical association measures typically trade-off the degree to which generally frequent terms are scored highly due to the significant weight of evidence resulting from high co-occurrence counts, or penalized due to the high independent probability of co-occurrence of generally frequent terms. The t-score tends to prioritise generally frequent words, while pointwise mutual information often over-estimates the significance of co-occurrence of words with low overall frequencies (Evert, 2005).

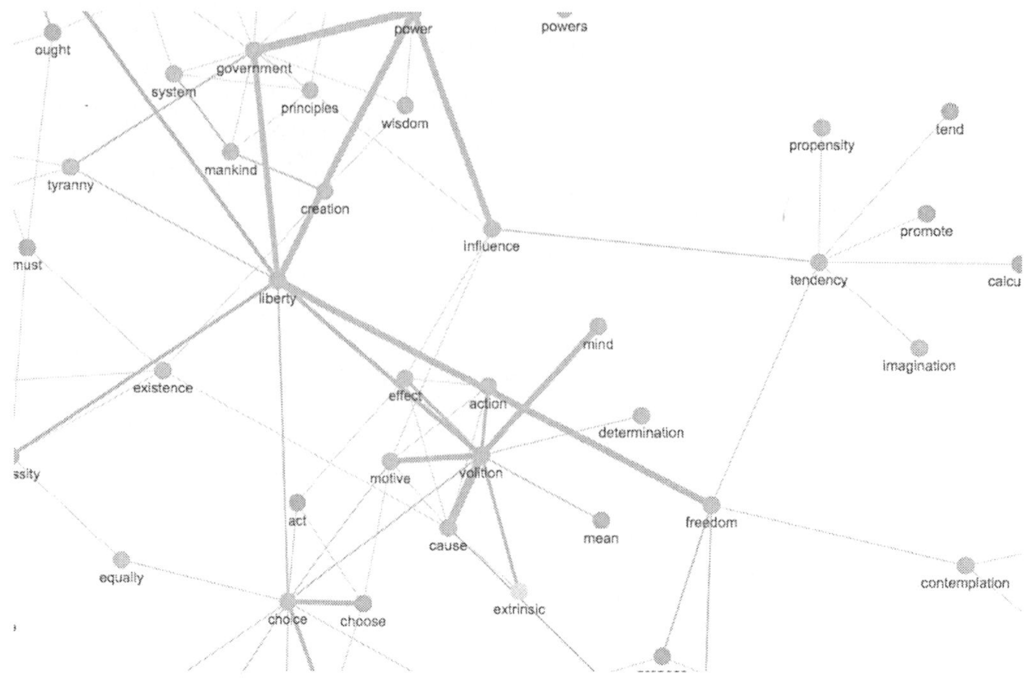

Figure 4: Joint neighbourhood network of the terms *freedom* and *liberty* from the 1795 – 1800 portion of the Eighteenth Century Collections Online corpus. Color indicates dominant part-of-speech; edge width indicates log t-score association. An online demo is available here: `http://52.207.96.220:3838/ecco-network-1/`. This demo also provides interactive interfaces to igraph's clique-finding and shortest-path functions applied to the semantic network derived from ECCO.

2.3 Centrality measures

Beyond network visualisation, many standard network analysis methods may be applied to semantic networks to discover the most important nodes and clusters in the graph. The table below shows the highest scoring words by two commonly-used network centrality measures — eigenvector centrality and betweenness centrality — for the libertarian and socialism subreddits. While further work is needed to go beyond face-validity, the terms seem to reflect common concerns in the ideological communities from which the semantic network is constructed.

Libertarian		Socialism	
eigen	betweeness	eigen	betweeness
detention_N	law_N	class_N	class_N
detainee_N	government_N	production_N	capitalism_N
facility_N	tax_N	revolution_N	party_N
administration_N	libertarian_N	struggle_N	socialism_N
detain_V	pay_V	relation_N	revolution_N
congress_N	year_N	movement_N	movement_N
law_N	state_N	commodity_N	society_N
amendment_N	libertarianism_N	labor_N	production_N
prosecute_V	business_N	socialism_N	war_N
authorize_V	get_V	capitalism_N	union_N
charter_N	rate_N	value_N	state_N
judge_N	crime_N	mode_N	think_V
section_N	amendment_N	development_N	power_N
senate_N	marriage_N	party_N	struggle_N
suspect_N	insurance_N	participation_N	time_N
combatant_N	property_N	produce_V	work_V
trial_N	war_N	contradiction_N	system_N
conviction_N	case_N	society_N	say_V
restore_V	regulation_N	communism_N	value_N

3   Conclusion

This paper presents an interactive web visualisation system for exploring conceptual associations derived from syntactic and textual lexical co-occurrence data. The method is motivated by the need for descriptive and exploratory methods for investigating the linguistic context of essentially contested contests in political discourse. A demonstration is presented showing the usage of political concepts in ideologically partisan comments in an online community, and an interface to neighborhood network plots and clique-detection for a portion of the Eighteenth Century Collections Online corpus. Future extension of this work will diachronically and synchronically compare modern usage of particular contested concepts in online social communities with that of political actors from records such as Hansard, and extend the analysis beyond visualisation to make further use of network analysis techniques such as community detection and centrality measures.

References

Berlin, I. (1958). Two concepts of liberty.

Blinder, S. and W. L. Allen (2015). Constructing immigrants: Portrayals of migrant groups in british national newspapers, 2010–2012. *International Migration Review*.

Budge, I. (2001). Validating party policy placements. *British Journal of Political Science 31*(01), 179–223.

De Bolla, P. (2013). *The architecture of concepts: The historical formation of human rights*. Fordham Press.

Evert, S. (2005). The statistics of word cooccurrences: word pairs and collocations.

Ferguson, J. (2010). The uses of neoliberalism. *Antipode 41*(s1), 166–184.

Finlayson, A. (2007). From beliefs to arguments: Interpretive methodology and rhetorical political analysis. *The British Journal of Politics and International Relations 9*(4), 545–563.

Freeden, M. (1994). Political concepts and ideological morphology. *Journal of Political Philosophy 2*(2), 140–164.

Fruchterman, T. M. and E. M. Reingold (1991). Graph drawing by force-directed placement. *Software: Practice and experience 21*(11), 1129–1164.

Gallie, W. B. (1955). Essentially contested concepts. In *Proceedings of the Aristotelian society*, Volume 56, pp. 167–198. JSTOR.

Gray, J. N. (1980). On negative and positive liberty. *Political Studies 28*(4), 507–526.

Grimmer, J. (2010). A bayesian hierarchical topic model for political texts: Measuring expressed agendas in senate press releases. *Political Analysis*, 1–35.

Grimmer, J. and B. M. Stewart (2013). Text as data: The promise and pitfalls of automatic content analysis methods for political texts. *Political analysis*, 267–297.

Gruenenfelder, T. M., G. Recchia, T. Rubin, and M. N. Jones (2015). Graph-theoretic properties of networks based on word association norms: implications for models of lexical semantic memory. *Cognitive science*.

Honnibal, M., M. Johnson, et al. (2015). An improved non-monotonic transition system for dependency parsing. In *EMNLP*, pp. 1373–1378.

Iyyer, M., P. Enns, J. Boyd-Graber, and P. Resnik (2014). Political ideology detection using recursive neural networks. In *Proceedings of the Association for Computational Linguistics*, pp. 1113–1122.

Jackendoff, R. (2010). *Meaning and the lexicon: the parallel architecture, 1975-2010*. Oxford University Press.

Kilgarriff, A., V. Baisa, J. Bušta, M. Jakubíček, V. Kovář, J. Michelfeit, P. Rychlý, and V. Suchomel (2014). The sketch engine: ten years on. *Lexicography 1*(1), 7–36.

Koselleck, R. (1989). Linguistic change and the history of events. *The journal of Modern history 61*(4), 650–666.

Laver, M., K. Benoit, and J. Garry (2003). Extracting policy positions from political texts using words as data. *American Political Science Review 97*(02), 311–331.

Levy, O., Y. Goldberg, and I. Dagan (2015). Improving distributional similarity with lessons learned from word embeddings. *Transactions of the Association for Computational Linguistics 3*, 211–225.

Lopes, C. T., M. Franz, F. Kazi, S. L. Donaldson, Q. Morris, and G. D. Bader (2010). Cytoscape web: an interactive web-based network browser. *Bioinformatics 26*(18), 2347–2348.

MacCallum, G. C. (1967). Negative and positive freedom. *The Philosophical Review 76*(3), 312–334.

Monroe, B. L., M. P. Colaresi, and K. M. Quinn (2008). Fightin'words: Lexical feature selection and evaluation for identifying the content of political conflict. *Political Analysis 16*(4), 372–403.

Oppenheim, F. E. (1961). Dimensions of freedom: An analysis.

Oppenheim, F. E. (1983). Political concepts: A reconstruction.

Pustejovsky, J., P. Anick, and S. Bergler (1993, June). Lexical semantic techniques for corpus analysis. *Comput. Linguist. 19*, 331–358.

Quinn, K. M., B. L. Monroe, M. Colaresi, M. H. Crespin, and D. R. Radev (2010). How to analyze political attention with minimal assumptions and costs. *American Journal of Political Science 54*(1), 209–228.

Reinert, M. (1993). Les mondes lexicaux et leur logiqueà travers l'analyse statistique d'un corpus de récits de cauchemars. *Langage et société 66*, 5–39.

Sagi, E., D. Diermeier, and S. Kaufmann (2013). Identifying issue frames in text. *PLoS one 8*(7), e69185.

Shneiderman, B. and A. Aris (2006). Network visualization by semantic substrates. *IEEE Transactions on Visualization and Computer Graphics 12*(5), 733–740.

Skinner, Q. (1969). Meaning and understanding in the history of ideas. *History and theory 8*(1), 3–53.

Skinner, Q. (2012). *Liberty before liberalism*. Cambridge University Press.

Slapin, J. B. and S.-O. Proksch (2008). A scaling model for estimating time-series party positions from texts. *American Journal of Political Science 52*(3), 705–722.

Steyvers, M. and J. B. Tenenbaum (2005). The large-scale structure of semantic networks: Statistical analyses and a model of semantic growth. *Cognitive science 29*(1), 41–78.

Van Atteveldt, W. (2008). Semantic network analysis: Techniques for extracting, representing, and querying media content. *PhD Thesis*.

Distributional Lesk: Effective Knowledge-Based
Word Sense Disambiguation

Dieke Oele
CLCG
Rijksuniversiteit Groningen
The Netherlands
d.oele@rug.nl

Gertjan van Noord
CLCG
Rijksuniversiteit Groningen
The Netherlands
g.j.m.van.noord@rug.nl

Abstract

We propose a simple, yet effective, Word Sense Disambiguation method that uses a combination of a lexical knowledge-base and embeddings. Similar to the classic Lesk algorithm, it exploits the idea that overlap between the context of a word and the definition of its senses provides information on its meaning. Instead of counting the number of words that overlap, we use embeddings to compute the similarity between the gloss of a sense and the context. Evaluation on both Dutch and English datasets shows that our method outperforms other Lesk methods and improves upon a state-of-the-art knowledge-based system. Additional experiments confirm the effect of the use of glosses and indicate that our approach works well in different domains.

1   Introduction

The quest of automatically finding the correct meaning of a word in context, also known as Word Sense Disambiguation (WSD), is an important topic in natural language processing. Although the best performing WSD systems are those based on supervised learning methods (Snyder and Palmer, 2004; Pradhan et al., 2007; Navigli and Lapata, 2007; Navigli, 2009; Zhong and Ng, 2010), a large amount of manually annotated data is required for training. Furthermore, even if such a supervised system obtains good results in a certain domain, it is not readily portable to other domains (Escudero et al., 2000).

As an alternative to supervised systems, knowledge-based systems do not require manually tagged data and have proven to be applicable to new domains (Agirre et al., 2009). They only require two types of information: a set of dictionary entries with definitions for each possible word meaning, and the context in which the word occurs. An example of such a system is the Lesk algorithm (Lesk, 1986) that exploits the idea that the overlap between the definition of a word and the definitions of the words in its context can provide information about its meaning.

In this paper, we propose a knowledge-based WSD method that is loosely based on the Lesk algorithm exploiting both the context of the words and the definitions (hereafter referred to as glosses) of the senses. Instead of counting the number of words that overlap, we use word- and sense embeddings to compute the similarity between the gloss of a sense and the context of the word. The strong point of our method is that it only requires large unlabeled corpora and a sense inventory such as WordNet, and therefore does not rely on annotated data. Also, it is readily applicable to other languages if a sense inventory is available.

2   Related work

In the past few years, much progress has been made on learning word embeddings from unlabeled data that represent the meanings of words as contextual feature vectors. A major advantage of these word embeddings is that they exhibit certain algebraic relations and can, therefore, be used for meaningful semantic operations such as computing word similarity (Turney, 2006), and capturing lexical relationships (Mikolov et al., 2013).

A disadvantage of word embeddings is that they assign a single embedding to each word, thus ignoring the possibility that words may have more than one meaning. This problem can be addressed by associating each word with a series of sense-specific embeddings. For this, several methods have been proposed in recent work. For example, in Reisinger and Mooney (2010) and Huang et al. (2012), a fixed number of senses is learned for each word that has multiple meanings by first clustering the contexts of each token, and subsequently relabeling each word token with the clustered sense before learning embeddings.

Although previously mentioned sense embedding methods have demonstrated good performance, they use automatically induced senses. They are, therefore, not readily applicable to NLP applications and research experiments that rely on WordNet-based senses, such as machine translation and information retrieval and extraction systems (see Morato et al. (2004) for examples of such systems). Recently, features based on sense-specific embeddings learned using a combination of large corpora and a sense inventory have been shown to achieve state-of-the-art results for supervised WSD (Rothe and Schütze, 2015; Jauhar et al., 2015; Taghipour and Ng, 2015).

Our system makes use of a combination of sense embeddings, context embeddings, and gloss embeddings. Somewhat similar approaches have been proposed by Chen et al. (2014) and Pelevina et al. (2016). The main difference to our approach is that they automatically induce sense embeddings and find the best sense by comparing them to context embeddings, while we add gloss embeddings for better performance. Inkpen and Hirst (2003) apply gloss- and context vectors to the disambiguation of near-synonyms in dictionary entries. Also Basile et al. (2014) use a distributional approach, however, it requires a sense-tagged corpus while our system does not rely on any tagged data.

3   Method

Our WSD algorithm takes sentences as input and outputs a preferred sense for each polysemous word. Given a sentence $w_1 \ldots w_i$ of i words, we retrieve a set of word senses from the sense inventory for each word w. Then, for each sense s of each word w, we consider the similarity of its lexeme (the combination of a word and one of its senses (Rothe and Schütze, 2015) with the context and the similarity of the gloss with the context.

For each potential sense s of word w, the cosine similarity is computed between its gloss vector G_s and its context vector C_w and between the context vector C_w and the lexeme vector $L_{s,w}$. The score of a given word w and sense s is thus defined as follows:

$$\text{Score}(s, w) = cos(G_s, C_w) + cos(L_{s,w}, C_w) \tag{1}$$

The sense with the highest score is chosen. When no gloss is found for a given sense, only the second part of the equation is used.

Prior to disambiguation itself, we sort the words by the number of senses is has, in order that the word with the fewest senses will be considered first. The idea behind this is that words that have fewer senses are easier to disambiguate (Chen et al., 2014). As the algorithm relies on the words in the context which may themselves be ambiguous, if words in the context have been disambiguated already, this information can be used for the ambiguous words that follow. We, therefore, use the resulting sense of each word for the disambiguation of the following words starting with the "easiest" words.

Our method requires lexeme embeddings $L_{s,w}$ for each sense s. For this, we use AutoExtend (Rothe and Schütze, 2015) to create additional embeddings for senses from WordNet on the basis of word embeddings. AutoExtend is an auto-encoder that relies on the relations present in WordNet to learn embeddings for senses and lexemes. To create these embeddings, a neural network containing lexemes and sense layers is built, while the WordNet relations are used to create links between each layer. The advantage of their method is that it is flexible: it can take any set of word embeddings and any lexical database as input and produces embeddings of senses and lexemes, without requiring any extra training data.

Ultimately, for each word w we need a vector for the context C_w, and for each sense s of word w we need a gloss vector G_s. The context vector C_w is defined as the mean of all the content word representations in the sentence: if a word in the context has already been disambiguated, we use the corresponding sense embedding; otherwise, we use the word embedding. For each sense s, we take its gloss as provided in WordNet. In line with Banerjee and Pedersen (2002), we expand this gloss with the glosses of related meanings, excluding antonyms. Similar to the creation of the context vectors, the gloss vector G_s is created by averaging the word embeddings of all the content words in the gloss.

4 Experiments

The performance of our algorithm was tested on both Dutch and English sentences in an all-words setup. Our sense inventory for Dutch is Cornetto (Vossen et al., 2012) while, for English, we use WordNet 1.7.1 (Fellbaum, 1998). In Cornetto, 51.0% of the senses have glosses associated with them and in the Princeton WordNet, almost all of them do. The DutchSemCor corpus (Vossen et al., 2013) is used for Dutch evaluation and, for English, we use SemCor (Fellbaum, 1998). For both languages, a random subset of 5000 manually annotated sentences from each corpus was created. Additionally, we test on the Senseval-2 (SE-2) and Senseval-3 (SE-3) all-words datasets (Snyder and Palmer, 2004; Palmer et al., 2001)[1].

We build 300-dimensional word embeddings on the Dutch Sonar corpus (Oostdijk et al., 2013) using word2vec CBOW (Mikolov et al., 2013), and create sense- and lexeme embeddings with AutoExtend. For English, we use the embeddings from Rothe and Schütze (2015)[2]. They lie within the same vector space as the pre-trained word embeddings by Mikolov et al. (2013)[3], trained on a part of the Google News dataset, which contains about 100 billion words. This model (similar to the Dutch model) contains 300-dimensional vectors for 3 million words and phrases.

We evaluate our method by comparing it with a random baseline and Simplified Lesk with expanded glosses (SE-Lesk) (Kilgarriff and Rosenzweig, 2000; Banerjee and Pedersen, 2002). Additionally, we compare our system to a state-of-the-art knowledge-based WSD system, UKB (Agirre and Soroa, 2009), that, similar to our method, does not require any manually tagged data. UKB can be used for graph-based WSD using a pre-existing knowledge base. It applies random walks, e.g. Personalized PageRank, on the Knowledge Base graph to rank the vertices according to the context. We use UKBs Personalized PageRank method word-by-word with WordNet 1.7 and eXtended WordNet for English, as this setup yielded the best results in Agirre and Soroa (2009). For Dutch, we use the Cornetto database as input graph.

We do not compare our system to the initial results of AutoExtend (Rothe and Schütze, 2015) as they tested it in a supervised setup using sense embeddings as features. However, as is customary in WSD evaluation, we do compare our system to the most frequent WordNet sense baseline, which is notoriously difficult to beat due to the highly skewed distribution of word senses (Agirre and Edmonds, 2007). As this baseline relies on manually annotated data, which our system aims to avoid, we consider this baseline to be semi-supervised and therefore an upper bound.

For Dutch, the manually annotated part of DutchSemCor is balanced *per sense* which means that an equal number of examples for each sense is annotated. It is therefore not a reliable source for computing the most frequent sense. Alternatively, similar to Vossen et al. (2013), we derive sense frequencies by using the automatically annotated counts in DutchSemCor[4], assuming that the automatic annotation

---

[1] For SenseEval-2, we used conversions from WordNet 1.7 to 1.7.1 from http://web.eecs.umich.edu/ mihalcea/downloads.html

[2] http://www.cis.lmu.de/ sascha/AutoExtend/

[3] https://code.google.com/p/word2vec/

[4] In DutchSemCor senses are annotated with an SVM, trained on the manually annotated part of the corpus, see Vossen et al. (2013) for more details.

sufficiently reflects the true distribution for this purpose. The most frequent sense baseline for Dutch is, therefore, lower as compared to the English one, where the most frequent sense of a word is fully based on manual annotation.

5   Results

The results of the evaluation of our method (Lesk++) for both Dutch and English can be found in Table 1. Accuracy is calculated by dividing the number of words that were disambiguated correctly, as compared to the sense tagged corpus, by the total amount of polysemous words. Results are in bold when statistically significant over the baselines at $p < 0.05$.

| | Dutch | English | | |
	DSC	SC	SE-2	SE-3
ES-Lesk	31.3%	45.2%	47.1%	43.4%
UKB	35.7%	41.2%	51.4%	47.4%
Lesk++	**42.1%**	53.5%	52.1%	49.3%
Random	27.1%	33.6%	35.8%	30.1%
MFS	37.0%	**69.9%**	**59.7%**	**59.5%**

Table 1: Results on DutchSemCor (DSC), SemCor (SC) Senseval-2 (SE-2) and Senseval3 (SE-3)

For both Dutch and English, our method performs significantly better than SE-Lesk and the random baseline for all tasks. Also, our system performs better than UKB on both SemCor and DutchSemCor. On DutchSemCor, it outperforms the most frequent baseline.

5.1   Effects of sorting, lexemes, and glosses

The main idea behind our method is a simple combination of two cosine similarity scores. In a second experiment, we evaluate the effects of both of these scores by using them separately. Additionally, we examine the use of sorting the words by its number of senses before disambiguation.

We compare our final results with a system where similarity is only computed between the context and gloss vector and with a system that only computes the cosine distance between the context and the lexeme (only the first and the second part of Equation 1 respectively). Both systems are tested without and with (+S) sorting. The results of this third experiment on the sense tagged corpora for Dutch (DSC) and English (SC) can be found in Table 2.

	Lesk++	Lex	+S	Gloss	+S
DSC	42.1%	38.3%	38.6%	41.5%	41.6%
SC	53.5%	42.7%	47.0%	52.8%	52.6%

Table 2: Effects of lexemes, glosses and sorting. The second and the fourth column show results of a system that only uses the lexeme (Lex) or gloss vectors (Gloss) respectively. In the third and last column sorting (+S) is added.

For Dutch, the results indicate that sorting the words by its number of senses by itself is not very effective compared to the system that does not use this module. The use of glosses, on the other hand, seems to be very effective while the combination of both measures yields the best results. The effect of the gloss vectors is even stronger for English, which can be explained by the fact that the English WordNet has a higher gloss coverage. Also, for English, although both sorting and glosses are effective, the combination performs better.

5.2 Comparison of Different Domains

To examine the robustness of our system in different domains, we evaluate it on different parts of Dutch-SemCor. We randomly took 5000 manually annotated sentences from each of the four largest subsets of the corpus. The results of this experiment for the all-words task can be found in Table 3. On every subsec-

	dl	st	wp	np
SE-Lesk	27.7%	30.4%	28.8%	29.4%
UKB	30.5%	32.1%	37.3%	33.8%
Lesk++	**36.8%**	**36.8%**	**45.6%**	40.3%
Random	24.2%	23.5%	28.2%	25.7%
MFS	30.6%	33.3%	35.8%	**42.9%**

Table 3: Results for the Dutch all-words task on a random subset of each of the four largest datasets from DutchSemCor: discussion lists (dl), subtitles (st), Wikipedia (wp) and newspapers (ns).

tion of the DSC dataset, our method outperforms SE-Lesk, the random baseline and UKB. Furthermore, our method outperforms the most frequent baseline on three of them. The newspapers subsection forms an exception, probably because it belongs to a more general domain (Agirre et al., 2014).

6 Discussion

The difference in results for Dutch and English can possibly be explained by the coverage of the datasets. The Cornetto coverage is about 60%, compared to Princeton Wordnet, with an average polysemy of 1.07 for nouns, 1.56 for verbs and 1.05 for adjectives while, for English it is 1.24 for nouns, 2.17 for verbs and 1.40 for adjectives. Also, not all Dutch senses have corresponding glosses while most of the English ones do. As our method relies greatly on gloss vectors, this could affect its performance.

Our WSD approach combines a lexical knowledge base with word- and sense embeddings. The results of our experiments show that the use of embeddings can help improve other Lesk methods (Kilgarriff and Rosenzweig, 2000; Banerjee and Pedersen, 2002). An obvious next step would be to see whether other extensions that do not require manually tagged data are compatible as well. For example, Vasilescu et al. (2004) shows improvements by pre-selecting context words using the WordNet hierarchy. Also, the method of Miller et al. (2012) could be used to first expand the glosses and/or the context before using our adaptation of the Lesk system.

7 Conclusion

In this paper we propose an extension to the Lesk algorithm which uses sense, gloss and context embeddings to compute the similarity of word senses to the context in which the words occur. Although our approach is a straightforward extension to the Lesk algorithm, it achieves better performance compared to Lesk and a random baseline and outperforms, or yields similar performance to, a state-of-the-art knowledge-based system. For Dutch, it outperforms all other systems including the most frequent sense on three out of four subsets. A second experiment confirms the effects of gloss vectors while the results of a final experiment indicate that our method works well in different domains. The main advantage of our method is its simplicity which makes it fast and easy to apply to other languages. It furthermore only requires unlabeled text and the definitions of senses, and does not rely on any manually annotated data, which makes our system an attractive alternative for supervised WSD.

References

Agirre, E., O. L. De Lacalle, and A. Soroa (2009). Knowledge-based WSD on specific domains: Performing better than generic supervised WSD. In *Proceedings of the 21st International Joint Conference on Artifical Intelligence*, pp. 1501–1506.

Agirre, E. and P. Edmonds (2007). *Word Sense Disambiguation: Algorithms and Applications* (1st ed.). Springer Publishing Company, Incorporated.

Agirre, E., d. O. L. Lacalle, and A. Soroa (2014). Random walks for knowledge-based word sense disambiguation. *Computational Linguistics 40*(1), 57–84.

Agirre, E. and A. Soroa (2009). Personalizing PageRank for word sense disambiguation. In *Proceedings of the 12th Conference of the European Chapter of the ACL*, pp. 33–41.

Banerjee, S. and T. Pedersen (2002). An adapted Lesk algorithm for word sense disambiguation using WordNet. In *Proceedings of the Third International Conference on Computational Linguistics and Intelligent Text Processing*, pp. 136–145.

Basile, P., A. Caputo, and G. Semeraro (2014). An enhanced Lesk word sense disambiguation algorithm through a distributional semantic model. In *Proceedings of the 25th International Conference on Computational Linguistics*, pp. 1591–1600.

Chen, X., Z. Liu, and M. Sun (2014). A unified model for word sense representation and disambiguation. In *Proceedings of the 2014 Conference on Empirical Methods in Natural Language Processing*, pp. 1025–1035.

Escudero, G., L. Màrquez, and G. Rigau (2000). An empirical study of the domain dependence of supervised word sense disambiguation systems. In *Proceedings of the 2000 Joint SIGDAT Conference on Empirical Methods in Natural Language Processing and Very Large Corpora*, pp. 172–180.

Fellbaum, C. (Ed.) (1998, May). *WordNet An Electronic Lexical Database*. Cambridge, MA ; London: The MIT Press.

Huang, E. H., R. Socher, C. D. Manning, and A. Y. Ng (2012). Improving word representations via global context and multiple word prototypes. In *Proceedings of the 50th Annual Meeting of the Association for Computational Linguistics*, pp. 873–882.

Inkpen, D. Z. and G. Hirst (2003). Automatic sense disambiguation of the near-synonyms in a dictionary entry. In *Computational Linguistics and Intelligent Text Processing, 4th International Conference*, pp. 258–267.

Jauhar, S. K., C. Dyer, and E. H. Hovy (2015). Ontologically grounded multi-sense representation learning for semantic vector space models. In *The 2015 Conference of the North American Chapter of the Association for Computational Linguistics*, pp. 683–693.

Kilgarriff, A. and J. Rosenzweig (2000, May). English senseval: report and results. In *Proceedings of the Second International Conference on Language Resources and Evaluation*, Athens, Greece. European Language Resources Association (ELRA).

Lesk, M. (1986). Automatic Sense Disambiguation Using Machine Readable Dictionaries: How to Tell a Pine Cone from an Ice Cream Cone. In *Proceedings of the 5th Annual International Conference on Systems Documentation*, SIGDOC '86, New York, NY, USA, pp. 24–26. ACM.

Mikolov, T., K. Chen, G. Corrado, and J. Dean (2013). Efficient estimation of word representations in vector space. *CoRR*.

Mikolov, T., W. Yih, and G. Zweig (2013). Linguistic regularities in continuous space word representations. In *Human Language Technologies: Conference of the North American Chapter of the Association of Computational Linguistics, Proceedings*, pp. 746–751.

Miller, T., C. Biemann, T. Zesch, and I. Gurevych (2012). Using distributional similarity for lexical expansion in knowledge-based word sense disambiguation. In *Proceedings of COLING 2012*, pp. 1781–1796.

Morato, J., M. N. Marzal, J. Llorns, and J. Moreiro (2004). Wordnet applications. In *Proceeding of the Second Global Wordnet Conference*.

Navigli, R. (2009, February). Word sense disambiguation: A survey. *ACM Computing Surveys 41(2)*, 10:1–10:69.

Navigli, R. and M. Lapata (2007). Graph connectivity measures for unsupervised word sense disambiguation. In *Proceedings of the 20th International Joint Conference on Artificial Intelligence*, pp. 1683–1688.

Oostdijk, N., M. Reynaert, V. Hoste, and I. Schuurman (2013). *The Construction of a 500-Million-Word Reference Corpus of Contemporary Written Dutch*, pp. 219–247. Berlin, Heidelberg: Springer Berlin Heidelberg.

Palmer, M., C. Fellbaum, S. Cotton, L. Delfs, and H. T. Dang (2001). English tasks: All-words and verb lexical sample. In *The Proceedings of the Second International Workshop on Evaluating Word Sense Disambiguation Systems*, pp. 21–24.

Pelevina, M., N. Arefiev, C. Biemann, and A. Panchenko (2016). Making sense of word embeddings. In *Proceedings of the 1st Workshop on Representation Learning for NLP*, pp. 174–183.

Pradhan, S. S., E. Loper, D. Dligach, and M. Palmer (2007). SemEval-2007 task 17: English lexical sample, SRL and all words. In *Proceedings of the 4th International Workshop on Semantic Evaluations*, pp. 87–92.

Reisinger, J. and R. J. Mooney (2010). Multi-prototype vector-space models of word meaning. In *Proceedings of the 11th Annual Conference of the North American Chapter of the Association for Computational Linguistics*, pp. 109–117.

Rothe, S. and H. Schütze (2015). AutoExtend: Extending word embeddings to embeddings for synsets and lexemes. In *Proceedings of the 53rd Annual Meeting of the Association for Computational Linguistics and the 7th International Joint Conference on Natural Language Processing*, pp. 1793–1803.

Snyder, B. and M. Palmer (2004, July). The english all-words task. In R. Mihalcea and P. Edmonds (Eds.), *Senseval-3: Third International Workshop on the Evaluation of Systems for the Semantic Analysis of Text*, pp. 41–43.

Taghipour, K. and H. T. Ng (2015, May–June). Semi-supervised word sense disambiguation using word embeddings in general and specific domains. In *Proceedings of the 2015 Conference of the North American Chapter of the Association for Computational Linguistics: Human Language Technologies*, pp. 314–323.

Turney, P. D. (2006). Similarity of semantic relations. *Computational Linguistics, Volume 32, Number 3, September 2006*.

Vasilescu, F., P. Langlais, and G. Lapalme (2004). Evaluating variants of the Lesk approach for disambiguating words. In *Proceedings of the Fourth International Conference on Language Resources and Evaluation*.

Vossen, P., A. Görög, R. Izquierdo, and A. van den Bosch (2012, may). Dutchsemcor: Targeting the ideal sense-tagged corpus. In *Proceedings of the Eight International Conference on Language Resources and Evaluation*, pp. 584–589.

Vossen, P., R. Izquierdo, and A. Görög (2013). Dutchsemcor: in quest of the ideal sense-tagged corpus. In G. Angelova, K. Bontcheva, and R. Mitkov (Eds.), *Recent Advances in Natural Language Processing*, pp. 710–718.

Vossen, P., I. Maks, R. Segers, H. d. v. Vliet, M.-F. Moens, K. Hofmann, E. T. K. Sang, and M. de Rijke (2013). *Cornetto: A Combinatorial Lexical Semantic Database for Dutch*, pp. 165–184. Berlin, Heidelberg: Springer Berlin Heidelberg.

Zhong, Z. and H. T. Ng (2010). It makes sense: A wide-coverage word sense disambiguation system for free text. In *Proceedings of the ACL 2010 System Demonstrations*, ACLDemos '10, pp. 78–83.

Unsupervised Induction of Compositional Classes for English Adjective-Noun Pairs

Wiebke Petersen
Düsseldorf University, SFB 991
petersen@phil.uni-duesseldorf.de

Oliver Hellwig
Düsseldorf University, SFB 991
ohellwig@phil-fak.uni-duesseldorf.de

Abstract

The paper examines how adjectival modification classes can be detected by applying unsupervised methods on adjective-noun co-occurrence data. It evaluates a k-means baseline, two graphical models, and a recently introduced bidirectional clustering algorithm against HeiPLAS, a manually annotated gold standard for hidden modificational classes. The paper shows that the bidirectional clustering algorithm performs best on this task, and discusses how the results of the unsupervised approaches can be employed for building a frame-based inventory of adjectival modification.

1 Introduction

Recent years have witnessed an increasing interest in computational models of compositionality that operate on vector-space representations (Baroni and Zamparelli, 2010; Guevara, 2010) or neural word embeddings (Socher et al., 2011; Mikolov et al., 2013). While many of these studies deal with the problem of predicting the distribution of compound phrases from the distributions of their elements, comparatively few of them examine which classes of compositional mechanisms are reflected by the learned models. The present paper focusses on adjectival modification and aims at uncovering adjective clusters with common modificational patterns.

The approach followed in this paper is frame-based. We assume that the meaning of a noun concept is represented by recursive attribute-value structures (Pustejovsky, 1995; Petersen, 2007; Löbner, 2014). Adjectives operate on these structures by (i) simply specifying the value of a single attribute or by (ii) enriching the concept structure by additional attributes and constraints. Examples of (i) are most property denoting adjectives with an intersective reading like 'red ball', where the adjective restricts the value range of the attribute COLOR to the value 'red'. Note that the noun concept may offer more than one adequate attribute like in 'red pen', where 'red' either specifies the color of the pen or the color of the writing of the pen. Examples of (ii) are, among many others, relational A+N phrases such as 'presidential speech' (not every speech given by the current president is presidential, i.e., a speech given at a private party[1]) and modal A+N phrases such as 'fake meat' (fake meat is no meat and lacks important attributes of meat).

Although linguistic research has proposed various classification schemes for adjectives, none of them reflects the modificational patterns of a frame-based approach, to our knowledge. They are either constructed from a lexicographic perspective, and aim at capturing fine-grained meaning distinctions (e.g., Hundsnurscher and Splett, 1982) that do not result in different modificational patterns from a frame perspective; or they focus on the semantics of adjective modification, but propose only a coarse distinction into major patterns like 'property' or 'relational' (e.g. Dixon, 2010). Furthermore, only a few of the

---

[1]See Anderson and Löbner (2017) for a frame based approach to relational adjectives.

proposed classification schemes are based on empirical evidence from larger corpora (e.g., Raskin and Nirenburg, 1995). As none of the proposed linguistic classifications is based on or suited for a frame perspective on adjectival modification, we intend to provide empirical evidence for adjectival classifications without resorting to linguistic theories, and test which quantitative methods are most suited for the unsupervised induction of compositional classes.

We hypothesize that the selectional restrictions of A+N pairs result from the attribute-value structures of the involved concepts, and that a clustering based on such A+N pairs may provide insights into these structures. We therefore focus on four unsupervised models that are able to cluster adjectives on the basis of the nouns they modify, and to induce latent compositional classes from A+N co-occurrence in this way. Apart from a baseline k-means clustering, we test two graphical models (Rooth et al., 1999; Séaghdha and Korhonen, 2014) and a recently proposed bidirectional clustering algorithm (Petersen and Hellwig, 2016). The graphical and bidirectional models were chosen, because they have proven to be effective tools in former studies on compositionality. The resulting clusters are compared with a gold data set that consists of attribute-adjective-noun triples and was originally designed for a semi-supervised attribute assignment task (HeiPLAS; Hartung, 2015). The data set is not fully appropriate for our task, as it only covers modificational patterns of type (i), i.e., adjectives specifying attribute values in noun frames. In spite of this restriction, it will turn out that bidirectional clustering slightly outperforms the k-means baseline and the two graphical models that were designed for the unsupervised induction of latent semantic classes.

The rest of the paper is organized as follows. Section 2 gives an overview of related research in NLP. Section 3 describes the training corpus, its preprocessing, and the structure of the evaluation data set. Section 4 sketches the applied models, and Section 5 presents an evaluation of the results.

2 Related Research

One important track of research in the field of computational approaches to semantic composition deals with predicting composed expressions on the basis of their atoms, either using vector space models (Mitchell and Lapata, 2008; Baroni and Zamparelli, 2010) or, more recently, relying on pretrained word embeddings (Socher et al., 2011; Dima, 2016). A group of studies with a stronger linguistic motivation examines which or how many compositional mechanisms are active in forming composed expressions (Tratz and Hovy, 2010; Hartung, 2015), and how the active mechanisms can be predicted using machine learning techniques (Hartung and Frank, 2011; Dima and Hinrichs, 2015). Most relevantly for our task, Hartung et al. (2017) aim at predicting hidden attributes of A+N phrases. The authors train a flat neural network that learns an embedded representation of an A+N phrase from the word embeddings of its components. The trained model is applied to the HeiPLAS data, and the hidden attribute is predicted using nearest neighbor search with the learned compositional embedding.

3 Data

A+N pairs are obtained by parsing the 2013 English news dump from www.statmt.org (Bojar et al., 2014) using the Stanford CoreNLP dependency parser (Manning et al., 2014), and extracting the lemmas of all sequences of the form JJ-[NN|NE|NNS]. By this method, we obtain 1,048,653 A+N pairs with 8,392 adjective lexemes, 17,560 noun lexemes, and 430,256 unique combinations of A+N; the density of the co-occurrence matrix is 0.002919691.

We use the HeiPLAS data set (Hartung, 2015) for evaluating the received adjective clusters. The design of HeiPLAS is linguistically motivated by a classification into basic, event- and object-related adjectives introduced by Boleda (2007) (refer to Hartung (2015, 57–59) for a short overview). Adjectives and the attributes they modify are extracted from the anchor structure of WordNet, and ambiguous cases were manually validated by a group of native speakers (Hartung, 2015, 98ff.). Therefore, the set of attributes available in HeiPLAS primarily reflects the linguistic intuition and the lexicographic aim underlying WordNet. The data set consists of 1,598 triples of the form (attribute, adjective, noun), such as (VOLUME, big, voice) or (BEAUTY, repulsive, mask) with 849 distinct adjectives, 923 distinct nouns, and 253 distinct attributes. Due to its structure, the coverage of HeiPLAS is limited to basic adjectives, which denote attribute values of nouns ("blue car" for COLOR, "big house" for SIZE). The attributes in HeiPLAS are derived from WordNet attribute nouns, and were validated in a manual classification step. In order to use HeiPLAS as a gold standard for the evaluation of clusters of adjectives, we interpret the attributes as class labels. Thus, for each triple *(adj,attr,noun)* in HeiPLAS, we classify the adjective *adj* as belonging to the class *attr*.

4   Models

The paper compares four unsupervised models that can be used to cluster adjectives on the basis of the nouns they modifiy. **Rooth-LDA**[2] denotes a graphical model of compositionality that interprets each A+N pair as an independent observation (Rooth et al., 1999). During generation, the model samples a hidden topic variable z. Subsequently, adjective and noun distributions are sampled based on the value of z, resulting in the following joint probability of adjective a and noun n (Séaghdha and Korhonen, 2014, 602):[3]

$$p(a, n) = \sum_z p(a|z)p(n|z)p(z)$$

We use the Gibbs sampler described in Séaghdha and Korhonen (2014, 605–606) for training the model. The symmetric priors of the distributions are estimated using a grid search on held-out data, in order to maximize the Adjusted Rand Index (Hubert and Arabie, 1985) of the detected adjective clusters when compared with the gold standard provided by HeiPLAS (details in Section 5). The grid search produces the following values: $\alpha = 0.001, \beta = 0.01, \gamma = 0.1$. It is important to note that the chosen hyperparameter optimization method feeds in an element of supervision to the graphical model, because its parameters are tuned to reproduce the HeiPLAS classes. We will come back to this point in the evaluation.

Lex-LDA splits the generative process for an A+N pair into two separate subprocesses in order to deal with lexicalized and truly compositional A+N pairs (Séaghdha and Korhonen, 2014, 603-606). While the association between adjective and noun is modelled through their conditional probability in lexicalization mode, the model uses a topic model in non-lexicalized or compositional mode. The decision between lexicalized and compositional mode is directed by an adjective specific parameter σ_a that is learned from the data along with the model:

$$p(n|a) = \underbrace{\sigma_a p_{lex}(n|a)}_{\text{lexicalized}} + \underbrace{(1 - \sigma_a) \sum_z p(n|z)p(z|a)}_{\text{compositional}}$$

We implement the Gibbs sampler described in Séaghdha and Korhonen (2014, 606). As noted in Séaghdha and Korhonen (2014, 605), this model poses the potential problem that hidden topics are not generated when the lexicalized subprocess is active. The symmetric priors are estimated in the same way as for Rooth LDA, above, resulting in $\alpha = 0.001, \beta = 0.1, \gamma = 0.01$. Using the gap statistics (Tibshirani et al., 2001) on pretrained GloVe vectors (Pennington et al., 2014) for English adjectives, we choose $k = 250$ hidden topics for training both graphical models.

Contrary to the two graphical models, the bidirectional clustering (**BidirClus**, Petersen and Hellwig (2016)) operates on a vector space matrix (VSM; Turney and Pantel, 2010) constructed from adjectives (rows) and the nouns they co-occur with (columns). In BidirClus, adjectives are first clustered on the basis of nouns they co-occur with. The centers of clusters detected in this way replace the adjective rows in the VSM, and the same process is repeated for the transposed VSM, such that nouns are clustered on the basis of adjectives in the second step. This process is repeated until no further clusters can be constructed from the semantic space.

---

[2]This model was first described in Rooth et al. (1999). We adhere to the naming proposed in Séaghdha (2010).

[3]As we are only interested in adjectives and nouns, we slightly adapted the notation found in Séaghdha and Korhonen (2014).

More specifically, the distributional distance between items in rows r_i and r_j, which are adjectives in the first step, is measured using their Jaccard distance:

$$d_{ij} = 1 - \frac{|\vec{r_i} \wedge \vec{r_j}|}{|\vec{r_i} \vee \vec{r_j}|}$$

In addition, an LDA topic model (Blei et al., 2003) with $k = 15$ hidden topics is built from the VSM. The topic similarity θ_{ij} of rows r_i and r_j is calculated from the Θ values of the LDA model:

$$\theta_{ij} = \left(\sum_{k=1}^{K=15} (\Theta_{ik} - \Theta_{jk})^2 \right)^{\frac{1}{2}}$$

The final similarity score d_{ij}^{lda} of rows r_i and r_j is calculated as the product of Jaccard distance and topic similarity:

$$d_{ij}^{\text{lda}} = d_{ij} \cdot \theta_{ij}$$

In each iteration of BidirClus, new clusters are created from the 5% of rows that have the highest combined similarity scores d_{ij}^{lda}. New clusters R are constructed from transitive closures detected in the top 5%, and their distributional representation $\vec{R}$ is calculated using the following majority function:

$$\vec{R_k} = \begin{cases} 1 & \text{if } \sum_{\vec{r} \in R} r_k \geq \frac{|R|}{2} \\ 0 & \text{else} \end{cases}$$

The respective rows of the matrix are replaced by the new distributional representation $\vec{R}$, which means that the number of rows in the VSM is reduced by $|R| - 1$ in this step. It should be noted that Bidir-Clus does not allow for multiple semantic readings of adjectives or nouns, because each item is assigned to a single cluster while building the transitive closure.[4]

As a baseline model for comparison, we use k-means clustering with the expected number of clusters set to $k = 250$.

5   Evaluation and Results

We evaluate the outcomes of the three models against HeiPLAS using Rand Index (RI; Rand, 1971) and Adjusted Rand Index (ARI; Hubert and Arabie, 1985). The two graphical models (Rooth-LDA, Lex-LDA) generate a hidden class variable z for each A+N pair, which denotes the (anonymous) compositional mechanism activated for this pair.[5] Because we are interested in clustering A's on the basis of their modificational properties, we operate directly with the sampled values of this class variable z. We average the counts of z for each A+N pair at every 20th iteration after a burn-in period of 100 iterations. Using z for labeling A+N pairs provides an elegant solution for clustering polysemous A's, because a single A can be labeled with different values of z, depending on which N it is combined with. However, the bidirectional clustering algorithm does not differentiate between semantic readings of the same A, but assigns each A to a single class. In order to provide a fair comparison of the three models, the evaluation of the two graphical models is broken down to the A level: Given the adjective set $\mathcal{A}$, noun set $\mathcal{N}$ and set of hidden topics $\mathcal{Z}$, let lda : $\mathcal{A} \times \mathcal{N} \rightarrow \mathcal{Z}$ be the partial function that models the topic assignment of LDA. We define $Z_A = \arg\max_{Z \in \mathcal{Z}} |\{N \in \mathcal{N} : \text{lda}(A, N) = Z\}|$ and assign each A to the class corresponding to Z_A.

---

[4] We are currently testing a new version of BidirClus that accounts for multiple readings by using a more flexible clustering strategy than transitive closure.

[5] For details on z see Figure 2 in Séaghdha and Korhonen (2014, 602) for Rooth-LDA, and Figure 3 in Séaghdha and Korhonen (2014, 603) for Lex-LDA. Note that for Lex-LDA the value of z is only defined if the model is in the class-based mode ($s_i = 0$).

Model	RI	ARI
k-means	0.9352	0.1778
Rooth-LDA (uninf.)	0.9668	0.3007
Rooth-LDA (optim.)	0.9669	0.3208
Lex-LDA (uninf.)	0.9719	0.3097
Lex-LDA (optim.)	0.9715	0.3150
BidirClus, 'leaf'	**0.9762**	**0.3472**
BidirClus, 'topmost'	0.9688	0.3215

Table 1: Evaluation of the four clustering models on the HeiPLAS dataset; uninf.: model uses an uninformed symmetric prior; optim: model uses a symmetric prior optimized on a held-out set of A+N pairs. RI: Rand Index; ARI: Adjusted Rand Index

BidirClus produces deeply nested, hierarchical clusterings that need to be transformed into hard, non-hierarchical clusterings for comparison with the other models. Following Petersen and Hellwig (2016), we report results for two brute force evaluation modes. In the mode 'topmost', each adjective obtains the label of the largest cluster containing it, and in the mode 'leaf' it obtains the label of the smallest non-singleton cluster containing it.

Table 1 reports Rand Index (RI) and Adjusted Rand Index (ARI) for the k-means baseline and the three more specialized methods.[6] Both graphical models and the bidirectional clustering clearly outperform k-means in terms of RI and ARI, while they generate similar coefficients when compared to each other. As noted above, however, the hyperparameters of Rooth-LDA and Lex-LDA were optimized using HeiPLAS data with the objective of maximizing their ARI on the HeiPLAS data set. To compare the influence of this optimization on model performance, we have repeated the training of Rooth-LDA and Lex-LDA with uninformed symmetric priors of 0.01 (settings marked with 'uninf.'). The respective results in Table 1 show that hyperparameter optimization gives both models a slight, but noticeable advantage over the uninformed versions. If one compares only the unsupervised models, the uninformed versions of Rooth-LDA and Lex-LDA are outperformed by BidirClus.

A closer look at the HeiPLAS gold standard reveals that the evaluated models may actually perform better than expressed by the values in Table 1. In several cases, the models capture frame semantic properties of adjectives that were not relevant for designing and building the HeiPLAS data set. The adjectives 'exceptional' and 'extraordinary', for example, are grouped into one cluster by BidirClus, while HeiPLAS labels 'exceptional' with the attribute COMMONNESS and 'extraordinary' with ORDINARINESS ('extraordinary beauty', 'extraordinary capacity') or MODERATION ('extraordinary desire'), as can be seen in the following list of HeiPLAS attributes and their associated adjectives:

COMMONNESS uncommon, common, special, exceptional, popular, rare, average

ORDINARINESS ordinary, remarkable, extraordinary, average, everyday, routine

MODERATION immoderate, reasonable, intermediate, extreme, moderate, modest, conservative, over-the-top, abnormal, average, exaggerated, excessive, exorbitant, extraordinary, outrageous, unreasonable

Looking into traditional lexicons, Merriam-Webster describes 'exceptional' by (a) forming an exception, (b) better than average, and (c) deviating from the norm and 'extraordinary' by (a) going beyond what is usual, regular, or customary and (b) exceptional to a very marked extent.[7] Although there is a subtle lexicographic distinction between 'extraordinary' and 'exceptional', they are often used synonymously in actual language use, and are even explicitly marked as synonyms by the Merriam-Webster.

---

[6]The Rand Index measures the probability that the automatic clustering agrees with the HeiPLAS classes on a randomly chosen pair of adjectives. The Adjusted Rand Index is a version of the Rand Index that is corrected for chance. As the values of the latter are less easy to interpret (they may take negative values), we have decided to present both indices.

[7]www.merriam-webster.com

A further example of an adjective pair that is not contained in one attribute cluster in HeiPLAS, but grouped together by BidirClus is 'current' and 'future'. HeiPLAS labels 'current' with the attribute CURRENTNESS and 'future' with TIMING. From a frame perspective, both adjectives specify the temporal relation of the modified noun and the utterance time ('current prize' versus 'future prize'). Related considerations apply to the pair 'impossible' and 'tricky', where HeiPLAS labels 'impossible' and its opposite 'possible' with POSSIBILITY, and 'tricky' with DIFFICULTY (along with adjectives such as 'troublesome' or 'challenging'). In a frame-based approach one reading of 'impossible' would place the adjective on the maximum on the difficulty scale.

On the whole, we could identify 32 pairs of adjectives that are, from a frame perspective, grouped correctly by the bidirectional clustering, but assigned to different groups in HeiPLAS. The main reason for the divergence between HeiPLAS and the unsupervised approach is the fact that HeiPLAS is derived from WordNet. WordNet focusses on modelling fine grained lexicographic distinctions, which may not necessarily be reflected in actual language use (Navigli, 2009). In the cases just described, BidirClus seems to succeed in grouping adjectives that belong to the same value ranges from a less fine grained, frame semantic perspective.

If one looks at the cases where pairs of adjectives are grouped in one class in HeiPLAS, but end up in different classes by BidirClus, the main weakness of the current implementation of BidirClus becomes obvious. Because BidirClus clusters into disjoint classes, meaning variants of adjectives are not captured. While, for example, 'right' is found in the same class APPROPRIATENESS as 'appropriate' and 'inappropriate' in HeiPLAS, BidirClus clusters 'right' together with 'left' in a group consisting of directional adjectives.

The results indicate two main lines of future research. First, BidirClus must be adapted in order to account for meaning variants, either by a preprocessing step that disambiguates adjectives and nouns, or by a less strict update procedure of the co-occurrence matrix. Second, a more dedicated gold standard is required. This gold standard should be based on a frame semantic perspective of A+N modification. It should provide data not only for attribute value specifying adjectives such as HeiPLAS, but for more complex frame modification patterns as triggered by relational or modal adjectives (see Section 1). Such a gold standard will serve for tuning and optimizing unsupervised models, as described in this paper. In addition, the gold standard itself and improved models derived from it will provide more fine grained empirical evidence for linguistic research in modificational structures of adjectives and nouns.

Acknowledgment

This work was supported by the DFG Collaborative Research Centre 991, "The Structure of Representations in Language, Cognition, and Science", University of Düsseldorf. In addition, we would like to thank the anonymous reviewers for their comments on the paper.

References

Anderson, C. and S. Löbner (2017). Roles and the lexical semantics of role-denoting relational adjectives. Abstract submitted to 12th International Tbilisi Symposium on Logic, Language, and Computation.

Baroni, M. and R. Zamparelli (2010). Nouns are vectors, adjectives are matrices: Representing adjective-noun constructions in semantic space. In *Proceedings of EMNLP*, Boston, pp. 1183–1193.

Blei, D. M., A. Y. Ng, and M. I. Jordan (2003). Latent Dirichlet Allocation. *Journal of Machine Learning Research 3*, 993–1022.

Bojar, O., C. Buck, C. Federmann, B. Haddow, P. Koehn, J. Leveling, C. Monz, P. Pecina, M. Post, H. Saint-Amand, R. Soricut, L. Specia, and A. Tamchyna (2014). Findings of the 2014 Workshop on Statistical Machine Translation. In *Proceedings of the Ninth Workshop on Statistical Machine Translation*, pp. 12–58.

Boleda, G. (2007). *Automatic Acquisition of Semantic Classes for Adjectives*. Ph. D. thesis, Pompeu Fabra University.

Dima, C. (2016). On the compositionality and semantic interpretation of English noun compounds. In *Proceedings of the 1st Workshop on Representation Learning for NLP*, pp. 27–39.

Dima, C. and E. Hinrichs (2015). Automatic noun compound interpretation using deep neural networks and word embeddings. In *Proceedings of the 11th International Conference on Computational Semantics*, pp. 173–183.

Dixon, R. W. (2010). Where have all the adjectives gone? In *Where have All the Adjectives Gone? And Other Essays in Semantics and Syntax*, pp. 1–62. Berlin: De Gruyter Mouton.

Guevara, E. (2010). A regression model of adjective-noun compositionality in distributional semantics. In *Proceedings of the 2010 Workshop on Geometrical Models of Natural Language Semantics*, pp. 33–37.

Hartung, M. (2015). *Distributional Semantic Models of Attribute Meaning in Adjectives and Nouns*. Ph. D. thesis, University of Heidelberg.

Hartung, M. and A. Frank (2011). Exploring supervised LDA models for assigning attributes to adjective-noun phrases. In *Proceedings of the 2011 Conference on Empirical Methods in Natural Language Processing*, pp. 540–551.

Hartung, M., F. Kaupmann, S. Jebbara, and P. Cimiano (2017). Learning compositionality functions on word embeddings for modelling attribute meaning in adjective-noun phrases. In *Proceedings of the 15th Meeting of the European Chapter of the ACL (EACL)*.

Hubert, L. and P. Arabie (1985). Comparing partitions. *Journal of classification 2*(1), 193–218.

Hundsnurscher, F. and J. Splett (1982). *Semantik der Adjektive im Deutschen: Analyse der semantischen Relationen*. Westdeutscher Verlag.

Löbner, S. (2014). Evidence for frames from human language. In T. Gamerschlag, D. Gerland, R. Osswald, and W. Petersen (Eds.), *Frames and Concept Types*, Volume 94 of *Studies in Linguistics and Philosophy*, pp. 23–67. Springer International Publishing.

Manning, C. D., M. Surdeanu, J. Bauer, J. Finkel, S. J. Bethard, and D. McClosky (2014). The Stanford CoreNLP natural language processing toolkit. In *ACL System Demonstrations*, pp. 55–60.

Mikolov, T., I. Sutskever, K. Chen, G. S. Corrado, and J. Dean (2013). Distributed representations of words and phrases and their compositionality. In *Advances in Neural Information Processing Systems*, pp. 3111–3119.

Mitchell, J. and M. Lapata (2008). Vector-based models of semantic composition. In *Proceedings of 46th Annual Meeting of the ACL*, pp. 236–244.

Navigli, R. (2009). Word sense disambiguation: A survey. *ACM Comput. Surv. 41*, 10:1–10:69.

Pennington, J., R. Socher, and C. D. Manning (2014). GloVe: Global vectors for word representation. In *Proceedings of the 2014 EMNLP*, pp. 1532–1543.

Petersen, W. (2015/2007). Representation of concepts as frames. In T. Gamerschlag, D. Gerland, R. Osswald, and W. Petersen (Eds.), *Meaning, Frames, and Conceptual Representation*, Volume 2 of *Studies in Language and Cognition*, pp. 43 – 67. Düsseldorf University Press. Reprint with comments. Originally published 2007 in The Baltic International Yearbook of Cognition, Logic and Communication, Vol. 2.

Petersen, W. and O. Hellwig (2016). Exploring the value space of attributes: Unsupervised bidirectional clustering of adjectives in German. In *Proceedings of the COLING*, pp. 2839–2848.

Pustejovsky, J. (1995). *The Generative Lexicon*. Cambridge, MA: MIT Press.

Rand, W. M. (1971). Objective criteria for the evaluation of clustering methods. *Journal of the American Statistical Association 66*, 846–850.

Raskin, V. and S. Nirenburg (1995). Lexical semantics of adjectives. *New Mexico State University, Computing Research Laboratory Technical Report, MCCS-95-288.*

Rooth, M., S. Riezler, D. Prescher, G. Carroll, and F. Beil (1999). Inducing a semantically annotated lexicon via EM-based clustering. In *Proceedings of the 37th Annual Meeting of the ACL*, pp. 104–111. Association for Computational Linguistics.

Séaghdha, D. and A. Korhonen (2014). Probabilistic distributional semantics with latent variable models. *Computational Linguistics 40*(3), 587–631.

Séaghdha, D. O. (2010). Latent variable models of selectional preference. In *Proceedings of the 48th Annual Meeting of the ACL*, pp. 435–444.

Socher, R., C. C. Lin, C. Manning, and A. Y. Ng (2011). Parsing natural scenes and natural language with recursive neural networks. In *Proceedings of the 28th International Conference on Machine Learning*, pp. 129–136.

Tibshirani, R., G. Walther, and T. Hastie (2001). Estimating the number of data clusters via the Gap statistic. *Journal of the Royal Statistical Society B 63*, 411–423.

Tratz, S. and E. Hovy (2010). A taxonomy, dataset, and classifier for automatic noun compound interpretation. In *Proceedings of the 48th Annual Meeting of the ACL*, pp. 678–687.

Turney, P. D. and P. Pantel (2010). From frequency to meaning: Vector space models of semantics. *Journal of Artificial Intelligence Research 37*(1), 141–188.

There's no 'Count or Predict' but task-based selection for distributional models

Martin Riedl and Chris Biemann
Universität Hamburg, Germany
{riedl,biemann}@informatik.uni-hamburg.de

Abstract

In this paper, we investigate the differences between prediction-based (word2vec), dense count-based (GloVe) and sparse count-based (JoBimText) semantic models. We evaluate the models, which were selected because they can all be computed efficiently on large data, based on word similarity tasks and a semantic ranking task both for verbs and nouns. We demonstrate that prediction-based models yield higher scores than the other two models at determining a similarity score between two words. To the contrary, sparse count-based methods perform best in the ranking task. Further, sparse count-based methods benefit more from linguistically informed contexts, such as dependency relations. In summary, we highlight differences of popular distributional semantic representations and derive recommendations for their usage.

1   Introduction

With the steady growth of textual data, NLP methods are required that are able to process the data efficiently. In this paper, we focus on efficient methods that are targeted to compute distributional models that are based on the distributional hypothesis of Harris (1951). This hypothesis claims that words occurring in similar contexts tend to have similar meanings. In order to implement this hypothesis, early approaches (Hindle, 1990; Grefenstette, 1994; Lin, 1997) represented words using count-based vectors of the context. However, such representations are very sparse, require a lot of memory and are not very efficient. In the last decades, methods have been developed that transform such sparse representations into dense representations mainly using matrix factorization. With word2vec (Mikolov et al., 2013), an efficient prediction-based method was introduced, which also represents words with a dense vector. However, also sparse and count-based methods have been proposed that allow an efficient computation, e.g. (Kilgarriff et al., 2004; Biemann and Riedl, 2013). A more detailed overview of semantic representations can be found in (Lund and Burgess, 1996; Turney and Pantel, 2010; Ferrone and Zanzotto, 2017).

In this work, we explore different aspects between three different methods for computing similarities: similarity computations that use sparse symbolic vectors for similarity computations, dense vector based methods that are based on co-occurrences and prediction-based methods. For this, we aim to focus on efficiently computable methods and selected SKIP and CBOW from word2vec, GloVe and JoBimText. Based on these methods we want to explore different aspects: 1) which method performs the best global similarity scoring using word pair similarity datasets 2) which method performs the best local ranking of most similar terms for a query term 3) which context works best for the different methods and 4) are there differences in the performance when evaluating on verbs and nouns.

2   Related Work

One of the first comparisons between count-based and prediction-based distributional models was performed by Baroni et al. (2014). For this, they consider various tasks and show that prediction-based word embeddings outperform sparse count-based methods and dense count-based methods used for computing distributional semantic models. The evaluation is performed on datasets for relatedness, analogy, concept categorization and selectional preferences. The majority of word pairs considered for the evaluation consists of noun pairs. However, Levy and Goldberg (2014b) showed that dense count-based methods, using PPMI weighted co-occurrences and SVD, approximates neural word embeddings. Levy et al. (2015) showed in an extensive study the impact of various parameters and show the best performing parameters for these methods. The study reports results for various datasets for word similarity and analogy. However, they do not evaluate the performance on local similarity ranking tasks and omit results for pure count-based semantic methods. Claveau and Kijak (2016) performed another comparison of various semantic representation using both intrinsic and extrinsic evaluations. They compare the performance of their count-based method to dense representations and prediction-based methods using a manually crafted lexicon, SimLex and an information retrieval task. They show that their method performs better on the manually crafted lexicon than using word2vec. For this task, they also show that a word2vec model computed on a larger dataset yields inferior results than models computed on a smaller corpus, which is contrary to previous findings, e.g. (Banko and Brill, 2001; Gorman and Curran, 2006; Riedl and Biemann, 2013). Based on the SimLex task and the extrinsic evaluation they show comparable performance to the word2vec model computed on a larger corpus.

In this work, we do not focus on the best performing systems for each dataset, like e.g. retrofitting embeddings (Kiela et al., 2015; Rothe and Schütze, 2015), but want to carve out the difference of existing methods for computing distributional similarities.

3 Methods for Distributional Semantics

For the efficient and scalable similarity computation, we select SKIP and CBOW from word2vec as prediction-based, GloVe as dense count-based[1] and JoBimText as sparse count-based method.

Word2Vec

We use the SKIP-gram model, which predicts for a word the neighboring words within a symmetric window of w. Considering the CBOW model, a word is predicted by its neighboring words. For the computation, we use the implementation by Mikolov et al. (2013)[2]. In addition, we use the extension of word2vec, which was introduced by Levy and Goldberg (2014a)[3] and allows to use arbitrary contexts for computing dense vector representations for similarity computations.

Global Vectors (GloVe)

As dense count-based approach, we select GloVe (Pennington et al., 2014).[4] GloVe achieves its representation based on logarithmic co-occurrences between words and context. This representation is learned using matrix factorization methods.

JoBimText (JBT)

We consider JoBimText (Biemann and Riedl, 2013) as symbolic count-based method[5] that produces word similarities encoded in a distributional thesaurus (DT, cf. Lin, 1998). The method is based on a term-context representation and can handle arbitrary contexts. For an efficient computation it considers

---

[1]In this study, we consider GloVe as a dense count-based method. Although GloVe uses a classifier in order to optimize its cost function, it is based on co-occurrence statistics and does not predict contexts from words directly, as performed in word2vec.

[2]https://code.google.com/archive/p/word2vec/

[3]https://bitbucket.org/yoavgo/word2vecf

[4]https://nlp.stanford.edu/projects/glove/

[5]http://sf.net/p/jobimtext/

several pruning techniques and uses Lexicographer's Mutual Information (LMI) (Evert, 2005) to determine relevant contexts per word. In addition, we show results when using the frequency (freq) for ranking which turned out to perform well in Padró et al. (2014). For each term the 1000 contexts with the highest LMI score or frequency are kept. Additionally, contexts are removed that co-occur with more than 1000 terms. The similarity score is only computed between terms that share at least one context and is based on the logarithmic sum of the reciprocal value of the number of terms a context co-occurs (log). Furthermore, we computed similarity scores by using solely the number of contexts two terms share (one).

4 Experimental Setting

For performing the studies, we rely on two different evaluation methods. First, we show results based on datasets that contain averaged similarity scores for word pairs annotated by humans. We use SimLex-999 (Hill et al., 2015), which consists of 999 word pairs, formed by 666 noun, 222 verb and 111 adjective pairs and the SimVerb-3500 dataset (Gerz et al., 2016) which comprises of 3500 verb pairs. The evaluation scores are computed using the Spearman rank correlation coefficient between the gold standard scores and the similarity scores obtained with the semantic methods. These evaluations validate the ability of semantic methods to provide similarity scores that demonstrate the performance for a global ranking between word pairs scores. We name this task as a 'global ranking task' as the semantic models have to provide a score between two given word pairs and the evaluation score is computed by the correlation between similarity scores given by the model and averaged similarity scores given by humans.

In a so-called local ranking task, we will evaluate how well semantic models can retrieve the most similar words for a given term. For this, we sample 1000 low-, middle- and high frequent nouns and verbs. In order to compute the semantic similarities between the most similar terms, we use the WordNet Path measure (Pedersen et al., 2004) and perform an evaluation that is similar to the one used by Biemann and Riedl (2013). This Path measure is the shortest reciprocal distance + 1 between two words based on the IS-A path.

The computation of the various models is performed using a dump of English Wikipedia that comprises of 35 million sentences. The similarities are computed on raw tokenized text, then on lemmatized and POS-tagged tagged text and finally using dependency parses[6] as context representation, which has been shown to work well for computing similarities (Lin, 1997; Biemann and Riedl, 2013; Levy and Goldberg, 2014a). Whereas the tokens and lemmas can be processed with all methods, the dependency parses can only be used with a modification of word2vec (Levy and Goldberg, 2014a) and JBT.

5 Word Similarity Evaluation

In this section, we show the Spearman correlations for the different models using SimLex and SimVerb[7]. First, we perform the computation of the models on raw text (see Table 1). Using various parameters for both word2vec models[8], we observe the best results for the SimLex dataset when computing both SKIP and CBOW with 500 dimensions, using random sampling ($s = 1E^{-5}$), 10 negative examples and a word window size of 1 (W1). This is in line with Melamud et al. (2016), who mostly obtain the highest scores for word similarity tasks when using a comparably high number of dimensions. For GloVe we obtain the best results with the same parameters as for word2vec: we use a window size of 1 and 500 dimensions.[9] The CBOW model performs best on the SimVerb dataset but does not yield the best scores for the verbs in SimLex. However, we could not detect much differences between the two sets, as we observe a correlation of 0.9177 for 90 verb pairs that are shared in both datasets. GloVe performs best on

---

[6] We use the Stanford dependency parser (de Marneffe et al., 2006)

[7] All word pairs not contained in the model are scored with zero.

[8] We tested different values for random sampling ($s = \{0, 1^{-5}\}$), dimension size ($d = \{100, 200, 500\}$), window size ($w = \{1, 5, 10, 15\}$) and negative examples ($n = \{0, 5, 10\}$

[9] We tested various window sizes ($w = \{1, 2, 5, 10, 15\}$) and various number of dimensions ($d = \{50, 100, 200, 500\}$).

	Method	SimLex				SimVerb
		all	NN	VB	JJ	
raw text	SKIP W1 100	0.3105	0.3488	0.1630	0.4345	0.2113
	SKIP W1 500	**0.3908**	0.4223	0.2616	0.5324	0.2656
	SKIP W5 500	0.3364	0.3758	0.1741	0.4531	0.2335
	CBOW W1 100	0.3159	0.3529	0.1683	0.4575	0.2121
	CBOW W1 500	0.3901	0.4193	0.2638	0.5284	**0.2677**
	CBOW W5 500	0.3427	0.3821	0.1698	0.4798	0.2339
	GloVe W1 100	0.2359	0.2367	0.1633	0.3567	0.1565
	GloVe W1 500	0.3055	0.2832	**0.2679**	**0.5359**	0.1903
	JBT freq one	0.2940	0.3934	0.0576	0.3742	0.1469
	JBT freq log	0.3085	0.4032	0.0726	0.4071	0.1599
	JBT LMI one	0.3140	0.4113	0.0741	0.4144	0.1763
	JBT LMI log	0.3306	**0.4231**	0.0942	0.4328	0.1889
lemma	SKIP W1 500	**0.4024**	0.4465	0.2041	0.5347	0.3012
	CBOW W1 500	0.3997	0.4409	0.2037	0.5353	**0.3023**
	GloVe W1 500	0.3751	0.3786	**0.2411**	0.5437	0.3017
	JBT LMI log	0.3784	**0.4583**	0.2100	0.3906	0.2961
dep.	SKIP W1 500	0.3480	0.4089	**0.2678**	0.3220	0.2552
	JBT LMI log	**0.3869**	**0.4475**	0.2649	**0.3841**	**0.3276**

Table 1: Spearman correlation with SimLex and SimVerb for models computed on tokenized text.

adjectives and verbs for the SimLex dataset, but cannot reach the highest scores on the SimVerb dataset. Although, JBT is not optimized for global similarity scoring, as it does not compute normalized similarity scores between two terms, the correlation scores are are highest for the SimLex's nouns. In contrast to Padró et al. (2014), computing JBT by using the frequency (JBT freq log and JBT freq one) for ranking relevant contexts does not yield the best performance. Here the highest scores are achieved using LMI with a logarithmic scoring, which confirms the findings by Riedl (2016). As the selected parameters also performed best for the lemmatized and dependency-parsed data, we restrict the presentation of results to this setting in the remainder.

Inspecting the correlation scores on the lemmatization-based models equipped with POS-tags we observe a similar trend. In general, we examine higher scores than with raw text. For the entire SimLex and SimVerb dataset we again observe the best performance with the prediction-based models. In contrast to the previous evaluations, the scores from the JBT LMI log are closer to the highest correlation scores of CBOW. Again the best scores for verbs and adjectives are retrieved using GloVe.

Using dependency parses as context, we spot the best performance with JBT LMI log. For the SimVerb dataset, we get even higher results than using the best performing CBOW model using lemmas. Using the dependency-based SKIP model performs well for the SimLex verbs, but apart from that cannot even outperform the word2vec models computed on raw text.

6 Word Ranking Evaluation

In this section, we use the WordNet-based evaluation in order to show the performance of the methods based on a local similarity ranking. Here, we focus on the methods with its best performing parameters and show results for lemma and POS-based models and dependency-based models. Table 2 shows results for nouns and verbs for different frequent bands for the top $N = \{1, 5, 10, 50, 100\}$ highest ranked words. For low- and mid-frequent nouns the best scores up to the top 10 most similar nouns are achieved with the SKIP model. Beyond considering more than the 10 most similar terms the JBT model performs best. Whereas, up to the 50 most similar nouns, the performance of the different models is comparable, we observe performance drops for the top 100 ranked words for GloVe and SKIP in comparison to JBT.

	Method	freq	1	5	10	50	100
nouns	SKIP W1 500	high	0.3613	0.2759	0.2373	0.1326	0.0751
	GloVe W1 500	high	0.2612	0.2412	0.2266	0.1821	0.1439
	JBT LMI log	high	**0.3821**	**0.3007**	**0.2649**	**0.2013**	**0.1802**
	SKIP W1 500	mid	**0.2480**	**0.1887**	0.1649	0.1138	0.0736
	GloVe W1 500	mid	0.2270	0.1612	0.1429	0.1133	0.0980
	JBT LMI log	mid	0.2377	0.1828	**0.1660**	**0.1362**	**0.1249**
	SKIP W1 500	low	**0.1891**	**0.1461**	0.1320	0.0816	0.0477
	GloVe W1 500	low	0.1423	0.1174	0.1092	0.0864	0.0618
	JBT LMI log	low	0.1798	0.1508	**0.1392**	**0.1166**	**0.1062**
verbs	SKIP W1 500	high	0.4718	0.3384	0.2866	0.1574	0.0956
	GloVe W1 500	high	**0.4882**	**0.3683**	0.3217	0.2462	0.1864
	JBT LMI log	high	0.4611	0.3651	**0.3286**	**0.2686**	**0.2498**
	SKIP W1 500	mid	**0.3689**	0.2524	0.2139	0.1129	0.0676
	GloVe W1 500	mid	0.3286	0.2352	0.2111	0.1741	0.1481
	JBT LMI log	mid	0.3437	**0.2705**	**0.2520**	**0.2167**	**0.2052**
	SKIP W1 500	low	0.2481	0.1766	0.1469	0.0653	0.0354
	GloVe W1 500	low	0.1950	0.1768	0.1665	0.1276	0.0878
	JBT LMI log	low	**0.2544**	**0.2246**	**0.2140**	**0.1904**	**0.1773**

Table 2: Results of the lemma-based models for the WordNet-based evaluation showing results for the top N most similar words.

Considering the high frequent nouns the best performance is always obtained with the JBT model. For verbs Glove achieves the highest scores for when using the top 1 to 5 most similar terms for high frequent verbs. However, similar to the results based on nouns the best performance for the 10, 50 and 100 most similar terms ist gained using the JBT model.

Using dependency parses as context, we obtain the overall highest scores using JBT (see Table 3). Again, the modified SKIP model cannot compete with the count-based method and performs even inferior to the lemma and POS-tag based models.

	Method	freq	1	5	10	50	100
nouns	SKIP W1 500	high	0.3760	0.2889	0.2546	0.1907	0.1665
	JBT LMI log	high	**0.4004**	**0.3143**	**0.2776**	**0.2148**	**0.1929**
	SKIP W1 500	mid	0.1990	0.1630	0.1507	0.1308	0.1216
	JBT LMI log	mid	**0.2898**	**0.2214**	**0.1989**	**0.1585**	**0.1451**
	SKIP W1 500	low	0.1420	0.1288	0.1230	0.1061	0.0913
	JBT LMI log	low	**0.2634**	**0.2012**	**0.1815**	**0.1431**	**0.1300**
verbs	SKIP W1 500	high	0.4073	0.3011	0.2656	0.2153	0.1973
	JBT LMI log	high	**0.4948**	**0.3729**	**0.3305**	**0.2660**	**0.2494**
	SKIP W1 500	mid	0.2842	0.2201	0.2012	0.1770	0.1683
	JBT LMI log	mid	**0.3980**	**0.3026**	**0.2699**	**0.2193**	**0.2072**
	SKIP W1 500	low	0.2076	0.1781	0.1714	0.1589	0.1482
	JBT LMI log	low	**0.3214**	**0.2597**	**0.2363**	**0.2007**	**0.1919**

Table 3: WordNet Path scores for semantic models that use dependency parses as context

7   Data Analysis

When examining the most similar words, we detected some further properties of each models. Exemplarily, we show the five most similar terms to the noun "access" using the POS-tagged and lemmatized models in Table 4. First, we observe that not all similar terms are nouns and in addition it seems, that

SKIP W1 500		GloVe W1 500		JBT LMI log	
access#VB	0.73	accessible#JJ	0.80	connection#NN	27.08
accessible#JJ	0.65	provide#VB	0.80	connectivity#NN	22.72
accessibility#RB	0.64	allow#VB	0.78	link#NN	14.62
accessibility#NN	0.64	enable#VB	0.78	exposure#NN	13.58
wifus#NN	0.61	available#JJ	0.75	entry#NN	12.11

Table 4: Most similar words for the noun "access".

in comparison to JBT, SKIP and GloVe favor less frequent words. These effects are explored in the following.

Frequency of Similarities

To explore the frequencies of similar words, we compute the average frequency for the top $N = \{1, 10, 100, 200\}$ most similar words for the sampled candidates. In addition, we use the relative frequency in relation to the frequency of the queried word. Among all frequency bands and for verbs and nouns we observe a consistent pattern, as shown in Figure 1. For nouns, the SKIP and CBOW similar

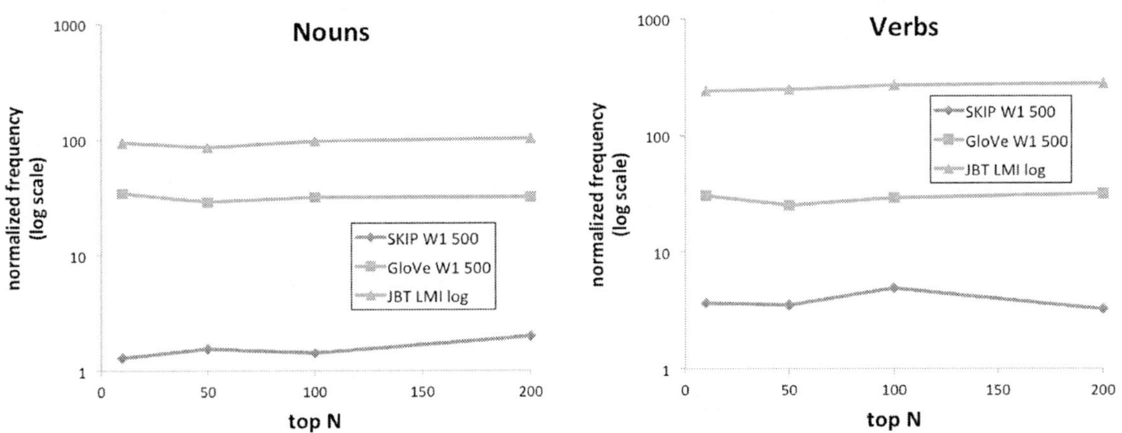

Figure 1: Normalized average frequency for the top N most similar words for 3000 nouns (left) and 3000 verbs (right) for the semantic models computed using lemmas and POS information.

words are on average 3 times more frequent than the queried term. Schnabel et al. (2015) also describe that the frequency of the similarities stay in the same frequency region and attribute this effect to the cosine similarity. Using GloVe the similar nouns are on average 20 times more frequent and for JBT we retrieve words that are on average 100 times more frequent than the queried word. For verbs, we obtain consistently higher average similarities. However, the pattern is similar to the one observed with nouns.

Keeping the same POS

Next, we examine the stability of the most similar terms in respect to the POS of the candidate term. For this we use the lemmatized and dependency-based models in order to determine the percentage of similar words that keep the same POS-tag. This reveals how good the most similar words stay in their same grammatical function and is e.g. relevant when trying to replace unknown words in machine translation or for POS-tagging and dependency parsing, where the grammatical function should be the same. We show the ratio of all 3000 selected nouns for the top $N = \{1, 10, 50, 100\}$ first entries in Table 5. Using the lemmatized models, we obtain the highest POS consistency among the similar terms using JBT, followed by GloVe and SKIP after a large margin. The dependency parses-based models show a

context	Method	1	10	50	100
	SKIP W1 500	0.6077	0.5550	0.5060	0.4834
lemmas	GloVe W1 500	0.5137	0.5382	0.5446	0.5408
	JBT LMI log	**0.9997**	**0.8969**	**0.8762**	**0.8650**
dependen-	SKIP W1 500	0.9703	**0.9687**	**0.9559**	**0.9450**
cies	JBT LMI log	**1.0000**	0.9486	0.9258	0.9139

Table 5: Percentage of the top N most similar terms for nouns that keep the same POS-tag

different trend: here the SKIP model pertains mostly in the same POS class and yields higher scores than the JBT approach.

8 Conclusion

In this paper, we have shown the differences between efficiently computable semantic methods of three different classes: sparse count based, dense count-based and dense prediction-based models. For global similarity ranking, we advise using the SKIP or CBOW method when processing raw and lemmatized text, which obtain the best overall results on SimLex and SimVerb. In general, we observe performance increases when using lemmatized text rather than raw text. Using dependency parses, only the JBT model improves and yields the best result for verbs. Using SKIP with dependency parse context no improvements are gained and the performance is mostly worse than using raw text. Based on the local similarity ranking, we recommend using the JBT model, which yields the best overall performance both for nouns and verbs. In addition, using dependency parses as context results in further improvements. When requiring more than the top 50 most similar terms for query term, we would not advise using the dense vector representations, as both GloVe and word2vec perform poorly. Based on tasks where words in text should be replaced with words of the same grammatical function (e.g. lexical substitution, machine translation) using either JBT with all context or SKIP using dependency parses is advised, as word and lemma based GloVe and SKIP favor similarities to words of another POS. Furthermore, SKIP and CBOW favor to extract similar terms of the same frequency as the queried word, whereas similar words obtained with JBT are on average 176 times more frequent. For tasks like text simplification however, providing more frequent words is favored as frequent words are more likely to be known.

In future work, we would like to evaluate further methods like Random Indexing, SVD-based methods, and DM (Padó and Lapata, 2007) and enhance the evaluation by extrinsic ones. In addition, we want to conceive a method that integrates the advantages of all discussed methods.

References

Banko, M. and E. Brill (2001). Scaling to very very large corpora for natural language disambiguation. In *Proceedings of 39th Annual Meeting of the Association for Computational Linguistics*, Toulouse, France, pp. 26–33.

Baroni, M., G. Dinu, and G. Kruszewski (2014). Don't count, predict! A systematic comparison of context-counting vs. context-predicting semantic vectors. In *Proceedings of the 52nd Annual Meeting of the Association for Computational Linguistics (Volume 1: Long Papers)*, Baltimore, MA, USA, pp. 238–247.

Biemann, C. and M. Riedl (2013). Text: Now in 2D! a framework for lexical expansion with contextual similarity. *Journal of Language Modelling 1*(1), 55–95.

Claveau, V. and E. Kijak (2016). Direct vs. indirect evaluation of distributional thesauri. In *Proceedings of COLING 2016, the 26th International Conference on Computational Linguistics: Technical Papers*, Osaka, Japan, pp. 1837–1848.

de Marneffe, M.-C., B. Maccartney, and C. D. Manning (2006). Generating typed dependency parses from phrase structure parses. In *Proceedings of the International Conference on Language Resources and Evaluation*, LREC 2006, Genova, Italy, pp. 449–454.

Evert, S. (2005). *The Statistics of Word Cooccurrences: Word Pairs and Collocations*. Ph. D. thesis, Institut für maschinelle Sprachverarbeitung, University of Stuttgart.

Ferrone, L. and F. M. Zanzotto (2017). Symbolic, distributed and distributional representations for natural language processing in the era of deep learning: a survey. *CoRR abs/1702.00764*.

Gerz, D., I. Vulić, F. Hill, R. Reichart, and A. Korhonen (2016). SimVerb-3500: A Large-Scale Evaluation Set of Verb Similarity. In *Proceedings of the 2016 Conference on Empirical Methods in Natural Language Processing*, Austin, Texas, pp. 2173–2182.

Gorman, J. and J. R. Curran (2006). Scaling distributional similarity to large corpora. In *Proceedings of the 21st International Conference on Computational Linguistics and the 44th annual meeting of the Association for Computational Linguistics*, ACL 2006, Sydney, Australia, pp. 361–368.

Grefenstette, G. (1994). *Explorations in Automatic Thesaurus Discovery*. Norwell, MA, USA: Kluwer Academic Publishers.

Harris, Z. S. (1951). *Methods in Structural Linguistics*. Chicago: University of Chicago Press.

Hill, F., R. Reichart, and A. Korhonen (2015). SimLex-999: Evaluating Semantic Models with (Genuine) Similarity Estimation. *Computational Linguistics 41*(4), 665–695.

Hindle, D. (1990). Noun classification from predicate-argument structures. In *Proceedings of the 28th Annual Meeting on Association for Computational Linguistics*, ACL 1990, Pittsburgh, PA, USA, pp. 268–275.

Kiela, D., F. Hill, and S. Clark (2015, September). Specializing word embeddings for similarity or relatedness. In *Proceedings of the 2015 Conference on Empirical Methods in Natural Language Processing*, Lisbon, Portugal, pp. 2044–2048.

Kilgarriff, A., P. Rychlý, and D. T. Pavel Smrz (2004). The sketch engine. In *Proceedings of the 11th EURALEX International Congress*, Lorient, France, pp. 105–115.

Levy, O. and Y. Goldberg (2014a). Dependency-based word embeddings. In *Proceedings of the 52nd Annual Meeting of the Association for Computational Linguistics (Volume 2: Short Papers)*, Baltimore, MD, USA, pp. 302–308.

Levy, O. and Y. Goldberg (2014b). Neural word embedding as implicit matrix factorization. In *Advances in Neural Information Processing Systems 27*, NIPS 2014, pp. 2177–2185.

Levy, O., Y. Goldberg, and I. Dagan (2015). Improving distributional similarity with lessons learned from word embeddings. *Transactions of the Association for Computational Linguistics 3*, 211–225.

Lin, D. (1997). Using syntactic dependency as local context to resolve word sense ambiguity. In *Proceedings of the 35th Annual Meeting of the Association for Computational Linguistics and Eighth Conference of the European Chapter of the Association for Computational Linguistics*, ACL 1998/EACL 1997, Madrid, Spain, pp. 64–71.

Lin, D. (1998). Automatic retrieval and clustering of similar words. In *Proceedings of the 17th international conference on Computational linguistics*, COLING 1998, Montreal, Quebec, Canada, pp. 768–774.

Lund, K. and C. Burgess (1996). Producing high-dimensional semantic spaces from lexical co-occurrence. *Behavior Research Methods, Instruments, & Computers 28*(2), 203–208.

Melamud, O., D. McClosky, S. Patwardhan, and M. Bansal (2016). The role of context types and dimensionality in learning word embeddings. In *Proceedings of the 2016 Conference of the North American Chapter of the Association for Computational Linguistics: Human Language Technologies*, NAACL-2016, San Diego, CA, USA, pp. 1030–1040.

Mikolov, T., K. Chen, G. Corrado, and J. Dean (2013). Efficient Estimation of Word Representations in Vector Space. In *Proceedings of the International Conference on Machine Learning*, ICLR 2013, Scottsdale, AZ, USA, pp. 1310–1318.

Padó, S. and M. Lapata (2007). Dependency-based construction of semantic space models. *Computational Linguistics 33*(2), 161–199.

Padró, M., M. Idiart, A. Villavicencio, and C. Ramisch (2014). Nothing like good old frequency: Studying context filters for distributional thesauri. In *Proceedings of the 2014 Conference on Empirical Methods in Natural Language Processing*, EMNLP 2014, Doha, Qatar, pp. 419–424.

Pedersen, T., S. Patwardhan, and J. Michelizzi (2004). WordNet::Similarity: measuring the relatedness of concepts. In *Demonstration Papers at HLT-NAACL 2004*, Boston, MA, USA, pp. 38–41.

Pennington, J., R. Socher, and C. D. Manning (2014). GloVe: Global Vectors for Word Representation. In *Proceedings of the 2014 Conference on Empirical Methods in Natural Language Processing*, EMNLP 2014, Doha, Quatar, pp. 1532–1543.

Riedl, M. (2016). *Unsupervised Methods for Learning and Using Semantics of Natural Language*. Ph. D. thesis, Technische Universität Darmstadt, Germany.

Riedl, M. and C. Biemann (2013). Scaling to large[3] data: An efficient and effective method to compute distributional thesauri. In *Proceedings of the 2013 Conference on Empirical Methods in Natural Language Processing*, EMNLP 2013, Seattle, WA, USA, pp. 884–890.

Rothe, S. and H. Schütze (2015). AutoExtend: Extending Word Embeddings to Embeddings for Synsets and Lexemes. In *Proceedings of the 53rd Annual Meeting of the Association for Computational Linguistics*, ACL 2015, Beijing, China, pp. 1793 – 1803.

Schnabel, T., I. Labutov, D. Mimno, and T. Joachims (2015). Evaluation methods for unsupervised word embeddings. In *Proceedings of the 2015 Conference on Empirical Methods in Natural Language Processing*, Lisbon, Portugal, pp. 298–307.

Turney, P. D. and P. Pantel (2010, January). From frequency to meaning: vector space models of semantics. *Journal of Artificial Intelligence Research 37*(1), 141–188.

Role Semantics for Better Models of Implicit Discourse Relations

Michael Roth
Department of Language Science and Technology, Saarland University
`mroth@coli.uni-sb.de`

Abstract

Predicting the structure of a discourse is challenging because relations between discourse segments are often implicit and thus hard to distinguish computationally. I extend previous work to classify implicit discourse relations by introducing a novel set of features on the level of semantic roles. My results demonstrate that such features are helpful, yielding results competitive with other feature-rich approaches on the PDTB. My main contribution is an analysis of improvements that can be traced back to role-based features, providing insights into why and when role semantics is helpful.

1 Introduction

Understanding natural language texts involves, inter alia, correctly identifying coherent segments and the relations that hold between them. Recognizing discourse relations is an important part of this process because such relations not only conceptualize which parts of a text belong together but also *how* they are related. Apart from direct applications in text analysis (e.g., discourse parsing), recognizing discourse relations has further proven a useful preprocessing step for a range of downstream tasks (Louis et al., 2010; Guzmán et al., 2014; Narasimhan and Barzilay, 2015; Chandrasekaran et al., 2017, inter alia).

From a computational perspective, it has been shown that recognizing discourse relations can be performed with high accuracy when explicit discourse markers are available (Pitler et al., 2008). However, classifying relations without explicit markers, so-called *implicit* discourse relations, has persisted as a difficult task to date (cf. Xue et al., 2016). One of the main challenges, as identified in Lin et al. (2009), is the need to perform inference over two discourse segments. In this paper, I propose a new set of features based on semantic roles to address this challenge. These features are meant to provide a shallow form of semantic representation, which might help a classifier to make better informed classification decisions. I argue that role semantic representations are particularly well-suited for this task because different types of discourse relations are defined over the propositions that they connect. For example, definitions in the Penn Discourse TreeBank 2.0 annotation manual (Prasad et al., 2007) explicitly refer to role-level concepts such as events, situations and involved participants. In Rhetorical Structure Theory (Mann and Thompson, 1988), some definitions contain references to concepts akin to *proto-roles* (e.g. "someone's deliberate action"). To illustrate the usefulness of role semantics for the classification of implicit discourse relations, consider the two sentenes shown in Example (1):

(1) a. "Mr. Brady phoned Mr. Greenspan, ..."
    b. "He continued to work the phones through the weekend."
       Relation: then, *Temporal.Asynchronous.Precedence*   (source: `wsj_2413.pdtb`)

In terms of frame-semantic representation (Fillmore, 1976), the roles involved in the second sentence can be identified as an `Ongoing_activity` (the argument of "continue"), a definite `Duration` and a pronominal `Agent`.[1] These cues indicate a sequence of situations with the same actor, making it likely that a *Temporal* relation holds to the previous sentence.

---

[1] Roles based on FrameNet, see `http://framenet.icsi.berkeley.edu/`.

2 Discourse Relation Classification with Feature-rich Models

The task addressed in this paper is to determine the discourse relations that hold between two implicitly related discourse segments. In this section, I introduce a combined model for this task that aggregates outputs from multiple simpler models (2.1), each of which uses only one type of feature. I then introduce new feature sets based on semantic roles (2.2).

2.1 Model and Previous Features

My motivation for a model combination derives from the observation that different types of features from the literature greatly vary with respect to the associated number of feature instances and how well they generalize. Consequently, there is no unique set of hyperparameters (e.g. level of regularization, thresholding) that works best for all feature types. The proposed combined model consists of two steps to make use of information from inherently diverse feature types. First, I train simple discourse relation classifiers that only use one feature type each. Outputs from multiple classifiers are then combined using averaging as a simple but effective form of model combination.[2]

I formalize the classification of an instance i with respect to a discourse relation r as follows. Given a set of n feature types, feature values are extracted and a set of simple classifiers $c_{r,1} \ldots c_{r,n}$ are trained. At test time, each classifier outputs an individual score $score_{c_{r,j}}(i) \in [0, 1]$. Decisions of multiple classifiers are then aggregated by computing the arithmetic mean of the individual scores. As single classifiers, I use logistic regression models with L2 loss, as implemented in the LIBLINEAR toolkit (Mu-Chu et al., 2015). Accordingly, the aggregated model predicts a relation r for instance i iff $\frac{1}{n}\Sigma_{j=1...n} score_{c_{r,j}}(i) > 0.5$.

The following list provides an overview of all feature sets from the literature that I reimplemented for the described approach, and gives the total number of features for each type.

First/Last.   Set of indicators for the first and last words in each discourse segment. In case of Example (1), instances of this feature set include `1:FIRST:Mr.`, `2:FIRST:He`, etc. (for details, see Pitler et al., 2009). ca. 74 000 features

Dates and number.   Indicator features for the number of date and number expressions in each discourse segment (e.g. `1:DATE:0`; see Pitler et al., 2009). ca. 10 000

Production rules.   Features on production rules used to construct each discourse segment's constituency tree (e.g. `1:S_NP_VP`; see Lin et al., 2009). ca. 78 000

Verb features.   Indicators for the main verb, its tense/modality and average verb phrase length (e.g. `1:VERB:phone`, `2:TENSE:past`; see Park and Cardie, 2012). ca. 20 000

Coreference.   Set of features that indicate coreferring mentions, as predicted by Stanford CoreNLP (Lee et al., 2013), across two related discourse segments (see Rutherford and Xue, 2014). ca. 10 000

Brown clusters.   Feature sets indicating precomputed Brown cluster IDs (Turian et al., 2010) of words occurring in each discourse segment (e.g. `2:11100110`; see Braud and Denis, 2015). 200–6 400

Pairwise Brown clusters.   Pairwise Brown cluster IDs indicating word pairs across two related discourse segments (e.g. `11110110x11000100`; see Braud and Denis, 2015). up to 10 million

---

[2]Sum/averaging is used here because of its simplicity and robustness (Kittler et al., 1998). Due to the small development set size, methods with additional parameters may tend to overfit.

2.2 Features based on Semantic Roles

As new features, I propose to utilize the semantic roles identified in a pair of discourse segments. I define two variants of this feature type: one based on FrameNet (Ruppenhofer et al., 2010) and one based on PropBank (Palmer et al., 2005). All features are computed automatically using a state-of-the-art semantic role labeler (Roth, 2016; Roth and Lapata, 2016). Each variant includes both raw labels as well as a combination of the label and the filler word to which the label is assigned. To reduce sparsity, filler words are always represented by pre-computed Brown cluster IDs (Turian et al., 2010). The list below provides additional details as well as example instances based on the sentences shown in Example (1).

FrameNet roles. This feature set indicates all frame elements that are identified in a pair of related discourse segments. For instance, two frame element fillers are identified in the phrase *he continued to work*: *he* is the `Agent` of the frame evoked by the verb *work*, and *work* itself fills the `Ongoing_activity` element of the frame evoked by *continue*. To compute features for *he*, the Brown cluster ID of the word is looked up (`11100110`) and it is determined that the word occurs in the 2nd discourse segment in Example (1). Accordingly, the indicator features that represent *he* and its semantic role in this case are `2:Agent` and `2:Agent:11100110`.[3]   ca. 37 000

PropBank roles. Analogous to the FrameNet features, this feature set consists of indicators for Prop-Bank labels. Because argument labels in PropBank (A0...A5) are only meaningful with respect to a given predicate, I define two conjoined versions of this feature type: one takes into account the predicate's class in VerbNet (Kipper et al., 2008) and one the predicate lemma itself (e.g., `2:work-73.2_A0` and `2:work_A0:11100110`, resp.). In each variant, predicate-independent labels (modifiers such as time and location) are optionally considered in the same representation format.   ca. 560 000

3   Experiments

I evaluate the proposed model on version 2.0 of the Penn Discourse Treebank (PDTB, Prasad et al., 2008). To ensure a fair comparison, I use the same preprocessing and weighting techniques as well as the same data instances as previous work (Rutherford and Xue, 2014; Braud and Denis, 2015). That is, each instance is a pair of implicitly related discourse segments as annotated in the PDTB corpus. Sections 2–20 of the corpus are used for training, 21–22 for testing, and all other sections for development.

Baseline and comparison models.   I use three variants of the proposed model to directly examine the utility of semantic roles and combining classifiers. The first two models are instances of the feature-rich model described in Section 2, with hyperparameter tuning and feature selection done on the training and development sets: *AverageFeats* uses a combination of feature sets described in subsection 2.1, whereas *AverageFeats+SRL* also uses the role-level features from subsection 2.2. Note that for each type of role set at most one feature representation is chosen. All feature sets are selected based on the best performance on the development set. The third model, *AllFeats*, is a baseline logistic regression classifier that uses all best development feature sets at the same time.

For comparison, I consider a range of current state-of-the-art models. The best feature-rich models (Rutherford and Xue, 2014; Braud and Denis, 2015) use a range of binary indicator features largely identical to the features described in Section 2.1. The most notable difference to this work is that Rutherford and Xue use a small list of coreference patterns in addition to features that simply indicate coreferring mention counts. Neural-network models (Zhang et al., 2015; Liu and Li, 2016; Qin et al., 2016) use attention or convolution mechanisms to identify important words and word spans in each discourse segment. They then predict the discourse relation based on a composition function applied over representations of important words. All of the comparison models use the same training and test instances as this work and are directly comparable.

---

[3] I also experimented with feature conjunctions in order to explicitly model semantic interactions between two discourse segments. However, such conjuctions consistently reduced development performance, probably due to sparsity.

	comp	cont	exp	temp
Neural network models				
Zhang et al. (2015)	33.2	52.0	69.6	30.5
Liu and Li (2016)	36.7	54.5	70.4	**38.8**
Qin et al. (2016)	**41.6**	**57.3**	**71.5**	35.4
Recent feature-rich models				
Rutherford and Xue (2014)	<u>39.7</u>	54.4	<u>70.2</u>	28.7
Braud and Denis (2015)	36.4	55.8	67.4	29.3
This work's models				
AverageFeats	36.3	55.9	69.4	30.5
AverageFeats+SRL	37.0	<u>56.3</u>	69.4	<u>32.1</u>
AllFeats	34.5	51.3	60.4	26.8

Table 1: One-vs-all results in F_1-score on the four PDTB top-level relations (*comp*arison, *cont*ingency, *exp*ansion and *temp*oral). Best overall results are marked in bold, best results by feature-rich models are underlined.

Role name	Position	Weight
Request	segment 1	+1.13061
Addressee	segment 1	+0.90852
Relative_time	segment 1	+0.85555
Stuff	segment 2	+0.79267
Success_or_failure	segment 2	+0.69008
Unattr_information	segment 2	+0.66578
Agent	segment 1	+0.39992
Agent	segment 2	−0.68378

Table 2: List of indicator features on FrameNet frame elements that received a high weight for recognizing the discourse relation Contingency.

Results. Table 1 lists F_1-scores for each of the top-level relations in the PDTB test set. Note that multiple relation types can apply to one relation instance. Hence, instead of one 4-way classification, this task is traditionally separated into four binary tasks. The results show that *AverageFeats* performs competitively with other feature-rich models for discourse relation classification. Additional features on semantic roles improve performance for all but one relation. In the cases in which semantic roles are helpful, both FrameNet-based and PropBank-based feature sets are selected. Two of the four scores by *AverageFeats+SRL* represent the best reported results with a feature-rich model. The performance of *AllFeats* is consistently worse than those of other recent models. This complies with my hypothesis that hyperparameters tuned for one single model do not generalize well across different feature types.

Discussion. One advantage of simple classification models based on binary features is that predictions based on learned feature weights can easily be interpreted. In the following, I take a closer look at classification instances that the model *AverageFeats+SRL* got correct but that were misclassified by the other models. The weights of the features that apply in these examples provide insights as to how and when semantic roles are beneficial. For simplicity, I focus the discussion on FrameNet roles (i.e. frame element types).

For the implicit relation *Contingency*, the learned feature weights indicate that its prediction becomes more likely when an `Agent` is identified in the first discourse segment (high positive feature weight) but not in the second segment (negative feature weight). This seems to reflect the fact that most of these relations connect a cause and a result, as shown for instance in Example (2).

(2) "...traders can buy or sell even when they don't have a customer order ... [*as a result*] liquidity becomes a severe problem for thinly traded contracts ..." (`wsj_2110.pdtb`)

Semantic roles are helpful in such cases because they provide a means to distinguish events initiated by someone (the cause) from simple states (the result). A list of features that seem to contribute to this distinction, as identified by their associated feature weights, are given in Table 2.

The feature weights assigned in role-based classifiers for other discourse relations are overall smaller and thus harder to interpret. Still, certain trends can be observed. For example, I find that co-occurrences of specific roles in both connected discourse segments may indicate a *Comparison*. Example (3) shows one such instance, in which the role `Purpose` has been identified in both segments (assigned feature weight: $+0.117$). Other roles, for which the same pattern of weights are observed include, among others, `Theme` ($+0.435$) and `Businesses` ($+0.254$).

(3) "Her goal: to top 300 ad pages ... [*but*] whether she can meet that ambitious goal is still far from certain." (`wsj_2109.pdtb`)

Concerning the *Temporal* relation, high feature weights are learned for specific FrameNet roles, such as `Activity_start` in the first discourse segment ($+1.654$) and `Process_end` in the second segment ($+1.116$). Even though these feature weights seem to be intuitive, they only lead to marginal improvements to the absolute classification performance, presumably because textual order in discourse not necessarily represents linear temporal order ("before" vs. "after"). Higher gains could be achieved if training and evaluation was performed on more specific relation annotations but such instances are too rare in practice for the feature-rich classifiers to learn robust generalizations: For example, the current version of the Penn Discourse Treebank contains a total of only 151 implicit relation instances of the discourse relation *Temporal.Asynchronous.Succession.*

4   Related Work

The task of predicting implicit discourse relations was first introduced in the context of implicit and explicit relation classification (Marcu and Echihabi, 2002). Pitler et al. (2009) were the first to address implicit relations specifically. They applied a Naive Bayes model with a range of binary features. Follow-up work examined different methods for feature selection (Lin et al., 2009; Park and Cardie, 2012) as well as novel feature types based on pairs of word classes/clusters, entity mentions, and word embeddings (Biran and McKeown, 2013; Louis et al., 2010; Braud and Denis, 2015). Further improvements were made via multi-task learning (Lan et al., 2013) and training data expansion (Rutherford and Xue, 2015).

In recent years, a myriad of neural-network based models have been proposed for the task of recognizing implicit discourse relations (Ji and Eisenstein, 2014; Zhang et al., 2015; Liu and Li, 2016; Qin et al., 2017, inter alia). Models of this kind have a high expressive power and generally outperform methods that rely on manual feature engineering. However, being able to trace back improvements to individual features was key to my discussion in Section 3. Recent results in downstream NLP tasks indicate that neural network models can perform better when incorporating binary features (Cheng et al., 2016; Sennrich and Haddow, 2016, inter alia).

5   Conclusions

I proposed a simple model combination for discourse relation classification that aggregates outputs from multiple classifiers. Several classifiers use novel features based on automatic semantic role labeling. I have shown that such features improve classification performance and provide shallow insights into relationships between role semantics and discourse semantics.

In the future, I plan to apply more sophisticated methods of model ensembling. I would like to investigate whether neural network approaches to discourse relation classification can also benefit from structural information in the form of semantic roles. I believe this to be a promising research direction especially because of the small size of available training data, which presumably makes it difficult for a neural network to learn any higher level structures by itself.

Acknowledgements

This research was supported in part by the Cluster of Excellence "Multimodal Computing and Interaction" of the German Excellence Initiative, and a DFG Research Fellowship (RO 4848/1-1).

References

Biran, O. and K. McKeown (2013). Aggregated word pair features for implicit discourse relation disambiguation. In *Proceedings of the 51st Annual Meeting of the Association for Computational Linguistics (Volume 2: Short Papers)*, Sofia, Bulgaria, pp. 69–73.

Braud, C. and P. Denis (2015). Comparing word representations for implicit discourse relation classification. In *Proceedings of the 2015 Conference on Empirical Methods in Natural Language Processing*, Lisbon, Portugal, pp. 2201–2211.

Chandrasekaran, M. K., C. Demmans Epp, M.-Y. Kan, and D. Litman (2017). Using discourse signals for robust instructor intervention prediction. In *31st AAAI Conference on Artificial Intelligence*, San Francisco, California. to appear.

Cheng, H.-T., L. Koc, J. Harmsen, T. Shaked, T. Chandra, H. Aradhye, G. Anderson, G. Corrado, W. Chai, M. Ispir, et al. (2016). Wide & deep learning for recommender systems. In *Proceedings of the 1st Workshop on Deep Learning for Recommender Systems*, Boston, Massachusetts, pp. 7–10.

Fillmore, C. J. (1976). Frame semantics and the nature of language. In *Annals of the New York Academy of Sciences: Conference on the Origin and Development of Language and Speech*, Volume 280, pp. 20–32.

Guzmán, F., S. Joty, L. Màrquez, and P. Nakov (2014). Using discourse structure improves machine translation evaluation. In *Proceedings of the 52nd Annual Meeting of the Association for Computational Linguistics (Volume 1: Long Papers)*, Baltimore, Maryland, pp. 687–698.

Ji, Y. and J. Eisenstein (2014). Representation learning for text-level discourse parsing. In *Proceedings of the 52nd Annual Meeting of the Association for Computational Linguistics (Volume 1: Long Papers)*, Baltimore, Maryland, pp. 13–24.

Kipper, K., A. Korhonen, N. Ryant, and M. Palmer (2008). A large-scale classification of english verbs. *Language Resources and Evaluation Journal 42*(1), 21–40.

Kittler, J., M. Hatef, R. P. Duin, and J. Matas (1998). On combining classifiers. *IEEE Transactions on Pattern Analysis and Machine Intelligence 20*(3), 226–239.

Lan, M., Y. Xu, and Z. Niu (2013). Leveraging synthetic discourse data via multi-task learning for implicit discourse relation recognition. In *Proceedings of the 51st Annual Meeting of the Association for Computational Linguistics (Volume 1: Long Papers)*, Sofia, Bulgaria, pp. 476–485.

Lee, H., A. Chang, Y. Peirsman, N. Chambers, M. Surdeanu, and D. Jurafsky (2013). Deterministic coreference resolution based on entity-centric, precision-ranked rules. *Computational Linguistics 39*(4), 885–916.

Lin, Z., M.-Y. Kan, and H. T. Ng (2009). Recognizing implicit discourse relations in the Penn Discourse Treebank. In *Proceedings of the 2009 Conference on Empirical Methods in Natural Language Processing*, Singapore, pp. 343–351.

Liu, Y. and S. Li (2016). Recognizing implicit discourse relations via repeated reading: Neural networks with multi-level attention. In *Proceedings of the 2016 Conference on Empirical Methods in Natural Language Processing*, Austin, Texas, pp. 1224–1233.

Louis, A., A. Joshi, and A. Nenkova (2010). Discourse indicators for content selection in summarization. In *Proceedings of the SIGDIAL 2010 Conference*, Tokyo, Japan, pp. 147–156.

Louis, A., A. Joshi, R. Prasad, and A. Nenkova (2010). Using entity features to classify implicit discourse relations. In *Proceedings of the SIGDIAL 2010 Conference*, Tokyo, Japan, pp. 59–62.

Mann, W. C. and S. A. Thompson (1988). Rhetorical structure theory. Toward a functional theory of text organization. *Text 8*(3), 243–281.

Marcu, D. and A. Echihabi (2002). An unsupervised approach to recognizing discourse relations. In *Proceedings of 40th Annual Meeting of the Association for Computational Linguistics*, Philadelphia, Pennsylvania, pp. 368–375.

Mu-Chu, L., C. Wei-Lin, and L. Chih-Jen (2015). Fast matrix-vector multiplications for large-scale logistic regression on shared-memory systems. In *IEEE International Conference on Data Mining*, Atlantic City, New Jersey.

Narasimhan, K. and R. Barzilay (2015). Machine comprehension with discourse relations. In *Proceedings of the 53rd Annual Meeting of the Association for Computational Linguistics and the 7th International Joint Conference on Natural Language Processing (Volume 1: Long Papers)*, Beijing, China, pp. 1253–1262.

Palmer, M., D. Gildea, and P. Kingsbury (2005). The Proposition bank: An annotated corpus of semantic roles. *Computational Linguistics 31*(1), 71–106.

Park, J. and C. Cardie (2012). Improving implicit discourse relation recognition through feature set optimization. In *Proceedings of the 13th Annual Meeting of the Special Interest Group on Discourse and Dialogue*, Seoul, South Korea, pp. 108–112.

Pitler, E., A. Louis, and A. Nenkova (2009). Automatic sense prediction for implicit discourse relations in text. In *Proceedings of the Joint Conference of the 47th Annual Meeting of the ACL and the 4th International Joint Conference on Natural Language Processing of the AFNLP*, Suntec, Singapore, pp. 683–691.

Pitler, E., M. Raghupathy, H. Mehta, A. Nenkova, A. Lee, and A. Joshi (2008). Easily identifiable discourse relations. In *Coling 2008: Companion volume: Posters*, Manchester, United Kingdom, pp. 87–90.

Prasad, R., N. Dinesh, A. Lee, E. Miltsakaki, L. Robaldo, A. K. Joshi, and B. L. Webber (2008). The Penn Discourse TreeBank 2.0. In *Proceedings of the Sixth International Conference on Language Resources and Evaluation (LREC-2008)*, Marrakesh, Marocco.

Prasad, R., E. Miltsakaki, N. Dinesh, A. Lee, A. Joshi, L. Robaldo, and B. Webber (2007). The penn discourse treebank 2.0 annotation manual. Technical report.

Qin, L., Z. Zhang, and H. Zhao (2016). A stacking gated neural architecture for implicit discourse relation classification. In *Proceedings of the 2016 Conference on Empirical Methods in Natural Language Processing*, Austin, Texas, pp. 2263–2270.

Qin, L., Z. Zhang, H. Zhao, Z. Hu, and E. Xing (2017). Adversarial connective-exploiting networks for implicit discourse relation classification. In *Proceedings of the 55th Annual Meeting of the Association for Computational Linguistics (Volume 1: Long Papers)*, Vancouver, Canada, pp. 1006–1017. Association for Computational Linguistics.

Roth, M. (2016). Improving frame semantic parsing via dependency path embeddings. In *Book of Abstracts of the 9th International Conference on Construction Grammar*, Juiz de Fora, Brazil, pp. 165–167.

Roth, M. and M. Lapata (2016). Neural semantic role labeling with dependency path embeddings. In *Proceedings of the 54th Annual Meeting of the Association for Computational Linguistics (Volume 1: Long Papers)*, Berlin, Germany, pp. 1192–1202.

Ruppenhofer, J., M. Ellsworth, M. R. L. Petruck, C. R. Johnson, and J. Scheffczyk (2010). FrameNet II: Extended Theory and Practice. Technical report, International Computer Science Institute.

Rutherford, A. and N. Xue (2014). Discovering implicit discourse relations through brown cluster pair representation and coreference patterns. In *Proceedings of the 14th Conference of the European Chapter of the Association for Computational Linguistics*, Gothenburg, Sweden, pp. 645–654.

Rutherford, A. and N. Xue (2015). Improving the inference of implicit discourse relations via classifying explicit discourse connectives. In *Proceedings of the 2015 Conference of the North American Chapter of the Association for Computational Linguistics: Human Language Technologies*, Denver, Colorado, pp. 799–808.

Sennrich, R. and B. Haddow (2016). Linguistic input features improve neural machine translation. In *Proceedings of the First Conference on Machine Translation*, Berlin, Germany, pp. 83–91.

Turian, J., L.-A. Ratinov, and Y. Bengio (2010). Word representations: A simple and general method for semi-supervised learning. In *Proceedings of the 48th Annual Meeting of the Association for Computational Linguistics*, Uppsala, Sweden, pp. 384–394.

Xue, N., H. T. Ng, S. Pradhan, A. Rutherford, B. Webber, C. Wang, and H. Wang (2016). Conll 2016 shared task on multilingual shallow discourse parsing. In *Proceedings of the CoNLL-16 shared task*, Berlin, Germany, pp. 1–19.

Zhang, B., J. Su, D. Xiong, Y. Lu, H. Duan, and J. Yao (2015). Shallow convolutional neural network for implicit discourse relation recognition. In *Proceedings of the 2015 Conference on Empirical Methods in Natural Language Processing*, Lisbon, Portugal, pp. 2230–2235.

Representation Learning for Answer Selection with LSTM-Based Importance Weighting

Andreas Rücklé[†] and **Iryna Gurevych**[†‡]

[†]Ubiquitous Knowledge Processing Lab (UKP)
Department of Computer Science, Technische Universität Darmstadt
[‡]Ubiquitous Knowledge Processing Lab (UKP-DIPF)
German Institute for Educational Research
`www.ukp.tu-darmstadt.de`

Abstract

We present an approach to non-factoid answer selection with a separate component based on *BiLSTM* to determine the importance of segments in the input. In contrast to other recently proposed attention-based models within the same area, we determine the importance while assuming the independence of questions and candidate answers. Experimental results show the effectiveness of our approach, which outperforms several state-of-the-art attention-based models on the recent non-factoid answer selection datasets InsuranceQA v1 and v2. We show that it is possible to perform effective importance weighting for answer selection without relying on the relatedness of questions and answers. The source code of our experiments is publicly available.[1]

1 Introduction

Answer selection is an important subtask of question answering (QA) that enables choosing one final answer from a list of candidate answers in regard to the input question (Feng et al., 2015; Wang and Nyberg, 2015). QA itself can be divided into factoid QA, which enables the retrieval of facts, and non-factoid QA, which enables finding of complex answer texts (e.g. descriptions, opinions, or explanations). Answer selection for non-factoid QA is especially difficult because we usually deal with user-generated content, for example questions and answers extracted from community question answering platforms or FAQ websites. As a consequence, candidate answers are complex multi-sentence texts with detailed information. Two examples are shown in Figures 2 and 3.

To deal with this challenge, recent approaches employ attention-based neural networks to focus on segments within the candidate answer that are most related to the question (Tan et al., 2016; Wang et al., 2016). For scoring, dense vector representations of the question and the candidate answer are learned and the distance between the vectors is measured. With attention-based models, segments with a stronger focus are treated as more important and have more influence on the resulting representations.

Using the relatedness between a candidate answer and the question to determine the importance is intuitive for correct candidate answers because the most important segments of both texts are expected to be strongly related. However, we also deal with a large number of incorrect candidate answers where the most important segments are usually dissimilar to the question. In such cases, the relatedness does not correlate with the actual importance. Thus, different methods for determining the importance could lead to better representations, especially when dealing with incorrect candidate answers.

In this work, we therefore determine the importance of segments in questions and candidate answers with a method that assumes the independence of both items. Our approach uses *CNN* and *BiLSTM* for representation learning and employs a separate network component based on *BiLSTM* for importance weighting. Our general concept is similar to self-attention mechanisms that have recently been integrated

---

[1]`https://github.com/UKPLab/iwcs2017-answer-selection`

to models for natural language inference and sentiment classification (Lin et al., 2017; Liu et al., 2016). They however employ feedforward components to derive importance values and deal with classification problems. In contrast, we directly compare learned representations with a similarity measure and derive the importance using a separate $BiLSTM$, which was motivated by the effectiveness of stacked models in answer selection (Tan et al., 2016; Wang and Nyberg, 2015).

We evaluate our approach on two non-factoid answer selection datasets that contain data from a community question answering platform: InsuranceQA v1 and InsuranceQA v2. In comparison to other state-of-the-art representation learning approaches with attention, our approach achieves the best results and significantly outperforms various strong baselines. An additional evaluation on the factoid QA dataset WikiQA demonstrates that our approach is well-suited for other scenarios that deal with shorter texts. In general, we show that it is possible to perform effective importance weighting in non-factoid answer selection without relying on the relatedness of questions and candidate answers.

2   Related Work

Earlier work in answer selection relies on handcrafted features based on semantic role annotations (Shen and Lapata, 2007; Surdeanu et al., 2011), parse trees (Wang and Manning, 2010; Heilman and Smith, 2010), tree kernels (Moschitti et al., 2007; Severyn and Moschitti, 2012), discourse structures (Jansen et al., 2014), and external resources (Yih et al., 2013).

More recently, researchers started using deep neural networks for answer selection. Yu et al. (2014), for example, propose a convolutional bigram model to classify a candidate answer as correct or incorrect. Similar but more enhanced, Severyn and Moschitti (2015) use a CNN with additional dense layers to capture interactions between questions and candidate answers, a model that is also part of a combined approach with tree kernels (Tymoshenko et al., 2016). And Wang and Nyberg (2015) incorporate stacked $BiLSTMs$ to learn a joint feature vector of a question and a candidate answer for classification.

Answer selection can also be formulated as a ranking task where we learn dense vector representations of questions and candidate answers and measure the distance between them for scoring. Feng et al. (2015) use such an approach and compare different models based on CNN with different similarity measures. Based on that, models with attention mechanisms were proposed. Tan et al. (2016) apply an attentive $BiLSTM$ component that performs importance weighting before pooling based on the relatedness of segments in the candidate answer to the question. Dos Santos et al. (2016) introduce a two-way attention mechanism based on a learned measure of similarity between questions and candidate answers. And Wang et al. (2016) propose novel ways to integrate attention inside and before a GRU.

In this work, we use a different method for importance weighting that determines the importance of segments in the texts while assuming the independence of questions and candidate answers. This is related to previous work in other areas of NLP that incorporate self-attention mechanisms. Within natural language inference, Liu et al. (2016) derive the importance of each segment in a short text based on the comparison to a average-pooled representation of the text itself. Parikh et al. (2016) determine intra-attention with a feedforward component and combine the importance of nearby segments. And Lin et al. (2017) propose a model that derives multiple attention vectors with matrix multiplications. Within factoid QA, Li et al. (2016) weight the importance of each token in a question with a feedforward network and perform sequence labeling.

In contrast to those, we apply this concept to answer selection, we directly compare vector representations of questions and candidate answers, and we use a separate *BiLSTM* for importance weighting.

3   Representation Learning for Answer Selection

We formulate answer selection as a ranking task. Given a question q and a pool A of candidate answers, the goal is to re-rank A according to a scoring function that judges each candidate answer $a \in A$ for relevancy in regard to q. The best-ranked candidate answer is then selected. For scoring we learn dense vector representations of q and a and calculate the similarity between those vectors.

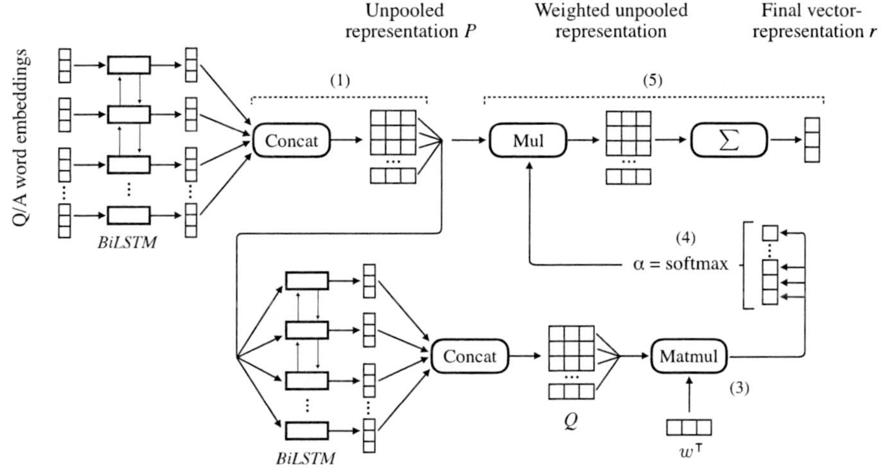

Figure 1: The network structure of LW with $BiLSTM$ to learn the unpooled representation (LW_{BiLSTM}). Numbers in parentheses refer to the related Equations.

Basic BiLSTM Model   The best-performing models for representation learning in non-factoid answer selection are usually based on $BiLSTMs$ (Tan et al., 2016; Dos Santos et al., 2016). Thus, we build our own approach on a variation of such model. To obtain a representation for an input text we apply an $LSTM$ on the concatenated d-dimensional word embeddings $E \in \mathbb{R}^{l \times d}$ of the input text with length l in forward direction and in backward direction. As a result, we obtain two matrices $H^{\rightarrow}, H^{\leftarrow} \in \mathbb{R}^{l \times c}$ that contain the state vectors of each recurrence (c is the $LSTM$ cell size). We define the unpooled representation P as the row-wise concatenation of both matrices and create a fixed-size dense vector representation r of the question or candidate answer by applying 1-max pooling:

$$P_i = [H_i^{\rightarrow}, \; H_i^{\leftarrow}] \tag{1}$$

$$r_j = \max_{1 < i < l} (P_{i,j}) \tag{2}$$

where $P \in \mathbb{R}^{l \times 2 \cdot c}$ and $r \in \mathbb{R}^{2 \cdot c}$.

We can also use CNN for learning text representations. In this case, P contains the values of all filter operations applied on all n-grams in the input text and the dense vector representation r is calculated with 1-max pooling as before. Formal definitions can be found in (Feng et al., 2015; Dos Santos et al., 2016).

LSTM-Based Importance Weighting (LW)   The basic $BiLSTM$ model is often extended with different attention mechanisms that utilize the relatedness between questions and candidate answers to focus on the most relevant segments of the texts (Tan et al., 2016; Wang et al., 2016; Dos Santos et al., 2016). In contrast, we perform importance weighting while assuming the independence of both items. As a consequence, we do not rely on the relatedness to determine the importance.

Our approach LW is an extension to simple representation learning models and can be used instead of 1-max pooling. We first create an encoding of the importance for each segment in the unpooled representation P of a prior component (e.g. the basic $BiLSTM$) by applying an additional, separate $BiLSTM$. We obtain the concatenated output states $Q \in \mathbb{R}^{l \times 2 \cdot c}$ of this $BiLSTM$ where the ith row Q_i contains the state vectors that encode the importance of the ith row in P. We then reduce each row Q_i to a scalar v_i and apply softmax on the vector v to obtain scaled importance values that sum to 1.0:

$$v_i = w^{\mathsf{T}} Q_i \tag{3}$$

$$\alpha = softmax(v) \tag{4}$$

Dataset	Train	Valid	Test	Candidates	Correct Answers	Answer Length
	Questions	Questions	Questions	per Question	per Question	in Tokens
InsuranceQA v1	12,887	1,000	3,600	500.0	1.4	96.5
InsuranceQA v2	12,889	1,592	1,625	500.0	1.6	111.8
WikiQA	873	126	243	9.8	1.2	25.2

Table 1: Dataset statistics.

where $w \in \mathbb{R}^c$ are learned network parameters for the reduction operation, $v_i \in \mathbb{R}$ is the (unscaled) importance value of the ith segment in P, and $\alpha \in \mathbb{R}^l$ is the resulting importance vector (or attention vector). Applying softmax is important because we do not want more accumulated importance for longer texts compared to shorter texts. Finally, we reduce P to a fixed-size dense vector representation r according to our importance vector α:

$$r_j = \sum_{i=1}^{l} \alpha_i P_{i,j} \tag{5}$$

In contrast to average pooling or 1-max pooling, this operation allows different segments in the input to contribute to r with different strengths (having more or less influence on r). A visualization of LW that uses $BiLSTM$ to learn the unpooled representation P is shown in Figure 1.

In general, we always use shared network weights to learn the unpooled representation P of questions and candidate answers as it is more effective compared to using separate network weights (Feng et al., 2015). Within the components of LW we however use separate network weights, which allows the network to learn different importance weighting behavior for questions and candidate answers. We analyze the impact of this choice later in Section 5.

4 Experimental Setup

Training   We define the loss $\mathcal{L}$ as follows:

$$\mathcal{L} = max\left(0,\ m - s(r^q, r^{a+}) + s(r^q, r^{a-})\right)$$

where r^q is the learned question representation, r^{a+} and r^{a-} are learned representations of correct and incorrect candidate answers, s is cosine similarity, and m is the desired margin between the similarities. Because such triples are not pre-defined in our datasets, we construct them during training. For a pair of question and correct answer we randomly sample 50 incorrect candidate answers from the whole training set and select the candidate with the highest similarity according to our currently trained model.

Datasets   We evaluate our models on the two recent non-factoid answer selection datasets InsuranceQA v1 and InsuranceQA v2 (Feng et al., 2015). In general, both datasets contain more than 15,000 questions and the candidate answers are long multi-sentence texts. Even though InsuranceQA v1 and v2 were crawled from the same community question answering website, they model different setups due to a different sampling strategy that was used to create the candidate answer pools. Whereas in InsuranceQA v1 the pools were created randomly (plus the correct answers), the pools in InsuranceQA v2 were created by querying a search engine to retrieve candidate answers that are lexically similar to the question.[2]

In addition, we also test our approaches on the factoid answer selection dataset WikiQA, which was constructed by means of crowd-sourcing through the extraction of sentences from Wikipedia articles (Yang et al., 2015). We use this dataset to test our models within the different scenario of factoid answer selection that deals with significantly shorter texts. The dataset statistics are listed in Table 1.

---

[2] Since the correct answers were not separately inserted in InsuranceQA v2, the pools are not guaranteed to contain a correct answer. We discard all questions without any correct answer in the associated pool of candidate answers.

Model	Valid	Test
AttentiveBiLSTM (Tan et al., 2016)	68.9	66,9
IABRNN (Wang et al., 2016)	69.1	67.0
AP_{BiLSTM} (Dos Santos et al., 2016)	68.4	69.1
CNN	60.5	58.3
BiLSTM	68.2	65.7
CNN+BiLSTM	68.5	67.3
BiLSTM+BiLSTM	67.5	66.3
LW_{CNN}	70.0	67.9
LW_{BiLSTM}	**70.9**	**70.0***

Table 2: Experimental results on InsuranceQA v1 (accuracy). * = significant improvement against our other models ($p < 0.05$, Wilcoxon test).[3]

Model	Valid	Test
AP_{BiLSTM} (reimplementation)	32.2	31.9
CNN	24.4	24.4
BiLSTM	32.4	31.1
CNN+BiLSTM	33.0	31.4
BiLSTM+BiLSTM	31.2	32.0
LW_{CNN}	33.5	33.7
LW_{BiLSTM}	**35.4**	**36.9***

Table 3: Experimental results on InsuranceQA v2 (accuracy). * = significant improvement against all other models ($p < 0.05$, Wilcoxon test).

Models and Baselines   We evaluate LW with $BiLSTM$ (LW_{BiLSTM}) and CNN (LW_{CNN}) to learn the unpooled representations. As baselines we employ $BiLSTM$ and CNN with 1-max pooling and the stacked variants $CNN+BiLSTM$ and $BiLSTM+BiLSTM$, which use a $BiLSTM$ with 1-max pooling to process the unpooled representation P of the prior component.

A comparison against the stacked models is particularly important because they employ the same components as LW_{CNN} and LW_{BiLSTM}, but use a different network structure.

Neural Network Setup   We performed grid search over several hyperparameter combinations and found the optimal choices to be similar to hyperparameters of previous work. The cell size of all $LSTMs$ is 141 (each direction), and the number of filters for all $CNNs$ is 400 with size 3. The only exception is $CNN+BiLSTM$ with 282 filters and a cell size of 282. We use the Adam optimizer (Kingma and Ba, 2015) with a learning rate of $4 \cdot 10^{-4}$ and a margin $m = 0.2$. We initialize the word embeddings with off-the-shelf 100-dimensional uncased GloVe embeddings (Pennington et al., 2014) and optimize them further during training. Dropout of 0.3 was applied on the representations before comparison.

We chose different hyperparameters for WikiQA, which we do not list here due to space restrictions. Details can be found in our public source code repository.

5   Experimental Results

InsuranceQA v1   Our evaluation on InsuranceQA v1 allows us to compare our approach against a broad list of recently published attention-based models. Table 2 shows the results of our evaluation where we measure the ratio of correctly selected answers (accuracy). We observe that by adding LW to either CNN or $BiLSTM$ we can significantly improve the answer selection performance by 9.6% and 4.3% respectively. This clearly shows that LW is effective and can be used to extend basic models to learn better representations of questions and candidate answers. Additionally, LW models are more effective than stacked models due to the different network structure that we use to explicitly learn importance weights. Stacked models are less effective because they need to carry the full representation through all components. Overall, LW_{BiLSTM} significantly outperforms all our other tested models. LW_{BiLSTM} also achieves the best results compared to other state-of-the-art representation learning approaches with attention such as the two-way attention model AP_{BiLSTM}, which derives attention from a learned measure of similarity between questions and answers. This clearly shows that we can successfully perform importance weighting without relying on the relatedness of questions and answers.

It is important to mention that Wang and Jiang (2017) very recently experimented with a novel

---

[3] We did not have access to the predictions of other top-performing approaches, hence, we report significance against our own models. We note that the differences are however within the usual margins of this dataset.

Model	MAP	MRR
AP_{CNN} (Dos Santos et al., 2016)	0.6886	0.6957
$ABCNN$ (Yin et al., 2016)	0.6921	0.7127
$IABRNN$ (Wang et al., 2016)	**0.7341**	**0.7418**
CNN	0.6204	0.6365
$BiLSTM$	0.6174	0.6310
$CNN+BiLSTM$	0.6560	0.6737
$BiLSTM+BiLSTM$	0.6735	0.6789
LW_{CNN}	**0.7102**	**0.7240**
LW_{BiLSTM}	0.6941	0.7039

Table 4: Experimental results on WikiQA compared to recent approaches with attention.

Model	InsuranceQA		WikiQA	
	V1	V2	MAP	MRR
LW_{CNN} / shared	67.8	**34.0**	0.6992	0.7112
LW_{CNN} / sep.	**67.9**	33.7	**0.7102**	**0.7240**
LW_{BiLSTM} / shared	68.5	36.1	0.6854	0.6954
LW_{BiLSTM} / sep.	**70.0**	**36.9**	**0.6941**	**0.7039**

Table 5: Experimental results with shared vs. separate LW weights.

method that achieves state-of-the-art results on the InsuranceQA v1 dataset.[4] Instead of learning dense vector representations, they classify pairs of questions and candidate answers with a compare-aggregate model that performs comparisons on the word level, aggregates this information with CNN, and uses additional layers to determine the classification result. Because their approach is not learning dense vector representations, we did not directly compare against it. It would however be possible to use our approach in their framework to compare segments of weighted unpooled representations.

InsuranceQA v2 The evaluation on InsuranceQA v2 allows us to compare our models within a more realistic answer selection scenario due to the different creation of candidate answer pools. Because there are no previously published results, we re-implemented Attentive Pooling with $BiLSTM$ (AP_{BiLSTM}) as proposed by Dos Santos et al. (2016) for a better comparison.[5] We report the experimental results in Table 3. Similar to our previous findings, LW significantly improves the answer selection performance of CNN and $BiLSTM$. In contrast, AP_{BiLSTM} only achieves minor improvements against $BiLSTM$. We expect this to be an effect of the more realistic candidate answer pools where all incorrect candidates are lexically similar to the question. Because AP_{BiLSTM} uses an explicitly learned measure of similarity between questions and candidate answers to determine the importance, it assigns high scores to lexically similar incorrect candidate answers. On the other hand, our experimental results suggest that LW is not affected by this issue. As a consequence, our best model LW_{BiLSTM} significantly outperforms all other approaches, showing that importance weighting without relying on the relatedness of questions and answers is very effective within the realistic answer selection scenario of InsuranceQA v2.

Since our best observed accuracy on this dataset is significantly lower than on InsuranceQA v1, we tried to determine the actual usefulness of our approach. We manually labeled the first 100 incorrectly selected answers of $BiLSTM$ and LW_{BiLSTM} for correctness, where a candidate answer is correct if it contains the information that was requested in the question. In the case of LW_{BiLSTM}, 50 answers were labeled as correct, and for $BiLSTM$ the number of correct labels is 44. The improvement of LW_{BiLSTM} is often driven by a sharp question focus, which enables to better retrieve answers that contain the requested information. These numbers indicate that the actual usefulness of our models is higher than the reported accuracy scores. The primary issue is the number of missing labels in the dataset, which is a result of the different sampling strategy and the lack of manual relevance annotations. We however did not notice any particular consequences from this situation beyond under-estimating the model performance.

WikiQA Experiments on WikiQA allow us to test our proposed approach within a different scenario that deals with considerably shorter texts. Following Yang et al. (2015), we measure MAP and MRR within our evaluation. The results are listed in Table 4.

Similar to our results on both InsuranceQA datasets, the addition of LW substantially improves the answer selection performance. Neither the reduced length of the answers nor the significantly reduced

---

[4]They evaluated many different variations of their approach and achieve a maximum accuracy of 74.3%.

[5]Our re-implementation achieves similar results on InsuranceQA v1 as reported by (Dos Santos et al., 2016).

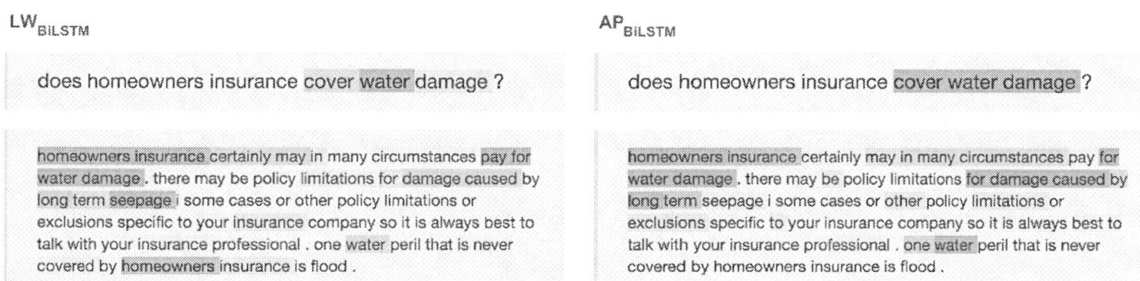

Figure 2: A visualization of the attention weights of LW_{BiLSTM} and AP_{BiLSTM} for a question and a correct answer. Red colors visualize the relative importance.

size of the training data has a noticeable influence on the performance. Compared to the stacked models, the performance increase of LW models is also considerable. Even though our best model LW_{CNN} does not achieve state-of-the-art results on this dataset (the best results are currently achieved by Wang and Jiang (2017) with 0.7433 MAP), we note that it performs on the same level as other top-performing attention-based models. This suggests that our approach can be suitably applied to scenarios that are different to non-factoid answer selection.

Separate vs. Shared LW Network Weights   To measure the impact of our choice to use separate LW parameters for questions and candidate answers, we re-ran all experiments with shared parameters and provide a comparison in Table 5.

We observe that using separate LW parameters leads to improvements in 5 out of 6 cases, where LW_{BiLSTM} obtains the biggest gains of up to 1.5% accuracy. This suggests that learning separate parameters for the importance weighting of questions and candidate answers can lead to better representations. Even though this is intuitive because questions and answers are different types of texts, previous work has shown that using separate network parameters usually results in performance declines (Feng et al., 2015). However, since we still use shared parameters to learn the unpooled representations and only use separate parameters in LW, our approach does not suffer from the same optimization issues.

6   Analysis

Importance Weights   We qualitatively analyzed the importance weights of LW_{BiLSTM} and AP_{BiLSTM} using an end-to-end QA framework with attention visualization (Rücklé and Gurevych, 2017) and configured it to use InsuranceQA v2. In general, we oberserved that for pairs of questions and correct candidate answers, the most important segments determined by LW_{BiLSTM} and AP_{BiLSTM} are very similar. An example is given in Figure 2. We also noticed two important attributes of LW that contribute to the previously reported improvements.

First, for incorrect candidate answers with high lexical similarity to the question, LW_{BiLSTM} often focusses on segments that happen to be unrelated and thus creates dissimilar representations (desired). In contrast, AP_{BiLSTM}, by design, focusses on similar segments and creates similar representations (undesired). An example is shown in Figure 3, where our approach strongly focusses on a segment within the question that corresponds to the word *when*. This requires candidate answers to have a similar focus in order to achieve a high score (e.g. by describing a date).[6] Since this is not the case for the presented incorrect candidate answer, the representations are dissimilar and the score is low. This allows LW to better handle incorrect candidate answers.

And second, we found that LW_{BiLSTM} very strongly focusses on few highly relevant segments that are well-suited to describe the overall topic of the text. This leads to representations that are strongly based on individual aspects and allows the model to filter out noise more effectively because irrelevant segments

---

[6]Our approach sometimes focusses on words indicative for the question type (wh-type words), but this is not always the case. If an important noun is present in the question, LW most often focusses on that (e.g. *fire, water, electricity*).

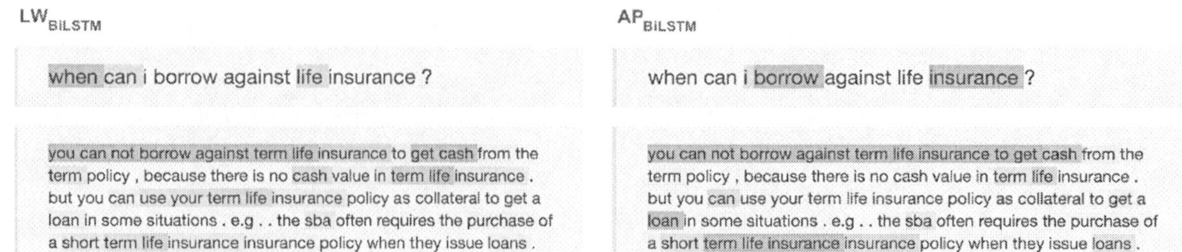

Figure 3: A visualization of the attention weights of LW_{BiLSTM} and AP_{BiLSTM} for a question and an <u>incorrect</u> candidate answer (with high lexical similarity). Red colors visualize the relative importance.

receive lower relative importance. We quantitatively analyzed this property by measuring the strength of the importance weights for all answers in InsuranceQA v2. For each individual question/answer pair (correct or incorrect) we determined the maximum values of the importance weights with LW_{BiLSTM} and AP_{BiLSTM}. Interestingly, LW_{BiLSTM} derives at least one importance weight greater or equal 0.10 within 77% of all answers, and one importance weight greater or equal 0.20 within 24% of all answers.[7] AP_{BiLSTM} on the other hand does not apply such a strong focus (0% of cases; a very small number). As a consequence, LW can better ignore irrelevant content because it strongly focusses on few important segments within the relatively long texts found in InsuranceQA v2.

Error Analysis and Limitations The most common error we observed is related to important aspects of the question that are not addressed in the selected answer. The question *"What is a renters insurance declaration page?"*, for example, contains the aspects *what* (question type), *renters insurance*, and *declaration page*. When LW_{BiLSTM} fails, it usually selects an answer that differs in only one aspect. For the previous question, our approach selects an answer that describes what the *auto insurance* declaration page is (a similar topic). The reason is the inability of LW to focus on all important aspects of the question separately. This can also be observed in our previous example in Figure 2, where our approach focusses on the aspects *cover* and *water damage* but ignores *homeowners insurance*. In this case our approach would not be able to effectively differentiate between candidate answers that write about *renters insurance* instead of *homeowners insurance*.

To tackle this issue, future work could add a separate classification step after ranking that discards any top-ranked answers that do not cover all aspects of the question.

7   Conclusion

In this work, we presented an approach to non-factoid answer selection that determines the importance of segments within questions and answers while assuming the independence of both items. Our experimental results on the two non-factoid answer selection datasets InsuranceQA v1 and v2 show that our approach is effective and substantially outperforms various strong baselines and different state-of-the-art attention-based approaches. Our additional evaluation on WikiQA demonstrates that our proposed approach is also suitable for different scenarios with shorter texts. We showed that it is possible to perform effective importance weighting for answer selection without relying on the relatedness of questions and answers.

Acknowledgements

This work has been supported by the German Research Foundation as part of the QA-EduInf project (grant GU 798/18-1 and grant RI 803/12-1). We gratefully acknowledge the support of NVIDIA Corporation with the donation of the Tesla K40 GPU used for this research. Some calculations for this research were conducted on the Lichtenberg high performance computer of the TU Darmstadt.

---

[7]Segments with a related importance weight of 0.10 have a high influence on the representation (10%).

References

Dos Santos, C., M. Tan, B. Xiang, and B. Zhou (2016). Attentive Pooling Networks. *arXiv preprint*.

Feng, M., B. Xiang, M. R. Glass, L. Wang, and B. Zhou (2015). Applying deep learning to answer selection: A study and an open task. In *2015 IEEE Workshop on Automatic Speech Recognition and Understanding (ASRU)*, pp. 813–820.

Heilman, M. and A. N. Smith (2010). Tree edit models for recognizing textual entailments, paraphrases, and answers to questions. In *Human Language Technologies: The 2010 Annual Conference of the North American Chapter of the Association for Computational Linguistics*, pp. 1011–1019. Association for Computational Linguistics.

Jansen, P., M. Surdeanu, and P. Clark (2014). Discourse complements lexical semantics for non-factoid answer reranking. In *Proceedings of the 52nd Annual Meeting of the Association for Computational Linguistics (ACL)*, pp. 977–986. Association for Computational Linguistics.

Kingma, D. P. and J. L. Ba (2015). Adam: a Method for Stochastic Optimization. In *3rd International Conference on Learning Representations (ICLR)*.

Li, P., W. Li, Z. He, X. Wang, Y. Cao, J. Zhou, and W. Xu (2016). Dataset and Neural Recurrent Sequence Labeling Model for Open-Domain Factoid Question Answering. *Arxiv preprint*.

Lin, Z., M. Feng, C. N. Dos Santos, M. Yu, B. Xiang, B. Zhou, and Y. Bengio (2017). A Structured Self-attentive Sentence Embedding. *5th International Conference on Learning Representations (ICLR)*.

Liu, Y., C. Sun, L. Lin, and X. Wang (2016). Learning Natural Language Inference using Bidirectional LSTM model and Inner-Attention. *Arxiv preprint*.

Moschitti, A., S. Quarteroni, R. Basili, and S. Manandhar (2007). Exploiting syntactic and shallow semantic kernels for question answer classification. In *Proceedings of the 45th Annual Meeting of the Association of Computational Linguistics (ACL)*, pp. 776–783. Association for Computational Linguistics.

Parikh, A. P., O. Täckström, D. Das, and J. Uszkoreit (2016). A Decomposable Attention Model for Natural Language Inference. In *Proceedings of the 2016 Conference on Empirical Methods in Natural Language Processing (EMNLP)*, pp. 2249–2255. Association for Computational Linguistics.

Pennington, J., R. Socher, and C. Manning (2014). Glove: Global vectors for word representation. In *Proceedings of the 2014 Conference on Empirical Methods in Natural Language Processing (EMNLP)*, pp. 1532–1543. Association for Computational Linguistics.

Rücklé, A. and I. Gurevych (2017). End-to-end non-factoid question answering with an interactive visualization of neural attention weights. In *Proceedings of the 55th Annual Meeting of the Association for Computational Linguistics-System Demonstrations (ACL)*, pp. 19–24. Association for Computational Linguistics.

Severyn, A. and A. Moschitti (2012). Structural relationships for large-scale learning of answer re-ranking. In *Proceedings of the 35th International ACM SIGIR Conference on Research and Development in Information Retrieval (SIGIR)*, pp. 741–750. ACM.

Severyn, A. and A. Moschitti (2015). Learning to rank short text pairs with convolutional deep neural networks. In *Proceedings of the 38th International ACM SIGIR Conference on Research and Development in Information Retrieval (SIGIR)*, pp. 373–382. ACM.

Shen, D. and M. Lapata (2007, June). Using semantic roles to improve question answering. In *Proceedings of the 2007 Joint Conference on Empirical Methods in Natural Language Processing and Computational Natural Language Learning (EMNLP-CoNLL)*, pp. 12–21. Association for Computational Linguistics.

Surdeanu, M., M. Ciaramita, and H. Zaragoza (2011). Learning to rank answers to non-factoid questions from web collections. *Computational Linguistics 37*(2), 351–383.

Tan, M., C. Dos Santos, B. Xiang, and B. Zhou (2016). Improved representation learning for question answer matching. In *Proceedings of the 54th Annual Meeting of the Association for Computational Linguistics (ACL)*, pp. 464–473. Association for Computational Linguistics.

Tymoshenko, K., D. Bonadiman, and A. Moschitti (2016). Convolutional neural networks vs. convolution kernels: Feature engineering for answer sentence reranking. In *Proceedings of the 2016 Conference of the North American Chapter of the Association for Computational Linguistics: Human Language Technologies (NAACL-HLT)*, pp. 1268–1278. Association for Computational Linguistics.

Wang, B., K. Liu, and J. Zhao (2016). Inner attention based recurrent neural networks for answer selection. In *Proceedings of the 54th Annual Meeting of the Association for Computational Linguistics (ACL)*, pp. 1288–1297. Association for Computational Linguistics.

Wang, D. and E. Nyberg (2015). A long short-term memory model for answer sentence selection in question answering. In *Proceedings of the 53rd Annual Meeting of the Association for Computational Linguistics and the 7th International Joint Conference on Natural Language Processing (ACL-IJCNLP)*, pp. 707–712. Association for Computational Linguistics.

Wang, M. and C. Manning (2010). Probabilistic tree-edit models with structured latent variables for textual entailment and question answering. In *Proceedings of the 23rd International Conference on Computational Linguistics (COLING)*, pp. 1164–1172.

Wang, S. and J. Jiang (2017). A Compare-Aggregate Model for Matching Text Sequences. *5th International Conference on Learning Representations (ICLR)*.

Yang, Y., W.-t. Yih, and C. Meek (2015). Wikiqa: A challenge dataset for open-domain question answering. In *Proceedings of the 2015 Conference on Empirical Methods in Natural Language Processing (EMNLP)*, pp. 2013–2018. Association for Computational Linguistics.

Yih, W.-T., M.-W. Chang, C. Meek, and A. Pastusiak (2013). Question answering using enhanced lexical semantic models. In *Proceedings of the 51st Annual Meeting of the Association for Computational Linguistics (ACL)*, pp. 1744–1753. Association for Computational Linguistics.

Yin, W., H. Schütze, B. Xiang, and B. Zhou (2016). Abcnn: Attention-based convolutional neural network for modeling sentence pairs. *Transactions of the Association of Computational Linguistics (TACL) 4*, 259–272.

Yu, L., K. M. Hermann, P. Blunsom, and S. Pulman (2014). Deep Learning for Answer Sentence Selection. In *NIPS Deep Learning Workshop*.

Skip-Prop: Representing Sentences with One Vector Per Proposition

Rachel Rudinger, Kevin Duh, Benjamin Van Durme
Johns Hopkins University
{rudinger,kevinduh,vandurme}@cs.jhu.edu

Abstract

We introduce the notion of a multi-vector sentence representation based on a "one vector per proposition" philosophy, which we term *skip-prop* vectors. By representing each predicate-argument structure in a complex sentence as an individual vector, skip-prop is (1) a response to empirical evidence that single-vector sentence representations degrade with sentence length, and (2) a representation that maintains a semantically useful level of granularity. We demonstrate the feasibility of training skip-prop vectors, introducing a method adapted from *skip-thought* vectors, and compare skip-prop with "one vector per sentence" and "one vector per token" approaches.

1 Introduction

The length and complexity of written natural language sentences is highly variable. Sentences from New York Times (NYT) stories (August 1997), for example, contain on average 23 tokens, with a standard deviation of 12. By information-theoretic measures, too, natural language sentences convey differing amounts of information (Hale, 2003; Genzel and Charniak, 2002). It is natural to suppose, then, that methods in computational linguistics that aim to learn fixed-size semantic representations of sentences, i.e., with vectors of fixed dimension, may be limited in their expressiveness or efficiency. Indeed, on many NLP tasks for which neural sentence embedding methods have been adapted, degraded performance on longer input sentences is commonly observed: in machine translation (Cho et al., 2014), question-answering (Kumar et al., 2016), and semantic role labeling (Zhou and Xu, 2015), for example.

Motivated by these observations, we introduce *skip-prop vectors*, a method for learning multi-vector sentence representations following a "one vector per proposition" strategy. Our approach is based on the *skip-thought* method of Kiros et al. (2015), which combines neural sequence-to-sequence models (Sutskever et al., 2014) with a skip-gram-like training objective (Mikolov et al., 2013) to obtain general-purpose sentence representations as a fixed-size vector. Skip-prop capitalizes on the idea that a complex sentence may be represented in terms of the simpler sentences, or *propositions*, that constitute it.

2 Motivation

There are many potential motivations for taking a "one vector per proposition" approach to representing the meaning of a sentence. As discussed in §1, it has been observed that NLP approaches that embed an entire sentence into a single, fixed-size vector may degrade in performance on longer sentences. One answer to this problem is to use finer-grained, multi-vector sentence representations that can grow with sentence complexity. Indeed, most neural (or otherwise continuous-space) models of sentences provide some finer-grained vector representations, most notably at the token level (i.e., standard RNN implementations), sub-token level (Sennrich et al., 2016), character-level (Kim et al., 2016), and syntactic constituent level (Dyer et al., 2016), and are often used in task-specific attention mechanisms. For many tasks involving search or attention, however, such as open question-answering or document-level analysis, preserving each such intermediate representation may be prohibitively expensive.

In comparison to other fine-grained, multi-vector representations, skip-prop offers two advantages: (1) the number of propositions (and hence vectors) per sentence is relatively few, and (2) the proposition is its own interpretable unit of meaning. Figs. 1 and 2 illustrate the granularity-expense tradeoff between one-vector-per sentence, proposition, and token representations. One sentence on average corresponds to 3.5 propositions and 22.8 tokens.[1] Which point in this tradeoff is optimal is likely a task-specific matter; by training *skip-prop* vectors, however, we introduce a new point in this tradeoff scale.

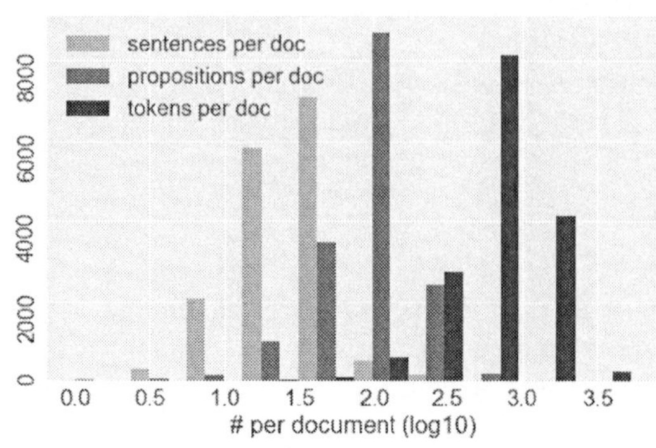

Figure 1: Histogram shows typical NYT documents contain more propositions than sentences, and many more tokens than propositions. (Log scale x-axis.)

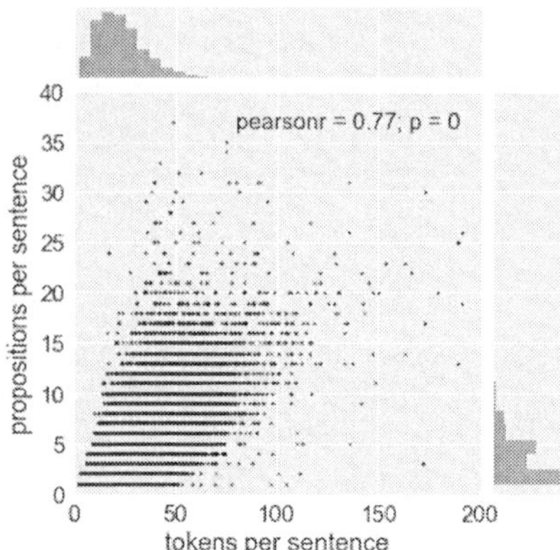

Figure 2: Scatter plot shows longer sentences contain more propositions. Most sentences contain fewer than 50 tokens, and fewer than 8 propositions.

3   Background

Sequence-to-Sequence Models Sequence-to-sequence (seq-to-seq) models are a class of neural networks that compute the conditional probability of an output sequence given an input sequence, i.e., $P(y_1...y_n|x_1...x_m)$. They have been applied to many tasks in NLP (Bahdanau et al., 2014; Vinyals et al., 2015; McClosky et al., 2006), though here we train them to encode multi-vector sentence representations.

Typical seq-to-seq models consist of two recurrent neural networks (RNNs): an *encoder* and *decoder*, which iterate over the input and output sequences, respectively. The final hidden state of the encoder RNN, h_m, is passed as the initial state to the decoder RNN. Thus, the vector h_m is a representation of the entire input, and the decoder computes the conditional distribution: $P(y_1...y_n|x_1...x_m) = P(y_1...y_n|h_m) = \prod_{i=1}^{n} P(y_i|y_{<i}, h_m)$. We train skip-prop with a multi-encoder, multi-decoder variant of seq-to-seq (§4), borrowing aspects of the skip-thought vector model (Kiros et al., 2015).

Sentences to Propositions Our method of learning a "one vector per proposition" representation relies on the use of PredPatt[2], a publicly-available tool for predicate-argument analysis of sentences, run atop Universal Dependency parses.[3] PredPatt extracts predicate-argument structures, or *propositions*, from sentences, including those arising from embedded clauses within the sentence. (See example in Fig. 3.) Though formal accounts of what constitutes a *proposition* may vary (McGrath, 2014), here we refer to a single extracted pattern as a *proposition*, comprising one fully-specified predicate-argument structure.

```
?a extracts ?b from ?c        ?a extracts ?b from ?c
    ?a:   PredPatt                ?a:   PredPatt
    ?b:   predicates              ?b:   arguments
    ?c:   text                    ?c:   text
```

Figure 3: An analysis of the sentence "PredPatt extracts predicates and arguments from text." Two propositions are extracted (when option to resolve conjunctions is enabled).

---

[1] Note that a binary parse of a sentence with N tokens has N-1 non-leaf nodes.

[2] `https://github.com/hltcoe/PredPatt` (commit eb42a8e, run with all flags enabled)

[3] Our method for training *skip-prop* vectors is in principle extensible to any language with UD parsers.

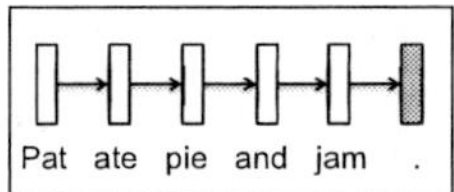

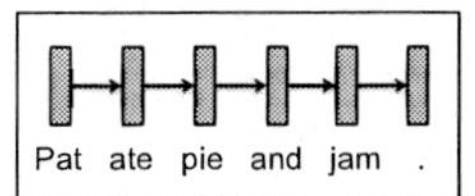

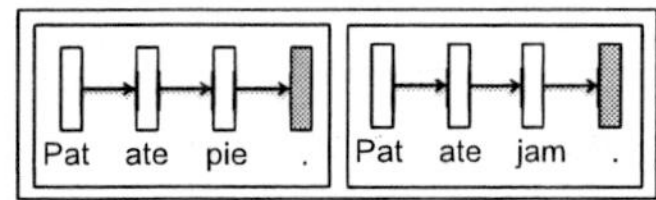

Figure 4: Left to right, encoders for ST, STA, and SP models. Each vertical rectangle represents the LSTM hidden state, h. Only shaded states are visible to the decoders. SP has one encoder per proposition.

Linearization We use a simple method to linearize each extracted proposition into a sequence of tokens so that each may be encoded by a linear-chain RNN. Specifically, each argument variable (?a, ?b...) in the predicate pattern is replaced with the argument it stands for. Thus, linearizing the extraction in Fig. 3 yields "PredPatt extracts predicates from text" and "PredPatt extracts arguments from text."

4 Models

We compare **skip-prop vectors** (SP) with two other representations: **skip-thought vectors** (ST) as "one vector per sentence," and **skip-thought vectors with attention** (STA) as "one vector per token." (Fig 4.)

These models' architectures have many overlapping components, which we present in a unified fashion, drawing distinctions across models as necessary. Each model is a variant of seq-to-seq (encoder-decoder), trained on sentence tuples, (s_l, s_c, s_r), where sentences s_l and s_r are the left (previous) and right (next) context sentences of sentence s_c in a text document, following the approach of Kiros et al. (2015). The *encoder* (one or more RNNs) computes a representation of s_c and passes it to a left RNN decoder and a right RNN decoder, which compute $P(s_l|s_c)$ and $P(s_r|s_c)$, respectively. Together, the two decoders determine the total loss of the network: $-log(P(s_l|s_c)) + -log(P(s_r|s_c))$. We refer to this as the "skip-thought objective" (in contrast with the "autoencoder objective," described below). The gradient of each network parameter with respect to this loss is computed using backpropagation, and all parameters are updated according to the Adam optimization algorithm for stochastic gradient descent.

For notation, we say sentences s_l, s_c, and s_r consist of L, C, and R tokens, each. The tokens of s_c are $w_c^1, ..., w_c^C$ with corresponding embeddings $x_c^1, ..., x_c^C$. For skip-prop, s_c is preprocessed with PredPatt (§3), generating propositions $\pi_1, ..., \pi_P$. A proposition π_p is a sequence of C_p tokens $w_p^1, ..., w_p^{C_p}$.

Encoder Both skip-thought models (ST and STA) use the same encoder: one RNN with a long short-term memory (LSTM) cell (Hochreiter and Schmidhuber, 1997). At time step t, the LSTM cell applies its recurrent update equations to its previous state, (c^{t-1}, h^{t-1}), and an input, x^t, to yield its new state, (c^t, h^t). The final hidden state of the encoder, h^C, represents the entire input sequence s_c.

Skip-prop uses an identical LSTM architecture in its encoder; however, because skip-prop has P input sequences (i.e., one per proposition π_p, instead of just one for the full sentence s_c), it uses P *identical copies* of this LSTM (with shared parameters) to encode each proposition. Thus, the P encoders of skip-prop yield P final-state representations, $h_1^{C_1}, ..., h_P^{C_P}$, to be passed to the decoders. An attention mechanism is used in the skip-prop decoders to accommodate this variable number of vectors passed from the encoder (see below). The dimensionality of h and x is 256 for all models.

Decoder The ST, STA, and SP models all use two LSTM-based decoders, with the same basic architecture as the LSTM encoder (see above). In each model, the left and right decoders are identical (though with separate parameters), so we sometimes drop the l and r subscripts. For clarity, d_t denotes the *decoder* hidden state, akin to h_t in the encoder. For models ST and STA, the decoder's hidden state is initialized as the final hidden encoder state, i.e. $d_0 = h_C$; in SP, d_0 is a trainable parameter. The dimensionality of the hidden decoder states d is the same as the encoder state for all models (256). Each decoder computes the probability of an output sequence, i.e. s_l or s_r, conditioned on the encoder's representation of s_c (§3). For the right-hand decoder, specifically,

$$P(y_i|y_{<i}, h_m) = P(w_r^t|w_r^{<t}, h^C) = P(w_r^t|d_t) = \text{softmax}(d_t^\mathsf{T} W_d) \tag{1}$$

Model	Skip-Thought Obj.			Autoencoder Obj.		
	train	dev	test	train	dev	test
Skip-Thought (ST)	171.32	223.72	216.00	74.22	87.63	88.60
Skip-Thought w/ Attn. (STA)	152.89	204.51	199.16	2.04	2.20	2.22
Skip-Prop (SP)	169.29	213.01	206.29	29.69	41.42	43.21

Table 1: Average per-token perplexity, both with skip-thought and autoencoder objectives.

where W_d is an output vocabulary embedding matrix, also a trainable parameter.

Attention Mechanism The decoder described in the previous section is modified in the case of models STA and SP with an attention mechanism. Our attention mechanism is adapted from Vinyals et al. (2015). At each time step in the decoder, a weighted average over a set of vectors passed from the encoder is dynamically computed. In STA, this set is all encoder hidden states $h_1...h_C$; in SP, it is the final hidden state of each encoder (one per proposition), i.e. $h_{C_1} ... h_{C_P}$. The weighted average at decoder time t is computed according to Vinyals et al. (2015):

$$a_i^t = \text{softmax}_i(v^\mathsf{T}\tanh(W_1 h_i + W_2 d_t)) \quad (2) \qquad d_t' = h_1 a_1^t + h_2 a_2^t + ... + h_C a_C^t \quad (3)$$

where W_1, W_2, and v are learnable parameters. The resulting vector d_t' is concatenated with d_t to create a new decoder output, though the hidden state as passed to the next time step remains unchanged. A result of this concatenation step, the output embedding matrix (W_d) in STA and SP is doubled in dimension.

Autoencoder Variant We train a second version of each model with an autoencoder-like objective in place of the skip-thoughts objective. That is, rather than use two decoders to predict the left and right context sentences, use a single decoder to predict the original sentence that was fed to the encoder (s_c). The autoencoder variant of each model is designated with the suffix -AUTO.

5 Experiments

Data All training, development, and test data consist of articles from the NYT portion of the Concretely Annotated Gigaword corpus labeled "story" (Ferraro et al., 2014). Train is 100K random sentence triples from Aug. 1997 NYT stories; development is 5K random sentence triples from Sept. 1997; and test is 5K random sentence triples from Oct. 1997. The vocabulary is approximately 39K tokens from Sept. 1997 NYT with minimum frequency of 15. Each model is trained for one epoch on the entire train set using mini-batches of size 1. As described in §4, a sentence triple (s_l, s_c, s_r) consists of a contiguous set of three sentences from a news story: a "left," "center," and "right" sentence. For the qualitative nearest-neighbor experiments, two datasets are used: (1) a 100K superset of the NYT development set (Sept. 1997), and (2) all sentences from the SICK corpus (Marelli et al., 2014).

Results As a preliminary evaluation of *skip-prop* vectors, we present both quantitative and qualitative results. These results show that (1) it is feasible to train *skip-prop* vectors with our proposed method, and (2) some notion of semantic similarity over propositions is preserved in this representation.

Table 1 shows the perplexity attained by each model. Here, perplexity is computed either from the two decoders' predictions of the left and right context sentences (skip-thought objective), or one decoder's prediction of the original sentence (autoencoder objective). In all cases, the *skip-prop* models score in between skip-thought and skip-thought with attention models. This is not surprising: the skip-prop decoder has, on average, access to more vectors than the skip-thought decoder, but fewer than the skip-thought with attention decoder.[4] (See Figs. 4 and 1.) This kind of result supports the plausibility

---

[4]This result is particularly magnified under the autoencoder objective, where the skip-thought with attention model attains very low perplexity by learning to attend to the token it needs to decode at each step.

of *skip-prop* vectors as a sentence representation that successfully trades off between the size and cost of one-vector-per-sentence strategies (ST) and one-vector-per-token strategies (STA).

Table 2 shows the qualitative results of a nearest neighbor search for both *skip-thought* and *skip-prop* vectors. We use both in-domain and out-of-domain data: 100K sentences from our NYT development set, and about 40K sentences from the SICK corpus (Marelli et al., 2014). Both query sentences are a random sentence from NYT or SICK with a correct predicate-argument analysis. The corresponding query propositions are each an extracted proposition from the query sentence.

The results in Table 2 suggest that skip-prop vectors provide a useful level of granularity for representing sentence meaning. For example, the NYT query sentence contains multiple salient propositions (?a owns ?b, ?a will jettison ?b, etc.). While the skip-thought representation must pack all of this information into a single vector, skip-prop vectors allow us to represent each proposition *individually*. Accordingly, in the corresponding NYT query proposition, we see that it is possible to isolate a particular proposition of interest (?a owns ?b) and find nearest-neighbors of that proposition, without regard to rest of the sentence's content. This allows a more targeted search using skip-prop vectors.

NYT Query Sentence: H&R Block Inc. , which owns 80 percent of CompuServe , will jettison a business it 's been trying to unload for more than a year .

(ST) New Mexico would notify New York when they release convicted murderers into the Empire State ; New York would notify New Mexico .

(ST-AUTO) IAI Balanced Fund is for investors who want a little bit of everything , Hoelting said .

(SP) The Air Line Pilots Association and US Airways management have been at odds over the labor contract since for more than a year .

(SP-AUTO) H&R Block Inc. , which owns 80 percent of CompuServe , rose 11/16 to 40 7/8 .

NYT Query Proposition: *H&R Block Inc.* **owns** *80 percent of CompuServe*

(SP) H&R Block Inc. , the Kansas City , Missouri , *tax preparation company* that **owns** *80 percent of CompuServe* , will save on taxes by minimizing its gain on the sale .

(SP-AUTO) *Charterhouse* **owns** *80 percent of HRC* , while Accor owns the rest .

SICK Query Sentence: The woman with a black hat is wearing sunglasses

(ST) The blonde girl with the pink top is smiling and wearing funny glasses with a large nose attached

(ST-AUTO) the black and white dog is running outdoors

(SP) *The man with brown hair* **is wearing** *sunglasses* and is sitting listlessly at a table with cans of soda and other drinks

(SP-AUTO) *The woman* is sitting on a bench and **is wearing** a gray jacket and *black pants*

SICK Query Proposition: *a hat* **is/are black**

(SP) A dog and a black man are running through brown leaves [*a man* **is/are black**]

(SP-AUTO) A bride with a black veil is looking down [*a veil* **is/are black**]

Table 2: 1-best nearest-neighbor search over sentences and propositions, using vectors from trained skip-thought (ST) and skip-prop (SP) encoders. Both training objectives, "skip-thought" and "autoencoder" (-AUTO) are compared. Resulting nearest-neighbor propositions are shown within the full sentence they were extracted from; however, only the proposition's **predicate** and *arguments* are represented in its vector. Scoring by cosine similarity.

6 Conclusion

In this paper, we have proposed *skip-prop* vectors, a multi-vector sentence representation that extends the approach of *skip-thought* vectors (Kiros et al., 2015), to represent sentences according to a *one-vector-per-proposition* strategy. We have discussed how skip-prop vectors offer a potential solution to the observed issue of RNN performance degradation on longer sequences, allowing the sentence representation to grow roughly with its length or information content. We have also demonstrated how skip-prop vectors offer a new trade-off point between one-vector-per-sentence and one-vector-per-token strategies, balancing representation size (number of vectors) with performance (test perplexity), at a meaningful level of granularity (the proposition). Test perplexity results indicate that the skip-prop representation is feasible to train, while qualitative results suggest that skip-prop vectors capture some notion of meaning at the proposition level. We believe that this set of attributes makes skip-prop vectors a potentially suitable representation for tasks like question-answering, summarization, or machine reading, and hope to pursue such applications in future work.

Acknowledgments

This work is supported by the National Science Foundation Graduate Research Fellowship under Grant No. DGE-1232825, DARPA LORELEI, the Johns Hopkins Human Language Technology Center of Excellence (HLTCOE), and the Johns Hopkins Center for Language and Speech Processing (CLSP). We would also like to thank Sheng Zhang, Pushpendre Rastogi, and three anonymous reviewers for their feedback. Any opinions expressed in this work are those of the authors.

References

Bahdanau, D., K. Cho, and Y. Bengio (2014). Neural machine translation by jointly learning to align and translate. *CoRR abs/1409.0473*.

Cho, K., B. van Merrienboer, D. Bahdanau, and Y. Bengio (2014, October). On the properties of neural machine translation: Encoder–decoder approaches. In *Proceedings of SSST-8, Eighth Workshop on Syntax, Semantics and Structure in Statistical Translation*, Doha, Qatar, pp. 103–111. Association for Computational Linguistics.

Dyer, C., A. Kuncoro, M. Ballesteros, and N. A. Smith (2016, June). Recurrent neural network grammars. In *Proceedings of the 2016 Conference of the North American Chapter of the Association for Computational Linguistics: Human Language Technologies*, San Diego, California, pp. 199–209. Association for Computational Linguistics.

Ferraro, F., M. Thomas, M. R. Gormley, T. Wolfe, C. Harman, and B. Van Durme (2014). Concretely annotated corpora. In *AKBC Workshop at NIPS*.

Genzel, D. and E. Charniak (2002). Entropy rate constancy in text. In *Proceedings of the 40th Annual Meeting of the Association for Computational Linguistics*.

Graff, D. and C. Cieri (2003). English gigaword corpus. *Linguistic Data Consortium*.

Hale, J. (2003). The information conveyed by words in sentences. *Journal of Psycholinguistic Research 32*(2), 101–123.

Hochreiter, S. and J. Schmidhuber (1997, November). Long short-term memory. *Neural Comput. 9*(8), 1735–1780.

Kim, Y., Y. Jernite, D. Sontag, and A. M. Rush (2016). Character-aware neural language models. In *Proceedings of the Thirtieth AAAI Conference on Artificial Intelligence*, AAAI'16, pp. 2741–2749. AAAI Press.

Kiros, R., Y. Zhu, R. R. Salakhutdinov, R. Zemel, R. Urtasun, A. Torralba, and S. Fidler (2015). Skip-thought vectors. In C. Cortes, N. D. Lawrence, D. D. Lee, M. Sugiyama, and R. Garnett (Eds.), *Advances in Neural Information Processing Systems 28*, pp. 3294–3302. Curran Associates, Inc.

Kumar, A., O. Irsoy, P. Ondruska, M. Iyyer, J. Bradbury, I. Gulrajani, V. Zhong, R. Paulus, and R. Socher (2016, 20–22 Jun). Ask me anything: Dynamic memory networks for natural language processing. In M. F. Balcan and K. Q. Weinberger (Eds.), *Proceedings of The 33rd International Conference on Machine Learning*, Volume 48 of *Proceedings of Machine Learning Research*, New York, New York, USA, pp. 1378–1387. PMLR.

Marelli, M., S. Menini, M. Baroni, L. Bentivogli, R. Bernardi, and R. Zamparelli (2014). A sick cure for the evaluation of compositional distributional semantic models. In *LREC*, pp. 216–223.

McClosky, D., E. Charniak, and M. Johnson (2006, June). Effective self-training for parsing. In *Proceedings of the Human Language Technology Conference of the NAACL, Main Conference*, New York City, USA, pp. 152–159. Association for Computational Linguistics.

McGrath, M. (2014). Propositions. In E. N. Zalta (Ed.), *The Stanford Encyclopedia of Philosophy* (Spring 2014 ed.). Metaphysics Research Lab, Stanford University.

Mikolov, T., I. Sutskever, K. Chen, G. S. Corrado, and J. Dean (2013). Distributed representations of words and phrases and their compositionality. In C. J. C. Burges, L. Bottou, M. Welling, Z. Ghahramani, and K. Q. Weinberger (Eds.), *Advances in Neural Information Processing Systems 26*, pp. 3111–3119. Curran Associates, Inc.

Napoles, C., M. Gormley, and B. Van Durme (2012). Annotated gigaword. In *Proceedings of the Joint Workshop on Automatic Knowledge Base Construction and Web-scale Knowledge Extraction*, pp. 95–100. Association for Computational Linguistics.

Sennrich, R., B. Haddow, and A. Birch (2016). Neural machine translation of rare words with subword units. In *Proceedings of the 54th Annual Meeting of the Association for Computational Linguistics (Volume 1: Long Papers)*, pp. 1715–1725. Association for Computational Linguistics.

Sutskever, I., O. Vinyals, and Q. V. Le (2014). Sequence to sequence learning with neural networks. In Z. Ghahramani, M. Welling, C. Cortes, N. D. Lawrence, and K. Q. Weinberger (Eds.), *Advances in Neural Information Processing Systems 27*, pp. 3104–3112. Curran Associates, Inc.

Vinyals, O., L. u. Kaiser, T. Koo, S. Petrov, I. Sutskever, and G. Hinton (2015). Grammar as a foreign language. In C. Cortes, N. D. Lawrence, D. D. Lee, M. Sugiyama, and R. Garnett (Eds.), *Advances in Neural Information Processing Systems 28*, pp. 2773–2781. Curran Associates, Inc.

Zhou, J. and W. Xu (2015, July). End-to-end learning of semantic role labeling using recurrent neural networks. In *Proceedings of the 53rd Annual Meeting of the Association for Computational Linguistics and the 7th International Joint Conference on Natural Language Processing (Volume 1: Long Papers)*, Beijing, China, pp. 1127–1137. Association for Computational Linguistics.

Handling Multiword Expressions in Causality Estimation

Shota Sasaki, Sho Takase, Naoya Inoue, Naoaki Okazaki, Kentaro Inui
Tohoku University
{sasaki.shota, naoya-i, okazaki, inui}@ecei.tohoku.ac.jp
takase.sho@lab.ntt.co.jp

Abstract

Previous studies on causality estimation mainly aquire causal event pairs from a large corpus based on lexico-syntactic patterns and coreference relations, and estimate causality by a statistical method. However, most of the previous studies assume event pairs can be represented by a pair of single words, therefore they cannot estimate multiword causality correctly (e.g."tired"-"give up"). In this paper, we create a list of multiword expressions and extend an existing method. Our evaluation demonstrates that the proper treatment of multiword expression events is effective and the proposed method outperforms the state-of-the-art causality estimation model.

1 Introduction

This paper addresses *causality estimation*, the task of estimating the strength of causality between two sentences. For example, consider the following two sentences:

(1) a. John was tired of the customer service.
    b. John gave up using the product.

The task is to estimate that sentence (1a) is more causally related to sentence (1b) than non-causally related sentences such as "John opened a door.". Causality estimation is considered as an essential component of common sense reasoning.

A conventional approach to causality estimation is to construct a statistical model of causality relying on a large corpus in a semi-supervised manner. The main idea is two-fold: (i) collect causally related *word pairs* (e.g. *typhoon-die*) by exploiting the contextual proximity or discourse markers and (ii) apply them to a correlation measure (Chambers and Jurafsky, 2008; Luo et al., 2016) or a supervised classifier (Riaz and Girju, 2014; Granroth-Wilding and Clark, 2016).

A key limitation of the previous studies is that they model causality in terms of *word pairs*, not taking into account the causality represented by multiword expressions. For example, in example (1), a causality estimation model is expected to consider the causality between *tired* and *gave up* (i.e. *stop something*). However, the previous models consider only word pairs; therefore, it would improperly estimate the causality based on word pairs such as *tired-give* and *tired-up*. Because each individual word in multiword expressions might have a completely different meaning from the whole, it is crucial to solve this problem.

To address the above issue, this paper proposes a method that can estimate the causality between events represented by multiword expressions. Specifically, we obtained the list of multiword expressions from Wiktionary[1] to acquire the causality of multiword expressions from a corpus. Our experiments demonstrate that the proposed method outperforms the state-of-the-art method on Choice of Plausible Alternatives (COPA) (Roemmele et al., 2011), which can be regarded as a variant of causality estimation.

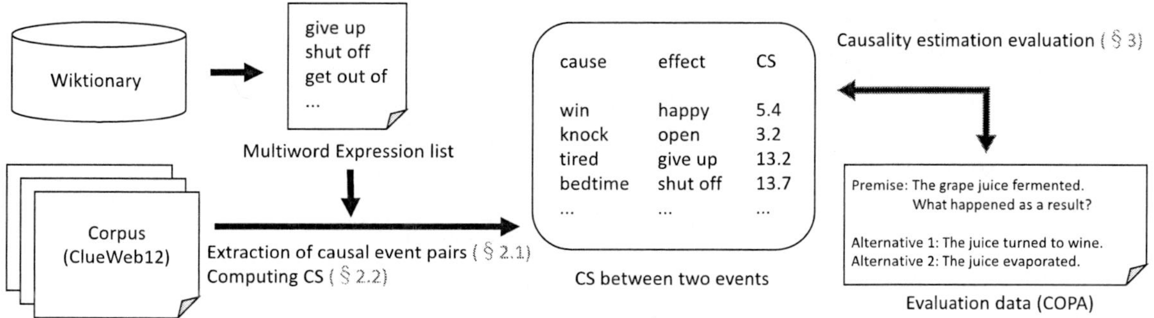

Figure 1: An overview of the proposed method.

2 Proposed Method

Following Luo et al. (2016), we extract a pair of causal events from a corpus by using causal markers (e.g. "B because A"), and model the strength of causality by using *Causal Strength* as a statistical measure. During the extraction of causal event pairs, the proposed method considers a multiword expression as a unit of an event as well as a single word. Figure 1 illustrates an overview of the proposed method.

2.1 Extraction of Causal Event Pairs

Considering that a template-matching approach is relatively successful in causality estimation (Luo et al., 2016), we first extract sentences matching a predefined template from a corpus. A template consists of a causal marker and two slots A, B, where A, B indicates cause and effect, respectively (e.g. "B because A"). This study uses the list of templates provided by Luo et al. (2016).

Suppose that the following sentence is matched with a template "Because A, B":

(2) [Because] <u>John was tired of the customer service</u>$_A$, <u>John gave up using the product</u>$_B$.

From each slot, we extract nouns, verbs, adjectives and adverbs defined in WordNet (Fellbaum, 1998)[2]. In the sentence above, this yields {tired, customer, service} from A and {give, up, use, product} from B. Finally, we take the Cartesian product of these two sets, which yields the causal word pairs such as (tired_c, give_e), (tired_c, up_e) and (tired_c, use_e), to obtain all possible pairs of cause and effect words.

As exemplified above, most of the previous studies including Luo et al. (2016) assume that any events can be represented by a single word, measuring associations on word pairs. However, this assumption does not hold for causality represented by multiword expressions (e.g. "give up" in the above example). To identify events represented by multiword expressions correctly, we make a list of multiword expressions from Wiktionary[3], a publicly available dictionary edited by Wiktionary community members. In this study, we focus only on multiword predicates (MWPs), predicates consisting of multiple words (e.g., "give up"). To create the list of MWPs, we extracted 33,274 verb Wiktionary entries whose titles consist of two or three words. By using this list, we acquire a causal event pair represented by multiword expressions (e.g. (tired_c, give up_e)) in addition to single-word event pairs (e.g. (tired_c, give_e) and (tired_c, up_e)).

2.2 Causal Strength

After extracting causal event pairs, we estimate causality between events. In this paper, we use *Causal Strength* (henceforth, CS) proposed by Luo et al. (2016). Causal Strength is similar to pointwise mutual information (PMI) but more superior in modeling causality, combining two factors: the necessary factor

---

[1] https://en.wiktionary.org/

[2] During the extraction, all words are lemmatized and lowercased.

[3] https://en.wiktionary.org/wiki/Wiktionary:Main_Page

and the sufficient factor. Formally, for a causal event i_c and a effect event j_e, the two factors are defined by the following equations:

$$\mathrm{CS}_{\mathrm{nec}}(i_c, j_e) = \frac{p(i_c|j_e)}{p^\alpha(i_c)} = \frac{p(i_c, i_e)}{p^\alpha(i_c)p(j_e)}, \tag{1}$$

$$\mathrm{CS}_{\mathrm{suf}}(i_c, j_e) = \frac{p(j_e|i_c)}{p^\alpha(j_e)} = \frac{p(i_c, i_e)}{p(i_c)p^\alpha(j_e)}, \tag{2}$$

where $\mathrm{CS}_{\mathrm{nec}}(i_c, j_e)$ is the necessary factor, $\mathrm{CS}_{\mathrm{suf}}(i_c, j_e)$ is the sufficient factor, and α is a hyper-parameter. We set $\alpha = 0.66$, the same value as Luo et al. (2016); Wettler and Rapp (1993). By using $\mathrm{CS}_{\mathrm{nec}}(i_c, j_e)$ and $\mathrm{CS}_{\mathrm{suf}}(i_c, j_e)$, Causal Strength is defined as,

$$\mathrm{CS}(i_c, j_e) = \mathrm{CS}_{\mathrm{nec}}(i_c, j_e)^\lambda \mathrm{CS}_{\mathrm{suf}}(i_c, j_e)^{1-\lambda}, \tag{3}$$

where λ is a hyper-parameter.

3 Experiment

To examine the necessity of proper treatment of multiword expressions, we compare the proposed method against existing causality estimation models, and conduct an ablation study.

3.1 Dataset

To extract causal event pairs, we used the ClueWeb12[4], a large-scale corpus consisting of 700 million documents crawled from the Web. We evaluated the proposed method on the task of Choice of Plausible Alternatives (COPA) (Roemmele et al., 2011), which is a widely-used benchmark of commonsense-reasoning models. Each COPA problem consists of a *premise* sentence and two *alternative* sentences as follows:

> **Premise:** The grape juice fermented. *What happened as a result?*
> **Alternative 1:** The juice turned to wine.
> **Alternative 2:** The juice evaporated.

The task is to choose the most plausible alternative as either the cause or effect of the given premise (e.g. Alternative 1 in the above example). For our evaluation, we used the publicly available COPA dataset[5], which consists of 500 development and 500 test problems.

3.2 Settings

We evaluate the proposed model against four existing baseline models: (i) "Random", a random baseline model, (ii) "PMI" (Roemmele et al., 2011), modeling the causality between two word pairs in terms of their co-occurrences within a particular window-size on Project Gutenberg corpus[6], (iii) "PMI-EX" (Gordon et al., 2011), the improved version of PMI using millions of personal stories extracted from the Weblogs and (iv) "CS w/o MWP" (Luo et al., 2016), the state-of-the-art system of COPA that achieved an accuracy of 70.2%.

We use Stanford CoreNLP (Manning et al., 2014) for POS tagging and lemmatization. The hyper-parameter λ in the Causal Strength method is tuned from 0.0 to 1.0 in increments of 0.1 on the development set; see Table 1 for the actual values used in this experiment.

Cause   John was tired of the customer service.

Effect   John gave up using the product.

Causal event pairs

3.21 (tired_c, give_e)
2.25 (tired_c, up_e)
13.2 (tired_c, give_up_e)
...

Figure 2: The outline of causality estimation between two sentences.

Table 1: Results of COPA evaluation.

Method	Corpus	Accuracy (%)
Random		50.0
PM I (Roemmele et al., 2011)	Project Gutenberg	58.8
PMI-EX (Gordon et al., 2011)	Personal stories	65.4
CS w/o $\text{MWP}_{\lambda=1.0}$ (Luo et al., 2016)	Causal Net	70.2
CS w/o $\text{MWP}_{\lambda=0.8}$	ClueWeb12	69.9
CS w/ $\text{MWP}_{\lambda=0.7}$	ClueWeb12	**71.2**

3.3 Estimating Causality between Sentences

Let S_c and S_e be a sentence describing cause and effect, respectively. We first pre-process the sentences by lemmatization and removal of stop words[7], and then extract content words (nouns, verbs, adjectives and adverbs included in WordNet (Fellbaum, 1998))[8] from the sentences. As in the extraction of causal word pairs (see Sec. 2.1), the proposed method extracts a multiword expression as a single word if it is found in the list of multiword expressions. Let $W(S)$ be the words extracted from S by this procedure. The causality score between S_c and S_e is then calculated as,

$$\text{Score}(S_c, S_e) = \frac{1}{|W(S_c)||W(S_e)|} \sum_{w_i \in W(S_c)} \sum_{w_j \in W(S_e)} \text{CS}(w_i, w_j). \tag{4}$$

For example, in Figure 2, $W(S_c) = \{\text{tired, customer, service}\}$ and $W(S_e) = \{\text{give, up, give\_up, use, product}\}$ hold; therefore, $\text{Score}(S_c, S_e)$ is given by $(3.21 + 2.25 + 13.2 + ...)/(3 \cdot 5)$.

To solve a COPA problem, given a premise P and two alternatives A_1, A_2, we identify the most plausible alternative as A_i that maximizes $\text{Score}(P, A_i)$ for effect questions; $\text{Score}(A_i, P)$ for cause questions.

3.4 Results and Discussion

Table 1 shows the accuracy of the proposed model against the baselines on the 500 COPA test problems. The results indicate that the proposed method ("CS w/ MWP") outperformed the other existing models including CS, the state-of-the-art model of COPA (Luo et al., 2016) (by 1.0%). To see the effectiveness of the proper treatment of multiword-expression events, we also evaluated the proposed model without using the list of multiword expressions ("CS w/o MWP"). The results indicate that the proper treatment of multiword expression events significantly improves the accuracy of causality estimation (by 1.3%).

We manually analyzed how the proposed method improves the CS score on the COPA problems. The analysis revealed that the proper treatment of multiword expression events indeed rectifies the calculation of CS score in some COPA problems. For instance, consider the following problem:

---

[4]http://lemurproject.org/clueweb12/index.php
[5]http://people.ict.usc.edu/~gordon/copa.html
[6]http://www.gutenberg.org
[7]We used the list of stop words defined in Natural Language Toolkit: http://www.nltk.org/
[8]In addition, top-10 frequent words in a corpus are excluded (personal communication).

Premise: The father *shut off* the children's television. *What was the cause of this?*
Alternative 1: It was bedtime for the children.
Alternative 2: The children were watching cartoons.

In the premise, the multiword expression *shut off* represents an event of *to turn off*. However, each individual word, e.g. *shut* standing for *to close*, has a completely different meaning from the whole *shut off*. In this problem, the proposed model successfully estimates CS(bedtime$_c$, shut off$_e$)=13.7 as opposed to CS(bedtime$_c$, shut$_e$)=1.88. This indicates that the proposed model captures the causality represented by a multiword expression properly, i.e. the causality between "to shut off (electricity)" and "bedtime". Other such examples include (i) CS(wait$_c$, take a seat$_e$)=12.9 (c.f. CS(wait$_c$, take$_e$)=3.28, CS(wait$_c$, seat$_e$)=2.38) and (ii) CS(think$_c$, come up with$_e$)=5.23 (c.f. CS(think$_c$, come$_e$)=4.02).

To evaluate how well the proposed system identifies multiword expressions, we randomly extracted 50 multiword expressions identified by the system from the development set. The analysis of these instances reveals that 18.0% (9/50) of them were incorrectly recognized, where one typical error is exemplified by *jog on* in *"I jogged on the treadmill."*: *jogged on* standing for *jogging* here, is incorrectly identified as the idiom *jog on* standing for *"to continue with one's pursuit"*. To understand the potential effect of multiword expressions, we manually crafted the list of multiword expressions that are needed for solving the COPA test questions. The maximum accuracy[9] of the oracle system using the manually-crafted list was 71.0%, which suggests that the proposed method achieved almost equal score to the oracle score.

To gain further insights, we analyzed the remaining 82.0% (41/50) of correctly recognized multiword expressions. It reveals that proper causality estimation often requires the system to expand an event unit to another word as well as to recognize a multiword expression; for instance, when the causality between *"The stain came out of the shirt."* and *"I bleached the shirt"* is estimated, *stain come out*, rather than *come out*, is more appropriate as an event unit. Extending an event unit beyond a multiword expression would impose a severe data sparseness problem, which is to be addressed in our future work.

4   Related Work

Previous studies proposed a wide variety of approaches to causality estimation (Do et al., 2011; Kozareva, 2012; Riaz and Girju, 2014). Do et al. (2011) employed statistical measures such as PMI and inverse document frequency (IDF) from a corpus to model causality between events. Kozareva (2012) applied a bootstrap algorithm to acquire causal event pairs. Riaz and Girju (2014) extracted training data from FrameNet (Baker et al., 1998) to learn a classifier for a causal relation. However, these studies assume that an event is representable by a single word. Chambers and Jurafsky (2008)'s *Narrative Schema* uses a predicate-argument structure as an event unit, but a predicate is restricted to a single word.

Roemmele et al. (2011) introduced a baseline model of COPA that uses PMI between words on English documents in Project Gutenberg. Gordon et al. (2011) improved the baseline model introduced by Roemmele et al. (2011) by using personal stories extracted from Weblogs instead of Project Gutenberg. Luo et al. (2016) refined PMI to capture causality between events more accurately. In this paper, we employed the statistical measure proposed by Luo et al. (2016) because they achieved the state-of-the-art performance on the COPA dataset.

5   Conclusion

In this paper, we created the list of multiword expressions from Wiktionary, and proposed a method to capture causality of multiword expressions by extending the existing causality estimation model. We demonstrated the effectiveness of using a multiword expression list, reporting a new state-of-the-art

---

[9]We report a maximum accuracy because the manually created MWP list is specific to the test set and hence prevents us from tuning the hyper-parameter in the development set.

performance on COPA. Our future work include using a combination of a predicate and an object as a unit of a causal event.

References

Baker, C. F., C. J. Fillmore, and J. B. Lowe (1998). The berkeley framenet project. In *Proceedings of the 36th Annual Meeting of the Association for Computational Linguistics and 17th International Conference on Computational Linguistics, Volume 1*, pp. 86–90. Association for Computational Linguistics.

Chambers, N. and D. Jurafsky (2008). Unsupervised learning of narrative event chains. In *Proceedings of ACL-08: HLT*, pp. 789–797. Association for Computational Linguistics.

Do, Q., Y. S. Chan, and D. Roth (2011). Minimally supervised event causality identification. In *Proceedings of the 2011 Conference on Empirical Methods in Natural Language Processing*, pp. 294–303. Association for Computational Linguistics.

Fellbaum, C. (1998). *WordNet: An Electronic Lexical Database. Bradford Books.* MIT Press.

Gordon, A. S., C. A. Bejan, and K. Sagae (2011). Commonsense causal reasoning using millions of personal stories. In *Proceedings of the Twenty-Fifth AAAI Conference on Artificial Intelligence*, pp. 1180–1185. AAAI Press.

Granroth-Wilding, M. and S. Clark (2016). What happens next? event prediction using a compositional neural network model. In *Proceedings of the Thirtieth AAAI Conference on Artificial Intelligence*, pp. 2727–2733. AAAI Press.

Kozareva, Z. (2012). Cause-effect relation learning. In *Workshop Proceedings of TextGraphs-7: Graph-based Methods for Natural Language Processing*, pp. 39–43. Association for Computational Linguistics.

Luo, Z., Y. Sha, K. Q. Zhu, S. won Hwang, and Z. Wang (2016). Commonsense causal reasoning between short texts. In *Proceedings of the Fifteenth International Conference on Principles of Knowledge Representation and Reasoning*, pp. 421–430. AAAI press.

Manning, C., M. Surdeanu, J. Bauer, J. Finkel, S. Bethard, and D. McClosky (2014). The stanford corenlp natural language processing toolkit. In *Proceedings of 52nd Annual Meeting of the Association for Computational Linguistics: System Demonstrations*, pp. 55–60. Association for Computational Linguistics.

Riaz, M. and R. Girju (2014). Recognizing causality in verb-noun pairs via noun and verb semantics. In *Proceedings of the EACL 2014 Workshop on Computational Approaches to Causality in Language (CAtoCL)*, pp. 48–57. Association for Computational Linguistics.

Roemmele, M., C. A. Bejan, and A. S. Gordon (2011). Choice of plausible alternatives: An evaluation of commonsense causal reasoning. In *AAAI Spring Symposium: Logical Formalizations of Commonsense Reasoning*.

Wettler, M. and R. Rapp (1993). Computation of word associations based on the co-occurrences of words in large corpora. In *Proceedings of the 1st Workshop on Very Large Corpora*. Association for Computational Linguistics.

Vision and Language Integration: Moving beyond Objects

Ravi Shekhar, Sandro Pezzelle, Aurélie Herbelot,
Moin Nabi, Enver Sangineto, Raffaella Bernardi
University of Trento, Trento, Italy
{firstname.lastname}@unitn.it

Abstract

The last years have seen an explosion of work on the integration of vision and language data. New tasks like Image Captioning and Visual Questions Answering have been proposed and impressive results have been achieved. There is now a shared desire to gain an in-depth understanding of the strengths and weaknesses of those models. To this end, several datasets have been proposed to try and challenge the state-of-the-art. Those datasets, however, mostly focus on the interpretation of *objects* (as denoted by nouns in the corresponding captions). In this paper, we reuse a previously proposed methodology to evaluate the ability of current systems to move beyond objects and deal with attributes (as denoted by adjectives), actions (verbs), manner (adverbs) and spatial relations (prepositions). We show that the coarse representations given by current approaches are not informative enough to interpret attributes or actions, whilst spatial relations somewhat fare better, but only in attention models.

1 Introduction

Nouns are a crucial component of natural language sentences. It is not a coincidence that children first learn to use nouns and only afterwords expand their vocabulary with verbs, adjectives and other parts of speech (Waxman et al., 2013). Interestingly, the same development has taken place with Language and Vision models. Object classification has long been the main concern of the computer vision field, only then followed by action classification shared tasks. Recently, more ambitious competitions have been proposed, aiming to evaluate models' ability to connect whole sentences to images, through both Image Captioning (IC) or Visual Question Answering (VQA) tasks. Progress in this area has seemed swift and impressive, but the community is now scrutinising the results to understand whether enthusiasm is warranted. Several diagnostic datasets have been proposed with this goal in mind, highlighting various flaws in existing tasks (Johnson et al., 2017; Zhang et al., 2015). Our paper is a contribution to these efforts, showing that the field may have moved too fast from noun to sentence interpretation, overlooking difficulties in understanding other parts-of-speech.

Our paper expands the existing FOIL dataset (Shekhar et al., 2017). FOIL consists of a set of images matched with captions containing one single mistake. The mistakes are always nouns referring to objects not actually present in the image. The work demonstrates that the language and vision modalities are not truly integrated in current computational models, as they fail to spot the mistake in the caption and to correct it appropriately (humans, on the other hand, obtain almost 100% accuracy on those tasks). In the present paper, we exploit the FOIL strategy to evaluate Language and Vision models on a larger set of possible mismatches between language and vision. Beside considering nouns as possible 'foil' words, we also consider verbs, adjectives, adverbs and prepositions, as illustrated in Figure 1. The results obtained by state-of-the-art systems on this data demonstrate that current models are indeed little able to move beyond object understanding.[1]

---

[1] The data will be made available at: https://foilunitn.github.io/.

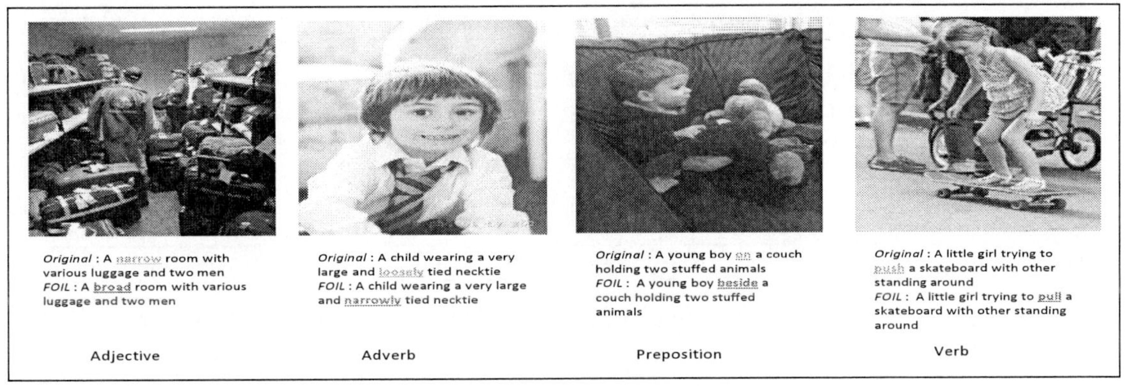

Figure 1: Sample image, corresponding original caption and the generated foil caption for the different parts of speech. The model has to be able to classify the caption as 'correct' or 'foil' (Task 1); detect the foil word in the foil caption (see words highlighted in red) (Task 2); and correct the foil word with an appropriate replacement (see words highlighted in green) (Task 3).

2 The FOIL methodology

We follow the methodology highlighted in Shekhar et al. (2017), which consists of replacing a single word in a human-generated caption with a 'foil' item, making the caption unsuitable to describe the original image. Given such replacements, the system should be able to perform three tasks: a) a *classification task* (T1): given an image and a caption, the model has to predict whether the caption is correct or inappropriate for the image (evaluating whether the model has a coarse understanding of the linguistic and visual inputs and their relations); b) a *foil word detection task* (T2): given an image and a foil caption, detect the foil word in the caption (evaluating whether the model reaches a fine-grained representation of the linguistic input); a *foil word correction task* (T3): given an image, a foil caption and the foil word, the model has to correct the mistake (verifying whether the model reaches a fine-grained representation of the image). Four models are tested on tasks 1-3: one baseline (a 'blind' model), and three state-of-the-art models from the Visual Question Answering (VQA) and Image Captioning (IC) literature.

Blind Model: this model is based on the caption only; in other words, the system does not have access to the visual data. The caption is modelled by an LSTM, fully connected to a hidden layer followed by a softmax to perform the classification. This blind baseline affords an evaluation of the 'language bias' of the data (i.e., the phenomenon by which a Language and Vision dataset can be suitably modelled using language only).

Discriminative VQA Models: two VQA models are used, namely the *LSTM + norm I* of Antol et al. (2015) and the Hierarchical Co-Attention model (*HieCoAtt*) of Lu et al. (2016). In *LSTM + norm I*, the text is represented by two stacked LSTMs and the image is represented by a normalisation of the last fully connected layer of VGG network (Simonyan and Zisserman, 2014). Both representations are projected onto a 1024-dimensional feature space. The combination of language and vision features is performed by point-wise multiplication followed by a fully connected and a softmax layer. *HieCoAtt* has a similar architecture, with the addition of an attention layer. Attention is provided to both image and text in alternation, in a hierarchical fashion.

Generative IC Model: we use the IC system of Wang et al. (2016) (henceforth, *IC-Wang*), which generates a word in a caption by considering both past and future contexts, using a bi-directional LSTM. *IC-Wang* consists of three modules: a CNN to encode the image, a text LSTM to encode captions, and a multimodal LSTM for mapping visual and text representations to a common space.

For T1, the models are directly trained to classify a given caption as 'good' vs. 'foil'. For T2 and T3, the model trained on T1 is adopted. For T2, we subsequently occlude one word (Goyal et al. (2016)) at a time and calculate the probability of the new caption to be good vs. foil. The model selects as foil word, the one which has generated the caption with the highest probability. For T3, we regress over all

	no. of unique images		no. of unique datapoints		no. of unique target::foil pairs	
	Train	Test	Train	Test	Train	Test
Noun*	22,101	15,435	73,076	37,381	236	194
Verb	6314	2788	7925	3353	268	219
Adjective	15,640	9009	20,720	11,900	80	62
Adverb	1011	451	1044	475	38	36
Preposition	8733	5551	24,665	15,755	101	89
TOT	22,101	15,435	127,430	68,864	723	600

Table 1: Statistics of the dataset. Here Noun* is a subset of FOIL-COCO used in Shekhar et al. (2017).

the target words on the position of the foil word and select the one which generates the caption with the highest probability to be "good". Due to the generative nature of IC models, adapting *IC-Wang* for the classification purpose is less straightforward. For T1, we generate all possible captions by subsequently predicting one word at a time provided all other words in the caption and the image. We compare the probability of these generated captions with the given caption. When the test caption probability is higher than generated captions probabilities, we classify the given caption as good caption, else as foil caption.

3 Dataset Creation

Following Shekhar et al. (2017), we aim at creating a dataset of images associated with both correct and foil captions, where the latter are obtained by replacing one word in the original text. Expanding on the original paper, our target/foil pairs do not merely consist of nouns. The introduced error can also be an adjective (an object's attribute), a verb (an action), a preposition (a relation between objects) or an adverb (a manner of action). In total, we produce 196,284 datapoints, each corresponding to an <image, original, foil> triple. The starting point for images and correct captions is Microsoft's Common Objects in Context (MS-COCO)(Lin et al. (2014)).

3.1 Creating new target/foil pairs

We describe below our procedure to expand the original dataset with new parts-of-speech.

Verbs: We use three resources: a) VerbOcean, a semi-automatically generated broad-coverage semantic network of verbs extracted from the Web by exploiting a pattern-based approach (Chklovski and Pantel (2004)); b) Computing Lexical Contrast (CLC), a resource of contrasting words selected from direct and indirect WordNet opposites, (Mohammad et al. (2013)); c) SimLex999, a set of related word pairs rated with respect to their similarity (Hill et al. (2016)). From VerbOcean and CLC, we extract all antonyms (e.g., *pull-push*). From SimLex999, we select those pairs with a similarity score lower than the average in the database (e.g., *allowing- preventing*). We end up with 902, 44, and 30 verb pairs from VerbOcean, CLC and SimLex999 respectively.

Adjectives and adverbs: As in the verb case, we use antonyms from CLC and we select pairs from SimLex999 which have a similarity score lower than average. We extract 46 and 127 adjectives pairs from CLC and SimLex999 respectively. All adverbial pairs come from CLC, and amount to 52 datapoints.

Prepositions: We extract prepositions from Berry et al. (1995), divided into three classes: place (e.g., *under*, *below*), direction (e.g., *inside*, *outside*) and device (e.g., *by*, *with*). Using these prepositions, we generate target/foil pairs by coupling prepositions which belong to the same class. We obtain a total of 206 pairs (110, 90 and 6 for place, direction and device respectively).

Nouns: The target/foil noun pairs are built using words that belong to the same category in MS-COCO (e.g., *bird/dog*, from the MS-COCO category ANIMAL). In order to obtain a balanced dataset across the various PoS, we only use a subset of the FOIL-COCO dataset of Shekhar et al. (2017). From

Table 2: Classification Task (T1). Overall (both original and foil captions) accuracy. Chance level 50%.

	Noun	Verb	Adjective	Adverb	Preposition	Total
Blind	57.39	77.90	83.10	54.62	70.88	75.48
LSTM + norm I	63.17	78.37	83.81	**55.84**	73.70	77.11
HieCoAtt	**64.46**	**81.79**	**86.00**	53.40	**74.91**	**79.09**
IC-Wang	47.59	34.93	28.67	44.92	32.68	31.58

the FOIL dataset, we retain the 37,536 images for which foil captions could be generated, using the target/foil pairs extracted from the resources mentioned above. Of the FOIL datapoints generated for the noun pairs, only those containing images used for the other PoS are selected. Hence, the number of unique images of the whole dataset is the same of those used for nouns (see Table 1 for details of the train/test set division.)

We use all word pairs in both directions (e.g. replacing *push* with *pull* and *pull* with *push*). We only use pairs for which target and foil are found in the original captions. This ensures that the model will not learn to recognise a foil caption simply by recording the presence of an unknown word. From each resource, we randomly split the target/foil pairs into training and test sets. The number of unique pairs per PoS is provided in Table 1.

3.2 Foil Caption Generation

From the word pair lists above, foil captions are generated from MS-COCO original captions. The foil captions are generated by replacing nouns are directly extracted from the FOIL dataset by Shekhar et al. (2017). In this case, for each original MS-COCO caption, several foil ones are generated and subsequently filtered using several heuristics. The aim of filtering is to prioritise salient objects in the image, and to minimise the language bias in the data. Ideally, these filters would have to be applied also for the generation of the foil caption for the other PoS, but we found that they reduced the size of our data in an unacceptably small size. As a consequence, the results we report are obviously affected by the language bias, as shown by the reasonable performance of a 'blind' model without access to visual data. However, as we will see, our broad claim is not affected by this heightened baseline. Details on the number of the unique images and of of datapoints generated for each PoS are reported in Table 1.

4   Experiments and Results

4.1   Results and Analysis

Table 2 reports the accuracy of the various models described in §2 for Task T1. The blind model's accuracy is well above chance level for all PoS, with lower results observed on the captions generated by noun and adverb replacement. Recall that for nouns, the language prior has been minimised, whereas the datapoints generated with verb, adjective and preposition replacements have some language prior that the models can exploit. The comparatively low performance on adverbs may be explained by the fact that all generated target/foil pairs are antonyms which behave very similarly from a distributional point of view (e.g. *upwards/downwards*, *partially/completely*, etc). *HieCoAtt* is the overall best performing model, but we note that it only outperforms the blind model by a few points. These numbers, however, do not show to which extent the models are able to avoid the trap of the dataset: Shekhar et al. (2017) showed that on the FOIL data, models tend to detect correct captions with reasonable accuracy but fail to identify the incorrect ones, leading to a large bias in classification. Taking this insight into account, for the rest of this paper, we focus on the accuracy of the systems in dealing with foil captions, across all three tasks.

Table 3: Classification Task (T1). Accuracy results of the foil captions only. Chance level 50%.

	Noun	Verb	Adjective	Adverb	Preposition
Blind	23.18	57.11	76.99	18.73	54.32
LSTM + norm I	36.17 (**+12.99**)	59.49 (+2.3)	77.48 (+0.49)	20.42 (+1.69)	57.53 (+3.21)
HieCoAtt	38.22 (**+15.04**)	57.94 (+0.83)	80.05 (+3.06)	14.73	61.92 (+7.6)
IC-Wang	43.32 (**+20.16**)	13.98	4.3	23.87 (+5.14)	21.43

Table 4: Foil Detection Task (T2) and Foil Correction Task (T3).

	Foil Detection Task (T2)					Foil Correction Task (T3)				
	Noun	Verb	Adj.	Adv.	Prep.	Noun	Verb	Adj.	Adv.	Prep.
Chance	23.25	**21.72**	**21.72**	**21.72**	21.72	1.38	0.22	2.04	2.04	4.34
LSTM + norm I	26.32	7.96	4.06	9.68	6.46	4.7	1.14	1.33	0.36	1.54
HieCoAttn	**38.79**	3.57	2.34	9.26	6.09	4.21	0.98	**2.48**	0.24	1.47
IC-Wang	27.59	8.67	9.23	12.56	**26.56**	**22.16**	**9.1**	1.61	**3.44**	**7.78**

As shown in Table 3, the blind model's accuracy is still reasonable on T1, but lower than chance for nouns and adverbs. In the case of nouns, the visual input helps obtaining a higher accuracy, whereas this is not the case for the other PoS. This could be due to the ability of vision models to 'see' objects but not their properties (adjectives) or relations (verbs, prepositions). It is a known shortcoming of such systems that they have difficulties in recognising anything that is not straightforwardly defined by a bounding box (Johnson et al. (2017)). *IC-Wang* performs very poorly on verbs, adjectives and prepositions, even though it is the best system for nouns. Other models improve minimally on the baseline, with prepositions getting the best improvement: +7% for *HieCoAtt*. When looking more in detail into this result, we observe that most instances in the preposition data indicate location: it is not surprising that an attention model would perform well on those, since it is trained to focus on particular areas of the image.

For task T2 (see Table 4), all models perform well under baseline on verbs, adjectives and adverbs. *IC-Wang* does however provide some improvement on prepositions. The reason for this may be that the system, being trained to generate sequences, has a better internal language model than other approaches. Whilst a good language model is unlikely to help in the case of content words, we can expect some benefits for function words. This trend has been observed in work on L2 error detection, where mistakes in words from closed classes are easier to spot and correct (Herbelot and Kochmar (2016)).

For task T3 (see Table 4), improvements over the baseline are minimal. *IC-Wang* performs best overall, but at a level well below its achievement on nouns. We do not only confirm that foil correction is hard, but that it is particularly challenging on parts-of-speech that represent attributes or relations. We note that *IC-Wang* improves more on prepositions than on adjectives and adverbs, confirming what was observed in T2 (i.e. closed classes are easier to deal with). But it also provides a good improvement on the verb baseline, which is puzzling given its inability to *spot* verb foils in T2.

5   Conclusion

Language and Vision integration has been studied in a fine-grained, but single-minded way, when focusing on objects (nouns). The level of events (sentences) has also received attention, but through coarse representations. Our work aims to highlight the importance of a fine-grained representation for all components of a sentence, including attributes and relations. Our results show that none of the current SoA models achieve this overall goal: attention models may have the right components to detect location (e.g., see locative prepositions), but some image captioning systems probably provide a better language model, in particular for closed-class words.

Acknowledgments

We gratefully acknowledge the support of NVIDIA Corporation with the donation of the GPUs used in our research.

References

Antol, S., A. Agrawal, J. Lu, M. Mitchell, D. Batra, C. L. Zitnick, and D. Parikh (2015). VQA: Visual Question Answering. In *International Conference on Computer Vision (ICCV)*. `https://github.com/VT-vision-lab/VQA_LSTM_CNN`.

Berry, C., A. Brizee, E. Angeli, and M. Ghafoor (1995). Prepositions for Time, Place, and Introducing Objects. `https://owl.english.purdue.edu/owl/owlprint/594/`.

Chklovski, T. and P. Pantel (2004). Verbocean: Mining the web for fine-grained semantic verb relations. In *EMNLP*, Volume 4, pp. 33–40.

Goyal, Y., A. Mohapatra, D. Parikh, and D. Batra (2016). Towards Transparent AI Systems: Interpreting Visual Question Answering Models . In *In Proceedings of ICML Visualization Workshop*.

Herbelot, A. and E. Kochmar (2016). Calling on the classical phone: a distributional model of adjective-noun errors in learners English. In *International Conference on Computational Linguistics (COLING)*.

Hill, F., R. Reichart, and A. Korhonen (2016). Simlex-999: Evaluating semantic models with (genuine) similarity estimation. *Computational Linguistics*.

Johnson, J., B. Hariharan, L. van der Maaten, L. Fei-Fei, C. L. Zitnick, and R. Girshick (2017). CLEVR: A Diagnostic Dataset for Compositional Language and Elementary Visual Reasoning. In *CVPR*.

Lin, T.-Y., M. Maire, S. Belongie, J. Hays, P. Perona, D. Ramanan, P. Dollár, and C. L. Zitnick (2014). Microsoft COCO: Common Objects in Context. In *European Conference on Computer Vision*, pp. 740–755. Springer.

Lu, J., J. Yang, D. Batra, and D. Parikh (2016). Hierarchical Question-Image Co-Attention for Visual Question Answering. In *Proceedings of NIPS 2016*. `https://github.com/jiasenlu/HieCoAttenVQA`.

Mohammad, S. M., B. J. Dorr, G. Hirst, and P. D. Turney (2013). Computing lexical contrast. *Computational Linguistics 39*(3), 555–590.

Shekhar, R., S. Pezzelle, Y. Klimovich, A. Herbelot, M. Nabi, E. Sangineto, and R. Bernardi (2017). FOIL it! Find One mismatch between Image and Language caption. In *ACL (to appear)*. https://arxiv.org/abs/1705.01359.

Simonyan, K. and A. Zisserman (2014). Very deep convolutional networks for large-scale image recognition. *arXiv preprint arXiv:1409.1556*.

Wang, C., H. Yang, C. Bartz, and C. Meinel (2016). Image captioning with deep bidirectional LSTMs. In *Proceedings of the 2016 ACM on Multimedia Conference*, pp. 988–997. ACM.

Waxman, S., X. Fu, S. Arunachalam, E. Leddon, K. Geraghty, and H. joo Song (2013). Are nouns learned before verbs? infants provide insight into a longstanding debate. *Child Dev Perspect 7*(3).

Zhang, P., Y. Goyal, D. Summers-Stay, D. Batra, and D. Parikh (2015). Yin and yang: Balancing and answering binary visual questions. *arXiv preprint arXiv:1511.05099*.

Can You See the (Linguistic) Difference?
Exploring Mass/Count Distinction in Vision

D. Addison Smith[1], Sandro Pezzelle[1],
Francesca Franzon[3], Chiara Zanini[4], Raffaella Bernardi[1,2]
[1]CIMeC, [2]DISI, University of Trento
[3]University of Padova
[4]University of Zürich
{first.last}@{unitn.it[1,2]|unipd.it[3]|uzh.ch[4]}

Abstract

This work explores the linguistic distinction between *count* and *mass* nouns in the visual modality. Since the former class typically refers to well-defined, countable objects, with the latter prototypically including less countable substances, we explore to which extent the linguistic distinction is grounded in the visual representations of the entities denoted by count/mass nouns. Using visual features extracted from a state-of-the-art Convolutional Neural Network (CNN), we show that the entities referred to as *mass* exhibit a lower variance both internally (i.e. intra-image) and externally (i.e. inter-image) compared to *count*. That is, various instances of substances are internally more homogeneous and externally more consistent to each other than are count. We compare variance across various CNN layers and show that it is indicative of the categorization when low-level features of the images are used, whereas any effect disappears when experimenting with higher-level, more abstract representations.

1 Introduction

The distinction between *mass* and *count* nouns is undoubtedly one of the most investigated topics in formal linguistics, at least since Cheng (1973) (see Fieder et al. (2014) for a brief review). At the simplest, descriptive level of analysis, mass nouns are usually paired with substances (e.g. water, flour, sand, etc.), cannot be inflected in plural form, and are preceded by indefinite determiners like 'some', 'much', 'a little', etc. In contrast, count nouns refer to isolable, well-defined objects (e.g. bicycle, house, tree, etc.), can take plural number, and are preceded by definite determiners like 'a/an', 'every', 'each', etc. Such a division is of course an oversimplification and leaves an uncertain zone in which semantic features do not map directly into morphosyntactic properties. In fact, nouns denoting the same referents may be used as mass in one language and as count in another (e.g. 'capelli' in Italian is countable, whereas 'hair' is mass). Moreover, nouns denoting aggregates like 'rice' or collections of semantically related objects such as 'furniture' or 'mail' may occur in mass contexts. While the status of these latter nouns is largely debated in literature (see Chierchia (1998); Doron and Müller (2010) for very opposite positions), substances in contrast are unanimously considered mass. Many theories have been proposed based either on the syntactic or the denotational aspects of the two groups (see among others Chomsky (1967); Allan (1980); Pelletier and Schubert (1989)). We do not enter into this debate and focus on a rather unexplored venue.

We investigate whether for the most prototypical cases, namely 'objects' for *count* and 'substances' for *mass*, the linguistic mass/count distinction is reflected in the perceptual properties of the referents. In support of a perceptual and conceptual, pre-linguistic difference between objects (usually denoted by count nouns in language) and substances (usually mass) are a number of studies reporting the ability of children to discriminate between them by relying solely on perceptual features of the entities, without using linguistic information (for a brief review see the introduction in Zanini et al. (2016)). To evaluate our hypothesis, we employ a computational model trained to classify objects in images. We test whether *mass-substance* images are internally (i.e. among the various regions of the same image) more homogeneous, and externally (i.e. among the various instances of the same entity) more consistent compared to entities denoted by count nouns (see Figure 1). In other words, 'substances' should be distinguished from 'objects' by means of the lower *variance* of their visual features (somewhat similar to Kiela et al. (2015) in a lexical entailment detection task). Though similar with respect to shape, entities denoted by count nouns are likely to be very different with respect to many other low-level visual features (surface, texture, color, etc.). As a consequence, they would require higher-level operations to be recognized and classified as belonging to a particular entity class.

Figure 1: Left: images representing the count noun 'building'. Right: images representing the mass noun 'flour'. As can be noted, the former exhibits much more variability compared to the latter, both internally (i.e. among regions of the same image) and externally (i.e. among different images of the same entity).

Notable works have advanced the understanding of the perceptual cues linked to material recognition (Sharan (2009); Sharan et al. (2014)). To our knowledge, the present study is the first attempt to investigate the mass/count distinction in vision as linked to a linguistic perspective, namely the relationship between visual features and a grammaticalized opposition attested in language. The motivation is indeed different from the group of studies taking into account the distinction between *things* and *stuff* in the computer vision community (Tighe and Lazebnik (2010, 2013); Mottaghi et al. (2014); Caesar et al. (2016)). Caesar et al. (2016), for example, recently proposed an enriched version of the popular COCO dataset (Lin et al. (2014)) containing pixel-level annotation for *stuff* in addition to the source annotation for *things*. In this resource, however, the *stuff* class does not align with the *mass* category defined linguistically. To illustrate, it contains nouns like 'mirror', 'door', 'table', 'tree', 'mountain', and 'house', which are *count* nouns from a linguistic perspective. As a consequence, using existing resources is not feasible for our purposes. To test our hypothesis, we thus collect images representing objects and substances by relying on an existing lexical resource where countability annotation is available for English nouns. We then extract visual features from various layers of a pretrained state-of-the-art Convolutional Neural Network (CNN) and compute intra-image (i.e. between the various regions of an image) and inter-image (i.e. between different images depicting the same entity) variance at each layer. We show that visual features extracted from images depicting mass nouns exhibit a significantly lower intra-image variance compared to those representing count nouns, when computed at the early layers of the network (encoding low-level visual features). That is, mass nouns refer to simpler, more homogeneous entities compared to the more varied representations of count nouns. Moreover, at the early layers mass nouns are also more consistent between instances of the same object compared to count (i.e. lower inter-image variance). Consistent with our expectations, any effect disappears when experimenting with higher-level visual features extracted from the last layers of the network.

2   Dataset

To obtain mass/count categorization of nouns, and more specifically categorization of their respective senses, the Bochum English Countability Lexicon (BECL) (Kiss et al. (2016)) is used. This resource maps synsets within WordNet (Miller (1995)) to their respective countability classes, with noun senses annotated as either *mass*, *count*, *both*, or *neither* based on a series of syntactic patterns. The annotation occurs at the sense level, and a given noun can therefore have various senses belonging to distinct countability classes. Since our intention is to approach the matter from a vision perspective, we first check how many of the labeled synsets are available within ImageNet (Deng et al. (2009)), with an additional requirement that the images have available bounding box annotations. Among the available synsets are 36 *mass*, 58 *both*, and a remarkable 686 *count*.[1] This could well be a byproduct of the fact that count nouns are seemingly easier to annotate with bounding boxes given that they are discrete instances and are more often present in the foreground of an image. For this reason it could also be argued that more pictures are taken of count objects in general, which could explain the synset availability bias within ImageNet with regard to mass/count nouns.

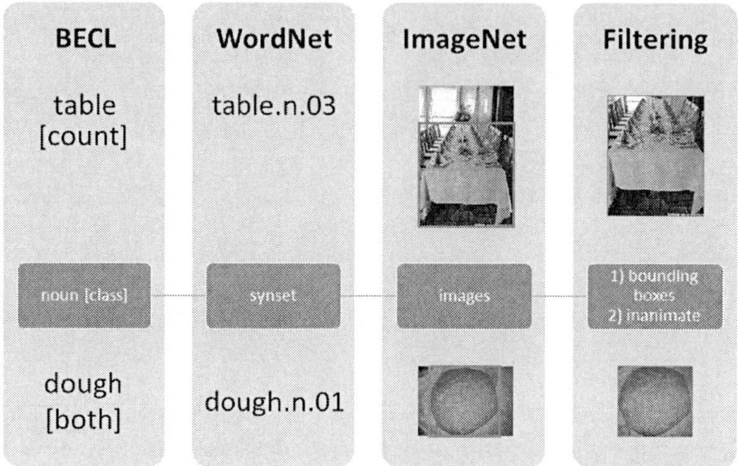

Figure 2: Various steps performed in building the dataset.

Investigation into the synsets annotated as *mass* reveals entities such as various sports ('soccer', 'basketball', etc.) whose corresponding images depict countable entities such as players or balls. We also encounter collective nouns such as 'equipment', 'furniture', 'luggage', 'housing', and 'artwork', which are merely collections of countable objects. The *both* category is therefore more suitable for our purposes given that the senses fit the prototypical idea of a mass noun as a substance. This *both* categorization in BECL is intuitive given that mass nouns can also be used in count contexts, i.e. 'two wines' which would refer either to two glasses (containers) of wine or perhaps to two different types of wine. In any case, nouns contained in this class ('flour', 'sugar', 'grain', etc.) are also viable from a vision perspective given their propensity for bounding box annotations. Since the *both* category captures mass-substance nouns, we henceforth refer to it simply as mass. Of these 58 mass noun senses none are animate, and so to avoid any possible confounding effects due to animacy we also constrain the countable objects to be inanimate, choosing the 58 most frequent where frequency is a BECL metric based on the Open American National Corpus (OANC). Images for the 58 + 58 synsets are downloaded and cropped according to bounding box annotations. Figure 2 illustrates the various steps followed to build the dataset, with descriptive statistics of the dataset reported in Table 1.

---

[1] We do not consider *neither* senses as they are very few and we do not find them useful for our purposes.

	#syns	#uniq_nouns	#imgs (avg)	#imgs (range)	OANC_freq (avg)	OANC_freq (range)
mass	58	56	214.66	64 - 705	112.6	10 - 447
count	58	53	303.93	60 - 1467	1435.16	33 - 4121

Table 1: Descriptive statistics of the dataset. From left to right, (1) number of synsets, (2) number of unique nouns among synsets, (3) average number of images per synset, (4) min, max number of images per synset, (5) average linguistic (OANC) frequency of the noun, (6) min, max frequency of the noun.

3 Experiments

To investigate the progression from the low-level, more concrete image features to the more abstract representations, we use a deep Convolutional Neural Network (CNN). This state-of-the-art CNN, namely the VGG-19 model (Simonyan and Zisserman (2014)), is pretrained on ImageNet ILSVRC data (Russakovsky et al. (2015)). VGG-19 consists of 5 blocks of convolutional layers (hence, *Conv*), each followed by a max pooling layer which extracts the most relevant features and hence reduces the dimensions of the feature vector. After the fifth convolutional block, 3 fully-connected layers (*fc*) are implemented. We evaluate 4 out of the 5 convolutional blocks (*Conv2-Conv5*) by extracting the outputs of the first and last layers for each block[2] and the output of the 3 fully-connected layers (*fc6*, *fc7*, and *fc8*). Convolutional layers are expected to capture low-level features (e.g. edges, texture, color, etc.) while the fully-connected layers compute abstract ones (see LeCun et al. (2015)). We check at which layer the *mass* and *count* synsets significantly differ with respect to their variance.

Figure 3: Toy representation of the two types of variance computed, i.e. *intra-* and *inter*-image.

Two types of variance are computed for all cropped images of a given synset: *intra*-vector (intra-image) variance and *inter*-vector (inter-image). See Figure 3 for a toy representation of both types of variance.

Intra-image After extracting and storing the feature vector for an image of a given synset at a given layer of the CNN, the variance of the feature vector is computed and subsequently averaged with the variances for all other images of the synset. This provides us with the mean *intra*-image variance, or the average variability within a single image of a given synset. This constitutes a measure of the relative homogeneity of the object, and picks up on the general complexity of the corresponding noun/sense.

Inter-image For the second type of variance, *inter*-vector variance, feature vectors for all images of a given synset are first extracted and stored from a given layer of the neural network. In this case, we calculate 'vertical' or column-wise variance among each individual dimension for all images of the synset, after which the dimension variances are averaged. This provides us with the *inter*-image variance, or the variability between distinct images of the same synset, which is a measure of the relative consistency

---

[2]Due to computational constraints, we do not consider the first *Conv1* block, which has approximately 3.2M dimensions.

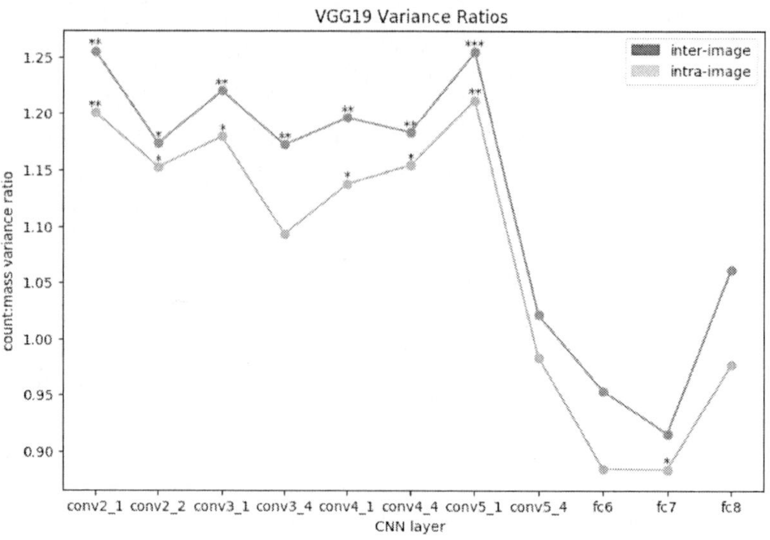

Figure 4: Difference between mass/count variance through the various layers of the network in both *intra-* (orange) and *inter-* (blue) settings. *** refers to a significant difference at p<.001, ** at p<.01, * at p<.05.

between instances of a given entity and its corresponding noun/sense.

Both types of variance are computed using the original, full-size vectors as extracted from the network.[3] That is, we do not employ any dimensionality reduction technique that could cause information loss affecting the variance values. To determine whether there is a significant difference between *mass* and *count* nouns, a two-tailed t-test is performed for each type of variance and for each layer of the CNN.

4   Results

We find both *intra*-image and *inter*-image variances to be significantly lower for *mass* nouns as compared to *count* nouns throughout all tested convolutional layers up until *Conv5_1*, with only one exception (*intra*-image variance in *Conv3_4*). From *Conv5_4*, in contrast, the difference becomes no longer significantly different, again with just one exception (*intra*-image variance in *fc7*).

Figure 4 shows this pattern of results obtained across the investigated layers. For visualization purposes, we plot the *ratio* between count and mass variance at each layer. As can be seen, this value is higher than 1 through the early layers, showing that count variance is higher than mass variance. Most importantly, within these layers (encoding low-level visual features) the difference in variance is overall very significant (as shown by the stars on the top of each 'node'). Throughout the convolutional blocks, the ratio indicating the difference between the two classes increases after the max pooling step is applied. This process ends at *Conv5_1*, when the more abstract visual features start to be computed by the network. Here, we observe quite a big drop in the count/mass ratio, showing that the two variances first become very similar and eventually 'change sign' (i.e. mass variance becomes higher than count). However, the difference in variance within these layers is generally not significant. Interestingly, at the last steps, especially at *fc8*, the ratio between the two variances stabilizes around 1, likely indicating that visual representations at this stage are abstract enough not to encode any information about the mass/count distinction. Zooming into the layers, *Conv5_1* turns out to be the layer where the difference in variance between mass/count synsets is highest for both settings (see Figure 5).

In Table 2 we report top-10 highest variance and bottom-10 lowest variance synsets obtained from

---

[3] Vector size ranges from 1.6M dimensions of *Conv2* to 1K dimensions of *fc8*.

Conv5_1 intra- variance		Conv5_1 inter- variance	
top-10	bottom-10	top-10	bottom-10
magazine_01 (c)	range_04 (c)	magazine_01 (c)	egg_yolk_01 (m)
salad_01 (m)	dough_01 (m)	shop_01 (c)	range_04 (c)
shop_01 (c)	mountain_01 (c)	salad_01 (m)	dough_01 (m)
church_02 (c)	mesa_01 (c)	machine_01 (c)	mountain_01 (c)
machine_01 (c)	flour_01 (m)	church_02 (c)	mesa_01 (c)
floor_02 (c)	milk_01 (m)	stage_03 (c)	milk_01 (m)
press_03 (c)	glacier_01 (m)	press_03 (c)	flour_01 (m)
stage_03 (c)	butter_01 (m)	floor_02 (c)	butter_01 (m)
pasta_01 (m)	egg_yolk_01 (m)	brunch_01 (m)	glacier_01 (m)
brunch_01 (m)	floor_04 (c)	building_01 (c)	sugar_01 (m)

Table 2: Synsets with highest (top-10) and lowest (bottom-10) variance in both *intra-* and *inter-* settings. Underlined synsets are those belonging to the lesser-represented class in a given column. The bottom-10 columns are presented starting from lowest variance and in ascending order.

this *Conv5_1* layer. As expected, most synsets in the top-10 columns belong to the count class (c), with synsets in the bottom-10 being mostly included in the mass class (m). Moreover, it can be noted that most of the synsets in the *intra-* setting also appear in the *inter-* setting, sometimes with an almost perfect alignment. Finally, by looking at the nouns that fall outside the expected pattern, we foresee some interesting cutting-edge cases (i.e. mass in top-10, count in bottom-10). 'Mountain' and 'range' (here with the sense of 'a series of hills or mountains'), for instance, are count nouns whose visual texture is intuitively homogeneous, as well as 'salad' and 'pasta' which are mass nouns referring to entities that consist *de facto* of many isolable parts, and thus vary more on average across instances.

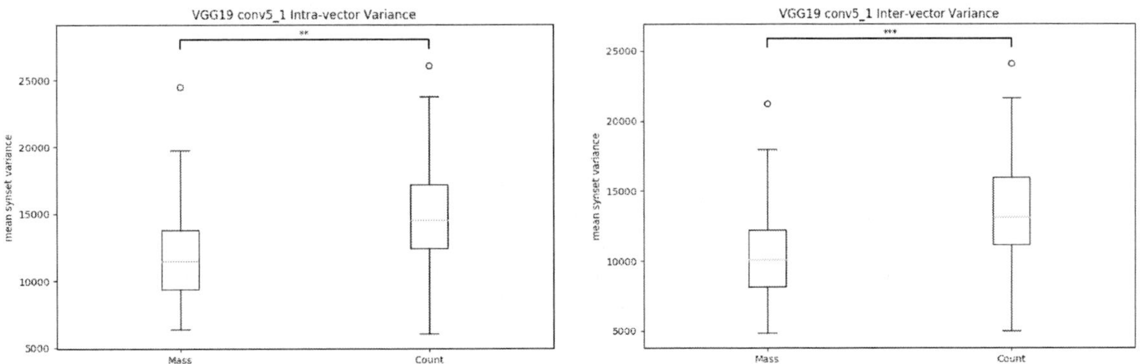

Figure 5: Boxplots reporting distribution of synset variance in both *intra-* (left) and *inter-* (right) setting for *Conv5_1* layer. Mass/count variance distribution is reliably different at p<.01 (left) and p<.001 (right).

5 Discussion

We show that mass-substance nouns have significantly lower intra- and inter-image variance than do count nouns, which is shown throughout the early convolutional layers of a state-of-the-art CNN. This could be useful in applications such as Visual Question Answering (VQA) or image caption generation, where a proper understanding of countability can lead to better responses and descriptions.

With that said, we can also see that there are cases which lie somewhere in the middle, exhibiting visual properties belonging to the opposing mass/count class. Interestingly, count nouns which are labeled as 'stuff' in the *things* vs. *stuff* distinction, namely 'mountain', 'door', etc. (see Introduction), are found to behave more like mass in our experiments. More in general, there seems to be a visual *continuum* ranging from mass-substance all the way to count nouns. Similarly, recent studies in linguistics point to the fact that the distribution of nouns with respect to their syntactic contexts of occurrence is not consistent with a dichotomist division of the lexicon in two clear-cut classes of 'mass' and 'count' nouns (Zanini et al. (2016)). Also, metalinguistic judgments collected in various languages point to an interpretation of mass and count nouns as poles of a continuous distribution (Kulkarni et al. (2013)). Further investigations on the relation between the visual features of referents and cross-linguistic features are thus desirable.

Finally, the outcome showing lower variance for mass nouns in the inter-image setting might seem surprising, given that count nouns should overall refer to more well-defined objects, and thus more consistent in shape. However, this pattern of results is confirmed by literature dealing with object recognition in humans (Cichy et al. (2016)), where it is proposed that shape is a somewhat higher-level cognitive feature. In fact, when perceiving the real world, each visual experience of an entity is almost unique, due to changes in things such as orientation, lighting, and distance. This lack of invariance does not obstruct object recognition in the human observer, but its mechanisms are yet to be fully understood (DiCarlo et al. (2012)).

Acknowledgments

We kindly acknowledge Raquel Fernandez, Angeliki Lazaridou, Roberto Zamparelli, and Marco Marelli for their valuable insights and feedback. We are grateful to the Erasmus Mundus European Master in Language and Communication Technologies (EM LCT) for the scholarship provided to the first author. Moreover, we gratefully acknowledge the support of NVIDIA Corporation with the donation of the GPUs used in our research.

References

Allan, K. (1980). Nouns and countability. *Language*, 541–567.

Caesar, H., J. Uijlings, and V. Ferrari (2016). COCO-Stuff: Thing and Stuff Classes in Context. *arXiv preprint arXiv:1612.03716.*

Cheng, C. Y. (1973). Response to Moravcsik. In J. Hintikka, J. M. E. Moravcsik, and P. Suppes (Eds.), *Approaches to Natural Language*, pp. 286–288. Dordrecht: Reidel.

Chierchia, G. (1998). Reference to kinds across language. *Natural language semantics* 6(4), 339–405.

Chomsky, N. (Ed.) (1967). *Aspects of the Theory of Syntax*. Cambridge. Mass: MIT Press.

Cichy, R. M., A. Khosla, D. Pantazis, A. Torralba, and A. Oliva (2016). Comparison of deep neural networks to spatio-temporal cortical dynamics of human visual object recognition reveals hierarchical correspondence. *Scientific reports 6.*

Deng, J., W. Dong, R. Socher, L.-J. Li, K. Li, and L. Fei-Fei (2009). Imagenet: A large-scale hierarchical image database. In *Computer Vision and Pattern Recognition, 2009. CVPR 2009. IEEE Conference on*, pp. 248–255. IEEE.

DiCarlo, J. J., D. Zoccolan, and N. C. Rust (2012). How does the brain solve visual object recognition? *Neuron 73*(3), 415–434.

Doron, E. and A. Müller (2010). The cognitive basis of the mass-count distinction: Evidence from bare nouns. *Abstract. The Hebrew University of Jerusalem and University of Sao Paolo.*

Fieder, N., L. Nickels, and B. Biedermann (2014). Representation and processing of mass and count nouns: a review. *Frontiers in psychology 5*.

Kiela, D., L. Rimell, I. Vulic, and S. Clark (2015). Exploiting image generality for lexical entailment detection. In *Proceedings of the 53rd Annual Meeting of the Association for Computational Linguistics (ACL 2015)*, pp. 119–124. ACL.

Kiss, T., F. J. Pelletier, H. Husic, J. M. Poppek, and R. N. Simunic (2016). A Sense-Based Lexicon for Count and Mass Expressions: The Bochum English Countability Lexicon. In *Proceedings of LREC*.

Kulkarni, R., S. Rothstein, and A. Treves (2013). A statistical investigation into the cross-linguistic distribution of mass and count nouns: Morphosyntactic and semantic perspectives. *Biolinguistics 7*, 132–168.

LeCun, Y., Y. Bengio, and G. Hinton (2015). Deep learning. *Nature 521*(7553), 436–444.

Lin, T.-Y., M. Maire, S. Belongie, J. Hays, P. Perona, D. Ramanan, P. Dollár, and C. L. Zitnick (2014). Microsoft COCO: Common objects in context. In *European Conference on Computer Vision*, pp. 740–755. Springer.

Miller, G. A. (1995). Wordnet: a lexical database for English. *Communications of the ACM 38*(11), 39–41.

Mottaghi, R., X. Chen, X. Liu, N.-G. Cho, S.-W. Lee, S. Fidler, R. Urtasun, and A. Yuille (2014). The role of context for object detection and semantic segmentation in the wild. In *Proceedings of the IEEE Conference on Computer Vision and Pattern Recognition*, pp. 891–898.

Pelletier, F. J. and L. K. Schubert (1989). Mass expressions. In *Handbook of philosophical logic*, pp. 327–407. Springer.

Russakovsky, O., J. Deng, H. Su, J. Krause, S. Satheesh, S. Ma, Z. Huang, A. Karpathy, A. Khosla, M. Bernstein, et al. (2015). ImageNet large scale visual recognition challenge. *International Journal of Computer Vision 115*(3), 211–252.

Sharan, L. (2009). *The perception of material qualities in real-world images*. Ph. D. thesis, Massachusetts Institute of Technology.

Sharan, L., R. Rosenholtz, and E. H. Adelson (2014). Accuracy and speed of material categorization in real-world images. *Journal of vision 14*(9), 12–12.

Simonyan, K. and A. Zisserman (2014). Very deep convolutional networks for large-scale image recognition. *arXiv preprint arXiv:1409.1556*.

Tighe, J. and S. Lazebnik (2010). Superparsing: scalable nonparametric image parsing with superpixels. *Computer Vision–ECCV 2010*, 352–365.

Tighe, J. and S. Lazebnik (2013). Superparsing. *International Journal of Computer Vision 101*(2), 329–349.

Zanini, C., S. Benavides-Varela, R. Lorusso, and F. Franzon (2016). Mass is more: The conceiving of (un) countability and its encoding into language in 5-year-old-children. *Psychonomic Bulletin & Review* (24), 1330–1340.

Sense Embeddings in Knowledge-Based
Word Sense Disambiguation

Loïc Vial   Benjamin Lecouteux
Didier Schwab
GETALP – LIG – Univ. Grenoble Alpes
{loic.vial, benjamin.lecouteux, didier.schwab}
@univ-grenoble-alpes.fr

Abstract

In this paper, we develop a new way of creating sense vectors for any dictionary, by using an existing word embeddings model, and summing the vectors of the terms inside a sense's definition, weighted in function of their part of speech and their frequency. These vectors are then used for finding the closest senses to any other sense, thus creating a semantic network of related concepts, automatically generated. This network is hence evaluated against the existing semantic network found in WordNet, by comparing its contribution to a knowledge-based method for Word Sense Disambiguation. This method can be applied to any other language which lacks such semantic network, as the creation of word vectors is totally unsupervised, and the creation of sense vectors only needs a traditional dictionary. The results show that our generated semantic network improves greatly the WSD system, almost as much as the manually created one.

1   Introduction

In Natural Language Processing (NLP), Word Sense Disambiguation (WSD) aims at assigning the most probable sense of a word in a document, given a pre-defined sense inventory. State of the art methods in WSD are often supervised systems, as stated by Navigli (2009), which are trained thanks to a great quantity of sense usage examples coming from sense-annotated corpora. The trained model is then used to tag a word with the sense that appears to be the most correct given its context. Unsupervised and knowledge-based methods, on the other hand, have the advantage that they require much less resource to work, and in particular no sense-annotated corpora. Hence they offer a wider coverage more easily, as they do not need to *learn* a sense from an example in order to assign it to a word. In addition, unsupervised and knowledge-based methods are generally the only usable systems to work for disambiguating another language than English. Indeed, sense-annotated corpora are very expensive resources to produce, and almost practically inexisting for every other languages [1]. For this reason, this paper will focus on a knowledge-based method, and on a novel approach that improves its performance in an unsupervised manner, by using word embeddings.

Word embeddings are a set of methods which aim to represent words as vectors. Several recent state of the art methods such as Mikolov et al. (2013)'s Word2Vec, Pennington et al. (2014)'s GloVe and Levy and Goldberg (2014)'s dependency-based vectors have proven to be very useful in many NLP tasks, like Machine Translation, Word Similarity tasks, and even in WSD, where word embeddings are also parts of some recent methods, such as Chen et al. (2014), Iacobacci et al. (2016) or Yuan et al. (2016).

In this paper, we are going to produce sense embeddings, i.e. vectors which represent senses present in the lexical database Princeton WordNet (Miller, 1995). The methodology used to create these vectors is described in section 2. Other methods exist for computing sense embeddings, such as in Iacobacci et al.

---

[1] Less than ten different languages have at least one corpus sense annotated with WordNet, as listed in `http://globalwordnet.org/wordnet-annotated-corpora/`

(2015) for example, who learn a distributional representation of senses through sense-annotated corpora and Word2Vec, but it presupposes a good WSD system, which is already able to sense-annotate precisely. Our sense vectors are hence evaluated by comparing their performance when used as a semantic network for a knowledge-based WSD system described in section 3.1.

The sense embeddings will be used for expanding the gloss of every sense in WordNet, by concatenating the gloss of the most related senses, in a similar way than Banerjee and Pedersen (2002)'s Extended Lesk algorithm does, but instead of considering that two senses are related because they share a lexical or semantic relation in the WordNet network, we consider two senses to be related if their vector's cosine similarity reaches a certain threshold. In the experiments in section 4, we evaluate our method on two different English all-words disambiguation tasks: first, we learn the best value of the similarity threshold on a task, then, this value is tested on the other task. The scores shown are hence the ones we obtain for the latter task, and thereafter, we perform the opposite.

The method could be applied to any language for which it exists a dictionary and a set a unannotated corpora. However, it is evaluated on an English task for at least two reasons: First, it will be easier to compare our results to other systems, since the main WSD evaluation campaigns also use WordNet. Second, we wanted to compare the benefits of different pre-existing word embeddings models to our system, and the most popular ones are trained on English corpora.

2 Creation of Sense Embeddings

Our model for representing a dictionary's sense vector relies on an existing word embeddings model, and on the sense's definition in the dictionary. In practice, our method is very similar to the one presented by Ferrero et al. (2017), who create sentence vectors for a cross-language semantic textual similarity task. Our sense vector is computed as the normalized sum of all the terms' vectors present in the sense's definition, weighed in function of their part of speech (noun, verb, adjective or adverb), and also weighed by their inverse document frequency (IDF), i.e. the inverse of the number of occurrence in the entire dictionary. More formally, we denote:

- $D(S) = \{w_0, w_1, w_2, \ldots, w_n\}$ the definition of sense S in the dictionary

- $pos(w_n) = \{n, v, a, r\}$ the part of speech of the term w_n (noun, verb, adjective or adverb)

- $weight(pos)$ the weight associated with a specific part of speech

- $idf(w_n)$ the IDF value of w_n, computed as $\log(\frac{N_{tot}}{N(w_n)})$, with N_{tot} being the total number of definitions in the dictionary (206,941 in WordNet 3.0), and $N(w_n)$ the number of definitions containing at least one occurrence of the word w_n.

The definition of the vector of the sense S, denoted $\phi(S)$ is hence the following:

$$\phi(S) = \sum_{i=0}^{n} (\phi(w_n) \times weight(pos(w_n)) \times idf(w_n))$$

$\phi(S)$ is then normalized, in order to be the same length as the vectors contained in the word embeddings model (generally the length is 1). The chosen POS weights are the same that Ferrero et al. (2017) used for representing English and Spanish sentences, but they can be trained as parameters of the model.

We generated five sense embeddings models, all created for every sense of WordNet 3.0, but exploiting a different word embeddings model. The five word embeddings model that we used are:

1. The pre-trained word vectors available on the Web page of the original Mikolov et al. (2013)'s Word2Vec [2]. This model was trained on about 100 billion words from Google News datasets. The vocabulary size is about 3 million words and phrases, and the vectors have a dimension of 300.

2. The pre-trained Pennington et al. (2014)'s GloVe [3], trained on 42 billion words from Common

---

[2] https://code.google.com/archive/p/word2vec/
[3] https://nlp.stanford.edu/projects/glove/

Crawl. The vocabulary size is about 2 million words, and the vectors have a dimension of 300.

3. The pre-trained Levy and Goldberg (2014)'s dependency-based word embeddings [4]. The training was done on Wikipedia. The vocabulary size is about 175,000 words, and the dimension is 300.

4. The best *predict* vectors created in Baroni et al. (2014) [5]. The vectors have a dimension of 400 and the vocabulary size is about 300,000.

5. Finally, the best *reduced count* vectors also created in Baroni et al. (2014) [5], of dimension 500, and with the same vocabulary than the previous model.

In the experiments section, we compare the performance of each of the embeddings model in our WSD system extension. All five sense embeddings models are publicly released on our GitHub[6].

3   Evaluation in Knowledge-Based WSD

The generated vector representation of senses will be evaluated on a WSD task, as a supplementary resource for a knowledge-based method. The idea is to use the embeddings model as a semantic network, which is able to fetch senses related to another sense. These related senses will then contribute to the similarity measure used in the WSD system, in the same manner than Banerjee and Pedersen (2002)'s usage of the semantic network integrated in WordNet.

3.1   Disambiguation Algorithm

The knowledge-based WSD system that is used to compare the performance of the semantic network is built as two pieces: the Local Algorithm, which computes a score of similarity for a pair of senses, and the Global Algorithm, which searches for the best combination of senses at the document level, using the local algorithm.

The global algorithm is a heuristic that will avoid to compute every possible combination of senses in the document, because this would lead to an uncomputable number of calls to the local algorithm (the average number of senses per word, to the power of the number of words in the document).

The heuristic used in our system is an implementation of the Cuckoo Search Algorithm, as research done by Vial et al. (2017) on Global Algorithms shows that it is among the best global algorithm for this kind of knowledge-based WSD system. Our implementation uses as parameters a single cuckoo, a Levy location of 5 and a Levy scale of 0.5, as described as the best parameters in Vial et al. (2017). In all of our experiments, we set the number of iterations to be a very large number (300,000), so the results do not differ notably from an execution to another. In addition, we compute the mean of 10 complete executions when giving a score, and we ensure a low standard deviation (generally < 0.1) so the end result is stable and reliable.

The local algorithm is the central element of the system and this is where the usage of the semantic network will occur. As a baseline, we are going to use the original Lesk measure, also called gloss overlap measure. This algorithm returns, as a similarity score, the number of words in common in the two senses' definition. Formally, if we denote $D(S) = \{w_1, w_2, \ldots, w_n\}$ the definition of S, then the Lesk measure between sense S_1 and sense S_2, denoted $Lesk(S_1, S_2)$ is the following:

$$Lesk(S_1, S_2) = |D(S_1) \cap D(S_2)|$$

As a second baseline, and in order to compare the quality of our produced semantic network, we will also use the Extended Lesk measure, described in Banerjee and Pedersen (2002). This measure consider not only the definition of the target sense, but also the definition of every sense that have a relation to the

---

target sense (hyperonymy, hyponymy, etc.). Let's denote $rel(S)$ the set of senses related to S, through an explicit link in WordNet, then the Extended Lesk measure between sense S_1 and sense S_2, denoted $ExtLesk(S_1, S_2)$ is the following:

$$ExtLesk(S_1, S_2) = |(D(S_1) \cup D(rel(S_1))) \cap (D(S_2) \cup D(rel(S_2)))|$$

3.2 Gloss Expansion Through Sense Embeddings

Our method for using our sense embeddings model produced in section 2 is to extend the Lesk algorithm in a way similar to Banerjee and Pedersen (2002), that is by also considering the related senses when computing the similarity of two senses.

Because our sense vectors are created from the vectors of the terms used in the dictionary's glosses, the impact of these terms is huge. This is why for our expansion, we will take into account the most similar senses not using solely the cosine similarity, because this would blindly fetch some unrelated senses that are described using the same kind of wording. We also filter on the lemma's vector of the target sense in the word embeddings space, so the fetched senses will also be close to the *idea* of the sense's lemma, as captured by the word embeddings model. As a recall, operations between a sense vector and a word vector are possible because the sense vector is, in essence, only a weighted sum of word vectors.

Let's denote $rel(S, \delta_1, \delta_2)$ the set of senses related to S. δ_1 is the threshold cosine similarity value on the **lemma**'s vector, below which we do not consider a sense as related. δ_2 is the threshold cosine similarity value on the **sense**'s vector, below which we do not consider a sense as related. *Senses* is the set of all the senses in the dictionary. *cosine* is the cosine similarity operator. The formula for computing $rel(S, \delta_1, \delta_2)$ is the following:

$$rel(S, \delta_1, \delta_2) = \{S' \mid cosine(\phi(lemma(S)), \phi(S')) > \delta_1, cosine(\phi(S), \phi(S')) > \delta_2\}$$

Finally, the formula for our new local algorithm for the WSD system, which we will be denoted as $VecLesk(S_1, S_2, \delta_1, \delta_2)$, can be written almost exactly as the Extended Lesk:

$$VecLesk(S_1, S_2, \delta_1, \delta_2) = |(D(S_1) \cup D(rel(S_1, \delta_1, \delta_2))) \cap (D(S_2) \cup D(rel(S_2, \delta_1, \delta_2)))|$$

In the following section, we are going to evaluate this new local algorithm on two WSD all-words tasks, in regards with the Lesk and the Extended Lesk baselines.

4 Experiments

In order to see how our sense embeddings model performs as a semantic network, we use it for a lexical expansion of the dictionary's glosses, for improving the Lesk local algorithm of our WSD system.

Our expansion considers the related senses regarding two cosine similarity threshold: δ_1, filtering out senses based on their similarity with the target sense's lemma vector, and δ_2, filtering out senses based on their similarity with the target sense vector.

These two parameters have to be set in some way, so we chose two WSD tasks: SemEval 2007 task 7 (Navigli et al., 2007), and SemEval 2015 task 13 (Moro and Navigli, 2015), and we estimated the best set of parameters on a task, then tested this set of parameters on the other. The reason why we chose these two tasks is that they are of the same nature, i.e. both all-words WSD tasks, and that the task 7 of SemEval 2007 is largely used in most WSD articles, so it is easier to put the results in perspective.

All five word embeddings models mentioned in section 2 are evaluated separately. And the parameters δ_1 and δ_2 have been estimated by testing every values in the range $[0.5, 0.9]$ with steps of 0.1.

The results of the best parameters estimation on SemEval 2007 task 7 and on SemEval 2015 task 13 is in Table 1. The comparison of our method on both tasks in regards with the baselines and a state of the art system is in Table 2.

Word Embeddings Model	baroni_c		baroni_p		deps		glove		word2vec	
Parameters	δ_1	δ_2	δ_1	δ_2	δ_1	δ_2	δ_1	δ_2	δ_1	δ_2
Best values on SemEval 2007	0.6	0.6	0.5	0.5	0.6	0.8	0.5	0.6	0.5	0.6
Best values on SemEval 2015	0.5	0.8	0.5	0.6	0.6	0.8	0.5	0.7	0.5	0.6

Table 1: Estimation of parameters δ_1 and δ_2 on SemEval 2007 task 7 and SemEval 2015 task 13.

System	SemEval 2007 F1 score	SemEval 2015 F1 score
Chen et al. (2014)	75.80%[7]	
Lesk baseline	68.70%	50.65%
ExtLesk baseline	78.01%	61.42%
VecLesk (baroni_c)	**75.29%**	58.02%
VecLesk (baroni_p)	73.52%	53.46%
VecLesk (deps)	73.02%	56.40%
VecLesk (glove)	73.00%	**59.01%**
VecLesk (word2vec)	73.30%	57.00%

Table 2: Comparison of our results on SemEval 2007 task 7 and SemEval 2015 task 13 for each word embeddings model used, in regards with the Lesk and Extended Lesk baselines and a state of the art method that uses similar resources than us. The parameters δ_1 and δ_2 used in VecLesk are taken from the parameter estimation of Table 1 **from the other task**, not the one that is tested.

The results show that our extension improves greatly the score of the Lesk measure, which is at least around +5% for the worst combination of word embeddings model and parameters, on SemEval 2007, and around +7% for the best combination. On SemEval 2015, the worst extension still improves the score by +3%, and the best one gives +9%. Our extension does not reach the score of the Extended Lesk baseline however. Which is a sign that our semantic network is probably less relevant than the explicit links found in WordNet.

An interesting data is the difference of score obtained by the different word embeddings model. The best result on SemEval 2007 uses Baroni et al. (2014)'s count vectors, and the score is 2% higher than the second best word embeddings model's score (using Baroni et al. (2014)'s predict vectors). This tends to show that the "older" approach of word embeddings creation, i.e. counting-based vectors, are in some cases a better choice than the predicting models. However, on SemEval 2015, the best model is GloVe. Baroni's count vectors is a close second though. The fluctuation of the results in function of the model used may be because of the different natures of the word embeddings models, or due to the different corpora they were trained on. In any cases, our extension works with any model, systematically raising the score from the Lesk baseline.

The comparison of our system to the best existing method to our knowledge that uses the same kind of resources than us (i.e. a dictionary and unannotated corpora), shows that our extension achieves state of the art results on methods using such few resources. The score achieved by Chen et al. (2014) has to be treated with caution, because they learned a threshold parameter δ similarly to us, for their construction of vectors, however they estimated their best parameter and tested on the same corpus, leading to an obvious bias. Note that in the same conditions, when we use the best set of parameters learned on this same task, our method reaches a score of 77.08% on SemEval 2007.

---

[7]The referenced article's score is biased, since the authors' system learns a parameter $\delta \in [-0.1, 0.3]$ comparable to our, but directly during the testing phase. The score ranges from 72.10% to 75.80% depending on the value of their δ.

5 Conclusion

In this article, we created a Sense Embeddings model, representing every sense of a dictionary, based on the words contained in their gloss and using an existing Word Embeddings model. Our method of construction essentially computes the sum of the gloss terms' vectors, weighted in function of their part of speech and their inverse frequency. We created five sense embeddings models, each one of them relying on different word embeddings model. They are available publicly on our GitHub[8].

The models are then used as a semantic network for improving a knowledge-based WSD system, based on the Lesk algorithm. The idea is to take into account the closest senses to a target sense in our semantic network, in order to disambiguate it, in the same manner as Banerjee and Pedersen (2002) do using the related senses information built in WordNet.

The resulting extended WSD system performs systematically better than its unextended baseline counterpart, improving the score from about +3% for the worst extension, to about +9% for the best one.

This article uses WordNet as a dictionary, and evaluations are performed on two English all-words WSD tasks, because it is easier to compare the performance and the robustness of the method, as the majority of the researches in WSD uses this language. However, the whole process of sense embeddings creation and Lesk extension can be easily adapted to many language, requiring only a set of unannotated corpora, and a typical dictionary, thus, giving the possibility to create an efficient WSD system, even for a poorly resourced language.

---

[8]`https://github.com/getalp/WSD-IWCS2017-Vialetal`

References

Banerjee, S. and T. Pedersen (2002, February). An adapted lesk algorithm for word sense disambiguation using wordnet. In *CICLing 2002*, Mexico City.

Baroni, M., G. Dinu, and Kruszewski (2014, June). Don't count, predict! a systematic comparison of context-counting vs. context-predicting semantic vectors. In *Proceedings of the 52nd Annual Meeting of the Association for Computational Linguistics (Volume 1: Long Papers)*, Baltimore, Maryland, pp. 238–247. Association for Computational Linguistics.

Chen, X., Z. Liu, and M. Sun (2014, October). A unified model for word sense representation and disambiguation. In *Proceedings of the 2014 Conference on Empirical Methods in Natural Language Processing (EMNLP)*, Doha, Qatar, pp. 1025–1035. Association for Computational Linguistics.

Ferrero, J., L. Besacier, D. Schwab, and F. Agnès (2017, August). CompiLIG at SemEval-2017 Task 1: Cross-Language Plagiarism Detection Methods for Semantic Textual Similarity. In *Proceedings of the 11th International Workshop on Semantic Evaluation (SemEval 2017)*, Vancouver, Canada.

Iacobacci, I., M. T. Pilehvar, and R. Navigli (2015). Sensembed: Learning sense embeddings for word and relational similarity. In *In Proceedings of ACL*, pp. 95–105.

Iacobacci, I., M. T. Pilehvar, and R. Navigli (2016, August). Embeddings for word sense disambiguation: An evaluation study. In *Proceedings of the 54th Annual Meeting of the Association for Computational Linguistics (Volume 1: Long Papers)*, Berlin, Germany, pp. 897–907. Association for Computational Linguistics.

Levy, O. and Y. Goldberg (2014). Dependency-based word embeddings. In *Proceedings of the 52nd Annual Meeting of the Association for Computational Linguistics, ACL 2014, June 22-27, 2014, Baltimore, MD, USA, Volume 2: Short Papers*, pp. 302–308.

Mikolov, T., I. Sutskever, K. Chen, G. S. Corrado, and J. Dean (2013). Distributed representations of words and phrases and their compositionality. In C. Burges, L. Bottou, M. Welling, Z. Ghahramani, and K. Weinberger (Eds.), *Advances in Neural Information Processing Systems 26*, pp. 3111–3119. Curran Associates, Inc.

Miller, G. A. (1995). Wordnet: A lexical database. *ACM Vol. 38*(No. 11), p. 1–41.

Moro, A. and R. Navigli (2015, June). Semeval-2015 task 13: Multilingual all-words sense disambiguation and entity linking. In *Proceedings of the 9th International Workshop on Semantic Evaluation (SemEval 2015)*, Denver, Colorado, pp. 288–297. Association for Computational Linguistics.

Navigli, R. (2009). Wsd: a survey. *ACM Computing Surveys 41*(2), 1–69.

Navigli, R., K. C. Litkowski, and O. Hargraves (2007, June). Semeval-2007 task 07: Coarse-grained english all-words task. In *SemEval-2007*, Prague, Czech Republic, pp. 30–35.

Pennington, J., R. Socher, and C. D. Manning (2014). Glove: Global vectors for word representation. In *Empirical Methods in Natural Language Processing (EMNLP)*, pp. 1532–1543.

Vial, L., A. Tchechmedjiev, and D. Schwab (2017). Comparison of global algorithms in word sense disambiguation. *CoRR abs/1704.02293*, 1–22.

Yuan, D., J. Richardson, R. Doherty, C. Evans, and E. Altendorf (2016). Semi-supervised word sense disambiguation with neural models. In *COLING 2016*.

LexSubNC: a Dataset of
Lexical Substitution for Nominal Compounds

Rodrigo Wilkens[1], Leonardo Zilio[1], Silvio Cordeiro[2,3],
Felipe S. F. Paula[2], Carlos Ramisch[3], Marco Idiart[4], Aline Villavicencio[2]

[1]CENTAL, Université catholique de Louvain (Belgium)
[2]Institute of Informatics, Federal University of Rio Grande do Sul (Brazil)
[3]Aix Marseille Université, CNRS, LIF UMR 7279 (France)
[4]Institute of Physics, Federal University of Rio Grande do Sul (Brazil)
`{rodrigo.wilkens,leonardo.zilio}@uclouvain.be`
`{silvio.cordeiro,carlos.ramisch}@lif.univ-mrs.fr`
`{felipesfpaula,marco.idiart,alinev}@gmail.com`

Abstract

In the context of NLP tasks such as text simplification, lexicons containing information about semantically related words are an important resource for evaluating the quality of the system output. Existing resources containing lexical substitutes have been built with a focus on single words. In this paper, we present a lexical substitution dataset for Portuguese nominal compounds. The compounds have varying degrees of compositionality, conventionality and frequency, and we investigate the impact of these characteristics on the suggestions of lexical substitution made by native speakers. No strong correlations are found for these factors on the number or type of responses provided. However, a significant effect of compositionality is found in the use of one of the component words (head or modifier) as a substitute. The resulting resource, LexSubNC, contains over 1,500 manually validated substitutes for 180 compounds, further classified according to the type of response.

1   Introduction

In tasks involving lexical substitution, alternatives need to be identified for a given target word (McCarthy and Navigli, 2007, 2009), usually in a particular context. Candidates can be chosen to maximize word properties that are relevant for the particular task, such as unigram and n-gram frequencies, concreteness, imageability, and conventionality. Depending on the target word, more than one possible alternative substitution may fulfill the criteria and produce an acceptable result (e.g. *acquire/buy/purchase a painting*). Resources such as thesauri, containing semantically related words (Fellbaum, 1998; Lin, 1998), and word norms, with information about word properties (Nelson et al., 2004), may be used to inform these tasks.

Various initiatives for collecting word norms resulted in datasets such as the South Florida Association Norms (Nelson et al., 2004), SimLex-999 (Hill et al., 2015), Hyperlex (Vulić et al., 2016) and Rare Words (Luong et al., 2013). These resources form valuable gold standards for evaluating the quality of a variety of tasks and applications, including text simplification and machine translation. However, they often concentrate on single words as targets.

The collection of norms for longer units is particularly challenging due to the arbitrary interactions between their member words, particularly if they involve multiword expressions (MWEs), such as nominal compounds or verbal idioms. Available MWE datasets often target specific types of MWEs such as verb-particle constructions (McCarthy et al., 2003) and noun compounds (Reddy et al., 2011), and tend to focus on numerical scores that model compositionality and conventionality. Resources with lexical substitutes or paraphrases for MWEs are rare and often only include compositional expressions (Hendrickx et al., 2013).

However, MWEs may also involve some degree of semantic or statistical idiosyncrasy with respect to regular combinations (Baldwin and Kim, 2010) and these may have an impact on the quality of the collected data. For instance, there may be less agreement among annotators for an idiomatic nominal compound like *Black Friday* as it may be perceived as being related to various different concepts like *Friday*, *promotion* and *Thanksgiving*, which may all be possible substitutes for the compound but are not synonyms among themselves.

In this paper we introduce LexSubNC, a dataset that contains the responses of human annotators about lexical substitutes for a set of nominal compounds of varying degrees of compositionality, frequency and conventionality in Brazilian Portuguese. The raw data was collected using a dedicated web interface, allowing the participation of many volunteer non-expert native speakers. The responses were then manually validated and classified according to the particular semantic relations involved. We examine the impact of factors like frequency, conventionality and compositionality on the number and type of responses collected for the construction of the dataset.[1]

LexSubNC is potentially useful for the evaluation and development of several NLP tasks and applications. For example, it could be used to tune the development of distributional semantic models that maximize the similarity between an MWE and its substitutes, similarly to what is currently done for single words (Hill et al., 2015; Levy et al., 2015). It could also be used for the evaluation of machine translation methods that focus on non-compositional expressions, similarly to what is currently done for instance in METEOR (Denkowski and Lavie, 2014). For automatic text simplification, paraphrases could be used to replace non-compositional expressions by more explicit paraphrases (Specia et al., 2012).

This paper is structured as follows: we discuss similar resources and the techniques used to collect them (§2), and describe the protocol used for collecting human responses (§3). The responses are analyzed for possible correlations between characteristics of the compounds and the responses provided (§4). We finish with conclusions and a discussion of future work (§5).

2   Related Work

A variety of protocols have been adopted for collecting specific word norms, usually targeting single words. For the lexical substitution of single words in English, McCarthy and Navigli (2007) asked annotators to provide up to three substitutes, preferably also single words, for 210 target words (nouns, verbs, adjectives and adverbs) in 10 sentences each, in a total of 2.100 sentences. They adopted no fixed inventory of words for the task, and the results reflected this inherent variation, as several substitutes are possible for a specific target in a particular context. This dataset was later used as the starting point for rating the alternatives provided in terms of simplicity (Specia et al., 2012).

Lexical substitution datasets for languages other than English include a dataset for German containing substitutes for 153 target words (51 nouns, 51 adjectives, and 51 verbs) in 2,040 sentences (Cholakov et al., 2014). Cholakov et al. (2014) also collected information about the difficulty of the annotation from a pilot study, where 78% of the tasks were considered of easy or medium difficulty. For multilingual lexical substitution Mihalcea et al. (2010) asked annotators to find Spanish alternatives for English words in a given context, allowing the presence of multiword substitutes.

Related resources that target MWEs include collecting paraphrases, which can be used as a form of MWE substitution. Due to the particular structure of nominal compounds, their semantics can often be approximated using paraphrasing verbs and prepositions in combination with their component nouns (Lauer, 1995; Nakov, 2008; Butnariu et al., 2010; Hendrickx et al., 2013). Nakov (2008) collected annotations for about 250 noun compounds, where the annotators were asked to use the component words of a compound along with verbs and prepositions to form paraphrases (e.g., *malaria mosquito* is a *mosquito that **causes** malaria*). Girju et al. (2005) model similar information using a restricted set of categories from a semantic inventory. Arguing for a less restricted task, Hendrickx et al. (2013) requested free paraphrases from the annotators for 355 compounds in English. The paraphrasing terms could have

---

[1] The full resource is publicly available at `http://pageperso.lif.univ-mrs.fr/~carlos.ramisch/?page=downloads/compounds&lang=en`.

any part of speech, as long as the resulting paraphrase was a well-formed noun phrase. In all of these cases, the compounds were compositional: they could be paraphrased using combinations of their parts, and lexical substitution could be performed for each component individually.

Other MWE datasets contain compositionality assessment, and, as a consequence, they also include idiomatic cases. Datasets for nominal compound compositionality are available in English (Reddy et al., 2011; Ramisch et al., 2016; Farahmand et al., 2015), German (Roller et al., 2013), Portuguese and French (Ramisch et al., 2016), and for noun-verb expressions in Basque (Gurrutxaga and Alegria, 2013). For instance, Reddy et al. (2011) collected numerical scores for 90 English nominal compounds regarding their compositionality. Data for each compound and component word was gathered through crowdsourcing using a 6-point scale ranging from totally idiomatic (0) to fully compositional (5). Ramisch et al. (2016) extended this set with additional compounds and also applied it to other languages, generating a total of 180 compounds per language for English, Portuguese, and French. Farahmand et al. (2015) performed a similar dataset collection with 1,048 compounds annotated for compositionality and conventionality by 4 expert judges using a binary scale. However, these do not contain information about lexical substitutes. Moreover, to date, no analysis has been published on the impact of compositionality on the selection of substitutes. This paper examines this question for the substitutes proposed for compounds of varying degrees of compositionality in Brazilian Portuguese.

3 Materials and Methods

As the basis for LexSubNC, we use the set of 180 nominal compounds consisting of a noun and an adjective in Brazilian Portuguese described by Ramisch et al. (2016). They include two morphosyntactic configurations: adjective-noun, such as in *alto mar* (lit. *high sea* [international waters]), and noun-adjective, such as *vinho branco* (lit. *wine white* [white wine]). To investigate possible effects of familiarity, conventionality and compositionality in the quality of the human responses about lexical substitutes, all compounds have been annotated with corpus frequency, association strength and compositionality information.

Frequency is used as a predictor of human *familiarity* with a word, assuming that the higher the frequency the more familiar the compound. The association strength is used as an indication of the *conventionality* of a compound, with the assumption that the higher the strength, the more conventional the compound is. This follows the agreement between association measures and conventionality found by Farahmand et al. (2015). In this work we use pointwise mutual information (PMI, Church and Hanks (1990)), an association measure widely used for MWEs. 12Both frequency and PMI are calculated based on counts from a combined corpus of around 1.91 billion tokens. The corpus is formed by a concatenation of the brWaC (Wagner Filho et al., 2016; Boos et al., 2014), the Brazilian Corpus (Berber Sardinha et al., 2008), and the Portuguese Wikipedia. For *compositionality* we use the scores collected by Ramisch et al. (2016). This ensures a balance of compositionality, since the dataset was designed to contain 60 compositional (e.g., *acampamento militar* – lit. *camp military* [military camp]), 60 partly compositional (e.g., *círculo vicioso* – lit. *circle vicious* [vicious circle]), and 60 idiomatic cases (e.g., *bode expiatório* – lit. *goat expiatory* [scapegoat]).

To collect lexical substitutes for nominal compounds suggested by native speakers, we invited 86 volunteer native speakers of Brazilian Portuguese to participate in the task. All participants were undergraduate and graduate students in computer science and linguistics. Prior to starting the annotation, they were required to take a training session in which examples of compounds in sentences were presented along with the expected responses.

During the annotation, participants were asked to first read 3 sentences selected from corpora. Our hypothesis is that, by reading the sentences, annotators will think about the sense of the compound. Moreover, dispersion due to polysemy is avoided,[2] since the sentences were manually selected so that a single sense of the compound is represented.

---

[2]Polysemous compounds are rare but do exist, for example, *braço direito* can mean *right-hand man*, that is, a reliable assistant, or literally *right arm* as a body part.

The annotators were then asked to provide between 3 and 5 substitutes per compound, preferably single words. A minimum of three substitutes was required to allow for a greater diversity of answers per user and per compound. This requirement proved to be too strict, as many annotators complained that sometimes it is extremely difficult to find more than one substitute per compound.

The annotation interface is shown in Figure 1. Each compound was shown on a separate screen, so that, after submitting the answers, the annotator could choose to continue annotating or to stop contributing. A simplified login procedure ensured that the same annotator did not annotate the same compound twice. We estimate that each compound took 1-3 minutes to annotate, therefore this design allowed for a good flexibility, adapting to the each annotator's availability.

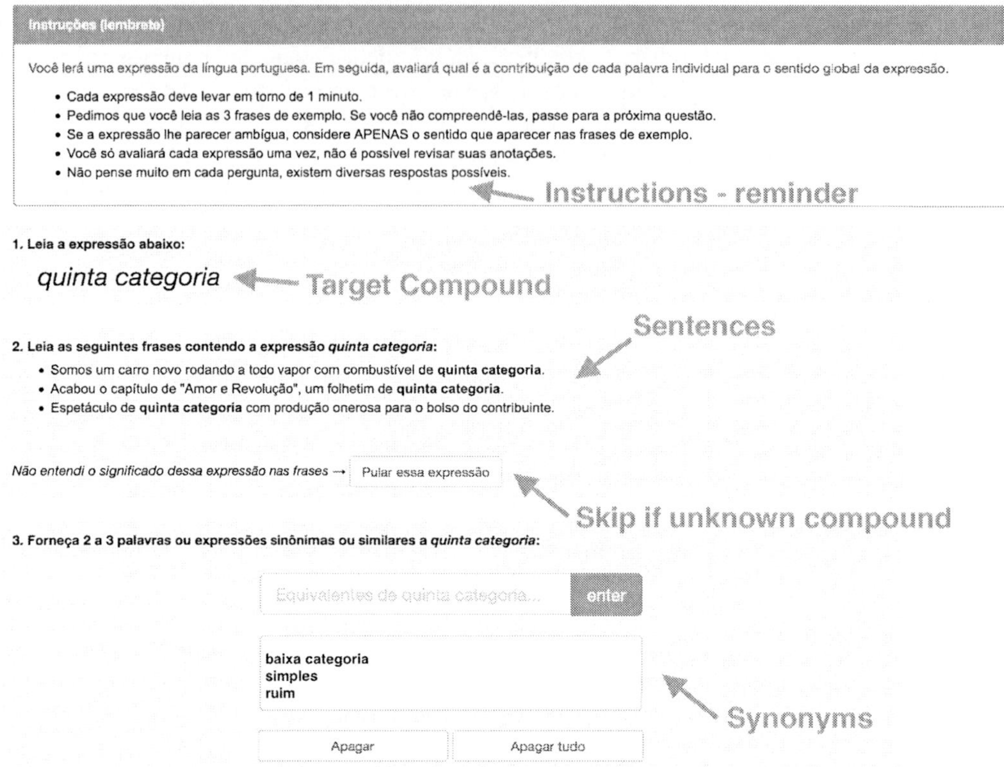

Figure 1: Annotation interface for lexical substitutes.

4 Results

A total of 5,546 responses were collected for the 180 target compounds, with 3,715 unique responses, which were manually verified by a linguist. From these, any response that could not be considered a substitute for the compound was removed: responses that expressed opinions or judgments about the compound (e.g., *país conivente com falcatruas* [country that indulges scams] for *paraíso fiscal* – lit. *paradise fiscal* [tax haven]), that used semantically related but distinct concepts (e.g., *binóculo* [binoculars] for *olho mágico* – lit. *eye magic* [peephole]) and that were tentative explanations (e.g., *recipiente de presente secreto* [recipient of secret gift] for *amigo secreto* – lit. *friend secret* [secret Santa]). One of the possible reasons for invalid cases is that users needed to enter at least three responses for a compound before being able to start the next task. The valid responses were manually classified by the expert according to the following categories:

- Synonyms: this class distinguishes between single-word synonyms ($\mathbf{Syn}_{word}$, like *microchip* for *circuito integrado* – lit. *circuit integrated* [integrated circuit]) and multiword synonyms ($\mathbf{Syn}_{MWE}$, such as *pronto-atendimento* [urgent care] for *pronto-socorro* – lit. *ready help* [emergency services]). Moreover, where applicable, the synonyms were further identified as head (**head**, as in *vinho* [wine] for *vinho branco* [white wine]) or modifier (**mod**, as in *doce* [sweet] for *algodão-doce* – lit. *cotton sweet* [cotton candy]) of the compound.

- Near synonyms: this class identified semantically related responses, such as hypernyms, meronyms, and hyponyms, distinguishing between single word ($\mathbf{NearSyn}_{word}$, like *comida* [food] for *batata-doce* – lit. *potato sweet* [sweet potato]) and multiword near synonyms ($\mathbf{NearSyn}_{MWE}$, e.g., *carne de peixe* [fish meat] for *carne branca* – lit. *meat white* [white meat]).

- Paraphrases (**Paraphrases**) or definitions (**Definitions**): these two classes were used for rewrites or explanations about the target compound (e.g., *arma que não é de fogo* [weapon that is not a firearm] for *arma branca* – lit. *weapon white* [white weapon] or *passagem de ano* [passage from one year to another] for *ano-novo* – lit. *year new* [new year]).

Table 1 displays the number of total and unique responses per category, along with the number of target compounds that received responses in each category. Table 2 shows the number of cases for which the head or the modifier were proposed as substitutes for the compound.

	# Total Responses	# Unique Responses	# Target Compounds
Syn_{word}	966	318	99
Syn_{MWE}	1,257	684	159
$\mathrm{NearSyn}_{word}$	315	150	83
$\mathrm{NearSyn}_{word}$	303	183	96
Paraphrases	54	47	24
Definitions	166	162	90
Total	3,061	1,544	

Table 1: Substitutes classified

The average number of responses per class ranges from 1 to 4.3 types and 2 to 9.5 tokens. Some compounds had more responses than others, from 14 (for *banho turco* – lit. *bath Turkish* [Turkish bath]) to 45 (for *reta final* – lit. *straight-line final* [final stretch]). The number of annotators that agreed on a response varied from 2 to 16. Indeed, the distribution of responses confirms the suggestion of Hendrickx et al. (2013) for not using a fixed inventory of options and allowing participants to propose free paraphrasing, as most responses were unique and proposed only once for the target compounds.

	# Total Responses	# Unique Responses	# Target Compounds
Head	232	56	56
Mod	5	2	2

Table 2: Heads and modifiers as substitutes

To examine whether the familiarity, conventionality and compositionality of the compounds had any impact on the number and variety of valid lexical substitutes obtained, we measured their correlation using the Spearman coefficient, reported in Table 3. We found no effect for the total number of responses. In other words, the fact that a compound is more familiar, conventional or compositional does not necessarily correlate with the number of different substitutes it has. We found a significant mild effect for either the head or the modifier being used as response, which was positively correlated with the compositionality of the compound. In other words, the heads or modifiers were used as responses more often for the compositional cases (e.g. *água* [water] for *água mineral* – lit. *water mineral* [mineral water]).

	Frequency	PMI	Compositionality
Total number of responses	0.09	-0.03	0.08
Synonyms and near synonyms	0.05	0.10	0.16*
Head or modifier	0.02	0.18*	0.41**

Table 3: Spearman Correlation Coefficient for responses collected. Significance levels marked as * for $p \leq 0.05$ and ** for $p \leq 0.01$.

This is not surprising given that, in compositonal compounds, the meaning of the whole can be derived from the meaning of the component words to some extent.

The resulting resource, LexSubNC, contains over 1,500 manually validated substitutes for 180 compounds classified according to the type of response and annotated for frequency, PMI and compositionality.

5   Conclusions and Future Work

In this paper we presented LexSubNC, a dataset of lexical substitutes for nominal compounds in Brazilian Portuguese. The dataset contains 180 compounds, annotated with frequency, PMI and compositionality. For each compound, the dataset contains information about different substitutes, their classification and the number of times they were proposed by the annotators. We analyzed the responses so as to determine if the frequency, conventionality or compositionality of a compound had any impact on the responses given by the human annotators. The results obtained suggest that no such effects can be found for either of these factors, apart from a mild correlation between the head or the modifier used as a response and the compositionality of a compound. The resulting dataset can be used for a variety of tasks, including as a gold standard for the evaluation of the output of lexical simplification and machine translation systems.

As future work, we plan on ranking the responses according to simplicity as substitutes for these particular compounds. This would result in a resource not only for lexical substitution, but also for lexical simplification. In addition, we plan on collecting annotations on whether these compounds are concrete or abstract, so as to verify whether there is any interaction between the analyzed variables and the concreteness of compounds. Finally, we will also collect scores for the similarity of the responses, which will result in a gold standard of lexical similarity scores.

Acknowledgments

Financial support from the projects: BEWARE 1610378 and 1510637, CNPq 312114/2015-0, 423843/2016-8, PARSEME (COST IC1207), PARSEME-FR (ANR-14-CERA-0001), ORFEO (ANR-12-CORP-0005). We would also like to thank all volunteer annotators for their valuable contribution.

References

Baldwin, T. and S. N. Kim (2010). Multiword expressions. In N. Indurkhya and F. J. Damerau (Eds.), *Handbook of Natural Language Processing* (2 ed.)., pp. 267–292. Boca Raton, FL, USA: CRC Press, Taylor and Francis Group.

Berber Sardinha, T., J. Moreira Filho, and E. Alambert (2008). O corpus brasileiro. *Comunicaçao ao VII Encontro de Lingüistica de Corpus*.

Boos, R., K. Prestes, A. Villavicencio, and M. Padró (2014). brWaC: a WaCky corpus for Brazilian Portuguese. In *International Conference on Computational Processing of the Portuguese Language*, pp. 201–206. Springer.

Butnariu, C., S. N. Kim, P. Nakov, D. Ó Séaghdha, S. Szpakowicz, and T. Veale (2010, July). Semeval-2 task 9: The interpretation of noun compounds using paraphrasing verbs and prepositions. In *Proceedings of the 5th International Workshop on Semantic Evaluation*, Uppsala, Sweden, pp. 39–44. Association for Computational Linguistics.

Cholakov, K., C. Biemann, J. Eckle-Kohler, and I. Gurevych (2014). Lexical substitution dataset for German. In *LREC*, pp. 1406–1411.

Church, K. W. and P. Hanks (1990, March). Word association norms, mutual information, and lexicography. *Computational Linguistics 16*(1), 22–29.

Denkowski, M. and A. Lavie (2014). Meteor universal: Language specific translation evaluation for any target language. In *Proceedings of the EACL 2014 Workshop on Statistical Machine Translation*.

Farahmand, M., A. Smith, and J. Nivre (2015, June). A multiword expression data set: Annotating non-compositionality and conventionalization for English noun compounds. In *Proceedings of the 11th Workshop on Multiword Expressions*, Denver, Colorado, pp. 29–33. Association for Computational Linguistics.

Fellbaum, C. (Ed.) (1998, May). *WordNet: An Electronic Lexical Database (Language, Speech, and Communication)*. MITPRESS. 423 p.

Girju, R., D. Moldovan, M. Tatu, and D. Antohe (2005). On the semantics of noun compounds. *Computer speech & language 19*(4), 479–496.

Gurrutxaga, A. and I. n. Alegria (2013, June). Combining different features of idiomaticity for the automatic classification of noun+verb expressions in Basque. In *Proceedings of the 9th Workshop on Multiword Expressions*, Atlanta, Georgia, USA, pp. 116–125. Association for Computational Linguistics.

Hendrickx, I., Z. Kozareva, P. Nakov, D. Ó Séaghdha, S. Szpakowicz, and T. Veale (2013, June). Semeval-2013 task 4: Free paraphrases of noun compounds. In *Proceedings of *SEM 2013, Volume 2 – SemEval*, pp. 138–143. ACL.

Hill, F., R. Reichart, and A. Korhonen (2015). Simlex-999: Evaluating semantic models with (genuine) similarity estimation. *Computational Linguistics 41*(4), 665–695.

Lauer, M. (1995). How much is enough?: Data requirements for statistical NLP. *CoRR abs/cmp-lg/9509001*.

Levy, O., Y. Goldberg, and I. Dagan (2015). Improving distributional similarity with lessons learned from word embeddings. *Transactions of the Association for Computational Linguistics 3*, 211–225.

Lin, D. (1998). Automatic retrieval and clustering of similar words. In *Proceedings of the 17th international conference on Computational linguistics-Volume 2*, pp. 768–774. Association for Computational Linguistics.

Luong, T., R. Socher, and C. Manning (2013). Better word representations with recursive neural networks for morphology. In *Proceedings of the Seventeenth Conference on Computational Natural Language Learning*, pp. 104–113. Association for Computational Linguistics.

McCarthy, D., B. Keller, and J. Carroll (2003, July). Detecting a continuum of compositionality in phrasal verbs. In *Proceedings of the ACL 2003 Workshop on Multiword Expressions: Analysis, Acquisition and Treatment*, Sapporo, Japan, pp. 73–80. Association for Computational Linguistics.

McCarthy, D. and R. Navigli (2007). Semeval-2007 task 10: English lexical substitution task. In *Proceedings of the 4th International Workshop on Semantic Evaluations*, pp. 48–53. Association for Computational Linguistics.

McCarthy, D. and R. Navigli (2009). The English lexical substitution task. *Language resources and evaluation 43*(2), 139–159.

Mihalcea, R., R. Sinha, and D. McCarthy (2010). Semeval-2010 task 2: Cross-lingual lexical substitution. In *Proceedings of the 5th International Workshop on Semantic Evaluation*, SemEval '10, Stroudsburg, PA, USA, pp. 9–14. Association for Computational Linguistics.

Nakov, P. (2008). Paraphrasing verbs for noun compound interpretation. In *Proc. of the LREC Workshop Towards a Shared Task for MWEs (MWE 2008)*, pp. 46–49.

Nelson, D. L., C. L. McEvoy, and T. A. Schreiber (2004). The University of South Florida free association, rhyme, and word fragment norms. *Behavior Research Methods, Instruments, & Computers 36*(3), 402–407.

Ramisch, C., S. R. Cordeiro, L. Zilio, M. Idiart, A. Villavicencio, and R. Wilkens (2016). How naked is the naked truth? A multilingual lexicon of nominal compound compositionality. In *Proc. of ACL 2016*. ACL. To appear.

Reddy, S., D. McCarthy, and S. Manandhar (2011, November). An empirical study on compositionality in compound nouns. In *Proceedings of The 5th International Joint Conference on Natural Language Processing 2011 (IJCNLP 2011)*, Chiang Mai, Thailand.

Roller, S., S. Schulte im Walde, and S. Scheible (2013, June). The (un)expected effects of applying standard cleansing models to human ratings on compositionality. In *Proceedings of the 9th Workshop on Multiword Expressions*, pp. 32–41. ACL.

Specia, L., S. K. Jauhar, and R. Mihalcea (2012). Semeval-2012 task 1: English lexical simplification. In *Proceedings of the 6th International Workshop on Semantic Evaluation, SemEval@NAACL-HLT 2012, Montréal, Canada, June 7-8, 2012*, pp. 347–355.

Vulić, I., D. Gerz, D. Kiela, F. Hill, and A. Korhonen (2016). Hyperlex: A large-scale evaluation of graded lexical entailment. *arXiv*.

Wagner Filho, J., R. Wilkens, L. Zilio, M. Idiart, and A. Villavicencio (2016). Crawling by readability level. In *Proceedings of 12th International Conference on the Computational Processing of Portuguese (PROPOR)*.

Exploring Soft-Clustering for German (Particle) Verbs across Frequency Ranges

Moritz Wittmann
iteratec GmbH
Moritz.Wittmann@iteratec.de

Maximilian Köper
Institut für Maschinelle Sprachverarbeitung
Universität Stuttgart
koepermn@ims.uni-stuttgart.de

Sabine Schulte im Walde
Institut für Maschinelle Sprachverarbeitung
Universität Stuttgart
schulte@ims.uni-stuttgart.de

Abstract

In this paper we explore the role of verb frequencies and the number of clusters in soft-clustering approaches as a tool for automatic semantic classification. Relying on a large-scale setup including 4,871 base verb types and 3,173 complex verb types, and focusing on synonymy as a task-independent goal in semantic classification, we demonstrate that low-frequency German verbs are clustered significantly worse than mid- or high-frequency German verbs, and that German complex verbs are in general more difficult to cluster than German base verbs.

1   Introduction

Semantic classifications are of great interest to computational linguistics, specifically regarding the pervasive problem of data sparseness in the processing of natural language. Such classifications have been used in applications such as *word sense disambiguation* (Dorr and Jones, 1996; Kohomban and Lee, 2005; McCarthy et al., 2007), *parsing* (Carroll et al., 1998; Carroll and Fang, 2004), *machine translation* (Prescher et al., 2000; Koehn and Hoang, 2007; Weller et al., 2014), and *information extraction* (Surdeanu et al., 2003; Venturi et al., 2009), among many others.

Aiming for not only a hard assignment of word types to semantic classes but potentially distinguishing between various word senses, soft-clustering approaches have been exploited as the main tool for automatic semantic classification, e.g., Rooth et al. (1999); Schulte im Walde (2000); Korhonen et al. (2003); Iosif and Potamianos (2007); Köper and Schulte im Walde (2016). Most recently, sense-distinguishing classification approaches have also been defined for predict models by using multi-sense embeddings, e.g., Biemann (2006); Lau et al. (2012); Neelakantan et al. (2014); Li and Jurafsky (2015).

In general, clustering efforts are motivated by specific tasks or applications, so it is difficult to provide universal recommendations regarding the optimal clustering setup. This paper nevertheless addresses clustering parameters that are presumably of general importance on the meta level: Focusing on synonymy as a task-independent goal in semantic classification, we provide an extensive clustering setup to explore the role of verb frequency ranges across various numbers of clusters. The contributions of this paper are two-fold: We demonstrate that (1) low-frequency German verbs are clustered significantly worse than mid- or high-frequency German verbs, and that (2) German complex verbs are in general more difficult to cluster than German base verbs. While (1) the effect of clustering low-frequency target verbs has been investigated by a restricted number of earlier approaches, e.g. Schulte im Walde (2000); Korhonen et al. (2003); Schulte im Walde (2006); Scarton et al. (2014), (2) might be considered as general knowledge but has –as far as we are aware of– not explicitly been proven before.

2 Data and Algorithm

Using *DECOW* (Schäfer and Bildhauer, 2012; Schäfer, 2015) as one of the currently largest German web corpora, we extracted all base verbs and particle verbs from version *DECOW14*. The corpus sentences were morphologically annotated and parsed using *SMOR* (Faaß et al., 2010), *MarMoT* (Müller et al., 2013) and the MATE dependency parser (Bohnet, 2010). Relying on the morphological annotation, and after disregarding prefix verbs (i.e., non-separable complex verbs), we extracted a total of 4,871 base verb types and 3,173 particle verb types.

As vector spaces for the verbs, we relied on *word2vec* (Mikolov et al., 2013) using a symmetrical window of sizes 3 and 10. The underlying corpus was again *DECOW14*. We applied a min-frequency threshold of 50, the dimensionality was set to 400, and we used 10 corpus iterations and 15 negative samples. Other parameters were set to default.

For soft clustering, we used *Non-negative matrix factorization (NMF)*, a factorisation approach with an inherent (soft) clustering property (Ding et al., 2005). NMF has been applied successfully to other NLP tasks before, such as document clustering (Xu et al., 2003), topic number estimation (Yokoi, 2013), and preposition classification (Köper and Schulte im Walde, 2016). We applied the NMF algorithm from the *LAML* (Linear Algebra and Machine Learning) Java library, version 1.6.2 (Qian, 2016).

3 Clustering Experiments

3.1 Clustering Setup

In all clustering experiments, we clustered the German verbs using Non-negative Matrix Factorization with k-Means initialisation. We distinguished the following parameters.

- *Verb set*: We clustered (i) either the base verbs, or (ii) the particle verbs, or (iii) both base and particle verbs, to explore differences for simplex vs. complex verbs.

- *Frequency ranges*: The verbs were sorted by their corpus frequencies, and then split into three equally sized bins, to distinguish between low-, mid- and high-frequency verbs. We clustered only verbs from the same frequency range (LOW, MID, HIGH), or all verbs at the same time.

- *Verb vector spaces*: We applied two different vector spaces, relying on window sizes of 3 vs. 10.

- *Number of clusters*: We used 50, 100, and 250 clusters.

- *Number of iterations*: We let the clustering algorithm perform a maximum of 500 iterations (or less if it converged successfully).

Due to the combination of all parameters used, a total of 24 clusterings can be obtained for each of the three verb sets. For one parameter combination, the clustering algorithm failed to produce an output: base verbs, all frequencies, vectors relying on a window size of 3, and splitting into 250 clusters. The Java library used did not provide any reasons or explanations in the event of failure.

3.2 Clustering Evaluations

As mentioned in the introduction, clustering efforts are motivated by specific tasks or applications, so it is difficult to provide universal recommendations regarding the optimal clustering setup. However, we consider synonymy in cluster analyses as a meta-level goal for clustering approaches, because synonymy represents the strongest type of semantic relatedness. We therefore focus on the ability of the cluster analyses to detect synonymy as a task-independent goal in semantic classification, cf. Section 3.2.1. As a more task-specific evaluation for semantic classification we also assess the ability of the cluster analyses to predict the degree of compositionality of the particle verbs, cf. Section 3.2.2. Considering a strong compositionality of a particle verb regarding its base verb as a case of near-synonymy, the second evaluation targets a semantic relatedness between the complex and the simplex verbs that is not too different to the synonymy evaluation, yet more task-oriented.

3.2.1 Evaluation: Synonymy

We assess the cluster analyses on their ability to contain pairs of synonymous verbs in the same clusters. As basis for the evaluation, we use synonyms provided by the German online synonym dictionary *Duden*[1]. The dictionary contained 2,158 of our particle verbs (with an average of 19 synonyms), and 3,303 of our base verbs (with an average of 13 synonyms). Some examples are listed below:

aussehen   *ausblicken, ausschauen, ausspähen, beobachten, entgegensehen, erwarten, spähen, umherblicken, ausgucken, luchsen, ähneln, anmuten, erscheinen, scheinen, vorkommen, wirken, sehen, suchen, umsehen*

zugestehen   *akzeptieren, bewilligen, billigen, einwilligen, erlauben, genehmigen, gestatten, gewähren, zubilligen, zuerkennen, konzedieren, legitimieren, sanktionieren, tolerieren, zugutehalten, absegnen, unterschreiben, abnicken, stattgeben*

erklären   *aufzeigen, auseinanderlegen, auseinandersetzen, ausführen, darlegen, definieren, entwickeln, erläutern, erörtern, konkretisieren, veranschaulichen, verdeutlichen, zeigen, exemplifizieren, explizieren, klarlegen, klarmachen, verdeutschen, verklickern, verkasematuckeln, auslegen, begründen, belegen, deuten, kommentieren, motivieren, rechtfertigen, fundieren, interpretieren, legitimieren, substanziieren, aufklären, einweihen, informieren, unterrichten, anbringen, anmelden, ausdrücken, äußern, aussprechen, bekennen, bekunden, eröffnen, formulieren, melden, mitteilen, sagen, verlautbaren, vorbringen, kundgeben, kundtun, offenbaren, unterbreiten, verkünden, verkündigen, artikulieren, dokumentieren, verbalisieren, angeben, ausweisen, bescheinigen, bezeichnen, deklarieren, kennzeichnen, einsetzen, einstehen, eintreten, zustimmen, starkmachen, enthüllen, offenbaren, outen*

siegen   *bezwingen, gewinnen, schlagen, triumphieren*

Across the clusters within a cluster analysis, we check for all pairs of verbs whether they represent synonyms according to our gold standard or not, and compute precision, recall and the harmonic f-score.

As NMF clustering provides a membership score $x \geq 0$ for each verb and each cluster, we assume that the higher the membership score of a verb for a certain cluster, the more likely the verb is to be part of it. Before running the synonym evaluation, we thus apply an inclusion threshold in order to decide for each verb whether it is considered to be in a cluster or not. Since there is no maximum membership score, and since the values lie on different scales depending on the clustering parameters, determining the ideal membership threshold for each of the clusterings is not straightforward. We therefore employ a brute-force solution: after finding the largest membership score t_{max} for a specific cluster analysis, the synonym evaluation is applied to all non-negative thresholds in the set $t_{max} - k \cdot 0.001, k \in \mathbb{N}_0$. For example, if the largest membership value in a clustering is 0.8916, the synonym evaluation is applied to all thresholds in the set $\{0.8916, 0.8906, 0.8896, ..., 0.0036, 0.0026, 0.0016, 0.0006\}$.

For a given threshold value, the synonym evaluation counts all verb pairs given by the clustering. Two verbs are considered a pair if they share one or more clusters. Since verbs are included in more clusters as the threshold is lowered, we add an abort condition: as soon as 50% of all possible verb pairs are present in the clustering, the threshold is not lowered any further.

See Figure 1 for a small-scale example, listing all symmetric verb pairs for the gold standard and the clustering, marking the correct pairs among the clustering pairs, and calculating precision, recall and f-score. Since the clusterings in our experiments cover thousands of verbs, the actual number of verb pairs in our clusterings is large. This results in f-scores on a very low magnitude, which is not important for our evaluation, however, as the scores are used to compare clustering parameter variations, rather than providing impressive evaluation scores.

---

[1] `www.duden.de`

Gold Standard

V_1	V_{100}	V_{200}	V_2	V_{500}	
V_2	V_{50}	V_{100}	V_1	V_{201}	
V_3	V_{10}	V_{20}	V_{75}	V_5	V_4 V_{120}
V_4	V_3	V_5	V_{65}		
V_5	V_3	V_4	V_{80}	V_{85}	V_{86}

Gold Standard Pairs

$(V_1\,V_{100})\ (V_1\,V_{200})\ (V_1\,V_2)\ (V_1\,V_{500})\ (V_2\,V_{50})$
$(V_2\,V_{100})\ (V_2\,V_{201})\ (V_3\,V_{10})\ (V_3\,V_{20})\ (V_3\,V_{75})$
$(V_3\,V_5)\ (V_3\,V_4)\ (V_3\,V_{120})\ (V_4\,V_5)\ (V_4\,V_{65})$
$(V_5\,V_{80})\ (V_5\,V_{85})\ (V_5\,V_{86})$

Clustering

C_1	C_2	C_3	C_4
V_1	V_1	V_3	V_3
V_2		V_4	V_4
		V_6	V_5
		V_7	V_1
			V_7
			V_8

Clustering Pairs

$(V_1\,V_2)\ (V_3\,V_4)\ (V_3\,V_6)\ (V_3\,V_7)\ (V_4\,V_6)$
$(V_4\,V_7)\ (V_6\,V_7)\ (V_3\,V_5)\ (V_1\,V_3)\ (V_3\,V_8)$
$(V_4\,V_5)\ (V_1\,V_4)\ (V_4\,V_8)\ (V_1\,V_5)\ (V_5\,V_7)$
$(V_5\,V_8)\ (V_1\,V_7)\ (V_1\,V_8)\ (V_7\,V_8)$

$$\text{Precision} = \frac{\text{Clustering Pairs} \cap \text{Gold Standard Pairs}}{\text{Clustering Pairs}} = \frac{4}{19} \approx 0.211$$

$$\text{Recall} = \frac{\text{Clustering Pairs} \cap \text{Gold Standard Pairs}}{\text{Gold Standard Pairs}} = \frac{4}{18} \approx 0.222$$

$$\text{F-Score} = \frac{2 \times \text{Precision} \times \text{Recall}}{\text{Precision} + \text{Recall}} \approx 0.216$$

Figure 1: Small-scale example of verb pair evaluation.

As an alternative to the brute-force search for the best inclusion threshold, we also apply a method for assigning verbs to their top n clusters, with $1 \leq n \leq \frac{N}{2}$ and N representing the total number of clusters. In this variant, verbs are added to the n clusters with the highest membership scores. For example, suppose that in a clustering of verbs into 6 clusters, verb v_1 has the membership values 0.7, 0.4, 0.45, 0.2, 0.5, and 0.8 for clusters 1 to 6 respectively. For $n = 1$, the verb will be included only in cluster 6, for $n = 2$, it will be considered part of clusters 6 and 1, and for $n = 3$, it belongs to clusters 6, 1, and 5. This variant is referred to as *top-n evaluation*, whereas the previously described method is referred to as *threshold evaluation*.

3.2.2 Evaluation: Compositionality

In this evaluation, we predict the degree of compositionality of the complex particle verbs, i.e., the degree of relatedness between the particle verbs and their corresponding base verbs (such as *abnehmen − nehmen* 'take over − take', and *anfangen − fangen* 'begin − catch'). We assume that if a particle verb and its base verb tend to co-occur in the same cluster within a cluster analysis, then the particle verb is semantically transparent, rather than opaque. The predictions are evaluated against an existing dataset of human ratings on German particle verb compositionality (Bott et al., 2016). The gold standard contains a total of 400 particle verbs across 11 particle types and 3 frequency bands.

Similarly to the evaluation metric described in the previous section, the compositionality evaluation is also applied to all thresholds in the set $t_{max} - k \cdot 0.001, k \in \mathbb{N}_0$, with t_{max} being the largest inclusion value found in the clustering, as well as to all top-n cluster assignments with $1 \leq n \leq \frac{N}{2}$. For each pair of particle verb and base verb, e.g., *abnehmen – nehmen*, we then compare the assignment of the two verbs to the same vs. different clusters in two different ways.

- *Pointwise Mutual Information (PMI)*:

    We calculate $\log \frac{p(PV,BV)}{p(PV)p(BV)}$, with $p(PV, BV)$ the proportion of clusters containing both the particle verb PV and the base verb BV, and $p(PV)$ and $p(BV)$ the proportions of clusters containing the particle and base verbs individually. The proportions are relative to the total number of clusters, so $p(PV, BV) = 0.2$ means that 20% of the clusters contain both PV and BV. A high PMI means that a pair tends to occur in the same clusters rather than in different ones.

- *Cosine similarity between average cluster centroid vectors*:

    For each cluster, we calculate the centroid vector as the average over all verb vectors in that cluster. In addition, we calculate average cluster centroid vectors for all verbs, as the average over all centroid vectors a verb has been assigned to. Then, each two verbs are compared by calculating the cosine of the angle between the respective average cluster centroid vectors. A high cosine similarity means that a pair tends to occur in the same clusters, or that the clusters in which the two verbs occur have similar centroids.

In the final evaluation step, we compute the correlation between the PV–BV similarity predictions relying on PMI/cosine in comparison to the gold standard ratings, using Spearman's Rank-Order Correlation Coefficient ρ (Siegel and Castellan, 1988).

4 Results

In the following, we present the results of our clustering experiments and evaluations. Please (a) remember that the f-score values for the synonym evaluation are in a very low range because they assess a comparably large number of verb pairs across 4,871 base verbs and 3,173 particle verbs within the cluster analyses; and (b) note that the compositionality evaluation is carried out on a subset of only 400 particle verbs for which the gold standard contains compositionality ratings.

Figure 2 presents the synonymy evaluation f-score values when clustering all particle and base verbs in 50, 100 and 250 clusters. With an increasing threshold (x-axis), a smaller number of verbs is included in the clusters. The resulting quality of the cluster analyses differs across the different numbers of clusters, as one would have expected. For 50 and 100 clusters, the correlation decreases with an increasing threshold along the x-axis, so a more general inclusion is better, but for 250 clusters, the clusters are better when they contain less verbs. As the different scales on the y-axis across the three plots show, overall a smaller number of clusters with generous assignment is best.

Table 1 zooms into the differences of clustering low-, mid, high-frequency or all verbs, regarding base verbs (BVs), particle verbs (PVs) and both BVs and PVs. For each cell, we show the best result across thresholds/top-n and vector spaces. For low- and mid-frequency verbs, we did not assess the compositionality evaluation because less than 10% of the particle verbs and corresponding base verbs from the gold standard were found in the clustering, regardless of the inclusion threshold or the top-n value used.

The results in the table demonstrate the following differences:

- The results for high-frequency verbs are generally better than for low- and mid-frequency verbs, demonstrating that target frequency (and, most probably, less sparse data) matters.

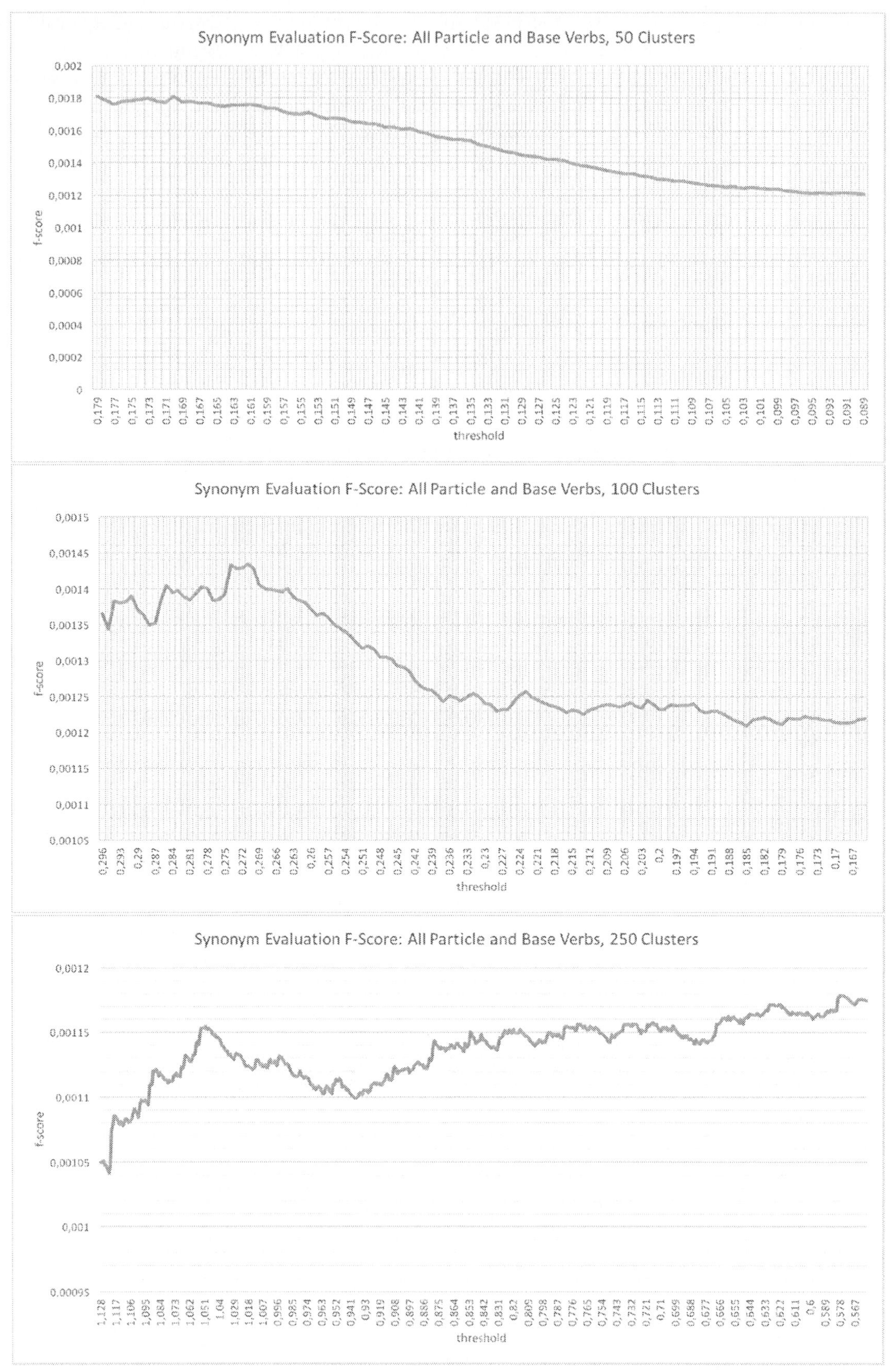

Figure 2: Synonymy f-score results for all verbs and 50/100/250 clusters.

Evaluation: synonymy (threshold)

Frequency	ALL			HIGH			MID			LOW		
Clusters	50	100	250	50	100	250	50	100	250	50	100	250
BVs	**.00640**	.00412	.00370	**.02337**	.01559	.01606	**.00955**	.00480	.00277	**.00212**	.00103	.00090
PVs	.00126	.00076	.00068	.01170	.00602	.00736	.00072	.00025	.00022	.00009	.00004	.00003
BVs+PVs	.00181	.00143	.00118	.01420	.00823	.00925	.00225	.00101	.00084	.00012	.00007	.00004

Evaluation: synonymy (top-n)

Frequency	ALL			HIGH			MID			LOW		
Clusters	50	100	250	50	100	250	50	100	250	50	100	250
BVs	**.01169**	.00736	.00428	**.03006**	.02271	.01999	**.01007**	.00514	.00324	**.00255**	.00144	.00099
PVs	.00217	.00124	.00119	.01335	.00616	.00788	.00088	.00026	.00018	.00004	.00003	.00003
BVs+PVs	.00368	.00351	.00214	.01935	.01206	.00917	.00239	.00152	.00101	.00012	.00007	.00004

Evaluation: compositionality (threshold)

Frequency	ALL			HIGH		
Clusters	50	100	250	50	100	250
BVs+PVs (PMI)	.274***	.183***	.248***	**.468****	.220*	.281**
BVs+PVs (Cos)	**.334*****	.264***	.287***	.439**	.301***	.283**

Evaluation: compositionality (top-n)

Frequency	ALL			HIGH		
Clusters	50	100	250	50	100	250
BVs+PVs (PMI)	.259***	.297***	**.377*****	**.421*****	.378***	.398***
BVs+PVs (Cos)	.197***	.186***	.203***	.311***	.257**	.207*

Table 1: Results across evaluations and clustering parameters (* = p$\leq$0.05, ** = p$\leq$0.01, *** = p$\leq$0.001).

- The results for base verbs are generally better than for particle verbs (only applicable to the synonym evaluation), demonstrating that particle verbs are harder to assess semantically than base verbs, presumably because they are more ambiguous.

- Confirming insights from Figure 2, the results for clusterings with 50 clusters are generally better than for clusterings with 100 or 250 clusters.

- For predicting particle verb compositionality, PMI generally works better than the cosine.

- (not shown in the table:) There is no strong tendency for one of the vector spaces (i.e., using a window of 3 vs. 10 words) outperforming the other.

5 Conclusion

We provided an extensive clustering setup and focused on synonymy as a task-independent goal in semantic classification, in order to explore the role of verb frequency ranges across various numbers of clusters. We demonstrated that (1) low-frequency German verbs are clustered significantly worse than mid- or high-frequency German verbs, and that (2) German complex verbs are in general more difficult to cluster than German base verbs. While (1) the effect of clustering low-frequency target verbs has been investigated by a restricted number of earlier approaches, (2) might be considered as general knowledge but has –as far as we are aware of– not explicitly been proven before.

Acknowledgments

The research was supported by the DFG Collaborative Research Centre SFB 732/D12 *"Sense Discrimination and Regular Meaning Shifts of German Particle Verbs"* (Maximilian Köper, Moritz Wittmann), the DFG Research Grant SCHU-2580/2 *"Distributional Approaches to Semantic Relatedness"* (Moritz Wittmann), and the DFG Heisenberg Fellowship SCHU-2580/1 (Sabine Schulte im Walde).

References

Chris Biemann. 2006. Chinese Whispers: An Efficient Graph Clustering Algorithm and Its Application to Natural Language Processing Problems. In *Proceedings of the 1st Workshop on Graph-Based Methods for Natural Language Processing*. Stroudsburg, PA, USA, pages 73–80.

Bernd Bohnet. 2010. Top Accuracy and Fast Dependency Parsing is not a Contradiction. In *Proceedings of the 23rd International Conference on Computational Linguistics*. Beijing, China, pages 89–97.

Stefan Bott, Nana Khvtisavrishvili, Max Kisselew, and Sabine Schulte im Walde. 2016. $G_h$ost-PV: A Representative Gold Standard of German Particle Verbs. In *Proceedings of the 5th Workshop on Cognitive Aspects of the Lexicon*. Osaka, Japan, pages 125–133.

John Carroll and Alex C. Fang. 2004. The Automatic Acquisition of Verb Subcategorisations and their Impact on the Performance of an HPSG Parser. In *Proceedings of the 1st International Joint Conference on Natural Language Processing*. Sanya City, China, pages 107–114.

John Carroll, Guido Minnen, and Ted Briscoe. 1998. Can Subcategorisation Probabilities Help a Statistical Parser? In *Proceedings of the 6th ACL/SIGDAT Workshop on Very Large Corpora*. Montréal, Canada, pages 118–126.

Chris Ding, Xiaofeng He, and Horst D. Simon. 2005. On the Equivalence of Nonnegative Matrix Factorization and Spectral Clustering. In *Proceedings of the SIAM International Conference on Data Mining*. Newport Beach, CA, USA, pages 606–610.

Bonnie J. Dorr and Doug Jones. 1996. Role of Word Sense Disambiguation in Lexical Acquisition: Predicting Semantics from Syntactic Cues. In *Proceedings of the 16th International Conference on Computational Linguistics*. Copenhagen, Denmark, pages 322–327.

Gertrud Faaß, Ulrich Heid, and Helmut Schmid. 2010. Design and Application of a Gold Standard for Morphological Analysis: SMOR in Validation. In *Proceedings of the 7th International Conference on Language Resources and Evaluation*. Valletta, Malta, pages 803–810.

Elias Iosif and Alexandros Potamianos. 2007. A Soft-Clustering Algorithm for Automatic Induction of Semantic Classes. In *Proceedings of the 8th Interspeech Conference*. Antwerp, Belgium, pages 1609–1612.

Philipp Koehn and Hieu Hoang. 2007. Factored Translation Models. In *Proceedings of the Joint Conference on Empirical Methods in Natural Language Processing and Computational Natural Language Learning*. Prague, Czech Republic, pages 868–876.

Upali S. Kohomban and Wee Sun Lee. 2005. Learning Semantic Classes for Word Sense Disambiguation. In *Proceedings of the 43rd Annual Meeting on Association for Computational Linguistics*. Ann Arbor, MI, pages 34–41.

Maximilian Köper and Sabine Schulte im Walde. 2016. Automatic Semantic Classification of German Preposition Types: Comparing Hard and Soft Clustering Approaches across Features. In *Proceedings of the 54th Annual Meeting of the Association for Computational Linguistics*. Berlin, Germany, pages 256–263.

Anna Korhonen, Yuval Krymolowski, and Zvika Marx. 2003. Clustering Polysemic Subcategorization Frame Distributions Semantically. In *Proceedings of the 41st Annual Meeting of the Association for Computational Linguistics*. Sapporo, Japan, pages 64–71.

Jey Han Lau, Paul Cook, Diana McCarthy, David Newman, and Timothy Baldwin. 2012. Word Sense Induction for Novel Sense Detection. In *Proceedings of the Conference of the European Chapter of the Association for Computational Linguistics*. Avignon, France, pages 591–601.

Jiwei Li and Dan Jurafsky. 2015. Do Multi-Sense Embeddings Improve Natural Language Understanding? In *Proceedings of the Conference on Empirical Methods in Natural Language Processing*. Lisbon, Portugal, pages 1722–1732.

Diana McCarthy, Sriram Venkatapathy, and Aravind K. Joshi. 2007. Detecting Compositionality of Verb-Object Combinations using Selectional Preferences. In *Proceedings of the Joint Conference on Empirical Methods in Natural Language Processing and Computational Natural Language Learning*. Prague, Czech Republic, pages 369–379.

Tomas Mikolov, Ilya Sutskever, Kai Chen, Greg S. Corrado, and Jeff Dean. 2013. Distributed Representations of Words and Phrases and their Compositionality. In *Advances in Neural Information Processing Systems 26*. Lake Tahoe, Nevada, USA, pages 3111–3119.

Thomas Müller, Helmut Schmid, and Hinrich Schütze. 2013. Efficient Higher-Order CRFs for Morphological Tagging. In *Proceedings of the 2013 Conference on Empirical Methods in Natural Language Processing*. Seattle, Washington, USA, pages 322–332.

Arvind Neelakantan, Jeevan Shankar, Alexandre Passos, and Andrew McCallum. 2014. Efficient Nonparametric Estimation of Multiple Embeddings per Word in Vector Space. In *Proceedings of the 2014 Conference on Empirical Methods in Natural Language Processing*. Doha, Qatar, pages 1059–1069.

Detlef Prescher, Stefan Riezler, and Mats Rooth. 2000. Using a Probabilistic Class-Based Lexicon for Lexical Ambiguity Resolution. In *Proceedings of the 18th International Conference on Computational Linguistics*. Saarbrücken, Germany, pages 649–655.

Mingjie Qian. 2016. LAML. `https://github.com/MingjieQian/LAML`.

Mats Rooth, Stefan Riezler, Detlef Prescher, Glenn Carroll, and Franz Beil. 1999. Inducing a Semantically Annotated Lexicon via EM-Based Clustering. In *Proceedings of the 37th Annual Meeting of the Association for Computational Linguistics*. Maryland, MD, pages 104–111.

Carolina Scarton, Lin Sun, Karin Kipper-Schuler, Magali Sanches Duran, Martha Palmer, and Anna Korhonen. 2014. Verb Clustering for Brazilian Portuguese. In Alexander Gelbukh, editor, *Proceedings of the 15th International Conference on Intelligent Text Processing and Computational Linguistics*. Kathmandu, Nepal, pages 25–39.

Roland Schäfer. 2015. Processing and Querying Large Web Corpora with the COW14 Architecture. In *Proceedings of the 3rd Workshop on Challenges in the Management of Large Corpora*. Mannheim, Germany, pages 28–34.

Roland Schäfer and Felix Bildhauer. 2012. Building Large Corpora from the Web Using a New Efficient Tool Chain. In *Proceedings of the 8th International Conference on Language Resources and Evaluation*. Istanbul, Turkey, pages 486–493.

Sabine Schulte im Walde. 2000. Clustering Verbs Semantically According to their Alternation Behaviour. In *Proceedings of the 18th International Conference on Computational Linguistics*. Saarbrücken, Germany, pages 747–753.

Sabine Schulte im Walde. 2006. Experiments on the Automatic Induction of German Semantic Verb Classes. *Computational Linguistics* 32(2):159–194.

Sidney Siegel and N. John Castellan. 1988. *Nonparametric Statistics for the Behavioral Sciences*. McGraw-Hill, Boston, MA.

Mihai Surdeanu, Sanda Harabagiu, John Williams, and Paul Aarseth. 2003. Using Predicate-Argument Structures for Information Extraction. In *Proceedings of the 41st Annual Meeting of the Association for Computational Linguistics*. Sapporo, Japan, pages 8–15.

Giulia Venturi, Simonetta Montemagni, Simone Marchi, Yutaka Sasaki, Paul Thompson, John McNaught, and Sophia Ananiadou. 2009. Bootstrapping a Verb Lexicon for Biomedical Information Extraction. In Alexander Gelbukh, editor, *Linguistics and Intelligent Text Processing*, Springer, Heidelberg, pages 137–148.

Marion Weller, Sabine Schulte im Walde, and Alexander Fraser. 2014. Using Noun Class Information to model Selectional Preferences for Translating Prepositions in SMT. In *Proceedings of the 11th Conference of the Association for Machine Translation in the Americas*. Vancouver, Canada, pages 275–287.

Wei Xu, Xin Liu, and Yihong Gong. 2003. Document Clustering Based on Non-negative Matrix Factorization. In *Proceedings of the 26th Annual International ACM SIGIR Conference on Research and Development in Information Retrieval*. Toronto, Canada, pages 267–273.

Takeru Yokoi. 2013. Topic Number Estimation by Consensus Soft Clustering with NMF. In Tai-Hoon Kim, Young-Hoon Lee, Byeong Ho Kang, and Dominik Slezak, editors, *Future Generation Information Technology*, Springer, volume 8105 of *Lecture Notes in Computer Science*, pages 63–73.

Towards Semantic Modeling of Contradictions and Disagreements: A Case Study of Medical Guidelines

Wlodek Zadrozny
Department of Computer Science, UNC Charlotte
wzadrozn@uncc.edu

Hossein Hematialam
Department of Computer Science, UNC Charlotte
hhematia@uncc.edu

Luciana Garbayo
Departments of Philosophy and Medical Education, U. of Central Florida
Luciana.Garbayo@ucf.edu

Abstract

We introduce a formal distinction between contradictions and disagreements in natural language texts, motivated by the need to formally reason about contradictory medical guidelines. This is a novel and potentially very useful distinction, and hasn't been discussed so far in NLP and logic. We also describe a NLP system capable of automated finding contradictory medical guidelines; the system uses a combination of text analysis and information retrieval modules. We also report positive evaluation results on a small corpus of contradictory medical recommendations.

1   Introduction

This is a programmatic paper (and work in progress) motivated by the challenge of automatically identifying and representing contradictions in medical guidelines. In this paper we take the perspective of building a natural language understanding system that can properly represent disagreements. On the practical side, we expect this research to eventually result in a larger solution that can provide decision support for patients and physicians, and help identify and reason with contradictory advice in their specific cases. However, proposed solution apply more generally to natural language semantics.

Contributions: This paper makes the following novel contributions:

- A novel formal analysis of types of contradictions in text. Namely, we introduce and formally characterize the distinction between *contradictions* and *disagreements*. This distinction is generally applicable to all semantic processing of natural language text, and is orthogonal to other typologies of contradictions, e.g. De Marneffe et al. (2008).

- A proposal for an architecture and a method for identifying contradictions and disagreement in medical guidelines (viewed as self-standing documents, and ignoring, in this paper, all epistemological issues in expert disagreements, Garbayo (2014))

- Preliminary results from an implemented system showing the feasibility of the proposed approach. (Section 3)

Motivation: Disagreements in medical guidelines raise uncertainty in disease screening and treatment. Uncertainty derived from the lack of guidelines consistency among different expert groups is confusing for patients, and also contributes to overdiagnosis. For example, the ACOG recommends that women

over age 40 get a mammography annually, but the USPSTF recommends clinicians base screening decisions for women aged 40 to 49 on the womens individual risk profile and preferences. We can see two
different actions recommended by two guideline sets for women aged 40 to 49. We'll see other examples
below.

A Brief Overview of the Proposed Approach: For the sake of simplicity, we will focus on analyzing the
guidelines pairwise. Thus with two texts of guidelines for the same condition we propose the following:

1. Identify candidate sentences pertaining to the same condition or the same action;

2. Compute candidate contradictions and disagreements (using techniques of information retrieval
   and statistical language modeling);

3. Identify the specific contradictions and disagreements computationally, using different, deeper
   modes of analysis based on semantic representation informed by *formal representations of disagreements and contradictions*;

4. A method for automated automated reasoning with disagreements and contradictions in computational settings, focused on the identification areas of agreement and disagreement, including their
   provenances.

2   Formal representation of disagreement and contradiction

We need a formal representation of contradictory guidelines in order to be able to reason about them. This
section proposes, to our knowledge for the first time in formal semantics, a way to reason with partially
contradictory information based on a formal distinction between disagreements and contradictions, and
formalized using a combination of propositional calculus and lattice theory.

Let's consider a few examples of actual sentences containing disagreements or contradictions. For
clarity of exposition we will always present contradictions between pairs of documents, such as guidelines.

Example 1. We will use an example from a CDC table comparing "Breast Cancer Screening Guidelines
for Women" provided by seven different accredited medical bodies. [1] There we find contradictory recommendations for *"women aged 50 to 74 with average risk"* coming from two (of the seven) different
organizations):

    (a) *Screening with mammography and clinical breast exam annually.*
    (b) *Biennial screening mammography is recommended.*

Example 2. Consider the question about the recommended number of minutes of physical activity.
Again, the guidelines might differ [2] : One organization recommending a minimum of 150 minutes per
week, and another 150-300 minutes week (we simplify the recommendation a bit here). Clearly, someone exercising 30 min per day, 6 days a week satisfies both guidelines. The guidelines don't agree 100%,
but intuitively they are not 100% contradictory either.

Disagreements vs. contradictions: To capture the intuitive distinction between Examples 1 and 2, we
say that two guidelines are *contradictory* if it is impossible for both guidelines to be followed (at the
same time). And two guidelines are in *disagreement* if there are patients where the two guidelines are
possible to be followed, and patients for which this is impossible. As it turns out we can represent this
distinction formally, in logic, making it broadly applicable in semantics, using the following idea:

- *Contradiction* is present if there is no model for the joint theory expressed in two text segments
  (coming from different guidelines);

---

[1] https://www.cdc.gov/cancer/breast/pdf/BreastCancerScreeningGuidelines.pdf

[2] https://www.supertracker.usda.gov/physicalActivityInfo.aspx. https://www.cdc.gov/
healthyweight/physical_activity/

- *Disagreement* is present, if the sets of models, for the predicates present in both text segments, are different for each segment, but a model can be created satisfying both segments.

The requirement that for disagreements the predicates are present in both segments means that we are aiming at modeling the same or similar relations; and the existence of a common model requires some thought about how to represent the meaning of both segments. We want to reflect the idea that any two propositions that are neither contradictory nor equivalent are in disagreement, *provided they talk about similar relations*. To model this similarity we need a formalism.

Formalization: We start by assuming that at least initially we do not need full power of first order logic (FOL) or a stronger logical system. So the basis of our representation will be a formal language of propositions. Thus we do not have variables or quantifiers. However, to be able to reflect the disagreements we need to augment it with a representation of parameters.]

For example, we would like to be able distinguish between a recommendation of a minimum of 30 minutes of daily exercise and another one of 20 minutes; and at the same time we need to be able to notice that both recommendations pertain to the recommended dose (time) of exercise.

To this end we assume that our representation language contains propositional symbols $p, q, r, ..., p_1, p_2, ...$ and symbols representing parameters a, b, c, a_1, a_2, etc. We have special parameters $o_1, o_2, ...$ which later will be used to represent the provenance of recommendations. This will allow us to find the sources of contradictions and disagreements. We assume the standard inference rules of propositional logic. The added parameters obviously don't extend the power of the system beyond propositional calculus. To reason about disagreements we will need to introduce additional rules of inference.

Example 1 continued: Let p stand for *screening mammography is recommended*; o_1, o_2 represent the provenance of the recommendations (a) and (b) respectively; and a, b stand for *annually* and *biennally*. We then have the formal representation of the respective guidelines as $p(a, o_1)$ and $p(b, o_2)$.

We need means to formally represent the fact that these guidelines are contradictory. This cannot simply be due to having different constants/parameters inside the parentheses (and ignoring the o's). To see this point, consider a similar representation of doses of daily recommended exercise. Here, we would also have two distinct provenances and two distinct values; however, intuitively we could recognize a disagreement and not a contradiction, since anyone exercising 30 minutes or more is also exercising 20 minutes or more.

To proceed we need to make two additional assumptions, namely that no particular guidelines document can have internal contradictions. That is, the set of all $p_i(a_j^i, o)$ for a particular o is never contradictory (viewed as statements in classical propositional logic).

And the second assumption is that the parameters come in different sorts, which we will represent by capital letters followed by a colon, e.g. $A : a_1$. More importantly, we assume elements of any particular sort form a *lattice* (or at least *meet semi-lattice*). That is, for any set of parameters of a particular sort (e.g. time, duration, dosage, etc.) $a_1 \wedge a_2$ is defined, and every such lattice has a minimal element $\perp$.

In the example representations of the mammography guidelines, the meet of *biennial* and *annual* is $\perp$, since biennial events cannot be annual and vice versa. However, the meet of "20 minutes or more" and "30 minutes or more" is the latter, because if you exercise e.g. 40 minutes you satisfied the requirement "20 minutes or more" of exercise. This mechanism allows us to make a formal distinction between contradictions and disagreements:

$p(A\colon a_1, o_1)$ and $p(A\colon a_2, o_2)$ are *contradictory* if $a_1 \wedge a_2 = \perp$

$p(A\colon a_1, o_1)$ and $p(A\colon a_2, o_2)$ *disagree* if taking $a_1 \wedge a_2 = a$, we have $a \neq \perp$ and either $a \neq a_1$ or $a \neq a_2$.

These definitions are naturally extended to multi-parameter cases by defining the contradiction as a

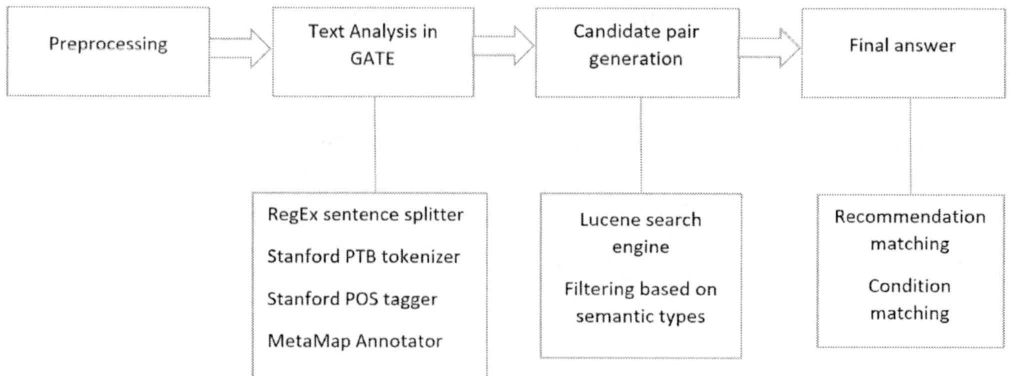

Figure 1: The architecture used to evaluate extraction of contradictions in medical guidelines

situation, where the meet of at least one type of parameters is $\perp$; and the disagreement, when there's no contradiction, and at least one type of parameter contains a disagreement.

To do some elementary reasoning about disagreement we need an inference rule capable of relating two formulas with different parameters, and to keep track of provenances we need to allow propositions with multiple labels, e.g. $\{o_1, o_2\}$. This is nicely combined in a single inference rule:

$$\frac{p(A\colon a_1, o_1), p(A\colon a_2, o_2)}{p(A\colon a_1 \wedge a_2, \{o_1, o_2\})} \text{ Lattice } \wedge$$

If the formula p has more than one parameter, we apply this rule for each parameter separately. With this inference rule we are getting the following:

- The set of derivable (using the above rule) contradictory propositions corresponds to the ones that have $\perp$ as at least one parameter.

- The set of disagreements corresponds to the derivable propositions with two or more provenance parameters and a disagreement for one or more sorts.

- For any fixed provenance o we have the full power of power of inference rules of propositional calculus applied to sentences of the form $p(a, o)$ where a stands for a collection of parameters of different sorts.

3 Finding contradictions and disagreements

Having solved the problem of formally representing contradictions and disagreement, and having created a formal method of keeping track of their provenances, we now focus on the language understanding part.

The results presented in this section are preliminary in two ways: First, we have not completed a translation from a semantic representation produced by NLP tools to a logical form amenable to reasoning with the parameterized propositional logic of the previous section. We assume this can be done using existing methods, as described in publications ranging from standard textbooks (Bird et al. (2009)) to complex NLP architectures (McCord et al. (2012)). Obviously, we intend to prove that this indeed is possible. Second, our methods for finding contradictions and disagreements, even though not trivial, very likely can be improved. Nevertheless the results are promising.

Figure 1 shows a novel architecture consisting of several well known components. We follow the approach presented in the Introduction: we use the text analysis tools for feature generation and concept identification. The Lucene search engine is used to for finding similar sentences based on indexed semantic features (and words). For examples, given the query "mammography is recommended for women age 40-49" we search multiple guidelines and identify sentences for further analysis. This analysis done through recommendation matching ('mammography recommended') and condition matching ('age 40-49', or 'age') allows the system to decide if given guidelines document recommends a procedure or not. Similarly, we can identify partial matches, e.g. 'age 40-49' and 'age over 40'.

Evaluation: At this point we only evaluated this method on finding agreement and disagreement on twelve example recommendations sentences and breast cancer screening guidelines produced by seven different medical organizations. [3] This gives us only 84 data points. However, the results are promising: The system produced only four errors (two false positives and two false negatives), thus on this – admittedly simple – data set achieved an impressive accuracy of 95%.

4   Summary, comparisons, and ongoing work

Summary: Motivated by analysis of medical guidelines we introduced the formal distinction between disagreements and contradictions. We presented a new system for finding both, and results of a preliminary evaluation. The new formal representation and the general architecture of the system are potentially broadly applicable to NLP, for example to question answering, where an answer can be extracted from texts that disagree on details, but broadly provide the same answer or recommend the same action. Many obstacles remain: we do not have reliable ways of converting longer texts intended for human reading into semi-structured representation suitable for text mining (for example dealing with tables); in evaluation we used simple sentences, but texts might contain information in multiple sentences, and thus increasing the difficulty of matching, and necessitating the need to combine partial information. And while solutions to these problems exist, they are not perfect, and will likely decrease the accuracy of our system.

Comparisons: We want to acknowledge prior work on representing contradictions in NLP, e.g. De Marneffe et al. (2008) and Kloetzer et al (2013). The former containing a taxonomy of linguistic expressions of contradiction, potentially useful when dealing with the linguistic diversity of the guidelines. The latter showing methods for large scale acquisition of contradictory patterns. We believe such distributional methods might add coverage to our approach and complement the IR method we are currently using. Neither of these works makes a formal distinction between contradictions and disagreements. On the formal side, clearly there is a big body of work on contextualizing the truth of propositions, for example in modal logic and para-consistent logics [4]. We even found, accidentally, a 1969 paper on 'topological logic' Rescher and Garson (1969), which parameterizes propositions in several ways, but does not use lattices of parameters – this seems to be our original contribution.

Ongoing work: We are pursuing several extensions of this work. On the medical side, we are exploring opportunities to apply the results of this semantic disagreement analysis to medical practice, developing an epistemic analysis of expert disagreement (Garbayo (2014)), extended to medical simulation (Karnon et al. (2012), Garbayo and Stahl (2017)). On the language processing side, we will be evaluating the current system on linguistically more complex sets of guidelines. This will require additional text pre-possessing and dealing with information spread out in multiple sentences. We have done before work Hematialam and Zadrozny (2016) on extracting condition and action expressions in medical guidelines for sinusitis, hypertension and asthma, with acceptable results. We plan to evaluate our current work by adding guidelines for the same conditions issued by other medical organizations. In addition, we will be looking at the potential of this work to be applied more broadly to the interpretation of text, and on the formal side into other models of contradictions; for example, dealing with contradictory medical or other diagnoses would require adding Bayesian reasoning.

---

[3] `https://www.cdc.gov/cancer/breast/pdf/BreastCancerScreeningGuidelines.pdf`

[4] `https://plato.stanford.edu/entries/possible-worlds/`, and `https://plato.stanford.edu/entries/logic-paraconsistent/`

Acknowledgments. The authors would like to thank James Stahl of the Department of Internal Medicine, Dartmouth College, for discussions of contradictions in medical guidelines. Also, we want to thank the referees for their questions and comments resulting in clarifications added to the paper.

References

Bird, S., E. Klein, and E. Loper (2009). *Natural Language Processing with Python* (1st ed.). O'Reilly Media, Inc.

De Marneffe, M.-C., A. N. Rafferty, and C. D. Manning (2008). Finding contradictions in text. In *ACL*, Volume 8, pp. 1039–1047.

Garbayo, L. (2014). *Epistemic Considerations on Expert Disagreement, Normative Justification, and Inconsistency Regarding Multi-criteria Decision Making*, pp. 35–45. Cham: Springer International Publishing.

Garbayo, L. and J. Stahl (2017, Mar). Simulation as an ethical imperative and epistemic responsibility for the implementation of medical guidelines in health care. *Medicine, Health Care and Philosophy 20*(1), 37–42.

Hematialam, H. and W. Zadrozny (2016). Text mining of medical guidelines. In *Proc. of the Twenty-Ninth Intern. Florida Artificial Intelligence Res. Soc. Conf.; FLAIRS-29 Poster Abstracts*. AAAI.

Karnon, J., J. Stahl, A. Brennan, J. J. Caro, J. Mar, and J. Mller (2012). Modeling using discrete event simulation. *Medical Decision Making 32*(5), 701–711. PMID: 22990085.

Kloetzer et al, J. (2013). Two-stage method for large-scale acquisition of contradiction pattern pairs using entailment. *EMNLP*, 693–703.

McCord, M. C., J. W. Murdock, and B. K. Boguraev (2012). Deep parsing in Watson. *IBM Journal of Research and Development 56*(3.4), 3–1.

Rescher, N. and J. Garson (1969). Topological logic. *The Journal of Symbolic Logic 33*(4), 537–548.

An Evaluation of PredPatt and Open IE
via Stage 1 Semantic Role Labeling

Sheng Zhang
Johns Hopkins University
zsheng2@jhu.edu

Rachel Rudinger
Johns Hopkins University
rudinger@jhu.edu

Benjamin Van Durme
Johns Hopkins University
vandurme@cs.jhu.edu

Abstract

PredPatt is a pattern-based framework for predicate-argument extraction. While it works across languages and provides a well-formed syntax-semantics interface for NLP tasks, a large-scale and reproducible evaluation has been lacking, which prevents comparisons between PredPatt and other related systems, and inhibits the updates of the patterns in PredPatt. In this work, we improve and evaluate PredPatt by introducing a large set of high-quality annotations converted from PropBank, which can also be used as a benchmark for other predicate-argument extraction systems. We compare PredPatt with other prominent systems and shows that PredPatt achieves the best precision and recall.

1   Introduction

PredPatt[1] (White et al., 2016) is a pattern-based framework for predicate-argument extraction. It defines a set of interpretable, extensible and non-lexicalized patterns based on Universal Dependencies (UD) (de Marneffe et al., 2014), and extracts predicates and arguments through these manual patterns. Figure 1 shows the predicates and arguments extracted by PredPatt from the sentence: *"Chris, the designer, wants to launch a new brand."*

(1) [Chris, the designer] **wants** [to launch a new brand]
(2) [Chris, the designer] **to launch** [a new brand]
(3) [Chris] **be** [the designer]

Figure 1: Predicates and arguments extracted by PredPatt.[2]

The underlying predicate-argument structure constructed by PredPatt is a directed graph, where a special dependency ARG is built between a predicate head token and its arguments' head tokens, and the original UD relations are retained within predicate phrases and argument phrases. For example, Figure 2 shows the directed graph for the predicate-argument extraction (1) and (2) in Figure 1.

Compared to other existing systems for predicate-argument extraction (Banko et al., 2007; Fader et al., 2011; Angeli et al., 2015), the use of manual language-agnostic patterns on UD makes PredPatt a well-founded component across languages. Additionally, the underlying structure constructed by PredPatt has been shown to be a well-formed syntax-semantics interface for NLP tasks: Zhang et al. (2016) utilizes PredPatt to extract possibilistic propositions in automatic common-sense inference generation. White et al. (2016) uses PredPatt to help augmenting data with *Universal Decompositional Semantics*. Zhang et al. (2017) adapts PredPatt to data generation for cross-lingual open information extraction.

However, the evaluation of PredPatt has been restricted to manually-checked extractions over a small set of sentences (White et al., 2016), which lacks gold annotations to conduct an objective and reproducible evaluation, and inhibits the updates of patterns in PredPatt.

---

[1] PredPatt is publicly available at https://github.com/hltcoe/PredPatt

[2] The predicates are colored blue, and the arguments are colored purple with brackets.

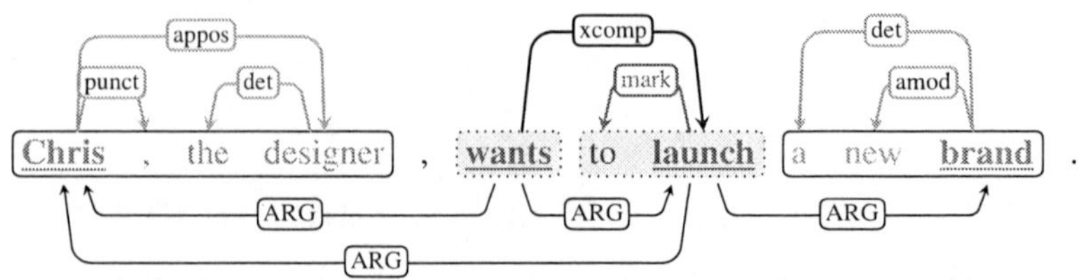

Figure 2: Underlying predicate-argument structure constructed by PredPatt. The predicates are colored blue in dotted cycles with gray background. The arguments are colored purple in solid cycles. The head tokens of predicates and arguments are underlined in bold. A special dependency ARG is built between a predicate head token and its arguments head tokens. The UD relations are kept within predicates and arguments. The relations between predicate head tokens are also kept. The upper relations are UD. The lower relations are ARG relations added by PredPatt.

In this work, we aim to conduct a large-scale and reproducible evaluation of PredPatt by introducing a large set of gold annotations gathered from PropBank (Palmer et al., 2005). We leverage these gold annotations to improve PredPatt and compare it with other prominent systems. The evaluation results demonstrate that we make a promising improvement on PredPatt, and it significantly outperforms other comparing systems. The scripts for creating gold annotations and evaluation are available at: https://github.com/hltcoe/PredPatt/tree/master/eval

2   Creating Gold Annotations

Open Information Extraction (Open IE) and Semantic Role Labeling (SRL) (Carreras and Màrquez, 2005) are quite related: semantically labeled arguments correspond to the arguments in Open IE extractions, and verbs often match up with Open IE relations (Christensen et al., 2011). Lang and Lapata (2010) has acknowledged that the SRL task can be viewed as a two stage process of (1) recognizing predicates and arguments then (2) assigning semantics. Therefore, predicate-argument extraction (i.e., Open IE) should primarily be considered the same as the first of two stages of SRL, and expert annotated SRL data would be an ideal resource for evaluating Open IE systems. This makes PropBank (Palmer et al., 2005) a natural choice from which we can create gold annotations for Open IE, Here, we choose to use expert annotations from PropBank, as compared to the recent suggestion to employ non-expert annotations as a means of benchmarking systems Stanovsky and Dagan (2016). Another advantage of choosing PropBank is that PropBank has gold annotations for UD which lays the important groundwork for evaluating UD-based patterns in PredPatt.

In this work, we create gold annotations for predicate-argument extraction by converting PropBank annotations on English Web Treebank (EWT) (LDC2012T13) and the Penn Treebank II Wall Street Journal Corpus (WSJ) (Marcus et al., 1994).[3] These two corpora have all verbal predicates annotated, and are used to evaluate PredPatt in different perspectives: EWT is the corpus where the gold standard English UD Treebank is built over, which enables an evaluation and analysis of PredPatt patterns; WSJ is used to evaluate PredPatt in a real-world scenario where we run SyntaxNet Parser[4] (Andor et al., 2016) on the corpus to generate automated UD parses as input of PredPatt.

Table 1 shows the statistics of the auto-converted gold annotations for predicate-argument extraction on EWT and WSJ. We convert the PropBank annotations for all verbal predicates in these two corpora, and ignore roles of directional (DIR), manner (MNR), modals (MOD), negation (NEG) and adverbials (ADV), as they aren't extracted as distinct argument but instead are folded into the complex predicate by PredPatt and other systems for predicate-argument extraction (Banko et al., 2007; Fader et al., 2011; Angeli et al., 2015). For EWT, we select 13,583 sentences that have the version 2.0 of the gold UD annotations.[5] The resulting annotations on these two corpora contain over 94K extractions.

---

[3] PropBank annotations are available at: https://github.com/propbank/propbank-release
[4] SyntaxNet Parser is trained on the UD Treebank which has no overlap with WSJ.
[5] English Universal Depedency Treebank is available at: http://universaldependencies.org

Corpus	#sentence	#predicate	#unique_verb	#avg_arg_per_pred
EWT	13,583	21,479	4,336	2.0
WSJ	36,432	73,076	7,880	2.1

Table 1: Statistics of the gold annotations on EWT and WSJ.

3   Improving PredPatt

PredPatt is a pattern-based system, comprising an extensible set of clean, interpretable linguistic patterns over UD parses. By analyzing PredPatt extractions in comparison with gold annotations (Sec. 2), we are able to refine and improve PredPatt's pattern set. From the auto-converted gold annotations, we create a held-out set by randomly sampling 10% sentences from EWT. We then update the existing PredPatt patterns and introduce new patterns by analyzing PredPatt annotations on the held-out set.

PredPatt extracts predicates and arguments in four stages (White et al., 2016): (1) predicate and argument root identification, (2) argument resolution, (3) predicate and argument phrase extraction, and (4) optional post-processing. We analyze PredPatt extraction in each of these stages on the held-out set, and make 19 improvements to PredPatt patterns. Due to lack of space, we only highlight one improvement for each stage below.

Fixed-MWE-pred: The UD version 2.0 introduces a new dependency relation `fixed` for identifying fixed function-word "multiword expressions" (MWEs). To accommodate this new feature, we add patterns to identify the MWE predicate and its argument. As shown in Figure 3, the predicate root in this case is the dependent of `fixed` that is tagged as a verb (i.e., "opposed"); the root of its argument is the token which indirectly governs the predicate root via the `case` and `fixed` relation (i.e., "one").

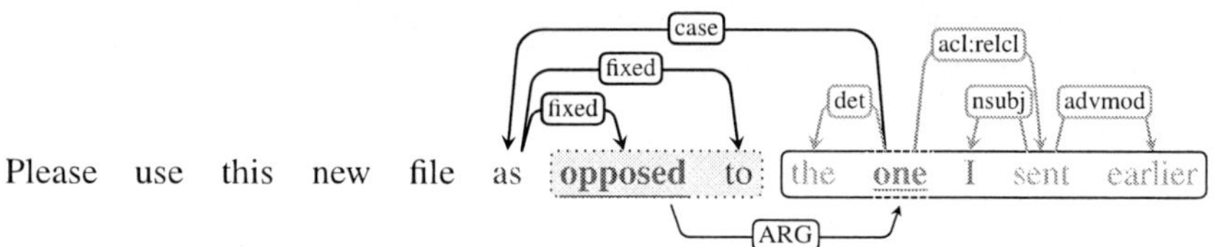

Figure 3: Example for add argument for `fixed` MWE predicates.

Cut-complex-pred: The existing patterns take clausal complements (`ccomp` and `xcomp`) as *predicatives* of complex predicates in the argument resolution stage, where the arguments of the clausal complement will be merged into the argument set of their head predicate. For example, in the sentence "*Chris, the designer, wants to launch a new brand*", PredPatt merges the argument "*a new brand*" of the predicate "*to launch*" into the argument set of the complex predicate "*wants to launch*". As a result, only the complex predicate, "[Chris, the designer] **wants to launch** [a new brand]", will be extracted. It ignores the possibility of the clausal complement itself being a predicate. Here, we add a cutting option; when turned on, it will cut the complex predicate into simple predicates as shown in Figure 1.

Prep-separation: By default, PredPatt considers prepositions to belong to the predicate, while PropBank places preopositions within the span of their corresponding argument. Either behavior may be preferable under different circumstances, so we make preposition placement a new configurable option of PredPatt.

Borrow-subj-for-conj-of-xcomp: PredPatt contains a post-processing option for distributing a single `nsubj` argument over multiple predicates joined by a `conj` relation. PredPatt also contains a pattern assigning subject arguments to predicates introduced by open clausal complement (`xcomp`) relations, according to the theory of obligatory control (Farkas, 1988). We introduce a new post-processing option that combines these two patterns, allowing an argument in subject position to be distributed over multiple `xcomp` predicates that are joined by a `conj` relation, as illustrated in Figure 4.

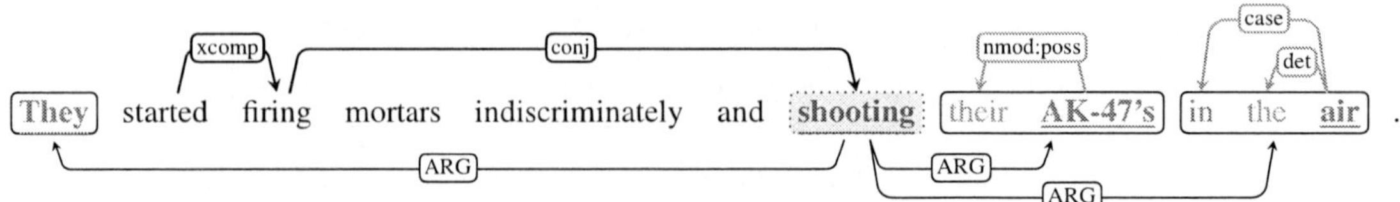

Figure 4: Example for borrowing subject from the conjunction of open clausal complement.

4   Evaluation

In this section, we evaluate the original PredPatt (PredPatt v1) and the improved PredPatt (PredPatt v2) on the English Web Treebank (EWT) and the Wall Street Journal corpus (WSJ), and compare their performance with four prominent Open IE systems: OpenIE 4,[6] OLLIE (Mausam et al., 2012), ClausIE (Del Corro and Gemulla, 2013), and Stanford Open IE (Angeli et al., 2015).

4.1   Precision-Recall Curve

We compare PredPatt with four prominent Open IE systems which are also built for predicate-argument extraction. To allow some flexibility, we compute the precision and recall of different systems by running the scripts used in Stanovsky and Dagan (2016),[7] where an automated extraction is matched with a gold extraction based on their token-level overlap. Figure 5 and Figure 6 show the Precision-Recall Curves for different systems on EWT and WSJ.[8] When tested on EWT which has gold UD parses (Figure 5), PredPatt v1 and v2 outperforms the other systems by a significant margin in both precision and recall. When tested on WSJ where only automated UD parses are available (Figure 6), ClausIE achieves a recall that is slightly better than PredPatt v1, but PredPatt v2 still shows the best performance across all systems.

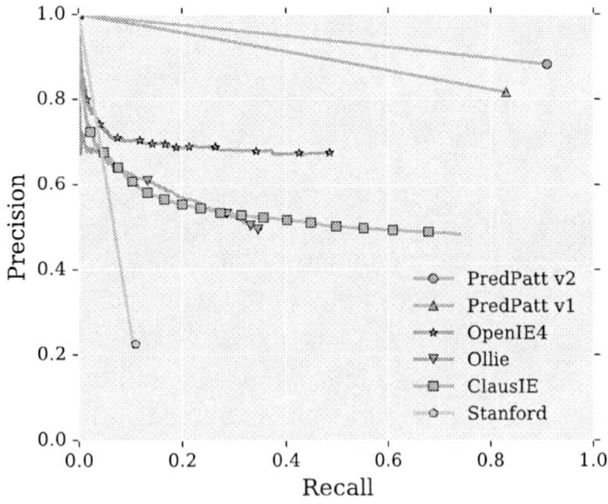

Figure 5: Precision-Recall Curve for different systems on EWT w/ gold UD.

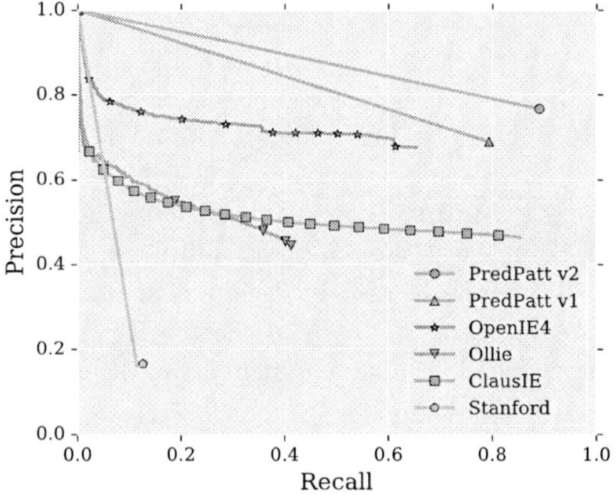

Figure 6: Precision-Recall Curve for different systems on WSJ w/ automated UD.

4.2   Extraction Head Agreement

The rich underlying structure in PredPatt (see Figure 2) contains head information for predicates and arguments, which enables a precision-recall metric based on the agreement of head information. Similar

---

[6]OpenIE 4 is available at: https://github.com/allenai/openie-standalone.

[7]The scripts are available at: https://github.com/gabrielStanovsky/oie-benchmark.

[8] Studies of PredPatt confidence prediction have been done before, but the current system does not output them. In this evaluation, we assign 1.0 confidence score to all PredPatt extractions.

to He et al. (2015), we first match an automated predicate with a gold predicate if they both agree on their head.[9] With two matched predicates, we then match an automated argument with a gold argument if the automated argument head is within the gold argument span.

We evaluate the precision and recall by a loose macro measure: For the i-th extractions that have two matched predicates, let the argument set of the gold predicate be A_i, and the argument set of the automated predicate be $\hat{A}_i$. The number of matched arguments is represented by $|A_i \cap \hat{A}_i|$. Then the precision is computed by Precision $= \frac{1}{N} \sum_{i=1}^{N} |A_i \cap \hat{A}_i|/|\hat{A}_i|$, and the recall is computed by Recall $= \frac{1}{N} \sum_{i=1}^{N} |A_i \cap \hat{A}_i|/|A_i|$. Table 2 shows the evaluation results of PredPatt v1 and v2 on EWT and WSJ. PredPatt v2 modestly increases the precision by 2.3 on EWT and 0.9 on WSJ, and increases the recall by 1.6 on EWT and 0.2 on WSJ.

	EWT		WSJ	
	PredPatt v1	PredPatt v2	PredPatt v1	PredPatt v2
Precision	77.5	79.8 (**+2.3**)	62.1	63.0 (**+0.9**)
Recall	88.0	89.6 (**+1.6**)	84.9	85.1 (**+0.2**)

Table 2: Precision and Recall based on the agreement of head information.

4.3   Statistics of Argument Span Relations

Besides the precion-recall oriented metrics, we impose another metric to further measure the argument span relations. Following in same notations in § 4.2, for the i-th extractions that have an automated predicate and a gold predicate matched with each other, let an argument in the gold argument set be $\alpha \in A_i$, and an argument in the automated argument set $\beta \in \hat{A}_i$. We categorize the automated extractions into four sets according to their arguments relation to the gold arguments.

$$
\begin{aligned}
S_{\text{same}} &= \{(A_i, \hat{A}_i) \mid \forall \alpha \in A_i. \exists \beta \in \hat{A}_i. \text{span}(\alpha) = \text{span}(\beta)\} \\
S_{\text{superset}} &= \{(A_i, \hat{A}_i) \mid \forall \alpha \in A_i. \exists \beta \in \hat{A}_i. \text{span}(\alpha) \subseteq \text{span}(\beta)\} \setminus S_{\text{same}} \\
S_{\text{subset}} &= \{(A_i, \hat{A}_i) \mid \forall \alpha \in A_i. \exists \beta \in \hat{A}_i. \text{span}(\alpha) \supseteq \text{span}(\beta)\} \setminus S_{\text{same}} \\
S_{\text{overlap}} &= \{(A_i, \hat{A}_i) \mid \forall \alpha \in A_i. \exists \beta \in \hat{A}_i. \text{span}(\alpha) \cap \text{span}(\beta) \neq \emptyset\} \setminus (S_{\text{same}} \cup S_{\text{superset}} \cup S_{\text{subset}})
\end{aligned}
$$

Table 3 shows the proportion of PredPatt extractions in different sets. As we expected, compared to WSJ, more extractions on EWT fall into S_{same}, which shows that PredPatt works better on gold UD parses. In contrast to PredPatt v1, PredPatt v2 on EWT increases extractions in S_{same} by 12.97%, which contributes to the most increase of S_{subset}; on WSJ, PredPatt v2 decreases extractions in S_{subset} by 13.89%, which leads the major increases of S_{same} and S_{superset}. There are still over 10% extractions not belonging to any of these four sets. Case analysis shows that the inconsistent extractions are mainly caused by incorrect borrowing of arguments for compound predicates or predicates under obligatory control, missing arguments for passive/active verbs that act as adjectival modifiers, etc. These cases are not easily reachable via UD analysis, but leave room for further improvement on PredPatt.

	EWT		WSJ	
	PredPatt v1	PredPatt v2	PredPatt v1	PredPatt v2
Same	63.77	76.74 (**+12.97**)	41.56	52.03 (**+10.47**)
Superset	2.74	4.15 (**+1.41**)	8.64	14.10 (**+5.46**)
Subset	18.31	5.82 (**-12.49**)	28.63	14.74 (**-13.89**)
Overlap	0.78	0.39 (**-0.39**)	2.16	1.06 (**-1.10**)
Other	14.40	12.90 (**-1.50**)	19.01	18.07 (**-0.94**)

Table 3: Proportion of PredPatt extractions in different sets.

---

[9]In the current settings, the head of a gold predicate is the verb token in the predicate.

5 Conclusions

We introduce a large-scale benchmark for predicate-argument extraction by converting manual annotations from PropBank. Based on the benchmark, we improve PredPatt patterns, and compare PredPatt with four prominent Open IE systems. The comparison shows that PredPatt significantly outperforms the other systems. The evaluation results demonstrate that we improve the performance of PredPatt in both precion-recall and the argument span relation with the gold annotations. As for further work, we see the confidence score estimater for PredPatt extractions as a desirable target, so that the quality of extractions can be controlled. Additionally, we would like to further improve the PredPatt patterns by analyzing more PredPatt extractions in comparison with gold annotations.

Acknowledgments

Thank you to the anonymous reviewers for their feedback, as well as the colleague Tim Vieira. This work was supported in part by the JHU Human Language Technology Center of Excellence (HLTCOE), DARPA LORELEI, and the National Science Foundation. The U.S. Government is authorized to reproduce and distribute reprints for Governmental purposes. The views and conclusions contained in this publication are those of the authors and should not be interpreted as representing official policies or endorsements of DARPA or the U.S. Government.

References

Andor, D., C. Alberti, D. Weiss, A. Severyn, A. Presta, K. Ganchev, S. Petrov, and M. Collins (2016, August). Globally normalized transition-based neural networks. In *Proceedings of the 54th Annual Meeting of the Association for Computational Linguistics (Volume 1: Long Papers)*, Berlin, Germany, pp. 2442–2452. Association for Computational Linguistics.

Angeli, G., M. J. Johnson Premkumar, and C. D. Manning (2015, July). Leveraging linguistic structure for open domain information extraction. In *Proceedings of the 53rd Annual Meeting of the Association for Computational Linguistics and the 7th International Joint Conference on Natural Language Processing (Volume 1: Long Papers)*, Beijing, China, pp. 344–354. Association for Computational Linguistics.

Banko, M., M. J. Cafarella, S. Soderland, M. Broadhead, and O. Etzioni (2007). Open information extraction from the web. In *Proceedings of the 20th International Joint Conference on Artifical Intelligence*, IJCAI'07, San Francisco, CA, USA, pp. 2670–2676. Morgan Kaufmann Publishers Inc.

Carreras, X. and L. Màrquez (2005). Introduction to the conll-2005 shared task: Semantic role labeling. In *Proceedings of the Ninth Conference on Computational Natural Language Learning*, pp. 152–164. Association for Computational Linguistics.

Christensen, J., S. Soderland, O. Etzioni, et al. (2011). An analysis of open information extraction based on semantic role labeling. In *Proceedings of the sixth international conference on Knowledge capture*, pp. 113–120. ACM.

de Marneffe, M.-C., T. Dozat, N. Silveira, K. Haverinen, F. Ginter, J. Nivre, and C. D. Manning (2014). Universal stanford dependencies: A cross-linguistic typology. In *LREC*, Volume 14, pp. 4585–4592.

Del Corro, L. and R. Gemulla (2013). Clausie: clause-based open information extraction. In *Proceedings of the 22nd international conference on World Wide Web*, pp. 355–366. ACM.

Fader, A., S. Soderland, and O. Etzioni (2011, July). Identifying relations for open information extraction. In *Proceedings of the 2011 Conference on Empirical Methods in Natural Language Processing*, Edinburgh, Scotland, UK., pp. 1535–1545. Association for Computational Linguistics.

Farkas, D. F. (1988). On obligatory control. *Linguistics and Philosophy 11*(1), 27–58.

He, L., M. Lewis, and L. Zettlemoyer (2015, September). Question-answer driven semantic role labeling: Using natural language to annotate natural language. In *Proceedings of the 2015 Conference on Empirical Methods in Natural Language Processing*, Lisbon, Portugal, pp. 643–653. Association for Computational Linguistics.

Lang, J. and M. Lapata (2010, June). Unsupervised induction of semantic roles. In *Human Language Technologies: The 2010 Annual Conference of the North American Chapter of the Association for Computational Linguistics*, Los Angeles, California, pp. 939–947. Association for Computational Linguistics.

Marcus, M., G. Kim, M. A. Marcinkiewicz, R. MacIntyre, A. Bies, M. Ferguson, K. Katz, and B. Schasberger (1994). The penn treebank: Annotating predicate argument structure. In *Proceedings of the Workshop on Human Language Technology*, HLT '94, Stroudsburg, PA, USA, pp. 114–119. Association for Computational Linguistics.

Mausam, M. Schmitz, R. Bart, S. Soderland, and O. Etzioni (2012). Open language learning for information extraction. In *Proceedings of Conference on Empirical Methods in Natural Language Processing and Computational Natural Language Learning (EMNLP-CONLL)*.

Palmer, M., D. Gildea, and P. Kingsbury (2005). The proposition bank: An annotated corpus of semantic roles. *Computational linguistics 31*(1), 71–106.

Stanovsky, G. and I. Dagan (2016, November). Creating a large benchmark for open information extraction. In *Proceedings of the 2016 Conference on Empirical Methods in Natural Language Processing*, Austin, Texas, pp. 2300–2305. Association for Computational Linguistics.

White, A. S., D. Reisinger, K. Sakaguchi, T. Vieira, S. Zhang, R. Rudinger, K. Rawlins, and B. Van Durme (2016, November). Universal decompositional semantics on universal dependencies. In *Proceedings of the 2016 Conference on Empirical Methods in Natural Language Processing*, Austin, Texas, pp. 1713–1723. Association for Computational Linguistics.

Zhang, S., K. Duh, and B. Van Durme (2017, April). Mt/ie: Cross-lingual open information extraction with neural sequence-to-sequence models. In *Proceedings of the 15th Conference of the European Chapter of the Association for Computational Linguistics: Volume 2, Short Papers*, Valencia, Spain, pp. 64–70. Association for Computational Linguistics.

Zhang, S., R. Rudinger, K. Duh, and B. Van Durme (2016). Ordinal common-sense inference. *arXiv preprint arXiv:1611.00601*.

Association for Computational Linguistics
209 N. Eighth Street
Stroudsburg, Pennsylvania 18360

ISBN 978-1-5108-5283-9